Diverse Learners with Exceptionalities

Culturally Responsive Teaching in the Inclusive Classroom

Diverse Learners with Exceptionalities

Culturally Responsive Teaching in the Inclusive Classroom

Gwendolyn Cartledge
The Ohio State University

Ralph Gardner, III
The Ohio State University

Donna Y. Ford
Vanderbilt University

Merrill
is an imprint of

Upper Saddle River, New Jersey
Columbus, Ohio

Library of Congress Cataloging in Publication Data

Cartledge, Gwendolyn
　Diverse learners with exceptionalities : culturally responsive teaching in the inclusive classroom / Gwendolyn Cartledge, Ralph Gardner, III, and Donna Y. Ford.
　　　p. cm.
　　Includes bibliographical references and index.
　　ISBN-13: 978-0-13-114995-3
　　ISBN-10: 0-13-114995-4
　1. Inclusive education—United States. 2. Children with social disabilities—Education—United States. 3. Minorities—Education—United States. I. Gardner, Ralph. II. Ford, Donna Y. III. Title.
　　LC1201.C37 2009
　　371.9′046—dc22

2007027164

Vice President and Executive Publisher: Jeffery W. Johnston
Executive Editor: Ann Castel Davis
Editorial Assistant: Penny Burleson
Production Editor: Sheryl Glicker Langner
Production Coordination: Carol Singer, GGS Book Services
Photo Coordinator: Valerie Schultz
Design Coordinator: Diane C. Lorenzo
Cover Design: Jason Moore
Cover Image: Photodisc by Getty Images
Production Manager: Laura Messerly
Director of Marketing: Quinn Perkson
Marketing Coordinator: Brian Mounts

This book was set in Optima by GGS Book Services. It was printed and bound by Hamilton Printing. The cover was printed by Phoenix Color Corp.

Chapter Opening Photo Credits: Scott Cunningham/Merrill, pp. 2, 228, 254; Anne Vega/Merrill, pp. 24, 71, 210, 280; Todd Yarrington/Merrill, pp. 54, 130; David Buffington/Getty Images, Inc.—Photodisc, p. 100; David Mager/Pearson Learning Photo Studio, p. 158; Laima Druskis/PH College, pp. 188, 304; Anthony Magnacca/Merrill, p. 330.

Copyright © 2009 by Pearson Education, Inc., Upper Saddle River, New Jersey 07458.
All rights reserved. Printed in the United States of America. This publication is protected by Copyright and permission should be obtained from the publisher prior to any prohibited reproduction, storage in a retrieval system, or transmission in any form or by any means, electronic, mechanical, photocopying, recording, or likewise. For information regarding permission(s), write to: Rights and Permissions Department.

Pearson® is a registered trademark of Pearson plc
Merrill® is a registered trademark of Pearson Education, Inc.

Pearson Education Ltd.
Pearson Education Singapore Pte. Ltd.
Pearson Education Canada, Ltd.
Pearson Education—Japan

Pearson Education Australia Pty. Limited
Pearson Education North Asia Ltd.
Pearson Educación de Mexico, S.A. de C.V.
Pearson Education Malaysia Pte. Ltd.

Merrill
is an imprint of

10 9 8 7 6 5 4 3 2 1
ISBN-13: 978-0-13-114995-3
ISBN-10:　　0-13-114995-4

Preface

Children from culturally and linguistically diverse (CLD) backgrounds disproportionately make up special education and at-risk populations. School data consistently show that certain segments of this group have the highest rates of school failure and the poorest postschool outcomes of all the students in our schools. School failure not only is a problem for the individual learner but is extremely challenging for educators and costly to the larger society. As our communities increase in diversity, there is a corresponding urgent need to attend to school practices that will enable us to minimize the effects of disabilities and greatly reduce the risk status of students in the most vulnerable groups.

Risk status for many CLD learners begins at birth and, without intervention, systematically worsens through the development years. Our research and experiences convince us not only that these students can learn, but also, with appropriate interventions, that the risk status for these students can in some cases be eliminated and in others minimized. In addition to more intensive and systematic instruction, these students would benefit from learning environments that are affirming and nurturing, leading the students to embrace their student roles and value themselves as learners. To achieve these conditions, in addition to acquiring effective teaching skills, teachers need a greater understanding of their CLD learners as well as of themselves.

The purpose of this text is to help preservice and inservice professionals to identify learning challenges unique to CLD populations and to determine ways these conditions might be altered to promote the school, and later life, success of the CLD learner. The intent of this text is to help teachers understand the urgency associated with teaching CLD learners, the importance of being proactive, and the specific strategies that are most likely to be effective with this population. Rather than interject a chapter, section, or an occasional reference to the CLD learner, this book is designed to focus extensively on this population. Widespread school failure cannot be an option for the fastest-growing segment of our pupil population.

In terms of diversity, we recognize that no group is monolithic and that within any particular group there are several subgroups. For example, Hispanic Americans include individuals from several different countries such as Cuba, Mexico, Puerto Rico, and other countries in Central and South America. We also are aware that Hispanic Americans are often referred to as Latinos/as, but in our review of the relevant literature we have not discerned a particular preference. Therefore, in the interest of uniformity we will use the term *Hispanic Americans* throughout this text. Following the same reasoning, we have chosen to use terms such as *African American* instead of *Black* and *European American* instead of *White*. On the few occasions when we do use alternative terms, such as *Black* or *White*, we are reflecting the work of another author rather than our own. *Asian Americans* is the term that we have elected to use for Asian and Pacific Islanders, and we use *Native Americans* to refer to American Indians/Alaska Natives. Although these latter groupings conform to those of the U.S. Bureau of Statistics, we recognize that there are some groups who do not fit neatly into these categories. To some extent we address the cultural and language differences of learners who fall outside of these categories in discussions of recent immigrants.

To refer to the entire group of ethnically and racially diverse learners, we use the terms *CLD* or *CLDE*. *CLD* refers to students or families who have not been classified as exceptional. *CLDE* (culturally and linguistically diverse with exceptionalities) refers to those students who either have been diagnosed with disabilities or are designated as being gifted/talented.

The authors of this text represent a wide spectrum of applied and professional experience. In addition to having taught children with and without disabilities, we have an extensive background as producers and consumers of the research literature. Much of our work has centered on the culturally diverse population with exceptionalities, ranging from low-incidence groups to the gifted and talented. Some of our most recent efforts have focused on preventing learning and behavior problems among young CLD learners within inclusive environments. Elements of that work have been incorporated into this text.

The targeted audience for this text includes preservice and inservice educators who are preparing to teach or serve CLD learners with and at risk for disabilities. Considering the growing presence of CLD learners in all of our schools, coursework on this topic would be appropriate for all new school personnel. The text emphasizes the need for skilled, culturally competent general educators who are able to put into place effective preventive strategies and special education interventionists who work in concert with general educators to increase the academic and behavioral growth of CLDE learners within general education settings. Equally important are culturally competent educators who can identify and nurture intellectual gifts in CLD learners.

Organization of the Book

There are 14 chapters in this book. The first chapter provides an overview of racial and cultural differences in our society, the corresponding diversity in our schools, and the impact of these factors on teaching and learning. Chapter 2 continues this description of diversity in terms of disability categories and emphasizes how CLD groups are disproportionately affected by disabilities. This chapter also discusses the legislation that is so critical to the education of CLD populations with exceptionalities. Chapter 3 further builds on the first two chapters by discussing ways that multiculturalism can be built into classroom instruction, how to create equitable classrooms, and how to provide for recent immigrants and their families. Social behavior is the focus of chapters 4 and 5. In chapter 4, teachers are helped to create disciplined environments and use management strategies that enable students to become more disciplined and effective learners. Chapter 5 provides a model and strategies for using the child's culture as a means for teaching social skills.

Chapter 6 offers a profile of CLD families, their particular orientation to the schools, their perspective on disabilities, and ways to work effectively with CLD parents of children with exceptionalities. Issues of assessment and evaluation, which are particularly germane to the identification, placement, and instruction of CLD learners, are the focus of chapter 7. Chapter 8 presents community services, providing a discussion of their importance to CLDE learners and how they might be utilized for maximum benefit. Methods of instruction are the content of chapters 9 and 10. Chapter 9 gives the reader the fundamental principles of effective instruction as encompassed in a five-step process. It presents effective instruction methods in an applied form with various strategies for teaching basic skills and content subjects. These chapters emphasize techniques for teaching this curriculum to CLDE learners.

Self-determination and self-advocacy are the focus of chapter 11. Strategies in this chapter emphasize students developing organization, goal-setting, and self-regulation skills to become successful learners. The critical importance of early intervention, particularly for low-socioeconomic CLD families, is the topic of chapter 12. The chapter discusses interventions from infancy to kindergarten and the promising effects of evidence-based interventions. CLD learners have the poorest outcomes in transitioning from school to postsecondary environments. Chapter 13 details the special transition problems for CLD learners and offers strategies for more effective interventions. The final chapter of this book, chapter 14, focuses on CLD gifted learners. This chapter discusses giftedness, why CLD learners tend to be underidentified, and how teachers might better identify and retain CLD students with gifts.

Chapter Format

Each of the chapters in this book includes a set of pedagogical elements designed to increase the readability and utility of the text.

Questions and strategies. The chapters begin with a brief introduction followed by a set of questions that the reader should be able to answer by the end of the chapter. After the questions, where appropriate, a set of teaching strategies is provided, which the reader should expect to find in the chapter.

Vignettes. Near the beginning of each chapter is a vignette about a CLD learner with or at risk for a disability. These cases are partially based on students we have known. They are realistic situations, and in several vignettes we purposely chose particularly challenging situations in order to make the point that regardless of circumstances, given genuine effort and appropriate interventions, all students can be helped to improve. To the extent possible, these cases are extended throughout the chapter and used as illustrations of suggested strategies.

Teaching tips. These are a listing of recommended steps that teachers should take to effect some desired outcome. The tips could also be viewed as brief how-to summaries of the preceding text.

Applications. These are brief narratives describing how the preceding text might be applied with a CLD learner.

Summaries. The chapter summaries are written to reflect the questions presented at the beginning of the text with the intention of facilitating the reader's understanding of the chapter and fuller understanding of the main concepts presented.

Related learning activities. Each chapter ends with a set of related learning activities that the reader might pursue. These applied activities could give the reader real-life experience in addressing the learning issues of special-needs CLD learners.

Acknowledgments

Textbooks are much easier to conceive than to complete. Although we believed in this project from its inception, we were not totally prepared for all the twists and turns our lives would take in the process. Granted this was mostly forward movement, even positive changes contribute to stress and create the need for course adjustments. Even more important were the occasional reality checks to make sure we were appropriately aligned with each other and our intended constituency. These were intense and somewhat grueling periods. Nevertheless, we have found this to be a rewarding growth experience, facilitated immensely by the highly capable personnel at Merrill.

We are most grateful to Allyson Sharp, the executive editor, whose vision and expertise helped us to conceptualize and develop most of this book. Allyson's keen insights, professionalism, exceptional abilities, and drive not only helped us over the initial glitches typical of any new endeavor but also enabled us to remain on course for a fairly timely completion. We were more than disappointed when Allyson was transferred to a new assignment and location, but she assured us that her replacement, Ann Davis, would be every bit as helpful, supportive, and effective. And, as usual, Allyson was right. We are equally grateful to Ann for her skill in working closely with us to finalize this book. We appreciate her special insights and perspectives, which, we believe, helped us to see the book more holistically and undoubtedly led to a better product.

We would also like to thank the reviewers: Beverly Argus-Calvo, The University of Texas at El Paso; Isaura Barrera, University of New Mexico; Debbie Case, Southwestern Oklahoma State University; Mary G. Curtis, University of Texas at Brownsville; Blanche Jackson Glimps, Tennessee State University; Linda A. Gregg, College of Santa Fe; Harold William Heller, University of South Florida, St. Petersburg; Placido A. Hoernicke, Fort Hays State University; Maurice Miller, Indiana State University; Claudia Peralta Nash, Boise State University; Crystal Pauli, Dakota State University; Elissa Wolfe Poel, New Mexico State University; Janet Steck, University of Toledo; Rita van Loenen, Arizona State University; Sandra Warren, East Carolina University.

Brief Contents

PART 1 Foundation of Diversity in Special Education — 1

1. Understanding Diversity — 2
2. Understanding the Culturally and Linguistically Diverse Exceptional Learner — 24

PART 2 Creating Culturally Responsive, Equitable, and Inclusive Classrooms — 53

3. The Culturally Responsive Inclusive Classroom — 54
4. The Disciplined CLDE Learner — 70
5. Socially Skilled CLDE Learners — 100
6. Culturally Responsive Collaborations with CLD Families — 130
7. Culturally Responsive Assessment of CLDE Learners — 158
8. Culturally Responsive Community-Based Interventions — 188

PART 3 Culturally Responsive Instruction — 209

9. Understanding Effective Instruction for CLDE Learners — 210
10. Implementing Effective Instruction in Inclusive Classrooms for CLDE Learners — 228
11. Creating Self-Directed CLDE Learners — 254
12. Early Interventions for the CLDE Learner — 280
13. Effective Postsecondary Transitions for CLDE Learners — 304

PART 4 Special Issues for Special Populations — 329

14. Gifted and Talented CLDE Learners — 330

Contents

PART 1   **Foundation of Diversity in Special Education**   1

1   Understanding Diversity   2
    Introduction 2
    Race and Ethnicity 3
        How Diverse Is the United States? 3
    The Real Village: 2000 Census Data 5
        Racial and Ethnic Diversity in the United States 5
        How Diverse Are Teachers and Students? 6
        Educational Implications: What Is Culture and Why Does It Matter? 10
    How Do We Define Culture? 11
    What Function Does Culture Serve? 14
    A Model of Culture: What Are Some Specific Dimensions of Culture? 15
    How Do I Become a Culturally Responsive Educator? 18
    Summary 21
    Activity: If the World Were a Village . . . 21
    References 21

2   Understanding the Culturally and Linguistically Diverse Exceptional Learner   24
    Special Education and Diversity 25
    Special Education Law 25
        Section 504 of Rehabilitation Act of 1973 25
        Individuals with Disabilities Education Act 27
        What Is Specified in the Early Childhood Legislation? 27
        No Child Left Behind 29
    Special Education Services in General Education Classes 29
    What Is Bilingual Education? 30
    What Are the Special Placement Issues for the CLDE Learner? 31
    What Are the Categories of Exceptionality and the Unique Issues for CLDE Learners? 32
        What Are High-Incidence Disabilities? 32
        What Are Low-Incidence Disabilities? 43
        Gifted Education 48
    Summary 48
    Related Learning Activities 48
    References 49

PART 2 Culturally Responsive, Equitable and Inclusive Classrooms — 53

3 The Culturally Responsive Inclusive Classroom — 54
How Have Our Schools Changed? 55
What Is the Role of Culture in Schooling? 55
How Does Diversity Impact Education? 56
What Are Culturally Responsive Classrooms? 58
  Content Integration 59
  Knowledge Construction 59
  Equity Pedagogy 59
  Empowering School Culture 59
How Can We Appreciate Diversity in the Classroom? 60
How Do We Implement Culturally Responsive Lessons? 61
How Can We Provide Culturally Responsive Education for English Language Learners? 63
  Can CLDE Learners Become Efficient English Language Learners? 64
  Immigration 65
  How Do We Involve Families of English Language Learners? 66
Summary 67
Related Learning Activities 67
References 67

4 The Disciplined CLDE Learner — 70
Culture and the Disciplined Environment 71
  What Is the Relationship Between Culture and Social Behavior? 72
  How Does the Culture of the School Affect Children's Social Behavior? 72
What Are the Discipline Issues in Our Schools? 75
  What Are Some Discipline Issues with Regard to Special Populations? 75
What Is Effective Culturally Responsive Discipline? 79
How Can We Be Proactive in Addressing Disciplinary Issues for CLDE Learners? 82
  How Do We Provide Culturally Responsive Functional Behavior Assessments? 82
  How Do We Create Positive School Environments? 92
Summary 97
Related Learning Activities 97
References 97

5 Socially Skilled CLDE Learners — 100
What Do We Need to Know to Teach Social Skills? 101
What Are the Social Behaviors of CLDE Students? 102

Hispanic Americans 102
Native Americans 103
Asian Americans 103
African Americans 104

What Are the Social Skill Needs of Students with Exceptionalities? 106

How Can We Use the Child's Culture to Teach Social Skills? 107
The Traditional Culture and Social Skill Instruction 107
How Can We Use Culturally Specific Literature to Teach Social Skills? 109
Language and Social Skill Development 109

What Is a Model for Culturally Responsive Social Skills Instruction? 111
Basic Model 111
How Do We Provide Culturally Responsive Social Skill Instruction? 111

How Do We Provide Peer-Mediated Interventions for CLDE Learners? 116

How Do We Teach Social Skills According to Gender? 121
What Are the Social Skill Needs According to Gender? 121
How Do We Teach Gender-Specific Social Skills? 121

What Are the Social Skill Needs According to Sexual Orientation? 122

What Are the Social Skill Curriculums? 124

Summary 125

Related Learning Activities 125

References 126

6 Culturally Responsive Collaborations with CLD Families 130

What Is the Home–School Relationship? 131
How Are Home–School Relationships Perceived? 132
What Is the Role of Families in Pupil Achievement? 133

What Role Have Families Had in the Schooling of Children with Exceptionalities? 134
How Have Families Been Perceived? 134
How Do Families React to the Presence of Disabilities? 134
What Are the Implications of Federal Legislation for CLD Families of Children with Disabilities? 135

What Are Some Special Issues for CLD Families of Children with Exceptionalities? 136
What Are Family Perceptions? 136
What Are Trust Issues? 136
What Is Family Adaptation? 136
How Do Goals Differ? 137
What Are Some Different Parenting Issues? 137
What Are Some Economic Issues? 138
What Are the Cultural Discontinuities? 139

How Do We Promote CLD Family Involvement in the Schools? 140

How Do We Empower CLD Families and Schools? 140
What Are Empowered Schools? 140
How Do We Empower Parents Through Parent Education? 141
How Do We Empower Families Through Parent Skill Development? 142
How Do We Empower Families Through Home-Based Learning? 142

How Can We Communicate Effectively with CLD Parents? 145
How Do We Build Positive and Respectful Relationships? 145
How Do We Communicate Regularly with Families? 148
How Do We Communicate Regularly Through Writing? 149
How Can We Handle Difficult Situations Constructively? 150

What Is Parental Advocacy for CLDE Children? 151
What Is the Historical Perspective? 151
What Are Advocacy Resources? 152

Summary 154

Related Learning Activities 155

References 155

7 Culturally Responsive Assessment of CLDE Learners — 158

What Are the Special Issues of Standardized Testing for CLDE Groups? 160
Intelligence Tests: What Are Some General Issues and Concerns? 161
What Are the Major Criticisms of Using Tests with CLDE Groups? 163
How Do Personal Biases Affect Testing of CLDE Learners? 168

The Bigger Picture: What Is Assessment and How Does Assessment Differ from Testing? 169

What Are Some Key Features of Culturally Responsive Assessment? 171

How Can We Address High-Stakes Testing of CLDE Learners? 174
What Are High-Stakes Tests? 174
How Do We Help CLDE Students Perform on High-Stakes Tests? 175
What Are Some Additional High-Stakes Testing Considerations for CLDE Students? 176

Where Do We Go from Here? Assessment Principles 178
Nondiscriminatory Assessment Principles 178

Where Do We Go from Here? Educational Implications 180

Summary 183

Related Learning Activities 184

References 184

8 Culturally Responsive Community-Based Interventions — 188

What Is Inclusion in a Community Setting? 189

How Can Inclusive Community Activities for CLDE Learners Be Provided During After-School Hours? 190

What Are the Benefits of After-School Programs for CLDE Learners? 191
    School-Age Childcare 192
    Youth Development Programs 194
    What Are Educational After-School Programs for CLDE Learners? 194

How Can We Serve CLDE Students Through Community-Based Programs? 196

Community-Based Inclusion and the Law 197

Why Do CLDE Learners Benefit from Well-Designed Community-Based Programs? 198
    An Example of a Community-Based Program for CLDE Learners: Project D.E.L.T.A.A. 200

How Can We Make Community-Based Interventions More Culturally Responsive? 201
    Inclusive Games 202
    Cooperative Teaming 203
    Peer Buddy Systems 203

Planning for Individuals with Severe Disabilities 204

Religious Institutions 204

Summary 205

Related Learning Activities 205

References 206

PART 3 Culturally Responsive Instruction   209

9 Understanding Effective Instruction for CLDE Learners   210

What Is Effective Instruction? 211

What Is the Legislative Impact on Effective Instruction? 212

Effective Instruction: A Five-Step Process 213
    What Are Effective Assessments for CLDE Learners? 213

Effective Instruction: Translating Assessment Data into Instructional Objectives 216

Effective Instruction: Standards and Strategies 217
    What Are the Professional Standards for Effective Instruction? 217
    Effective Instruction: An Evidence-Based Practice 217
    What Are Effective Instruction Strategies? 218

Effective Instruction: Progressive Monitoring 220

Effective Instruction: Maintenance and Generalization 220
    Maintenance 220
    Generalization 220

What Are Some Special Considerations for Effective Instruction of CLDE Learners? 221
    Teacher Quality 221
    Low Expectations 221
    Culturally Specific Strategies 222

Summary 224
Related Learning Activities 224
References 225

10 Implementing Effective Instruction in Inclusive Classrooms for CLDE Learners   228

What Should Be Taught? 230
How Do We Provide Reading Instruction to CLDE Learners? 230
   What Is the Reading Profile of CLDE Learners? 230
   What Reading Skills Should Be Taught CLDE Learners? 232
   How Do We Teach Older Struggling Readers? 235
   How Can We Provide Multicultural Reading Materials? 237
How Do We Help CLDE Students Develop Writing Skills? 239
How Do We Help CLDE Students Develop Math Skills? 241
   How Do We Make Math Materials and Instructional Formats Appropriate for CLDE Learners? 243
Teaching Other Academic Content to CLDE Learners 245
   Lectures 245
   Choral Responding 246
   Response Cards 246
   Peer Tutoring 247
How Can Teachers Know If Their Instruction Is Effective with CLDE Learners? 247
   What Are Other Factors Impacting the Inclusive Educational Environment? 248
Summary 250
Related Learning Activities 250
References 250

11 Creating Self-Directed CLDE Learners   254

How Do We Help CLDE Students Become More Effective Learners? 256
How Do We Help CLDE Students Develop Self-Directed Preparedness Skills? 256
   Why Teach Organization and Preparedness Skills? 256
   How Do We Teach for Student Organization and Preparedness? 258
   How Do We Help Improve Homework Performance? 259
How Do We Help CLDE Students Develop Study Skills? 262
   Why Teach Study Skills? 262
   What Are Study Skills? 263
   A Sample Study Skill 263
How Do We Help CLDE Students Develop Note-Taking Skills? 265
   Why Teach Note-Taking Skills? 265
   What Are Specific Note-Taking Strategies? 265
How Do We Help CLDE Students Improve Their Academic Self-Management Skills? 268
   How Do We Teach Students to Set Goals? 268
   How Do We Teach Students to Self-Monitor Their Academic Behavior? 270

Summary 276
Related Learning Activities 277
References 277

12 Early Interventions for the CLDE Learner — 280

Why Provide Early Interventions for Young Children With or At Risk for Disabilities? 281

What Are the Conditions That Place Infants and Toddlers At Risk? 282

Why Is Early Intervention Important for Culturally Diverse Learners With or At Risk for Exceptionalities? 283
 What Is the Impact of Poverty Among CLDE Populations? 283
 What Are the Special Birth Risks of CLD Populations? 286

What Interventions Are Available for Infants to Three-Year-Old Children? 288
 Intervening with At-Risk Infants and Toddlers 288
 How Can Early Head Start Best Serve CLD Learners? 290

What Interventions Are Available for 3- to 5-Year-Old CLD Children? 292
 How Can Head Start Best Serve CLD Learners? 292
 How Do We Upgrade Early Childhood Programs? 293

How Can We Reduce Special Education Placements of CLDE Learners Through Early Intervention? 295
 How Can We Prevent Special Education Placements Through Early Reading Intervention? 295

Summary 299
Related Learning Activities 300
References 300

13 Effective Postsecondary Transitions for CLDE Learners — 304

What Are the Transition Needs of Special Populations? 305
 What Are the Transition Needs of Students with Disabilities? 306
 What Are the Transition Needs According to Gender? 306
 What Are the Transition Needs According to Cultural and Linguistic Diversity? 307

How Do We Prepare CLDE Students to Make Successful Transitions? 308
 What Are Self-Determination Skills? 309
 How Do We Prepare CLDE Students to Assume Leadership Roles in Transition Planning? 311
 How Do We Teach Self-Determination Skills? 313

How Do We Develop Self-Determination Skills with CLDE Learners? 315
 How Can Teachers Become More Flexible in Teaching for Transitions? 315
 How Can We Mentor Students for Transitions? 316
 How Can We Provide CLDE Students Person-Centered Planning? 317
 How Can We Use Culturally Specific Literature in Teaching for Transitions? 318

How Can We Help Students Transition to Postsecondary
Environments? 319
How Do We Provide Career Education for CLDE Learners? 320
What Is the Role of Vocational Training for CLDE Learners? 322
How Can We Promote Independent Living for CLDE Learners? 323

Summary 324

Related Learning Activities 325

References 325

PART 4   Special Issues for Special Populations — 329

14   Gifted and Talented CLDE Learners — 330

Who Are Gifted and Talented Students? 333

Underrepresentation: What Are the Contributing Factors Associated
with Recruitment and Retention? 335

What Are Some Barriers to Recruiting and Retaining CLDE Learners
in Gifted Education? 336
Cultural Misunderstanding 336

How Does Deficit Thinking Influence Assessment, Policy,
and Practice? 340
Extensive Reliance on Tests 340
Psychometric-Based Definitions and Theories 342
Achievement-Based Definitions and Theories 342
Inadequate Policies and Practices 343

What Changes Should Be Made for Recruitment and Retention
Interventions? 344
Adopt Contemporary Definitions and Theories 345
Adopt Culturally Sensitive Instruments 345

How Do We Identify and Serve Underachievers
and Low-Socioeconomic-Status Students? 347

Where Do We Go from Here? 349
Provide Multicultural Preparation for Educators 349
Provide a Multicultural Education for Gifted Students 349
Develop Home–School Partnerships 351
Conduct Ongoing Evaluation 351

Summary 354

Related Learning Activities 355

References 355

Index — 359

Note: Every effort has been made to provide accurate and current Internet information in this book. However, the Internet and information posted on it are constantly changing, so it is inevitable that some of the Internet addresses listed in this textbook will change.

About the Authors

Gwendolyn Cartledge, Ph.D., is a professor at The Ohio State University, School of Physical Activity and Educational Services, special education programs. She has had an extensive teaching career in both the public schools and higher education, teaching learners with and without disabilities in both suburban and urban public school settings. A faculty member at OSU since 1986, her professional teaching, research, and writings have centered on students with mild disabilities, the development of social skills, and early intervention and prevention of learning and behavior problems through effective instruction with particular emphasis on urban and culturally/linguistically diverse learners. Gwendolyn has researched these topics extensively, as documented in her writings that include the coauthored books *Teaching Social Skills to Children and Youth*, 3rd Edition (1995), *Cultural Diversity and Social Skills Teaching: Understanding Ethnic and Gender Differences* (1996), and *Teaching Urban Learners* (2006). She also has published two social skills curricula, *Taking Part* (1991) and *Working Together* (1994), and numerous articles in professional journals. Her work has been recognized by The Ohio State University for Fostering the Success of Black Students (1991) and for Distinguished Teaching (2003), and by The Ohio Council for Exceptional Children (OH-CEC) for Leadership and Distinguished Service (1996; Ohio Teacher Education Division-TED) and as the Educator of the Year (2006).

Ralph Gardner, III, Ph.D., is an associate professor of special education at The Ohio State University. He is a researcher and teacher educator. Ralph earned his Ph.D. from The Ohio State University in Special Education/Applied Behavior Analysis in 1989 after seven years of teaching children with learning and behavior disabilities. He has authored numerous publications on educating children with disabilities and children at risk for school failure. Ralph remains involved in the educational programs of exceptional children through his participation in inservice and research activities in schools, especially urban schools. His current research interests are effective reading instruction for urban learners and classroom management strategies. Ralph was recognized by The Ohio State University with the Distinguished Teaching Award (1992).

Donna Y. Ford, Ph.D., is a professor of education and human development at Vanderbilt University. She teaches in the Department of Special Education. Professor Ford conducts research primarily in gifted education and multicultural/urban education. Dr. Ford's work has been recognized by various professional organizations: Research Award from the Shannon Center for Advanced Studies; the Early Career Award and the Career Award from The American Educational Research Association; Early Scholar Award from The National Association for Gifted Children; and the Esteemed Scholarship Award from The National Association of Black Psychologists. She is the author of *Reversing Underachievement Among Gifted Black Students* (1996) and coauthor of *Multicultural Gifted Education* (1999), *In Search of the Dream: Designing Schools and Classrooms That Work for High Potential Students from Diverse Cultural Backgrounds* (2004), and *Teaching Culturally Diverse Gifted Students*. Donna is a board member of the National Association for Gifted Children, has served on numerous editorial boards, and has an extensive record of professional publications and presentations.

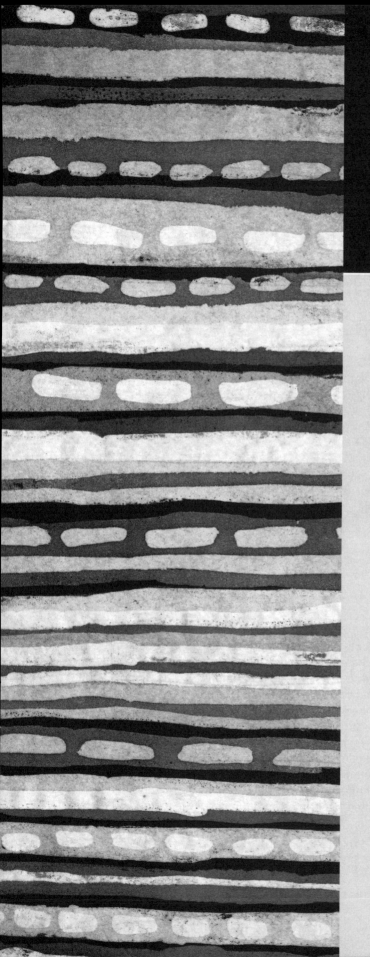

PART 1

Foundation of Diversity in Special Education

Chapter 1

Understanding Diversity

Introduction

The world is shrinking at an incredible pace, and as a result our communities and schools are daily becoming more diverse than ever before. With these changes come differences in cultural worldviews, beliefs, values, customs, and traditions. This multitude of differences among people has important implications for educators.

This chapter presents an overview of racial and ethnic diversity in the United States and in its schools. We focus specifically on the impact of culture or cultural differences on teaching and learning. The first two sections present an overview of demographics, beginning with a summary of racial and ethnic diversity in the United States and then focusing on diversity in school settings. The third section goes behind these numbers and percentages to describe the concept of "culture" and presents a dimension of culture based on research, theory, and practice to shed light on how culture affects teaching and learning, including relationships, expectations, and communication. As you read the chapter, you should consider several questions:

1. How does the increasing diversity of the United States impact the demographics of schools?
2. Why is it important for educators to be aware of racial, ethnic, and cultural diversity?

3. What are the potential dangers of educators being color-blind (culture-blind) and otherwise pretending that groups are not culturally different?
4. What are the benefits of educators being culturally responsive or competent?
   a. How do educators benefit when they are aware of and appreciate cultural diversity among students?
   b. How do culturally and linguistically diverse exceptional (CLDE) students benefit when they are affirmed as culturally diverse individuals?
   c. How do European American students and educators benefit when they are helped to be culturally aware and responsible citizens?

Race and Ethnicity

How Diverse Is the United States?

As described by Census data, the number of people and the percentage of racial and ethnic groups may be overwhelming and difficult to comprehend. In Figure 1–1, "If the World Were a Village of 1,000 People...," Dona Meadows simplifies these data and

FIGURE 1–1 If the world were a village of 1,000 people

If the world were a village of 1,000 people, it would include:

- 584 Asians
- 124 Africans
- 95 East and West Europeans
- 84 Latin Americans
- 55 Soviets (including for the moment Lithuanians, Latvians, Estonians and other national groups)
- 52 North Americans
- 6 Australians and New Zealanders

The people of the village have considerable difficulty in communicating:

- 165 people speak Mandarin
- 86 English
- 83 Hindi/Urdu
- 64 Spanish
- 58 Russian
- 37 Arabic

That list accounts for the mother tongues of only half the villagers. The other half speaks (in descending order of frequency) Bengali, Portuguese, Indonesian, Japanese, German, French, and 200 other languages.

In this village of 1,000 there are:

- 329 Christians (among them 187 Catholics, 84 Protestants, 31 Orthodox)
- 178 Moslems

(continued)

FIGURE 1-1 (continued)

- 167 "non-religious"
- 132 Hindus
- 60 Buddhists
- 45 atheists
- 3 Jews
- 86 all other religions
  - One-third (330) of the 1,000 people in the world village are children and only 60 are over the age of 65. Half the children are immunized against preventable infectious diseases such as measles and polio.
  - Just under half of the married women in the village have access to and use modern contraceptives.
  - This year 28 babies will be born. Ten people will die, 3 of them for lack of food, 1 from cancer; 2 of the deaths are of babies born within the year. One person of the 1,000 is infected with the HIV virus; that person most likely has not yet developed a full-blown case of AIDS.
  - With the 28 births and 10 deaths, the population of the village next year will be 1,018.
  - In this 1,000-person community, 200 people receive 75% of the income; another 200 receive only 2% of the income.
  - Only 70 people of the 1,000 own an automobile (although some of the 70 own more than one automobile).
  - About one-third have access to clean, safe drinking water.
  - Of the 670 adults in the village, half are illiterate.

The village has 6 acres of land per person, 6,000 acres in all, of which

- 700 acres are cropland
- 1,400 acres pasture
- 1,900 acres woodland
- 2,000 acres desert, tundra, pavement, and other wasteland
- The woodland is declining rapidly; the wasteland is increasing. The other land categories are roughly stable.

The village allocates 83% of its fertilizer to 40% of its cropland—that owned by the richest and best-fed 270 people. Excess fertilizer running off this land causes pollution in lakes and wells. The remaining 60% of the land, with its 17% of the fertilizer, produces 28% of the food grains and feeds 73% of the people. The average grain yield on that land is one-third the harvest achieved by the richer villagers.

In the village of 1,000 people, there are:

- 5 soldiers
- 7 teachers
- 1 doctor
- 3 refugees driven from home by war or drought

The village has a total budget each year, public and private, of over $3 million—$3,000 per person if it is distributed evenly (which, we have already seen, it isn't).

Of the total $3 million:

- $181,000 goes to weapons and warfare
- $159,000 for education
- $132,000 for health care

The village has buried beneath it enough explosive power in nuclear weapons to blow itself to smithereens many times over. These weapons are under the control of just 100 of the people. The other 900 people are watching them with deep anxiety, wondering whether they can learn to get along together; and if they do, whether they might set off the weapons anyway through inattention or technical bungling; and, if they ever decide to dismantle the weapons, where in the world village they would dispose of the radioactive materials of which the weapons are made.

Source: Dona Meadows. http://www.gdrc.org/uem/1000-village.html (retrieved January 22, 2007). Also see David J. Smith's 2004 book for children entitled *If The World Were a Village: A Book About the World's People.*

illustrates how diverse we truly are as a nation. Her synopsis captures the reality of diversity relative to race and ethnicity, as well as socioeconomic status and other variables. Study Figure 1–1 carefully and then proceed to the related activity.

The Real Village: 2000 Census Data

As Figure 1–1 indicates, the world is smaller and more diverse than we might think. And if projections come true, our schools will be even more diverse in both the near and distant future. The United States and its 15,000-plus school districts are diverse, especially relative to race, ethnicity, and socioeconomic status. Ten years ago, a teacher in a school district that had few CLDE students, say 5%, could conceivably find herself teaching in the same school district that is now comprised primarily of students who are Hispanic, African American, and Asian American. Just how diverse is our nation?

Racial and Ethnic Diversity in the United States

Every decade, the United States conducts a population census. The first U.S. Census was taken in 1790 under the direction of Secretary of State Thomas Jefferson. At the time, the Census counted 3.9 million inhabitants, of whom 80.7% were European American and 19.3% were Black (1.5% free and 17.8% enslaved) (AAGEN Briefing, 2003).

Counting the population by race and ethnicity is not an easy task. For more than 20 years, the Office of Management and Budget (OMB) has sought to provide a common language to promote uniformity and comparability of data on race and ethnicity for the U.S. population. These data are needed to monitor equal access in housing, education, employment, and other areas for populations that historically had experienced discrimination and differential treatment because of race or ethnicity (OMB, 1997). The following sections describe each group, but first we must explain the concepts of race and ethnicity.

According to the federal government, "race" and "ethnic origin" are two separate and distinct concepts (U.S. Census Bureau, 2001). Specifically, the federal government maintains that Hispanics may be of any racial group. According to the OMB (1997),

> The categories represent a social-political construct designed for collecting data on the race and ethnicity of broad population groups in this county, and are not anthropologically or scientifically based (p. 2).

Further, the federal government maintains that racial and ethnic categories should not be interpreted as being primarily biological or genetic in reference. That is, race and ethnicity may be thought of in terms of social and cultural characteristics, as well as ancestry (p. 2).

Since the 1990 Census, the standards have been heavily scrutinized and criticized by those who do not believe that they reflect the nation's increasing diversity, which has been extensively influenced by immigration and interracial marriages. While one can argue about the construct of "race" and the groups subsequently placed in each racial category, the most confusing standard is the "Hispanic" category. The federal government has not set forth a convincing argument or case for designating Hispanics as an ethnic group. Be that as it may, however, we use the federal standards in this text and chapter.

In 1997, the OMB announced revised standards for federal data on race and ethnicity. The minimum categories for race are now American Indian or Alaska Native, Asian or Pacific Islander, Black or African American, Native Hawaiian or Other Pacific Islander, and White. The federal government recognized only one "ethnic" group: Hispanic or Latino (U.S. Census Bureau, 2004). On July 1, 2004, 98% of all U.S. residents (289.2 million people) belonged to one of these five racial groups. White Americans comprised the largest group, at 80.4%. Hispanic or Latino represented the second-largest group at 14.1%, followed closely by Blacks

TABLE 1-1 2000 census data profiles of U.S. population

White Population

Census 2000 reported that the U.S. population on April 1, 2000, was 284.1 million. Of the total, 77.1%, or 216.9 million people, reported themselves as "White." This term refers to people having origins in any of the original peoples of Europe, the Middle East, or North Africa. It includes people who reported only "White" or wrote in such entries as Irish, German, Italian, Lebanese, Near Easterner, Arab or Polish.

The majority of White Americans live in the South (34%). Others are distributed somewhat evenly in other regions—Midwest (25%), West (21%), and Northeast (20%). New York, Los Angeles, Chicago, and Houston have the largest White populations (U.S. Census Bureau, 2001).

African American Population

Census 2000 reported that 12.3% (34.7 million) of the U.S. population on April 1, 2000, was Black or African American. Unlike other racial or ethnic groups, Blacks have been included in every Census report since 1790. This group includes people having origins in any of the Black race groups of Africa, specifically people who wrote in the entries African American, Afro American, Nigerian, and Haitian. Over half of Blacks live in the South (54.8%), followed by the Midwest (18.8%), Northeast (17.6%), and West (9.6%) (U.S. Census, 2001). In terms of actual numbers, large urban cities such as New York, Chicago, Detroit, and Philadelphia have the largest number of African Americans. However, when looking at the percentages of Blacks, Gary (85.3%), Detroit (82.8%), Birmingham (74%), Jackson (71.1%), New Orleans (67.9%), Baltimore (65.2%), Atlanta (62.1%), Memphis (61.9%), Washington, DC (61.3%), and Richmond (58.1%) are predominantly Black (p. 7).

American Indian and Alaska Native Population

American Indians were first counted in the 1860 Census, but in a limited way. Those individuals on reservations and in American Indian Territory were not counted. This changed in the 1890 Census. Alaska Natives have been counted since 1880, but it was not until 1940 that they were reported under the "American Indian" category. Several changes have occurred in each census, but Census 2000 combined the groups. The American Indian and Alaska Native population represented 1.5% of the U.S. population in Census 2000, a total of 4.1 million people. The combined term refers to people having origins in any of the original peoples of North and South America, including Central America.

The majority of this group resides in the West (43%), followed by the South (31%), Midwest (17%), and Northeast (9%). The largest numbers live in California, Oklahoma, Arizona, Texas, and New Mexico. The largest American Indian tribal groupings are Cherokee (729,533), Navajo (298,197), Latin American Indian (180,940), Choctaw (158,774), Sioux (153,360), Chippewa (149,669), Apache (96,833), Blackfeet (85,750) Iroquois (80,822), and Pueblo (74,085), respectively.

"Hispanic or Latino"

The 1970 Census was the first to include a separate question regarding Hispanic origin. During that time, the options were "Mexican, Puerto Rican, Cuban, Central or South American, or other Spanish." "Latino" appeared on

or African Americans at 12.8%. Asians (4.2%), and Native Hawaiian and other Pacific Islander (1.5%) represented the remaining racial groups. Table 1–1 presents 2004 Census data on the U.S. population, including geographic location, percentages, and trends.

How Diverse Are Teachers and Students?

While the U.S. and student populations have changed dramatically in terms of diversity, the teaching population is very homogeneous. In fact, the teaching force seems to be decreasing in racial and ethnic diversity. This fact carries important implications and raises such questions as

1. How can I, as an educator, appreciate, respect, and affirm the cultures of my students?
2. How does my view of diverse students influence our relationships and understanding of each other?

the census form for the first time in 2000. After several iterations, the federal government now uses the term. This is the fastest-growing group in the United States, having increased by 59.9% between 1990 and 2000 (from 22.4 million to 35.3 million during this period) (U.S. Census, 2001). The Hispanic/Latino population represented 12.5% of the U.S. population in 2000, numbering some 35.3 million people. Of this group, most are Mexican (58.5%) and Puerto Rican (9.6%). This group also includes Spaniards, Cubans, Central Americans, Dominicans, and others. Most live in the West (43.5%), followed by the South (32.8%), Northeast (14.9%) and Midwest (8.9%). It is noteworthy that one fourth of the West is comprised of Hispanics (24.3%) (U.S. Census, 2001).

Asian Population

The 1790 Census collected data on race but made no distinction for people of Asian descent. Data have been collected on the Chinese population since the 1860 Census and on the Japanese population since the 1870 Census. In 1910, other Asian groups were included, namely, Filipinos and Koreans. Until 1970, collection of data on Asians had been intermittent. Interestingly, in the 1970 Census, Asian Indians were classified as "White," while the Vietnamese population was classified as "other" relative to race (U.S. Census, 2002).

As of Census 2000, of the 284.1 million U.S. citizens, 3.6% were Asian. Census 2000 defines Asians as people having their origins in any of the original peoples of the Far East, Southeast Asia, or the Indian subcontinent (e.g., Cambodia, China, India, Japan, Korea, Malaysia, the Philippine Islands, Thailand, Pakistan, and Vietnam). Most Asian populations reside in the West (46.8%), 20.7% reside in the Northeast, 18.8% live in the South, and 11.7% live in the Midwest. Over half of the Asian population lives in three states—California, New York, and Hawaii. In terms of actual numbers, most Asians live in New York, Los Angeles, San Jose, and San Francisco, respectively. However, in terms of percentages, 67.7% of Hawaii is Asian, and 53.69% of Daly City (California), 39.8% of Fremont (California), and 34.2% of Sunnyvale (California) is Asian. In 2000, Chinese was the largest Asian group in the U.S., followed by Filipino, Asian Indian, Vietnamese, Korean, and Japanese (U.S. Census, 2002, p. 9).

Native Hawaiian and Other Pacific Islander Population

In 1960, the year after Hawaii became the 50th state, two separate categories were included on the decennial census questionnaire for the state of Hawaii only: "Hawaiian" and "Part Hawaiian." In 1980 and 1990, other distinctions were made. According to Census 2000, this group represents 0.3% of the U.S. population. Specifically, 874,414 people are in this group, including 399,000 who reported themselves as Pacific Islander only. The total Pacific Islander population refers to such groups as Native Hawaiian, Guamanian, and Fijian. Relative to within-group differences, Pacific Islanders differ in language and culture. They are of Polynesian, Micronesian, and Melanesian cultural backgrounds (U.S. Census, 2001, p. 2), with most being Polynesian (e.g., Native Hawaiian, Samoan), followed by Micronesian (e.g., Guamanian or Chamorro, Marshallese), and Melanesian (e.g., Fijian) (U.S. Census, 2001, p. 9).

Over three fourths of this group (76.3%) reside in the West. The remainder live in the South (12.8%), Midwest (5.6%), and Northeast (5.2%). Most of the Native Hawaiian and Other Pacific Islanders live in Hawaii and California (58%). More than 100,000 live in Honolulu, Long Beach, Los Angeles, San Diego, and New York.

---

3. How does my view of diversity and culture influence assessment, curriculum and instruction?
4. How can I become a culturally responsive or competent educator?

Teacher Diversity (or Lack Thereof). The data below presents findings from the Common Core of Data (CCD) "State Nonfiscal Survey of Public Elementary/Secondary Education: School Year 2001–02." Data for this annual NCES (National Center for Education Statistics) survey are collected directly from state education agencies and include the total number of students, teachers, and graduates in the United States. Data from the 2001–2002 CCD survey provide answers to many questions about public elementary and secondary education, including the following:

- How many students were enrolled in public elementary and secondary schools?
- What was the racial/ethnic background of students enrolled in public schools?
- How many teachers worked in public elementary and secondary schools?

- How many and what kinds of staff worked in public elementary and secondary schools?
- How many students graduated from public high school during the previous school year?
- How many students were educated in the Department of Defense (DoD), Bureau of Indian Affairs (BIA), and outlying area schools? (Data on DoD, BIA, and outlying area schools are discussed separately. These data are not included in national totals.)

About 3.0 million full-time-equivalent teachers provided instruction in public elementary and secondary schools in the 2001–2002 school year. Among this group, 56.3% (1.7 million) were elementary school teachers (including prekindergarten and kindergarten teachers), 36.0% (1.1 million) were secondary school teachers, and 7.8% (232,654) were teachers who taught ungraded classes or were not assigned a specific grade (Figure 1–2). Eight states had over 100,000 teachers (California, Florida, Illinois, New Jersey, New York, Ohio, Pennsylvania, and Texas). Two of these, California and Texas, had over a quarter million teachers each.

While there was an 11.5% increase in students between the 1991–1992 and 2001–2002 school years, there was a 21.2% increase in the number of teachers during this period. As with the number of students, Nevada also had the largest percentage increase in the number of teachers (69.0%). Only the District of Columbia and one state had a decrease in the number of teachers between these two school years, the number of teachers declining by 22.0% in the District of Columbia and by 4.1% in West Virginia.

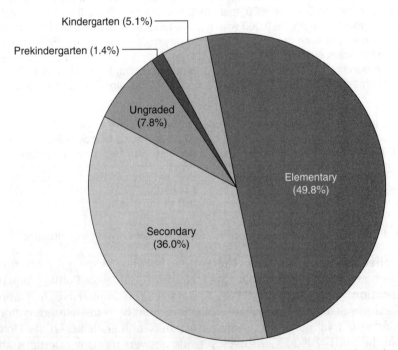

FIGURE 1–2 Percentage of public elementary and secondary teachers, by level of instruction: School year 2001–2002

Note: Detail may not sum to total because of rounding.

Source: U.S. Department of Education, National Center for Education Statistics, Common Core of Data (CCD), "State Nonfiscal Survey of Public Elementary/Secondary Education," 2001–2002.

Despite the increasing racial and cultural diversity in the pupil population, the typical classroom teacher is a European American female.

The typical teacher in the public school system is a European American female of middle-class status, making up between 87 to 90% of the workforce. During the 1990s, African American students accounted for 16% of public school enrollment, while the percentage of African American teachers stood at half that, with 8% (National Center for Education Statistics, 1996). As of 2001, teachers were predominantly European American (90%), with only 6% of teachers being African American and 5% being Hispanic or other (National Education Association, 2003, p. 8).

Pupil Diversity *How many students were enrolled in public elementary and secondary schools?* In the 2001–2002 school year, there were 47.7 million students enrolled in public elementary and secondary schools in the 50 states and the District of Columbia. Of these students, 26.3 million (55.2%) were in prekindergarten through Grade 6, an additional 20.9 million (43.9%) were in Grades 7 through 12, and the remaining 0.6 million (1%) were ungraded students. Not including prekindergarten or ungraded classes, Grade 9 had the most students and Grade 12 had the fewest. The 47.7 million students enrolled in the 2001–2002 school year represent an 11.5% increase in the number of students being served in the public elementary and secondary school system since the 1991–1992 school year.

What was the racial/ethnic background of students enrolled in public schools? In the 2001–2002 school year, racial/ethnic data were reported for 47.4 million of the 47.7 million students enrolled in public elementary and secondary schools in the 50 states and the District of Columbia. White, non-Hispanic students made up the majority of students (60.3%), followed by Black, non-Hispanic and Hispanic students (17.2 and 17.1%, respectively) (Figures 1–3 and 1–4). Asian/Pacific Islander students made up 4.2% and American Indian/Alaska Native students made up 1.2% of the public school population.

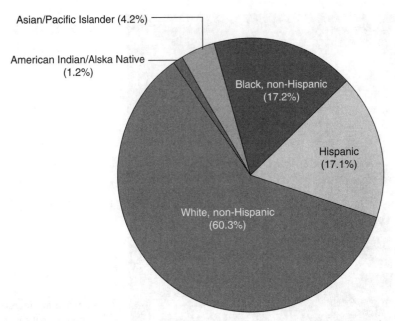

FIGURE 1-3 Percentage of public elementary and secondary students, by race/ethnicity: School year 2001–2002

Note: Detail may not sum to total because of rounding.

Source: U.S. Department of Education, National Center for Education Statistics, Common Core of Data (CCD), "State Nonfiscal Survey of Public Elementary/Secondary Education," 2001–2002; Young, B. (2002). Public school student, staff and graduate counts by state: School year 2001–02. *Education Statistics Quarterly, 5*(2), http://nces.ed.gov/programs/quarterly/vol_5/5_2/q3_4.asp, retrieved 5/29/2004.

In six states (California, Hawaii, Louisiana, Mississippi, New Mexico, and Texas) and the District of Columbia, 50% or more of students were non-White. Black, non-Hispanic students made up more than 50% of all students in the District of Columbia and Mississippi. New Mexico reported 51.0% of its students as Hispanic, and Hawaii reported 72.3% of its student body as Asian/Pacific Islander. No state reported a majority of its public school student body as American Indian/Alaska Native, but in Alaska 25.5% of students were designated as American Indian/Alaska Native. Four states (Maine, New Hampshire, Vermont, and West Virginia) reported that over 90% of their students were White, non-Hispanic.

Educational Implications: What Is Culture and Why Does It Matter?

Later in this book, we present data on the demographics of programs for exceptional learners, both special education students and gifted education students. In both fields, there is considerable debate about the over- and underrepresentation of CLDE students. In special education, the concerns center on the disproportionate representation or overrepresentation of diverse students; in gifted education, concerns center on the underrepresentation of diverse students. As we will argue later, one possible explanation for these discrepancies is that teachers who are ill-prepared to work with CLDE students are not likely to see their strengths. Thus, these teachers are more likely to refer CLDE students (particularly African American males) for special education services but less likely to refer them for gifted education services. This is particularly true for African American, Native American, and Hispanic American students. Both situations relate to teacher expectations for CLDE students, for in both instances, expectations are low or negative.

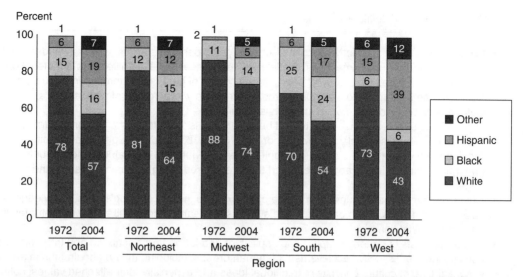

FIGURE 1-4 Minority enrollment: Percentage distribution of the race/ethnicity of public school students enrolled in kindergarten through 12th grade, by region: Fall 1972 and 2004

Note: Detail may not sum to totals because of rounding. Includes all public school students enrolled in kindergarten through 12th grade. Black includes African American and Hispanic includes Latino. Race categories exclude Hispanic origin unless specified. In 1994, the survey methodology for the Current Population Survey (CPS) was changed and weights were adjusted. In 2003, the categories for race changed on the CPS, allowing respondents to select more than one race. Respondents who selected more than one race were placed in the "other" category for the purposes of this analysis.

Source: U.S. Department of Commerce, Bureau of the Census, Current Population Survey (CPS), October 1972 and 2004 Supplements, previously unpublished tabulation (December 2004).

How Do We Define Culture?

The term *culture* originates from the Latin word *cultura* or *culturus*, as in "agri cultura," the cultivation of soil. Overtime, other meanings became attached to the word. From its root meaning of an "activity," *culture* came to mean a condition, a state of being cultivated (Freilich, 1989). There are many definitions of culture (See Figure 1–5) and the question "What is culture?" has intrigued scholars in various disciplines for decades. Because it contains both concrete and abstract components (Ting-Toomey, 1999; Ting-Toomey & Oertzel, 2001), culture is an enigma. The study of culture has ranged from a focus on architecture and landscape to the study of the implicit principles and values to which a group of members subscribe (Ting-Toomey & Oertzel, 2001).

Ting-Toomey (1999) defined culture as "a complex frame of reference that consists of patterns or traditions, beliefs, values, norms, and meanings that are shared in varying degrees by interacting members of a community" (p. 10). More specifically, D'Andrade (1984) offered the following definition:

> [Culture is] learned systems of meaning, communicated by means of nature language and other symbol systems... and capable of creating cultural entities and particular senses of reality. Through these systems of meaning, groups of people adapt to their environment and structure interpersonal activities.... Cultural meaning systems can be treated as a very large diverse pool of knowledge, or partially shared cluster of norms, or as intersubjectively shared, symbolically created realities (p. 116).

This definition of culture, and others, captures three points worth noting. First, culture refers to a diverse pool of knowledge, shared realities, and clustered norms that constitute

FIGURE 1-5 Sample definitions of the term *culture*

- Culture refers to the cumulative deposit of knowledge, experience, beliefs, values, attitudes, meanings, hierarchies, religion, notions of time, roles, spatial relations, concepts of the universe, and material objects and possessions acquired by a group of people in the course of generations through individual and group striving.
- Culture is the systems of knowledge shared by a relatively large group of people.
- Culture is communication, communication is culture.
- Culture in its broadest sense is cultivated behavior; that is the totality of a person's learned, accumulated experience, which is socially transmitted, or more briefly, behavior through social learning.
- A culture is a way of life of a group of people—the behaviors, beliefs, values, and symbols that they accept, generally without thinking about them, and that are passed along by communication and imitation from one generation to the next.
- Culture is symbolic communication. Some of its symbols include a group's skills, knowledge, attitudes, values, and motives. The meanings of the symbols are learned and deliberately perpetuated in a society through its institutions.
- Culture consists of patterns, explicit and implicit, of and for behavior acquired and transmitted by symbols, constituting the distinctive achievement of human groups, including their embodiments in artifacts; the essential core of culture consists of traditional ideas and especially their attached values; culture systems may, on the one hand, be considered as products of action, on the other hand, as conditioning influences upon further action.
- Culture is the sum total of the learned behaviors of a group of people that are generally considered to be the tradition of that people and are transmitted from generation to generation.
- Culture is a collective programming of the mind that distinguishes the members of one group or category of people from another.

Source: Web page for I.M. Choudhury. See http://www.tamu.edu/classes/cosc/choudhury/culture.html, retrieved January 24, 2007.

the learned systems of meanings in a particular society. Second, these learned systems of meanings are shared and transmitted through daily interactions among members of the cultural group and from one generation to the next. Third, culture facilitates the capacity of members to survive and adapt to their external environment (Ting-Toomey, 1999).

Hofstede (1991) is credited with creating the analogy "the body is the hardware and culture is the software." Just as a MacIntosh and an IBM are both computers and serve the same functions, but do so in different ways due to different software, so it is with different groups of people. All people eat and sleep—eating and sleeping are universal—but do so in different ways. Different groups eat different foods (pork vs. beef vs. no meat) for a variety of reasons (celebration, tradition, folklore) and in different ways (fork vs. chopsticks; utensils vs. hands). Further, traditions relative to the foods selected and their significance vary from group to group (e.g., on January 1, New Year's Eve or Day, some eat greens, which represent "money"; pork, which represents "health"; and black-eyed peas, which represent "luck"). All people cook or prepare food, but different groups use different ingredients. Some use herbs, others do not; some use lard, others dare not. All people sleep, but some groups have communal sleeping arrangements, and not every cultural group sleeps on a mattress. In short, the acts of eating and sleeping are universal, but they are influenced by culture.

Conceptually, culture can also be described by an iceberg analogy (see Figure 1-6). The part of the iceberg above the surface of the water represents cultural artifacts—music, fashion, and art, for example. The part below the surface is termed "invisible culture" or "deep culture"; deep culture includes traditions, beliefs, values, norms, and symbolic meanings. Deep culture, using the computer analogy, is the software.

Culturally shared traditions include myths, legends, ceremonies, and rituals (e.g., celebrating holidays in certain ways) that are passed on, verbally and nonverbally, from one

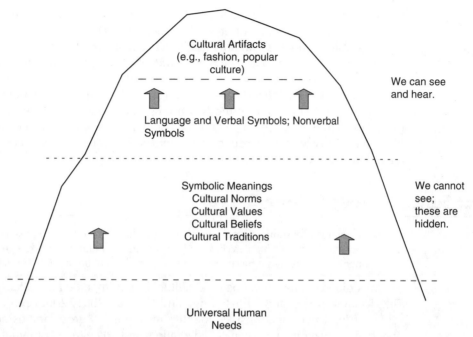

FIGURE 1-6 Culture as an iceberg
Source: Adapted from Ting-Toomey, 1999.

generation to another. *Culturally shared beliefs* are fundamental assumptions that people hold to closely and without question. These beliefs can encompass the concept of time, the meaning of life and death, and the meaning of space. They provide the explanatory logic for behavior and the goals to be desired and achieved in life. *Cultural values* are the set of priorities that guide such notions as good and bad, fair and unfair, and right and wrong. Cultural values also include views on individual competitiveness versus group harmony or collectiveness. *Cultural norms* are the collective expectations of what constitutes "proper" or "improper" behavior in a given situation and guide the scripts to be followed (e.g., how we greet someone; how we introduce ourselves; how we eat; how we show gratitude; how we discipline children; how we treat the elderly, etc.).

Scholars contend that our ignorance of different traditions, beliefs, values, and norms can produce unintentional clashes between people or groups with different traditions, beliefs, values, and norms or rules. We may not even notice that we have violated another culture's norms in a particular situation. The concept of two icebergs colliding illustrates this point. For example, a teacher may celebrate Christmas and offer a gift to a child who does not celebrate or believe in Christmas; a child may offer beef to a teacher who holds cows sacred, as do Hindus in India; a teacher may consider prearranged marriages to be "wrong" and share this opinion with a child whose family believes in the practice; a teacher may make the okay sign to a child who regards this sign as an insult; a teacher may go to a funeral wearing black when wearing black is unacceptable in the group's culture.

In a wonderfully enlightening book entitled *I Felt Like I Was from Another Planet* (Dresser, 1994), foreign students new to the United States undergo such cultural blunders or clashes. Their experiences of adjusting to a new culture, one that was very different from their indigenous culture, were what scholars refer to as *culture shock*, a term first coined by Oberg (1960). We will return to this discussion later.

According to Storti (1989), Americans who travel to another country and, thus, to another culture often experience culture shock, which is defined as severe, sometimes traumatic, difficulty in adjusting to another culture, that occurs when individuals are away from their native environment and are immersed in another environment. Although the notion of culture shock is primarily used relative to international encounters, it can also be applied to intranational ones, such as a student encountering another student or teacher whose values, traditions, and norms conflict with his own due to age differences, economic differences, regional differences, language differences, gender differences, or some other factor. A child reared in the North might have difficulty understanding the Gullah dialect of a child from certain parts of the South, for example. A teacher from a high socioeconomic status (SES) background might hold work-ethic values that conflict with those of a child from a low SES background.

What Function Does Culture Serve?

> Behavior does not somehow carry its meaning within it; meaning is imposed upon it (or not) by those who observe it.... What is a behavior in one culture, such as a gesture, is in fact not behavior—because it has no meaning—in another culture. (Storti, 1999, pp. 10, 11)

In addition to understanding what culture is, it is important to understand its functions. Ting-Toomey (1999) and Ting-Toomey and Oertzel (2001, 2006) proposed that culture serves at least five functions: (1) identity meaning; (2) group inclusion; (3) intergroup boundary regulation; (4) ecological adaptation; and (5) cultural communication.

Identity meaning function. Culture provides the frame of reference for answering the most fundamental question of each human being: Who am I? Stated another way, cultural beliefs, norms, and values provide the anchoring points by which we attribute meanings and significance to our identities (Ting-Toomey, 1999; Ting-Toomey & Oertzel, 2006). For example, several studies have demonstrated that middle-class European Americans frequently value individual initiative and achievement. Competent or successful people are those who take personal initiative to realize their potential. In particular, those who realize their dreams despite difficult circumstances are admired and considered successful. But these individualistic values may not be shared by other cultures, which instead may value cooperation and believe in a "we-us-our" philosophy that places a high premium on group cohesion and collective strivings.

Group inclusion function. Culture serves the group inclusion function of satisfying one's need for membership affiliation and belonging. Thus, culture creates a comfort zone in which people experience in-group inclusion and in-group/out-group differences. Within our own group, we experience safety, inclusion, and acceptance. We tend to speak the same language, share similar values, and are able to read the nonverbal moods and cues of others in our group. Conversely, when interacting with members from other groups, we have to defend, justify and/or explain our actions; we have to be on the alert; we tend to "stand out," resulting in "us-them" conflicts.

Intergroup boundary regulation function. This function shapes our in-group and out-group attitudes when we deal with people who are culturally different. Culture helps us to form evaluative attitudes, which may be positive- or negative-valenced emotions, towards others who are in or out of our group. In other words, we tend to hold favorable attitudes towards those who are like us, resulting in a certain degree of ethnocentrism. Further, we tend to experience a range of emotions—frustration and bewilderment, for instance—when we are violated by the norms of others, such as being misunderstood and/or not accepted by others.

Ecological adaptation function. Culture is dynamic rather than static. People are also dynamic and change with different situations. This function, therefore, facilitates the adaptation process of the self to the cultural community and between the community and the larger environment. Referring to the iceberg analogy described earlier, surface-level cultural elements (e.g., fashion, music, art) change at a faster pace than deep-level cultural elements (e.g., values, beliefs, norms). Change is also based on the extent to which behaviors are compatible with a given cultural group. That is, groups reward behaviors that are compatible with their values, beliefs, and norms and sanction those that are not. The extent to which an individual seeks group approval will influence how and how much that person endeavors to change.

Cultural communication function. This function represents coordination between culture and communication. Culture affects communication and communication affects culture.

Having reviewed definitions as well as several proposed functions of culture, we present a more concrete discussion in the next section, where we present a model of culture with specific attention to its dimensions and sample scenarios to illustrate each point.

A Model of Culture: What Are Some Specific Dimensions of Culture?

> What's special about people from other cultures is not simply that they are different from you, but the *degree* to which they are different. (Storti, 1999, p. 2)

Several publications—Storti (1989, 1998, 1999), Ting-Toomey (1999), Hofstede (1980, 1991) Hofstede and Bond (1984), Hall (1959, 1981, Hall and Hall (1987), and Ting-Toomey and Oertzel (2001, 2006), among others—have presented research-based models and theories of culture. Because space limitations do not permit a detailed discussion of each model, we present a synthesis of these models here with a major focus on interpretations of Hofstede's extensive research in a practical guide by Storti (1999). This section presents five dimensions of culture: concept of self; personal versus social responsibility; concept of time; locus of control; and styles of communication. These dimensions, all having at least two extreme poles, are not to be interpreted as dichotomous; they are continuous. But for the sake of space and clarity, the following discussion and examples focus on the extreme or opposite orientations of each dimension. Behaviors can fall anywhere along the continuum, however, with some at the center of the continuum. (For an extensive discussion of research that summarizes where specific cultural groups fall along the continua, see Hofstede, 1980, 1991; Storti, 1998, 1999; Ting-Toomey, 1999; Ting-Toomey & Oertzel, 2001, 2006.) The following five dimensions are also not an exhaustive list of cultural dimensions; again, readers are referred to Hofstede, Storti, and Ting-Toomey.[1]

Concept of Self. People from different cultures have different notions of personal identity, spanning a wide range of alternatives, from collectivism at one end to individualism at the other.

- *Individualism.* At this end of the continuum, the smallest unit of survival is the individual. People who are primarily individualistic identify mostly with the self, and the needs of the individual are satisfied before those of the group. Looking after oneself,

---

[1]Other dimensions are management style (authoritarian vs. democratic); power distance orientations; attitude toward work (achievement vs. quality of life); key to productivity (results vs. harmony); source of power (achieved vs. ascribed), and more.

being self-sufficient, guarantees the well-being of the group. Independence and self-reliance are emphasized and valued, and personal freedom is highly desired.
- *Collectivist.* At this end, the primary group, often the immediate family, is the smallest unit of survival. One's identity is largely a function of one's membership and role in the group. The survival and success of the group ensures the well-being of the individual, so that in considering the needs and feelings of others, one protects oneself. Harmony and interdependence of group members are stressed and valued, and there is relatively little psychological or emotional distance between group members. This is a "we-us-our" orientation.

SCENARIO: What conflicts might ensue when Ms. Jones tends towards individualism, while Jerome tends towards collectivism? Ms. Jones is likely to value individual effort and independent work, while Jerome is likely to enjoy working in groups, helping others, and asking questions of classmates. When Ms. Jones posts students' grades, Jerome is uncomfortable. If he gets a high grade and his friend gets a low grade, Jerome is not pleased. He sometimes blames himself for not being more helpful to his friends.

Personal Versus Social Responsibility. People in every culture wrestle with how to balance personal responsibilities to family, close friends, and colleagues with responsibility to the larger society (including out-groups). We present two opposing poles, universalism and particularism.

- *Universalism.* At this end of the pole, people believe there are certain absolutes that apply, regardless of the circumstances or situation. What is right is always right, and rules should be applied to everyone in similar situations. Being fair means treating everyone alike and not making exceptions, even for family and friends. Personal feelings are laid aside in order to be objective in judging situations.
- *Particularism.* At this end, how one behaves in a given situation depends on the circumstances—what is right in one situation may not be right in another. Family and friends are treated the best and the rest of the world can take care of itself. The belief is that exceptions will always be made for certain groups and to be fair is to treat everyone as unique. Personal feelings should not be laid aside, but, rather, relied upon.

SCENARIO: Mr. Richards is no nonsense when it comes to rules; they are meant to be followed at all times. Therefore, students must follow his guidelines and requirements when writing assignments; students who deviate from the prescribed outline lose points. Tyrone dislikes such structure; he is not as linear in his thinking style and likes to play with ideas. He does not believe there is only one way to write a paper.

Concept of Time. Another way that cultures differ is how people conceive of and handle time and how their concept of time affects their interactions with each other. The two poles of this continuum are monochronic and polychronic orientations to time.

- *Monochronic.* At this end, time is viewed as a commodity; it is quantifiable and there is a limited amount of it. Therefore, people consider it essential to use time wisely and not waste it. A premium is placed on efficiency, as demonstrated by a sense of urgency that seems to loom over people. When one is monochronic, time is the independent variable; people are the dependent variable—people change and adjust to suit the demands of time; the amount of time does not change. Accordingly, efficiency

means doing one thing at a time and doing it well and interruptions are considered a nuisance.
- *Polychronic.* Time is limitless and not quantifiable when one's orientation is polychronic. There is always more time, and people are never too busy. Time is the servant and tool of people, and it is adjusted to suit the needs of people. Schedules and deadlines often get changed, and people may have to do more than one thing at a time—a sign of being efficient, maximizing time, and using time wisely. It is not necessary to finish one thing before moving on to something else. There is no such thing as an interruption.

SCENARIO: Mr. Ogbu (who prefers to be called Brother Ogbu) loves being around people; he spends each morning talking to students in an attempt to set a positive tone for the day. And he is often late for meetings, as he spends time greeting all students in the hallway. To Mark, Mr. Ogbu is wasting time. When the bell rings, Mr. Ogbu needs to start the lesson immediately, and he should never be late or miss appointments. His job is to teach, not waste time socializing.

Locus of Control. Cultural groups differ in the degree to which they view their place vis-à-vis the external world, particularly relative to the degree to which they believe that human beings can control or manipulate their own destiny. Two poles, internal and external, are described next.

- *Internal.* The locus of control here is primarily internal, meaning within the individual. People at this end of the continuum believe there are few givens in life, that few things or circumstances have to be accepted as they are and cannot be changed. They believe that there are no limits to what they can do or become, if they set their minds to it and take the steps necessary to achieve goals. Life is what you do, which represents an activist orientation. (You make your own luck. Where there's a will, there's a way. Every problem has a solution.)
- *External.* This locus of control is largely external, outside of the individual. Some things in life are predetermined. Individuals thus believe there are limits beyond which one cannot go, and there are certain givens that cannot be changed and must be accepted. One's success is a combination of one's effort and good fortune. Life is part of what happens to you, which represents a more fatalistic orientation. (That's the way things are. Unhappiness is a part of life.)

SCENARIO: Mrs. Lightfoot enjoys teaching, believing she is blessed to be in this profession. This was her destiny. So when students are difficult (e.g., resist learning), she does not give up on them. Mr. Melvin respects the hard work involved in teaching, but he has other plans. Although he enjoys helping others, he will be more prosperous economically if he majors in engineering. Why settle for hard work and little pay when you can work hard and earn lots of money?

Styles of Communication. Communication is the sending and receiving of messages. What people say, how they say it, and what they don't say are all deeply affected by culture (Storti, 1999). As described next, the dimension on which people differ the most is that of directness in communicating. The differences between the two poles of directness and indirectness account for more cross-cultural misunderstandings than any other single factor (Storti, 1999, p. 91). In addition to directness, communication styles fall along a continuum between high and low context.

- *Indirect.* Groups in the indirect cultures tend to infer, suggest, and imply rather than say things directly. There is a tendency toward indirectness and away from confrontation. In-group members have an intuitive understanding of each other. (People tell you what they think you want to hear; you may have to read between the lines to grasp what someone is saying.)
- *High-context.* Context cultures involve intuitive understanding. In high-context cultures, words are not needed or necessary to convey messages; nonverbal communication is often enough. (What you do is just as important or more important than what you say.) People are sensitive to the setting or environment and are watchful of the behaviors of others. (Actions speak louder than words.) Personal space, touching, eye contact, affect, tone when speaking, and other nonverbal cues receive much attention because they help to communicate messages. Researchers have found that high-context cultures tend to be collectivist, as described earlier.
- *Direct.* Direct cultures tend to be more individualist. People need to spell things out, that is, people need to be explicit in communicating their desires, likes, dislikes, and feelings. People say exactly what they mean rather than suggest or imply. Thus, the spoken word carries most of the meaning. (*Yes* means "yes," *no* means "no." You should not read anything into what is not said or done.)
- *Low-context.* In low-context cultures, the primary mode of communication is verbal. Contextual cues, unique situations, and special circumstances are less likely to be noticed because of the reliance on what is said rather than what is done.

SCENARIO: Mr. Livingston is very direct in giving students feedback on assignments. And if they don't like the assignment or textbook, they need to say so. If students don't understand what has been taught, they should ask questions. Lei holds Mr. Livingston and teachers in reverence. If she does not understand the lesson, it is her fault. To ask him a question would suggest that he is not a good teacher. She asks few questions and does not admit when she is confused. ("No" can mean "yes.")

How Do I Become a Culturally Responsive Educator?

In order for teachers to provide an effective multicultural curriculum for culturally and linguistically diverse (CLDE) students, it is necessary for them to become culturally competent. Such scholars as Geneva Gay, Gloria Ladson-Billings, Jacqueline Irvine, Sonia Nieto, Barbara Shade, Linda Darling-Hammond, and others have provided detailed information and readings on culturally competent teachers.

Becoming culturally competent requires teachers to demonstrate knowledge of the history of students of color, societal racism, language, affirmation of minority students, multicultural education, and the role of community and family (Banks, 2006; Darling-Hammond, 2006; Darling-Hammond & Bransford, 2005; Gay, 2002, 2003; Hale, 2001; Howard, 2006; Irvine, 2003; Irvine & Armento, 2001; Ladson-Billings,1997, 2001, 2005a, 2005b; Spradlin & Parsons, 2008; Villegas & Lucas, 2002). Culturally competent teachers possess self-awareness and self-understanding, cultural awareness and understanding, and social responsiveness and responsibility and are able to provide appropriate teaching techniques and strategies. They recognize the differences between their students and themselves and strive to become nonjudgmental (e.g., Ford, 2005; Ford & Harris, 1999; Ford & Milner, 2005; Howard, 2006; Ladson-Billings, 2005b).

Anne Vega/Merrill

Differences in communication styles is one means for distinguishing cultural groups.

Culturally competent teachers develop meaningful relationships with their students of color (Gay, 2000, 2002; Ladson-Billings, 1997, 2005a; Villegas & Lucas, 2002). They demonstrate social responsiveness and responsibility by increasing racial harmony within their classrooms, decreasing the negative beliefs and attitudes of European American students toward minority students, and demanding respect for individual differences (Ford, 2005; Ford & Milner, 2005). Education teachers who are culturally competent recognize institutional barriers that prevent students of color from obtaining an equal education. They have an understanding of how the traditional practices of education often conflict with the values of these students. These teachers engage students by providing a multicultural curriculum utilizing culturally congruent teaching methods to help students to understand concepts and content (Banks, 2006; Darling-Hammond, 2006; Gay, 2000, 2002, 2003; Harmon, 2002; Irvine, 2003; Ladson-Billings, 2005a, 2005b).

Figure 1–7, which is based on the work of Storti (1999), presents one model of cultural competence for consideration. His four levels range from a complete lack of cultural awareness and competence (level 1, blissful ignorance) to unconscious, somewhat natural skills in negotiating different cultures (level 4, spontaneous sensitivity). After reviewing the model, determine at what level you are in terms of each of the major racial and ethnic groups. What are the benefits and disadvantages of staying at your current level(s) with each group? Which racial or ethnic group(s) do you feel most competent with? Which group(s) gives you the most challenges? What can you do to become more culturally competent with each major group? As we have just described, becoming a culturally responsive educator is an ongoing process. It is a conscious and deliberate decision that takes much effort and practice. It is also the first step in creating culturally responsive classrooms.

> Each of us is like everybody else in some ways (universal behaviors), like the people in our culture (cultural behaviors), and like no one else at all (personal behaviors). Storti (1999, p. 16)

Some educators are uncomfortable when labels are used to characterize groups or behaviors. Some of us have been conditioned or encouraged to be "culture-blind," as

FIGURE 1-7 A model of cultural competence: Levels/stages of cultural awareness

	Incompetence	Competence
Unconscious	**Blissful Ignorance** **Level 1** You are not aware that cultural differences exist between you and another person. It does not occur to you that you may be making cultural mistakes or that you may be misinterpreting much of the behavior going on around you.	**Spontaneous Sensitivity** **Level 4** You no longer have to think about what you are doing in order to be culturally sensitive (in a culture you know well). Culturally appropriate behavior comes naturally to you, and you trust your intuition because it has been reconditioned by what you know about cross-cultural interactions.
Conscious	**Troubling Ignorance** **Level 2** You realize that there are cultural differences between you and another person, but you understand very little about these differences. You know there's a problem, but don't know the magnitude of it. You are worried about whether you'll ever figure out these differences in others.	**Deliberate Sensitivity** **Level 3** You know there are cultural differences between people, you know some of the differences, and you try to modify your own behavior to be sensitive to these differences. This does not come naturally, but you make a conscious effort to behave in culturally sensitive ways. You are in the process of replacing old intuitions with new ones.

Source: Adapted from Storti (1998).

reflected in the statement "I don't see differences, all people are the same." In terms of labeling, even the words *intelligent* and *gifted* are controversial, both within the field of gifted education and outside it. Some educators feel that labels strip individuals of their personal, unique identity. We argue that labeling to the extreme can indeed result in all-or-nothing thinking, such as the belief that all Black students have a polychronic conception of time or that all Koreans are indirect when communicating their ideas. Such all-or-nothing thinking goes beyond labeling and results in stereotyping, defined as inflexible beliefs—beliefs about groups that are resistant to change, even when data contradict the beliefs (Hewstone, 1989).

We have, therefore, avoided summarizing research on group differences along the five dimensions described in this chapter. However, hundreds of studies have examined group differences along these cultural dimensions and reported consistent group patterns relative to the concept of time, concept of self, locus of control, and so forth. These patterns help us to make generalizations, but our generalizations must be flexible. What do we mean by the label or concept "gifted"? What do we mean when we describe a child as "intelligent" or "retarded" or "behavior disordered"? Certain characteristics, certain generalizations, come to mind when these terms are applied to a person. For instance, an intelligent child may be one who is a logical thinker, an abstract thinker, and a problem solver; a creative child may be original, expressive, and like playing with ideas. And so it is with cultural differences, as presented in the aforementioned scenarios. All people share universal needs, such as the need for food, water, safety, and shelter. But some groups eat, sleep, and live in dwellings in ways that are different from those of others. These group differences, whatever they are, must not be ignored, negated, minimized, or trivialized by educators. That is to say, acknowledging group differences is acknowledging cultural differences. For the sake of our nation's increasingly diverse student population, educators must seek to become culturally aware, knowledgeable, sensitive, and competent.

Summary

Achieving competence in any area, discipline, or field is a lifelong endeavor, one that takes time, patience, determination, and commitment. Becoming a culturally competent educator is no exception. As we work with CLDE students, it is important to remember that our schools are very diverse and becoming more so every day. Diversity is here to stay. It is, therefore, important for educators to avoid attempting to be color-blind; they must recognize cultural diversity in all its manifestations and attempt to understand, appreciate, and work with those who come from different cultures. Despite the extensive diversity that exists in our nation and our schools, some educators do not appreciate those who are different. When we resist or in any way refuse to become culturally competent, we run the risk of neglecting our responsibility to those entrusted to our care. It is important to understand that CLDE students benefit when their teachers appreciate, understand, and respect them. Just as important, teachers must recognize how they, too, benefit from being culturally aware, sensitive, respectful, and competent.

Activity: If the World Were a Village...

1. Collect data on the current demographics of your local school district. Focus on race and ethnicity, language, socioeconomic level (e.g., free and reduced lunch), and so on.
   a. Collect data on the demographics of your local school district from 10 years ago. How has the school district changed? If changes continue, how diverse might the school district be 10 years from now?
   b. Interview a school administrator or educator. How have they responded to these demographic changes in terms of policies and curriculum, for example?
   c. Recommend some ways that the district might respond to these changes in order to meet students' needs.

OR

2. Visit the school district from which you graduated.
   a. What are the current demographics?
   b. How is this different from the year in which you graduated?
   c. What changes, if any, do you predict for the school in the next 10 years?
   d. Interview a school administrator or educator. How have they responded to these changes?
   e. Recommend some ways that the district might respond to these changes in order to meet students' needs.

References

Baldwin, A. Y. & Vialle, W. (1999). *The many faces of giftedness: Lifting the masks.* Belmont, CA: Wadsworth.

Banks, J. A. (2006). *Cultural diversity and education: Foundations, curriculum and teaching.* Boston: Allyn & Bacon.

Castellano, J. A. (2003). *Special populations in gifted education: Working with diverse gifted learners.* Boston: Allyn & Bacon.

Culture. Retrieved January 24, 2007 from http://www.tamu.edu/classes/cosc/choudhury/culture.html

D'Andrade, R. (1984). Cultural meaning systems. In R. Shweder & R. LeVine (Eds.), *Culture theory: Essays on mind, self, and emotion,* 89–119. Cambridge, UK: Cambridge University Press.

Darling-Hammond, L. (2006). *Powerful teacher education.* New York: Jossey-Bass.

Darling-Hammond, L. & Bransford, J. (Eds.). (2005). *Preparing teachers for a changing world: What teachers should learn and be able to do.* New York: Jossey-Bass.

Dresser, N. (1994). *I felt like I was from another planet: Writings from personal experience.* New York: Addison-Wesley.

Ford, D. Y. (1998). The under-representation of minority students in gifted education: Problems and promises in recruitment and retention. *The Journal of Special Education, 32*(1), 4–14.

Ford, D. Y. (2005). Welcoming all students to room 202: Creating culturally responsive classrooms. *Gifted Child Today, 28,* 28–30, 65.

Ford, D. Y. & Harris J. J., III. (1999). *Multicultural gifted education.* New York: Teachers College Press.

Ford, D. Y., Harris J. J., III, Tyson, C. A., & Frazier Trotman, M. (2002). Beyond deficit thinking: Providing access for gifted African American students. *Roeper Review, 24*(2), 52–58.

Ford, D. Y. & Milner, H. R. (2005). *Teaching culturally diverse gifted students.* Waco, TX: Prufrock Press.

Ford, D. Y., Moore J. L., III, & Milner, H. R. (2005). Beyond cultureblindness: A model of culture with implications for gifted education. *Roeper Review, 27*(2), 97–103.

Frasier, M. M., Hunsaker, S. L., Lee, J., Mitchell, S., Cramond, B., Krisel, S., Garcia, J. H., Martin, D., Frank, E., & Finley, V. S. (1995a). *Core attributes of giftedness: A foundation for recognizing the gifted potential of minority and economically disadvantaged students.* Storrs, CT: The National Research Center on the Gifted and Talented, The University of Connecticut.

Frasier, M. M., Hunsaker, S. L., Lee, J., Finley, V. S., Garcia, J. H., Martin, D., & Frank, E. (1995b). *An exploratory study of the effectiveness of the staff development model and the research-based assessment plan in improving the identification of gifted economically disadvantaged students.* Storrs, CT: The National Research Center on the Gifted and Talented, The University of Connecticut.

Frasier, M. M., Hunsaker, S. L., Lee, J., Finley, V. S., Frank, E., Garcia, J. H., & Martin, D. (1995c). *Educators' perceptions of barriers to the identification of gifted children from economically disadvantaged and limited English proficient backgrounds.* Storrs, CT: The National Research Center on the Gifted and Talented, The University of Connecticut.

Frasier, M. M., Garcia, J. H., & Passow, A. H. (1995). *A review of assessment issues in gifted education and their implications for identifying gifted minority students.* Storrs, CT: The National Research Center on the Gifted and Talented, The University of Connecticut.

Frasier, M. M., Martin, D., Garcia, J., Finley, V. S., Frank, E., Krisel, S. & King, L. L. (1995). *A new window for looking at gifted children.* Storrs, CT: The National Research Center on the Gifted and Talented, The University of Connecticut.

Freilich, M. (1989). Introduction: Is culture still relevant? In M. Freilich (Ed.), *The relevance of culture.* New York: Morgan & Garvey.

Gay, G. (2000). *Culturally responsive teaching: Theory, research, and practice.* New York: Teachers College Press.

Gay, G. (2002). Culturally responsive teaching in special education for ethnically diverse students: Setting the stage. *International Journal of Qualitative Studies in Education, 15*(6), 613–629.

Gay, G. (Ed.). (2003). *Becoming multicultural educators: Personal journey toward professional agency.* San Francisco, CA: Jossey-Bass.

Hale, J. (2001). *Learning While Black: Creating Educational Excellence for African American Children.* Baltimore: The Johns Hopkins University Press, 256 pages.

Hall, E. T. (1959). *The silent language.* New York: Doubleday.

Hall, E. T. (1981). *Beyond culture* (2nd ed.). Garden City, NY: Anchor Press/Doubleday.

Hall, E. T., & Hall, M. (1987). *Hidden differences: Doing business with the Japanese.* Garden City, NY: Anchor Press/Doubleday.

Harmon, D. (2002). They won't teach me: The voices of gifted African American inner-city students. *Roeper Review, 24*(2), 68–75.

Hewstone, M. (1989). Changing stereotypes with disconfirming information. In D. Bar-Tal, C. Graumann, A. Kruglanski, & W. Stroebe (Eds.), *Stereotyping and prejudice: Changing conceptions.* New York: Springer Verlag.

Hofstede, G. (1980). *Culture's consequences: International differences in work-related values.* Beverly Hills, CA: Sage.

Hofstede, G. (1991). *Cultures and organizations: Software of the mind.* London: McGraw-Hill.

Hofstede, G., & Bond, M. (1984). Hofstede's culture dimensions. *Journal of Cross-Cultural Psychology, 15,* 417–433.

Howard, G. R. (2006). *We can't teach what we don't know: White teachers, multiracial schools.* New York: Teachers College Press.

Irvine, J. J. (2003). *Educating teachers for a diverse society: Seeing with the cultural eye.* New York: Teachers College Press.

Irvine, J. J., & Armento, B. (2001). (Eds.). *Culturally responsive teaching: Lesson planning for elementary and middle grades.* Boston: McGraw-Hill.

Ladson-Billings, G. J. (1997). *The dreamkeepers: Successful teachers of African-American children.* San Francisco, CA: Jossey-Bass.

Ladson-Billings, G. J. (2001). *Crossing over to Canaan: The journey of new teachers in diverse classrooms.* San Francisco, CA: Jossey-Bass.

Ladson-Billings, G. J. (2005a). Is the team all right? Diversity and teacher education. *Journal of Teacher Education, 56*(2), 229–234.

Ladson-Billings, G. J. (2005b). *Beyond the big house: African American educators on teacher education.* New York: Teacher College Press.

National Education Association. (2003, August). *Status of the American Public School Teacher 2000–01.* Washington, DC: Author.

Oberg, K. (1960). Culture shock and the problems of adjustment to new cultural environments. *Practical Anthropology, 7,* 170–179.

Office of Management and Budget (1997), "Recommendations form the Interagency Committee for the Review of the Racial and Ethnic Standards to the Office of Management and Budget Concerning Changes to the Standards for the Classification of Federal Data on Race and Ethnicity, Notice," *Federal Register,* Vol. 62, No. 131, 36844–36946.

Smith, D. J. (2002). If the world were a village: A book about the world's people. Toronto, Canada: Kids Can Press, LTD.

Spradlin, L. K., & Parsons R. D. (2008). *Diversity matters: Understanding diversity in schools.* Belmont, CA: Thomson Wadsworth.

Storti, C. (1989). *The art of crossing cultures.* Yarmouth, ME: Intercultural Press.

Storti, C. (1998). *The art of crossing cultures* (2nd ed.). Yarmouth, ME: Intercultural Press.

Storti, C. (1999). *Figuring foreigners out: A practical guide.* Yarmouth, ME: Intercultural Press.

Ting-Toomey, S. (1999). *Communicating across cultures.* New York: Guilford Press.

Ting-Toomey, S., & Oertzel, J. G. (2001). *Managing intercultural conflict effectively.* Beverly Hills, CA: Sage.

Ting-Toomey, S., & Oertzel, J. G. (Eds.). (2006). *The Sage Handbook of conflict communication: Integrating theory, research, and practice.* Beverly Hills, CA: Sage.

U.S. Census Bureau. (2004). *Race and Hispanic origin in 2004.* Population profile of the United States: Dynamic version. Washington, DC: Author.

U.S. Department of Education. (1993). *National excellence: A case for developing America's talent.* Washington, DC: Author.

U.S. Department of Education. (1998). *Talent and diversity: The emerging world of Limited English Proficient students in gifted education.* Washington, DC: Author.

U.S. Department of Education, National Center for Education Statistics. (1996). *Findings from the Condition of Education 1996, No. 8, Preparation for Work,* NCES 97-373. Washington, DC: Author.

U.S. Department of Education, National Center for Education Statistics (2000). *School and staffing survey, 1999–2000 public school teacher questionnaire and public charter school teacher questionnaire.* Washington, DC: Author.

U.S. Department of Education, National Center for Education Statistics (2003). *Statistics and trends in the education of Blacks.* Washington, DC: Author.

Villegas, A. M., & Lucas, T. (2002). *Educating culturally responsive teachers: A coherent approach.* New York: SUNY Press.

Chapter 2

Understanding the Culturally and Linguistically Diverse Exceptional Learner

This chapter provides an overview of special education laws, the categories of exceptionality, and the unique challenges experienced by culturally and linguistically diverse learners with exceptionalities (CLDE). Special attention is given to the challenges that occur across exceptionalities for CLDE learners. After reading this chapter, the reader should be able to answer the following questions.

1. What is the critical legislation in special education for children with disabilities and their families?
2. What are high- and low-incidence disabilities?
3. Who is the culturally and linguistically diverse learner with exceptionalities?
4. Which special education categories have disproportionate numbers of CLDE learners?
5. What are some additional challenges for CLDE learners across the different exceptionalities?
6. Why is disproportionality a concern in special education?

Special Education and Diversity

The Individuals with Disabilities Education Improvement Act (IDEIA/IDEA 2004) mandates that all children are entitled to a "free and appropriate" education. Children who have disabilities come from every socioeconomic, cultural, and linguistic group within the United States. Accurately determining the educational needs of children and identifying the appropriate resources to meet those needs is a complex challenge for educators. IDEA mandates that children with disabilities receive special education services under designated categories, albeit many children do not always fit neatly into the designated categories. Although educational services are better determined by the child's needs than the category label, special education categories do serve important functions, such as allowing professionals to more easily communicate with each other and families about the meaningful differences in children's learning and behavior (Heward, 2006). Additionally, special education categories provide a vehicle by which resources can be allocated and monitored through the federal, state, and local education bureaucracies.

Special Education Law

The Supreme Court's decision in the *Brown v. the Board of Education of Topeka, Kansas* case (1954) set a legal standard that separate was not equal. By ruling that schools segregated by race were inherently unequal and therefore unconstitutional, the Court set off a chain of events that has dramatically reshaped the American education system. The success of minorities in achieving equal educational status in the eyes of the Court energized advocates for children with disabilities. Parents of children with disabilities used the legal and legislative systems to promote their struggle to ensure that children with disabilities were granted their right to a free and appropriate education.

One of the first legislative milestones was Section 504 of the Rehabilitation Act of 1973, which provides for specialized services to children with special needs. This law was quickly followed by passage of the Education of All Children Act in 1975 (later renamed Individuals with Disabilities Education Act—IDEA). Prior to this legislation, many schools provided minimal, if any, educational services for children with disabilities (Yell, Rogers, & Rogers, 1998). More recently, school systems have been under the mandate of No Child Left Behind (NCLB), which requires that school districts provide effective instruction for all children, including students with disabilities, and demonstrate the effects of the instruction through annual testing. This legislation notwithstanding, there is still much to be done to make this ideal a reality for *all* children, especially children with disabilities from diverse backgrounds.

Section 504 of Rehabilitation Act of 1973

Since the 1970s schools have been required to provide specialized education services to all children with disabilities. Section 504 of the Rehabilitation Act of 1973 (P.L. 93-112) requires that schools provide accommodations to children with special needs, including those with disabilities (see Figure 2-1). This is civil rights legislation designed to prevent discrimination

FIGURE 2-1 Section 504 of the Rehabilitation Act of 1973

Sometimes children with special needs do not qualify for special education services. What options are available for those children? The child may be eligible for a "504 Plan." Section 504 of the Rehabilitation Act of 1973 is a federal statute that protects individuals with disabilities from discrimination in programs that receive federal funds. All institutions and programs receiving federal funds, including public schools, public and private institutions, where students receive financial assistance (i.e., colleges and universities) fall under this law.

What is a 504 Plan?

It is an intervention plan specifically designed for a child with a disability who is experiencing difficulty in a regular education setting. A 504 Plan is a legal document but is not the same as an Individualized Education Program (IEP). The goal of the 504 Plan is to prevent discrimination based on a student's disability. An IEP is designed to provide a free, appropriate public education (FAPE) in the least restrictive environment. The child is provided accommodations using a 504 Plan (e.g., additional time on tests) so he or she can fully and fairly participate in classroom activities.

Who qualifies?

A 504 Plan is applied to a person "otherwise qualified" if the person is able to meet the requisite academic standards, with or without accommodations. The person must have a physical or cognitive impairment that limits one or more of the major life activities (i.e., self-care, walking, seeing, hearing, performing manual tasks, speaking, breathing, working, and learning). Children do not need to have the specific disability designation such as autism, specific learning disabilities, or serious emotional disturbances that are required for special education placement. There does however, need to be a documentation of the disability. Children with a health disability such as ADD, ADHD, or diabetes will usually need to have a physician's diagnosis.

Does every school district have 504 Plans?

Yes; because all public schools receive federal funds, they are subject to this law. Like special education services provided under the Individuals with Disabilities Act (IDEA), services provided under Section 504 of the Rehabilitation Act are at no cost to families.

What is the referral process for a 504 Plan?

A child can be referred by a parent, teacher, administrator, or self. For example, parents can contact their child's school principal or counselor, who will be able to tell you the specific procedures for making a referral. After a formal referral is made a meeting is usually set up involving you and your child's teachers, principal, counselors and other relevant support staff. If a need for a 504 Plan is determined, then the special accommodations for your child are agreed on and the document is signed.

What are accommodations?

Accommodations are tactics or tools designed to eliminate the disadvantage your child may be experiencing when participating in activities. For example, a child may need additional time on tests/quizzes due to cognitive processing difficulties.

Some possible accommodations are:

- Note taker during class
- Extra time to take quizzes and tests
- Assistive technology in regular classroom
- Additional transition time between classes
- Allowance for health-related absences
- Have tests/quizzes read out loud and/or respond orally
- Assignments sheets that are signed by teachers and parents
- Take tests/quizzes in a quiet area away from the classroom
- Extended time on written reports/essays/research papers

Where can I find additional information?

Further information about the 504 Plan is available on the EdLaw website, http://www.edlaw.net/publications/epubs.html, or through the ERIC Clearinghouse on Disabilities and Gifted Children at 1-800-328-0272.

Source: National Association for Education of African American Children with Learning Disabilities (2007). Section 504 Rehabilitation Act of 1973. Retrieved September 23, 2007 from http://www.charityadvantage.com/aacld/Sec504RehabActof1973.asp

against children with disabilities in school (i.e., general education classrooms), work, or the community.

An evaluation of a child with a disability is conducted usually using existing data such as school and/or medical records. Once it is agreed that a child could benefit from a 504 Plan, the team must determine the appropriate accommodations, which are to be designed to meet the unique needs of the child. For example, a child with an orthopedic disability might need to change classes at a different time than the rest of the students to avoid being pushed around in crowded hallways. A child with a learning disability who can read but requires more time to read may be given additional time on a test. Or a child with an emotional disability might be placed on a behavior contract that stipulates he or she must stay on task and complete assignments to a certain level in order to earn a designated reward.

Individuals with Disabilities Education Act

Congress passed the Education of All Handicapped Children Act (P.L. 94-142, later renamed Individuals with Disabilities Education Act—IDEA) in 1975. IDEA requires states to aggressively seek and provide appropriate educational services for children with disabilities and has dramatically changed how education is provided to them. The law has been reauthorized five times since 1975; however, the six guiding principles have not changed over the years (see Figure 2–2).

In 2004, the Individuals with Disabilities Education Improvement Act (IDEIA) was passed. IDEIA continues to guarantee special education services for children with disabilities. It also assures that parents can fully participate in educational decision making for their child, continues established federal guidelines for identification procedures, and confirms that education services are to be available at the public's expense. Key to IDEA/IDEIA is multifactored evaluation and the Individualized Education Program (IEP). The multifactored evaluation is used to determine if the child's unique educational needs require specialized services.

What Is Specified in the Early Childhood Legislation?

The Individuals with Disabilities Education Act (IDEA), when originally passed in 1975, authorized services for all children with disabilities, birth through 21 years. Priority was given to school-aged students without services and to individuals with severe disabilities in inappropriate placements. Services for preschool children were optional and available only in a few states where state and local authorities took the initiative to provide preschool programs (Umansky & Hooper, 1998). Congress passed a major amendment in 1986, P.L. 99-457, which not only continued services for 3- to 5-year-old preschool children with disabilities but also included services for infants and toddlers with or at risk for disabilities. School programs for 3- to 5-year-olds, however, did not become mandated for all states until the reauthorization of IDEA in 1991. This meant that 3- to 5-year-old children with disabilities would receive the same rights as school-age children (see Table 2–2). The 1991 reauthorization also increased funds to states and local school agencies for preschool programs under Section 619 of Part B of IDEA.

In the 2004 reauthorization of IDEA section on infants and toddlers with disabilities, Part C (formerly Part H in IDEA 1997), asserts the *urgent and substantial* need to provide services to this population. It particularly focuses on minimizing or reducing the impact of the disability, on empowering the family to utilize services, and on enhancing the ability of agencies to fully service all populations, particularly those from diverse backgrounds.

FIGURE 2–2 IDEA's six principles

Zero reject All children are entitled to an education, including those with disabilities. Public schools are required to educate all children regardless of the type of or severity of their disability. All school-age children with disabilities that meet the criteria for special education services must be provided appropriate educational services without cost to the family.

Nondiscriminatory assessment Educators must assess children for special education using unbiased, multifactored methods. Assessment measures cannot discriminate based on culture, race, or language. Children should be assessed in their native language. Further, a single assessment tool cannot be used to make the special education placement determination. Ortiz (2002) recommends that a comprehensive framework for nondiscriminatory assessment include the following steps:

1. Assess and evaluate the learning ecology.
2. Assess and evaluate language proficiency.
3. Assess and evaluate opportunity for learning.
4. Assess and evaluate educationally relevant cultural and linguistic factors.
5. Evaluate, revise, and retest hypotheses.
6. Determine the need for and language(s) of assessment.
7. Reduce bias in traditional testing practices.
8. Utilize authentic and alternative assessment procedures.
9. Evaluate and interpret all data within the context of the learning ecology.
10. Link assessment to intervention. (Ortiz, 2002, p. 1332)

Free, appropriate public education All children with disabilities are entitled to a public education at no expense to the family. An Individualized Education Program (IEP) must be developed for each child in special education to meet that child's unique characteristics.

Least restrictive environment Children with disabilities are to be educated with their typically developing peers to the greatest extent possible. Children with disabilities should be removed to separate classrooms or schools only when they are unable to receive an appropriate education in the general education classroom due to the nature and/or severity of the child's disability.

Due process Parents and children with disabilities are entitled to due process safeguards. Schools must obtain parental consent to begin initial assessment for special education placement. Parental consent must be obtained for placement decisions. Schools must make all education records for children with disabilities accessible to the parents. If parents of a child with a disability disagree with the assessment of their child, they can obtain an additional assessment at the school district's expense. Parents have the right to a due process hearing if they disagree with a placement evaluation, identification, or services or if they disagree with the school determination. If parents are successful in their due process or court case, they are entitled to attorney fees.

Parent participation Schools must actively seek out and collaborate with parents and students with disabilities to develop and implement education services.

Legislation for Infants and Toddlers. Services for infants and toddlers with disabilities or at risk for developmental delays are an important feature of P.L. 99-457. A notable difference for this age group is the increased role for families that includes not only collaboration with professionals but services to the whole family as part of the intervention plan. Smith, Gartin, Murdick, and Hilton (2006) observe that the plan focuses on the family and its ability to support itself as well as on the child with a disability. They suggest that the development of this plan should be preceded by (1) an assessment of the family's ability to provide and care for the child; (2) the identification of family routines that would provide learning experiences for the child; and (3) a functional assessment of the child's development relative to the family's goals, concerns, and priorities.

The Individualized Family Service Plan (IFSP) is similar to the IEP but differs in that it provides for a multidisciplinary assessment of the infant/toddler and the infant's/toddler's

---

IDEA 2004

Services for Infants and Toddlers with Disabilities

(1) Minimize developmental delay,

(2) Reduce special education costs by minimizing the need for special education services once these infants and toddlers reach school age,

(3) Maximize the potential for these individuals to live independently,

(4) Enhance families' abilities to meet the needs of their infants and toddlers with disabilities, and

(5) Enhance the capacity of state and local agencies and service providers to identify, evaluate, and meet the needs of all children, particularly minority, low-income, inner city, and rural children, and infants and toddlers in foster care (IDEA, 2004).

---

family. The IFSP is to be developed promptly after assessment, it is put in place with parental consent, it is reviewed regularly with the family at 6-month intervals or more frequently, if needed, and is evaluated yearly. If the parents do not consent to the entire plan, only the parts with parental approval are implemented.

No Child Left Behind

In 2001, Congress passed No Child Left Behind (NCLB) legislation. NCLB is the reauthorization by Congress of the Elementary and Secondary Education Act (ESEA 2002). The NCLB law requires states to measure the progress of all students, including those with disabilities, in important content areas (e.g., reading, math, science) each academic year. A school district may exempt a maximum of 5% of its students with disabilities and 5% of English as a Second Language (ESL) students from the annual testing, thereby requiring 95% of the students with disabilities and ESL students to participate in the assessment of the school district's performance in meeting the NCLB standards for academic achievement. This can place a disproportionate burden on urban school districts, which often have higher percentages of poor children, ESL students, and children with special needs—all factors that are associated with lower academic achievement.

NCLB encourages teachers to emphasize scientifically based instructional strategies in order to raise academic standards (U.S. Department of Education, 2003). However, there is ongoing debate about what constitutes empirically validated instructional strategies.

Special Education Services in General Education Classes

The previously noted special education legislation has attempted to protect children with special needs from discrimination in general education classrooms. The various reauthorizations of IDEA/IDEIA have mandated that children with disabilities be instructed in the least restrictive environment (LRE). Sometimes the terms *LRE* and *inclusion* are used interchangeably, but they do not have the same meaning. LRE refers to the instructional environment that is closest to (and includes) the general education classroom where the student with disabilities can receive an appropriate education. LRE is interpreted for each child based on the child's special needs. For example, James is a child with spina bifida; his LRE is the general education classroom with assistive technology. Clarinda, a teenager with a

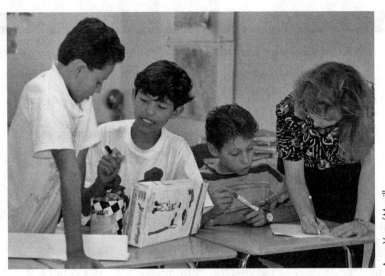
Explicit one-on-one instruction is often necessary to maximize academic gains.

learning disability, is in general education classes for math, social studies, and science but receives reading and language arts instruction in a special education resource room. Both settings are examples of LRE for these students.

Inclusion means educating all children with disabilities in their neighborhood schools in the general education classroom (Wood, 2006). In other words, inclusion means that students receive their specialized instruction with their nondisabled peers. It also means that students with disabilities in inclusive classrooms have access to the general education curriculum. Regardless of where students with disabilities are educated, teachers must provide special education services. Heward (2003) describes special education as "individually planned, specialized, intensive, and goal-directed instruction. When practiced most effectively and ethically, special education is also characterized by the use of research-based teaching methods, the application of which is guided by direct and frequent measures of student performance" (p. 38).

What Is Bilingual Education?

The U.S. Supreme Court decided in the *Lau v. Nichols* case of 1975 that appropriate education requires children to receive instruction in a language they can comprehend. In 1968, the U.S. Congress enacted P.L. 90-257, which supports the use of both the child's native language and English for instruction. The most recent revision of this law occurred with the passage of No Child Left Behind in 2001.

Educators have a special responsibility to promote an understanding of diversity since the schools are often one of the first places where children encounter persons who are from different cultural and linguistic backgrounds. As the number of children from culturally and linguistically diverse families increases (Santos, Corso, & Maude, 2006), teachers will need to be prepared for children whose first language is not English.

The development of language skills is usually uneven. Typically, children will develop the ability to converse in English much more quickly than they will develop the ability for academic learning in English (Moran & Hakuta, 1995). This phenomenon poses additional instructional obstacles for children who are nonnative speakers of English and/or at-risk for a disability. Teachers must not only instruct using empirically validated strategies, they should constantly probe the students to ensure that what has been presented has been accurately received by the children. How can teachers determine if their students who are English Language Learners (ELL) have accurately received what they have instructed? They must build into their instruction ongoing assessments to determine if their students have an accurate understanding of the content and that the students can use the information appropriately.

One ongoing concern is that ELLs are overrepresented in special education (Artiles & Ortiz, 2002; McCollin & O'Shea, 2006). Torrez-Guzman, Abbate, Brisk, and Minaya-Rowe (2002) found that ELL students in bilingual programs had significantly higher academic achievement than those not receiving bilingual education. Montecel and Cortez (2002) found that effective bilingual programs help decrease the achievement gap; a minimum of 4 years of bilingual education is recommended for maximum results (Baca & Cervantes, 2004). The increasing number of ELLs (especially Spanish-speaking students) in American schools requires that effective programs be in place to meet the needs of these students (Krashen & McField, 2005).

What Are the Special Placement Issues for the CLDE Learner?

Special education includes all students who need specialized instruction (i.e., children who have disabilities and/or who are gifted and talented). Under IDEA 2004 (P.L. 108-446), as in previous authorizations of the special education law, children with disabilities must be qualified and given a specific special education label to receive services. The exception is education for the gifted, which is not federally mandated. Students who are gifted and talented typically must be recommended and qualified for services based on school district and/or state standards.

The qualification process for IDEA requires a nondiscriminatory evaluation. Therefore, when a disability is suspected, the assessment process involves a multifactored evaluation, which means that children are assessed using various evaluation tools and strategies to accurately determine their abilities and minimize possible discriminatory factors inherent in any single assessment tool. For example, intelligence quotient (IQ) tests are the best single predictor of student academic success; however, as discussed in chapter 7 of this text and noted elsewhere (e.g., Heward, 2006; Venn, 2004), IQ tests can be culturally biased. Similarly, student work can be a valuable means of assessment, but the type of work requested by the teacher limits which skills the learner can demonstrate. Therefore, a more accurate picture of the student's abilities is most likely obtained through multiple assessments, including intelligence tests, standardized achievement tests, criterion-referenced measures, student products, parent interviews, and observations. The multifactored evaluation is an essential tool in accurately identifying children with disabilities, especially CLD learners. In addition to using multiple assessment measures, multiple evaluators should also be used, representing various professions. Thus, the assessment team might include parents, general educators, special educators, school psychologists, administrators, and other relevant professionals such as speech and hearing specialists, occupational and physical therapists, social workers, physicians, rehabilitation specialists, and so forth. The team analyzes the information and comes to a consensus about whether the student needs special education services.

One reason the multifactored evaluation is critical for students from culturally and linguistically diverse backgrounds is because of the mismatch that can exist between these learners and the culture of the schools they attend (Ishil-Jordan, 1997; Nieto, 2000). Educators need to carefully analyze the impact of cultural and linguistic incompatibilities that can exist between CLD learners and schools (Gollnick & Chinn, 2002; Hernandez, 2001). In assessing CLD learners for special education placement it is important to assess language proficiency, opportunities for learning, cultural factors (e.g., does the culture value group or individual achievement), and linguistic factors (e.g., what is the child's first language) and to judiciously interpret the assessment information in terms of the learning environment (Ortiz, 2002).

Once a student is determined to be qualified for special education services, that child is given an exceptionality label. The student then receives individualized education services as prescribed in the Individualized Education Plan (IEP). A student designated as gifted and talented receives advanced instruction.

What Are the Categories of Exceptionality and the Unique Issues for CLDE Learners?

Children with exceptionalities are assessed, given exceptionality labels, and provided specialized instruction. This text will use three general groupings of exceptionalities: high-incidence disability categories (i.e., specific learning disabilities, communication disabilities, behavior disorders, and mental retardation), low-incidence disability categories (i.e., sensory disabilities, physical disabilities, and autism), and gifted and talented. Each of these broad groupings provides unique challenges and opportunities for CLDE learners.

What Are High-Incidence Disabilities?

There is extensive debate concerning the overrepresentation/disproportionality of CLDE learners in the categories of high-incidence disabilities (Artiles & Zamora-Duran, 1997; Obiakor et al., 2002). There are two primary issues: (1) Are CLD children being accurately assessed for the existence of disabilities (Obiakor et al., 2002; Rueda, 1997; Skiba, Simmons, Ritter, Kohler, & Wu, 2003) and (2) are CLD children receiving an appropriate education (Skrtic, 2003).

What Is Disproportionality? African Americans, especially African American males, are given the special education label of behavior disorder/serious emotional disturbances or mild mental retardation at a much higher frequency than their percentage in the school-age population (Hosp & Reschly, 2004). Native Americans and Hispanics also have a higher frequency of special education placement in specific learning disabilities (Hosp & Reschly, 2004). Further, Finn (1982) found that the lack of bilingual programs in a school district increases the possibility that Hispanic children will be placed in special education programs. Twenty years after Finn's study, researchers analyzing California urban school, districts found elementary limited English Language Learners in English language immersion programs were three times more likely to be placed in a "resource specialist program" (Artiles, Rueda, Salazar, & Higareda, 2002). Krashen and McField's (2005) review of bilingual education research concluded that bilingual programs were important to the success of limited ELLs. There is also controversy about how Hispanic American students are assessed and placed in education programs, particularly programs that lack academic rigor (Executive Summary, 2006; Antrop-Gonzalez, Velez, & Garrett, 2004). Conversely, Asian Americans are underrepresented in high-incidence disability categories and overrepresented in gifted education (Patton, 1997).

With the exception of Asian American students, CLD children tend to perform less well on every academic measure (National Center for Educational Statistics, 2000).

Attributing these patterns solely to racial, language, gender, and/or religious differences would be a mistake and would imply inherent differences based on a single attribute. Further, the assessment and placement process for children in special education remains an inexact science (Utley & Obiakor, 2001). The fact is there is no clear explanation in the professional literature as to why these patterns occur along racial, gender, and linguistic lines. One common rationale is that CLD children are more likely to live in poverty (Proctor & Dalaker, 2002) and that it is poverty that places the children at higher risk for poor school outcomes. In other words, ethnicity can serve as a proxy for socioeconomic status. Hosp and Reschly (2004), however, wrote, "although economic and demographic variables share a degree of variability, they are not always interchangeable" (p. 187). Clearly, poverty does play an important role in school outcomes for children, but poverty alone does not explain the disproportionate representation of minorities in special education (see chapter 12 for a more extensive discussion on poverty). African and Native Americans were more likely to be identified with disabilities if they attended wealthier than poorer school districts (Executive Summary, 2006).

The fact is that disproportionality is a complicated multilayer issue involving not only the special education designation but also where education is provided and the quality of education. Parrish (2002) found significant variability across states in regard to the identification of Hispanic Americans as SLD. That is, Hispanic Americans in Pennsylvania were 43% more likely to be labeled SLD compared to European American students, but in Montana, Hispanic Americans were 71% less likely than European American students to receive the SLD label. In contrast, Hallahan et al. (2007), comparing learning disabilities data for 1984–85 through 2001–02 using coefficients of variation, found that SLD was the least variable of the special education categories from state to state (including low-incidence categories). They therefore concluded that using state-to-state variability data to criticize SLD placements is largely unfounded. Although Hallahan and colleagues did not analyze the data across ethnicity, their results do raise questions about how educators should look at the state-by-state data in special education.

Educators need to develop standard procedures for analyzing special education prevalence data before the issue of overrepresentation of minorities can be understood and addressed. As stated earlier, disproportionality is multifaceted and is at least partly dictated by where students are educated (i.e., low- or higher-income districts). Once identified, minorities (i.e., African, Hispanic, and Native Americans) are more likely to be educated in restrictive environments, that is, away from the general education classroom (Executive Summary, 2006). The shortage of special education teachers means that children in special education (especially in classrooms for the behaviorally disordered) are at increased risk of having teachers who are not fully certified (Billingsley, Fall, & Williams, 2006). Peske and Haycock (2006) state that poor and minority children tend to be disproportionately instructed by the less experienced, out-of-certification area, or uncertified teachers.

It is important that trends in unfavorable student outcomes not be ignored, for ignoring these trends of disproportionality and poor achievement would be to accept large failure rates for children based on ethnicity and/or poverty. The acceptance of failure is not prevalent in any other area of American life and should not be acceptable in education either. These trends warn us that what we are doing in schools is not working for many students and that changes need to be made, if the goal is really "to leave no child behind." Educators must seek pedagogy that will improve outcomes for children regardless of their cultural, linguistic, or socioeconomic background. If educators are to use the cultural diversity in schools to an advantage, then careful analysis and planning of how culture can be incorporated in classrooms is critical (Hallahan & Kauffman, 2000).

Specific Learning Disabilities. A specific learning disability (SLD) as defined under IDEA is a disorder in one or more of the basic psychological processes involved in understanding or in using language, spoken or written, which may manifest in an imperfect ability to listen, think, speak, read, write, spell, or do mathematical calculations. SLD is often thought to result from conditions that can impact academic achievement, such as perceptual disabilities, brain injury, minimal brain dysfunction, dyslexia, and developmental aphasia.

SLD is the largest category of special education; approximately 49% of children receiving services under IDEA are included in it, with boys substantially outnumbering girls (U.S. Department of Education, 2005). By definition, students with SLD have academic difficulties; the areas of greatest difficulty are, first, reading (Hallahan & Kauffman, 2000; Moats, 2000) followed by written language (Graham & Harris, 2005; Hessler, 2005) and math (Crawley, Parmar, Foley, Salmon, & Roy, 2001). Children with SLD are also at a higher risk for behavioral problems than their typical peers (Cullinan, 2002).

What are the special concerns for CLDE learners with SLD? As noted previously, SLD is the largest special education category, comprising nearly 50% of all the disabilities (see Table 2–1). As Table 2–1 shows, there is some evidence of disproportionality for Native and Hispanic American students. In their respective groups more than half (i.e., 56% and 58%) are diagnosed as SLD. Clearer evidence of disproportionality is revealed by the U.S. Department of Education (1999) data that shows Native American students making up 1.0% of the student population and Hispanic Americans 14.2% but these

TABLE 2–1 Disability distribution, by race/ethnicity, of students ages 6 through 21 served under IDEA: 2001

Disability	American Indian/ Alaska Native	Asian/ Pacific Islander	Black (non-Hispanic)	Hispanic	White (non-Hispanic)	All Students Served
Specific learning disabilities	56.0	42.1	45.4	58.9	48.1	49.2
Speech or language impairments	16.8	25.1	14.6	17.7	20.0	18.6
Mental retardation	8.2	9.4	17.4	8.1	8.6	10.3
Emotional disturbance	7.7	5.0	11.3	5.0	8.0	8.1
Multiple disabilities	2.3	2.7	2.1	2.0	2.2	2.2
Hearing impairments	1.1	3.0	1.0	1.6	1.1	1.2
Orthopedic impairments	0.8	1.8	0.9	1.3	1.4	1.3
Other health impairments	4.4	4.4	4.3	3.2	7.0	5.8
Visual impairments	0.4	0.8	0.4	0.5	0.4	0.4
Autism	0.8	4.1	1.4	1.1	1.8	1.7
Deaf-blindness	0.0	0.1	0.0	0.0	0.0	0.0
Traumatic brain injury	0.3	0.4	0.3	0.3	0.4	0.4
Developmental delay	1.2	1.0	0.9	0.4	0.8	0.8
All disabilities	100.0	100.0	100.0	100.0	100.0	100.0

U.S. Department of Education, Office of Special Education Programs, Data Analysis System (DANS), Table AA15 in vol. 2. Data are for the 50 states, D.C., Puerto Rico, and the outlying areas.

Source: U.S. Department of Education (2005) *25th Annual Report to Congress on the Implementation of the Individuals with Disabilities Education Act for 2003,* Office of Special Education and Rehabilitative Services, Vol. I, Washington DC: Author.

TABLE 2–2 Percentage of students ages 6 through 21 served by disability and race/ethnicity in the 1998–99 school year

Disability	American Indian	Asian/ Pacific Islander	Black (non-Hispanic)	Hispanic	White (non-Hispanic)
Specific learning Disabilities	1.4	1.4	18.3	15.8	63.0
Speech and language Impairments	1.2	2.4	16.5	11.6	68.3
Mental retardation	1.1	1.7	34.3	8.9	54.1
Emotional disturbance	1.1	1.0	26.4	9.8	61.6
Multiple disabilities	1.4	2.3	19.3	10.9	66.1
Hearing impairments	1.4	4.6	16.8	16.3	66.0
Orthopedic impairments	.8	3.0	14.6	14.4	67.2
Other health impairments	1.0	1.3	14.1	7.8	75.8
Visual impairments	1.3	3.0	14.8	11.4	69.5
Autism	.7	4.7	20.9	9.4	64.4
Deaf-blindness	1.8	11.3	11.5	12.1	63.3
Traumatic brain injury	1.6	2.3	15.9	10.0	70.2
Developmental delay	.5	1.1	33.7	4.0	60.8
All disabilities	1.3	1.7	20.2	13.2	63.6
Resident population	1.0	3.8	14.8	14.2	66.2

Source: U.S. Department of Education, Office of Special Education Programs, Data Analysis System (DANS).

groups disproportionately comprising 1.4% and 15.8%, respectively, of the SLD population. African Americans, who make up 14.8% of the school students and 18.3% of the SLD population, are also represented disproportionately in this category. See Table 2–2 for a breakdown across disability categories of the students served under IDEA.

Educators must be careful when assessing CLDE learners for learning disabilities and take into account linguistic and sociocultural factors. For some students, particularly English language learners, a language barrier might inhibit accurate assessment; educators need to assess whether the child has a learning disability in his or her first language (Ortiz, 2002). Ideally, the assessor would be both expert in educational assessment and fluent in the child's first language. Unfortunately, this dual expertise is rare, making the process complex. Some CLD learners come to school with significant language and cognitive skill deficits as a result of environmental factors. The preferred course of action under these conditions would be intensive instruction designed to ameliorate the deficits and eliminate or minimize the need for SLD services. But sociocultural factors compound the disabilities of CLDE learners. These students typically need even more resources and more specialized instruction than their non-CLD peers. Figure 2–3 lists some instructional resources across disability categories available on the internet.

Behavior Disorders. For years educators of children with behavior problems have been trying to reach a consensus on a definition of behavior disorders. Heward (2003) lists several reasons why it has been difficult to achieve a consensus:

- Disordered behavior is a social construct.
- Various theories use different concepts and terminology that do not promote a uniform meaning.

FIGURE 2-3 Resources

A guide to learning disabilities for the ESL classroom teacher, http://www.kyoto-su.ac.jp/information/tesl-ej/ej01/a.4.html

ADA home page: information and technical assistance on the Americans with Disabilities Act, http://www.usdoj.gov/crt/ada/adahom1.htm

ADD Resources, http://www.addresources.org/

On-line Asperger Syndrome and support, http://www.udel.edu/bkirby/asperger/

American Foundation for the Blind, http://www.afb.org/

American Sign Language Browser, Michigan State University, http://commtechlab.msu.edu/sites/aslweb/browser.htm

Asheville speech and language disorders, http://www.ashevillespeech.com/span.html

The Association for Persons with Severe Handicaps, http://tash.org/

The ARC (formerly, the Association of Retarded Citizens), http://www.thearc.org/info-mr.html

Autism resources, http://www.vaporia.com/autism/

The Brain Injury Association of America, http://www.biausa.org/Pages/splash.html

Center for Immigration Studies, http://www.cis.org/

CHADD: Children and Adults with Attention-Deficit/Hyperactivity Disorder, http://www.chadd.org/

Council for Children with Behavior Disorders http://www.ccbd.net/

DeafBlindInfo.org, http://www.deafblindinfo.org/

Hoagies' Gifted Education Page, http://www.hoagiesgifted.org/gifted_101.htm

Information on Disabilities and Gifted Children, http://ntidwell@aacld.org/

National Association for Gifted Children, http://www.nagc.org/

National Center on the Gifted and Talented, University of Connecticut, http://ntidwell@aacld.org/

National Association on Deafness and Other Communication Disorders, http://www.nidcd.nih.gov/

National Association for Educating African American Children with Disabilities, ntidwell@aacld.org

National Federation of the Blind, http://www.nfb.org/

Office of Special Education: Categorical Information (2006), Curry School of Education at the University of Virginia http://curry.edschool.virginia.edu/sped/projects/ose/categories/

The President's Committee on People with Intellectual Disabilities, http://www.acf.hhs.gov/programs/pcpid/index.html

United Cerebral Palsy, http://www.ucp.org/ U.S. Census 2000, http://www.census.gov/main/www/cen2000.html

---

- Expectations and norms differ across cultural and ethnic groups.
- Sometimes behavior disorders occur in conjunction with other disabilities.

Generally, the term *behavior disorders* refers to a pattern of behavior that is extreme, chronic, and unacceptable because of social and cultural expectations (IDEA, 2005). The federal law defines behavior disorders in the following manner:

(i) The term means a condition exhibiting one or more of the following characteristics over a long period of time and to a marked extent, which adversely affects educational performances;
 (A) An inability to learn that cannot be explained by intellectual, sensory, or health factors;
 (B) An inability to build or maintain satisfactory relationships with peers and teachers;
 (C) Inappropriate types of behavior or feelings under normal circumstances;

(D) A general pervasive mood of unhappiness or depression; or
(E) A tendency to develop physical symptoms or fears associated with personal or school problems.
(ii) The term includes children who are schizophrenic. The term does not include children who are socially maladjusted unless it is determined that they are emotionally disturbed (45 CFR 121a.5[b][8] [1978]).

This definition of behavior disorders has been controversial, mainly due to its exclusion of children who are socially maladjusted, a category interpreted as conduct disorders (Hallahan & Kauffman, 2000) and an exclusion opposed by the Council for Children with Behavior Disorders (CCBD). The controversy is partly reflected in the various terms used to label this category. *Emotionally disturbed* is the label currently used in the federal legislation, but many professionals in the field prefer to use *behaviorally disordered* (Kauffman, 2005). The category of emotional disturbance or behaviorally disordered makes up 8.1% of all disabilities (see Table 2–1). The estimates of school-age children with behavior disorders vary but conservatively at least 2% of students are in this category. The U.S. Department of Education reports 1% of students receive services within the category (Kauffman, 2005). Authorities like Kauffman argue that services should be extended to many more students than the current 1%.

It is not always possible to determine why students have behavior disorders. Some children come to school already exhibiting chronic behavior problems; others seem to develop problem behaviors during their school years. The behavior problems fall into two general classifications—internalizing (e.g., tending to isolate themselves, spending time daydreaming rather than interacting with peers, depression) and externalizing (e.g., disturbing class, arguing, fighting, lying, stealing, tantrums). Children who enter adolescence with a pattern of aggressive behavior are at increased risk for dropping out of school, delinquency, and using drugs (Lipsey & Derzon, 1998; Walker, Colvin, & Ramsey 1995).

What are the special concerns for CLDE learners with behavior disorders? The percentage of African American students (11.3%) who received special education services under the behavior disorder label is considerably higher than that of any other ethnic group (see Table 2–1). From Table 2–2, it can be seen that African American students make up 14.8% of the student population but 26.4% of those within the category of emotional disturbance or behavior disorders. Since the behavior disorders category is heavily weighted toward males (Cullinan, 2002), the vast majority of African American students labeled BD are males. Boys tend to engage in externalizing behaviors, whereas girls are more prone to internalizing behaviors (Talbott & Thiede, 1999). Ishil-Jordan (1997) argues that one factor placing African American males at greater risk for the BD label is a cultural tendency to be more socially demonstrative. She goes on to indicate that Asian Americans are at a lower risk of BD placement due to their tendency toward internalizing behaviors. But the overrepresentation of African Americans categorized as behavior disordered has been a contentious issue among educators and other professionals (Artiles & Zamora-Duran, 1997).

One strategy for accurately identifying CLDE learners as BD is to have persons familiar with the child's culture participate in assessing and interpreting the child's behavior within the environmental context (Ishil-Jordan, 1997). Not only is accurate identification an ongoing concern but also the quality of instruction. Some teachers emphasize behavior management at the expense of academic instruction, thereby negatively impacting academic achievement (Gardner & Miranda, 2001). CLDE learners with BD need both effective academic and social behavior interventions.

Mental Retardation. The American Association on Mental Retardation (AAMR) defines mental retardation in the following way:

> Mental retardation refers to substantial limitations in present functioning. It is characterized by significantly subaverage intellectual functioning, existing concurrently with related limitations in two or more of the following applicable adaptive skill areas: communication, self-care, home living, social skills, community use, self-direction, health and safety, functional academics, leisure, and work. Mental retardation manifests before the age of 18 (AAMR Ad Hoc Committee on Terminology and Classification, 1992, p 5).

Typically, individuals given the mental retardation label are further classified by the severity of their retardation. The subclassifications are primarily guided by the individual's IQ score or by the level of support the individual needs. For example, when classifying persons by IQ scores, the four categories are mild mental retardation (IQ 50–55 to 70), moderate mental retardation (35–40 to 50–55), severe mental retardation (20–25 to 35–40), and profound mental retardation (below 20–25) (Grossman, 1983). The majority of schools use the IQ classification to describe children with mental retardation. In 1992, the AAMR changed the classification system to one describing differences among persons with mental retardation based on the level of support required. The classifications are intermittent or as needed support, limited or consistent support for a limited time, extensive or consistent support in some settings, and pervasive or constant intensive support in multiple settings (see Table 2–3).

What are the special concerns for CLDE learners with mental retardation? Students receiving special education services under the mental retardation label make up about 10.3% of all children in special education. Among African Americans the category accounts for 17% of all disabilities (see Table 2–1). This is a higher proportion than for the other racial/ethnic groups. Table 2–2, for example, shows African Americans make up 34.3% of the mental retardation population, which is more than twice what would be expected according to their representation in the student population. It also means that African Americans are more than twice as likely to be labeled mentally retarded as European American students (National Research Council, 2002). This overrepresentation of African American children is of concern to educators and other professionals.

TABLE 2–3 Definition of level of support for persons with mental retardation

Intermittent	Supports on an "as needed basis." Characterized by episodic nature, person not always needing the support(s), or short-term supports needed during life-span transitions (e.g., job loss or an acute medical crisis). Intermittent supports may be high or low intensity when provided.
Limited	An intensity of supports characterized by consistency over time and time-limited but not of an intermittent nature, may require fewer staff members and less cost than more intense levels of support (e.g., time-limited employment training or transitional supports during the school-to-adult period).
Extensive	Supports characterized by regular involvement (e.g., daily) in at least some environments (such as work or home) and not time-limited (e.g., long-term support and long-term home living support).
Pervasive	Supports characterized by their constancy and high intensity provided across environments: potential life-sustaining nature. Pervasive supports typically involve more staff members and intrusiveness than do extensive or time-limited supports.

Source: From AAMR Ad Hoc Committee on Terminology and Classification, *Mental Retardation: Definition, classification, and Systems of Support*, 9th ed., 1992, p. 26), Washington, DC: Author.

The greatest number of children and the greatest percentage of African Americans are classified as mild mentally retarded, which is the classification system most schools prefer. The mild–moderate or severe–profound system primarily uses the IQ score as a basis for classification, but the relevancy of IQ tests for CLD learners has been much criticized (Hilliard, 1980; Rueda, 1997). Recommendations are that other types of assessments be included, such as portfolio assessments, when determining if children, especially CLD learners, should be labelled mentally retarded (Rueda, 1997). Concerns over the suitability of IQ tests are not limited to their use with African Americans. Venna (2004) recommends that the Binet and Weschler IQ tests in particular be avoided with children who have English as a second language because these two tests are highly verbal. The Binet and Weschler were mostly normed on middle-class European American children and thus tend to favor those children (Venna, 2004).

Looking further into the problem of the disproportionate number of African Americans categorized as mildly mentally retarded, Greenwood, Hart, Walker, and Risley (1994) found that many children in urban schools were consistently receiving poor academic instruction. Ineffective instruction is one of the critical factors impacting the pattern of behavior (i.e., poor academic performance) that Greenwood et al. called developmental retardation. Children in inner-city schools were more likely to have lower rates of academic engagement then their suburban peers. The consequences of not appropriately preparing large groups of children to participate successfully in society might be grave, possibly leading to higher crime rates and increased numbers of individuals dependent on social agencies.

Speech or Language Impairments. Speech and language make up a system of communication that allows people to encode (send) and decode (receive) information. Communication between people is important in all aspects of life (Owens, 2001). At its most basic level, communication involves a person sending information, a person receiving information, and the receiver responding to the information. The ability to communicate allows a person to tell information, explain, make requests, express feelings, and ask questions. People who have difficulty communicating with others have less access to and fewer choices in the environment than their more typical peers.

The American Speech-Language-Hearing Association (ASHA) (1993) defines a communication disorder as an impairment in the ability to receive, send, process, and comprehend concepts or verbal, nonverbal, and graphic systems. Communication disorders may occur in the hearing, language, and/or speech processes and can be present at birth or acquired later. The disorders will vary in severity among individuals. A speech disorder is an impairment of the articulation of speech sounds, fluency, and/or voice (Hallahan & Kauffman, 2000), such as

- An articulation disorder
- Fluency disorder
- Voice disorder

A language disorder is impaired comprehension and/or use of spoken, written, and/or other symbol systems (Hallahan & Kauffman, 2000) in the following areas:

- Phonology—language sounds and rules for sounds
- Morphology—the structure of words and the construction of word forms
- Syntax—the rules governing the order and combination of words to form sentences and the relationships among the elements within a sentence
- Semantics—meaning of words and sentences
- Pragmatics—the system that combines the language components in functional and socially appropriate communication

Although language development is very complex, most children learn to talk during their toddler years. Typical children begin to use words from their parents'/caregivers' language at about 18 months (Owens, 2002). By the time children are 5 years old they typically have a vocabulary of from 1,500 to 2,000 words and use the words in sentences. Six-year-old children will show evidence in their speech of all the complex forms of adult speech (Owens, 2002).

What are the special concerns for CLDE learners with communication disorders? Of all students receiving special education services 18% do so under the speech and language impairment label. Table 2–1 shows that this is the second greatest category of need, following SLD, for all groups. In terms of disproportionality, Table 2–2 shows slightly elevated rates of speech and language impairment among African American and European American (non-Hispanic) students.

Language development is influenced by a variety of factors, including race, ethnicity, socioeconomic class, education, geography, and peers (Payne & Taylor, 2002). Every language has dialects, and teachers must be sensitive to the various dialects represented in their classroom. Because a student's English differs from Standard English does not necessarily mean that the student has a communication disorder (Battle, 1998; Van Keulen, Weddington, & DeBose, 1998); that is, if the student is following the language rules of the dialect, then the child does not have a disorder. The child, however, can benefit from the teacher modeling Standard English and providing positive feedback on the child's development in Standard English because the development of Standard English skills is important for success in society. If the child speaks a dialect but does not follow the language

TABLE 2–4 AD/HD student percentages in disabilities categories

Distribution of parent-reported student ADD/ADHD by primary disability category (SEELS uses the acronym AD/HD for these students): 2000–2001

Primary IDEA Category (SEELS did not sample students with developmental delay.)	Percentage of ADD/ADHD Students Served (Total does not equal 100 due to rounding.)
Specific learning disabilities	41
Speech/language impairments	15
Mental retardation	11
Emotional disturbance	14
Hearing impairments	1
Visual impairments	0
Orthopedic impairments	1
Other health impairments	12
Autism	2
Traumatic brain injury	0
Multiple disabilities	2
Deaf-blindness	0
Total	99

Source: SEELS Parent Survey, U.S. Department of Education, *25th Annual Report to Congress on the Implementation of the Individuals with Disabilities Education Act for 2003*, Office of Special Education and Rehabilitative Services, Vol. I, 2005, Washington DC: Author.

rules of that dialect, he or she will need to be further assessed by someone familiar with the dialect to determine if in fact a communication disorder exists.

Attention Deficit/Hyperactivity Disorders (ADHD). ADHD is not a recognized category under IDEA, but children with ADHD can be served under the other health impairments category if their distractibility negatively impacts their academic performance. Many children also receive services under the high-incidence disability categories of SLD and BD. Special Education Elementary Longitudinal Study (SEELS) data (U.S. Department of Education, 2005), which is based on parent reports, indicate that overall 27% of students with disabilities have ADD/ADHD (see Table 2–4).

Children with ADHD chronically have trouble focusing their attention and repeatedly engage in purposeless behavior. They have limited ability to concentrate and a tendency to emit impulsive behaviors. It should be noted that there are times when all children have difficulty maintaining attention and engage in meaningless behaviors. Whether or not a child's behavior indicates the presence of ADHD is determined by using the criteria found in the *Diagnostic and Statistical Manual of Mental Disorders, Text Revision* (DSM-IV-TR) (American Psychiatric Association, 2000). ADHD is a medical diagnosis, and, therefore, a physician needs to receive regular information about behavior and academic performance in school in order to closely monitor a child's progress. Despite efforts to quantify aspects of ADHD (see Table 2–5), there remains some subjectivity in the diagnosis. The evaluation process typically includes a medical examination, clinical interviews, and teacher and parent rating scales (Barkley, 1998).

It is estimated that from 3% to 5% of the school-age population has ADHD (American Psychiatric Association, 2000). Males are more likely to be diagnosed with ADHD than females, raising the question of gender bias in evaluation (Barkley, 1998). The number of CLDE learners with ADHD is not easy to determine since ADHD is not a recognized category and the students receive services across a variety of other special education categories.

TABLE 2–5 Diagnostic criteria for attention

Diagnostic Criteria

A. Choose behaviors from column 1 or column 2 below:

Six (or more) of the following symptoms of **inattention** have persisted for at least 6 months to a degree that is maladaptive and inconsistent with developmental level:	Six (or more) of the following symptoms of **hyperactivity-impulsivity** have persisted for at least 6 months to a degree that is maladaptive and inconsistent with developmental level:
• Often fails to give close attention to details or makes careless mistakes in schoolwork, work, or other activities • Often has difficulty sustaining attention in tasks or play activities • Often does not seem to listen when spoken to directly • Often does not follow through on instructions and fails to finish schoolwork, chores, or duties in the workplace (not due to oppositional behavior or failure to understand instructions) • Often has difficulty organizing tasks and activities • Often avoids, dislikes, or is reluctant to engage in tasks that require sustained mental effort (such as schoolwork or homework)	*Hyperactivity* • Often fidgets with hands or feet or squirms in seat • Often leaves seat in classroom or in other situations in which remaining seated is expected • Often runs about or climbs excessively in situations in which it is inappropriate (in adolescents or adults, may be limited to subjective feelings of restlessness) • Often has difficulty playing or engaging in leisure activities quietly • Is often "on the go" or often acts as if "driven by a motor" • Often talks excessively

(continued)

TABLE 2-5 (continued)

• Often loses things necessary for tasks or activities (e.g., toys, school assignments, pencils, books, or tools) • Is often easily distracted by extraneous stimuli. • Is often forgetful in daily activities	***Impulsivity*** • Often blurts out answers before questions have been completed • Often has difficulty awaiting turn • Often interrupts or intrudes on others (e.g., butts into conversations or games)

B. Some hyperactive-impulsive or inattentive symptoms that caused impairment were present before age 7 years.

C. Some impairment from the symptoms is present in two or more settings (e.g., at school [or work] and at home).

D. There must be clear evidence of clinically significant impairment in social, academic, or occupational functioning.

E. The symptoms do not occur exclusively during the course of a Pervasive Developmental Disorder, Schizophrenia, or other Psychotic Disorder and are not better accounted for by another mental disorder (e.g., Mood Disorder, Anxiety Disorder, Dissociative Disorder, or a Personality Disorder).

Specify Type:

- **Attention-Deficit/Hyperactivity Disorder, Combined Type:** if both Criteria A1 and A2 are met for the past 6 months
- **Attention-Deficit/Hyperactivity Disorder, Predominantly Inattentive Type:** if Criterion A1 is met but Criterion A2 is not met for the past 6 months
- **Attention-Deficit/Hyperactivity Disorder, Predominantly Hyperactive-Impulsive Type:** if Criterion A2 is met but Criterion A1 is not met for the past 6 months
- For individuals (especially adolescents and adults) who currently have symptoms that no longer meet full criteria, "In Partial Remission" should be specified.

Retrieved February 21, 2006, from Internet Mental Health, http://www.mentalhealth.com/dis1/p21-ch01.html

High-Incidence Disabilities Summary. Learners with high-incidence disabilities make up the vast majority (approximately 80%) receiving instruction under IDEA. The precise number of learners with high-incidence disabilities is difficult to determine due to the inclusion of the mental retardation category. Identifying children with high-incidence disabilities is of concern to avoid having cultural and linguistic differences become determining factors in labeling. A further challenge to educators is the fact that many CLDE learners attend poor, ill-equipped schools (Kozol, 1991).

TEACHING TIPS

High-Incidence CLDE Learners

1. Assessments of CLDE learners need to be multifactored, without cultural bias, and involve significant persons from the learner's culture in order to avoid inappropriate diagnosis/placment.
2. Effective bilingual education is needed for ELLs to reduce overidentification.
3. Emphasis should be placed on opportunities for CLDE learners to be educated in general education environments with access to the general education curriculum.
4. Teachers of CLDE learners need to be highly qualified and fully prepared for these assignments.
5. Where indicated, intensive early interventions for CLDE learners should be provided to minimize disabilities and disproportionality.

Alessandra's Story

Alessandra is a 16-year-old deaf high school student. She attends a high school on the opposite side of town from her home, where she lives with her parents, Mr. and Mrs. Ruiz, and two younger brothers in a working-class neighborhood. She is the only person in her family who is deaf. In fact, she is the first person in her extended family to be deaf. Her brothers attend the neighborhood schools and often have friends visit after school or on the weekend. Both of her parents work outside the home.

Alessandra feels closer to her mother and enjoys the time they spend together even though communication is difficult. The parents include Alessandra in all of the family activities, but sometimes she still feels left out. Since no one in her family is fluent in sign language, she often finds herself observing family discussions without really understanding what is being communicated. Her parents did take a sign language class where they learned the signs for family members, colors, and common objects in the home. However, trying to communicate effectively with Alessandra is difficult using a combination of basic signs, notes, and lipreading. Often there are miscommunications that are frustrating for everyone.

The family regularly attends church but even this is not enjoyable for Alessandra because there is no sign language interpreter available. Alessandra enjoys her friends at school but she lives a great distance from them and since she is not driving yet she must depend on her parents to take her to visit or on her friends being dropped off at her house. Alessandra loves her girl cousins. They do not know sign language either but they still have fun together whenever the extended family gets together. Her cousins take the time to make sure she knows what is happening.

At school Alessandra is the only deaf Hispanic student in her class. There are two Hispanic boys in the hearing-impaired program but both are only in the ninth grade. She has made friends with the other deaf girls in the class, three European Americans and one African American. They spend every moment they can talking about the important social issues of adolescence. Alessandra also enjoys calling her friends on her TTY/TDD when she is at home.

Alessandra often feels she is left out and becomes easily frustrated and annoyed. Alessandra's mother senses her daughter's frustration but is unsure of what to do.

What Are Low-Incidence Disabilities?

Low-incidence disabilities categories discussed in this text are hearing disabilities, visual disabilities, physical disabilities (including other health disabilities), and autism. These areas of disabilities all require a medical evaluation and designation along with a special education assessment. Disproportionality occurs in low-incidence categories (e.g., overrepresentation of Asian/Pacific Islanders in autism and hearing impairment), yet there is less controversy because the identification process tends to be more objective than in high-incidence disabilities.

Hearing Impairments. Hearing impairment involves a hearing loss severe enough to negatively impact the student's education. A student who is deaf is unable to use hearing to understand speech. A student who is hard of hearing has a hearing loss that is great enough to require some adaptation. Children who have hearing loss are at a tremendous disadvantage in terms of developing language skills unless the children are born to parents proficient in sign language (Chamberlain & Mayberry, 2000). Most children with hearing impairments are born to hearing parents without sign language skills (Calderon, 2000).

There are two basic types of hearing loss, conductive and sensorineural (Lewis & Doorlag, 2006), which can be bilateral (both ears) or unilateral (one ear). Abnormalities in the middle or outer ear can cause a conductive loss. For example, the ear canal may not be completely formed, which inhibits the auditory information from getting to the inner ear. Most

Teachers of CLD students with hearing impairments must understand the culture of the deaf, and the learner's minority culture.

conductive hearing losses are correctable with surgery or medical treatment. These children usually benefit from amplification from hearing aids. Sensorineural hearing loss occurs in the inner ear, often involving damage to the nerve fibers. Sensorineural hearing loss is usually not correctable by surgery or medical intervention. Some children's hearing loss is a mixture of conductive and sensorineural. Children who have prelingual deafness (i.e., before language development) need to acquire language, whereas children with a postlingual loss need to retain language while developing new language skills (Heward, 2006).

Children who are deaf generally have difficulty across all academic areas. About 30% of deaf students leave school functionally illiterate (Paul & Jackson, 1993), and so the development of literacy skills is an ongoing concern for educators. Educators have long debated over the best way to educate children with hearing impairments (HI) (Woolsey, Harrison, & Gardner, 2004). Some strongly advocate an oral approach; others advocate a manual approach. Total communication, which involves the use of signed English and oral strategies, is the strategy most used in educating children with HI.

What are the special concerns for CLDE learners with hearing impairments? Hearing impairments make up from 1% to 3% of all the disabilities listed in Table 2–1. In terms of disproportionality, Table 2–2 shows small to modest elevations for all four minority groups (i.e., Native, Asian, African, and Hispanic Americans).

Hearing impairments present some unique challenges for CLDE learners. The impairment may isolate individuals from the hearing population, making it difficult for them to interact with and learn from other members of their culture. If the CLDE child must communicate with sign language, then the child might be restricted to interacting with only a few individuals in the community who have the skills needed for conversations that go beyond the most rudimentary level. European American deaf persons must face the challenge of negotiating between the deaf culture and the majority hearing culture; CLDE deaf persons must negotiate among the deaf culture, their ethnic culture, the majority hearing culture, and their deaf ethnic culture.

The fact that most parents of deaf children across all cultures do not use sign language at a conversational level makes the task of the CLDE learner with deafness so much more difficult, since parents often communicate their culture to their children during informal conversations that interpret life experiences to their children (Gollnick & Chinn, 2004). Educators of the deaf need to be sensitive to the special needs of CLDE learners and not only provide experiences for the children within a deaf culture context but also infuse cultural diversity into lessons and experiences. Among several national resources that can assist educators in addressing these unique needs are National Black Deaf Advocates, http://www.nbda.org/index.html; a gay and lesbian group named the Rainbow Alliance of the Deaf, http://www.rad.org/; a Native American group, Intertribal Deaf Council, http://www.deafnative.com/goals.htm; deaf Latino Organizations, http://www.deafvision.net/aztlan/resources/index.html; and the National Asian Deaf Congress, http://www.nadc-usa.org/chapters.html.

Visual Impairments. The legal definition of blindness is based on two factors: (1) visual acuity (ability to discriminate forms and shapes accurately) and (2) field of vision (the extent of peripheral vision) (Vaughn, Bos, & Schumm, 2003). Visual acuity of 20/200 or less is considered to be legally blind, as is a visual field range of 20 degrees or less. Blindness is a low-incidence disability and is more prevalent in adults than school-age children (Hallahan & Kauffman, 2000). Table 2–1 indicates that visual impairments make up from 0.4% to 0.8% of all disabilities for each ethnic or racial group.

Mobility and orientation are critical to the development of learners with visual impairments. Young children with visual impairments might be delayed in their development due to their uncertainty in exploring their environment. Parents who overly restrict their children's movement due to concerns about their safety may also slow their children's development.

Educationally, the most important consideration is determining the learner's functional vision (Lewis & Doorlag, 2006). Learners with visual impairments are typically placed in one of three categories—totally blind, functionally blind, and low vision (Hallahan & Kauffman, 2000). Totally blind means the learner receives no useful information visually and therefore must use other senses to acquire information and learn. Learners who are functionally blind receive so little information visually that they primarily learn from their auditory and tactile senses. Learners with low vision are able to learn primarily through sight and then enhance that information through their auditory and tactile senses. Learners with visual impairments tend to perform less well then their sighted peers on academic achievement assessments (Rapp & Rapp, 1992).

What are the special concerns for CLDE learners with visual impairments? As seen in Table 2–1, visual impairments are not disproportionate among any of the ethnic/racial minority groups. Like children with hearing impairments, CLD learners with visual impairments face mobility challenges that can inhibit their ability to interact with the community in general and their cultural community in particular. Both groups face barriers that may potentially prevent them from learning about and enjoying experiences related to their culture and linguistic background, which makes including individuals from diverse backgrounds in the classroom even more important.

Physical Disabilities. Students with physical disabilities have physical or health limitations that inhibit their education. The category of physical disabilities requires a medical diagnosis and ongoing medical supervision. These limitations might cause higher-than-normal absences (e.g., sickle-cell anemia) or require special services, materials, equipment, training, or facilities (e.g., epilepsy, muscular dystrophy) (Hallahan & Kauffman, 2000). Some students with physical disabilities may have a compromised skeletal structure (orthopedic) or central nervous system damage (neuromotor impairment). Other students with health problems might be served under the IDEA category of "other health impairment." In addition to ADHD discussed earlier in the chapter, such students might have asthma, diabetes, Human Immunodeficiency Virus (HIV) and Acquired Immunodeficiency Syndrome (AIDS), and so forth. Physical disabilities may coexist with other exceptionalities, including giftedness.

Teachers of children with physical disabilities need to establish effective communication with parents and their students' physicians due to the active nature of these disabilities, which can be potentially life threatening without appropriate and timely intervention. It is often necessary to create interdisciplinary teams that include professionals such as a physical therapists, adapted physical education teachers, occupational therapists, nurses, and paraprofessionals. Some students with disabilities have as a part of their IEP an individualized health care plan that prescribes specific health-related needs and interventions (Heward, 2006). Students with physical disabilities may also need assistive technology devices in order to function in the school environment (Lindsey, 2000). Students with physical disabilities may use low-tech devices, such as modified scissors, or they may use high-tech devices, such as augmentative communication devices. Some assistive technology, called *universal design assistive technology* (e.g., L-shaped door handles, curb cuts) (Lindsey, 2000), has become broadly integrated into society and is effectively used by everyone.

What are the special concerns for CLDE learners with physical disabilities? CLD families are more likely to live below the poverty level, placing them at increased risk for health-related problems such as asthma. Table 2–1 shows comparable levels of orthopedic and other health impairments for all groups, with ranges from 0.8% to 1.8% for orthopedic impairments and from 3.2% to 7.0% for other health impairments. A similar pattern is seen in Table 2–2, where the frequency of these impairments is consistent with the level of the resident population for each group. The one exception is the European American population, perhaps owing to the diagnosis of ADHD, which has increased quickly over the past few years.

Autism. Autism is a developmental disability that usually manifests during the preschool years (typically in the child's first three years). It is a disability that significantly impacts a child's verbal and nonverbal communication as well as social interactions. Children with autism may fall anywhere on a spectrum from mild to severe—*autism spectrum disorders* (ASD) is the umbrella term. There are five subcategories to autism:

1. Autism disorder—begins before the child is 3. Difficulty with typical social interactions. Impaired communication, including for some children the absence of vocal language. Stereotypic behavior.
2. Asperger syndrome—milder end of the autism spectrum. Problems with social interactions. Typically have average to above-average intellectual functioning.
3. Rhett syndrome—a neurological condition that manifests between 5 and 30 months. Stereotypic hand movements. Awkward or clumsy when walking; severe language and cognitive impairments.
4. Childhood disintegrative disorder—onset between 2 and 10 years of age. Difficulty with typical social interactions. Impaired communication, including for some children the absence of vocal language. Stereotypic behavior.
5. Pervasive developmental disorder—covers children who meet some but not all of the qualifying criteria for autism disorder (American Psychiatric Association, 2000).

What are the special concerns for CLDE learners with autism? The only area of disproportionality for Asian American learners, autism accounts for 4.1% of the disabilities found within the Asian/Pacific Islander group, a greater percentage than that for other groups (Table 2–1). Table 2–2 reveals that autism is also disproportional among African Americans. Although they are only 3.8% and 14.8% of the student population, respectively, Asian and African American students represent 4.7% and 20.9% of all students with autism.

Severe autism can have a devastating effect on a child' ability to interact with others and function in society. Like other low-incidence disabilities, autism can greatly restrict a child's ability to interact with the community. Services for students with autism provided in the

> ### TEACHING TIPS
>
> #### Low-Incidence CLDE Learners
>
> 1. Special effort should be made to incorporate the learner's specific culture into classroom lessons for students with sensory impairments. Identify famous/important persons from the learner's culture who have disabilities.
> 2. Due to poverty and other sociocultural factors, CLDE learners with physical and other health impairments may not have the same access to medical assistance as their more affluent peers. Therefore, teachers may need to monitor them more closely to proactively promote their overall well-being. Establish regular lines of communication between parents and medical personnel to provide ongoing assessment/information on the child's well-being.
> 3. Families of CLDE learners may need special training and assistance on how to advocate for their children (e.g., autism) in order to receive all available services. Teachers can assist in providing parents with contact information to professionals sensitive to their needs. Teachers can also provide opportunities for parents to meet and share information with other families.
> 4. Teachers can instruct parents and community institutions about effective teaching strategies for children with low-incidence disabilities so that the children can more fully participate in their communities. For example, a typically developing child from the same cultural background could be trained to be part of a buddy system, which pairs the child with a disability and a typical child for various activities or experiences. The buddy is trained to respond to the specific needs that the partner may have during the experience, including how to alert others if an emergency arises. A culturally specific buddy might help the child feel more connected to the cultural peer group.

home, school, and private facilities have substantially increased recently, but access to these services often depends on parental information and advocacy. Unfortunately, CLD parents often are not members of parent organizations that can provide critical information, and so educators and other professionals need to make a concerted effort to inform parents of available services, particularly early intervention.

Low-Incidence Disabilities Summary. Low-incidence disabilities can limit social opportunities because they present obstacles to communication, mobility, and accessibility. This can create a disconnect between the CLDE learners and their own cultures. In schools, children may be one of only a few students (or in some cases, the only one) from their culture. Therefore, teachers need to infuse lessons with cultural information and include information about members of diverse cultures. Because CLD learners are at increased risk of living in poverty, they may have limited access to health care (Artiles, Harry, Reschly, & Chinn, 2002). Limited health care may increase the the potential for health problems and/or inhibit the remediation of existing problems.

Alessandra's Story Continued

During Alessandra's IEP meeting, Mrs. Ruiz indicates that she is concerned about how easily Alessandra becomes frustrated and angry. Alessandra is in attendance at the meeting and as soon as Mrs. Ruiz's comments are communicated through sign language, Alessandra becomes upset. Alessandra tells her mother "she is always left out. It is hard for her to have friends over because of the distance, but she sees her brothers playing with friends in the neighborhood all the time. At home there is no one who can really communicate with her, and even when they go to Hispanic festivals, the food is good and the colorful clothes are beautiful but she really does not know what is going on and what everything means." Mrs. Ruiz begins to cry and the special education teacher says, "Let's think of some ways to help Alessandra feel more included."

Mrs. Ruiz, Alessandra, and the teacher work out a plan for Alessandra and her family. Mrs. Ruiz will begin to attend community sign language classes and Alessandra will tutor her. Mrs. Ruiz will also talk to Mr. Ruiz about attending. Regardless, Mrs. Ruiz will share what she learns with the rest of the family. The teacher tells them about the various deaf community activities available in the city. There is a deaf bowling league that many of the teenagers participate in that Alessandra could join. There are also deaf churches, including the same denomination that her family attends. Mrs. Ruiz says that she and her family will visit the deaf church but they will probably not join it. However, maybe once a month they can attend. Mrs. Ruiz will find out if Alessandra can participate in some of the youth activities there. Mrs. Ruiz also agrees that they should find interpreters when the family is going to attend Hispanic cultural activities so that Alessandra can better understand her culture. The teacher says that she will also work to bring into the school deaf Hispanic adults who can share some of their culture and experiences with the entire class. Finally, the teacher gives Mrs. Ruiz the contact information for some deaf Hispanic students who have already graduated and gone on to college at Gallaudet University. Mrs. Ruiz, Alessandra, and the teacher realize there is much work to be done if Alessandra is to become comfortable with her deafness and culture, but they have a plan to begin.

Gifted Education

Gifted students can be found at every grade level and across all socioeconomic, cultural, and linguistic groups. Students who are gifted and talented, like their peers with disabilities, need specialized instruction if they are to maximize their potential (Culross, 1997). Gifted education is a major concern for some CLDE populations (e.g., African, Hispanic, and Native Americans) due to their underrepresentation in this category. A full discussion of gifted and talented students is provided in chapter 14 of this text.

Summary

CLD children come from every socioeconomic level and linguistic background. CLDE learners are found in every category of special education and are both overrepresented and underrepresented in these categories. The disproportionate representation of CLDE learners in the area of high-incidence disabilities—specifically, mild mental retardation and behavior disorders—has been particularly controversial because of the level of subjectivity that is involved in the assessment process for high-incidence disability. It is yet unclear what role (if any) cultural differences play in the evaluation for special education. Another area of concern is the quality of instruction that CLDE learners receive.

CLDE learners have some unique challenges as a result of their cultural and linguistic differences, for example, navigating multiple cultures or losing access to information about their culture. Teachers need to be aware of these special challenges and assist CLDE learners to overcome the challenges.

Related Learning Activities

1. Interview CLDE adults about their educational experiences. Ask about challenges they faced and how they addressed them. What, if any, role did their diversity play in their education?

2. Review the data of your school/school district/state for disproportionality. Is disproportionality evident? If so, in which special education categories? Why do you think this phenomenon exists?

3. Review the documents from your state department of education. How does it define disproportionality? What programs, if any, does it provide to address this issue? How would you evaluate your state's plans?

4. Review the websites in Figure 2–3 to find information about a specific disability as well as instructional suggestions. You can do a unit on a specific disability in your classroom. Students can be involved in the unit by accessing the websites and identifying important information or activities.

5. Interview a teacher of CLDE students. Does the teacher feel the students' diagnoses fairly reflect their disabilities? Why or why not? Do these students present any special challenges due to their culture, such as language barriers? How do the teacher and school plan to address these challenges? What is the teacher's assessment of these interventions? What else does the teacher recommend that the school do?

References

American Association of Mental Retardation. (1992). *Mental retardation: Definition, classification, and systems of support* (9th ed.). Washington DC: Author.

American Psychiatric Association. (2000). *Diagnostic and statistical manual of mental disorders, text revision (DSM-IV-TR)*. Washington DC: Author.

American Speech-Language-Hearing Association. (1993). Definitions of communication disorders and variations. ASHA, *35* (Suppl. 10), 40–41. Washington DC: U.S. Department of Education and American Speech-Language-Hearing Association.

Antrop-Gonzalez, R., Velez, W., & Garrett, T. (2004). Challenging the academic (mis)categorization of urban youth: Building a case for Puerto Rican High Achievers. *Multiple Voices, 7*(1), 16–32.

Artiles, A. J., Harry, B., Reschly, D. J., & Chinn, P. C. (2002). Over-identification of students of color in special education: A critical overview. *Multicultural Perspectives 4*, 3–10.

Artiles, A. J. & Ortiz, A. A. (Eds.). (2002). *English language learners with special education needs: Identification, assessment, and instruction*. Arlington, VA: ERIC EC.

Artiles, A. J., Rueda, R. Salazar, J., & Higareda, I. (2002). English language learner representation in special education in California urban school districts. In D. Losen & G. Orfield (Eds.), *Racial inequality in special education* (pp. 11–136). Cambridge, MA: Harvard Educational Press.

Artiles, A. J., & Zamora-Duran, G. (1997). Disproportionate representation: A contentious and unresolved predicament. In A. J. Artiles, & G. Zamora-Duran (Eds.), *Reducing disproportionate representation of culturally diverse students in special and gifted education*. Reston, VA: Council for Exceptional Children.

Baca, L. M., & Cervantes, H. T. (2004). *The bilingual special education interface* (4th ed.). Upper Saddle River, NJ: Merrill/Prentice Hall.

Barkley, R. A. (1998). *Attention-deficit hyperactivity disorders: A handbook for diagnosis and treatment*. New York: Guilford Press.

Battle, D.E. (1998). *Communication disorders in multicultural populations* (2nd. ed.). Boston, MA: Butterworth-Heinemann.

Billingsley, B. S., Fall, A., & Williams, T. O., Jr. (2006). Who is teaching students with emotional and behavioral disorders? Profile and comparison to other special educators. *Behavioral Disorders, 37*(3), 252–264.

Calderon, R. (2000). Parental involvement in deaf children's education programs as a predictor of child's language, early reading, and social-emotional development. *Journal of Deaf Studies and Deaf Education, 5*, 140–155.

Chamberlain, C., & Mayberry, R. I. (2000). Theorizing about the relation between American Sign Language and reading. In C. Chamberlain, J. P. Morford, & R. I. Mayberry (Eds.), *Language acquisition by eye* (pp. 221–59). Mahwah, NJ: Erlbaum.

Crawley, J. E., Parmar, R. S., Foley, T. E., Salmon, S., & Roy, S. (Spring, 2001). Arithmetic performance of students: Implications for standards and programming. *Exceptional Children, 67*, 311–328.

Culross, R. R. (1997). Concepts of inclusion in gifted education. *Teaching Exceptional Children, 29*, 24–26.

Cullinan, D. (2002). *Students with emotional behavioral disorders; An introduction for teachers and other helping professionals*. Upper Saddle River, NJ: Merrill/Prentice Hall.

Executive Summary (2006). Racial inequality in special education: Executive summary for federal policy makers. Retrieved December 26, 2006, from http://www.civilrightsproject.harvard.edu/research/specialed/IDEA_paper02.php

Finn, J. D. (1982). Patterns in special education placement as revealed by the OCR surveys. In K.A. Heller,

W. H. Holtzman, & S. Messick (Eds.), *Placing children in special education: A strategy for equity* (pp. 322–381). Washington, DC: National Academy Press.

Gardner, R., III, & Miranda, A. H. (2001). Improving outcomes for urban African American students. *The Journal of Negro Education, 70,* 255–263.

Gollnick, D. M., & Chinn, P. G. (2004). *Multicultural education in a pluralistic society* (6th ed.). Upper Saddle River, NJ: Merrill/Prentice Hall.

Graham, S., & Harris, K. R. (2005). *Writing better: Effective strategies for teaching students with learning difficulties.* Baltimore, MD: Brookes.

Greenwood, C. R., Hart, B., Walker, D., & Risley, T. (1994). The opportunity to respond and academic performance revisited: A behavioral theory of developmental retardation and its prevention. In R. Gardner, III, D. M. Sainato, J. O. Cooper, T. E. Heron, W. L. Heward, J. Eshleman, & T. A. Grossi (Eds.), *Behavior analysis in education: Focus on Measurably superior instruction* (pp. 213–223). Pacific Grove, CA: Brooks/Cole.

Grossman, H. (Ed.). (1983). *Classification in mental retardation.* Washington DC: American Association on Mental Deficiency.

Hallahan, D. P., & Kauffman, J. M. (2000). *Exceptional learners: Introduction to special education* (8th ed.). Needham Heights, MA: Allyn & Bacon.

Hallahan, D. P., Keller, C. E., Matinez, E. A., Byrd, E. S., Gelman, J. A., & Fan, X. (2007). How variable are interstate prevalence rates of learning disabilities and other special education categories? A longitudinal comparison. *Exceptional Children, 2,* 136–146.

Hessler, T. (2005). *The effects of a writing template on the writing behaviors of high school students with learning disabilities.* Unpublished doctoral dissertation at The Ohio State University, Columbus, OH.

Hernandez, H. (2001). *Multicultural education: A teacher's guide to linking context, process, and content* (2nd ed.). Upper Saddle River, NJ: Merrill/Prentice Hall.

Heward, W. L. (2003). *Exceptional children: An introduction to special education* (7th ed.). Upper Saddle River, NJ: Merrill/Prentice Hall.

Heward, W. L. (2006). *Exceptional children: An introduction to special education* (8th ed.). Upper Saddle River, NJ: Merrill/Prentice Hall.

Hilliard, A. G. (1980). Cultural diversity and special education. *Exceptional Children, 46,* 584–588.

Hosp, J. L., & Reschly, D. J. (2004). Disproportionate representation of minority students in special education: Academic, demographic, and economic predictors. *Exceptional Children, 70,* 185–199.

Ishil-Jordan, S. R. (1997). When behavior differences are not disorders. In A. J. Artiles & G. Zamora-Duran (Eds.), *Reducing disproportionate representation of culturally diverse students in special and gifted education* (pp. 27–46). Reston, VA: Council for Exceptional Children.

Joseph, L., & Ford, D. Y. (Winter, 2006). Nondiscriminatory assessment: Consideration for gifted education. *Gifted Child Quarterly,* 50.

Kauffman, J. (2005). *Characteristics of emotional and behavioral disorders of children and youth* (8th ed.). Upper Saddle River, NJ: Merrill/Prentice Hall.

Kozol, J. (1991). Savage inequalities: Children in America's schools. New York: Harper.

Krashen, S. & McField, G. (2005). What works?: Reviewing the latest evidence on bilingual education. Language Learner. Retrieved July 27, 2007 from http://users.rcn.com/crawj/langpol/Krashen-McFiled.pdf

Lewis, R. B., & Doorlag, D. H. (2006). *Teaching special students in general education classrooms* (7th ed.). Upper Saddle River, NJ: Merrill/Prentice Hall.

Lindsey, J. D. (Ed.). (2000). *Technology & exceptional individuals* (3rd ed.). Austin, TX: Pro-Ed.

Lipsey, M. W., & Derzon, J. H. (1998). Predictors of violence or serious delinquency in adolescence and early adulthood: A synthesis of longitudinal research. In R. Loeber & D. P. Farrington (Eds.), *Serious and violent offenders: Risk factors and successful interventions* (pp. 6–105). Thousand Oaks, CA: Sage.

McCollin, M. J., & O'Shea, D. J. (2006). Improving literacy skills of students from culturally and linguistically diverse backgrounds. *Multiple Voices, 9,* 92–107.

Moats, L. C. (2000). Speech to print: Language essential for teachers. Baltimore, MD: Brookes.

Montecel, M. R., & Cortez, J. D. (2002). Successful bilingual education programs: Development and the dissemination of criteria to identify promising and exemplary practices in bilingual education at the national level. *Bilingual Research Journal, 26*(1), 4–21.

Moran, C. E., & Hukuta, K. (1995). Bilingual education: Broadening research perspective. In J. A. Banks, & C.A.M. Bank (Eds.) *Handbook of research on multicultural education.* (pp. 445–62). New York: Macmillan.

National Association for the Education of African American Children with Learning Disabilities Section 504 Rehabilitation Act of 1973. Retrieved July 26, 2007 from http://www.charityadvantage.com/aacld/Sec504RehabActof1973.asp

National Center for Education Statistics (2000). *Executive summary. Dropout rates in the United States: 1999.* Available: http://nces.ed.gov/pubs2001/droupout/

National Research Council, Committee on Minority Representation in Special Education, M.S. Donovan, & C.T. Cross (Eds.). (2002). *Minority students in special and gifted education.* Washington, DC: National Academy Press.

Nieto, S. (2000). *Affirming diversity: The sociopolitical context of multicultural education* (3rd ed.). New York: Addison-Wesley Longman.

Obiakor, F., Algozzine, B., Thurlow, M., Gwalla-Ogisi, N., Enwefa, S., Enwefa, R., & McIntosh, A. (2002). *Addressing the issue of disproportionate representation:*

Identification and assessment of culturally diverse students with emotional and behavioral disorders. Arlington, VA: Council for Children with Behavior Disorders.

Ortiz, S. O., (2002). Best practices in nondiscriminatory assessment. In A. Thomas & J. Grimes (Eds.). *Best Practices in School Psychology IV.* Bethesda, MD: National Association of School Psychologists.

Owens, R. E. (2001). *Language development: An introduction* (4th ed.). Boston, MA: Allyn & Bacon.

Owens, R. E. (2002). Development of communication, language, and speech. In G. H. Shames & N. B. Anderson (Eds.), *Human communication disorders: An introduction* (6th ed.) (pp. 28–69). Boston, MA: Allyn & Bacon.

Parrish, T. (2002). Disparities in the identification, funding, and provision of special education. In D. J. Losen & G. Orfield (Eds.), *Racial inequality in special education* (pp.15–38). Cambridge, MA: Harvard Educational Press.

Patton, J. M. (1997). Disproportionate representation in gifted programs: Best practices for meeting the challenge. In A. J. Artiles & G. Zamora-Duran (Eds.), *Reducing disproportionate representation of culturally diverse students in special and gifted education* (pp. 59–85). Reston, VA: Council for Exceptional Children.

Paul, P. V., & Jackson, D. (1993). *Towards a psychology of deafness* (2nd ed.). San Diego, CA: Singular.

Payne, K. T., & Taylor, O. (2002). Multicultural influences on human communication. In G. H. Shames & N. B. Anderson (Eds.), *Human communication disorders: An introduction.* (6th ed.) (pp. 106–140). Boston, MA: Allyn & Bacon.

Peske, H. G. & Haycock, K. (2006). Teaching inequality: How poor and minority students are shortchanged on teacher quality. *The Education Trust.* www.edtrust.org

Proctor, B. D., & Dalaker, J. (2002). *Poverty in the United States 2001* (U.S. Census Bureau, Current Population Reports P60–219). Washington DC: U.S. Government Printing Office.

Rapp, D. W., & Rapp, A. J. (1992). A survey of the current status of visually impaired students in secondary mathematics. *Journal of Visual Impairment and Blindness, 86,* 115–117.

Resnick, D. P., & Goodman, M. (1994). American Culture and the gifted. In P. O. Ross (Ed.), *National excellence: A case for developing America's talent. An anthology of readings* (pp. 109–121). Washington, DC: U.S. Department of Education, Office of Educational Research and Improvement.

Rueda, R. (1997). Changing the context of assessment: The move to portfolios and authentic assessment. In A. J. Artiles & G. Zamora-Duran (Eds.), *Reducing disproportionate representation of culturally diverse students in special and gifted education* (pp. 7–25) Reston, VA: Council for Exceptional Children.

Santos, R. M., Corso, R. M., & Maude, S. P. (2006). Meaningful participation of diverse constituents: The culturally and linguistically appropriate services institute. *Multiple Voices, 9,* 34–49.

Schwartz, W. (1997). Strategies for identifying the talents of diverse students. ERIC Digests #E122, ED410323. Retrieved March 2, 2006, from National Association for Gifted Children, http://www.nagc.org/index.aspx?id=203

Skiba, R. J., Simmons, A. B., Ritter, S., Kohler, K. R., & Wu, T. C. (2003). The psychology of disproportionality: Minority placement in context. *Multiple Voices, 6,* 27–40.

Skrtic, T. M. (2003). An organizational analysis of over-representation of poor and minority students in special education. *Multiple Voices, 6,* 41–57.

Smith, T. E. C., Gartin, B. C., Murdick, N. L., & Hilton, A. (2006). *Families and children with special needs: Professional and family partnerships.* Upper Saddle, NJ: Merrill Prentice Hall

Talbott, E. & Thiede, K. (1999). Pathways to antisocial behavior among adolescent girls. *Journal of Emotional and Behavioral Disorders, 7,* 31–39.

Torrez-Guzman, M. E., Abbate, J., Brisk, M. E., & Minaya-Rowe, L. (2002). Defining and documenting success for bilingual learners: A collective case study. *Bilingual Research Journal, 26*(1), 1–15.

U.S. Department of Education. (1999). *20th annual report to Congress on the implementation of the Individuals with Disabilities Education Act.* Washington, DC: Author.

U.S. Department of Education. (2003). *23rd Annual report to Congress on the implementation of the Individuals with Disabilities Education Act.* Washington, DC: Author.

U.S. Department of Education. (2005). *25th annual report to Congress on the Implementation of the Individuals with Disabilities Education Act for 2003.* Office of Special Education and Rehabilitative Services, Vol. I. Washington, DC: Author.

Umansky, W., & Hooper, S. R. (1998). Young children with special needs. (3rd ed.). New Jersey: Prentice Hall.

Utley, C. A., & Obiakor, F. E. (2001). Learning problems or learning disabilities of multicultural learners: Contemporary perspectives. In C. Utley & F. Obiakor (Eds.), *Special education, multicultural education, and school reform: Components of quality education for learners with mild disabilities* (pp. 90–117). Springfield, IL: Thomas.

Van Keulen, J. E., Weddington, G. T., & DeBose, C. E. (1998). *Speech, language learning, and the African American child.* Boston, MA: Allyn & Bacon.

Vaughn, S., Bos, C. S., & Schumm, J. S. (2003). *Teaching exceptional, diverse, and at-risk students in the general education classroom.* Boston, MA: Allyn & Bacon.

Venn, J. J. (2004). *Assessing students with special needs* (3rd ed.). Upper Saddle River, NJ: Merrill/Prentice Hall.

Walker, H. M., Colvin, G., & Ramsey, E. (1995). *Antisocial behavior in schools: Strategies and best practices*. Pacific Grove, CA: Brooks/Cole.

Wood, J. W. (2006). *Teaching students in inclusive settings: Adapting and accommodating instruction* (5th ed.). Upper Saddle, NJ: Merrill/Prentice Hall.

Woolsey, L. M., Harrison, T., Gardner, R., III. (2004). A preliminary examination of instructional arrangements, teaching behaviors, levels of academic responding of deaf middle school students in three different educational settings. *Education and Treatment of Children [special issue] 27*, 263–279.

Yell, M. L., Rogers, D., & Rogers, E. L. (1998). The legal history of special education: What a long, strange trip it's been! *Remedial and Special Education, 19*, 219–28.

PART 2

Culturally Responsive, Equitable and Inclusive Classrooms

Chapter 3

The Culturally Responsive Inclusive Classroom

This chapter builds on the information presented in chapter 1 of this book. It continues the discussion of the complex and daunting challenges faced by our schools and suggests ways of addressing their increasing diversity through multicultural education. In addition to adapting educational practices to the needs of traditional minorities, schools must also accommodate the unique needs presented by recent immigrant learners.

After reading this chapter, the reader should be able to answer the following questions:

1. What is the importance of culture in educating children?
2. What are the challenges of educating a culturally and linguistically diverse student population?
3. What are the benefits of having a culturally and linguistically diverse student population?
4. How can teachers treat each child in their classrooms in an equitable manner?
5. What are important resources for teachers in culturally diverse inclusive classrooms?
6. What is bilingual education?
7. How can teachers work more effectively with linguistically diverse learners?

By the end of this chapter, readers will obtain information on strategies to

1. Integrate multiculturalism into the classroom.
2. Provide culturally responsive education for English language learners.

How Have Our Schools Changed?

The commitment to provide an appropriate education for all children is relatively new. It was approximately 50 years ago when the U.S. Supreme Court ruled that the policy of separate but equal schools was unconstitutional (*Brown v. Board of Education, Topeka, Kansas*, 1954) thereby integrating the nation's classrooms. And it was just over 30 years ago that the right to a free and appropriate education (Education of All Handicapped Children Act, 1974, later renamed the Individuals with Disabilities Education Act, IDEA) was granted to children with disabilities. These two events caused fundamental changes in the education system. The Brown decision created more culturally and linguistically diverse classrooms, and IDEA dramatically increased the number of children with disabilities being served in schools. These two events—along with other factors, such as increased immigration—have resulted in record levels of diversity in our schools.

Increasingly, children in American schools are from culturally and linguistically diverse (CLD) families (Hoffman & Sable, 2006), which is particularly true in school districts in states that serve as entry points for arriving immigrants. Although the United States has long had significant numbers of descendants of Native Americans, Hispanics, and Africans, its culture and people have been largely European and Caucasian. Addressing the diversity of minority groups has been, historically, a challenge in U.S. schools, but the recent dramatic demographic changes have made the demands urgent and critical.

Diversity ought to be celebrated, for history clearly documents the valuable contributions made by every group, and future contributions to society can be maximized through quality education for all children. Thus, it is imperative that past practices of denying education to some be avoided so that all individuals, regardless of background or disabling condition, will be educated fully and equitably. In the 21st century, the federal government made a commitment to educate effectively all children (the No Child Left Behind Act, NCLB, 2001). Teachers must therefore be equipped with the skills to instruct children with and without disabilities as well as children from every ethnic and linguistic background.

What Is the Role of Culture in Schooling?

Educators need to provide a learning environment that is supportive and sensitive to the needs of their students. It would be impossible to create such a positive learning environment without taking into account cultural concerns. (Chapter 1 provided information on the definition and characteristics of culture.)

Children come to school already having begun the acculturation process. Cultures, by their very nature, create an environment in which children can begin to predict what to expect on a daily basis. For example, children become aware early in their development which behaviors will be rewarded and which punished in their culture. When placed in a significantly different environment, such as the school, children may become uneasy because they do not know what behavior is required to be successful in the new environment. Teachers can lessen children's anxiety by using terms, images, and customs that are familiar. For example, a teacher of Chinese children who are new to the country might label objects (e.g., desk, bookcase, clock, etc.) with both Chinese and English words to make the classroom more welcoming. Children of all backgrounds need to encounter aspects of their culture in the classroom, both in the visual displays and in the curriculum.

Culture is a complex concept and the behaviors and attitudes associated with culture are not always easily discerned, nor is the degree to which the child's background influences classroom learning easily determined. For many children, however, the gaps need to be bridged so that schools do not become foreign places for the CLD learner, but instead become inviting, nurturing entities where students learn and thrive. Thus, the question becomes one of how to incorporate the children's culture into the classroom so that it enhances instruction.

Cheveyo's Story

Cheveyo ("spirit warrior") is an 8-year-old Native American from the Hopi tribe. Cheveyo received his name, which was suggested by his paternal grandmother and aunts, on the 20th day after his birth in the Hopi tradition as the sun rose on the mesa.

Cheveyo is an active boy who likes to hunt and swim. He is a high-achieving student, consistently performing at the top of his class academically. Cheveyo's teacher believes he would benefit from being placed in a gifted program. However, Cheveyo is not always comfortable with his academic success despite encouragement by both parents and teachers. He does not like being set apart from his peers. He tries to avoid being differentiated from friends by not answering questions in class or sharing with his peers how well he does on tests and projects. Cheveyo struggles with pleasing his parents and wanting to be just like his friends.

Cheveyo and his parents have recently moved to Tucson from a pueblo in northeast Arizona, close to the Black mesa. In northeast Arizona Cheveyo was one of many Hopi children in the school. Now, Cheveyo will be attending a public school in Tucson, where for the first time he will be one of only a few Hopi children in a school. In fact, there are children from many different cultures attending the school. Cheveyo is a little nervous about the new school but has already met a couple of children in his new neighborhood and really likes them. He even met a girl who has the same passionate interest in plants and rocks that he has.

How Does Diversity Impact Education?

Perceptions of, and attitudes toward, cultural and linguistic diversity (CLD) often are rigorously based on a single attribute (i.e., race, ethnicity, or language) that is visible to others (Ishil-Jordan, 1997). There is a long history in this as well as many other countries of granting or restricting privileges based on such characteristics as race, country of origin, religion, or language. African Americans have historically had less access to certain privileges (e.g., education, housing, voting, jobs, etc.) based on their race. Both African Americans and

European Americans developed repertoires of written and unwritten customs regarding race and education. For example, some European Americans believed that African American students were not as academically capable as European American students, and that therefore teachers should not have the same academic expectations of African American students (Grant, 1916; Herrnstein & Murray 1994). How might lower expectations impact CLDE children? Lower teacher expectations might manifest in low rates of African American students being recommended for placement in gifted programs despite obvious indicators of giftedness. Ford (1995) for example, found in a statewide study in Virginia that even when African American students met the criteria to be placed in gifted programs, they were still less likely to be recommended for those programs then their European American peers.

How can educators place race, ethnicity, and linguistic differences in a proper context? Although these types of distinctions have their place in providing information about an individual, they are limited by their superficiality. The fact is many factors influence the behavior of an individual, and overreliance on any one of them may not yield the most useful information; Race, language, country of origin, religion, gender, or any single attribute of a person can lead to simplistic answers that do not provide clear information on the educational needs of individuals in the designated category.

Although there are behaviors common to specific cultures, it remains important to remember that cultures do not behave—individuals behave. A person's particular distinction (i.e., race, ethnicity, language) does not automatically indicate the degree to which the individual subscribes to the cultural norms of that group. Therefore, we cannot reliably predict an individual's behavior based solely on group distinctions, for no group is monolithic. There are many within-group differences, and there is always the danger of stereotyping when one overgeneralizes commonalities.

Although race, language, country of origin, and religious differences on their own do provide some information about individuals, these categories typically do not provide classroom teachers with the level of information required to provide meaningful academic instruction for students. A child whose ethnicity is Hispanic may be from any of many different cultures in South America, Mexico, or the Caribbean. The label gives some information about the child, such as the likelihood of his or her exposure to Spanish. However, the Hispanic label alone does not guarantee that the child is fluent in Spanish or even can speak Spanish at all. More valuable information about the child might be whether the child was born in the United States, what language is spoken at home, previous educational experiences, presence of a disability, and what skills the child currently possesses. This is the information that may further assist teachers in developing an overview of possible experiences and abilities of the child.

Knowing the ethnicity of a child is in some ways similar to knowing a child has been given the special education label. That label (e.g., specific learning disability) tells a teacher that the child has a higher probability of reading difficulties than a child without the label. However, additional information is needed because the SLD label does not guarantee that the child has reading problems. The learning disability might manifest itself in math, spoken language, or some other cognitive ability. In other words, educators need to regard ethnicity as potentially useful, but not decisive, information.

Why, then, is it important to track academic achievement and social behavior by race, ethnicity, language differences, and SES via schools, school districts, and states (see Table 3-1)? As discussed in chapter 2 of this text, when data are analyzed using these variables educators can determine important patterns of success or failure. What is it that the data reveal?

- African American, Hispanic, and Native American learners are at higher risk for receiving a special education disability label (specifically, high-incidence disabilities) (Artiles & Trent, 1994; Artiles, Trent, & Palmer, 2004; Obiakor, et al., 2002).

TABLE 3-1 Racial/ethnic composition of students ages 6 through 21 served under IDEA, Part B: 2001 [Data are for 50 states and District of Columbia.]

Hispanic	14.6
Black (not Hispanic)	20.5
Asian/Pacific Islander	1.9
American Indian/Alaska Native	1.3
White (not Hispanic)	61.7

While 16.6 percent of children between the ages of 6 and 21 in the general population are Hispanic and 15.1 percent are African American, according to 2001 population estimates, black students make up a larger proportion of students served under IDEA than do Hispanic students. [Population data are July 1 estimates for 2001, based on the 2000 decennial Census. The estimates were released by the Population Estimates Program, U.S. Census Bureau, Population Division in October 2003.]

Source: U.S. Department of Education, Office of Special Education Programs, Data Analysis System (DANS), Table AA15 in vol. 2.

- CLD learners (except for Asian Americans) are less likely to be placed in gifted education (Ford & Thomas, 1997; Losen & Orfield, 2002; Patton, 1997).
- CLD learners, especially those who are poor, are at increased risk of experiencing poor instruction (Losen & Orfield, 2002).
- Hispanic, Native American, and African American learners are at increased risk for dropping out of school and school suspension (Losen & Orfield, 2002).

The data reveal more about the educational system and its inequalities than about learners. The information thus becomes a useful tool in assisting educators to determine where and with whom educational environments need to be improved.

What Are Culturally Responsive Classrooms?

There is no magical solution based solely on ethnicity that will instructionally benefit all students. Instruction in each classroom needs to be empirically sound, utilizing evidence-based principles (see chapter 10 for a discussion of effective instruction). Although there are no silver bullets, teachers can enhance the classroom environment for each child through cultural sensitivity using basic multicultural education principles. Multicultural education, a reform movement that was born out of the failure of schools to adequately address the needs of CLD children (Sleeter, 1999), is meant to transform educational systems so that all children (males, females, exceptional children, and CLD children) can have an equal opportunity for academic success (Banks, 2006). It challenges educators to think differently about how they should educate children in a diverse democratic society (Lesson-Hurley, 1996). Multicultural education does not benefit just children from CLD families or children with exceptionalities; majority children are benefactors as well.

Multicultural education, carefully designed, should recognize the uniqueness of majority and minority children, better preparing children to live in a world with increasing diversity. Banks (2006) describes four dimensions of multicultural education: content integration, knowledge construction, equity pedagogy, and an empowering school culture.

Content Integration

Content integration involves using examples from various cultures to explain principles, theories, and concepts. The basic concepts, principles, and theories are not altered in any way, but the use of examples from diverse cultures can assist in making the instruction clearer for CLD children (Tam & Gardner, 1997). The teacher does not assume that an exemplar used to explain a concept is acceptable simply because it is common to most middle-class children. This is especially true with children who are learning English as a second language. A descriptive sentence in a story, such as "When James walked into the house, the first thing he did was *draw the drapes*," can be confusing. The teacher should question students (e.g., "What was the first thing that James did in the house? What does 'draw the drapes' mean?") to make sure that information is being received accurately. Idioms can be particularly difficult for children who are English language learners as well as for individuals with disabilities (e.g., hearing impairments, communication disorders, and mental retardation). The teacher must solicit responses from students to determine if they have an accurate understanding.

Knowledge Construction

Knowledge construction helps students understand how implicit assumptions, perspectives, and previous experience can influence how information is interpreted and constructed. Having children analyze an event from multiple perspectives can help them see how the same event can be interpreted in more than one way. For example, when studying World War II, Cheveyo's teacher might ask him to view the war from the perspective of a Jewish child. Cheveyo would need to try to determine what daily life might have been like for a Jewish child in Nazi Germany. Later, Cheveyo might be asked to view the war through the perspective of an Aryan German child. Cheveyo's lessons also might include information or stories about the roles that Native Americans and other groups played during this war.

Equity Pedagogy

Equity pedagogy encourages teachers to match the instruction to the learning styles of the children. Maybe the children are from a Native American culture where collectivism is an important value and many of the children's experiences involve working toward a common goal rather than an individual goal. Using peer-mediated instructional strategies could be effective and reassuring for children who are culturally more familiar with group tasks to achieve goals. Remember that Cheveyo closely identifies with his peers even at the expense of his educational opportunities. The teacher can incorporate that information into cooperative learning opportunities. This may encourage students to have a greater investment in the curriculum and their academic achievement.

Empowering School Culture

Schools that promote equity among students without respect to gender, cultural, ethnic, language, or SES differences are empowering to children (Vaughn, Bos, & Schumm, 2003). Educators need to establish a school environment that promotes acceptance of differences and is intolerant of bias or prejudice and work hard to become familiar with the communities in which their students live. Educators must know themselves and accept the premise that all children, including those with disabilities, can be empowered to see themselves as capable learners, especially those with disabilities, who are impoverished, and/or who are from disparaged or subjugated groups.

Cheveyo's Story Continued

Cheveyo's teacher, Mrs. Grooms, is an energetic young teacher who wants to use the diversity in her classroom as an asset. Mrs. Grooms has decided to use the upcoming Thanksgiving holiday as an opportunity to celebrate the contributions that the Indians and Pilgrims have made to society. She has selected several books about Native Americans and early settlers to read to the children. Mrs. Grooms has also decided to collaborate with another class and build a teepee as a way to teach the children about Native American lifestyle.

Mrs. Grooms knows that Cheveyo has recently moved from a reservation and as she is instructing the children about Native Americans, she says, "Cheveyo, you used to live on a reservation. Can you tell the class what you know about a teepee?" Cheveyo looks confused, so Mrs. Grooms repeats the question. Cheveyo looks around at all the children waiting to hear what he has to say. Cheveyo just drops his head on his desk and uses his arms to cover his face. Mrs. Grooms does not understand what has just happened, but she redirects the children back to herself and continues the lesson.

Cheveyo never lifts his head from his desk for the rest of the class and refuses to respond to Mrs. Grooms when she tries to talk to him. At the end of class, he quickly leaves without a word. Mrs. Grooms decides to talk to Mr. Liu, the principal, at the end of the school day about the perplexing behavior.

How Can We Appreciate Diversity in the Classroom?

Educators can use cultural and linguistic diversity to achieve their education goals, but infusing multicultural education into the curriculum is not easy. First, teachers must have excellent knowledge of the academic content to be taught. Second, teachers must purposefully plan lessons with the intent of including culturally sensitive information (Gollnick & Chinn, 2004). Third, since no one teacher can be from every cultural and linguistic group, teachers must assume the role of learners; that is, they should seek to learn about various culturally and linguistically diverse groups, especially those to which their students belong. Cheveyo's teacher, Mrs. Grooms, did achieve the first two steps: understanding the traditions surrounding Thanksgiving and the inclusion of culturally relevant information. However, she did not understand the differences among Native American tribal cultures.

Despite the potential for such errors as Mrs. Grooms's, it is important for teachers to purposefully incorporate culturally sensitive information into lessons. Even teachers who do not have CLD students in their classrooms should include multicultural education in their instruction in order to build understanding about diverse cultures and better prepare their students to live in an increasingly diverse America. Teachers can approach learning about diversity just as they do any other subject of interest. Some strategies for gathering information are the following:

1. Read books about the culture, both fiction and nonfiction. Try to read books that are written by an author who is a part of that culture.
2. Talk to individuals who are members of the culture. Tell them that you are interested in learning about their culture and ask them questions not only about their culture but also about barriers they face when interacting with the dominant culture or other cultural groups. This latter information will assist the teacher to know some of the challenges students might face and provide an opportunity to eliminate the

Explicit one-on-one instruction is often necessary to maximize academic gains.

challenges in the classroom or to help students develop skills to overcome the challenge.
3. Participate in community activities of CLD groups.
4. Talk to other teachers about how they have incorporated multicultural themes into the curriculum.
5. Ask CLD parents to share with the class their customs and traditions. Holidays and how they are celebrated vary across cultures. Sharing these varied experiences offers the opportunity for a class discussion of acceptance and tolerance.
6. Interview family members of the children in the class and note the within-group and across-group differences.
7. Permit children to take home tape recorders to interview family members about their most enjoyable family traditions. Permit children to share their experiences with the class.
8. Utilize web sites that can provide information about various cultures, such as the Cultural & Linguistically Appropriate Services web site (http://clas.uiuc.edu/links.html).
9. Develop a series of common home–school forms (e.g., homework log, social behavior feedback, upcoming events, parent permission, etc.) in the parents' home language and have them verified for accuracy by an adult fluent in the language. Use web-based translations with caution, for they may not always translate concepts accurately.
10. Use telephone voice mail for weekly homework assignments and school translators to provide messages in the families' home languages.
11. Graph important student academic behaviors (e.g., reading accuracy, math performance, quiz/tests scores, etc.) so that parents can see academic achievement visually.

How Do We Implement Culturally Responsive Lessons?

Including multicultural information in the curriculum should make the class more interesting for the students. It allows the teacher to use students' prior knowledge in order to teach new information, couching the new in the familiar. Teachers can begin with one class or academic content area and then eventually allow multiculturalism to permeate the entire curriculum. As with any new knowledge or skill, the teacher might not always get it right (remember Cheveyo's teacher). Teachers should readily acknowledge to students that they are attempting to incorporate multicultural themes into the curriculum. Sometimes students (especially middle and high school students) will reverse roles with the teacher to explain customs and beliefs, assisting the teacher on appropriate ways to present the specific cultural information. This can be a particularly effective way to motivate students and help them become invested in academic instruction.

Multiculturalism and special education are complementary. Both place the student, rather than the curriculum, at the center of instruction, which, to be considered effective, must have a positive impact on student achievement. The underlying principle of both multiculturalism and special education is not only that all children can learn but that all children can be taught effectively. Both include the idea that instruction should promote tolerance and acceptance of differences and that lessons should accommodate differences in a nonjudgmental way, showing how a single goal can be accomplished in multiple ways. For example, typical students might be given 20 minutes for a quiz while a student with a disability might be allowed 30 minutes, but both the typical students and the student with the disability are focused on demonstrating mastery of the same skill(s). Lessons should help students to better understand and resist racism, classism, sexism, and discrimination, including discrimination against those who are different due to disabilities, language, sexual preference, age, or weight. In the end, students should emerge from education that incorporates multiculturalism as productive members of society who believe in social justice and equality.

It is important to recognize that the subjugated status of children from diverse backgrounds in this society disproportionately places many of them at risk for failure in school and in later life (Losen & Orfield, 2002). Although these children should not be prejudged, culturally responsive education dictates that they be assessed immediately upon entering school to determine areas of specific strengths and special needs. Substantial pupil deficits are not an indication of potential failure, but rather of the need for greater effort on the part of educators. For example, a kindergarten class with 50% of its students lacking in preschool experiences and critical prereading skills such as phonemic awareness is likely to need more than the typical kindergarten readiness curriculum. The school should immediately adapt its staff and curriculum so that these students receive the intensive and appropriate instruction needed to be on grade level by the end of the school year.

By the same token, culturally responsive schools are aware that many talented students from minority groups go unidentified. These students' gifts and talents need to be nurtured, particularly if the students are impoverished, because often their communities and families do not have sufficient resources to provide the special advantages these children need. In these schools, educators should deliberately and diligently seek out children with promise and then work systematically to promote their special abilities. Culturally responsive schools do not make a priori negative assumptions about children. They are, however, willing and able to address the challenges that children may present due to differences of culture, socioeconomic status, and so forth. Approaches to these challenges are discussed throughout this book.

Cheveyo's Story Continued

Mrs. Grooms enters Mr. Liu's office at the end of the day and explains to him the lesson about Native Americans and what happened when she asked Cheveyo to talk about teepees. She thought it would be a wonderful opportunity for Cheveyo as a bright new student to share important information with the class. Mr. Lui listens carefully to Mrs. Grooms and compliments her on the selection of books and her efforts to include information about different cultures. Mr. Lui then explains to Mrs. Grooms (who is originally from St. Louis, Mo.) that Cheveyo is a Hopi Indian and that the Hopi do not live in teepees. Their traditional home is a pueblo and Cheveyo was probably very embarrassed to be called upon to explain something he did not know anything about.

Mrs. Grooms feels terrible that her attempt to be culturally responsive was so unsuccessful. Mr. Lui suggests that she contact Cheveyo's parents to explain the situation and apologize. Mr. Lui also suggests that she explain the error to the class as well. Mr. Lui then makes these suggestions for working with CLDE:

1. Always remember that within the large culturally and linguistically diverse groups (e.g., Native Americans) there is a great deal of diversity in terms of customs, beliefs, language, etc. . . . Therefore, you must be careful about making assumptions about any one child based on the large category.
2. Even if Cheveyo came from a tribe that historically lived in teepees and lived on a reservation, that does not mean he is personally familiar with teepees. It is dangerous to assume that because a person belongs to a particular group he or she is familiar with all of the customs or practices of that group, especially if those customs are not currently employed.
3. When working with CLDE students, it is better to encourage children to volunteer what they know about cultural practices than to put them on the spot with a direct question. So the question "Does anyone have information to share about teepees?" could have been posed to the entire class, thereby allowing Cheveyo and every other child an opportunity to respond or not respond.

Mrs. Grooms calls Cheveyo's family that evening and both explains and apologizes. Cheveyo's father is understanding and indicates he will talk with his son. He also says he will come to class and talk to the entire class about the customs of his Hopi tribe.

Mrs. Grooms decides that she needs to learn more about her students so that she can better incorporate the children's culture into the curriculum. She develops a four-part plan for herself. First, she will read books about each of the cultures represented in her classroom. Second, she will attend community activities of the various ethnic groups. Third, she will have all students bring in pictures and a narrative about their lives from birth to the present. Fourth, she will include information she learns about other cultures into future lessons.

How Can We Provide Culturally Responsive Education for English Language Learners?

Children who come to school with limited English proficiency present a unique challenge to educators. Schools are required to provide equal educational opportunities for all students (Coleman Report, 1968), and children who are bilingual have the right to be educated in the language in which they are more proficient (Artiles & Oritz, 2002). The U.S. Supreme Court further established language rights as a civil right in the *Lau v. Nichols* decision in 1974. Baca and Cervantes (2004) state, "... bilingual special education may be defined as the use of the home language and the home culture along with English in an individually designed program of special instruction for the student in

Educators must be prepared to work with the increasingly diverse U.S. student population.

an inclusive environment" (p.18). Bilingual education requires that educators provide instruction for students in a manner that best allows students to achieve academically while they are still mastering English with the goals of cognitive development, affective development, linguistic growth, and cultural enrichment (Baca & Cervantes, 2004). Thus, bilingual education focuses on developing the whole child as the child transitions into fluent English.

Can CLDE Learners Become Efficient English Language Learners?

There are two categories of second language development: concurrent (or simultaneous) and sequential (Baca & Cervantes, 2004). If a learner begins second language development prior to the age of 3, this is considered concurrent language development; beginning a second language after 3 years of age is considered sequential (Kessler, 1984).

The age of 3 is not viewed as educationally significant (Baca & Cervantes, 2004), but not enough is known about the development of a second language. Does second language development follow the same pattern as first language development? What is the precise effect of parents on the language development of their children? What educators do know is that language, like any skill, needs practice to develop. Therefore, social interaction is important (Ellis, 1999). Second language learners might have vastly different levels of opportunity to practice the second language. Some may only be able to practice their second language (English) during school hours; others may be able to practice at home or in their community after school. Older second language learners (sequential language development) may be able to use learning strategies to aid in the acquisition of the second language (Baca & Cervantes, 2004). Second language learners who are literate in their first language can use that knowledge to acquire the second language even when it uses a different alphabet (Nguyen, Shin, & Krashen, 2001).

Researchers have found that CLDE learners can learn a second language and learn to communicate and become literate in English (Kessler, 1984: Rondal, 2000). Contrary to a common belief, acquiring a second language does not inhibit the CLDE learner's academic development (Delpit, 2002; Wong Fillmore, 2000). CLDE learners are similar to their typical peers in that they are more able to acquire a second language if they have mastered their first language (Perozzi & Sanchez, 1992). Additionally, Wong Fillmore (2000) argues that it is better to have parents who are not fluent in English use their home language when speaking to their children rather than use only English. The unintended result of using only English to communicate may be broken parent-child communication and the possible loss of the family's home language.

Immigration

One reason for the increase of English language learners in U.S. schools is the unprecedented influx of immigrants (see Figure 3–1), especially from non-European countries (Camarota, 2005). There are approximately 35.2 million immigrants (legal and illegal) in the United States—12.1% of the total population—only slightly less then record of 14.7% reached in 1910 (Camarota, 2005). In the last 5 years, it is estimated that 7.9 million new

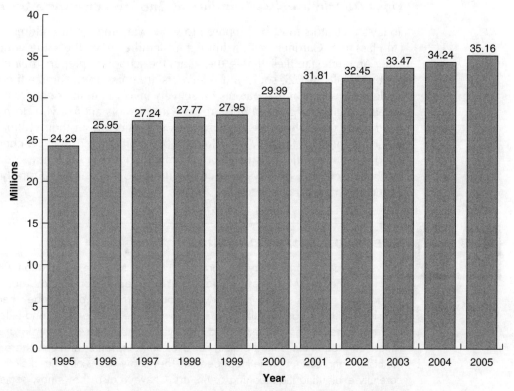

FIGURE 3–1 Number of Immigrants living in the United States, 1995–2005

Source: S. A. Camarota, December, 2005, Immigrants at Mid-decade: A Snapshot of America's Foreign-born Population in 2005, Center for Immigration Studies, retrieved February 4, 2006, from http://www.cis.org/ articles/2005/back1405.html

immigrants have arrived, with approximately 50% of than coming to the United States illegally (Camarota, 2005). As noted by Camarota (2005):

- Thirty-one percent of immigrants have not completed high school, about three-a-half times the rate of native-born Americans.
- The poverty rate for immigrant families is 18.4% compared to 11.7% for native-born American families.
- Immigration accounts for almost all of the increase in public school enrollment over the last two decades, approximately 10.3 million children.

Beginning with the first permanent settlement at Jamestown, America has historically been a nation of immigrants, who were primarily from Europe, with the notable exceptions of enslaved Africans (1619–1863) and Chinese laborers (mid- to late-1800s). Currently, immigrants are arriving in large numbers from Africa, Asia, Mexico, and South America (Camarota, 2005).

The current immigrant pattern has a direct impact on America's schools. In particular, those school districts located in large port cities (e.g., Boston, New York, Miami, San Diego, Los Angeles, Seattle, etc.) have been confronted with the problem of how to appropriately educate large numbers of children from culturally and linguistically diverse families, many of whom are English language learners. The CLDE learners among them are a heterogeneous group, like the rest of America's school-age population, ranging from those with severe disabilities to the highly gifted.

How Do We Involve Families of English Language Learners?

Today's educators must be prepared to work with immigrant children and their families (Al-Hassan & Gardner, 2002). Immigrant families have the same educational goals as other American families; that is, they want the schools to prepare their children to be productive adults in U.S. society. If educators are going to maximize the potential of their students, it is critical that parents be actively involved in their children's education. CLD parents, including parents who are new immigrants and/or who do not speak English, need to be given the same opportunities to participate in their children's education as other parents (Al-Hassan & Gardner, 2002). Parents can help teachers determine if a child is having difficulties because of limited English proficiency, a disability, or both. Further discussion of ways to increase the involvement of culturally diverse parents occurs in chapter 6 of this text.

Cheveyo's Story Continued

Cheveyo's father, Mr. *Masayesva* arrives at school to share information with the class about the Hopi tribe. Mr. *Masayesva* decided that this presentation would be an excellent opportunity to work with his son so that Cheveyo could learn more of the tribe's heritage. Father and son share with the class that the Hopi have lived in the same area of land at least since 500 A.D. and have the longest authenticated history of occupation of a single area by any Native American tribe in the United States. For over an hour, father and son share information about the history and custom of the Hopi people. They show works of art and clothing, with Cheveyo carefully explaining the meaning of the art. Cheveyo also shows how some Hopi live the traditional way while others live the same as most Americans. Cheveyo seems excited when talking about Hopi traditions. The other children eagerly ask questions and Mr. Masayesva patiently answers each one. At the end of the presentation, Cheveyo and Mr. *Masayesva* play Hopi music and teach the children a traditional Hopi dance.

Mrs. Grooms notices that all of the children seemed fascinated with the presentation and that Cheveyo's pride is obvious. She decides that she will give other families an opportunity to share their heritage with the class, which she feels will benefit all of the children. Mrs. Grooms develops a checklist she will share with the parents about what to cover in the presentation: important cultural/historical events, famous persons, lifestyle, holidays, clothes, food, and music.

Summary

Culture is an essential part of the human experience, providing a context in which individuals can live and socialize. Every person operates within some cultural context. Comprising the beliefs, history, customs, contributions, behaviors, and perspectives of an identified people, every culture has four basic characteristics: it is learned, shared, adapts, and is dynamic.

To accomplish the goal of providing an appropriate education for all children, educators must build bridges between home and school, the two most important environments for children. In order to infuse multiculturalism into the curriculum, teachers must be comfortable with their own backgrounds and abilities, be skilled in academic content, and be willing to learn about diverse cultures. Above all, they must possess a fundamental belief that all children can learn and hold high standards of excellence for each child. They should use the cultural information they acquire to enhance instruction for their students. Including culture in the curriculum is not easy, for it requires work and dedication. However, the rewards are children who are affirmed and encouraged.

Related Learning Activities

1. Read about the history of culturally and linguistically diverse populations and about famous individuals and events from the cultures represented in your classroom. Incorporate that information into lessons.

2. Attend community and religious gatherings of culturally and linguistically diverse populations. Ethnic festivals are wonderful places to sample diverse cultures. Encourage students in your class to attend ethnic festivals and to write about the experience.

3. Read children's books written by CLD authors to access the authors' perspective about events. Write about how an author's perspective on an event is different from or similar to what you might have felt in a similar situation.

4. Develop a list of CLD community contacts. The contacts should include individuals willing to come into your class and share information about traditions that are important to their culture. These individuals can also give you guidance on how cultural information can be included in the class lessons.

5. Develop a diversity calendar, noting special days for CLD groups and the meanings of the special days. Discuss the special days as they occur throughout the year. Provide opportunities for students to volunteer information about how they celebrate the special days with their families.

6. Have students write about their family culture. Divide them into groups of 3 or 4 and have them share their papers with each other. Try to arrange the groups so that students who normally sit together are not in the same group.

References

Al-Hassan, S., & Gardner, R., III. (2002). Involving parents of immigrant students with disabilities in the educational process. *TEACHING Exceptional Children, 34,* 52–58.

Artiles, A. J., & Ortiz, A. (2002). *English language learners with special education needs: Identification, assessment, and instruction.* McHenry, IL: Center for Applied Linguistics, Delta Systems Co. Inc.

Artiles, A. J., & Trent, S. C. (1994). Overrepresentation of minority students in special education: A continuing debate. *Journal of Special Education, 27,* 410–437.

Artiles, A. J., Trent, S. C., & Palmer, J. (2004). Culturally diverse students in special education: Legacies and prospects. In J. A. Banks & C. M. Banks (Eds.), *Handbook of research on multicultural education* (2nd ed., pp.716–735). San Francisco: Jossey-Bass.

Baca, L. M., & Cervantes, H. T. (2004). *The bilingual special education interface* (4th ed.). Upper Saddle River, NJ: Merrill/Prentice Hall.

Banks, J. A. (2006). *Cultural diversity and education foundations, curriculum and teaching* (5th ed.). Boston: Allyn & Bacon.

Camarota, S. A. (December 2005). *Immigrants at mid-decade: A snapshot of America's foreign-born population in 2005. Center for Immigration Studies.* Retrieved February 4, 2006, from http://www.cis.org/articles/2005/back1405.html

Coleman Report (1968). *Equality of educational opportunity.* Washington, DC: U.S. Office of Education as mandated by 1964 Civil Rights Act.

Delpit, L. (2002). No kinda sense. In L. Delpit & J. K. Dowdy (Eds.), *The skin that we speak: Thoughts on language and culture in the classroom* (pp. 33–48). New York: New Press.

Ellis, R. (1999). *Learning a second language through interaction.* Philadelphia, PA: John Benjamins.

Ford, D. Y. (1995). *A study of achievement and underachievement among gifted, potentially gifted, and average Black students.* Storrs, CT. The University of Connecticut, National Research Center for the Gifted and Talented.

Ford, D. Y., & Thomas, A. (1997). Underachievement among gifted minority students: Problems and promises. *ERIC Clearinghouse on Disabilities and Gifted Education.* Digest #E544. http://eric.hoagiesgifted.org

Gollnick, D. M., & Chinn, P. G. (2004). *Multicultural education in a pluralistic society* (6th ed.). Upper Saddle River, NJ: Merrill/Prentice Hall.

Grant, M. (1916). The passing of the great race; or, The racial basis of European history. New York: C. Scribner. Retrieved March 14, 2007, from http://books.google.com/books?vid=OCLC09053224&id=Q9cKAAAAIAAJ&pg=RA3-PA3&lpg=RA3-PA3&dq=The+passing+of+the+great+race%3B+or,+The+racial+basis+of+European+history

Herrnstein, R. J., & Murray, C. (1994). The bell curve: Intelligence and class structure in American life. New York: Free Press.

Hoffman, L., & Sable. J. (2006). *Public elementary and secondary students, staff, schools, and school districts: School year 2003–04* (NCES 2006-307). Washington, DC: National Center for Education Statistics, U.S. Department of Education.

Ishil-Jordan, S. R. (1997). When behavior differences are not disorders. In A. J. Artiles & G. Zamora-Duran G. (Eds.), *Reducing disproportionate representation of culturally diverse students in special and gifted education* (pp. 28–46). Reston, VA: Council for Exceptional Children.

Kessler, C. (1984). Language development in bilingual children. In N. Miller (Ed.), *Bilingualism and language disability* (pp. 26–54). San Diego, CA: College-Hill Press.

Lesson-Hurley, J. (1996). *The foundations of dual language instruction.* White Plains, NY: Longman.

Losen D. J., & Orfield, G. (2002). *Racial inequality in special education.* Cambridge, MA: Harvard Education Publishing Group.

Nguyen, A., Shin, F., & Krashen, S. (2001). Development of the first language is not a barrier to second language acquisition: Evidence from Vietnamese immigrants to the United States. *International Journal of Bilingual Education and Bilingualism, 4,* 159–164.

Obiakor, F., Algozzine, B., Thurlow, M., Gwalla-Ogisi, N., Enwefa, S., Enwefa, R., & McIntosh, A. (2002). *Addressing the issue of disproportionate representation: Identification and assessment of culturally diverse students with emotional and behavioral disorders.* Arlington, VA: Council for Children with Behavior Disorders.

Patton, J. M. (1997). Disproportionate representation in gifted programs: Best practices for meeting the challenge. In A. J. Artiles & G. Zamora-Duran (Eds.), *Reducing disproportionate representation of culturally diverse students in special and gifted education* (pp. 59–85). Reston, VA: Council for Exceptional Children.

Perozzi, J. A., & Sanchez, M. L. C. (1992). The effect of instruction in L_1 on receptive development of L_2 for bilingual children with language delay. *Language, Speech, and Hearing Services in Schools, 23,* 348–352.

Restoring Touch. Restoration: Reaching America's oldest cultures through practical acts of God's love. Retrieved August 11, 2007, from http://www.hopi.org.

Rondal, J. A. (2000). Bilingualism in mental retardation: Some prospective views. *Saggi: Child Development and Disabilities, 26*(1), 57–64. Retrieved March 7, 2006, from http://www.altonweb.com/cs/downsyndrome/index.htm?page=bilingualism.html

Sleeter, C. E. (1999). *Making choices for multicultural education: Five approaches to race, class, and gender* (3rd ed.). New York: John Wiley & Sons.

Tam, B., & Gardner, R., III. (1997). Multicultural education for students with behavioral disorders: Much to do about nothing or a real issue? *Addressing Cultural and Linguistic Diversity in Special Education: Issues and Trends, 2,* 1–11.

U.S. Department of Education (2003). 25th Annual Report to Congress on the Implementation of the Individuals with Disabilities Education Act. Washington, DC.

Vaughn, S., Bos, C. S., & Schumm, J. S. (2003). *Teaching exceptional, diverse, and at-risk students in the general education classroom.* (3rd ed.). Boston: Allyn & Bacon.

Wong Fillmore, L. (2000). Loss of family languages: Should educators be concerned? *Theory into Practice, 39,* 203–210.

Chapter 4

The Disciplined CLDE Learner

School discipline is essential to the effective schooling of all children regardless of cultural background, gender, or socioeconomic level. The negative disciplinary outcomes that disproportionately impact CLDE learners may be, in part, a function of the discontinuities that are so pervasive in our schools. Promoting student discipline requires developing an understanding of culturally based behaviors and the function of these behaviors, creating culturally responsive, caring school environments, developing orderly school environments, effectively teaching the desired behaviors while extinguishing undesired ones, and affirming students' strengths as well as reinforcing newly taught behaviors. The emphasis here is on the special issues surrounding disciplined culturally diverse learners with disabilities.

After reading this chapter, the reader should be able to answer the following questions:

1. How does the culture of the school positively or negatively influence the social behaviors of culturally diverse learners with exceptionalities?
2. What are the discipline problems in the schools and how do schools typically address them?
3. How can we differentiate discipline from punishment?

4. What are the unique discipline issues for students from culturally diverse backgrounds?
5. What are the features of effective discipline for culturally diverse students?
6. What are the IDEA specifications for the discipline of children with disabilities?
7. How can we conduct culturally responsive functional behavior assessments?
8. How can the model of Positive Behavioral Intervention Supports contribute to more positive school environments for culturally diverse learners?
9. How can we affirm culturally diverse students with and at-risk for disabilities?

By the end of this chapter readers will obtain information on strategies for:

1. Culturally responsive effective discipline.
2. Culturally responsive functional behavior assessments.
3. Culturally responsive positive school environments.
4. Culturally responsive pupil affirmations.

Culture and the Disciplined Environment

A guiding principle of special education, especially since the advent of PL 94-142, is that all children, regardless of disabling condition, have the right to a free and public education. The larger educational community also believes that every child has the right to be educated in a safe environment that is positive and conducive to learning. As a matter of fact, one of the explicit goals of the U.S. Department of Education is to ensure that all schools are safe, disciplined, and drug free (U.S. Department of Education, 2004). Schools are also challenged to provide a free and complete education for all children, including those with disabilities, without infringing on the rights of any student. Children who receive effective instruction are more likely to become adaptive in their behavior. Thus, removal from formal schooling not only deprives students of an academic education but also limits the opportunities for instruction that contributes to social competence. Effective schools are those that are able to provide high-quality academic and social instruction for all students within the least restrictive environment (LRE).

Lucas

Lucas is a 7-year-old second-grade student who has exhibited problem behaviors since he entered kindergarten. Lucas is not well liked by his peers, although he is rarely aggressive towards them physically. He does, however, taunt them and touches them inappropriately. Teachers mainly complain about Lucas's off-task, noncompliant, and disruptive behavior. When he wants the teacher's attention, he not only calls out the teacher's name without raising his hand and waiting to be called on, but if the teacher does not respond immediately, he will keep calling her or banging on the desk until she does attend to him. He also is quick to interrupt the teacher and others, talking over them as they speak. This behavior is so disruptive and annoying that the teacher often responds by sending Lucas out of the classroom or to in-school suspension.

Lucas is an African American male who is being reared by a single mother. He is an only child. His mother works for minimum wage and the family falls within the low socioeconomic level. His father is not in the home and, since his father has had a history of criminality, it is unclear how much contact Lucas has had with him. Lucas does spend his summers with his grandmother in another city, who the mother complains spoils him. Lucas attends school every day and is rarely absent. He is well groomed and cared for. It appears that Lucas is lacking a positive male influence in his life, including school, where nearly all of the staff is female and European American.

Academically, Lucas is about a half year below grade level in reading. Despite his troubling behavior, he does display a genuine desire to learn. When interviewed by one of his teachers, he stated that what he wanted most was to be able to read.

Lucas experiences alienation from his teachers, who consistently send him out of the classroom for disciplinary referrals, and his peers, who rarely elect to interact with him. He appears to be aware of his marginalized status, is increasingly demanding of others, and has not learned appropriate ways to solicit adult or peer attention. These are skills he needs to learn, but to this point the only actions by school personnel have been reactive with a focus on punishment.

Lucas's disruptive behavior and office referrals continued to increase and eventually he was referred to the school's intervention assistance team. The team pondered various options. Should Lucas be assessed for special education placement for behavior disorders? Would it be possible to maintain Lucas in a general education class? How might they reduce the number of disciplinary referrals he is receiving? How might they improve his positive interactions with others? What are some of Lucas's strengths that should be considered in this evaluation? These and other questions about Lucas, along with related interventions, will be discussed in this chapter.

What Is the Relationship Between Culture and Social Behavior?

As we note throughout this book, culture does not consist of a rigidly prescribed set of attributes that produce uniform behaviors among all members, but rather is a general framework through which we might view different groups. For example, if we viewed the traditional art of East Asian, West African, and Western European peoples, we could easily classify them according to their characteristic designs. But in closely examining the art within any one group, we would detect great variation. Likewise, children from culturally diverse groups present many physical and social similarities while exhibiting a wide array of individual differences. Nevertheless, educators can gain important insights into children's behaviors by understanding the powerful influence of cultural factors. The cultural differences may be so great that some children misinterpret the culture of the school and, in turn, school personnel may misperceive the culturally specific behaviors of the children.

How Does the Culture of the School Affect Children's Social Behavior?

Schools are primary socializing agents. They greatly influence the way children develop and the way they perceive themselves. Our schools largely reflect a European American or Western culture that emphasizes individualism, competition, and a Eurocentric curriculum

(Boykin, Tyler, Watkins-Lewis, & Kizzie, 2006; Cartledge & Milburn, 1996; Weinstein, Tomlinson-Clarke, & Curran, 2004). Culture is transmitted in the schools on both a formal and an informal basis, with the teacher playing a most important role in this process. Some important teacher characteristics include empathy, caring, healthy classroom climate, leadership skills, humor, and involvement with children's social relations (Gay, 2000; Monroe, 2005; Schneider, 1993). Compassion and flexibility are particularly important for teachers of culturally and linguistically diverse (CLD) students, who, regardless of the child's background or disability, must believe in the child's ability to make progress and refrain from assuming that all of the child's difficulties reside solely within the child.

As part of the "hidden curriculum," teachers, like parents, are powerful forces in shaping children's behaviors and serve as models for social development (Cartledge & Milburn, 1995; Digiovanni, 2004). Not all of the messages conveyed are constructive, however, particularly for CLD students and females. Irvine (1990), for example, observes that students may readily learn from this hidden curriculum that some children are favored by teachers while others are not, that well-dressed children are more likely to be called on than poorly dressed ones, that some children never succeed in gaining the favor of the teacher despite their best efforts, and that teachers display more favor towards children whose parents participate in the schools. Similarly, other professionals remind us of the way the hidden curriculum is weighted in favor of males (Digiovanni, 2004; Wren, 1999). According to Digiovanni, the scarcity of females and individuals of culturally diverse backgrounds in the written curriculum and visual displays sends powerful messages about how society views and values certain subgroups (i.e., females and minorities).

Classrooms are hierarchical in structure, the teacher is the focus of all communication, and children need to maintain their attention on the teacher (Ledlow, 1992). The common communication culture of the school may be at odds, however, with the experiences of many CLD children, who may be socialized at home in substantially different ways (Gay, 2000). For example, Ledlow mentions that teachers often felt Indian children were not paying attention because the children did not look at them or make behavioral responses indicative of listening. Along the same lines, Morse and Cole (2002) note that when a teacher scolds an African or Hispanic American student, the student will look away and the teacher may view that action as challenging her authority. Delpit (1995) points out the difference between the direct language used in African American communities and the indirect and veiled language typical of the European American middle-class school culture. Using indirect language in the form of questions such as "Are you out of your area?" or "Do you want to begin your work?" may be confusing to some students who are used to directions such as "Sit down and do not get up until I give you permission." Under these circumstances, students may view the teacher's directives as optional while the teacher perceives the student's behavior as willful and obstreperous.

One complaint about Lucas, the student in the scenario at the beginning of this chapter, was that he was noncompliant. His teacher, Ms. Norman, complained that Lucas either was slow to comply or that he failed to comply altogether. Observation in Ms. Norman's classroom showed that Lucas did indeed fail to comply in a timely fashion for approximately 30% of the time. It also revealed that Ms. Norman spoke in a soft, barely audible voice, that she delivered directives from across the room, and that she often gave instructions in the form of a question (e.g., Students would you like to take out your math books and get started on your work?). Observers determined that Ms. Norman needed to learn how to deliver precision requests (Rhode, Jenson, & Reavis, 1992). That is, to begin by standing close to Lucas and giving the direction in a quiet, firm voice with a nonquestion format, e.g., "Please take out your spelling book and begin working." If Lucas failed to comply within 5 seconds, she would return to his desk and say in the same voice, "I *need* you to start working." If Lucas remained noncompliant, she would repeat her directive with a warning of possible negative consequences such as a loss of 10 minutes of recess time. Lucas was to be praised when he responded immediately to Ms. Norman's directions. Ms. Norman learned that she was much more effective with Lucas and his classmates when she spoke to them using direct, firm, assertive, and positive language.

Critical messages also are communicated nonverbally to children through important aspects of the school culture, such as ability groupings. Schneider (1993) concluded from his research that when students are grouped on the basis of academic ability, social boundaries form between high- and low-achieving children, and these boundaries rarely break. Likewise, competitive environments are shown to increase the alienation of academically disadvantaged students, leading them to escape by dropping out of school. CLD students who are consistently tracked in low-ability or special education segregated classes and less often into advanced tracks are at a distinct disadvantage (Ferri & Connor, 2005) and begin to see themselves as inferior and low achievers (Cartledge & Milburn, 1996).

Authorities on culturally responsive interventions typically recommend greater use of cooperative groupings, which are more in line with the cultural backgrounds of many of these students (e.g., Boykin et al., 2006; Ellison, Boykin, Tyler, & Dillhunt, 2005; Gay, 2000). These researchers provide evidence that CLD students prefer collaborative interactions and that their learning is enhanced under these conditions. Ledlow (1992), for example, reports research showing that when given options for instructional structures, American Indian children were most responsive to one-on-one with the teacher or small-group work rather than whole-class or individual work. Cooperative and other peer-mediated formats have been found to be quite effective with students with disabilities (Fuchs et al., 2001) and with students from diverse backgrounds (Greenwood, 2004). Ms. Norman, for example, found that Lucas and his classmates thoroughly enjoyed their peer-tutoring activities. Although Lucas and several of his classmates were below grade level in reading, they were excited when they completed daily charts of their sight words and saw the progress that they were making. According to Ms. Norman, the students became more confident and began to show improvements both in their reading performance and in the interest they took in reading.

The culture of the school is often out of synch with the behavior of many of its students, particularly those with exceptionalities from CLD backgrounds. Culturally responsive schools recognize these differences and take the steps to learn about these students, helping them not only to be successful but also to thrive within these settings. To achieve this goal, an important first step is for school personnel to provide orderly learning environments for all students.

TEACHING TIPS

Culture and Social Behavior

1. Recognize that every child can progress, both socially and academically, regardless of cultural background.
2. Develop an understanding of the child's culturally based communication style.
3. Use direct but encouraging language to communicate with the CLDE learner.
4. Avoid rigid classroom structures (e.g., ability groupings) that constantly communicate an inferior status to CLDE students.
5. Use peer-mediated activities (e.g., cooperative learning and peer tutoring) to create a community of learning for CLDE learners.

What Are the Discipline Issues in Our Schools?

Schools need to be safe and disciplined environments in order for learning to take place. Since the 1990s, considerable attention has been directed at school discipline and ways to make schools safe for all students. The anxiety resulting from several violent acts in our schools gave rise to *zero-tolerance* policies, which dictate punishing consequences for specified offenses (U.S. Department of Education, 1998). This concern also has led to the continuous national study of disciplinary conditions in our schools. A report on school crime and safety compiled from various national sources by the National Center for Education Statistics ([NCES] 2003) is intended to provide a profile of our schools. It notes that between 1995 and 2001 more violent victimizations of young people took place away from school grounds than at school. School crime, where students reported being victims of theft or violent acts, declined from 10% to 6%. However, there was no change in such school crimes as threats with weapons, assaults on teachers, or hate-related graffiti. Complaints of bullying, however, increased; reports rose to 8% from a previous low of 5% in 1999. Bullying was the number-one discipline problem reported by the public schools, followed by disrespect of teachers, verbal abuse of teachers, undesirable gang activity, undesirable cult extremism, and racial tensions. According to school type, middle schools were more likely than elementary or secondary schools to report bullying, verbal abuse of teachers, widespread disorder in the classrooms, and racial tensions. Gang and extremist cult activities were more likely to be reported by the high schools.

Schools have attempted to address these disciplinary problems mainly through dramatic increases in pupil suspensions and expulsions. Unfortunately, the research to date provides little or no evidence that suspensions or expulsions are effective in bringing about desired changes in student behavior (Cartledge, Tillman, & Talbert-Johnson, 2001; Mendez & Knoff, 2003; Morrison, Anthony, Storino, & Dillon, 2001). Furthermore, suspensions and expulsions are most likely to be counterproductive in that they (1) disenfranchise those with the greatest need for connectiveness and emotional support, (2) are inequitably implemented, and (3) are often given for minor infractions (Mendez & Knoff, 2003; Morrison et al. 2001; Sodak, 2003). Mendez and Knoff (2003) also argued that suspensions rarely are logically, functionally, or instructionally connected with the infractions that prompted the suspensions. They found that school suspensions increase substantially in middle school but then taper off in high school. Research by Morrison et al. shows that the most frequent reasons for office referrals were disruption, defiance, and physical contact. Extremely antisocial behaviors constituted a small number of referrals. Out-of-school suspension was the most common disciplinary action and it was often used for mild offenses such as disruption or fighting.

Recent provisions in the No Child Left Behind Act ([NCLB], 2001) authorize grants to states for programs in which suspended and expelled students can carry out community service. There are other provisions for mentoring programs so that individuals from the community could be trained to mentor youth at risk for educational failure or criminality, particularly those in rural or high-crime areas. The extent to which these options have been employed or are effective is yet to be determined.

What Are Some Discipline Issues with Regard to Special Populations?

What Are Discipline Concerns Relative to Race and Gender? The use of punishment has special relevance for males and ethnic/racial minorities, particularly African American males. Research literature shows that males and racial minorities are disproportionately referred for disciplinary actions (Skiba, Michael, Nardo, & Peterson, 2002). Although the violence that gave impetus to the current zero-tolerance policies in schools was mainly committed by nonminorities, it is CLD students who have been impacted most by these exclusionary policies. Zhan, Katsiyannis, and Herbst (2004) in analyzing national data gathered by the U.S. Department of Education over the period from 1998 to 2002 found an increasing trend in pupil exclusions. African and Native American students were most likely to be excluded and Hispanic American students had higher exclusion rates than European American students. The researchers also found differences according to geographical region, with more exclusions in the West than in the Midwest, Northeast, and South. Another finding was that the South had shorter exclusion periods. Whether these regional differences were due to factors such as greater availability of support services or to stronger belief in the beneficial effects of harsher penalties is not entirely clear.

More important than understanding regional differences is the need to examine reasons for the disproportionate number of referrals for CLD students (i.e., African, Native, and Hispanic American) compared to their European American counterparts. Monroe (2006) labels this difference the *discipline gap*. A common theme in the research literature is cultural discontinuities or the tendency for teachers to misperceive the culturally specific behaviors of some CLD students (Gay, 2000; Monroe, 2005, 2006; Morse & Cole, 2002). Monroe suggests as examples that teachers may view "overlapping" speech (or the failure to observe communication turn-taking) as disrespect, play fighting as authentic aggression, and ritualized humor as valid insults. All of these behaviors need to be viewed within a cultural context in order to determine the most appropriate response. A student who is punished for a misperceived culturally specific behavior is likely to react in anger. On the other hand, understanding and instruction could bring about the desired communication skills as well as a more empowered student.

Related to teacher misperceptions is the issue of teacher bias in the disproportionate referral of minority students (Downey & Pribesh, 2004; Skiba, Poloni-Staudinger, Simmons, Feggins-Azziz, & Chung 2005). Using a national data set, Downey and Pribesh matched students and teachers according to race and found some evidence of a race factor in teacher ratings that could not be explained by African American students being more resistant to the authority of European American teachers. These findings were consistent with previous matching studies, leading the authors to conclude "race continues to shape student-teacher dynamics in ways that turn out badly for black students" (p.279). Other researchers contend there is bias in the type of behaviors punished, in the type of punishment administered, and the severity of the penalties (Monroe, 2005; Morse & Cole, 2002; Skiba, 2002). Skiba, for example, argues that European American students are reprimanded for behaviors such as smoking and vandalism while African American students are referred for more nebulous behaviors such as excessive noise and disrespect.

Disciplinary referrals according to gender must also be examined. As noted earlier, males are more likely to be referred than females but referred students present somewhat different profiles by gender (Farmer, Goforth, Clemmer, & Thompson, 2004; Lo & Cartledge, 2007). In a study of the discipline problems of rural African American middle school students, Farmer et al. found many fewer females were accused of major offenses but referred females tended to have multiple problems that included academic, social skill, and emotional difficulties. These females were more likely to be viewed by teachers as troubled, more likely to be aggressive and involved in bullying, and less likely to be associated with popular students. On the other hand, many more boys were identified for major offenses but the males did not have as many accompanying problems or evidence the marginal status characteristic of girls. The authors suggest that social dominance and aggressive behaviors may be normative for these boys and that this profile heightens their peer social status. An additional interpretation may be that teachers are reluctant to refer girls, and only girls with the most severe behavior problems are subjected to disciplinary referrals. Some support for this position can be found in a similar phenomenon reported by Wehmeyer and Schwartz in 2001 who contended the disproportionate population of boys in special education is due partly to the disabilities of girls being overlooked.

Nevertheless, one may legitimately question the overrepresentation of boys, particularly minority males, in disciplinary actions. As noted in the Farmer et al. study (2004), many of these referrals may reflect relatively normative behaviors. Although they may not be adaptive for school success, the behaviors of these boys most likely could be managed in less severe, more culturally responsive ways. Other researchers have documented that the most frequently referred problems tend to be less serious offenses, such as insubordination, fighting, classroom disruption, and tardiness, rather than behaviors that result in destruction or danger (e.g., Lo & Cartledge, 2007; Putnam, Luiselli, Handler, & Jefferson, 2003; Skiba, Peterson, & Williams, 1997). In their study of an urban, predominantly African American elementary school, Lo and Cartledge found that African American males were the most vulnerable to disciplinary referrals and most likely to experience exclusionary disciplinary actions, that the exclusions systematically escalated over the course of the school year, and that there was no evidence the offending students or their peers benefited from these disciplinary actions. Punitive approaches alone, aiming to send a message to rule violators not to misbehave again, without corresponding interventions to help students develop positive behavioral competencies, are countraindicated. Such actions may actually worsen problem behaviors, further pushing students away from rather than enticing them toward educational systems (Morrison et al., 2001). Armed with this information, schools need to be proactive in intervening early to keep problem behaviors from developing or existing behaviors from worsening.

What Are the Discipline Concerns with Regard to Students with Disabilities? The underlying principle of special education is providing all individuals access to public education regardless of how they might differ from the general population (Howe & Miramontes, 1991). This commitment to "education for all" despite special needs has raised considerable controversy relative to student discipline. The Gun Free Schools Act ([GFSA], 1994) is based on the right of teachers to teach and of students to learn in gun-free environments. Zero tolerance and suspensions, which specify, for example, one-year mandatory expulsion for any student bringing firearms to school, are the most widely used form of discipline (Skiba, 2002). Special education advocates, on the other hand, contend that suspensions and expulsions for students with disabilities essentially violate their rights for free and public education (FAPE). Furthermore, they contend, students should not be excluded from school for acts that are manifestations of their disability.

These differences have led to the perception that there is a dual disciplinary system: one for students without disabilities and one for students with disabilities. The 2004 reauthorization of the Individuals with Disabilities Education Act (IDEA) continues to permit short-term disciplinary removals for students with disabilities of up to 10 days for minor infractions. Removals for more than 10 days would constitute a change in placement. However, the 2004 reauthorization authorized suspending students with disabilities for up to 45 *school* days (rather than the 45 days specified in the 1997 reauthorization) for more serious infractions, such as the possession of weapons or drugs or evidence of serious bodily harm to self and others. Special steps must be taken to make certain that the student continues to receive the educational services as designated on the individualized education program (IEP) (Skiba, 2002; Yell & Shriner, 1997). For these 45-school-day suspensions, students with disabilities can be placed in an interim alternative educational setting (IAES) to avoid cessation of educational placement. This assignment can be made without a ruling by a hearing officer. The parents may appeal the suspension decision, but the child is placed in the alternative setting while the appeal is pending.

An important aspect of expulsion proceedings for students with disabilities is the *Manifestation Determination*; the 2004 reauthorization stipulates that children with disabilities are not to be expelled for behaviors caused by or directly related to the disability or if the conduct in question is a direct result of the local education agency's failure to implement the IEP. In order to minimize exclusionary practices, especially for students with disabilities, the law does specify the use of functional behavior assessments and the development of individualized behavior plans to remedy problem behaviors. These procedures are discussed later in this chapter.

How Does Discipline Differ from Punishment for CLDE Learners? The term *discipline* is commonly associated with punishment, but a more wholesome perspective is to think of discipline as practices that create an orderly school environment in which students can willingly engage in learning (Smith & Misra, 1992) or as something that children possess rather than being something imposed upon them (Brendtro & Long, 1997). On the other hand, punishment is a consequence delivered after some behavior in order to decrease the frequency or probability of that behavior reoccurring (Algozzine & Kay, 2002). Punishment is an event that causes physical or emotional discomfort that is intended to stop a behavior, but not all aversive consequences will weaken or stop a behavior. In some cases, they may reinforce or strengthen a behavior. For many CLDE students, this may well be true. In schools where the majority of the CLDE students receive disciplinary referrals, the impact of disciplinary referrals is greatly reduced (e.g., Farmer et al., 2004; Lo & Cartledge, 2007). Part of the effect of exclusionary practices comes from the embarrassment that accompanies being singled out and removed from the classroom/school. But if exclusions are commonplace for most of the students in the school/subgroup, the potential effect of the stigma is possibly lost. As a matter of fact, for many students, particularly males who subscribe to cultural inversion, the reverse will be the case. These youngsters may take pride in their "outlaw" status and view these exclusions as a badge of honor (e.g., Ferguson, 2001). Furthermore, students may undertake to instigate exclusionary actions when they least want to participate in class.

Mild punishment procedures, used consistently, can be effective in eliminating some undesired behaviors, but punishment needs to be used sparingly, for several reasons. First, it needs to be balanced by positive consequences to be most effective. Positives should outnumber negative consequences. A standard of at least four positives to each negative might be a useful guideline. Positive consequences help students to see themselves as capable of being successful and will enable them to view authority figures more favorably.

Culturally diverse students respond positively to indications of teacher caring.

However, even though positive consequences can be effective in promoting desired behaviors, some CLDE students may respond inappropriately (e.g., with embarrassment) to positives such as social praise. As a result, they may stop doing the appropriate behavior once they are praised. Nevertheless, teachers need to continue to explore positive incentives that will keep the student moving in the desired direction. Instead of public praise, for example, the student and teacher might devise a behavior plan that involves private monitoring and rewarding of specified behaviors.

Unfortunately, schooling for CLDE learners tends to emphasize control strategies or punishment (Monroe, 2005) rather than positives, and praise is likely to be less genuine (Gay, 2000). Individuals who respond to students mainly in punishing ways become aversive to students and undermine their own ability to promote positive, constructive actions in these young people. Another reason to exercise caution in using punishment is that punishment alone rarely teaches alternative, socially desired behaviors. Lucas, for example, often practices a culturally specific behavior of "overlapping" speech, where he fails to follow the turn-taking rule during classroom conversations. He frequently interrupts others. Ms. Norman reprimands him and then sends him to in-school suspension for his persistent interruptions. Although Lucas often resents being sent out of the room when he is trying to say something, he still has not learned how to get the teacher's attention according to the culture of the classroom. Ms. Norman, on the other hand, needs strategies on how to *teach* Lucas to get attention and speak in class without getting in trouble.

Another consideration relative to punishment is that children might inadvertently learn undesirable lessons. When punishing consequences exceed positive ones, children may learn that the way to control their environment or have their needs met is through punitive or aggressive means. They also might resort to immoral deeds, such as lying or cheating, in order to avoid punishment. These outcomes actually exacerbate rather than ameliorate behavior problems. As punishing consequences increase, the student's maladaptive behaviors may escalate accordingly, which is particularly problematic for low-income CLDE learners who are likely to have limited options and less exposure to a variety of adaptive models. The excessive punishment these youths encounter is counterproductive, reinforcing the very behaviors we wish to extinguish.

An emphasis on punishment as the principal means of social development can also cause teachers to focus almost exclusively on undesirable behavior. As a result, they fail to attend to and encourage those strengths and talents that could conceivably counter some of the problem behaviors. A most important feature of culturally responsive interventions for CLDE students is creating a *constantly caring* school environment (Gay, 2000). Finally, teachers and other authority figures need to exercise self-control, since punishing actions may simply become a means to vent anger rather than to help the child redirect his or her behavior. Punishing consequences are periodically necessary, but they need to be administered in a calm manner with an emphasis on what the student needs to learn in order to behave more appropriately.

What Is Effective Culturally Responsive Discipline?

Unlike a punishment-only system, discipline is an approach designed to mold socially appropriate positive behavior through systematic planning, teaching, and evaluation. Reductive procedures may be part of a discipline plan, but they should not be the principal or dominant component of it. The integral components of culturally responsive discipline are cultural understanding, caring, fairness, skill in teaching adaptive behaviors, and commitment.

Cultural understanding means that teachers need to develop an understanding of their own culture as well as that of the students they teach. Weinstein et al. (2004) advised that teachers recognize their own ethnocentrism and bias, to understand that their worldview is not universal nor their cultural norms absolute. Children who have been socialized to look away rather than make eye contact when directed by an adult, for example, are not necessarily being disrespectful and should not be treated as such. Accordingly, Weinstein et al. suggested that teachers learn about their students, about their students' origins, education, relationship styles, discipline, views of time and space (e.g., punctuality), religion, food, health and hygiene, history, and traditions. In learning about their students, teachers would learn, for example, that many Mexican American students need to feel cared for before they can care about school.

Caring classroom environments may be the keystone of culturally responsive discipline. Gay (2000) wrote that within caring classrooms teachers demonstrate concern for children's emotional, physical, economic, and interpersonal environments. Caring teachers are those who demand high levels of performance from their CLD learners, who have high expectations, and who often are described as *warm demanders*. Additionally, according to Gay, these are teachers who listen to their students, respect them, are friendly both within and outside the classroom, and encourage their students to express themselves and to perform. Caring teachers make the effort to develop positive personal relationships with their students as well as help them to develop positive relationships among themselves. Accordingly, there are lots of smiles, positive touching, gentle teasing, and so forth. As a result, students feel a positive personal connection with their teachers. Gay gives an example of setting high expectations for social behavior and personal decorum through a model teacher. When encountering peer–peer conflict among CLD learners, this teacher would appeal to personal integrity and self-regard by using statements such as "Aren't you in my U.S.-period class? Using fisticuffs to solve problems is beneath your dignity. You are better than that," or "Young men (or women) don't behave that way." In contrast (Gay, 2000), uncaring teachers use excessive criticisms, reprimands, and disciplinary actions and are deficient in responding to and praising students. Based on anecdotal reports, Gay observes that CLD students are often seen "socializing, grooming themselves, and sleeping in classrooms when instruction is going on without some teachers being concerned about the inappropriateness of these behaviors" (p. 65).

Fairness is critical for discipline to be effective with CLDE populations. First, discipline needs to match the target behavior. Once Lucas has been taught the turn-taking procedures and the desired method for getting attention in the classroom, when an infraction occurs, a 5-minute time out from classroom interactions might be an appropriate reprimand, especially if accompanied by positives for speaking in turn during class. A half or full day of in-school suspension would be excessive for this misbehavior. In addition to producing understandable anger in the student, excessive suspensions may backfire in that these long periods outside of the classroom will become increasingly attractive and the student will miss valuable learning time, further adding to school failure.

Second, school personnel need to be careful that disciplinary measures do not convey a sense of privilege to select groups (Weinstein et al., 2004). Frequent and excessive punishment of African American males, for instance, not only reinforces stereotypes of their criminality but also suggests the school is failing to address the special needs of this segment of the school population. Weinstein et al. give the following example of racial unfairness in school discipline: African American males are suspended for 10 days for unsnapped overall straps (a cultural style) while European American males are permitted to wear pants with holes in the thighs (a cultural style) with impunity. Weinstein et al. predict that CLD students will withdraw psychologically and emotionally under oppressive systems that denigrate or dismiss them.

A third point about the way in which problem situations with CLD students are perceived and handled is that teachers often have preconceived notions about CLD students, expecting low achievement and more disruptive behavior (Gay, 2000). Gay also offers that teachers may contribute to the management problems of these students (particularly African and Hispanic American) by refusing to listen to the students' explanation of problem situations, administering harsher penalties, and ignoring comparable infractions of European and Asian American students.

Culturally appropriate management strategies also are critical to the effective discipline of CLDE learners. CLD children often have been socialized under forms of discipline that differ substantially from those of the schools. Native American parents, for example, often discipline their children through teachings and stories; their children consequently recoil at the harsh punitive measures frequently used in the schools (Dykeman, Nelson, & Appleton, 1995). Teachers need to appeal to the values and shared responsibilities of the culturally diverse group rather than simply press students to behave out of fear of punishment or promise of reward, which is typical practice in the schools (Weinstein et al., 2004). Weinstein et al. give an example of a teacher having difficulty teaching Haitian children until the teacher learned to express caring (e.g., the adults here like you and want you to be good children) instead of mainly appealing to emotional states (e.g., you appear angry). The teacher thus communicated caring as well as attempted to motivate the students to want to behave out of a sense of personal responsibility

Day-Vines and Day-Hairston (2005) also spoke of the importance of making personal connections with African American male adolescents so that they could receive corrective feedback appropriately. The authors describe the SSS strategy—stroke, stifle, and stroke—as an example of culturally responsive behavior management. With this procedure, the adult begins by affirming the student, which is followed by confronting the student with his misbehavior and giving corrective feedback. The sequence ends with another affirmation. For example, the student is observed using profanity in the school with another student. The authority figure calls the student aside and says, "Malik, you are such a tall handsome, intelligent, and articulate young man with a promising future. When others hear you use that language, I'm afraid they might not see your charm, good looks, and intelligence. Could you please help me by watching your language in class? I'm sure I'll be able to count on you because you emerge as a leader among your peers" (p. 241). The student feels good about this encounter with the authority figure and returns to class without further incident.

Teachers need to recognize not only when a student is engaging in a culturally specific behavior but also when there is a need for counterinstruction so that the student might be successful in school and the larger environment (Weinstein et al., 2004). In our previous example, Lucas engages in a culturally specific behavior of "overlapping" speech. This communication style is used extensively at home and he has difficulty controlling this behavior at school. Ms. Norman, his teacher, recognizes that punishment alone is neither helping Lucas to control his tendency to interrupt and speak over others nor teaching him how to express himself in the classroom in nondisruptive ways. In order to develop these skills, Ms. Norman needs to provide direct social skill instruction, as will be discussed in Chapter 5 of this text.

Commitment is the fifth component of culturally responsive discipline to be discussed in this chapter. Committed teachers not only demonstrate the caring behaviors described previously but also are resourceful and willing to try out culturally responsive strategies that are effective in helping students to be successful in school. Furthermore, committed teachers are persistent. They believe in the potential of their students, are dedicated to the success of their CLDE students, and, accordingly, are willing to try a variety of strategies to bring about positive outcomes. These teachers do not give up if initial efforts do not produce desired results. Committed teachers also recognize the benefit of high-quality instructional programs. Monroe (2005) observed that there is an inverse relationship between high rates of suspension/expulsion and pupil test scores. She suggests that

> **TEACHING TIPS**
>
> **Culturally Responsive Punishment and Discipline**
>
> 1. Minimize punishment, making certain that consequences are fair, brief, and directly related to the student's infraction.
> 2. Create caring classroom environments so that students know that you care about them and want them to be successful.
> 3. Emphasize positive relationships among students.
> 4. Listen to CLDE students and display respect for them.
> 5. Appeal to students' integrity and cultural backgrounds as reasons for being adaptive in their behavior.
> 6. Communicate high expectations to the students for academic and social behaviors.
> 7. Avoid disciplinary disproportionality according to culture/ethnicity and gender.

rigorous instruction is a good way to manage behavior and that the instructional material needs to be relevant, meaningful, and engaging.

How Can We Be Proactive in Addressing Disciplinary Issues for CLDE Learners?

The racial/ethnic and gender disparities in disciplinary referrals call for effective strategies to minimize behavior concerns in order to maintain CLDE students in the least restrictive environments. In addition to the aforementioned caring environment, recommended, empirically validated strategies include functional behavior assessments (FBA) and behavior intervention plans (BIP) (e.g., Reid & Nelson, 2002). It is recommended that these procedures be implemented widely as a preventive measure to avoid exclusionary practices (Scott & Nelson, 1999; Sugai, Lewis-Palmer, & Hagan-Burke, 1999–2000). This is particularly important with CLDE populations disproportionately affected by excessive referrals (e.g., African American males) but must be implemented taking culturally responsive factors into account.

How Do We Provide Culturally Responsive Functional Behavior Assessments?

Functional assessments are used to determine why a problem behavior is occurring and what interventions might be most effective in eliminating the disruptive behavior and in developing alternative adaptive behaviors. When we conduct a functional assessment, we are trying to determine the nature of the behavior, what causes it to occur, and what keeps it going (Sugai et al., 1999–2000). Functional assessments involve several steps, which at the minimum would include (1) forming a multidisciplinary team, (2) clearly specifying the problem behavior, and (3) developing a hypothesis about the behavior (Lo & Cartledge, 2006).

Multidisciplinary Team. Considering the type of observations and information needed, input from a multidisciplinary professional team as well as from parents and community members who know the child well is extremely important. Behavior specialists or school psychologists who have a working knowledge of functional assessments are primary members of this team. Other members might include the child's teachers, parents, clinicians such as counselors or speech professionals, and community members/professionals who know the child's behavior and culture. For CLDE learners, the team should be expanded to include culturally sensitive members (Duda & Utley, 2005). In Lucas's case, the team included the school social worker, who was African American and had a working knowledge of Lucas's cultural background. Also included was an African American community activist who knew the family and was invited by Lucas's mother to participate.

Assessment Information. Once the team is assembled and responsibilities assigned, the next step is to compile assessment information. The assessment may consist of both formal and informal methods and information derived from a variety of sources. For example, to ascertain how extensive and longstanding the behavior is, the professional team might review school records as well as informally converse with individuals in the school/community/home to determine if they are troubled by the behavior. Semistructured interviews of teachers and others using an instrument such as the one shown in Figure 4–1 (McConnell, 2001) give team members more specific details on what the behavior looks like, settings in which the behavior is most likely to occur, conditions that trigger the behavior, and what consequences most often follow the behavior. For example, after interviewing Ms. Norman about Lucas's off-task behavior, the team learned that (1) Ms. Norman was concerned that Lucas failed to attend to the task

FIGURE 4–1 Functional assessment interview form

Student: _____ Date: _____
Interviewer: _____

A. Describe the Behavior
   1. What is the behavior?
   2. How is the behavior performed?
   3. How often does the behavior occur?
   4. How long does the behavior last when it occurs?
   5. What is the intensity of the behavior when it occurs?
B. Define Setting Events and Environmental Factors that Predict the Behavior
   1. Classroom structure (physical)
   2. Class rules and behavioral expectations
   3. Instructional delivery methods (lecture, cooperative learning, labs, discussions, etc.)
   4. Instructional materials (textbooks, worksheets, hands-on activities, etc.)
   5. How are directions presented?
   6. Assessment techniques (multiple-choice tests, essay tests, etc.).
C. Define Specific Immediate Antecedent Events That Predict when the Behaviors are Most Likely to Occur
   1. When are the behaviors most likely to occur?
   2. When are the behaviors least likely to occur?
   3. Where are the behaviors most likely to occur?
   4. Where are the behaviors least likely to occur?
   5. During what activities are the behaviors most likely to occur?
   6. During what activities are the behaviors least likely to occur?
D. Identify Specific Consequences That Follow the Behavior
   1. What specific consequence is most likely to immediately follow the behavior?
   2. What seems to be the effect of the consequence on the student's behavior?
   3. Does the consequence remove the student from an uncomfortable situation?
   4. Is there consistency between the consequences given by the classroom teacher and the consequences given by other school staff?
   5. Is there consistent follow-through with all consequences both in the classroom and other school settings?

Source: Adopted and modified from *Functional Assessment Interview Form* by M. E. McConnell (2001) (pp. 97–98).

FIGURE 4–2 Student interview form

Student: _____ Date: _____
Interviewer: _____

What things do you generally do that get you in trouble at school?
_____
_____
_____

What are you doing when the behavior occurs and what usually happens afterward?
_____
_____
_____

When and where do the behaviors generally occur?
_____
_____
_____

How would you describe your behavior at school?
_____
_____
_____

What do you do when you get angry?
_____
_____
_____

What do you like most about school?
_____
_____

What things do you not like to do at school?
_____
_____

---

within 5 seconds of receiving her directions, (2) Lucas became quite disruptive if she did not respond to his requests for assistance immediately, (3) the behavior was most problematic during the reading period, (4) it was more likely to occur when she was busy instructing the other students, and (5) she typically responded to his off-task behavior by verbally reprimanding him and prodding him to return to his assignment.

The cultural relevance of this interaction was revealed when the differences between home and school communications with Lucas were considered. In contrast to his mother and grandmother, Ms. Norman was observed to be both inconsistent and indirect in her verbal interactions with Lucas. More than 50% of the time she responded to his inappropriate interruptions by answering his questions without reprimand, and on most of the other occasions she would deliver indirect reprimands, such as "Are you following my

What teacher behavior especially bothers you?
_____
_____

What are your favorite classes?
_____
_____

What classes are hard for you?
_____
_____

What can your teachers do to help you be more successful at school?
_____
_____

List some things you do best:
_____
_____

List some things you like most:
_____
_____

Additional Comments:
_____
_____

Source: Adopted and modified from *Student Interview Form* by M. E. McConnell (2001) (pp. 85–86).

directions?" Lucas had been socialized to the very direct language of authority figures. Although his parents (i.e., mother and grandmother) were direct and firm, being an only child meant that he did not have to wait for attention. Ms. Norman's indirect style and inconsistencies led Lucas to question her authority and to test the limits.

Using modified versions of the same instrument, similar interviews could be conducted with other important individuals, such as the art teacher, the school counselor, and Lucas's parents. If the student is sufficiently mature, it is particularly valuable to interview the student to find out how he or she perceives the behavior, the reasons for it, and how the student feels about school, peers, school subjects, and teachers (See Figure 4–2). Lucas's interview determined that he liked school, he wanted to learn to read, he would get angry with Ms. Norman when she did not help him right away, and he did not feel the other students in the class liked him, although he wanted them to like him. Instruments such as those provided by Kern, Dunlap, Clarke, and Childs (1994) and McConnell (2001) can be adapted for this purpose.

Lewis, Scott, and Sugai (1994) developed a Problem Behavior Questionnaire (Figure 4–3) that can further inform the team about the function a particular problem behavior can

(Text continues on page 88.)

FIGURE 4-3 Problem behavior questionnaire

Respondent Information

Student _____ DOB _____ Grade _____

Sex: M F   IEP: Y N

Teacher _____

School _____

Telephone _____

Date _____

Student Behavior

Please briefly describe the problem behavior(s).

DIRECTIONS: Keeping in mind a typical episode of the problem behavior, circle the frequency at which each of the following statements is true.

	Never	10% of the time	25% of the time	50% of the time	75% of the time	90% of the time	Always
1. Does the problem behavior occur and persist when you make a request to perform a task?	0	1	2	3	4	5	6
2. When the problem behavior occurs, do you redirect the student to get back to task or follow rules?	0	1	2	3	4	5	6
3. During a conflict with peers, if the student engages in the problem behavior, do peers leave the student alone?	0	1	2	3	4	5	6
4. When the problem behavior occurs, do peers verbally respond or laugh at the student?	0	1	2	3	4	5	6
5. Is the problem behavior more likely to occur following a conflict outside of the classroom (e.g., bus write-up)?	0	1	2	3	4	5	6
6. Does the problem behavior occur to get your attention when you are working with other students?	0	1	2	3	4	5	6

	Never	10% of the time	25% of the time	50% of the time	75% of the time	90% of the time	Always
7. Does the problem behavior occur in the presence of specific peers?	0	1	2	3	4	5	6
8. Is the problem behavior more likely to continue to occur throughout the day following an earlier episode?	0	1	2	3	4	5	6
9. Does the problem behavior occur during specific academic activities?	0	1	2	3	4	5	6
10. Does the problem behavior stop when peers stop interacting with the student?	0	1	2	3	4	5	6
11. Does the behavior occur when peers are attending to other students?	0	1	2	3	4	5	6
12. If the student engages in the problem behavior, do you provided one-to-one instruction to get the student back on task?	0	1	2	3	4	5	6
13. Will the student stop doing the problem behavior if you stop making requests or end an academic activity?	0	1	2	3	4	5	6
14. If the student engages in the problem behavior, do peers stop interacting with the student?	0	1	2	3	4	5	6
15. Is the problem behavior more likely to occur following unscheduled events or disruptions in classroom routines?	0	1	2	3	4	5	6

(continued)

FIGURE 4-3 (continued)

Problem Behavior Questionnaire Profile

DIRECTIONS: Circle the score given for each question from the scale below the corresponding question number (in bold).

Peers						Adults						Setting Events		
Escape			Attention			Escape			Attention					
3	**10**	**14**	**4**	**7**	**11**	**1**	**9**	**13**	**2**	**6**	**12**	**5**	**8**	**15**
6	6	6	6	6	6	6	6	6	6	6	6	6	6	6
5	5	5	5	5	5	5	5	5	5	5	5	5	5	5
4	4	4	4	4	4	4	4	4	4	4	4	4	4	4
3	3	3	3	3	3	3	3	3	3	3	3	3	3	3
2	2	2	2	2	2	2	2	2	2	2	2	2	2	2
1	1	1	1	1	1	1	1	1	1	1	1	1	1	1
0	0	0	0	0	0	0	0	0	0	0	0	0	0	0

Source: "The Problem Behavior Questionnaire: A Teacher-Based Instrument to Develop Functional Hypotheses of Problem Behavior in General Education Classrooms," by T. J. Lewis, T. M. Scott, & G. Sugai, 1994, *Diagnostique, 19,* pp. 103–115. Copyright © 1994 by the Hammill Institute on Disability. Reprinted with permission.

serve. If the teacher, for example, states that she *always* redirects the student to get back on task or to follow the rules when the problem behavior occurs, this is an indication that the problem behavior may be occurring to get the teacher's attention. After the questionnaire is completed and the items rated, the profile that emerges indicates whether the problem behavior occurs in order to escape some situation, such as avoiding peers or an undesired task, or to get attention from someone, such as the teacher or peers.

Direct observations of classroom behavior can help to pinpoint the times and conditions when the behavior most commonly occurs as well as the related events that serve as antecedents and consequences of the behavior. An A-B-C (Antecedent-Behavior-Consequence) recording form could be used to help the team understand the events that potentially trigger or reinforce the problem behavior. In the example given in Figure 4–4, the observer records Lucas's behavior for 40 minutes during reading. The record reveals that prior to Lucas's disruptions, Ms. Norman is trying to conduct the reading lesson with her attention directed to the entire class. Lucas's outbursts were followed by some attention from Ms. Norman intended to correct the disruptive behavior. It is quite possible that this attention was actually strengthening rather than reducing the disruptive behavior. Other observations made by the school psychologist show that Ms. Norman conducted a rather unstructured classroom. Even though Lucas might have been the most demanding student in the class, most other students also spoke out at will. Ms. Norman occasionally told them to wait until they were called upon, but she did not consistently enforce this rule. Students also tended to move about the classroom rather freely, seeking out Ms. Norman's attention as they desired.

The social worker was interested in observing the type of interactions that occurred between Lucas and Ms. Norman and if there was any indication of a personal bias. A review of school records revealed that Lucas was excluded from the classroom nearly every day. Observers within the classroom indicated few if any positives provided by

FIGURE 4–4 A-B-C observation recording form/results for Lucas

Student: <u>Lucas</u>   Date: <u>10/09/05</u>
Setting: <u>classroom (reading)</u>
Observer: <u>behavior specialist</u>
Starting time: <u>10:00 A.M.</u>
Ending time: <u>10:40 A.M.</u>

Time	Antecedents (A)	Behavior (B)	Consequences (C)
10:02	Ms. N reads and class follows along	Making noises, spacing around, asking where they were at	Ms. N walked over and pointed to the paragraph
10:03	Ms. N reads and class follows along	Flipping through pages, raised hand, then slammed the book down	Ms. N came over "what's wrong"
10:05	Ms. N came over "what's wrong"	Said he wanted to read out loud	Ms. N told him that he will have his turn
10:06	Ms. N reads out loud	Tearing up paper and shooting it at garbage can	Ms. N said to him "No more"
10:08	Ms. N reads out loud	Talking to a student, playing with notebook	Ms. N walked over and stood next to him
10:10	Ms. N reads out loud	Talking to another student	Ms. N reprimanded him "you need to pay attention"
10:15	Ms. N moves away from his desk	Continues talking to the student	Ms. N reprimanded him "Stop, that's a detention"
10:20	Ms. N reads	Playing with paper	Ms. N walked over and pointed to the place he should be looking at
10:26	Independent seatwork	Completed his work quietly	Ms. N remained sitting next to him
10:33	Ms. N teaches entire class	Hanging out of his seat, raising his hand	Ms. N called on him to answer the question
10:35	Ms. N asks the class a question	Raising his hand	Ms. N called on another student
10:36	Ms. N called on another student	Slammed his hands on his desk	Ms. N told him that he has to wait and it's others' turn
10:39	Ms. N told him that he has to wait and it's others' turn	Banging on desk louder and louder	Ms. N reprimanded "That's enough. You are going to the detention room."

Antecedents: Ms. Norman's attention was directed to the whole class or other students.

Consequences: Ms. Norman provided attention (verbal warnings, reprimands, or redirection) when Lucas exhibited off-task behaviors

Comments: <u>Antecedents</u>: Ms. Norman's attention was directed to the whole class or other students.
<u>Consequences</u>: Ms. Norman provided attention (verbal warnings, reprimands, or redirection) when Lucas exhibited off-task behaviors.

Ms. Norman to Lucas. Nearly all interactions were either neutral (e.g., giving directions) or negative (e.g., reprimands for some behavior).

The community activist shared with the team that although Lucas typically was seen in the community with no more than one or two friends, he was not known as a troublemaker. He moved about the neighborhood rather independently but could be depended upon to run errands for neighbors, if requested.

The assessment information based on interviews, ratings, and direct observations might be organized into a chart in order to produce a profile of Lucas's behavior within the school setting. Figure 4–5 is an example of such an organizational chart, which indicates that Lucas's problem behavior is most likely motivated by his desire for teacher attention.

FIGURE 4–5 Functional assessment for Lucas

Problem behavior: Off-task behavior

Antecedents of the Behavior	Problem Behavior	Consequences of the Behavior	Functions of the Behavior
• Unavailability of teacher attention • Whole-class reading instruction • Independent seatwork • Peers' provocation	Lucas yells out the teacher's name, bangs on his desk, lies on his chair, plays with noninstructional materials in his drawer, leaves his seat without permission, engages in conversations with peers, and initiates name-calling.	• Receives teacher attention in the forms of verbal warning and reprimands • Receives one-on-one adult attention in the forms of detention • Receives peer attention	• To obtain teacher attention • To obtain peer attention

Summary statement:

When given a reading activity in which teacher attention was directed to the whole group or other students, Lucas was most likely to engage in off-task behavior. His off-task behavior is often followed by teacher attention in the forms of verbal warning or reprimands and then detention when the problem behavior escalates. Lucas engaged in the off-task behavior to obtain teacher and peer attention.

Personal goals:

- Lucas wishes to be a good student, to have other students like him, and to have a special privilege to work with the teacher.
- Lucas feels that his teacher could help him control his behavior if she would call on him faster and more often.

Academic performance:

- Lucas likes and is good at math.
- Lucas performs one year below his grade level on reading. He enjoys reading, yet the reading instruction is too difficult for him.

Family and sociocultural issues:

- Lucas is socialized to use aggressive acts to solve conflicts.

Hypothesis About the Behavior. After gathering and reviewing the assessment information, the team will draw some hypotheses about the *function* the student's problem behavior serves. In Lucas's case, the team proposed that his aim was to get the teacher's attention. When she did not respond to his initial request, he became disruptive, which was usually followed by attention from Ms. Norman, albeit typically negative in form. To test out this hypothesis, the school psychologist observed Lucas under two conditions: (1) when Ms. Norman gave Lucas attention as he requested and (2) when she deliberately continued to work with other students and not attend to his constant requests. The psychologist also observed Lucas during times when Ms. Norman conducted her class as she did normally. The observations showed that Lucas typically became disruptive when Ms. Norman was working with other students and that his disruptive behavior persisted, increasing in intensity if Ms. Norman did not attend to him. These observations gave credibility to the previous hypothesis that the function of Lucas's disruptive behavior was his desire for the teacher's attention. The team noted that based on their observations and the fact that Lucas's behavior had escalated this year, Ms. Norman's informal teaching style and lack of positive interactions with Lucas were probably reinforcing his talk-out disruptions.

Also important were Lucas's strengths: his motivation for academic achievement, his skill in tutoring his peers, and his helpful behavior in his community. The committee determined that Lucas's behavior did not warrant a more restrictive placement and that Ms. Norman needed assistance in order to eliminate the exclusions so Lucas could maximize his schooling.

The intervention plan for Lucas evolved from the functional assessment. As shown in Figure 4–6, the goals are not only to reduce off-task behavior but also to teach Lucas how to attract the teacher's attention appropriately when it is genuinely needed. Additionally, this plan is designed to help Lucas become more academically successful and socially appropriate with peers. Equally important is the need for Ms. Norman to learn more effective, culturally responsive ways to interact with Lucas and her other students.

TEACHING TIPS

Culturally Responsive Functional Behavior Assessments

1. Functional behavior assessments need to be conducted by professional teams, not by classroom teachers alone.
2. Include on the assessment team persons familiar with the learner's cultural background and culturally specific behaviors.
3. Determine which, if any, of the problem behaviors are culturally specific and if counterinstruction is needed.
4. Assess the learner's classroom to determine factors, particularly teacher behaviors, that might contribute to the learner's problem behavior.
5. Assess the learner's strengths as well as problem behaviors.
6. Identify ways to promote more positive interactions between learner and classroom teacher.
7. Use the functional assessment to devise an intervention plan that increases adaptive behaviors and reduces punitive actions.

FIGURE 4-6 Behavior intervention plan for Lucas

Goals	Interventions	Methods of evaluation
1. To reduce Lucas's off-task behavior	• Teach Lucas appropriate on-task behavior. • Provide frequent teacher attention for Lucas's on-task behavior; ignore him when he is off-task. • Teach Lucas to self-monitor his own behavior. • Apply the behavioral consequences consistently. • Rearrange Lucas's desk to a close proximity to Ms. Norman. • Implement group-oriented contingency system. • Implement a "passport" system (check-in and check-out).	• Observe and record Lucas's off-task behavior daily. • Supervise Ms. Norman's use of consequences and behavior management system. • Monitor Lucas's use of self-monitoring.
2. To increase Lucas's appropriate solicitation of teacher attention	• Teach Lucas appropriate ways of soliciting attention. • Provide frequent teacher attention for Lucas's good behaviors. • Adopt attention-soliciting sign for Lucas to use when he needs teacher attention and waits for the teacher to come over.	• Observe and record Lucas's appropriate attention recruitment behavior daily.
3. To increase Lucas's involvement in academic instruction	• Implement effective reading instruction with high student response rates. • Train Lucas's mother to be a reading tutor, a home behavior manager, or an adult mentor.	• Conduct daily and weekly assessment on reading fluency and comprehension.
4. To increase Lucas's positive social interactions with peers	• Engage Lucas in peer-mediated repeated reading program. • Teach Lucas anger management and appropriate social interaction skills. • Train peers to ignore Lucas's inappropriate behaviors and to interact with Lucas when he demonstrates appropriate behaviors. • Train Lucas to be a cross-age tutor. • Train Lucas to be the playground monitor.	• Monitor Lucas's tutoring behavior and playground leadership behavior every session. • Monitor Lucas's interactions with peers.

How Do We Create Positive School Environments?

Children from diverse backgrounds are more likely to be impoverished, and poor children, for various reasons, are often characterized by externalizing problem behaviors, which may arise from the stressors resulting from depressed living conditions (Park, Turnbull, & Turnbull, 2002) or reflect the cultural differences in behavior management the child experiences between the style of parents at home and the style of school professionals. Culturally responsive schools are those that are effective in helping CLD students adapt their behavior in order to achieve school success. They also are schools that adapt to the needs of their students, are skilled in assessing what academic and social skills their students have not yet learned, and are effective in implementing the indicated interventions.

How Do We Create Positive Environments Through Positive Behavior Intervention Supports (PBIS)? Positive Behavior Intervention Supports (Lewis & Sugai, 1999; Sugai & Horner, 2005) is a proactive, positive approach to behavior management that can be effective in reducing disruptive student behaviors, facilitating adaptive student behaviors, and creating a positive classroom environment in which every student can participate and learn. This approach is particularly appropriate for CLD learners who have been overly exposed to zero-tolerance, punitive policies (Duda & Utley, 2005). PBIS is based on behavioral principles that call for analyzing the school environment and employing technologies that cause desired behaviors to occur and be maintained. It uses a problem-solving approach in which decisions about managing pupil behavior are based on the systematic assessment of disciplinary practices.

As applied, PBIS consists of a schoolwide planning process designed to provide a unified system of behavior management, featuring uniformity and consistency in efforts to create an environment that promotes desired pupil behavior throughout the school. Recognizing the differences in pupil behavior and based on the percentages of problem behavior typically found in schools, PBIS provides for three levels of behavior management: (a) primary or universal management strategies, (b) secondary or group support interventions, and (c) tertiary or individual support interventions (Lewis & Sugai, 1999; Sugai & Horner, 2005; Turnbull et al., 2002). The primary management strategies are applied to all students to establish a school culture of positive behaviors. The secondary and tertiary supports are applied to fewer students but at greater intensity, depending on the degree of behavior problems. Sugai and Horner have documented (2005) several examples of the successes of PBIS in which schools reduced their pupil problem behaviors by half and maintained the improvements for several years.

Primary level. Primary or universal management strategies are procedures designed to meet the needs of the majority of students who do not frequently present behavior problems. Strategies at this level are used to develop a common language and focus for all members of a school's staff. Activities include the development of a general mission statement and positively stated expectations for student behavior. To infuse culturally responsive principles in this universal management, school personnel would stress to the students that they care about them and want the children to employ these behaviors because they want what is best for the students. Teachers need to convey these principles in word and deed, displaying to students that they are trying to provide the best possible learning opportunities and modeling expectations of mutual respect. Additionally, school personnel need to appeal to the integrity of the students' heritage or traditions. For example, one African American school in Seattle, Washington, used modified Kwanzaa principles as the basis for their principles of social behavior (Gay, 2000). To promote a positive attitude toward school, they used the first principle of *Umoja* (unity)—having school spirit and good things to say about the school.

From these general expectations, specific methods can be developed to teach social behaviors that are consistent with schoolwide behavioral expectations, that encourage students to conduct themselves in a positive manner, and that discourage students from engaging in maladaptive behavior. Behavioral expectations are taught at the beginning of the school year. They are defined, modeled, enacted, practiced, and reinforced. Examples of behavioral expectations can be seen in the top row of the following chart. For each setting in the first column, specific overt responses are given that define that expectation. Additional specific behaviors could be identified for other school settings.

Setting	Be kind	Be safe	Be cooperative	Be respectful	Be peaceful
Cafeteria	Wait in the line in order	Walk	Sit at assigned table	Eat your food carefully Clean up after yourself	Use calm voices
Playground	Include all who want to play	Use equipment appropriately	Take turns	Keep game rules the same during the game	Return from playground quietly

In Lucas's classroom, Ms. Norman decided that all of the students should learn and practice classroom communication skills, such as appropriate attention-getting behavior and voice volume. As part of her instruction, she emphasized the pride the students should take in making their classroom an orderly place. Each day students would remind each other what they were to do if they wanted to speak or get the teacher's attention. They also modeled for their peers speaking in the appropriate voice tone. Students were complimented for showing ways to help make their classroom a good place to be and to work.

Secondary level. Intervention at the secondary level provides more direct and intense support. Social skills that students need to conduct themselves in a manner consistent with the school's behavioral expectations are taught. Social skill instruction is found to be more effective if used in combination with other behavioral management systems, such as classwide behavior management, self-management, and increased academic support. Students who are having difficulty resolving conflicts while playing on the playground, for example, would be engaged in small-group instructional sessions on how to manage playground conflict appropriately. Access to the playground would be contingent on the development of these skills. For social skill instruction to be most successful with CLDE learners, teachers need to connect the instruction to the students' backgrounds and make the target behaviors meaningful to students. Culturally responsive social skill instruction is discussed further in chapter 5 of this text.

Tertiary level. Students who fail to respond to primary and secondary supports require more intensive, individualized plans. A functional behavior assessment would be conducted from which an individualized behavior plan would emerge. Parents as well as other professionals would collaborate as needed. In Lucas's case, the intervention team determined that it was important to make the classroom a more nurturing place. In addition to individualized instruction on how to recruit the teacher's attention appropriately, the plan appealed to Lucas's leadership skills in the peer-tutoring activities. Ms. Norman began giving Lucas more positive attention and rewarding him with leadership positions in the classroom whenever he achieved a designated level of performance (e.g., having fewer than 3 talk-outs/interruptions in the morning in order to lead the class in their repeated reading practice activity in the afternoon). Lucas also was permitted to teach the other students how to use the teacher recruitment flag system when they needed the teacher. Lucas was assigned an African American male mentor as part of the university's mentoring program, and Ms. Norman was prompted in ways to develop more positive interactions with Lucas and to minimize disciplinary exclusions.

Lo and Cartledge (2006) provided research evidence of the beneficial effects of tertiary interventions with 4 elementary-aged inner-city African American males at risk for or with disabilities. The students were taught to monitor their own behavior and to solicit the teacher's attention appropriately in order to reduce off-task behavior and classroom disruption. The students learned to display more patience, to request the teacher's assistance appropriately, to display a sign for help if the teacher was unavailable at the time, and to keep working. The findings showed that the intervention had positive effects

> **TEACHING TIPS**
>
> **Culturally Responsive Positive School Environments**
>
> 1. Draw upon the CLDE's heritage and traditional background to identify schoolwide principles for desired behaviors.
> 2. Establish high behavioral standards and communicate through explicit instruction these expectations to all students.
> 3. When teaching skills at primary, secondary, and tertiary levels, emphasize the students' strengths and the responsibilities they can assume in contributing to the school and to others.
> 4. Develop and implement individual plans for students unsuccessful with secondary interventions.
> 5. Consistently communicate belief in and support for the CLDE student.

for all of the students, who were maintained successfully in their classrooms without referral to special education or more restrictive settings.

How Do We Affirm CLDE Students? In his 1992 book *Empowering African-American Males to Succeed,* Mychal Wynn stresses the power that teachers can exercise to bring out the best in their students. He asserts that our words are powerful and that "we can affirm success or we can affirm failure by what we say" (p. 97). He points out that our actions toward young people can help them to think of themselves as either achievers or failures. Wynn advises us to encourage our students to identify extraordinary goals and help students to see themselves as achieving these goals.

CLDE students and those at risk for disabilities need to be encouraged to persist with school and other worthwhile endeavors. An inordinate amount of attention is given to their "deficits," and we frequently overlook their strengths. Capitalizing on students' strengths can be an effective means of engaging these students in their schooling, making

Positive interventions are more powerful in shaping the behaviors of culturallly diverse learners than excessively punitive consequences.

Identifying positive and meaningful ways that students can contribute to others can be affirming and extremely effective in helping culturally diverse students embrace the schooling culture.

it meaningful to them, and helping to improve their overall self-regard. In our initial interview with Lucas, he told us that he wanted to learn to read. Although he was at the bottom of his class in reading, he persisted in his reading instruction and made the most progress of all the learners at risk for reading failure in his class. Despite his problems with peer-relationships, Lucas appeared to thrive within the peer-tutoring activities. He was ambitious and insisted on surpassing his peers in learning the reading material.

Lucas was also observed to be particularly patient and effective with students who were having more trouble in reading than he was. Lucas made good progress in second-grade reading. In third grade, to extend his behavioral and academic interventions, Lucas was assigned to be a cross-age tutor for one third-grade male with mild mental retardation and one first-grade female who needed practice at reading sight words. The tutees made very good progress and Lucas excelled under these conditions. His teachers continued to comment on the good academic and social progress he was making. When Lucas moved to the fourth grade, he was receiving satisfactory evaluations in social behavior and was only slightly behind the expected grade level in reading.

Teachers and researchers frequently complimented Lucas on the progress he was making in reading and what a good tutor he was. Lucas often would beam when he heard these statements. In fourth grade, Lucas asked to resume his cross-age tutoring activities. As he continued to make academic progress in his reading and in tutoring other students, he was encouraged to think of himself as a teacher, both as a current activity and as a future profession.

TEACHING TIPS

Affirming CLDE Students

1. Identify some interests and strengths of the CLDE student.
2. Help the CLDE student to develop the strengths and praise the student's progress.
3. Help the CLDE student to appropriately display talents to peers and adults.
4. Generously praise and recognize the CLDE student for strengths and accomplishments. Help the CLDE student to begin to see him- or herself according to strengths rather than according to deficits.

Summary

Creating disciplined students and school environments goes well beyond prescribing a set of punishment contingencies. Effective culturally responsive schools strive to maximize the potential of all students, anticipate behavior problems, and try to prevent them before they occur. A principal means for accomplishing this is through creating culturally responsive, caring environments. Teachers first develop an understanding of their own culture and then learn to study and respect the culture of their students. They develop and communicate caring attitudes toward their CLDE students, learn how to respond fairly to these behaviors, acquire culturally responsive management styles, and become committed to the success of their CLDE students. Culturally responsive procedures are incorporated into empirically validated interventions such as functional assessments and Positive Behavior Intervention Supports to bring about the best possible outcomes for CLDE students. Every effort needs to be taken to identify student strengths and affirm the student's continued progress.

Related Learning Activities

1. Select a classroom in your community that consists of students from racial/ethnic minorities as well as students with disabilities or at risk for disabilities. Identify two or three ways in which the classroom activities are at cross-purposes with the students' background culture (e.g., the teacher uses indirect language extensively) and/or two or three ways that the classroom is culturally responsive (e.g., the teacher presents a positively managed classroom where children with disabilities or from racially/ethnically different backgrounds do not experience punitive consequences disproportionately). What suggestions do you have to address those actions that are working at cross-purposes with the children's culture?

2. If possible, review the office disciplinary referrals of the children in a local school. Note the frequency of the referrals and the reasons for them. Note any differences according to the gender or cultural backgrounds of the students. How are these data being used to help the students become more adaptive in their behavior? Is there evidence of improvement for students with the most frequent referrals? If not, what are the implications for intervention based on these referrals?

3. Everytown Elementary School is an urban school in Citytown, U.S.A. At least 50% of its students have office referrals. Most of these referrals are due to verbal and physical fights on the playground. Design a schoolwide intervention that might address the excessive playground fighting. Detail in your plan, how school personnel might provide for a culturally responsive, caring environment.

4. Lucas, Adam, and Donald received extensive instruction from Mr. Williams, the counselor, on managing conflict on the playground. The boys have made considerable progress. Lucas likes to read, Adam likes to write, and Donald is a good artist. How could Mr. Williams use the boys' special interests and talents to promote these conflict management skills with other students in the school?

References

Algozzine, B., & Kay, P. (Ed.). (2002). *Preventing problem behaviors*. Thousand Oaks, CA: Corwin Press.

Arredondo, P., Toporek, R., Brown, S.P., Jones, J., Locke, D.C., Sanchez, J., & Stadler, H. (1996). Operationalization of the multicultural counseling competencies. *Journal of Multicultural Counseling and Development, 24*, 42–78.

Boykin, A. W., Tyler, K. M., Watkins-Lewis, K., & Kizzie, K. (2006). Culture in the sanctioned classroom practices of elementary school teachers serving low-income African American students. *Journal of Education for Students Placed At Risk, 11*, 161–173.

Brendtro, L. K., & Long, N. J. (1997). Punishment rituals: Superstition in an age of science. *Reclaiming Children and Youth, 6*(3), 130–135.

Cartledge, G., & Milburn, J. F. (1995). *Teaching social skills to children and youth*. Boston: Allyn & Bacon.

Cartledge, G., & Millburn, J. F. (1996). *Cultural diversity and social skills instruction: Understanding ethnic and gender differences*. Champaign, IL: Research Press.

Cartledge, G., Tillman, L. C., & Talbert-Johnson, C. (2001). Professional ethics within the context of student discipline and diversity. *Teacher Education Special Education, 24*, 25–37.

Day-Vines, N. L., & Day-Hairston, B.O. (2005). Culturally congruent strategies for addressing the behavioral needs of urban, African American male adolescents. *Professional School Counseling, 8*(3), 236–244.

Delpit, L. (1995). *Other people's children: Cultural conflict in the classroom.* New York: New Press.

Digiovanni, L. W. (2004). Feminist pedagogy and the elementary classroom. *Encounter: Education for Meaning and Social Justice, 17(3),* 10–15.

Downey, D. G., & Pribesh, S. (2004). When race matters: Teachers' evaluations of students' classroom behavior. *Sociology and Education, 77,* 267–282.

Duda, M. A., & Utley, C. A. (2005). Positive behavioral support for at-risk students: Promoting social competence in at-risk culturally diverse learners in urban schools. *Multiple Voices, 8,* 128–143.

Dykeman, C., Nelson, J. R., & Appleton, V. (1995). Building strong working alliances with American Indian families. *Social Work in Education, 17,* 148–158.

Ellison, C. M., Boykin, A. W., Tyler, K. M., & Dillhunt, M. L. (2005). Examining classroom learning preferences among elementary school students. *Social Behavior and Personality, 33,* 699–708.

Farmer, T. W., Goforth, J. B., Clemmer, J. T., & Thompson, J. H. (2004). School discipline problems in rural African American early adolescents: Characteristics of students with major, minor, and no offenses. *Behavioral Disorders, 29*(4), 317–336.

Ferguson, A. A. (2001). *Bad boys: Public schools in the making of black masculinity.* Ann Arbor: The University of Michigan Press.

Ferri, B. A., & Connor, D. J. (2005). Tools of exclusion: Race, disability, and (re)segregated education. *Teachers College Record, 107,* 453–474.

Fuchs, D., Fuchs, L., Yen, L., McMaster, K., Svenson, E., Yang, N., et al. (2001). Developing first-grade reading fluency through peer mediation. *Teaching Exceptional Children, 34,* 90–93.

Gay, G. (2000). *Culturally responsive teaching: Theory, research, & practice.* New York: Teachers College Press.

Greenwood, C. (October, 2004). Classwide peer tutoring learning management system (CWPT-LMS): Tools, findings, implications. Paper presented at the international meeting for the Council for Learning Disabilities, Las Vegas, NV.

Gun-Free Schools Act (GFSA) (1994). Title IV. Safe and Drug-Free Schools and Communities Act of 1994. U.S. Department of Education, Elementary and Secondary Programs.

Howe, R. R., & Miramontes, O. (1991). A framework for ethical deliberation in special education. *The Journal of Special Education, 25,* 7–25.

Irvine, J. (1990). *Black students and school failure: Policies, practices, and prescriptions.* New York: Greenwood.

Kern, L., Dunlap, G., Clarke, S., & Childs, K. E. (1994). Student-assisted functional assessment interview. *Diagnostique, 19,* 29–39.

Ledlow, S. (1992). Is cultural discontinuity an adequate explanation for dropping out? *Journal of American Indian Education, 31*(3), 21–35.

Lewis, T. J., Scott, T. M., & Sugai, G. (1994). The Problem Behavior Questionnaire: A teacher-based instrument to develop functional hypotheses of problem behavior in general education classrooms. *Diagnostique, 19,* 103–115.

Lewis, T. J., & Sugai, G. (1999). Effective behavior support: A systems approach to proactive school-wide management. *Focus on Exceptional Children, 31,* 1–24.

Lo, Y., & Cartledge, G (2006). FBA and BIP: Increasing the behavior adjustment of African American boys in schools. *Behavioral Disorders, 31,* 147–161.

Lo, Y., & Cartledge, G. (2007). Office disciplinary referrals in an urban elementary school. *Multicultural Learning and Teaching, 2*(1), 20–38.

McConnell, M. E. (2001). Functional behavioral assessment: A systematic process for assessment and intervention in general and special education classrooms. Denver, CO: Love.

Mendez, L. M. R., & Knoff, H. M. (2003). Who gets suspended from school and why: A demographic analysis of schools and disciplinary infractions in a large school district. *Education and Treatment of Children, 26,*30–51.

Monroe, C. R. (2005). Why are "bad boys" always black? Causes of disproportionality in school discipline and recommendations for change. *The Clearing House, 79,* 45–50.

Monroe, C. R. (Summer, 2006). Misbehavior or misinterpretation? Closing the discipline gap through cultural synchronization. *Kappa Delta Pi Record 42*(4), 161–165.

Morrison, G. M., Anthony, S., Storino, M., & Dillon, C. (2001). An examination of the disciplinary histories and the individual and educational characteristics of students who participate in an in-school suspension program. *Education and Treatment of Children, 24,* 276–293.

Morse, J., & Cole, W. (2002). Learning while black. *Time Europe, 159,* 1–4.

National Center for Education Statistics (2003). Indicators of School Crime and Safety, 2003. Institute of Education Sciences, U.S. Department of Education, http://nces.ed.gov/pubs2004/crime03/index.asp

No Child Left Behind (2001). Safe and Drug-Free Schools and Communities. Title IV, Part A. Preliminary Overview of Programs and Changes Included in the No Child Left Behind Act of 2001, http://www.ed.gov/nclb/overview/intro/progsum/sum_pg9.html

Noguera, P. A. (2003). School, prisons, and social implications of punishment: Rethinking disciplinary practices. *Theory Into Practice, 42,* 341–350.

Park, J., Turnbull, A. P., & Turnbull, H. R. (2002). Impacts of poverty on quality of life in families of children with disabilities. *Exceptional Children, 68*(2), 151–170.

Putnam, R. F., Luiselli, J. K., Handler, M. W., & Jefferson, G. L. (2003). Evaluating student discipline practices in a public school through behavioral assessment of office referrals. *Behavior Modifications, 27*, 505–523.

Reid, R., & Nelson, J. R. (2002). The utility, acceptability, and practicality of functional behavioral assessment for students with high-incidence problem behaviors. *Remedial and Special Education, 23*(1), 15–23.

Rhode, G., Jenson, W. R., & Reavis, H. K. (1992). *The tough kid book: Practical classroom management strategies.* Longmont, CO: Sopris West.

Schneider, B. H. (1993). *Children's social competence in context: The contributions of family, school, and culture.* Oxford, England: Pergamon.

Scott, T. M., & Nelson, C. M. (1999). Functional behavioral assessment: Implications for training and staff development. *Behavioral Disorders, 24*, 249–252.

Skiba, R. (2002). Special education and school discipline: A precarious balance. *Behavioral Disorders, 27*, 81–97.

Skiba, R. J., Michael, R. S., Nardo, A. C., & Peterson, R. (2002). The color of discipline: Sources of racial and gender disproportionality in school punishment. *The Urban Review, 34*(4), 317–342.

Skiba, R. J., Peterson, R. L., & Williams, T. (1997). Office referrals and suspensions: Disciplinary intervention in middle school. *Education and Treatment of Children, 20*, 295–315.

Skiba, R. J., Poloni-Staudinger, L., Simmons, A. B., Feggins-Azziz, R., & Chung, C.-G. (2005). Unproven links: Can poverty explain ethnic disproportionality in special education? *The Journal of Special Education, 39*, 130–144.

Smith, M. A., & Misra, A. (1992). A comprehensive management system for students in regular classrooms. *The Elementary School Journal, 92*(3), 353–371.

Sodak, L. C. (2003). Classroom management in inclusive settings. *Theory Into Practice, 42*, 327–333.

Sugai, G., & Horner, R. H. (2005) School wide positive behavior supports: Achieving and sustaining effective learning environments for all students. In W. L. Heward, T. E. Heron, N. A. Neef, S. M. Peterson, D. M. Sainato, G. Cartledge, R. Gardner, III, L. D. Peterson, S. B. Hersh, & J. C. Dardig (Eds.), *Focus on behavior analysis in education: Achievements, challenges, and opportunities* (pp. 90–102). Upper Saddle River, NJ: Prentice Hall/Merrill.

Sugai, G., Lewis-Palmer, T., & Hagan-Burke, S. (1999–2000). Overview of the functional behavioral assessment process. *Exceptionality, 8*, 149–160.

Turnbull, A. P., Edmonson, H., Griggs, P., Wickham, D., Sailor, W., Freeman, R., Guess, D., Lassen, S., McCart, A., Park, J., Riffel, L., Turnbull, R., & Warren, J. (2002). A blueprint for schoolwide positive behavior support: Implementation of three components. *Exceptional Children, 68*, 377–402.

U.S. Department of Education, National Center for Education Statistics (1998). *Violence and discipline problems in U.S. public schools: 1996–97.* NCES 98–030, by Sheila Heaviside, Cassandra Rowand, Catrina Williams, and Elizabeth Farris. Project Officers, Shelley Burns and Edith McArthur. Washington, DC: author.

U.S. Department of Education. (2004). Safe and drug-free school program—State grants program and national programs—2004. (http://www.ed.gov/about/reprts/annual/2004plan/edlite-safeanddrugfree.html.

Wehmeyer, M. L., & Schwartz, M. (2001). Disproportionate representation of males in special education services: Biology, behavior, or bias? *Education and Treatment of Children, 24*, 28–45.

Weinstein, C. S., Tomlinson-Clarke, S., & Curran, M. (2004). Toward a conception of culturally responsive classroom management. *Journal of Teacher Education, 55*, 25–38.

Wren, D. J. (1999). School culture: Exploring the hidden curriculum. *Adolescence, 34*(135), 593–596.

Wynn, M. (1992). *Empowering African-American males to succeed: A ten-step approach for parents and teachers.* Marietta, GA: Rising Sun Publications.

Yell, M. L., & Shriner, J. G. (1997). The IDEA Amendments of 1997: Implications for special and general education teachers, administrators, and teacher trainers. *Focus on Exceptional Children, 30*, 1–19.

Zhan, D., Katsiyannis, A., & Herbst, M. (2004). Disciplinary exclusions in special education: A 4-year analysis. *Behavioral Disorders, 29*(4), 337–347.

Chapter 5

Socially Skilled CLDE Learners

The purpose of this chapter is to present a model and strategies for teaching social skills to children and youth. To be most effective, we need to base our teaching on children's backgrounds, contemporary culture, and unique strengths. We also need to be aware of the conditions that will contribute the most to our efforts. Applications in this chapter emphasize learners with exceptionalities from culturally and linguistically diverse backgrounds.

By the end of this chapter, the reader should be able to answer the following questions:

1. What are the social skill needs of culturally and linguistically diverse exceptional learners?
2. What is a culturally responsive social skills training model?
3. What are the factors that make social skill instruction most effective?
4. How can we use peers to teach social skills?
5. How can we use the child's traditional culture to reinforce social skill instruction?
6. How can we use culturally diverse literature to reinforce social skill instruction?
7. What are children's social skill needs according to gender and sexual orientation?
8. How can we teach social skills according to gender and sexual orientation?
9. What are some of the curriculum programs that are useful in teaching social skills?

By the end of this chapter, readers will obtain information on strategies relative to:

1. A model for culturally responsive social skill instruction.
2. Procedures for peer-mediated social skill instruction.
3. Procedures for incorporating traditional cultural values into social skill instruction.
4. Procedures for using culturally relevant literature in social skill instruction.

What Do We Need to Know to Teach Social Skills?

Social skill instruction is proactive. That is, it is designed to prevent problem behaviors from occurring or to keep existing problems from worsening. Instead of waiting for problem behaviors to occur, which is the case with reactive strategies such as punishment, social skill instruction anticipates the behaviors that children need to acquire and attempts to equip children accordingly. This more positive approach not only fosters children's social development but can also make schools a more nurturing and attractive environment for both students and teachers.

Alberto

Alberto is an 8-year-old second grade student in Ms. Good's class. Alberto is of Hispanic/Latino background and he and his family are recent immigrants to the United States from Mexico. Alberto's family speaks Spanish to him at home but he has been in U.S. schools since he was 6 years old and he speaks and understands English fluently. Nevertheless, most of the children in the class are native English speakers and they often tease Alberto about his immigrant status and the fact that his parents do not speak English. Alberto hates being teased. There are not many other students in his school who are recent immigrants and who have a Hispanic/Latino background. He feels that the other students do not like him and he is beginning not to like school very much. Often when he is teased by one of his classmates he screams and tries to fight the students that teased him. This is disruptive to the entire class and undermines Alberto's academic performance.

Academically, Alberto is not doing well in school. He has reading and behavior problems, and testing last year resulted in a diagnosis of a learning disability (LD). He is more than a year behind in reading. He now receives instruction from the special education teacher for reading and math, but he is in Ms. Good's class, the general education second grade, for the rest of his academic and nonacademic subjects. Alberto has made some progress academically, but he still struggles with his behavior, particularly with his peer interactions.

Alberto comes from a family of five children; he is the oldest. Mr. and Mrs. Gonzales, Alberto's parents, have come to school to discuss Alberto's problems on at least two occasions, but these conferences have not been very successful. Despite the use of a translator, Ms. Good did not feel that the parents fully understood the problems nor did she feel that it was realistic that the parents alone would be able to solve the problems Alberto was experiencing in school. Ms. Good recognized that this was a problem-solving situation that called for home and school collaboration. The school team needed to consult with the family to construct a satisfactory plan to be implemented at school and at home.

In this situation, Ms. Good is challenged in two major ways. First of all, she not only wants to stop Alberto's fighting but also wants to help Alberto develop social skills that will enable him to respond more constructively to his classmates when he is teased. Among the various options that he needs to learn, such as making an assertive statement to his classmates, walking away, or seeking help from an authority figure, Ms. Good decided that she would first teach him how to ignore their taunts. In this case, the social skill objective would be: *When teased by his classmates, Alberto will refrain from having a tantrum and ignore the taunting by refusing to look at his classmates, refusing to say anything to them, and by thinking about something good that will happen to him if he does not cry or respond to his classmates.*

The second major objective was to eliminate the taunting and get the students to respond more positively to Alberto and each other. Thus, she wanted the class to improve their interpersonal social skills by *making positive rather than taunting statements to each other*. In teaching the students to be more positive with each other, Ms. Good decided to incorporate understandings of different cultures and the advantages of being multilingual.

What are the steps that Ms. Good should take to achieve these goals? This and other such questions will be addressed in the remainder of this chapter.

What Are the Social Behaviors of CLDE Students?

All children are more alike than they are different. Nevertheless, children from culturally and linguistically diverse (CLD) groups, particularly those from homes that subscribe to the traditional cultural ways of doing things, are likely to exhibit behaviors that challenge, baffle, or confuse their non-CLD teachers. As a result, these behavioral differences are likely to be viewed as social skill deficits and treated punitively or inappropriately. Children may then begin to feel devalued and seek affirmation from environments other than school.

In contrast to the individualistic culture of European Americans, the cultural roots of members of four major diverse groups—Asian, African, Hispanic, and Native American—are collectivist in orientation (e.g., Schneider, 1993; Shkodriani & Gibbons, 2001; Sosik & Jung, 2002), which is considered to promote certain behaviors or personality types (Triandis, 2001). Individualistic cultures stress competition and individual achievement, but collectivist cultures emphasize the group over the individual and their focus is on working for the interests of the group. Common to all of the CLD groups is an emphasis on the extended family and the family as a source of financial, emotional, and social support (Cartledge & Talbert-Johnson, 2004; Sanders, 1987; Turnbull, Blue-Banning, & Pereira, 2000).

Hispanic Americans

Its collectivist orientation is recognized within the Hispanic culture (e.g., Kopelowicz, 1998; Shkodriani & Gibbons, 2001), and the term *familismo* is used to emphasize the interdependence of extended families. Turnbull et al. (2000) studied friendship dyads of a child with and a child without a disability to determine how the Hispanic culture influenced their relationships. The researchers interviewed 11 Hispanic American children, their mutual friends, and family members. They determined that the relationships ranged from casual to intimate and that the child with the disability often gave as much emotional support as the child received. The source of friendships for these children tended to be the extended family network, particularly cousins. Based on their research, Turnbull et al. advise special educators to recognize the importance of the extended family to the quality and quantity of friendships for Hispanic children with disabilities. Consistent with these findings, Lampe, Rooze, and Tallent-Runnels (2001) found that fourth-grade Hispanic/Latino American students achieved more within cooperative learning groups than within the traditional instruction format.

In addition to their strong sense of group membership, Hispanic/Latino American students often are described as cooperative, quiet, and obedient (Cartledge & Talbert-Johnson, 2004). Their social skill difficulties typically are language based; students lack valuable communication skills such as seeming able to make assertive statements or offer an opinion. From their review of the literature, Cartledge and Talbert-Johnson observe that the number of Hispanic American students who move into adolescence plagued by many of the conditions of poverty/minority status—school failure, gang membership, substance abuse, and violence—is disproportionate.

Native Americans

Native Americans have a similar profile. For many traditional Native Americans, best friends and close peer relationships often evolve from extended families rather than from school or other interactions (Schneider, 1993). Best friends may live considerable distances from each other and may only interact on a periodic basis, but the family connection helps to define the importance and closeness of this relationship (Alberto, 1991). Children in these cultures are reared to respect adults, to seek their counsel, and to strive for independence, often performing very difficult tasks without assistance.

Sanders (1987) analyzed the difference between the Native American and Anglo American cultures and noted that compared to their majority counterparts, Native American children are more inclined to speak softly and at a slower rate, rely more on nonverbal communication, and prefer cooperative to competitive endeavors. Some strongly held Native American values include self-control and inner strength, living in harmony with nature and others, and generosity—sharing with others and keeping only enough to supply present needs (Horne & Leung, 2003; Sanders, 1987).

Asian Americans

Cartledge and Feng (1996) reported that in traditional Asian societies, the extended family is the basic family unit and children are socialized to be loyal to their families as well as to have harmonious relationships with others. Allegiance to the family unit increases rather than lessens as one moves into adulthood. Children's behaviors are considered to reflect on the family's dignity and there is great fear of losing face and bringing shame on one's family (Fessler, 2004). This orientation might result in social behaviors characterized by shyness, high anxiety, and an unwillingness to express opinions or feelings in public. In discussing the social behaviors of Hmong children, who have their cultural roots in Southeast Asia, Vang offered that many of these children may display passive, shy, reserved, and compliant behaviors in an effort to be respectful of others and unobtrusive. He also stated, "Many Hmong students rarely express their feelings, thoughts, opinions, and concerns in class because they have learned not to question adults and authority figures" (2003, p. 14). According to Vang, these children tend not to assert themselves, and this quiet demeanor may cause them to be overlooked in the classroom.

African Americans

As with the two preceding groups, the family is extremely important culturally in the African American community. The family structure is also extended and often viewed as a collective social network, emphasizing a sense of community and the survival of its members (Cartledge & Talbert-Johnson, 2004). The social support of kinship is an important factor in reducing family stress as well as in modifying acting out and shyness among the children (McCabe, Clark, & Barnett, 1999). Behaviors said to be characteristic of African American children include high key, animated, interpersonal, confrontational, intense, dynamic, and demonstrative (Irvine, 1990). Other sources say that these students are people-oriented, generous toward their peers, and receive positive ratings from their cross-race peers (Feng & Cartledge, 1996).

Teachers tend to perceive the social skills and problem behaviors of African American children less favorably than those of children of other races (Cartledge & Talbert-Johnson, 2004; Feng & Cartledge, 1996). But Feng and Cartledge found that African American children fared better under direct observation and peer reviews, where they enjoyed higher rates of cross-race initiations and positive peer ratings. Nevertheless, there was evidence of a need for these students to learn alternatives to verbal aggression and to improve conflict management skills.

Table 5–1 charts social profiles of these four groups and the related instructional implications.

TABLE 5–1 Cultural groups and social profiles

Characteristics	Hispanic American	African American	Native American	Asian American
Cultural Distinctions	• Religion major cultural factor • Strong gender roles • Machismo • Passivity and deference to others encouraged • Family unit sacred value • Bilingual • Interpersonal affective relationships cherished	• Religion/spirituality major cultural factor • Emphasis on relationships • Importance of music • Importance of extended family • Deference to elders and ancestors • Children encouraged to be tough • Special dialect/gestures, intragroup communication • Authoritarian child-rearing styles	• Spirituality major cultural factor • Over 400 tribes recognized in U.S • Encouraged to play freely with few restrictions until about age 10, when expected to assume many adult responsibilities • Cooperation among peers emphasized • More skilled individuals viewed as models, not competitors; • Emphasize aggression	• Family central focus of one's life and receives increasingly greater emphasis over one's lifetime • Children socialized to subjugate themselves to will of family • Emphasis on compliance

Characteristics	Hispanic American	African American	Native American	Asian American
Social Skills	• Rated as well mannered, shy, less competent with linguistically based social skills, i.e. initiates conversations, complimenting, describes feelings, participates in discussions, expresses opinions, initiates group activity • High rates of adolescent aggression and homicide	• Viewed as friendly and people-oriented • Consistently received lower teacher ratings on social skills and conflict management • Higher peer ratings • Feelings of alienation result in social disengagement • High rates of adolescent aggression and homicide	• Verbal among peers, more silent in classroom • Emphasize mastery, bravery, independence, harmony with nature and others, search for wisdom, and generosity • Rated as well mannered and less competent with linguistically based social skills • Development of academic-related behaviors, e.g., staying in school • Feelings of alienation may contribute to problems relative to substance abuse and suicide	• Typically receive highest ratings for self-control and cooperation • Relatively lower assertion ratings • Lower rates of verbal interaction • Tendency toward social isolation • Tendency not to question authority • Behavior problems likely to be overlooked • Adolescent alienation/ criminality
Instructional Implications	• More positive teacher attention needed—tend to get less. • Draw upon Hispanic/ Latino culture to teach social and academic skills, e.g., community-based programs or Hispanic folktales • Emphasize verbal assertiveness and self-confidence within dominant culture	• Begin instruction early in primary grades or preschool • Draw upon African American culture—music, literature • Emphasize peer-based strategies e.g., cooperative learning, peer mediation • Emphasize verbal assertiveness vs. verbal aggressiveness • Emphasize conflict management skills and alternatives to aggression • Put drug culture in proper perspective	• Create accepting, caring environments such as cooperative learning • Use Native American literature as means for transmitting culture and critical social learning • Capitalize on cultural orientation of caring behaviors • Focus on independent, self-management behaviors • Emphasize verbal assertiveness	• Direct instruction that incorporates teaching prompting and praise • Cooperative learning experiences, emphasizing peer collaboration rather than individual effort; heterogeneous groupings; and full equal participation for all members; avoid placing in stereotypical roles • Emphasize verbal assertiveness

What Are the Social Skill Needs of Students with Exceptionalities?

Social skill deficits are common among children with disabilities and most of the social skill research has centered on this population (Vaughn et al., 2003). Although many children with disabilities evidence good social development, some groups (i.e., behavior disorders, autism, and mental retardation) are defined and diagnosed by disorders of adaptive behavior. The research literature repeatedly documents the social perception and behavior problems of children with mild disabilities (i.e., learning disabilities, behavior disorders, attention deficit hyperactivity disorder, and mild mental retardation) (Forness & Kavale, 1996; Frankel & Feinberg, 2002; Kavale & Mostert, 2004; Nixon, 2001). In terms of these behaviors, children will display difficulties in social perception or in comprehending nonverbal cues, such as interpreting the facial expressions, voice tone, gestures, or feelings of others (Most & Greenbank, 2000). They also will have difficulty with problem solving, and when deliberating various options, they are likely to select the least socially desired behavior.

In terms of overt behaviors, many children with mild disabilities have inadequate affect or smiling, conversation skills, and conflict resolution skills. Nixon (2001) found that compared to typically developing agemates, students with attention deficit hyperactivity disorder (ADHD) had higher rates of off-task and disruptive behaviors. About 50% of the children with ADHD evidenced aggressive conduct and had more negative interactions with other aggressive children. They displayed social communication problems and nearly 50% of them reported being rejected by their peers.

The social development problems of children with sensory impairment are noted as well in the research literature (Andersson, Olsson, Rydell, & Larsen, 1999; Huurre & Aro, 1998; Sacks & Gaylord-Ross, 1989). Some researchers have estimated the maladjustment of children with hearing impairment to be greater than that of the typically developing population and contend that the social behaviors of these children are compromised within inclusive settings (Ridsdale & Thompson, 2002; Scott, Russell, Gray, Hosie, & Hunter, 1999). That is, authorities posit that language difficulties within integrated settings limit opportunities for social interaction and therefore impede social development. However, some of the existing research indicates that children with hearing impairment fared no worse socially in integrated than in segregated settings (Andersson et al., 1999; Cartledge, Cochran, & Paul, 1996; Cartledge, Paul, Jackson, & Cochran, 1991). As a matter of fact, there is some indication that students in inclusive settings may have more confidence in their social competence than those in segregated environments (Cartledge et al., 1996).

Difficulties in mobility and in controlling their environment have been regarded as giving rise to the social behavior problems of children with visual impairment. Their interpersonal difficulties include a tendency toward self-seclusion, an absence of smiling, and a lack of assertiveness. Researchers report a need to teach children with visual impairments certain behaviors, such as initiating and joining activities as well as physical orientation toward others (Huurre & Aro, 1998; Sacks & Gaylord-Ross, 1989).

The social needs of children with physical disabilities have received relatively little attention in the research literature, but Coster and Haltiwanger (2004) reported that these children evidence social assessment scores below the expected levels for same-grade peers. Social problems centered on social initiations and social interactions, which, according to the authors, is consistent with other research outcomes with this population. Furthermore, in contrast to other students with disabilities, the problems for children with physical disabilities may be more a function of environmental conditions and the lack of supports rather than social skill deficits within the children per se. Coster and Haltiwanger argue that teachers will need to do much more than simply arrange to place students with physical disabilities near typically developing students. Specific supports need to be put in

TABLE 5-2 Students with disabilities and characteristic social skill focus

Characteristic Social Skill Needs	Students with Mild Disabilities	Students with Moderate to Severe Disabilities	Students with Sensory and Physical Disabilities
Social Skills	• Social perception skills to read nonverbal cues • Problem-solving skills • Affect skills such as smiling • Social communication skills • Conflict-resolution skills • Peer-acceptance skills	• Self-care skills • Leisure skills • Social communication skills • Employability skills • Social interaction skills	• Conflict resolution skills (H-I) • Self-confidence skills • Sustained attention (H-I) • Self-assertion skills • Social initiation—joining others • Physical orientation to others (V-I)

place instead to ensure that students are engaged and have successful interactions with their peers. For example, in 2003 Mpofu employed a peer interaction intervention procedure in which students were assigned to a common-interest activity that required interaction with all group members. He found this to be more effective than providing academic support in enhancing peer social acceptance of adolescents with physical disabilities.

Self-care, leisure, communication, and employability skills tend to be the instructional focus for individuals with moderate to severe disabilities—moderate to severe mental retardation, pervasive developmental disorders (PDD) (i.e., autism, Asperger syndrome, Childhood Disintegrative Disorder, Rhett's Disorder, and PDD not otherwise specified) and childhood schizophrenia. By definition, these youngsters will have difficulties with social communication and interpersonal interactions. Children with autism, for example, tend to be unresponsive to the approach behaviors of others, have difficulty in communicating their needs, have an aloof manner, throw unexplainable tantrums, and have poor peer relationships (DiSalvo & Oswald, 2002; Laushey & Heflin, 2000). Table 5-2 gives an overview of these groups and their respective social skill needs. The existing research indicates that peers often perceive children with disabilities negatively and most of this rejection may be due to the social skill deficits of the children with disabilities (Gresham, 1981; Kemp & Carter, 2002; Miller, Cooke, Test, & White, 2003). The implications are that children with disabilities need to be helped to develop critical social skills and typically developing students need to be taught appropriate ways to interact with their peers with disabilities.

How Can We Use the Child's Culture to Teach Social Skills?

The Traditional Culture and Social Skill Instruction

Many children from culturally and linguistically different backgrounds would benefit from learning about their traditional culture and how they could incorporate these values in their daily lives. During her lifetime Esther Horne, a Native American educator, provided many valuable insights into American Indian culture and the implications for academic and social learning (Horne & Leung, 2003). Horne advised that we promote social competence in Indian children by teaching Indian values of bravery, individual freedom, generosity and sharing, adjustment to nature, and wisdom. According to Horne, *bravery* refers to being able to control oneself and live in harmony with others. Children learn that a brave person manages to control him- or herself even without adult supervision. This means that students work hard to exercise self-control in order to avoid the embarrassment of not being brave. Other teachings emphasize that when someone does something good, the whole group shares in that honor and that the focus is not on competing with others but on living in harmony with them.

Similarly, Delpit and White-Bradley (2003) advised teaching a traditional African value system as a means of developing the humanity, integrity, and thinking/leadership skills of poor African American children. One such value system is Ma'at, which began in ancient Egypt and then spread throughout Africa. It emphasizes the principles of truth, justice, harmony, balance, order, reciprocity, and righteousness. Delpit and White-Bradley describe an example of children studying these principles and then creating a quilt made up of pieces representing each principle. How students used the principles in their social interactions can be seen in the following excerpt from Delpit and White-Bradley's work:

> A student yanked Ayiesha's pencil from her hand. Ayiesha, typically confrontational in the past, looked over at the quilt, then turned to Terrence, the other student, and remarked, "I don't see any reciprocity here. Would you like it if I did that to you?" Without offering a verbal response, Terrence returned the pencil and then approached the teacher to request another. This kind of self-regulation occurred often and served to confirm the belief that the virtues of Ma'at could easily be understood and applied to the classroom setting, while providing a natural outlet for exercising student leadership. (p. 286)

Turnbull, Pereira (2000) et al. published a study in 2003 with examples of the cultural values of *respecto* (respect for personal dignity) and *personalismo* (personal integrity and personal attributes that make one a good person) to foster social relationships. Working with a youngster with special needs, one teacher began by building a trusting relationship. He first taught the student to engage appropriately in sports activities with adults and then to transfer those skills to playing with peers. In the course of these activities, he taught conflict management, anger control, eye contact, and appropriate language skills. The authors reported the student's substantial academic and social progress. In another case, the teacher established a special relationship with a teenage female by emphasizing her family relationships and leadership skills. The teacher engaged her in various community activities that were extended to the female's sister and mother. By highlighting the student's strengths, the teacher was able to foster bonding between this student and others in the class.

In some cases, the traditional values of CLD students may clash with those of the school. Teachers need to understand these traditional values and cultural differences in order to help the students make more satisfactory adjustments in the classroom. In describing Hmong students, for example, Vang (2003) relates that the Hmong are inclined not to ask for help with problems, believing that teachers should not be bothered. Their characteristic passivity is often due to the fact that they simply want to go along with existing activities or plans in order to show respect to others. Other reasons Vang gives for their not wanting to seek assistance are a reluctance to draw attention to having made a mistake for fear of bringing shame and humiliation to their families and their having learned not to question adults or authority figures.

Deference to authority, humility, and a tendency to avoid conflict are common traditional Asian traits that are somewhat at odds with the Western values of self-assertion and that may put the Asian American child at a distinct disadvantage in social situations in this society. Liang, Lee, and Ting (2002) contend that these traditional values may undermine Asian Americans in leadership roles in Western culture. Feng and Cartledge (1996) also found in their study of fifth-grade students that Asian American students were more inclined than European American or African American students to say that they would do nothing if treated unfairly by another person.

In addition to helping students understand that mistakes are inevitable, teachers need to encourage Asian American students to ask for help within academic and social situations.

Teachers should not assume that the student's silence is an indication that all is well and no assistance is needed. Paying close attention to class performance and social interactions, the teacher can determine when a student may need to be coached on how to request aid appropriately from the teacher or a peer, how to invite him- or herself into a peer social situation, how to assertively reprimand a peer for some wrongdoing, or how to report some unfair treatment to an authority figure. These are important skills for all children but may be particularly so for Asian American children whose traditional culture may not promote those traits that are important to social success in the American society.

How Can We Use Culturally Specific Literature to Teach Social Skills?

Literature can be an effective means of introducing and reinforcing social skill instruction for CLD students. Over the past three decades, many books have been published that authentically represent these populations. Many are redemptive and have excellent possibilities for teaching social skills. To deal with teasing and learning to make positive statements, for example, one attractive and appropriate book would be *The Woman Who Outshone the Sun* (Martinez, 1991). This is a Mexican tale from oral history about a woman who had special powers and understood the ways of nature. She shone brightly as the sun and absorbed the river's water and fishes in her hair. Because she was so different, the elders respected her, but others feared her and began to treat her cruelly. She left and took the river with her. The people begged her to return, which she did but advised them that they must "learn to treat everyone with kindness, even those who seem different from you" (p. 24). A Cherokee tale that addresses the importance of positive statements to others is *The First Strawberries* (Bruchac, 1993). The story makes the point that kind rather than harsh words bring about friendships and good relationships with others. *The Quarrelling Book* (Zolotow) and *The Meanest Thing to Say* (Cosby), for young children, are two other books that teachers might use for this purpose. A book for elementary-age children on the topic of teasing is *Angel Child, Dragon Child* (Surat, 1983). This is a story of a child from Viet Nam who is teased by other children for her dress and culture. One day the little girl gets into a fight with a child who is teasing her and the principal punishes them both by requiring the Vietnamese child to tell her story to the taunter, who was directed to write the story. After learning of her story, the entire school studied the Vietnamese culture and conducted a fund-raiser to bring the girl's mother from Viet Nam to join her family in this country.

Older readers also can find lessons on social development in books. Walter Dean Myers is particularly noted for his many books that focus on African American urban youth, especially males. Some examples are *Monster, Hoops,* and *Scorpions* and *Handbook for Boys* (2002), a novel specifically designed to provide guidelines for the successful social transition from boyhood to manhood. Another award-winning author is Virginia Hamilton, who has provided thought-provoking social development books for adolescents, such as *The Planet of Junior Brown* (1971). Prosocial hip-hop materials such as *The Winner Is . .* by LL Cool J (2002) provide an alternative format to books. This CD with accompanying text is intended to engage the student in academic/literary activities while simultaneously providing instruction on appropriate social skills such as sportsmanship and perseverance. Figure 5–1 gives guidelines for selecting books for social skill instruction.

Language and Social Skill Development

Language issues play a major role in the social development of children. The existing research on the social skills of many CLD students (e.g., Hispanic, Asian, and Native American) indicates that teachers often rate them as passive and their social skill difficulties

FIGURE 5-1 Guidelines for selecting books for social skill instruction

1. Provide a good match between the social skill being taught and the lessons within the story.
2. For explicit social skill instruction, avoid books/stories dominated by violence.
3. Choose books with simple, clear story lines so that the social skill main idea is easily understood.
4. Select brief stories that are easy to comprehend and will not consume excessive amounts of class time.
5. Select literature that is culturally diverse, representing cultures from around the world as well as the five major racial/ethnic groups within our society.
6. Stories should address gender issues, being careful to present males and females in empowered, nonstereotypical ways.
7. For less-skilled readers, try to select books with minimal text and/or that provide repeated refrains.

Source: Reprinted from, G. Cartledge and M. Kiarie, 2001, "Learning Social Skills Through Literature for Children and Adolescents," *Teaching Exceptional Children, 34,* 40–47.

as often language based (Cartledge & Loe, 2001). Language is key in social development/social interaction. Because so many CLD children are either English language learners (ELL) or come from homes where English is a second language, they may have classroom adjustment problems due to the difficulties encountered in trying to comprehend when one is not conversant with the language. Curran (2003) suggests that under these circumstances students who are English language learners are likely to tune the teacher out, begin speaking with someone who speaks a common language, or simply become engaged in other activities. Furthermore, if students sense that their native language and culture are disparaged, they may possibly react in antisocial ways. For all CLD students, including African American or Black students, the stress and strain of trying to adapt to a different or standard language may cause many to turn off or drop out of school.

To counter these problems, Curran (2003) recommends promoting within the classroom a strong sense of community and affirming linguistic diversity. This might be achieved by encouraging collaborative and cooperative activities across as well as within groups. Yates and Ortiz (1991) advise that instead of assigning ELL learners endless worksheet tasks where they work independently without interactions from others, these students be grouped into cooperative activities where they could benefit from both language and academic learning, as well as the opportunity to develop and refine critical social skills. School staff can affirm culturally and linguistically different children by acknowledging the value

Culturally specific literature can be used effectively to teach social skills to culturally diverse learners.

> **TEACHING TIPS**
>
> **Social Skill Instruction Through The Child's Culture**
>
> - Teach children about the traditional values of their heritage. Present these values as reasons for pride.
> - Use traditional values as the basis for constructing rules of socially appropriate behavior.
> - Use cultural values as a means for building strong relationships with students and their families.
> - Provide direct counterinstruction on cultural values that clash with the culture of the classroom.
> - Use the contemporary arts that reflect the child's culture to provide a forum for teaching social skills.
> - Identify music and literature from the child's culture that have explicit positive social skill messages.

of knowing more than one language and by getting to know the child and the child's culture and learning to speak the child's language (Curran, 2003).

What Is a Model for Culturally Responsive Social Skills Instruction?

Basic Model

Social skills training (SST) typically follows a social modeling paradigm: (1) identifying and providing a rationale for the skill, (2) modeling the skill, (3) providing for guided practice, (4) providing for independent practice, and (5) behavior generalization (Cartledge & Loe, 2001; Cartledge & Milburn, 1996; Goldstein & McGinnis, 1997; Walker, Ramsey, & Gresham, 2004). Social skills are positive behaviors and need to be framed in terms of what we want children to do. When we begin to teach social skills, we first must identify the behaviors we wish to teach and try to give students a reason for wanting to perform that behavior. Because the need typically emerges from problem situations, it is often necessary to think in terms of what behavior we want to stop as well as what behavior we want to develop. The following sections provide examples of infusing culturally responsive strategies into the components of social skill instruction.

How Do We Provide Culturally Responsive Social Skill Instruction?

Convincing children that they need to learn a social skill such as, for example, ignoring provocation from their peers, is not an easy task. We provide a rationale for the skill so they will understand how the skill, in contrast to their current behavior, will help them achieve their goals—in this case, to stop the teasing by classmates. There are various ways to provide a rationale, such as discussing the problem with the student, using a film or story about the problem situation, or just engaging the child in a problem-solving session to identify all the possible options for what to do when teased. Simple stories or puppet plays can be effective (e.g., Cartledge & Kleefeld, 1991; 1994). For CLDE students, teachers are advised to draw upon stories and materials that reflect the learner's culture, for example, the Mexican tale *The Woman Who Outshone the Sun* (Martinez, 1991).

APPLICATION

Ms. Good decided that she would use the story *The Woman Who Outshone the Sun* (Martinez, 1991), to reinforce with her students the practice of making positive statements to each other. Each page of the story is written in both English and Spanish. As she read the story, occasionally she would read a sentence in Spanish for Alberto to translate into English. In this role, Alberto was esteemed the "assistant teacher." After reading the story, the students discussed Lucia Zenteno, the main character, and identified something good about her. Each student wrote a positive statement about Lucia Zenteno and tacked it on the bulletin board, where there was a picture of a Spanish lady and the title "Positive Statements: The Woman Who Outshone the Sun." For social skill instruction the next day, the theme was continued with making positive statements about classmates. The teacher pulled one child's name from a hat and each child in the class had to write or dictate a positive statement about the target student. The statements were posted on the bulletin board. This practice continued each day until every child's name was drawn. Students received points for thinking of a positive statement about another child. One simple statement per week was selected for Spanish translation. Students who remembered the Spanish translation (e.g., *Malik lee bien*, "Malik reads well") at the end of the week received an additional point.

In addition to books, teachers might use clips of popular films that reflect the cultural background of their students and provide acceptable scenes of the skill being taught. Although care needs to be taken to avoid R- or X-rated material, the use of films and other media may be especially effective with CLDE adolescents (e.g., Gause, 2002; Morrell, 2002). Morrell describes how he used units on poetry, hip-hop, literature, and film to help urban adolescents develop concepts of social justice. After reviewing and analyzing the materials, the students left empowered to address problems within their own community.

Older students require authentic, realistic materials. One possibility is to use the real-life writings of young people, such as *The Freedom Writers Diary* (Gruwell, 1999), which has a series of personal entries by Hispanic/Latino and African American teens. Diary entry #17 relates one teen's experience of being taunted and physically abused by a group of girls because the teen was obese. After reading the essay, the teacher might engage students in a discussion of what the teen might do to get the taunting girls to stop. What should the obese girl's friends do to help her? What social skills do the taunting girls need to learn? These discussions should lead to a list of socially appropriate behaviors that need to be acquired by the student being taunted (e.g., walking away, seeking help), the taunting girls (e.g., positive statements to others, positive self-statements, empathy towards others), and the taunted girl's friends (e.g., helping others, supporting others). During and following the story, the trainer emphasizes the exact responses that the main character has to give in order to display the proper social skill.

Regardless of the materials used, discussion should evolve so that the desired social skill and related components are stressed. In responding to provocation, for example, learners should be helped to realize the beneficial effects of behaviors such as ignoring, walking away, or making an assertive statement. The class may decide to learn the skill of ignoring first. The trainer *models* the social skill to dramatize and highlight its components. That is, some mild barb or taunt is delivered (do not let children deliver these; the barbs might be previously taped by the trainer and played at this time), and the trainer (1) does not look at the hypothetical person, (2) does not say anything to that person, and (3) states out loud what the trainer is thinking in order to keep from reacting visually or orally. This third step is especially important because it helps students to understand that we can use self-statements to help us act in appropriate ways (e.g., "I'm not going to look at him because he's just trying to get me in trouble. If I don't get in trouble, I'll get 5 extra minutes at recess" or "I'll be able to stay in school and remain on the basketball team" or "These girls are trying to hurt me. I need to get away from them. I need someone to help me to find another way to get home"). In modeling self-statements, it is important that teachers identify the kinds of things that are important to students and the repercussions of inappropriate behavior. For example, one student may be most concerned about the loss of learning time in school, another about home punishment, another about the loss of video time, and still another about missing a pick-up game with friends. The enactment is modeled several times to make sure the students thoroughly understand the desired behavior. To further facilitate understanding, the teacher also presents negative models to help students to discriminate between desired and undesired actions that make up the skill of ignoring teasing.

In the next step of *guided practice*, students are given the opportunity to act out the social skill of ignoring. It is important that every child have the opportunity to display the social skill several times under the trainer's supervision. A critical feature of guided practice is to provide scenes and language that reflect the learner's cultural background. Moore, Cartledge, and Heckaman (1995), for instance, found that they had to change the social skills scenes and script in order to get and maintain the involvement of adolescent African American urban males diagnosed with behavior disorders. In teaching appropriate winning and losing behaviors, scenes were changed from school settings to playground pick-up games. Wording also was changed to local vernacular so that "Your J is broke" was used in place of "Your jump shot is no good." Similarly, "Your J is phat" replaced "Your jump shot is good." The researchers readily recognized the importance of collaborating with students to develop a curriculum that they could identify with and embrace. Following these changes, students participated more fully and substantial increases in the desired social skills resulted.

Appropriate responses are praised and inappropriate responses are corrected and reenacted immediately. Guided practice is continued until students are able to perform the social skill errorlessly without trainer prompting. Depending on the number of students and their abilities, this may involve several sessions over a period of weeks. Teachers might be wise to set some criterion that students must achieve before moving on to independent practice. For example, each student would have to display correctly the steps for ignoring three consecutive times to demonstrate competence for independent practice.

Skills taught to CLDE students need to be realistic and appropriate to their social situation. In the example from the *Freedom Writers Diary*, for instance, the taunted student's safety was in jeopardy. More important than ignoring in the context for CLDE students are assertiveness skills related to getting away and nonaggressive ways to protect themselves.

Once students display the ability to enact the target skills, they are then ready to participate in *independent practice* activities. For culturally responsive instruction, the same principle noted above for *guided practice* would apply. The scenes and language should reflect the learners' background as much as possible and be selected from the learners' experiences. Students can be involved in helping to construct these practice activities. In learning to ignore, for example, children could be assembled into small groups of three or four, depending on the age of the students and class size, with each child given a number from 1 to 3, according to the number of children in the group. The teacher could deliver or play a recording of a mild taunt for the entire class. The teaser is a stick figure drawn on a sheet of paper and positioned and pasted on a chair. Child number 1 in each group acts out the social skill according to the given steps. The other members of the group observe student number 1 and give praise/corrective feedback, as appropriate. Beforehand, the teacher has instructed that when students give feedback they are to either (1) tell the person "good job" or (2) tell the person the step they missed (e.g., "don't look at the person"). If a step is missed, the observer then says, "Try again." If the student misses the step the second time, the other student shows how to perform the sequence so the peer can imitate. The activity then continues with child number 2 and so forth until each child has had the opportunity to practice the skill. While students are practicing in small groups, the teacher circulates to make certain children are conducting their groups properly. This practice activity could be repeated for as many sessions as the trainer deems necessary for the students to become proficient in their responses.

Older students could collaborate with the teacher in generating several vignettes based on real-life episodes. Students then act out their responses in small groups as the objects of some taunting behavior. (Do not let students deliver the barbs or taunt each other.) Enactments should be structured so that they are positive and affirming for all students.

The final step in the teaching sequence is to achieve *behavior generalization*, or transferring the newly taught skill to different settings and maintaining it over time. That is, we want Alberto to demonstrate ignoring behaviors in other settings, such as on the playground, in the lunchroom, on the school bus, and at home as well as in the classroom where the behavior was taught. We also want the behavior to be maintained over time (i.e., for weeks, months, and years) after it was taught. To get this to occur, trainers need to teach for behavior generalization. This includes (1) praising the behavior profusely when it occurs in the natural environment and gradually fading the reinforcement; (2) teaching for overlearning—using trainers in other settings to prompt the desired behavior; (3) teaching students to monitor their own behavior in other settings; (4) teaching students to guide their own behavior through self-speech; (5) using mnemonics in the natural environment to remind students of the desired social skill; and (6) providing periodic booster sessions so that the behavior does not disappear from the learners' repertoire. In addition, an important feature of getting social skill instruction to stick with CLD students is teaching their traditional cultural values and encouraging them to adhere to the high standards of their traditional culture in their personal behavior. It also helps to reinforce this learning through culturally specific literature, as discussed previously.

In order to get behaviors to generalize to other settings and to be reinforced by significant others such as parents, teachers may need to make special efforts to establish and maintain positive relationships with the families. Teachers should refrain from being judgmental. Through a home–school partnership, the teacher can gain special insights into teaching the student and the parent may learn to reinforce the social behaviors critical to the child's school success.

Behavior generalization has been often studied by social skill researchers (Gresham, Sugai, & Horner, 2001). Gresham et al. note that many of the studies are conducted in pull-out, small-group settings, which do not match the conditions under which the child is expected to perform the skill. Although intensive small-group instruction is often warranted, the recommendation is to also provide instruction within the setting where the social skills are to be performed. That is, if Alberto is initially taught in a pull-out small group of three or four students how to ignore teasing, this instruction should then be moved into the classroom where the skill is taught to the entire class by the teacher.

Alberto Continued

Because Alberto's problem with peer provocation had persisted for more than a year and seemed to be worsening, it was decided that he first would be taught this skill in a small pullout group conducted by the special education teacher, Mr. Allen. Mr. Allen taught this skill to Alberto and two other students in the school who also were having difficulty with peer provocation. The sessions took place 3 times a week for approximately 30 minutes each session. The instruction lasted for 4 weeks, at which time Mr. Allen determined the three students could competently perform the steps without prompting from him and could discriminate between appropriate and inappropriate forms of the skill.

At this point, Mr. Allen and Ms. Good decided that the skill should be taught to all the students in Ms. Good's classroom so that the behavior would generalize across students. This also would help other students in the class who were exhibiting milder forms of the problem. Ms. Good was careful not to single out Alberto in any way, pointing out that we all have problems at times when others tease us and "ignoring" was something we all could learn to use. Alberto's teachers were wise to provide social skill instruction immediately while Alberto was still young, instead of waiting to see if he would grow out of his excessive reactions. Besides, other children could also benefit from this instruction.

The lessons would focus on the skills that Alberto and his peers needed most, that is, responding appropriately to teasing and making positive rather than taunting/unkind statements to others. Concentrating on the areas of greatest need, the teachers would intensify the lessons until they saw improvement in the skills. Both teachers had had university coursework in teaching social skills, but before embarking on this project, they met with the school's behavior consultant, who reviewed with them the instructional procedures for teaching the skills. The consultant observed the lessons, providing materials and feedback as needed. For example, one curriculum program, *Bully Proofing Your Elementary School* (Garrity, Jens, Porter, Sager, & Short-Camilli, 2004), would be especially appropriate for this class, considering the verbal bullying directed at Alberto and a few others. The behavioral consultant also assisted the teachers in assessing the effects of the instruction. Alberto and the other students were observed at targeted times throughout the school day to see how they responded to peer provocation or if they made positive statements to each other. Teachers and parents completed a simple rating scale directed only at behaviors related to the skills that were taught (i.e., appropriate responses to teasing and making positive statements to others). Finally, the behavior consultant interviewed Alberto and his classmates to find out how much progress the students felt they had made as a result of this instruction.

After 8 weeks of social skill instruction, the teachers felt the students evidenced considerable improvement. Nevertheless, both teachers continued weekly minisessions in which students were prompted to demonstrate the skills. They gave daily reminders of the specific skill steps and students continued to receive points when they were observed displaying the taught behavior.

TEACHING TIPS

Getting the Most from Social Skill Instruction

- Begin social skill training early in the primary grades when children are most receptive to behavior change.
- Gear instruction to the social skill deficits of the learner.
- Make sure social skill trainers are thoroughly trained and closely monitored to ensure that the instruction is implemented correctly.
- Evaluate the intervention according to the skills taught.
- Teach the behavior over an extended time period, making sure the learner has many opportunities to respond and practice the skill.

Sources: Bullis, Walker, & Sprague, 2001; Gresham et al., 2001; Kavale & Mostert, 2004; Lewis, Sugai, & Colvin, 1998.

> **TEACHING TIPS**
>
> **Basic Steps for Culturally Responsive Teaching of Social Skills**
>
> 1. Rationale: Help the learner to *want* to perform the skill.
>   a. Use a simple story reflecting learner's problem and culture and/or
>   b. Video vignette reflecting learner's problem and culture.
>   c. Discuss past events.
> 2. Model: Show the learner *how* to perform the skill.
>   a. Specify the responses that make up the skill.
>   b. Identify behaviors and self-statements that are culturally responsive.
>   c. Demonstrate each response.
>   d. Describe each response orally during enactment.
>   e. Provide negative and positive examples.
> 3. Guided Practice: Help the learner to *perform* the skill.
>   a. Direct the learner to imitate your model.
>   b. Use scenes and language from the learner's background.
>   c. Collaborate with the learner on scenes and scripts.
>   d. Give corrective and reinforcing feedback to the learner.
>   e. Permit each learner to act out the skill.
>   f. Make sure the learner knows what the skill is and what the skill is not.
>   g. Practice with the learner many times until the learner does not need the teacher's guidance.
> 4. Independent Practice: Give the learner the opportunity to practice the skill *independently*.
>   a. Practice through games.
>   b. Practice through role plays.
>   c. Provide for peer-mediated practice and provide cooperative activities.
>   d. Discuss the skill through books and films.
> 5. Behavior Generalization: Help the learner to perform the skill at *other times* and in *other settings*.
>   a. Request significant others such as teachers, parents, and peers to reinforce the skill.
>   b. Assign "homework" for the skill to be performed elsewhere.
>   c. Establish reinforcing contingencies for the skill to be performed elsewhere and over time.
>   d. Teach CLD learners about traditional values of their culture.
>   e. Assign culturally specific reading and writing activities that reinforce the skill.

How Do We Provide Peer-Mediated Interventions for CLDE Learners?

Social skill instruction emphasizes interpersonal skills and the research literature shows that peers can be quite effective in bringing about desired behavior changes (e.g., Blake, Wang, Cartledge, & Gardner, 2000; DiSalvo & Oswald, 2002; Laushey & Heflin, 2000; Prater, Serna, & Nakamura, 1999; Strain, Kerr, & Ragland, 1979). Peer-based strategies are especially important since there is good evidence that CLD learners prefer and succeed with such strategies (e.g., Boykin, Tyler, Watkins-Lewis, & Kizzie, 2006; Ellison, Boykin, Tyler, & Dillhunt, 2005).

Peer-based lessons can be effective with children of all ages. Lin (1996), for example, trained urban preschool students with disabilities to initiate social interactions with lower-functioning classmates with autism. Older students are better suited for the more formal, peer-mediated social skill lessons. Blake et al. (2000) prepared intermediate and middle school urban males with behavior disorders to teach social skills to their peers with behavior disorders. In these studies, the students learned to reduce their verbal aggression and to improve their game-playing behaviors. One rationale for this approach is that preadolescent and adolescent students, especially CLD students, often are more receptive to messages coming from their peers than from adult authority figures. It also is a means for making social skill instruction more attractive and engaging to young people.

In teaching about appropriate winning and losing, for example, the social skills trainer first taught the skill to the students and then trained one of the students to reteach the skill to his peers. The peer trainer was given a script like the one shown in Figure 5–2 to use in these lessons (Cartledge, Wang, Blake, & Lambert, 2002). These studies found that students not only improved in their social skills but also, in some cases, made even greater progress with the peer-directed instruction than with the adult instruction. They further showed that the gains persisted even after instruction was terminated. Students were helped to maintain these skills through self-monitoring where they recorded their behavior on self-recording sheets such as in Figure 5–3.

APPLICATION

After teaching her students social skills on learning to deal with teasing and on making positive statements to others, Ms. Good decided that it would be beneficial to get the students to apply these skills in everyday classroom activities. Alberto had made good progress in responding to teasing and Rodney was being much more positive to the other students, including Alberto. Three days a week the students participated in peer tutoring to practice that week's reading sight words and math facts. Ms. Good decided that on the other 2 days students would participate in "cross-ability" tutoring so that less skilled students would be tutored by their more skilled classmates.

Alberto, who was having difficulty in reading, was paired with Rodney, who was a good reader. Prior to the tutoring, Ms. Good reviewed with the students the steps for tutoring and how to make positive statements to each other. For example, Rodney praised Alberto each time he made a correct response and he helped Alberto each time he made an error. Following tutoring, Rodney thanked Alberto for being a good tutee and Alberto thanked Rodney for tutoring him. For 5 minutes following the tutoring session Alberto instructed Rodney and the other students in Spanish words, phrases, and sentences. Emphasis was placed on words and phrases that were positive, such as *Buen trabajo* ("great job"), *Tu eres buen trabajador* ("You're a good worker"), *Siga trabajando asi* ("Keep up the good work"), and *Me gusta como tu lees esto* ("I like the way you read that!"). Students were encouraged to use these phrases with their partners during their tutoring sessions. Ms. Good circulated around the room giving students points for tutoring appropriately and for using positive statements.

FIGURE 5-2 Student script for teaching social skills

Lesson Plan for Winning and Losing

Student Trainer Script

Begin by reviewing with students the story "The Race." Ask, "Who can tell us what the story is about?" Make sure the student tells what Turkey and Turtle did. REMEMBER TO GIVE YOUR CLASSMATES TIME TO THINK. SAY, "GOOD JOB" WHEN GIVEN A CORRECT ANSWER. SAY "TRY AGAIN" WHEN THE ANSWER IS NOT CORRECT.

Ask: "Why should we try to be good losers or winners?" (We get to play longer and have more fun; we make others and ourselves feel good.)

Review the steps for winning and losing.

When you win a game:

- Say, "thank you," if congratulated.
- Smile and shake hands.
- Say something nice to the other player
- Agree to a rematch, if asked.

When you lose a game:

Smile and say "congratulations."

- Shake the winner's hand.
- Say something nice about the game.
- Ask for a rematch, if you want one.

Ask if anyone else can think of other good things that they might say when they win or lose a game.

Role-play with one student how to be a good winner. Direct all the students to watch to see if you were a good winner. After the role-play, ask students to tell you if you followed each step and were a good winner. REMEMBER TO SAY "GOOD JOB" WHEN STUDENT GIVES CORRECT ANSWER.

Role-play with one student how to be a good loser. Direct all the students to watch to see if you were a good winner. After the role play, ask students to tell you if you followed each step and were a good winner. REMEMBER TO SAY "GOOD JOB" WHEN STUDENT GIVES CORRECT ANSWER.

Tell students they now will practice how to be good winners or losers. Tell students to get in their assigned pairs. Give one student in each pair a winner badge and the other student in the pair a loser badge. Give students the sheets with four tic-tac-toe grids on each sheet. Tell students to play the game and the person with the winner badge is to be the winner and the person with the loser badge is the loser. GIVE STUDENTS A FEW MINUTES TO PLAY THE GAME.

When you give the signal, each student with a loser badge is to stand and show everyone the correct steps when losing. Give another signal for the students with the winner badge to show the steps when winning.

Tell students to switch badges. Let students play the game again and demonstrate the way to win or lose a game.

Give students two more times to practice winning and losing with their partners. AGAIN REMEMBER TO PRAISE EACH STUDENT WHEN HE GIVES A CORRECT ANSWER. SHOW THEM THE RIGHT WAY AND ENCOURAGE THEM TO TRY AGAIN WHEN THEY ARE NOT CORRECT.

Thank the students for being good listeners and say, "It's time for our game sessions." Please go to your tables.

Source: Adapted from G. Cartledge, & J. Kleefeld, 1994, *Working Together: Building Children's Social Skills Through Folk Literature*, Circle Pines, MN: American Guidance Services.

Winning and Losing

When I won the game, I

❏ Said thank you when congratulated.

❏ Smiled and shook hands.

❏ Said something nice to the other players.

❏ Agreed to a rematch when asked.

When I lost the game, I

❏ Smiled and said congratulations.

❏ Shook the winner's hand.

❏ Said something nice about the game.

❏ Asked for a rematch, if I wanted one.

FIGURE 5-3 Student self-monitoring sheet

TEACHING TIPS

Peer-Mediated Interventions for Teaching Social Skills to CLDE Learners

- CLDE children can be effective social skill trainers for their peers.
- Train older/competent students to prompt less-skilled peers in social interaction behaviors.
- Peer trainers can serve as teachers to teach small groups of peers specific social skills.
- Teach the social skill to the entire class. Give the peer trainer a script to teach the skill to peers.
- Behaviors taught by peers are likely to be long-lasting.
- Students often enjoy being taught by peers.

APPLICATION

As the instruction in Alberto's classroom progressed on dealing with peer provocation and making positive statements to peers, Alberto's teachers decided to embellish their instruction through peer-mediated approaches, incorporating a "client as trainer" strategy. That is, they would use students who evidenced the most problems in these two skills as the initial trainers for the rest of the class. Therefore, Alberto would present activities on dealing with peer provocation, and another student, Rodney, who had been a leader in teasing Alberto and others, would present strategies on positive statements to others. In order to keep Alberto's and Rodney's selections from being perceived negatively, other students who were more socially competent and did not present these problems also served as peer trainers. As a matter of fact, over the course of the school year, all of the students in the class received the opportunity to serve as peer trainer for various social skills.

In his role as peer trainer, Alberto reviewed with the students the steps for ignoring peer teasing. Then he introduced an ignoring-teasing game. For this game, the class was divided into two teams of approximately 10 to 15 players each, depending on the size of the class. Each team received a set of cards, according to the number of players, with statements on one side of the card. Most of the cards had positive statements, such as "Good job, you completed your math assignment today." Five of the cards had mild barbs such as "Your joke wasn't very funny, ha, ha, ha!" A numeral from 1 to 5 was on the bottom right corner of each card that had a barb. All of the cards were placed statement side down and the students took turns selecting one of the cards. When a student got a card with a barb, the student stated and demonstrated the steps for ignoring teasing; that is, (1) not looking at the person, (2) not saying anything to the person, and (3) saying something to yourself that will help you to ignore the person.

Prior to the game, Alberto reminded the students how to perform the skill by modeling it for them. When the game started, Ms. Good served as the judge and Alberto the scorekeeper. When a player displayed the target behavior correctly, his team got the number of points given in the corner of the card. Once everyone had a turn, the cards were shuffled and the students would get to repeat the game until everyone got a chance to act out appropriate ignoring-teasing behavior. The game was continued over several sessions in order to give everyone a turn. The objective was to practice the target behavior but a team goal was to see which team got the most points. As coteacher, Alberto got to prompt students in the appropriate behaviors when directed to do so by the teacher. He also helped the teacher to deliver praise statements when students responded appropriately.

Culturally specific literature can be used effectively to teach social skills to culturally diverse learners.

How Do We Teach Social Skills According to Gender?

What Are Social Skill Needs According to Gender?

The social development research and literature repeatedly note the psychosocial differences between boys and girls (Burford, Foley, Rollins, & Rosario, 1996; Johnson et al. 2002; Litvak-Miller, & McDougall, 1997; Talbert-Johnson, Cartledge, & Milburn, 1996). Generally, girls are depicted as more nurturing and altruistic, preferring to interact in small, intimate groups and placing more emphasis than boys on social relationships. Girls tend to avoid overt conflict and are more likely to negotiate and cooperate in order to promote social harmony. Researchers also note that girls are inclined to defer to boys, often evidence less self-confidence, and tend to be less assertive than their male peers. Aggression among females is likely to be relational aggression where girls will use exclusionary strategies as a means of inflicting psychological harm to others. Girls are most likely to inflict this form of aggression on other girls, and it becomes most problematic during the middle school and high school years. Another important area of focus for girls tends to be a lack of assertiveness skills.

In contrast to girls, boys are more likely to employ self-serving strategies, with an emphasis on dominance and competition. Boys tend to be more overtly aggressive, to gain status through physical prowess, and to prefer large-group interactions rather than small-group intimacies. These groups are often hierarchical and have leaders who tell others what to do. Boys also were found more likely to be bullies and victims of bullies. Boys enjoy communicating with others through jokes or telling stories. They will challenge the stories of others and use egoistic language to brag about their accomplishments. Studies show boys often exhibit more self-confidence than girls, are likely to act independently, and tend to be more ambitious than girls. The following chart, based on a review of the sources given at the beginning of this section, gives a psychosocial profile of boys and girls.

How Do We Teach Gender-Specific Social Skills?

The strategies for teaching social skills according to gender issues is the same as those presented earlier in this chapter. It is important for teachers and others to recognize when they are inadvertently reinforcing some of these stereotypical behaviors. Physical aggression

TEACHING TIPS

Social Skill Characteristics According to Gender

Females	Males
Emphasis on social relationships	Emphasis on independence
Oriented toward small-group, intimate relationships	Large-group orientation
Emphasis on caring, sharing, altruistic behaviors	Short-term altruism, e.g., rescuing behavior; long-term altruism less likely
High levels of empathy	Lower levels of empathy
Inclined to defer to males	More use of coercive, dominant strategies
More likely to negotiate conflict and cooperate	More likely to engage in open conflict
Aggression expressed relationally	Aggression expressed overtly
Play in small, intimate groups	Large-group, hierarchical play with rules, dominance, and competition
Distinct Areas of Need for Social Skill Interventions	
Alternatives to relational aggression	Alternatives to overt aggression
Skills in assertiveness	Higher levels of empathy and prosocial behaviors

among boys, for example, is often overlooked or actually reinforced due to the notion that boys are prone to fight or are expected to learn how settle disputes physically. As a result, these youth may never learn alternatives to aggression and how to deal with conflict in more socially appropriate, nonviolent ways. The consequences of punishment for fighting are insufficient to curb the antisocial behaviors of aggression-prone youngsters; these students also need direct, systematic instruction on a series of aggression alternatives, such as learning to negotiate with others, to cooperate, to use assertive rather than aggressive words, to ignore the provocation of others, and so forth.

Another gender consideration is that under certain circumstances gender-specific groups might be preferred for social skill instruction. Middle school girls, for example, might benefit more from same-sex lessons on relational aggression, which would focus on learning to be more inclusive and generous with peers, particularly other females. By the same token, same-age males probably would gain more from lessons stressing social skill alternatives to overt aggression.

What Are the Social Skill Needs According to Sexual Orientation?

As young people move through childhood into adolescence, the peer group gains in importance. Trying to adjust becomes increasingly stressful, particularly for gay and lesbian youth (Cooley, 1998; Johnson & Johnson, 2000). At this point when adolescents are struggling with

APPLICATION

Ms. Good and Mr. Allen decided they would divide the students into gender groups to work on aggression, since the boys and girls tended to express aggression in different ways. Mr. Allen took the boys while Ms. Good took the girls. During his instruction, Mr. Allen decided to use the story, *Think Again* (Fresh, 2002), which is part of the Kid Hip Hop series published by Scholastic Books. It tells the story of two boys—one black, one white—who were verbally aggressive to each other because of differences in skin color. After joining the basketball team and being redirected by the coach, the boys learned to become best friends. They then began to help other students to understand why they should be friends and avoid violence. The story, focused on elementary-age boys is presented in the form of a rap with an accompanying CD.

Mr. Allen played the CD and projected the words on the classroom screen so the boys could "rap" along with the CD. They then discussed all the things that they could do to avoid fighting or violence. For example, the boys might decide that one thing they could do is to say something to the person who is trying to taunt them. Together, the class generated a rhyme that could be put in a rap, e.g., "When someone tries to start a fight, I will say, 'You know that's not right. Why don't we have a talk? That's better than throwing a rock.'"

Each day the boys discussed alternatives to aggression and then thought up rhymes to be used in their class rap. When completed, the boys performed their group rap for the girls in their class and other classes in the school. Alberto taught the boys how to speak at least one verse in Spanish.

---

identity issues, gay/lesbian youth have even greater challenges in dealing with their differences and trying to achieve acceptance among peers, school personnel, family members, and others. Cooley notes that the primary task of the adolescent homosexual is to adjust to the socially stigmatized role. Major stressors are the verbal and physical abuse that they receive from their peers. Gay and lesbian youth often experience violence in their homes; family members abuse them and may even eject them from the home, further subjecting them to more harm and exploitation as they attempt to survive in unprotected environments.

School professionals can help gay/lesbian youth and their families deal with the issue of sexual orientation in more satisfactory ways. The youth and the family should receive services from the school counselor or a community counselor in order to address the array of emotions that accompany an awareness of homosexuality (e.g., depression and anxiety). Classroom teachers need to create an atmosphere of acceptance of all students in the class regardless of differences and a zero-tolerance attitude toward taunting or verbal abuse of other students. The teacher needs to model acceptance, making certain that the

---

TEACHING TIPS

Teacher's Role with Gay and Lesbian Youth

1. Maintain a positive attitude of valuing and accepting all students.
2. Foster a zero-tolerance attitude toward peer abuse among students.
3. When appropriate and needed, present homosexuality as a fact of life in a nonjudgmental manner.
4. Teach social skills on dealing with provocation, on making positive statements, and on accepting individual differences.

student is seen as a valued individual, without projecting excessive favoritism and without drawing attention to a particular student's sexual orientation. On the other hand, homosexuality needs to be discussed as a fact of life in a nonjudgmental way. Social skill lessons that stress tolerance and positive interactions with others need to be an explicit part of the curriculum for the entire class. All students also need to participate in lessons on dealing with teasing or peer provocation.

What Are the Social Skill Curriculums?

Several formal curriculum programs offer detailed or scripted lessons for teaching social skills. Goldstein and McGinnis (1997; McGinnis & Goldstein, 1997; 2003) provide a series of programs for teaching social skills to preschool, elementary-age, and adolescent learners. The curriculum is skills based, using the skills training (SST) model, and lists specific skills to be taught at each age level. In addition to a text with specific guidelines for conducting training sessions, the programs contain workbooks or activity sets to provide for extended practice of the targeted skills.

As with the Goldstein and McGinnis series, many of the social skill curriculums focus on developing prosocial skills. However, as a consequence of the violent school events of the 1990s, some of the curriculum programs tend to focus more on reducing antisocial behavior. In *First Step to Success: Helping Young Children Overcome Antisocial Behavior,* Walker, Stiller, Golly, Kavanagh, Severson, and Feil (1997), for example, provide a curriculum targeting kindergarten-level children and specific strategies for helping to eliminate such antisocial behaviors as physical aggression, throwing tantrums, vandalism, and noncompliance. The strategies include teaching children skills at school and at home.

Another program designed to reduce antisocial behaviors is *Second Step: A Violence Prevention Curriculum* (Committee for Children, 2002, www.cfchildren.org). Designed for prekindergarten through middle school, the curriculum employs a skills training model and emphasizes (1) empathy, (2) impulse control and problem solving, and (3) emotional and anger management, and conflict resolution. Research findings support the program's effectiveness (e.g., Grossman, 1997), and the developers report success stories and case studies of positive effects in a variety of settings, including urban, suburban, and rural.

A series of instructional materials for early childhood to the secondary grades are designed to address peer–peer aggression in the form of bullying: *Bully Proofing in Early Childhood* (McCarnes, Nelson, & Sager, 2004), *Bully Proofing Your Elementary School* (Garrity, Jens, Porter, Sager, & Short-Camilli (2004), and *Bully Proofing Your Middle School* (Bonds, & Stoker, 2000). The lessons are designed to support victims as well as provide both victims and bullies the skills needed for more appropriate social interactions. A more comprehensive curriculum is provided in *The Tough Kid Social Skills Book* (Sheridan, 1995), which gives specific guidelines on how to assess and teach the skills as well as provides lessons on 10 basic social skills.

Culturally specific curriculums are rare. The typical teacher will have to adapt most curriculums for their CLD students. Taylor (1997) has developed one such curriculum for African American males. It uses a skills training model and identifies skills and instructional activities that are relevant to this population. Although most of the instructional objectives are broadly stated, the focus on African American males can be seen in skills such as learning how to show respect for females and expressing feelings, sympathy, and respect for others. The instructional strategies recommended by Taylor are similar to those recommended in this chapter and other curriculums (e.g., modeling, role playing, cooperative learning, and so forth); however, instruction is adapted to specific student needs, learning styles, and background. A focus unique to Taylor is the importance of African American male role models for this population. He advises recruiting male models from the community for regular mentoring activities in the schools as well as greater employment of African American males as teachers in the schools. Guidelines for helping parents to understand their role in promoting their son's appropriate social development are another special feature of this curriculum.

Hammond (1991), who also uses a skills training approach, provides a set of videotapes to address anger/aggression with African American youth. The tapes are gender and culturally specific and offer adaptive ways to deal with everyday provocations.

Summary

Social skills are socially approved positive behaviors that enable us to have our needs met while simultaneously contributing to the common good. Learners with exceptionalities may present social skill problems that interfere with their success within inclusive environments. These problem behaviors include poor problem solving, a tendency toward self-seclusion, attention deficits, and lack of assertiveness. Cultural and linguistic diversity adds another dimension to the problem of social skill development for children with exceptionalities. Children from diverse backgrounds may have social behaviors or traditions that differ from the culture of the school. Teachers need to understand the culture of their learners, identify ways in which traditional values can be used to specify more appropriate social behaviors, and provide counterinstruction when needed to help students benefit fully from their schooling.

Social skills are taught mainly through a social modeling paradigm in which teachers demonstrate to learners exactly how they are to perform the behavior and then provide the opportunity for students to practice and display the desired behavior frequently on subsequent occasions. Social skill instruction can be embellished and made more attractive through peer-mediated instruction as well as literature and music. Teachers need to match the social skill instruction to the specific needs of the students they serve. Every effort needs to be made to have students take ownership of learning these skills. Social skill instruction can be enhanced if it is provided early in a child's life, it is implemented correctly, students are engaged as collaborators, the instructional activities are culturally relevant, lessons are taught frequently and thoroughly, appropriate evaluation procedures are employed, and the skills are transferred to other settings and times.

In addition to culture, gender differences need to be considered when teaching social skills. On occasion, same-sex social skill instruction might be appropriate, especially when dealing with behaviors such as overt and relational aggression. Teachers also need to be aware of the special needs of students with a different sexual orientation. These students may need special professional interventions, but the classroom needs to be a positive environment where these students are not subjected to psychological or physical abuse.

Several social skill curriculums are available commercially. Teachers are advised to review these programs and select instructional activities according to the specific needs of their students. Culturally competent teachers can adapt these curriculum programs to the needs of their CLDE students as noted in this chapter.

Related Learning Activities

1. Observe a CLDE student in an inclusive setting during a non-teacher-directed period such as recess or lunch. Make special note of the student's peer interaction skills. For example, does the student initiate play activities or conversation with peers? Do peers invite the student to play or into their conversations? How does the student respond to peers? Does the student make positive comments to others? How does the student respond to negative peer comments? Based on your observations, what social skills do you feel the student needs to learn? What skills do you feel the student's peers need to learn?

2. Using the same target student, develop a social skill instructional sequence, following a social modeling paradigm, as discussed in this chapter. Specify in your instruction the special cultural factors that need to be considered and how your instruction will address these factors. Additionally, note the role that gender might play in the way the skills should be taught and how you plan to adjust the instruction for gender. Finally, specify the interventions you will provide the child's peers so that they might be more socially appropriate toward the target student and serve to model and reinforce the desired behaviors.

3. Review two or three existing social skill curriculums. Identify skill lessons that would be appropriate for teaching the desired skills to your targeted CLDE student and his or her peers. Determine what, if any, modifications are needed to make the lessons more culturally and gender appropriate for your targeted student.

4. Interview the student targeted in activity 1 above or select another student with disabilities. From your interview, find out if the student feels good about peer relationships. What does the student consider to be some of his or her social skill strengths? What problems does the student have with some of his or her friends? What does the student feel needs to be done to correct these problems? What social skills would the student like to develop?

References

Alberto, M. (1991). [Unpublished interview]. The Ohio State University, Columbus.

Andersson, G. Olsson, E., Rydell, A., Larsen, H. C. (1999). Social competence and behavioral problems in children with hearing impairment. *Audiology, 39,* 88–92.

Blake, C., Wang, W., Cartledge, G., & Gardner, R. (2000). Middle-school students with serious emotional disturbances (SED) serve as social skill trainers/reinforcers for peers with SED. *Behavioral Disorders, 25,* 280–298.

Bonds, M., & Stoker, S. (2000). *Bully proofing your middle school.* Longmont, CO: Sopris West.

Boykin, A. W., Tyler, K. M., Watkins-Lewis, K., & Kizzie, K. (2006). Culture in the sanctioned classroom practices of elementary school teachers serving low-income African American students. *Journal of Education for Students Placed At Risk, 11,* 161–173.

Bruchac, J. (1993). *The first strawberries: A Cherokee story.* New York: Penguin Putnam, Inc.

Bullis, M., Walker, H. M., & Sprague, J. R. (2001). A promise unfulfilled: Social skills training with at-risk and antisocial children and youth. *Exceptionality, 9,* 67–90.

Burford, H., Foley, L., Rollins, P., & Rosario, K. (1996). Gender differences in preschoolers' sharing behavior. *Journal of Social Behavior and Personality, 11,* 17–26.

Cartledge, G., Cochran, L., Paul, P. (1996). Social skill self-assessments by adolescents with hearing impairment in residential and public schools. *Remedial and Special Education, 17,* 30–36.

Cartledge, G., & Feng, H. (1996). *Asian Americans.* In G. Cartledge & J. F. Milburn (Eds.). *Cultural diversity and social skills instruction: Understanding ethnic and gender differences* (pp. 87–131). Champaign, IL: Research Press.

Cartledge, G., & Kiarie, M. (2001). Learning social skills through literature for children and adolescents. *Teaching Exceptional Children, 34,* 40–47.

Cartledge, G., & Kleefeld, J. (1991). *Taking part: Introducing social skills to children.* Circle Pines, MN: American Guidance Services.

Cartledge, G., & Kleefeld, J. (1994*). Working together: Building children's social skills through folk literature.* Circle Pines, MN: American Guidance Services.

Cartledge, G., & Loe, S. (2001). Cultural diversity and social skill instruction. *Exceptionality, 9,* 33–46.

Cartledge, G. & Milburn, J. F. (1995). *Teaching social skills to children and youth.* Boston, MA: Allyn & Bacon.

Cartledge, G., & Milburn, J. F. (1996). *Cultural diversity and social skills instruction: Understanding ethnic and gender differences.* Champaign, IL: Research Press.

Cartledge, G., Paul, P., Jackson, D., & Cochran, L. (1991). Teachers' perceptions of the social skills of adolescents with hearing impairment in residential and public school settings. *Remedial and Special Education, 12,* 34–39, 47.

Cartledge, G., & Talbert-Johnson, C. (2004). School violence and cultural sensitivity. In A. P. Goldstein & J. Close Conoley (Eds.), *School violence intervention handbook* (2nd ed., pp. 391–425). New York: Guildford Press.

Cartledge, G., Tillman, L. C., & Talbert-Johnson, C. (2001). Professional ethics within the context of student discipline and diversity. *Teacher Education Special Education, 24,* 25–37.

Cartledge, G., Wang, W., Blake, C. & Lambert, M. C. (Spring, 2002). Middle school students with behavior disorders as social skill trainers for peers. *Beyond Behavior,* 14–18.

Center for Mental Health in Schools. (2002). Bullying prevention. A center quick training aid. University of California, Los Angeles. http://smhp.psych.ucla.edu.

Cochran, L., & Cartledge, G. (1996). Hispanic Americans. In G. Cartledge & J. F. Milburn (Eds.), *Cultural diversity and social skills instruction: Understanding ethnic and gender differences* (pp. 245–296). Champaign, IL: Research Press.

Committee for Children (2002). *Second step: A violence prevention curriculum.* Seattle, WA: author.

Cool J., L. L. (2002). *And the winner is . . . .* New York: Scholastic Books.

Cooley, J. J. (1998). Gay and lesbian adolescents: Presenting problems and the counselor's role. *Professional School Counseling, 1,* 30–35.

Cooper, D., & Snell, J. L. (March, 2003). Bullying. *Educational Leadership*, 22–25.

Cosby, B. (1997). *The meanest thing to say: A little Bill book for beginning readers*. St. Paul, MN: Cartwheel.

Coster, W. J., & Haltiwanger, J. (2004). Social-behavioral skills of elementary children with physical disabilities included in general education classrooms. *Remedial and Special Education, 25*, 95–103.

Curran, M. E. (2003). Linguistic diversity and classroom management. *Theory into Practice, 42*, 334–340.

Delpit, L., & White-Bradley, P. (2003). Educating or imprisoning the sprit: Lessons from ancient Egypt. *Theory into Practice, 42*, 283–288.

DiSalvo, C. A., & Oswald, D. P. (2002). Peer-mediated interventions to increase the social interaction of children with autism: Consideration of peer expectancies. *Focus on Autism and other Developmental Disabilities, 17(4)*, 198–207.

Ellison, C. M., Boykin, A. W., Tyler, K. M., & Dillhunt, M. L. (2005). Examining classroom learning preferences among elementary school students. *Social Behavior and Personality, 33*, 699–708.

Feng, H., & Cartledge, G. (1996). Social skills assessment of inner city Asian, African, and European American students. *School Psychology Review, 25*, 227–238.

Fessler, D. M. T. (2004). The same in two cultures: Implications for evolutionary approaches. *Journal of Cognition & Culture, 4*, 207–262.

FitzGerald, S. (2003, April 15). Child bullies at risk for more violent behavior, study finds. *The Philadelphia Inquirer*. Retrieved from http://www.philly.com/mld/inquirer/living/education/5634167.htm

Forness, S. R., & Kavale, K. A. (1996). Treating social skill deficits in children with learning disabilities: A meta-analysis of the research. *Learning Disability Quarterly, 19*, 2–14.

Frankel, F., & Feinberg, D. (2002). Social problems associated with ADHD vs. ODD in children referred for friendship problems. *Child Psychiatry and Human Development, 33*, 125–146.

Fresh, D. E. (2002). *Think again*. New York: Scholastic, Cartwheel books.

Garrity, C., Jens, K., Porter, W., Sager, N., & Short-Camilli, C. (2004). *Bully proofing your elementary school*. Longmont, CO: Sopris West.

Gause, C. P. (October, 2002) Researcher points to pop culture for educating black youth. *Black Issues in Higher Education*, 18.

Goldstein, A. P., & McGinnis, E. (1997) *Skillstreaming the adolescent*. Champaign, IL: Research Press.

Gresham, F. (1981). Social skills training with handicapped children: A review. *Review of Educational Research, 5*, 139–176.

Gresham, F. M., Sugai, G., & Horner, R. H. (2001). Interpreting outcomes of social skills training for students with high-incidence disabilities. *Exceptional Children, 67*, 331–344.

Grossman, D. (1997). The effectiveness of violence prevention curriculum among children in elementary school. *Journal of the American Medical Association, 277*, 1605–1611.

Gruwell, E. (1999). *The freedom writers diary*. New York: Doubleday.

Hamilton, V. (1971). *The planet of Junior Brown*. New York: Simon and Schuster.

Hammond, W. R. (1991). *Dealing with anger: A violence prevention program for African American youth* [Videotape Program]. Champaign, IL: Research Press.

Horne, E. B., & Leung, C. B. (Summer, 2003). The development of identity and pride in the Indian child. *Multicultural Education*, 32–38.

Huurre, T. M., & Aro, H. M. (1998). Psychosocial development among adolescents with visual impairment. *European Child & Adolescent Psychiatry, 7*, 73–78.

Irvine, J. J. (1990). *Black students and school failure: Policies, practices, and prescriptions*. New York: Greenwood.

Johnson, C. C., & Johnson, K. A. (2000). High-risk behavior among gay adolescents: Implications for treatment and support. *Adolescence, 35*, 619–638.

Johnson, H. R., Thompson, M. J. J., Wilkinson, S., Walsh, L., Balding, J., & Wright, V. (2002). Vulnerability to bullying: Teacher-reported conduct and emotional problems, hyperactivity, peer relationship difficulties, and prosocial behavior in primary school children. *Educational Psychology, 22*, 553–556.

Kavale, K. A., & Mostert, M. P. (2004). Social skill interventions for individuals with learning disabilities. *Learning Disability Quarterly, 27*, 31–43.

Kemp, C., & Carter, M. (2002). The social skills and social status of mainstreamed students with intellectual disabilities. *Educational Psychology, 22*, 391–411.

Kopelowicz, A. (1998). Adapting social skills for Latinos with schizophrenia. *International Review of Psychiatry, 10*, 47–50.

Lampe, J. R., Rooze, G. E., & Tallent-Runnels, M. (2001). Effects of cooperative learning among Hispanic students in elementary social studies. *The Journal of Educational Research, 89*, 187–191.

Laushey, K. M., & Heflin, L. J. (2000). Enhancing social skills of kindergarten children with autism through the training of multiple peers as tutors. *Journal of Autism and Developmental Disorders, 30*, 183–193.

Lewis, T. J., Sugai, G., & Colvin, G. (1998). Reducing problem behavior though a school-wide system of effective behavioral support: Investigation of a school-wide social skills training program and contextual interventions. *School Psychology Review, 27*, 446–459.

Liang, C. T. H., Lee, S., & Ting, M. P. (2002). Developing Asian American leaders. *New Directions for Students Services, 97*, 81–89.

Lin, C-S. (1997). *The effects of peer-mediated social skills training on the social interactions of preschool children with special needs*. Columbus, OH: Unpublished doctoral dissertation, The Ohio State University.

Litvak-Miller, W., & McDougall, D. (1997). The structure of empathy during middle childhood and its relationship to prosocial behavior. *Genetic, Social and General Psychology Monographs, 123*, 303–325.

Lo, Y-Y., Loe, S. A., & Cartledge, G. (2002). The effects of social skill instruction on the social behaviors of students at risk for serious emotional disturbances. *Behavioral Disorders, 27*, 371–385.

Martinez, A. C. (1991). *The woman who outshone the sun*. San Francisco, CA: Children's Book Press.

McCabe, K. M., Clark, R., & Barnett, D. (1999). Family protective factors among urban African American youth. *Journal of Clinical Child Psychology, 28*, 137–150.

McCarnes, K., Nelson, K., & Sager, N.W. (2004). *Bully proofing your middle school*. Longmont, CO: Sopris West.

McGinnis, E., & Goldstein, A. P. (1997). *Skillstreaming the elementary school child*. Champaign, IL: Research Press.

McGinnis, E., & Goldstein, A. P. (2003). *Skillstreaming in early childhood*. Champaign, IL: Research Press.

Miller, M. C., Cooke, N. L., Test, D. W., & White, R. (2003). Effects of friendship circles on the social interactions of elementary age students with mild disabilities. *Journal of Behavioral Education, 12*(3), 167–184.

Moore, R., Cartledge, G., & Heckaman, K. (1995). The effects of social skill instruction and self-monitoring on anger-control, reactions-to-losing, and reactions-to-winning behaviors of ninth-grade students with emotional and behavioral disorders. *Behavioral Disorders, 20*, 253–266.

Morrell, E. (2002). Toward a critical pedagogy of popular culture: Literacy development among urban youth. *Journal of Adolescent and Adult Literacy, 48*, 72–77.

Most, T., & Greenbank, A. (2000). Auditory, visual, and auditory-visual perception of emotions by adolescents with and without learning disabilities and their relationship to social skills. *Learning Disabilities Research, 15*, 171–178.

Mpofu, E. (2003). Enhancing social acceptance of early adolescents with physical disabilities: Effects of role salience, peer interaction, and academic support interventions. *International Journal of Disability, Development and Education, 50*, 435–454.

Myers, W. D. (1981). *Hoops*. New York: Dell Publishing.

Myers, W. D. (1988). *Scorpions*. Cambridge, MA: Harper & Row.

Myers, W. D. (2001). *Monster*. New York: Harper Collins.

Myers, W. D. (2002). *Handbook for boys: A novel*. New York: Harper Collins.

Nixon, E. (2001). The social competence of children with attention deficit hyperactivity disorder: A review of the literature. *Child Psychology & Psychiatry Review, 6*, 172–179.

O'Connor, J. (1989). *Jackie Robinson and the story of all-black baseball*. New York: Random House.

Prater, M. A., Serna, L., & Nakamura, K. K. (1999). Impact of peer teaching on the acquisition of social skills by adolescents with learning disabilities. *Education and Treatment of Children, 22*, 19–35.

Ridsdale, J., & Thompson, D. (2002). Perceptions of social adjustment of hearing-impaired pupils in an integrated secondary school unit. *Educational Psychology in Practice, 18*, 21–34.

Sacks, S., & Gaylord-Ross, R. (1989). Peer-mediated and teacher-directed social skills training for visually impaired students. *Behavior Therapy, 20*, 619–638.

Sanders, D. (1987). Cultural conflicts: An important factor in the academic failures of American Indian students. *Journal of Multicultural Counseling and Development, 15*(2), 81–91.

Schneider, B. H. (1993). *Children's social competence in context: The contributions of family, school and culture*. Oxford, England: Pergamon.

Scott, C., Russell, P. A., Gray, C. D., Hosie, J. A., & Hunter, N. (1999). The interpretation of line of regard by prelingually deaf children. *Social Development, 8*, 412–426.

Sheridan, S. (2000). *Tough kid social skills book*. Longmont, CO: Sopris West.

Shkodriani, G. M., & Gibbons, J. L. (2001). Individualism and collectivism among university students in Mexico and the United States. *The Journal of Social Psychology, 135*, 765–772.

Skiba, R., & Fontanini, A. (2000). Bullying prevention. What works in preventing school violence. Safe and Responsive Schools Project Fact Sheet Series. Indiana Education Policy Center, Smith Research Center. Retrieved from http://www.indiana.edu/~iepc/welcome.html.

Sosik, J. J., & Jung, D. I. (2002). Work-group characteristics and performance in collectivistic and individualistic cultures. *The Journal of Social Psychology, 142*, 5–23.

Strain, P. S., Kerr, M. M., & Ragland, E. U. (1979). Effects of peer-mediated initiation and prompting/reinforcement procedures on the social behavior of autistic children. *Journal of Autism and Developmental Disorders, 9*, 41–54.

Surat, M. M. (1983). *Angel child, dragon child*. Milwaukee, WI: Raintree.

Talbert-Johnson, C., Cartledge, G., & Milburn, J. F. (1996). Social skills and the culture of gender. In G. Cartledge & J. F. Milburn (Eds.), *Cultural diversity and social skills instruction: Understanding ethnic and gender differences*, (pp. 297–352). Champaign, IL: Research Press.

Taylor, G. R. (1997). *Curriculum strategies: Social skills intervention for young African-American males.* Westport, CT: Praeger.

Triandis, H. C. (2001). Individualism-collectivism and personality. *Journal of Personality, 69,* 907–924.

Turnbull, A. P., Blue-Banning, M., & Pereira, L. (2000). Successful friendships of Hispanic children and youth with disabilities: An exploratory study. *Mental Retardation, 38,* 138–153.

Turnbull, A. P., Pereira, L., Blue-Banning, M. (May/June 2000). Teachers as friendship facilitators. *Teaching Exceptional Children, 32,* 66–70.

Vang, C. T. (Winter, 2003). Learning more about Hmong students. *Multicultural Education,* 10–14.

Vaughn, S., Kim, A., Morris-Sloan, C. V., Hughes, M. T., Elbaum, B., & Sridhar, D. (2003). Social skills interventions for young children with disabilities: A synthesis of group design studies. *Remedial and Special Education, 24,* 2–15.

Walker, H., Ramsey, E., & Gresham, F. (2004). *Antisocial behavior in school: Evidence-based practice.* Belmont, CA: Wadsworth/Thomson Learning.

Walker, H. M., Stiller, B., Golly, A., Kavanagh, K., Severson, H., & Feil, E. (1997). *First step to success: Helping young children overcome antisocial behavior.* Longmont, CO: Sopris West.

Yates, J. R., Ortiz, A. A. (1991). Professional development needs of teachers who serve exceptional language minorities in today's schools. *Teacher Education and Special Education, 14*(1), 11–18.

Zolotow, C. (1963). *The quarelling book.* New York: Harper and Row.

Chapter 6

Culturally Responsive Collaborations with CLD Families

The purpose of this chapter is to address the important interaction of families and schools, with a particular focus on reviewing the special relationships of CLD families who have children with exceptionalities. In addition to providing an authentic profile of these families, the chapter offers strategies for increasing family involvement with the school and family advocacy. After finishing this chapter, readers should be able to answer the following questions:

1. How have home–school relationships changed over the past 50 years?
2. What is family adaptation for CLD families who have children with disabilities?
3. What are the special issues encountered by CLD parents of children with exceptionalities?
4. In what ways might CLD families differ in their view of their children with disabilities compared to mainstreamed families?
5. What is meant by empowered CLD families and empowered schools?
6. How might schools foster effective home-based learning for CLD students with exceptionalities?

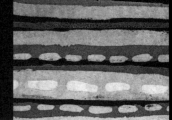

7. What strategies lead to effective communication with culturally and linguistically diverse families?
8. What family organizations advocate for the special needs of mainstreamed and culturally and linguistically diverse exceptional learners?

By the end of this chapter, readers will obtain information on strategies to:

1. Empower CLD parents through education and skill development.
2. Help CLD parents provide home-based instruction.
3. Communicate effectively with CLD parents.
4. Foster positive and supportive relationships with CLD parents.
5. Promote advocacy among CLD parents.

What Is the Home–School Relationship?

The importance of parent involvement and parenting practices to the success of children in the schools cannot be overstated. In the past three decades, at least two federal authorizations have helped to focus attention on the role of parents and families: (a) Public Law 94-142 in 1975 (now IDEIA, Individuals with Disabilities Education Improvement Act, 2004), giving parents of children with disabilities specific rights in the schooling of their children, and more recently (b) the "No Child Left Behind" law (U.S. Department of Education, 2001), giving parents the option to transfer their children from low- to higher-performing schools. Parents are acknowledged to be children's first teachers and they have the potential to be highly effective teachers. Indeed, in the early years of this society, parents were commanded to teach their children to read, but as this country became more industrialized and specialized, formal education became the law and the principal responsibility transferred from parents to professional educators. Nevertheless, the important function of families in education has not been dismissed: Many children begin school having been taught to read by their parents, and increasingly children are being homeschooled for their entire education, with highly favorable outcomes (Lines, 2001). Schools overwhelmingly expect families to inculcate their children with appropriate attitudes and provide children with the home-based learning experiences to ensure positive and problem-free learning at school.

As we examine the relative functions of families and schools and consider the increasing diversity of our society, a rather complex and somewhat ambiguous picture emerges. We need more precise understandings of family actions and pupil achievement, the type of family involvement/advocacy that needs to be promoted, and how to work most effectively with families that present diversity in terms of culture as well as exceptionalities. As our society changes, we experience corresponding changes in family types and structures. In order to be successful, schools need to change accordingly in the way they perceive families and the strategies they employ to engage the families of the students in their schools.

Marquis

Marquis is the third of Ms. Lewis's four children. He is in second grade and, in contrast to his two older sisters, Marquis is doing poorly in school. He is especially behind in reading; at the end of second grade, he is barely reading at the beginning of the first-grade level. Ms. Lewis is concerned about Marquis and occasionally asks his teachers how he is doing and what she should do. In the past, the teachers' comments were always the same: "Marquis is making slow progress and Ms. Lewis should read with him at home." Ms. Lewis says she and his sisters read with him at home, but she is not sure it is helping. She also assumes that part of his slowness is due to the fact that he is a boy: She does not expect boys to do as well as girls in school.

At the end of the year, the teachers call her in for a conference and tell her that they want to retain Marquis in second grade. Ms Lewis is adamant that he not be retained but the teachers insist on this. Eventually, Ms. Lewis relents because she does not know what else she might do.

The school scheduled a special education evaluation from which Marquis received a LD diagnosis. Despite the special education placement, Marquis is still severely behind his age-mates in reading. Ms. Lewis expresses disappointment with the teachers because she feels that they could have informed her earlier of Marquis's extremely poor performance. She now feels she is being poorly served by the school and is exploring ways to enroll her children in another school where they can be more academically successful.

What could the school do to help Ms. Lewis help Marquis? What special things might the school do to communicate more effectively with Ms. Lewis? How can Ms. Lewis learn to advocate for her son?

How Are Home–School Relationships Perceived?

Parent–school engagement differs greatly across our schools. Epstein (1995) makes the following observations about families and schools: (1) home–school involvement typically declines as students move through the grades; (2) home–school involvement is greater in more affluent communities; (3) parents of low socioeconomic children are contacted more often about problems; and (4) single parents, working parents, fathers, and parents who live long distances from the school are less involved. Epstein contends that most parents care, most teachers want families to be involved, and most students want their parents to be more knowledgeable about schooling. Families are underinvolved mainly because they are unskilled in how to accomplish this.

The way in which we view home–school relationships has altered over the years, paralleling the changes in the larger society. Summers, Gavin, Purnell-Hall, and Nelson (2003) describe the evolution of this relationship as occurring in four stages. First of all, there is the traditional, unilateral role wherein parents are expected to comply with the school's perceptions of the way to help their children succeed in school. That is, parents need to have high aspirations/expectations for their children's school success, participate in school activities, provide a supportive home environment, and communicate with their children about their school performance and achievement. This perspective does not encompass a model of a home–school *partnership* that gives parents a say in how their children are taught in the schools. The second stage described by Summers et al., is the Epstein (e.g., 1995) notion of overlapping spheres of influence: home, school, and community—all places where children learn. These spheres need to form partnerships and have frequent interactions so that children receive a common message. Epstein speaks of creating "family-like" schools where each child is made to feel special and all families are welcomed, not just those families who are easy to reach. Similarly, she recommends creating "school-like" families and communities where the importance of school and school-related activities is reinforced.

A third stage, according to Summers et al., is special education advocacy, whereby various parent organizations are instrumental in bringing about publicly supported school programs for their children with disabilities and in increasing the school's accountability for the progress of their children. A family-centered or family-support paradigm makes up the fourth and last stage. Here the focus is on empowering the family to be the primary decision-makers and on supporting the family/child according to their obvious needs. Other features of this model are that it is strengths-based so that educational goals and aspirations are built upon the families' strengths; it is flexible to address cultural diversity; and it requires sensitivity and respect to understand and appreciate the family's special stressors, particularly as they relate to children with exceptionalities.

What Is the Role of Families in Pupil Achievement?

Studies on family involvement indicate a positive effect on pupil achievement. Fan and Chen (2001) note the multidimensional aspect of home involvement, consisting of variables such as (a) parent–child communication (e.g., assistance with homework), (b) home supervision (e.g., providing an environment conducive to studying), (c) educational aspiration for children (e.g., valuing education), and (d) school contact and participation (e.g., attending school functions). The researchers found that past involvement correlated with achievement indicators such as grade point average or college success. The value that parents place on education appears to produce the strongest relationship with pupil achievement (Fan & Chen, 2001; Hill & Craft, 2003; The National Reading Panel, 2000). The National Reading Panel (2000) found that students who reported discussing their school studies at home had higher scores than those who reported not discussing their studies. It also found higher reading achievement among children who (a) spent $\frac{1}{2}$ to 1 hour daily on homework, (b) reported reading for fun daily, (c) had more types of reading materials at home, and (d) watched fewer than 3 hours of television daily.

One factor in assessing the impact of parent involvement on pupil achievement is socioeconomics. Hart and Risley (1995) analyzed the impact of parent language production on the language development of preschool children and found large differences between the verbal stimulation provided by middle-income parents compared to that provided by low-income parents. The middle- and low-income children showed corresponding differences in their language development. According to Hart and Risley, middle-income parents directed more than two times as many utterances at their children than did children of low-income parents. The researchers also observed that children in more affluent households encountered more words of encouragement from their parents than did children of lower-income parents. Affluent parents are more likely to have the resources and time to be involved in their children's schooling, and these children also are more likely to be higher achievers. Other studies show that families of higher-achieving children not only have slightly higher educational and financial resources but also report less extended depression and health impairments (Robinson, Weinberg, Redden, Ramey, & Ramey, 1998). This research supports the pivotal role of parents and points to the need to implement early intervention programs within the homes of low-income, CLD learners.

Socioeconomics are complicated by race, since racial minorities are disproportionately impoverished in this society (Fan & Chen, 2001; Hill & Craft, 2003). However, even within low-income minority (i.e., African American) groups, research evidence shows differential parenting between high- and low-achieving children. Gutman and McLoyd (2000) studied the strategies employed by low-income African American parents of high- and low-achieving students. They found that parents of high-achieving students used some specific strategies such as (1) organizing homework schedules, (2) creating math problems for their children, (3) assigning their children extra reading and writing lessons, and (4) providing tutoring in areas of deficit. They also found that parents of high-achieving students, compared to parents of low-achieving students tended to initiate more school contact, involved their children in more extracurricular and religious activities, and when problems occurred, were more inclined to contact the school immediately to work cooperatively to solve the problem. The researchers also observed that these parents readily praised their children's successes and provided support, rather than ridicule, when the children failed to reach their goals.

What Role Have Families Had in the Schooling of Children with Exceptionalities?

How Have Families Been Perceived?

Historically, a widely held view of families of children with disabilities was that the families were the cause of their children's disabilities, a belief that gave rise to the eugenics movement of the late 19th and early 20th centuries (Turnbull & Turnbull, 2001). Parents who gave birth to children who had mental, emotional, physical, or learning disabilities were considered to be unfit or genetically inferior. The eugenics movement set out to improve the human race through selective breeding procedures such as sterilizing and institutionalizing individuals with certain disorders. In this country, the eugenics movements impacted CLD families especially. Focusing on intelligence and intelligence test performance, the proponents of selective breeding targeted specific groups—for example, African Americans, Native Americans, the poor, and Eastern European Jews—for segregation and sterilization programs (Black, 2003). According to Black, this campaign resulted in the sterilization of 60 thousand Americans, many of whom did not become aware of this until decades later. The inhumane application of eugenics within Nazi Germany formally put a stop to the movement within this country, but such subsequent efforts as aggressively promoting birth control among CLD groups have aroused some lingering suspicion. Furthermore, as Turnbull and Turnbull observe, elements of parent blaming are still very much a reality and can serve as a barrier to home–school collaboration.

How Do Families React to the Presence of Disabilities?

There is disagreement about how families of children with disabilities deal with having a child with a disability. Some authorities theorize that parents of children with disabilities go through a "grief cycle," or mourning process, analogous to that from the death of a loved one (Turnbull & Turnbull, 2001). According to Moses (1989), parents typically have dreams for their children, and a child with disabilities often represents the death of those dreams, thus leading parents to grieve. The grief process encompasses the emotions of denial (e.g., refusing to accept the diagnosis), guilt (e.g., believing that the parent caused the disability), depression (e.g., turning one's anger inward), anger (e.g., externalizing one's anger—often toward the disabled child), and anxiety (e.g., becoming totally consumed in doing for others). This grief process is important, Moses argues, because it enables the individual to separate from the significant loss and emerge stronger emotionally.

Despite the intrinsic appeal and widespread endorsement of this view in the professional literature, Turnbull and Turnbull (2001) caution against applying it universally. First, the grief-cycle theory for the CLD population has not been scientifically validated and has a largely Eurocentric or European American middle-class perspective, which overlooks a significant portion of the population affected. Furthermore, the way in which parents respond to a child's disability will depend on a variety of factors, including the manner in which the diagnosis is presented. Parents may be more devastated, for example, by a diagnosis delivered by an insensitive, judgmental professional than if they received the same information from a supportive professional who was empathic and provided resources for other important services. Finally, the mourning theory for CLD families may be inadequate because it emphasizes a pathological (i.e., inherently diseased or disordered) view of parents and overlooks the views of culturally diverse families (Harry, 2002).

What Are the Implications of Federal Legislation for CLD Families of Children with Disabilities?

In this society, several decades of highly effective advocacy for families of children with disabilities have resulted in a series of federal laws that ensure educational services for their children. As discussed in chapter 2, the latest reauthorization of IDEIA 2004 strengthens the role of parents. The law articulates, for example, that parents are expected to be equal participants in the IEP process and notes that parents have the ability to provide critical information about their child's abilities, interests, performance, and history. The law makes clear that parents are expected to participate in discussing the child's need for special education and related supplementary services and aids. To strengthen their decision-making involvement, it encourages parents to participate in determining how their child will be involved in the general education curriculum as well as districtwide assessments. Parents are not only expected to be part of the team in developing the IEP but should also be informed they can invite any individual "with knowledge or special expertise" to serve on the team and can receive copies of the IEP without cost or having to request it. Furthermore, the meetings need to be scheduled in such a way as to facilitate the parents' attendance. The 2004 reauthorization of IDEIA allows parents to excuse (in writing) certain IEP team members from meetings, when appropriate. IEP meetings also may be conducted in alternative formats, such as videoconferencing or conference calls.

The expectation is that by increasing the input of parents and families in the child's education, the parents will assume major responsibility for monitoring the child's school program and progress and will keep records and participate in various forms of advocacy (Bauer & Shea, 2003). These increased expectations, however, do not necessarily match up with the changing structure of families. The contemporary family no longer conforms to the traditional model of the heterosexual married couple and children with a working father and a stay-at-home mother. Disproportionately, CLD families are unlikely to fit this profile. Over 70% of mothers are employed outside the home and 27% of family households are headed by single parents, so it is likely that the demands of these added responsibilities have siphoned off the energy and resources needed for in-school and home-based learning activities (Summers et al., 2003). The options were made even narrower for low-income families by the passage of the Personal Responsibility and Work Opportunity Reconciliation Act (welfare reform) of 1996 (Heyman & Earle, 2000). This legislation overwhelmingly affects single-parent families when the parent is forced to work outside the home. With full-time work or schooling and limited financial resources, these parents encounter major obstacles to school involvement.

Other family changes that certainly influence schooling, especially for CLD families, are the growing number of "blended" families resulting from the greater incidence of divorce and remarriage; the increase in single and never-married parents; the growing acceptance of same-sex couples rearing children as families; and the increased number of children being cared for by grandparents, other extended family members, or even foster parents. The federal regulations attempt to address this issue by defining parents as "persons acting in the place of a parent, such as a grandparent or stepparent with whom a child lives, as well as persons who are legally responsible for a child's welfare, and at the discretion of the State, a foster parent who meets the requirements specified in the law." Nevertheless, the current changes in the nature of the family can present real practical and legal difficulties for the schools (Summers et al., 2003) as well as possibly lead to a redefinition of what is meant by family involvement in the schooling of children.

What Are Some Special Issues for CLD Families of Children with Exceptionalities?

What Are Family Perceptions?

Diversity requires us to acknowledge differences in the way such parents are perceived, how their perceptions of their children and the schools differ, and the special limitations they experience in becoming involved in the schooling process. The previously noted "blaming" of families of children with disabilities appears to be intensified with this group, evolving into the "bashing" of culturally diverse families of children with disabilities. In the face of a history of discrimination, rejection, criticism, and poor services, many low-income CLD families tend to be reluctant to trust public agencies and schools (Unger, Jones, Park, & Tressell, 2001). Because the European American, middle-income family is typically viewed as the parenting model in this society, families from culturally diverse groups are relegated to a deficit model (Taylor & Whittaker, 2003; Thao, 2003). Harry (1992) argues that for African American parents, it is a double-deficit model, in that these families have been historically described pejoratively—involved in a "tangle of pathology," for example, and having children who are disproportionately identified for special education programs. She also proposes that due to the lower social position of many culturally diverse families in this society, it is difficult for those in the mainstream to see the strengths of families in this group (Harry, 2002).

What Are Trust Issues?

Teachers often complain that CLD parents are underinvolved in the schools and are not interested in their children (Thompson, 2003). Harry (1992) counters that instead of apathy, the behavior of these families may actually be a function of (1) the distrust they have of school personnel, (2) their perceptions that assessments are culturally biased, (3) the tendency of schools to make fewer contacts with CLD families than with majority families (i.e., European American), and (4) the perception that the schools are not acting as true partners in the IEP process. Other issues these parents have include the perception of overidentification of their children for special education programs (Townsend, Thomas, Witty, & Lee, 1996) and the undue stress of the everyday problems of living, which tends to lead poor CLD parents to place the full responsibility of their children's achievement on the schools (Paratore, 2001). Other researchers report that many Asian American parents tend to be even less involved in the schools than African American parents (Wu & Qi, 2005), but this underinvolvement is most likely due to their belief that they are not to interfere with the schools and should show their respect for teachers by not contacting them or challenging their actions (Huang, 1997; Lee & Manning, 2001).

What Is Family Adaptation?

The "grief cycle" seems to be less apparent in CLD families, based on evidence that certain African American and Hispanic/Latino families show greater resilience in terms of coping with a disability than European American families and are likely to use a broader scale for determining normalcy (Harry, 2002). According to Harry, CLD families are less likely to attach the disability label to mild disabling conditions such as learning disabilities, behavior disorders, or educable mental retardation. Children with mild disabilities may be considered a bit slow, but not disabled, based on the parent's perception of the child's ability to function in the home (Lian-Thompson & Jean, 1997). Some Asian American families are likely to disavow the presence of a learning disability or depression, tending to attribute these conditions either to a lack of effort or to lack of motivation (Huang, 1997).

How Do Goals Differ?

Families from diverse backgrounds may differ from the mainstream not only in the way they define their children but also in the goals that they have for their children and how they manage their children. Our society emphasizes preparing children for independence. Even individuals with disabilities, to the extent possible, are educated for independent living. An explicit feature of the IEP process is the development of transition plans with the expectation that the individual would acquire the academic, daily living, vocational, and social skills needed to be self-supporting and independent. Culturally diverse families may differ in their goals, and the question naturally arises of whose norms should be the goal in the normalization process (Bernhard, Lefebvre, Kilbride, Chud, & Lange, 1998; Harry, Rueda, & Kalyanpur, 1999). In qualitative studies of four families from various diverse backgrounds, Harry (1999) found that only one felt a normal life was living outside of one's biological family and that Spanish-speaking families expected their siblings to take care of the child with a disability. Because of this different understanding of independence, the above authors suggest that placement into inclusive settings is probably of lower priority for culturally diverse families. In contrast to white families, who make greater use of out-of-home planning, family extendedness is normal for CLD groups. For example, for Asians, the importance of the family increases, rather than lessens, as one becomes older (Cartledge & Milburn, 1996).

What Are Some Different Parenting Issues?

Parenting practices of culturally and linguistically diverse families are often misperceived and viewed dimly by the larger society. The more authoritarian methods observed in many African, Hispanic/Latino, and Asian American households are often viewed with concern. The schools and other authorities fail to see these actions as couched in a loving, nurturing culture and are inclined instead to label them as emotional or physical abuse. Although low-income African Americans, when compared to Asian Americans, were observed to use spankings more frequently, they also were more openly affectionate with their children and equal to Asians in holding positive attitudes toward their children (Wu & Qi, 2005). A study of middle-income African American families (Bradley, 1998) found that the most common disciplinary action was discussing the behavior with the child. These parents were more inclined to withdraw privileges, give warnings, and order the child not to perform the behavior than to use corporal punishment or ignore the child. Much of the African American parenting research has been conducted with low-income families and compared to middle-income European and Asian American families (Wu & Qi). Socioeconomic factors need to be considered before drawing conclusions about parenting styles.

Traditional values of immigrant populations also need to be taken into consideration. Thao (2003) reports from interviews with Mong parents that the parents desired to obtain respect from their children and permission from authorities to discipline their children according to the traditional Mong culture. These parents felt that the authorities helped their children to challenge them, further undermining the respect they desired from their children, the schools, and the general American population. They felt disrespected and devalued by the American authorities and society. Similar sentiments are found among many groups of recent immigrants, such as Somalians, who feared that their children would falsely claim abuse in order to free themselves from traditional Somali parenting customs (Phillips, 2003). Court rulings, no matter how minor, are regarded as undermining the authority of the family, placing the families at odds with their children, the schools, the courts, and social services.

Conflict between cultural differences and schools also occurs in Native American families. These parents tend to be more passive in their child-rearing practices and attempt to be respectful of their children's individuality and treat them more as young adults (Dykeman, Nelson, & Appleton, 1995; Harden & Hedgpeth, 2005). Storytelling is a common means of transmitting mores and the ways of doing things within the culture. When encountering the more confrontational and seemingly harsh methods used in the schools, Native American children may become frightened and withdraw (Dykeman et al., 1995). School personnel who have little cultural information about or understanding of the practices of culturally diverse families are likely to view these parents as inadequate or too passive. Bernhard et al. (1998), for example, studied teachers' attitudes toward the child-rearing practices of parents of young children from Asian, Mediterranean, Caribbean, and African backgrounds. The teachers saw the parents as being disinterested, felt that the child-rearing methods of the minority parents were too lax, and that the parents would spoil their children. On the other hand, parents often described themselves as being tired and felt that the teachers were not as receptive to their concerns over such issues as racial incidents in the school.

What Are Some Economic Issues?

Increasing cultural diversity in our society and schools will be accompanied by an increasing number of nontraditional families with fewer stay-at-home parents (Hodgkinson, 2002). Low-income CLD parents typically see education as a means to a better life for their children but often find their living conditions and the school climate substantially limit this opportunity

Schools need to learn of the family traditions of culturally diverse groups. Many Native Americans rely on storytelling and indirect teachings to socialize their children.

(Taylor & Whittaker, 2003; Thao, 2003). These families are disproportionately impacted by welfare reform and the decline of manufacturing jobs for unskilled individuals (Zhou, 2003). They are forced to work longer hours to meet the demands of their relatively large families, and these longer working hours mean less time to supervise their children and fewer opportunities to interact with the schools in the interest of their children. Zhou observes that poor youth who adopt the trappings of a youth culture perceived as adversarial (e.g., urban dress) are further disadvantaged because they are unlikely to be cushioned by the safety nets provided by more affluent families. Poor minority children are likely to be perceived as "bad," which is not the case for affluent youth engaging in the same behavior.

Poverty is a critical factor undercutting home–school alliances for Native Americans living on reservations, where there is a 45% poverty rate (Franklin, Waukechon, & Larney, 1995; Harden & Hedgpeth, 2005). The rural settings make easy access to the schools difficult, and families often have to deal with impassable roads, inclement weather, and time that it takes to get to the schools. Adolescents leave school and home in these communities at early ages (Dykeman et al., 1995; Franklin et al., 1995).

What Are the Cultural Discontinuities?

Many CLD families experience cultural discontinuities when attempting to communicate with the schools. Parents who are not skilled in English cannot easily do so, and competent translators frequently are not available. Using their children as translators often exacerbates a problem by pushing the child into the parental role and further increasing the parent's difficulties in supervising their children (Zhou, 2003).

Lee and Manning (2001) offer several suggestions for schools working with Asian American parents, such as using Asian parents as mentors for recent immigrant students, assisting the child with interpretations, and occasionally working with the parents. They also advise that Asian parents pay close attention to nonverbal communication, so teachers need to be careful not to convey to these parents impatience or lack of interest in the parents' concerns. Other recommendations include showing respect for the Asian culture within the classroom, avoiding the model minority stereotype since not all Asian Americans are high achievers, and helping parents access English learning programs in order to bridge any gaps that might exist between parents and their children. Many of these families come from a culture where personal problems are not shared outside of the home; they have difficulty with self-disclosure and often are afraid of "losing face" (Cartledge & Milburn, 1996; Taylor & Whittaker, 2003).

A recurring theme is that parents from culturally diverse backgrounds want schools to communicate to them with respect; they want school personnel to be honest with them, to present a no-blaming attitude, to be supportive, and to include them in the decision making for their children and for the schools. They also want to be included in school governance at a meaningful level (Dykeman et al., 1995; Robinson-Zanartu, Majel-Dixon, 1996; Townsend et al., 1996). Practitioners need to move away from the deficit model for culturally diverse families and toward a model emphasizing family empowerment and strength. Instead of focusing on inadequacies, professionals might seek out family strengths and make a deliberate effort to learn more about the family and its culture.

Although no group is a monolith, some shared commonalities of CLD families include extended families, mutual aid, fictive kinship, racial identity, and religious consciousness (Cartledge, Kea, & Simmons, 202). Families are often extended with multigenerational blood relatives assuming caretaking roles and pooling resources for the welfare of family members. These families may also include non-blood related (fictive kinship) individuals who also provide family support. CLD families typically take pride in their racial heritage, share common beliefs, and actively engage in their cultural religious practices.

Many culturally diverse parents, especially recent immigrants, would benefit from mentoring experiences with individuals of similar backgrounds and similar experiences.

How Do We Promote CLD Family Involvement in the Schools?

If schools hope to increase family involvement, particularly that of CLD families, they need to move beyond the traditional view that families should simply comply with the school. Instead, schools need to start where the families are, not where they want them to be (Simpson & Carter, 1993; Summers et al., 2003), and focus on supporting parents in addressing their needs (Norwood, Atkinson, Tellez, & Saladana, 1997). The idea is to *empower* parents so that they can act independently in their own and their children's best interests.

How Do We Empower CLD Families and Schools?

Empowerment is perhaps the greatest need of low socioeconomic CLD parents of children with exceptionalities. Turnbull and Turnbull (2001) define empowerment as the degree to which individuals are able to exercise control over their lives and to take action to get what they want. Additionally, this empowerment comes about from one's motivation and knowledge/skills. Motivation results from believing in one's capabilities, believing that one can employ those capabilities, believing that one's visions will materialize, and remaining energized, and persistent. Along with motivation, the empowerment requires a set of knowledge/skills that enable people to acquire information, apply problem-solving strategies, utilize coping/management skills, and communicate needs and wants effectively. When families and schools are both empowered, healthy collaborations can occur in the best interests of the students. If neither the schools nor the families are empowered, the situation tends to deteriorate into reciprocal blaming/bashing with little help for struggling students.

What Are Empowered Schools?

Empowered schools (i.e., personnel who are motivated, visionary, energized, skilled, resourceful, and so forth) can help families become empowered. At the first sign of difficulty in school or when families bring their concerns to the school, school personnel could communicate with them to define the possible problem, to seek solutions and design a plan of action, and to collaborate on their respective roles in carrying out the plan. Using Marquis as an example, when he began to fall behind in reading in kindergarten or first grade, an empowered school would have contacted the family to specify the learning problem, to describe intensified learning activities that would take place in the general education classroom, and to train the family in very specific strategies that could be employed at home to reinforce the school's effort. It also would have collaborated with the family in a short-term communication and monitoring system, thus enabling the school and family to closely monitor the progress being made in reading on a weekly basis. Such a system provides for a kind of synergy, allowing two units to act in concert, making the whole greater than the sum of its parts (Turnbull & Turnbull, 2001).

A major feature of empowerment is information, creating opportunities for families to acquire the knowledge and skills needed to manage their affairs competently (Dunst, Trivette, & Deal, 1994). Parents need information about the schools in which their children are enrolled, about federal education regulations, and about appropriate academic standards. In conversations with parents of children in an extremely poorly performing school, for example, one parent stated that her children were getting a better education than she ever did and another parent proudly stated that her children were smart because they were getting all A's. These comments raise questions about how much the parents knew about their children's schools and how academically competent their children actually were.

At an extremely low-achieving school, even the highest pupil evaluations would not assure a parent that the child is performing at grade level or competitive with age-mates within the district, in surrounding districts, or nationally. All parents, no matter where their children fall along the performance continuum, need to have a clear and precise understanding of their child's skills and age-level expectations so that they can advocate for their children from a position of knowledge and strength. Parents need accurate information about their children's status and advice on steps they might take to improve problem situations. Timing is extremely important. When children are permitted to persist in failing situations year after year, parents become discouraged and are much less likely to be engaged in a collaborative relationship for the schooling of their children.

How Do We Empower Parents Through Parent Education?

If parents are to become full partners in the schooling of their children, they will need assistance in understanding their roles (Koonce & Harper, 2005; Norwood et al., 1997). Norwood et al. describe a school-based parent education program designed to help African American urban parents acquire greater understanding of how they could have an impact on their children's learning. In this yearlong in-service project, they began by trying to build a sense of community with the parents by avoiding too formal language and dress. The content focused on parenting skills (positive behavior management, effective praise, nurturing children, child development, self-esteem, and stress management) and methods for fostering home-based learning (parents as partners, developing children's listening skills, engaging in parent-teacher conferences, helping with homework, study skills, fostering number and literacy skills). They introduced and emphasized cultural relevancy by presenting the training information from the cultural perspective of the parents, in this case African Americans. The issue of discipline, for example, was discussed in light of the history of discipline in the African American community, reflecting on the effectiveness of the parents' methods in the context of contemporary society. Each of the sessions ended with a review of the session and positive statements about oneself, one's children, and other participants. They also gave and received a supportive hug. These session closings were designed to be consistent with the attributes of spirituality, affection, and sociocentrism considered to be characteristic of the African American culture. According to the researchers, they made a point of always treating the parents with respect within a climate of trust and security, and the parents expressed satisfaction with the training as well as a willingness to continue to use the skills. Children of the 20 low-income parents who participated were reported to receive higher reading and math scores than did children of nonparticipating parents.

How Do We Empower Families Through Parent Skill Development?

Family-centered or empowerment approaches are designed to help families act independently (Dunst, et al., 1994). This requires school personnel to realize that home–school collaboration is an attitude, not an activity (Riggins-Newby, 2003) and that the process of parent involvement needs to be redefined so parent needs are given a priority by the schools. Riggins-Newby promoted productive relationships with families in a reading project in Humphries Elementary School in Atlanta, Georgia, by helping parents to upgrade their own literacy skills. A literacy coordinator visited homes to provide community literacy information and helped parents to get their GED so that they could help their children. The project also provided monthly workshops on taxes, job preparation, computer literacy, and so forth. Riggins-Newby reported that over a 5-year period, these activities resulted in greater home–school collaboration.

Lopez, Scribner, and Mahitivanichcha (2001), working with low-income migrant parents, provide another example of improving the home–school relationship through addressing parent skills and needs. The authors stress the importance of focusing on the needs of the families, being committed to them, and being willing to go the extra mile for these families. In qualitative studies of four migrant-impacted schools, the authors observed that substantive parental involvement is predicated on schools committing to meet the social, economic, and physical needs of the families. In these schools, personnel made the families a priority. They perceived migrant families as a permanent and important part of the school community and made the effort to establish "relational bonds" with migrant families. For example, at a time of a severe thunderstorm, school personnel cancelled classes and worked through the weekend to help the families with the special needs that resulted from the storm.

The schools involved parents in several different ways. Economic and physical needs were addressed by connecting parents to a network of social services and health systems. Some schools used prizes of hygiene products or of arts and crafts that the families could use to make things, which they then sold for additional income. These strategies were very effective because they addressed the immediate concerns of these families. School personnel were also genuine in their welcoming of migrant families. Instead of conducting meetings within a formal atmosphere, school personnel invited parents into less formal environments for informal chats to help them feel more comfortable. Professionals affirmed parents by commenting on the value the parents placed on education and the interest they took in their children's success in school. Schools provided education for the parents focused on either self-improvement (e.g., GED, vocational classes, English learning, citizenship classes) or their child's education.

How Do We Empower Families Through Home-Based Learning?

How Can Families Employ Home-based Activities to Support School Learning? Home-based learning activities can have a major impact on a child's school success even among low-income CLD children. Research shows, for example, that African American high-achieving students are more likely to come from homes where the parents make a deliberate effort to support their schooling (Clark, 1993; Gutman & McLoyd, 2000). In addition to providing the home-based learning activities reported earlier in this chapter, Gutman and McLoyd found that these parents also involved their children in more extracurricular and religious activities, praised their children for their successes, and continued to support, rather than ridicule, them when they failed to reach their goals. These parents initiated school contact more often and when problems occurred, they contacted school personnel immediately to solve the problems.

Fantuzzo and his colleagues (Fantuzzo, Davis, & Ginsburg, 1995; Heller & Fantuzzo, 1993) describe ways to provide parental support in their studies of fourth- and fifth-grade, low-socioeconomic, and academically at-risk African American urban students. Participating parents were permitted to provide rewards or incentives to their children based on their children's performance in classroom peer tutoring, observe their child's performance in the classroom, or serve as an assistant in their child's classroom (Heller & Fantuzzo, 1993). Those students who received peer tutoring plus parent involvement achieved the highest math scores and teacher ratings. Additionally, the authors report that the parents began to "perceive themselves as genuine partners in decision making concerning their children, and to be a part of their children's success" (p. 532). In a partial replication, Fantuzzo et al. (1995) again obtained superior math performance with the peer-tutoring plus parent-involvement group. The findings from these studies indicate that good instructional programs which foster high pupil response rates such as peer tutoring can boost academic achievement (e.g., Cooke, Heron, & Heward, 1983; Lo & Cartledge, 2004), but parent involvement appears to have a powerful additive effect.

How Can Parents Be Teachers?   It is frequently noted that parents are their children's first teachers, but empirical evidence of the positive effect of parental instruction is limited. One of the few existing investigations used parents to teach early literacy skills to their kindergarten children (Kraft, Findlay, Major, Gilberts, & Hofmeister, 2001). Children taught by their parents outperformed control-group peers on both the standardized and curriculum-based measures.

Although the Kraft et al. study (2001) was conducted using affluent, college-educated parents, similar findings are reported with low-income/diverse families with children at risk for or with disabilities. Anclien (2003) found that a parent-tutoring program benefited the math performance of six low-income and low-achieving fourth-grade students. Training the parents to tutor their children at home resulted in greater math achievement for these students and positive reviews from the parents on the assistance they received from the teacher. Bradley and Gilkey (2002) trained parents of poor children to use the Home Instructional Program for Preschool Youngsters (HIPPY) to develop readiness skills. Follow-up data on these children in Grades 3 and 6 showed that compared to peers who had other preschool experiences or no preschool experience, the children had fewer suspensions, better grades, higher test scores, and better behavior as rated by the classroom teacher. These studies of home-based instruction underscore the need to train and support parents in the skills to be taught.

Teachers often give parents general recommendations such as "read to your children" as a means of improving their children's performance in school. Such advice often leads parents to complain that schools are not giving them enough information to help their children at home (e.g., Koonce & Harper, 2005). Many parents, especially low socioeconomic CLD parents, often have limited academic skills and are not able to help their children without explicit directions (Slaughter-Defoe, 2000). The following application is an example of providing explicit, detailed directions to parents or extended family members for home-based tutoring.

APPLICATION

Home-Based Instruction

Ms. Lewis, Marquis's mother, Ms. Holmes, Marquis's second-grade teacher, and Mr. Green, the disability specialist, agreed to collaborate to devise a home-based instructional program for Marquis. The teachers advised Ms. Lewis that some of the annual reading goals for Marquis included reading second-grade passages at a minimum of 90 correct words per minute with comprehension and recognizing within 3 seconds all of the second-grade sight words. To help Marquis at home with these goals, his teachers taught Ms. Lewis how to tutor Marquis. The strategies focused on learning his weekly sight words and reading passages more fluently.

For learning his sight words, Ms. Lewis was given a set of 10 words (words for that week) and the following directions:

1. Set a timer for 5 minutes
2. Present the cards one at a time.
3. If the student is correct, say, "Great, that's right."
4. If the student is wrong, say, "Try again."
5. If still incorrect, tell the student the correct word and tell the student to say the word.
6. After going through all 10 cards, shuffle the cards and repeat until the timer rings.
7. Set the timer again and practice according to the above sequence for another 5 minutes.
8. At the end of the second 5 minutes, assess the student's knowledge by presenting each word. Give the student 3 seconds to say each word. Do not give the student the answers for missed words. Record the number of correct and incorrect words on the form and return the form in the folder to school with the student the following morning.

Ms. Holmes, the teacher, included in the card sets review words that Marquis had mastered previously. The recording form helped both the teachers and Marquis's mother keep track of the progress Marquis was making on his sight words.

For reading fluency, the disability teacher, Mr. Green, gave Ms. Lewis a 150-word passage that contained the sight words Marquis was learning for that week. Marquis was to read the passage as rapidly as possible, using a repeated reading strategy. Marquis read the passage repeatedly for 10 minutes, alternating paragraphs with his parent. If Marquis did not reach the goal of reading, he read the same paragraph on subsequent evenings until he was able to read the passage at 90 words per minute with fewer than 10 errors. His mother recorded his rate on the passage each evening. When Marquis met his goal, Mr. Green sent home another passage that contained the words Marquis was learning in school. In addition to reading the passage, Marquis was to answer five comprehension questions that Mr. Green provided for each passage. Mr. Green also gave Ms. Lewis a step-by-step written sequence of how she could get Marquis to read the passages.

Ms. Holmes and Mr. Green taught Ms. Lewis how to implement each of these strategies. Ms. Lewis practiced the strategies with Marquis in school in the presence of the teachers so that they could give her feedback on the procedures. The two strategies combined involved approximately 20 minutes per evening of tutoring for Marquis. The daily recording forms enabled Ms. Lewis to have a clear idea of the progress Marquis was making in his reading, and the scripted strategies helped her to determine exactly what she could do at home to help him make progress. Marquis and his mother were encouraged to spend another 10 minutes each evening reading from one of the books Marquis enjoyed, such as *The Watsons Go to Birmingham* (Curtis, 1995), *John Henry* (Lester, 1994), *I Dream of Trains* (Johnson, 2003). The teachers and Ms. Lewis met briefly but regularly, approximately every two weeks, to discuss Marquis, the strategies, and needed adjustments.

> **TEACHING TIPS**
>
> **Home-Based Instruction**
>
> 1. Provide parents with scripted, error-proof procedures that eliminate guesswork and enable parents to feel confident in their tutoring.
> 2. Provide one-on-one parent training in the procedure to eliminate confusion in the application.
> 3. Designate short instructional periods, generally less than 30 minutes. Often, 10 minutes of tutoring can be sufficient.
> 4. Assign tutoring activities using materials previously taught in the school. Avoid asking parents to attempt to teach novel academic material.
> 5. Use a daily reporting form to communicate with the parent what is expected and for the parent to use to report tutoring information.
> 6. Provide a system whereby parents can easily assess the child's progress on skills being taught.
> 7. Explore the possibility that an extended family member (e.g., grandparent) or older sibling might assist with tutoring if the parent is not available.

How Can We Communicate Effectively with CLD Parents?

Positive communication is the foundation upon which we are able to build productive home–school collaborations. Although some would contend that good communication skills are more of an art than science (Turnbull & Turnbull, 2001), all professionals can benefit from understanding and employing the communication structures that foster and strengthen relationships. To communicate effectively with parents, at the minimum, we need to (1) build good, respectful relationships; (2) communicate regularly with families; (3) handle angry situations constructively; and (4) skillfully relate to the culturally different family.

How Do We Build Positive and Respectful Relationships?

Many children, especially those with cognitive or behavioral disabilities, present special challenges to teachers, and teachers often see parents/families as the key to remedying these problems. These problems are exacerbated for CLD families, who may be suspicious of or intimidated by school personnel (Koonce & Harper, 2005; Robinson-Zanartu & Majel-Dixon, 1996; Thompson, 2003; Torres-Burgo, Reyes-Wasson, & Brusca-Vega, 1999), have language differences (Lee & Manning, 2001; Torres-Burgo et al., 1999), or believe they should not interfere with the work of the school (Lee & Manning, 2001; Wu & Qi, 2005). Teachers often interpret these communication barriers as indications of parental indifference, but that is typically not the case. Robinson-Zanartu and Majel-Dixon (1996), for instance, report that American Indian parents want to be involved in the education of their children but they generally feel that government school personnel do not respect the parents, their children, or their culture. CLD parents often express little satisfaction with the process of placing their children in special education (Robinson-Zanartu & Majel-Dixon, 1996; Torres-Bargo et al., 1999) and want the schools to make a deliberate effort to learn about them and their culture.

Recommendations for communicating effectively with CLD parents include the following:

1. Display respect for the parents and their children.
2. Make an effort to learn about the child's culture.
3. Learn about the goals the parents have for their child.
4. Accommodate language difficulties for parents with limited English.
5. Help parents access programs that would enable them to be more proficient in English.
6. Contact parents frequently, not just when problems arise, to convey the student's successes and your genuine interest in the student's welfare.

Al-Hassan and Gardner (2002) provide some specific suggestions for communicating with recent immigrant parents:

1. Ask learners and their families what language is spoken at home.
2. When possible, allow parents to have input about the foreign language interpreters (it is important that parents are comfortable with the interpreter).
3. Make an effort to greet parents in their native language. This shows respect and can assist in establishing rapport.
4. Make sure that foreign language interpreters are available for meeting when the parents are not fluent English speakers, even if the students are bilingual.
5. Provide important school information in writing for parents in their home language. Even if the parents are not literate in their home language, they can have people they trust review the information.
6. Provide opportunities for the parents to participate in their child's education program and help parents to understand that their participation is important.
7. Set up a school telephone system with voicemail messages to provide answers to the most common questions in the appropriate languages.
8. Set up accessible web pages for the immigrant families.
9. Aid the families in making contact with other families whose children have been successful.

Al-Hassan and Gardner also provide a list of resources for teachers (see Figure 6–1).

Externalizing the child's difficulties to the parents—assuming they are problem parents—will color perceptions of the family and undermine the ability to build viable relationships. To foster mutual respect, school personnel might invest time and effort in rapport-building and information-gathering/dissemination activities. One way this might be achieved is through informal contacts such as teacher-parent coffees or personal correspondence.

Prior to the beginning of the school year or certainly long before the target student begins to present special difficulties, the teacher might contact the parent for an informal conversation about the student and their respective expectations for the coming school year. In order to make this initial contact meaningful and to keep it focused, the teacher might make use of a conversation guide, such as the one provided by Turnbull and Turnbull (2001), which gives suggestions for getting information about the child (e.g., "What have been some school experiences in the past that have particularly helped Marquis feel good about himself?") and the family's visions for the child (e.g., "When you look to the future, what are your great expectations for Marquis' life? What are your greatest concerns?").

Another promising strategy for effective communication with CLD parents is sending introductory letters to students and their parents immediately prior to the beginning of the school year. Letters that are jargon free, written in an informal tone, and reflect an enthusiasm

FIGURE 6-1 Resources for working with CLD families

Helpful Resources on the World Wide Web

Beach Center on Families and Disability (http://www.beachcenter.org/). Conducts research and training to enhance families' empowerment and disseminates information to families, people with disabilities, educators, and the general public. Provides technical assistance to national network of parent-to-parent support programs.

The Center for Applied Linguistics offers on-line language and academic programs for recent immigrants (www.cal.org/crede/newcorner.htm).

Clearinghouse for Immigrants Education (CHIMME) (http://igc.ap.org/acas/sr_essi.htm): Selected readings. This is an interactive database and networking service that facilitates public access to literature, research, Internet resources, and reform strategies to promote the effective education of immigrant students.

Family Network on Disabilities of Florida, Inc. (http://fndf. org). A statewide alliance of people with disabilities, special needs, or at-risk children and their families. Its mission is to provide family-driven support, education, information, and advocacy.

National Clearinghouse for Bilingual Education (NCBE) (http://www.ncbe.gwu.edu/index.htm). Funded by the U.S. Department of Education's Office of Bilingual Education and Minority Languages Affairs to collect, analyze, and disseminate information relating to the effective education of linguistically and culturally diverse learners in the United States. Through this Web page you will have access to a variety of Internet resources relating to aspects of language, culture, and education. Through language and education links, you can also learn words, phrases, and holidays from around the world.

National Council on Disability (http://www.ned.gov/). Its purpose is to promote policies, programs, practices, and procedures that guarantee equal opportunity for all individuals with disabilities and those from diverse cultural backgrounds. Parents and teachers can have access to the Disabilities Act and other civil rights laws. NCD brochures online in several languages.

Northwest Regional Resource Center provides on-line seft-report checklists (www.nwrel. org/) for teachers and administrators to assess the school environment's friendliness toward immigrants.

Office of Bilingual Education and Minority Languages Affairs (http://www.edu. gov/offices/OBEMLA). OBEMLA's mission is to include various elements of school reform in programs designed to assist the language minority agenda. These include an emphasis on high academic standards, an improvement of school accountability, an emphasis on professional development, the promotion of family literacy, the encouragement of early reading, and the establishment of partnerships between parents and the community.

The Parent Advocacy Coalition of Educational Rights (PACER) serves families of children and adults with disabilities (http://www.pacer.org).

The Regional Resource and Federal Centers (RRFC) Network (http://www.dssc.org/frc/rrfc.htm). These centers are specially funded to assist state education agencies in the systemic improvement of education programs, practices, and policies that affect children and youth with disabilities. The RRCs help states and U.S. jurisdictions find integrated solutions for systemic reform, offering consultation, information services, technical assistance, training, and product development.

The Technical Assistance Alliance for Parent Centers (the Alliance) (http://www.taalliance.org), funded by the U.S. Department of Education, Office of Special Education Programs. Focuses on providing technical assistance for establishing, developing, and coordinating parent training and information projects under the Individuals with Disabilities Education Act. The Alliance is prepared to offer a variety of resources that will launch parent training and information centers into the 21st century.

Your Dictionary.com (http://www.yourdictionary. com). Offers online access to dictionaries in many languages.

Source: From "Involving Parents of Immigrant Students with Disabilities in the Educational Process" by S. Al-Hassan and R. Gardner III, *Teaching Exceptional Children, 34*(5), pp. 52–58. Copyright © 2002 by The Council for Exceptional Children. Reprinted with permission.

for teaching and a commitment to the student can be quite effective in creating a favorable impression of school personnel. This is particularly important with CLD families to help overcome feelings of suspicion or intimidation. One teacher wrote the following letter to each of her fifth-grade students one week before school started.

> Dear Marquetta,
>
> The first day of the new school year is coming closer. The room is cleaned and ready. I have been to school a little each day over the last two weeks trying to have everything in place. The only thing missing now is YOU! I am anxious to hear about your summer and to see how much you have grown and changed over the last three months. We will have lots of time that first day back for all of us to talk and share our adventures.
>
> We have a new physical education teacher and a new librarian. There may be a few other changes in the building, but those two people are the only ones I have met as of now.
>
> I am looking forward to seeing you all walk in here as mature and responsible fifth graders! Imagine that—your last year in elementary school! This should be an exciting year with lots of challenges and interesting experiences. I'll see you on Thursday August 31st.
>
> Sincerely,
>
> Mrs. F.

Mrs. F. also sent a letter to the parents of each of her students. Several of the parents commented on how much they appreciated receiving these letters, and Mrs. F. reported that the letters helped greatly in getting her home–school relationships off to a good start.

How Do We Communicate Regularly with Families?

Effective communication results from regularly scheduled and ongoing communication systems, which may take various forms, such as conferences, written communication, electronic communication (e-mail), telephone calls, and home visits. Parent-teacher conferences may be viewed as the backbone of the educational program for children with disabilities, especially because the parent is considered integral to the educational planning. CLD parents, particularly low-income parents, typically encounter more barriers to participating in school conferences than their nonminority counterparts. For instance, African American parents experience difficulties related to the scheduling of meeting times. A single parent who works full-time at minimum wage and uses public transportation would have considerable difficulty making meetings held at the school. Under these circumstances, school personnel, who have much more flexibility, might arrange to meet the parent in a more convenient location, such as in the community library or a coffee shop near the parent's home or work. CLD families often have high participation rates in their churches (Kim, Kim, & Kelly, 2006) and community centers, so these sites could be viable options for individual or group meetings.

Other possibilities are community agencies or local businesses that sometimes offer to transport parents to schools for evening meetings. Some parents who are reluctant to come to school for other reasons are likely to come if their children are participating in school productions. The developers of the *Second Step Curriculum* (Committee for Children, www.cfchildren.org) report a principal of an urban CLD school used such a strategy to increase parent involvement in its social skills program. Because parents were known to come to school when their children were performing, the staff devised a "Second Step Dinner Theater." Students at all grade levels were trained to act out the lessons. A parent meeting followed the production, where parents received information on the curriculum. This resulted in record parent attendance and other Dinner Theaters were planned to present the remainder of the curriculum. The presence of the CLD parent in the school helps to reinforce to the child the importance of schooling. The difficulty associated with contacting and engaging these parents suggests that schools might employ parent liaisons for this purpose. CLD parents from the community might be especially effective in this role.

Conferences with parents need to be thoroughly planned, positive, focused, and productive. School personnel need to prepare an agenda for the meeting that clearly identifies items that could be effectively addressed within the specified time of the meeting. For example, the purpose of the meeting might be to discuss the general education and special education assignments a student would need to receive for math and reading. Another part of the planning would be to determine where—child's home, school, or neutral location—the meeting would take place and who would participate. In addition to school personnel, parents should know that they can be accompanied by someone who is supportive and knowledgeable about the situation.

Meetings with CLD families need to stress a positive and committed tone. In discussing how to relate to CLD families, Kuykendall (1992) advised that conferences start with a statement of delight at having the child in the class and then follow this with two statements about the child's strengths. During the information giving, school personnel should remain positive about the child and the child's school program, highlighting as much as possible the gains the child has made and the potential for growth when other plans are implemented. Parents are encouraged to share the strengths of their children, as well as their perceptions of the child's needs. Throughout this interchange, school personnel are advised to listen empathetically and nonjudgmentally to the family's expression of feelings, avoid expressing frustration and anger directly at the parents, and use caring phrases such as "What is the best way to provide you with information about Marquis's progress in learning his sight words?" Additionally, school personnel would be wise to avoid defensiveness, arguing with parents, or belittling the child or other children during the conference. It is also important not to assume that parents will need, want, or be receptive to advice; personnel should wait until it is requested. At the end of the meeting, the main points should be summarized and everyone should know what is to be accomplished, who will assume responsibility for the various tasks, and what follow-up strategies and meetings will be. Following the meeting, written minutes might be shared with the student and other professionals. Such minutes can serve as a record for family meetings and aid in reflecting on pupil progress as well as the nature of the home–school collaboration.

How Do We Communicate Regularly Through Writing?

Although conferences are one of the most common forms of teacher-parent interaction, written communication allows for more frequent contacts. This is especially true if a routine form of written communication is employed. One example is the notebook system described by Williams and Cartledge (1997). The teacher in this article taught a class of African American students diagnosed with behavior disorders. The teacher devised a system of notebooks to be transported daily by the students between home and school. The teacher and parents recorded for each day messages in the notebooks about the students' academic and social behavior. In addition to communicating to the parents well-defined procedures for conducting the notebook system and being persistent, the teacher made certain that she conveyed to the parents that her primary interest was in helping the students progress in school. Over the course of the school year, the teacher found that the parents' responses to the notebook system increased in quantity and quality, especially as they became convinced

We build trusting and beneficial relationships with parents through regular and helpful meetings.

that the teacher was totally committed to helping their children become successful in school. Many parents expressed their gratitude for the system. This teacher exchanged the notebooks daily; teachers with larger classes might modify the system to sending them home on alternating days or every third day for each student. This notebook system can be especially attractive to those parents who do not always have transportation to the school or even a telephone with which to communicate with the teacher. For parents with inadequate literacy skills, tape recordings may be substituted for written communication and the assistance of school-based translators secured for non-English speakers. This system could be easily employed with parents who have access to e-mail.

Another option for written communication is newsletters. Newsletters are less personal but they can be excellent vehicles for communicating general news about the classroom, including upcoming classroom events, home learning activities, summaries of articles or books that might be of interest to parents, suggestions for community events that families might want to attend, and recognition of classroom volunteers and contributions. Newsletters present the opportunity to highlight student accomplishments or specific contributions to the newsletters. Making sure that each student gets some positive recognition in the newsletter increases the likelihood that all parents will read it, helping to foster productive home–school relationships. Other possibilities for newsletters include homework assignments, question/answer columns, and want ads for classroom volunteers. Newsletters can be specialized so that the entire newsletter could be devoted, for example, to one issue such as homework. Beginning at the upper elementary grades, students can assume primary responsibility for producing the newsletter under the supervision of the classroom teacher as a means of highlighting unique aspects of students' cultures, with students gathering the information and, whenever possible, writing the columns.

How Can We Handle Difficult Situations Constructively?

Even with the best of efforts, there are times when parties might lose control and situations might become difficult to handle. As emotions rise, reason tends to decline. Angry feelings and words are even more likely to emerge in CLD situations, where trust is fragile and cultural differences are pronounced. Under these conditions, it is probably best not to try to convince parents or other parties of the wisdom of a position. Instead, it would be best to use empathic language and attempt to de-escalate the situation in the interest of a future meeting under calmer, more reasoned circumstances. Suggestions that are generally recognized for dealing with angry parents include:

- Avoid arguing with parents or becoming defensive.
- Use reflective statements without being patronizing.
- Use a strategy of writing out parents' complaints.
- Share the list with parents and get corroboration.
- Adjust the list accordingly/add additional items.
- Proceed to discuss how each item will be addressed.
- Schedule a follow-up conference.
- Try not to take yourself too seriously.

What Is Parental Advocacy for CLDE Children?

What Is the Historical Perspective?

Beginning approximately at the middle of the 20th century, parents of children with disabilities started to organize in advocacy groups, such as the National Association for Retarded Children (now called Association for Retarded Citizens), the National Society for Autistic Children (now called the Autism Society of America), National Association for Down Syndrome, the Association for Children with Learning Disabilities (now called the Learning Disabilities Association of America), and the Federation of Families for Children's Mental Health. Turnbull and Turnbull (2001) describe the evolution of one such group, Association for Retarded Children, which began with small, independent groups that had sprung up throughout the country and came together in 1950 in Minneapolis to form the national organization. Membership in groups such as these certainly accounts for the phenomenal success parents have had in promoting the interests of their children.

Kenneth P. Davis/PH College

Culturally diverse parents can be empowered through learning about the educational rights of their children and in developing advocacy skills.

Although many parent groups originally organized to address concerns related to one specific disability such as mental retardation, more recently, parent centers that provide technical assistance and support for all disabilities have emerged. One such center is Pacer (http://www.pacer.org/about.htm). The Pacer Center, founded in 1977 by parents of children with disabilities, is designed to help parents and professionals understand issues relative to educating children as well as obtain needed assistance. Pacer is based in Minneapolis but is aligned with four regional centers located in New Hampshire, Ohio, Texas, and California, which work together with other groups. As part of their regular communications with parents and professionals, these centers provide information on new legislation, recent publications, educational resources, workshops, and community-based services.

What Are Advocacy Resources?

Historically, parent organizations have consisted largely of white, middle-class parents and few parents from culturally diverse or low socioeconomic backgrounds (Harry, 2002; Turnbull & Turnbull, 2001). To address this advocacy gap, parents of color have recently begun to organize to advocate for the learning needs of their children. One such example is the Mekye Center, founded by Nayo Watkins and based in Durham, North Carolina. In its executive summary the center states that its mission is to "serve the cause of children for whom learning difference and income/resources present particularly difficult obstacles in their efforts to become valued, achieving and contributing members of society. . . ." The Mekye Center is named in the memory of Watkins' son, who is described as being "intelligent, talented, sensitive, cheerful, big-hearted, and dyslexic." According to his mother, Mekye's journey was difficult; the difficulties led to depression and eventually to suicide at the age of 16. The center sees as its central focus a need to create a new model for the way in which we educate children with learning differences, particularly children of color. The Mekye Center offers opportunities for student tutoring, research, and parent workshops. The target audience is children from low- to modest-income homes, mostly children of color, with identified or suspected learning differences.

Another such organization is the National Association of the Education of African American Children with Learning Disabilities, founded in 2000 by Nancy Tidwell in Columbus, Ohio. Recognizing the unique issues encountered by children and their families from diverse backgrounds, part of her message to African American parents states:

> Many minority children have been misdiagnosed and inappropriately placed in special education but the reality is that the current legal process must be used to obtain the appropriate services and supports that every child is entitled to and needs for school and later success. *Parents should not resist evaluations for a child who is struggling but they should be vigilant, making sure that the findings are accurate and that the interventions rendered result in continuous academic and social progress.* (NAEAACLD, 2006 p. ii)

The overall focus of the NAEAACLD is to empower minority parents to become advocates by providing information. The major vehicles for informing parents are the NAEAACLD parent handbook, its web site (http://www.aacld.org), and workshops held in the Central Ohio area. The NAEAACLD is part of a network of mainstream organizations focused on learning disabilities that includes the Learning Disabilities Association of America (LDA), the International Dyslexia Association (IDA), the National Center for Learning Disabilities (NCLD), the Schwab Foundation, Council for Learning Disabilities (CLD), and the Division for Learning Disabilities (DLD).

A minority parent organization with a slightly different focus is Minding the Village (MTV, www.mindingthevillage.org), founded by Carmen D. Reynolds for the purpose of providing scholarship assistance for Northern Virginia minority students with diverse learning styles. Its mission is to advocate for disadvantaged, at-risk, minority students who learn differently, and its goal is to help parents find private schools that would teach their children more appropriately. The organization helps to raise funds for tuition as well as provides counseling and tutoring. The following articulates its perspective:

> Often students with diverse learning styles are labeled "a behavior problem," "unintelligent," "unmotivated," "unreachable," and/or "underachievers." We believe that these students would greatly benefit from the quality instruction and resources that are offered through private education: specifically, schools designed to teach children with diverse learning needs.

The preceding descriptions are examples of parent organizations established to help CLD parents of children with exceptionalities advocate more effectively for the educational success of their children. These groups are not restricted to families of color, but they do emphasize low socioeconomic status since such families experience the greatest difficulty in obtaining the resources needed to improve their children's schooling. Parents of culturally diverse backgrounds, especially low-income parents or those with language differences, might be more comfortable affiliating with parent organizations targeted to their specific subgroup, and this may be a way to engage otherwise reluctant parents in the advocacy process. To be most effective, however, minority parental advocacy groups need to build alliances with mainstream organizations to be totally informed and able to assist in lobbying efforts on issues of mutual concern.

APPLICATION

Parental Advocacy

Ms. Thomas, president of a chapter for African American students with learning disabilities, obtained funding to serve as a liaison to connect the families more closely with the school and project staff in the interest of school success for children from these families. Specifically, she focused on helping parents learn how they might advocate effectively for their children and how to develop effective relationships with school personnel. In consultation with the school staff, Ms. Thomas designed a series of six parent seminars: three held in the evening at the city's Urban League chapter, which was located within the neighborhood of most of these families, and three held during the lunch hour at Hilliard Elementary. The community sessions held at the Urban League were entitled "How to Advocate Effectively for Your Child," and the topic for the school-based meetings was "Building Relationships with Your School."

The sessions were problem-oriented. For example, parents felt the teachers gave vague, ambiguous suggestions such as "Read more with your son," advice the parents felt provided too little direction and thus was unhelpful. The consultants responded by helping these parents identify specific questions they might ask school personnel that would be more informative to the parents and helpful to their children. Instead of asking how M. is doing, for example (to which the teacher typically responded that he is making progress), the parents might inquire, "What skill did M. acquire this week?" "Did he reach the goal you had set for him for this time period?" "Specifically, what might I do at home to help him reach this goal?" "When could I meet with you so that you can show me how to practice this skill with him at home?" "What do you expect M. to be able to do in reading by the next grading period?" "What could you send home on a daily/weekly basis to help me monitor his progress toward that goal?"

Parents were advised to be assertive and focused, scheduling regular appointments with the teachers to monitor and revise these goals as appropriate. The answer to their child's reading difficulty was not simply another year of grade retention. They needed an explicit intervention plan leading to steady reading progress that could be monitored and reinforced easily by the child's parent.

> **TEACHING TIPS**
>
> **Parent Empowerment/Involvement**
>
> 1. Establish parent liaisons to help develop and maintain regular home–school communication. Preferably, use a parent of one of the children in the school who shares the cultural and socioeconomic background of the students.
> 2. Make direct contact with parents. If possible, make initial visits in the child's home or meet parents at a site in their community.
> 3. Avoid the temptation to dominate the conversation or "preach" to parents about how they could nurture the academic performance of their children. Try to listen to parents. After establishing trusting relationships, you will have good opportunities to help parents understand how they might contribute to their children's schooling.
> 4. Make sure parents know they are welcomed in the school. Parent centers in the school help to communicate this.
> 5. Take time to learn about the community and the child's culture. Invite parents to the school to give brief talks in class about special features of the child's culture.

Summary

Over the years, parents of children with disabilities have been powerful advocates and they currently play an integral role in the education of their children. CLD parents of children with exceptionalities have not always been involved in this process and often are not active participants in their children's schooling. Many CLD parents have a different perception of disabilities and the schools compared to mainstream parents.

A history of negative experiences has helped to undermine the relationship between CLD families and the schools. Other contributing factors may be a cultural tendency not to disclose personal or family matters, a concern that their children's problems are a reflection on their parenting skills, and an intimidating rather than a supportive school culture. Language-different parents are further limited by an inability to speak the language of the school or to understand the school's jargon.

School personnel are likely to view this apparent resistance as indifference and tend not to contact culturally diverse parents. But these families require direct contact and schools may need to make a special effort to engage in community outreach, extending themselves to places where parents congregate and respond most comfortably, including community centers and churches. Schools need to understand that parents from culturally diverse backgrounds need more, not less, contact.

There are several important considerations when communicating with families from diverse backgrounds. Begin interactions with positive statements about the child. Utilize competent translators if the parents are not fluent in English. Employ more frequent and detailed contacts with families where communication difficulties exist to make sure they understand the classroom demands in terms of academic and social behavior. Use homework assignments to reinforce skills taught at school, not to perform novel assignments where family members unfamiliar with the curriculum are not able to assist. Make every effort to understand the culture of the learner, appropriately interpreting nonverbal as well as spoken or written language. In some cultures, for example, silence only communicates respect and does not necessarily indicate agreement (Kea, 2002).

Schools are challenged to empower themselves as well as CLD parents of children with exceptionalities by responding respectfully and competently to the family's needs. Schools can help parents acquire personal development skills as well as learn how to nurture their children's school success. Empowered parents become informed and then act independently to achieve desired goals. These parents communicate effectively with the schools and advocate for their children. Parent organizations with a focus on CLD children with exceptionalities have begun to emerge in recent years, and schools could use these groups as a resource in working with CLD families of children with exceptionalities.

Related Learning Activities

1. As a class or small group, devise a semistructured parent interview consisting of a series of questions that can be used in interviewing a family of a child with exceptionalities. Get class approval of the interview form. Use the interview guide to conduct an interview (with permission) with a family from a culturally diverse background. Following the interview, analyze the information you obtained according to at least these points:
   a. What responses made by the family would you categorize as culturally specific? Why?
   b. What did you learn about the family that was contrary to your preconceived notions about this family/culture?
   c. What were some important strengths that you were able to identify about this family?
   d. What actions, in your opinion, should the school take to further empower this family?

2. Select either the preceding or another CLD family and identify an important area of skill development for the student with exceptionalities. Design a home-based learning program for this student that would reinforce the instruction the student is receiving in school. As part of this instructional program, be sure to specify at a minimum
   a. The skill to be learned.
   b. The goal for that skill.
   c. A script the family could use in teaching the skill.
   d. A home–school daily communication system for using the instruction.
   e. A recording system for monitoring the student's progress in reaching the goal.
   f. A reinforcement plan to be administered at home and school.

3. Contact a parent advocacy organization in your community. Review the agency's literature and interview one or two of its officers to obtain information about CLD parent participation. Among other things, identify the number of CLD parent participants; what groups these parents come from; how these parents participate; what, if any, the unique concerns of CLD parents are; and the degree to which the organization believes it is meeting the needs of CLD families.

4. Conduct research to identify a parent organization for children with exceptionalities that focuses on each of the major CLD groups: African, Asian, Hispanic, and Native American. For each of these groups, specify their overall purpose, goals, and main activities. If possible, indicate the degree to which the group is affiliated with mainstream parent groups with similar interests.

References

Al-Hassan, S., & Gardner, R., III (2002). Involving parents of immigrant students with disabilities in the educational process. *Teaching Exceptional Children, 34*(5), pp. 52–58.

Anclien, K. M. (2003). *The effects of daily parent-child practice of multiplication facts on student achievement.* Unpublished master's thesis, The Ohio State University. Columbus, OH.

Barbetta, P. M., & Heron, T. E. (1991). Project shine: Summer home instruction and evaluation. *Intervention in School and Clinic, 26,* 276–281.

Bauer, A. M., & Shea, T. M. (2003). *Parents and schools: Creating a successful partnership for students with special needs.* Upper Saddle River, NJ: Merrill/Prentice Hall.

Bernhard, J. K., Lefebve, M. L., Kilbride, K. M., Chud, G., & Lange, R. (1998). Troubled relationships in early childhood education: Parent-teacher interactions in ethno culturally diverse child care settings. *Early Education & Development, 9,* 5–28.

Black, E. (2003). *War against the weak: Eugenics and America's campaign to create a master race.* Retrieved November 6, 2006, from http://www.waragainsttheweak.com

Bradley, C. R. (1998). Child rearing in African American Families: A study of the disciplinary practices of African American parents. *Journal of Multicultural Counseling and Development, 26*(4), 273—279.

Bradley, R. H., & Gilkey, B. (2002). The impact of the home instructional program for preschool youngsters (HIPPY) on school performance in 3rd and 6th grades. *Early Education & Development, 13,* 301–311.

Cartledge, G., Kea, C., & Simmons-Reed, E. (2002). Serious emotional disturbance: Serving culturally diverse children and their families. *Journal of Child and Family Studies, 11*(1), 113–126.

Cartledge, G., & Milburn, J. F. (1996). *Cultural diversity and social skill instruction: Understanding ethnic and gender differences.* Champaign, IL: Research Press.

Clark, R. (1993). Homework-focused parenting practices that positively affect student achievement. In N. F. Chavkin (Ed.), *Families and schools in a pluralistic society* (pp. 85–105). Albany, NY: State University of New York Press.

Committee for Children. *Second Step.* www.cfchildren.org

Cooke, N. L., Heron, T. E., & Heward, W. L. (1983). *Peer tutoring: Implementing classwide programs in the primary grades.* Columbus, OH: Special Press.

Curtis, C. P. (1995). *The Watsons go to Birmingham—1963.* New York: Delacorte Press.

Dunst, C. J., Trivette, C. M., & Deal, A. G. (1994). Enabling and empowering families. In C. J. Dunst, C. M. Trivette, & A. G. Deal (Eds.), *Supporting and strengthening families* (pp. 2–11). Cambridge, MA: Brookline Books.

Dykeman, C., Nelson, J. R., & Appleton, V. (1995). Building strong working alliances with American Indian families. *Social Work in Education, 17,* 148–158.

Epstein, J. L. (May, 1995). School/family/community partnerships: Caring for the children we share. *Phi Delta Kappan,* 701–712.

Fan, X., & Chen, M. (2001). Parental involvement and students' academic achievement: A meta-analysis. *Educational Psychology Review, 13,* 1–22.

Fantuzzo, J. W., Davis, G. Y., & Ginsburg, M. D. (1995). Effects of parent involvement in isolation or in combination with peer tutoring on student self-concept and mathematics achievement. *Journal of Educational Psychology, 87,* 272–281.

Franklin, C., Waukechon, J., & Larney, P. S. (1995). Culturally relevant school programs for American Indian children and families. *Social Work in Education, 17,* 183–193.

Gutman, L. M., & McLoyd, V. C. (2000). Parents' management of their children's education within the home, at school, and in the community: An examination of African-American families living in poverty. *The Urban Review, 32* (1), 124.

Harden, B., & Hedgpeth, D. 2005, March 25. Minnesota killer chafed at life on reservation. *The Washington Post.* Retrieved August 10, 2007 from http://www.bluecorncomics.com/redlake.htm.

Harry, B. (1992). Restructuring the participation of African-American parents in special education. *Exceptional Children, 59,* 123–131.

Harry, B. (2002). Trends and issues in serving culturally diverse families of children with disabilities. *The Journal of Special Education, 36,* 131–138,147.

Harry, B., Rueda, R., & Kalyanpur, M. (1999). Cultural reciprocity in sociocultural perspective: Adapting the normalization principle for family collaboration. *Exceptional Children, 66,* 123–36.

Hart, B., & Risley, T. R. (1995). *Meaningful differences in the everyday experience of young American children.* Baltimore, MD: Paul H. Brookes.

Heller, L. R., & Fantuzzo, J. W. (1993). Reciprocal peer tutoring and parent partnership: Does parent involvement make a difference? *School Psychology Review, 22,* 517–534.

Heyman, S. J., & Earle, A. (2000). Low-income parents: How do working conditions affect their opportunity to help school-age children at risk? *American Educational Research Journal, 37,* 833–848.

Hill, N. E., & Craft, S. A. (2003). Parent-school involvement and school performance: Mediated pathways among socioeconomically comparable African American and Euro-American families. *Journal of Educational Psychology, 95,* 74–83.

Hodgkinson, H. L. (November/December, 2002). Dealing with diversity. *Principal,* 15–18.

Huang, G. (1997). Beyond culture: Communicating with Asian American children and families. Teachers College, Columbia University. Retrieved January 5, 2006, from CASAnet Resources website: http://www.casanet.org/library/culture/communicate-asian.htm

Johnson, A. (2003). *I dream of trains.* New York: Simon & Schuster.

Kea, C. (2002). Issues in family-school relationships. In G. Cartledge, K. Y. Tam, S. A. Loe, A. H. Miranda, M. C. Lambert, C. D. Kea, & E. Simmons-Reed (Eds.), *Culturally and linguistically diverse students with behavioral disorders* (pp. 45–53). CCBD Mini-Library Series. Arlington, VA: Council for Exceptional Children.

Kim, I. J., Kim, L. I. C., & Kelly, J. G. (2006). Developing cultural competence in working with Korean immigrant families. *Journal of Community Psychology, 34*(2), 149–165.

Koonce, D. A., Harper, W., Jr. (2005). Engaging African American parents in the schools: A community-based consultation model. *Journal of Educational and Psychological Consultation, 16*(1 & 2), 55–74.

Kraft, B. L., Findlay, P., Major, J., Gilberts, G., & Hofmeister, A. (2001). The association between a home reading program and young children's early reading skill. *Journal of Direct Instruction, 2,* 117–136.

Kuykendall, C. (1992). *From rage to home: Strategies for reclaiming Black & Hispanic students.* Bloomington, IN: National Educational Service.

Lee, G., & Manning, M. L. (Fall, 2001). Working with Asian parents and families. *Multicultural Education,* 23–25.

Lester, J. (1994). *John Henry.* Westport, CT: Puffin Books.

Lian-Thompson, S., & Jean, R. E. (1997). Completing the parent participation puzzle: Accepting diversity. *Teaching Exceptional Children, 30,* 46–50.

Lines, P. M. (September, 2001). *Homeschooling. ERIC Digest*. Eugene, OR: ERIC Clearinghouse on Educational Management (SJJ69850).

Lo, Y., & Cartledge, G. (2004). Total class peer tutoring and interdependent group-oriented contingency: Improving the academic and task-related behaviors of fourth-grade urban students. *Education and Treatment of Children, 27*, 235–262.

Lopez, G. R., Scribner, J. D., & Mahitivanichcha, K. (2001). Redefining parental involvement: Lessons from high-performing migrant-impacted schools. *American Educational Research Journal, 38*, 253–288.

Moses, K.(1989). *Shattered dreams and growth.* [Cassette] Resource Networks, Inc. (Available from Central Ohio Special Education Regional Resource Center, 470 Glenmont Avenue, Columbus, OH 43214, www.coserrc.org)

National Association of the Education of African American Children with Learning Disabilities (2006). *One child at a time: A parent handbook and resource directory for African American families with children who learn differently.* Columbus, OH: Author.

National Reading Panel (2000). *Report of the National Reading Panel: Teaching children to read.* U.S. Department of Health & Human Services, Public Health Service & National Institute of Child Health & Human Development. Retrieved June 1, 2004 from http://www.nichd.nih.gov/publications/nrp/smallbook.htm

Norwood, P. M., Atkinson, S. E., Tellez, K., & Saladana, D. C. (1997). Contextualizing parent education programs in urban schools: The impact on minority parents and students. *Urban Education, 32*, 411–432.

Paratore, J. R. (2001). *Opening doors, opening opportunities: Family literacy in an urban community.* Boston: Allyn & Bacon.

Phillips, J. (2003, August 3). Somalis fear children will falsely claim abuse. *The Columbus Dispatch*, Columbus, OH, pp. A1–A2.

Riggins-Newby, C. G. (2003). Families as partners. *The Education Digest, 68*, 23–24.

Robinson, N. M, Weinberg, R. A., Redden, D., Ramey, S. L., & Ramey, C. T. (1998). Family factors associated with high academic competence among former Head Start children. *Gifted Child Quarterly, 42*, 148–156.

Robinson-Zanartu, C., & Majel-Dixon, J. (1996). Parent voices: American Indian relationships with schools. *Journal of American Indian Education, 36*, 33–54.

Simpson, R. L., & Carter, W. J. (1993). Comprehensive, inexpensive, and convenient services for parents and families of students with behavior disorders: If only Sam Walton had been an educator. *Preventing School Failure, 37*, 21–25.

Slaughter-Defoe, D. T. (2000). *Early childhood development and school readiness: Some observations about "homework" for new-century working parents.* Paper presented at the Annual Meeting of the Voices for Illinois Conference, Chicago, IL, September 22, 2000 (ED 447 952).

Summers, J. A., Gavin, K., Purnell-Hall, T., & Nelson, J. (2003). Family and school partnerships: Building bridges in general and special education. *Advances in Special Education, 15*, 417–444.

Taylor, L. S., & Whittaker, C. R. (2003). *Bridging multiple worlds: Case studies of diverse educational communities.* Boston: Allyn & Bacon.

Thao, Y. J. (2003). Empowering Mong students: Home and school factors. *The Urban Review, 35*, 25–42.

The National Reading Panel. (2000). *Report of the national reading panel teaching children to read.* Rockville, MD: NICHD Clearinghouse.

Thompson, G. L. (2003). *What African American parents want educators to know.* Westport, CT: Praeger.

Torres-Burgo, N. T, Reyes-Wasson, P., & Brusca-Vega, R. (1999). Perceptions and needs of Hispanic and Non-Hispanic parents of children receiving learning disabilities services. *Bilingual Research Journal, 23*(4), 319–333.

Townsend, B. L., Thomas, D. D., Witty, J. P., & Lee, R. S. (1996). Diversity and school restructuring: Creating partnerships in a world of difference. *Teacher Education and Special Education, 19*, 102–118.

Turnbull, A., & Turnbull, R. (2001). *Families, professionals, and exceptionality: Collaborating for empowerment*, (4th ed.). Upper Saddle River, NJ: Merrill/Prentice Hall.

U.S. Department of Education. (2001). *No child left behind.* Washington, DC: Office of the Secretary.

Unger, D. G., Jones, C. W., Park, E., & Tressell, P. A. (2001). Promoting involvement between low-income single caregivers and urban early intervention programs. *Topics in Early Childhood Special Education, 21*, 197–212.

Williams, V., & Cartledge, G. (September/October, 1997). Passing notes to parents. *Teaching Exceptional Children, 30*, 30–34.

Wu, F., & Qi, S. (2005). *Parenting within cultural context: Comparisons between African-American and Asian-American parents.* Paper presented at the annual conference of American Educational Research Association, April 15, 2005, Montreal, Canada.

Zhou, M. (2003). Urban education: Challenges in educating culturally diverse children. *Teachers College Record, 105*, 208–225.

Chapter 7

Culturally Responsive Assessment of CLDE Learners

Assessment is the focal point in the classification, placement, and programming processes of special education and gifted education. Standardized intelligence and achievement tests have been the primary tools for determining eligibility for services (Ford & Joseph, 2006; Naglieri & Ford, 2005; Raymond, 2004; Spinelli, 2002). However, a great deal of controversy surrounds the use and usefulness of standardized tests in making decisions about students, particularly culturally and linguistically diverse learners with and without exceptionalities. The primary criticism focuses on intelligence tests rather than achievement tests; the argument frequently is that intelligence tests may be culturally biased and therefore contribute to the overrepresentation of CLDE students in special education programs and their underrepresentation in gifted education programs. In both situations, the contention is that CLDE learners are denied the opportunity to reach their full potential due to inappropriate labeling and placement.

This chapter presents a brief history of intelligence tests and their use with culturally and linguistically diverse exceptional learners. Because most of the research and debate have focused on African American and Hispanic American students (Herrnstein & Murray, 1994; Lynn, 2006; Rowe, 2005; Suzuki & Aronson, 2005), considerable attention is given to

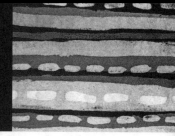

these two groups of learners. After this overview, we present a rationale for adopting culturally responsive assessment (CRA), a discussion of characteristics of CRA, and a discussion of relevant principles of CRA. We also address in this chapter high-stakes testing, based on assessments at the state level as mandated by federal legislation. The premise of this chapter is a simple one—that culturally responsive assessment holds much promise for ensuring equity and, thus, increasing the representation of students who are culturally and linguistically diverse in gifted education and, conversely, decreasing their representation in special education.

An underlying principle of this chapter is that teachers should have an understanding of how to proceed when they think that a CLDE learner is demonstrating academic problems or is in need of greater challenge. Thus, teachers need to be knowledgeable about the advantages, disadvantages, and limitations of all instruments used (tests, checklists, referral or nomination forms, and so on). Teachers need to be able to read and interpret test results so that they can actively and proactively participate in classification, placement, and program decisions on behalf of CLDE students. Teachers also need to know how students qualify for a specific classification and on what basis placement and programming have been determined. Likewise, they need to understand the credentials of those who do the testing or assessment, the tools used, and how the results factor into eligibility and program decisions (Raymond, 2004; Spinelli, 2002). Finally, teachers must consider these issues in terms of cultural and linguistic diversity.

Having made these assertions, we recognize that classroom teachers are not always directly involved in the administration and interpretation of standardized tests. However, they are involved in two other important ways. First, teachers are involved in the decision-making process by providing valuable anecdotal records, sharing their perceptions of students' skills and performance in the classroom, and sharing academic and behavioral data to help other educators and professionals make decisions about students (Raymond, 2004; Spinelli, 2002). Second, they are involved in teaching students based on identified needs as indicated by tests and other data.

This chapter addresses several questions that readers should consider and then be able to answer after finishing the chapter:

1. What are the primary concerns about using intelligence and achievement tests with students who are culturally and linguistically diverse?
2. What are some of the advantages and disadvantages of intelligence and achievement tests, particularly when used with culturally and linguistically diverse exceptional learners?
3. What is a test? What is the purpose of testing?
4. What is assessment and how is testing different from assessment?
5. What is culturally responsive assessment (CRA)? What does CRA "look like" when used with all students, especially CLDE students?
6. What are the benefits or advantages for students of culturally responsive assessment?
7. What are some of the key principles of culturally responsive assessment?
8. What alternative measures and assessment tools/strategies should be considered when assessing CLDE learners?

At the end of this chapter, readers will have a better understanding of and/or skill in recognizing:

1. Differences between testing and assessment.
2. Limitations of using traditional tests with CLDE students.
3. Alternative tests and assessment measures.
4. Steps to take for culturally responsive assessment.

Learning from Darnel: Making Decisions Based on Limited Information

Ms. Johnson had been working with Darnel, a second grader, since school began 2 months ago. She has referred him for special education screening because his verbal and written skills are low—lower than other students in the class. She was concerned that Darnel might need some type of assistance to improve his language-related skills. Darnel was above average in math and science and he was an eager, enthusiastic student. But his language skills were lagging, causing her much concern.

Test results indicated that Darnel indeed had above-average nonverbal or performance scores (IQ of 109) but below-average verbal scores (IQ of 87) on the intelligence test. Mr. Johnson and the principal wonder, based only on this test score, whether Darnel should receive special education services.

The special education evaluation team considers Darnel's other test scores, including subscales, but also examines Darnel's report cards from the current and previous school years, along with background information contained in the records. He often gets A's and B's. Previous teachers have reported that he is inquisitive and thoughtful in his responses to questions, readings, and activities. They do not appear to be as worried as Ms. Johnson about his low verbal skills; one teacher noted that she expects this to improve as Darnel progresses through school and gets exposure to literature and language on a consistent basis. Ms. Johnson is doubtful; she places more emphasis on the test scores than grades—actual performance. In her view, Darnel won't succeed academically without special education assistance.

The evaluation team looks at all of the information in Darnel's case file. They eventually conclude that Darnel does not seem to need special education services at this time. They recommend that the teacher place more emphasis on language-based activities in her class and believe that Darnel and other students will benefit greatly from this instructional modification.

What does Darnel's story tell you about making decisions based on one test score or on one piece of information? How is doing so justifiable and defensible? What are the advantages of collecting as much data as possible on students before making a decision about the need for special education services?

What Are the Special Issues of Standardized Testing for CLDE Groups?

For decades, standardized tests have been used to make decisions about students. Standardized tests—namely, intelligence and achievement tests—are viewed by many educators as a relatively inexpensive, effective, and objective way to make decisions about students. In schools, the purpose of these tools has been to measure academic progress, particularly what students have or have not learned from curriculum and instruction. More than ever before in our history, tests are being used to satisfy accountability requirements (e.g., Council for Exceptional Children, 2000; NCLB, 2001). In this era of high-stakes testing, teacher effectiveness is being measured by how well students perform on achievement and proficiency tests. In the next section, we present an overview of key issues surrounding the use of intelligence tests with CLDE learners. Following this discussion, we share options for alternative assessments and culturally responsive assessment principles.

Intelligence Tests: What Are Some General Issues and Concerns?

Intelligence tests were first introduced at the turn of the 20th century and since that time, educators, psychologists, and other professionals have battled over the issue of bias in traditional psychometric tests (Dent, 1996; Ford, 2004; Ford & Joseph, 2006; Puckett & Black, 2000). Intelligence testing among culturally and linguistically diverse groups, particularly African Americans, has had a consistent history of misunderstanding, controversy, misuse, and even abuse (see Gould, 1996; Herrnstein & Murray, 1994; Neisser et al., 1996). There have been moral indictments of labeling individuals, claims of cultural bias, and accusations of flagrant abuse of test scores (Groth-Marnat, 2003), as past and ongoing litigation gives witness to. It has been argued, for example, that once a student is assigned a label (e.g., mentally retarded, developmentally delayed), he or she will face lowered expectations from teachers, family members, other adults, and classmates. Conversely, if assigned the label of "gifted," students will often face high expectations. In the first instance, low expectations can lead to a self-fulfilling prophecy such that the student loses confidence in being a competent learner; in the second instance, high teacher expectations can lead to positive student outcomes, as over four decades of studies on the Pygmalion effect have found (see Rosenthal & Jacobson, 1992).

But despite decades of controversy, schools still rely heavily on tests to make decisions. Schools are the primary users of intelligence tests, and use these and other tests extensively for placement and programming decisions in special education and gifted education, as well as for promotion, graduation, and scholarship awards. Once referred for gifted education or special education screening, students will likely take some type of intelligence test. Davis and Rimm (2004) state that over 90% of schools use some type of test—most likely intelligence tests—to make placement decisions. Similarly, intelligence tests are used extensively for many categories of special education (mental retardation, learning disabilities, and developmental delay).

It is commonly believed that intelligence tests provide more valuable information about students' cognitive strengths and weaknesses, their potential for achieving academically, and the need for specialized educational services than do achievement and aptitude tests. Intelligence tests are thought to be particularly effective at predicting school performance or achievement (such as grade point average, probability for succeeding in college, and likelihood for doing well in high-level classes). They are also used to compare and sort students into performance levels (Spinelli, 2002) as seen in ability grouping and tracking. But in spite of their popularity and widespread use, a great deal of controversy surrounds the use—and usefulness—of intelligence tests for making decisions about culturally and linguistically diverse exceptional learners, regardless of whether they require gifted or special education services. The major criticisms are as follows:

1. Traditional intelligence tests have an inherent bias toward emphasizing convergent, analytical, and scientific modes of thought; this type of thinking may not be preferred or demonstrated by CLDE learners.

2. Intelligence tests measure a limited range of cognitive abilities and do not (cannot) measure the entire range of abilities that make up intelligence (Groth-Marnat, 2003; Sternberg, 2000);
3. Traditional intelligence tests do not adequately measure many cognitive abilities that contemporary theories and research specify as important in understanding learning and problem solving (Flanagan & Ortiz, 2001); they do not measure creativity, tacit knowledge, or street smarts, for example.
4. Intelligence tests are limited in their ability to make long-term predictions (Groth-Marnat, 2003); they may be ineffective at predicting performance in work settings, for example.
5. Intelligence tests are not measures of innate or fixed ability, and their use without other information in classifying students is questionable. Therefore, when interpreting test scores, especially those of CLDE learners, one must consider such variables as familiarity with taking paper-pencil tests, educational experiences, motivation, interests, learning styles, test anxiety, and language proficiency.
6. Traditional intelligence tests may not be appropriate to use with CLDE students due to such factors as norm group and norming procedures, format of the test, types of questions asked, and so forth.
7. Traditional intelligence tests may not be appropriate to use with linguistically diverse students due to the heavy emphasis on English language proficiency, specifically their high reliance on language (speaking rather than doing) to answer items.

Interestingly, many contemporary test developers have attempted to address these potential cultural nuances, but they allocate only a small section of their test manuals to discussing the challenges in using their instruments for assessing individuals of diverse cultures and language backgrounds (Esters, Ittenback, & Han, 1997). Thus, educators who administer, interpret, and use these tests may not be adequately prepared to understand and address factors that affect test performance, a few of which are presented in Figure 7–1.

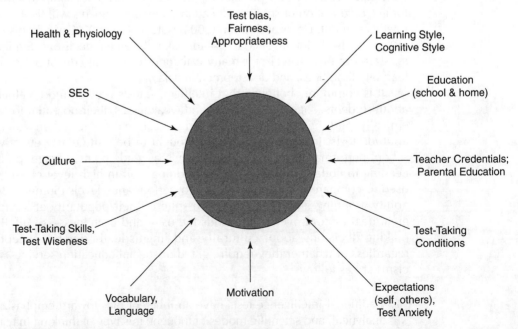

FIGURE 7–1 Sample factors that affect test performance

Much research and theory, as well as opinion, have been critical of using traditional intelligence tests with CLDE populations. The focus of there debates, particularly among those who oppose the use of tests with learners who are culturally and linguistically diverse, is on the issue of fairness and the discriminatory or disparate impact of standardized tests (Office for Civil Rights, 2005). Opponents often argue that such tests contribute to the underrepresentation of culturally and linguistically diverse students in gifted education and their overrepresentation in special education. For instance, Black students comprised 17.2% of the school population in 2002, but they made up only 8.4% of students in gifted education programs; likewise, Hispanic Americans represented 17.6% of the school population but comprised only 8.63% of the population in gifted education (U.S. Department of Education, 2002). We have presented data on the overrepresentation of CLDE learners in special education in other chapters in this text.

What Are the Major Criticisms of Using Tests with CLDE Groups?

Three overarching questions seem to capture the attention of educators when administering tests to CLDE groups: (1) Is the test biased against these students? (2) Is it fair and appropriate to use certain tests with CLDE students? and (3) will CLDE students be harmed or negatively impacted by the test results? At the center of all three questions is the notion of disparate impact. How do tests negatively affect CLDE students?

Referring back to Darnel, is it possible that he scored low due to test bias? Was the test fair to him? And could he have been harmed by his teacher's exclusive focus on his test scores, despite other information that could be taken into consideration (such as grades, former teacher comments, family background, exposure to a literacy-rich home and school environment)? The point is simple—the test we choose and how we use the information both have a profound impact on the decisions we make about students.

In contemporary psychology, *bias* is now viewed as a statistical concept that can be identified by statistical means. Bias is present when a test item has meanings or implications for a relevant, definable subgroup of test takers that are different from the meanings or implications for the remainder of the test takers. Specifically, when selecting a test and interpreting results, one must ask whether the test items have different meanings for European American students compared to CLDE learners.

Some educators do not believe that tests are biased (as may have been the case with Ms. Johnson), particularly in the statistical sense; others acknowledge that tests may be unfair and/or "culturally loaded." From a statistical standpoint, a test can be unbiased but still unfair. This issue cannot be ignored when we make decisions about students. Essentially, we must consider how fair a test is if a certain group consistently performs poorly on it. Further, when administering intelligence tests, educators must recognize the extent to which culture and cultural values have played a part in the construction of the tests from the very beginning (Flanagan & Ortiz, 2001; Gould, 1996). Neisser et al. (1996) asserted that the cultural environment—how people live, what they value, what they do—has a significant effect on the intellectual skills that are developed by individuals. Three test items may make this issue more conceptually concrete. Kaufman (1994) contended that the following items from the older versions of the Wecshler Adult Intelligence Scale (WAIS) and Wecshler Individual Scale for Children (WISC) reflect cultural values or loadings:

1. Why should we keep away from bad company?
2. Why should women and children be saved first in a shipwreck?
3. What should you do if someone smaller than you starts a fight with you?

What is the "correct" answer to these items? Why might Darnel and other CLDE students respond differently than non-CLDE students? For example, regarding the last item on fighting, why might some students respond that they should fight back? Such a response, by the way, would earn zero points.

In order to assess individuals from diverse cultural and language backgrounds in a more equitable manner, educators will need to come to terms with the fact that "intelligence cannot be tested independently of the culture that gives rise to the test" (Cole & Cole, 1993, p. 502). Stated differently, intelligence tests are not tests of intelligence in some abstract, culture-free way. They are measures of the ability to function intellectually by virtue of some knowledge and skills in the culture that they sample (Scarr, 1978). In an article subtitled "Why Ability Assessments Don't Cross Cultures," Greenfield (1997) maintained that intelligence tests are culturally loaded—students from different cultures perceive and respond differently to tests. Greenfield cited the seminal study on the Liberian Kpelle tribe by Cole, Gay, Glick and Sharp (1971), who took an object-sorting task to Liberia, where they presented the Kpelle participants with 20 objects to divide evenly into the linguistic categories of foods, implements, food containers, and clothing. Instead of performing the taxonomic sorts expected by the researchers, the Kpelle participants persistently made functional pairings. For example, rather than sorting objects into groups of tools and foods, they would put a potato and a knife together because "you take the knife and cut the potato" (p. 79). When asked to justify their functional pairings, participants stated "that a wise man could only do such and such" (Glick, 1968, p. 13). In total exasperation, the researchers finally asked, "How would a fool do it?" (p. 13). In response, the Kpelle paired the objects by taxonomy, resulting in four linguistically ordered categories. In other words, the researchers' criterion for *intelligent* behavior was the Kpelle participants' criterion for *foolish* behavior. What was "foolish" to the Kpelle was considered "intelligent" to the researchers.

Other investigations have explored the use of logical syllogisms with individuals from other cultures, especially cultures in which individuals are illiterate (Cole et al., Glick, 1971; Scribner, 1975, 1977). An example of a simple syllogism that may have been presented is "All oceans contain fish. The Atlantic is an ocean. Does it contain fish?" Researchers found that these individuals did not desire to solve the problems or make inferences because they had not observed the major premise (i.e., "All oceans contain fish") and did not want to assume it was true. Scribner (1977) argued that nonliterate peoples should not be perceived as illogical or unable to formulate hypotheses because they are unwilling to treat syllogisms as logical problems. If they could not verify the premises through direct observation or experience, nonliterate individuals felt uncomfortable providing a response to the question. He pointed out that specialized language genres, such as using verbal logical syllogisms, are familiar to those who have experienced solving story problems in which the answer must be derived from the relationships presented in the problem.

In their review of cross-cultural studies, Rogoff and Chavajay (1995) contended that "researchers cannot just assume, as we did before cross-cultural research, that a cognitive test reveals a general ability across tasks unrelated to people's experiences" (p. 863). These early and seminal studies as well as others (see Greenfield, 1966, 1997; Greenfield & Bruner, 1969; Sternberg, 2000) have called into question the cross-cultural validity of intelligence tests. Without deeper examination, the differences these studies found between cultural groups might have been interpreted as representing the cognitive deficiencies of one group in contrast to the superior cognitive abilities of another cultural group. The same can be said of comparison studies of the performance of two or more culturally diverse groups on IQ tests (e.g., Naglieri & Ford, 2005; Naglieri & Jensen, 1987; Taylor, Ziegler, & Partenio, 1984). These types of studies—if not interpreted responsibly—can imply a deficit model of performance if one group consistently performs better than another group. The numerous comparison studies of performance differences between

African Americans and European Americans on IQ tests are often based on a deficit model to start with, and, therefore, the outcomes are presented as differences in scores or performance levels without taking into account the cultural contexts in which these diverse groups developed. This is not to say that comparison studies should not be conducted, nor are we saying that tests do not yield useful information, but that they should be directed at a deeper, rather than a merely superficial, understanding of differences and similarities.

Scholars studying the role and influence of culture on test performance also contend that *it is not culture per se that acts as a biasing factor; rather, it is an individual's exposure to and familiarity (or lack thereof) with the test's underlying culture that affects performance on such tests* (Cummins, 1984; Figueroa, 1990; Matsumoto, 1994; Valdez & Figueroa, 1994). Flanagan and Ortiz (2001) coined the term *biasing effect* for this concept. They argue that the biasing effect operates whenever tests of intelligence that are developed and normed in one culture are given to individuals whose cultural backgrounds, experiences, and exposures are not similar to or consistent with those of the norm group against whom performance will be compared. In essence, idiosyncratic variations in the individual's culture and background can lower test performance. The test scores of students from diverse backgrounds are likely to be lower because the test samples only the cultural content related to mainstream experiences and not the full range of cultural content possessed by the individual (Flanagan & Ortiz, 2001; Valdez & Figueroa, 1994; Ford & Joseph, 2006; Ford & Whiting, 2006). Thus, while there is considerable research suggesting that many intelligence tests are technologically sound and appropriately normed and are not culturally *biased*, they are, nevertheless, culturally *loaded* and potentially unfair (Flanagan & Ortiz, 2001).

Cultural idiosyncratic variations can also exist with language. Much has been written about the appropriateness, usefulness, and fairness of administering intelligence tests to linguistically diverse students (i.e., bilingual or limited-English-proficient students). It is challenging to assess students' intellectual functioning when they have difficulty speaking and understanding English. It is common knowledge that test performance can be adversely affected by an individual's language proficiency (Flanagan & Ortiz, 2001).

In their review of popular tests, Flanagan and Ortiz (2001) categorized tests based on their degree of cultural loading and degree of linguistic demand. Tests can vary significantly on both dimensions; for example, a test can be high in linguistic demand but low or moderate in degree of cultural loading. Degree of cultural loading represents the extent to which a given test requires specific knowledge of or experience with mainstream U.S. culture. Degree of linguistic demand reflects the extent to which students must be English proficient and otherwise familiar with how language (vocabulary, definitions, homographs, homonyms, similarities, clichés, proverbs, etc.) is used in the United States. Therefore, tests can be linguistically biased, not because of any inherent structural defect, but because of the expectations and assumptions regarding the comparability of language proficiency among individuals taking the test. A student who is more proficient in English is likely to score higher on a test than someone who is less proficient in English. Further, the higher the linguistic demands of the test, the lower limited-English-proficient students are likely to score. Essentially, Flanagan and Ortiz (2001) maintain that

a. Tests of intelligence are constructed in ways that require or presume that a given level of language proficiency is present in the average individual that is sufficient to comprehend the instructions, formulate and verbalize responses, or otherwise use language ability in completing the expected task; and
b. In cases in which individuals are limited in English proficiency or for whatever reasons are not developmentally equivalent in language proficiency with the norm group against whom performance will be compared, the result will be bias.

FIGURE 7–2 Cultural loading and linguistic demands of two intelligence tests' subscales

	Low Degree of Cultural Loading	Moderate Degree of Cultural Loading	High Degree of Cultural Loading
Low degree of linguistic demand	Wechsler Matrix Reasoning	Wechsler Block Design, Symbol Search, and Digit Span	
	SB-IV Pattern Analysis	SB-IV Memory for Digits, Matrices, and Bead Memory	SB-IV Number Series
Moderate degree of linguistic demand	Wechsler Object Assembly	Wechsler Arithmetic	
	SB-IV Memory for Objects	SB-IV Quantitative	SB-IV Equation Building
High degree of linguistic demand			Wechsler Information, Similarities, Vocabulary, and Comprehension
			SB-IV Vocabulary, Verbal Relations, Absurdities, and Comprehension

Note: See Flanagan and Ortiz (2001) for a summary and analyses of other intelligence tests.

Figure 7–2 presents the cultural and linguistic demands of two widely used intelligence tests—the Wechsler Scales and the Stanford-Binet. Four subscales from both tests have high degrees of cultural loadings *and* linguistic demands. Conversely, the matrix reasoning and pattern analysis subscales have low degrees of cultural loading and linguistic demands. Finally, the mathematics subscales of both tests have moderate degrees of cultural loadings and linguistic demands.

Groth-Marnat (2003) and Gregory (1999) presented a thorough examination of the meaning of intelligence test scores and variables, traits, or characteristics measured by the various subscales. Their observations, which rely on descriptions of test subscales as presented in test manuals, indicate, as already noted, that intelligence tests are significantly influenced by culture, language, and schooling or educational exposure. Using the Wechsler Scales as a case in point, four subscales will be described here.

Information Subscale. The information subscale "samples types of knowledge that average persons with average opportunities should be able to acquire." This knowledge is usually based on overlearned material. "To score well, the individual must have been exposed to a highly varied past environment, have an intact long-term memory, and possess a wide range of interests" (Groth-Marnat, 2003, p. 166). Further, a high score on this subscale suggests that the examinee has "cultural interests, strong educational background, positive attitude toward school, and verbal ability. Low scores may show a lack of intellectual curiosity, cultural deprivation, or lack of familiarity with Western (American) culture" (p. 166). Gregory (1999) also notes that this subscale is influenced by cultural opportunities, richness of early environment, school learning, interests, and outside reading. Further, "the items query general knowledge normally available to individuals reared in the United States or Western Europe" (p. 81).

Comprehension Subscale. The comprehension subscale is thought to reflect the extent to which an individual "adheres to conventional standards, has benefited from past cultural opportunities, and has a well-developed conscience" (Groth-Marnat, 2003, p. 167). It requires verbal skills, a store of information (including proverbs), and how the individual uses this information to make decisions (e.g., Why do people take baths? Why should women and children be saved first in a shipwreck?). This subscale also requires "social judgment, knowledge of conventional standards of behavior, a grasp on social rules and regulations, as well as moral codes. A correct response requires accurate problem solving, good judgment, and abstract reasoning" (p. 167) and is influenced by overly concrete thinking (Gregory, 1999). In summarizing this subscale, Gregory (1999) noted that this subscale "measures degree of social acculturation, especially in the spheres of moral and ethical judgment. However, a high score does not mean a person will choose the 'right' action" (p. 84) when actually confronted with the situation.

Vocabulary Subscale. The vocabulary subscale is a test of accumulated verbal learning and represents an individual's ability to express a wide range of ideas with ease and flexibility. Sample items include: What is a horse? What does compassionate mean? According to Groth-Marnat (2003), "vocabulary generally reflects the nature and level of sophistication of the person's schooling and cultural learning. It is primarily dependent on the wealth of early educational environment, but is susceptible to improvement by later experience or schooling" (pp. 162–163). High scores suggest that the "person has a wide range of interest, a good fund of general information, and need for achievement; low scores suggest a limited educational background, poor language development, lack of familiarity with English, and/or poor motivation" (p. 163).

Similarities Subscale. The similarities subscale asks students to compare how two objects are alike [e.g., How are wood and coal alike? How are a ship and automobile alike? (See Miller-Jones, 1989)]. Correct responses require abstract reasoning (i.e., inductive reasoning and associative reasoning), verbal conceptual thinking, and skills in distinguishing essential from nonessential details (Groth-Marnat, 2003). To score well, the individual also requires strong verbal skills and information, as well as the ability to judge when a likeness is essential rather than trivial (Gregory, 1999).

As the descriptions of subscales suggest, intelligence tests are influenced by many variables, prominent among them are an individual's linguistic skills and background, educational experiences, and social and cultural experiences and learning (i.e., his/her familiarity with Western culture—rules, norms, standards of behavior, and so forth). Greenfield (1997) goes so far as to assert that "tests are not universal instruments; they are specific cultural genres" (p. 1122) because they reflect the values, knowledge, and communication strategies of their culture of origin. This makes them appropriate measures within their own culture, but ethnocentric when taken into a new culture. Helms (1992) and Miller-Jones (1989) made similar assertions and shared samples of additional test items that they thought were culturally loaded and, thus, unfair.

In summary, even with the most objective means and methods, bias exists in some form or another. An instrument whose vocabulary subscale contains words unfamiliar to a certain group might contain linguistic bias (e.g., "moor the boat" versus "dock the boat"); an instrument whose comprehensive subscale asks questions about experiences that are unfamiliar to students may contain experiential or content bias (e.g., "Why is it better to pay bills by check than with cash?" "If you were lost in the woods in the daytime, how would you find your way out?"). An instrument that is timed may be biased against individuals who have a different conception of time and who view and use time in different ways. Given that the goal of developing totally unbiased tests may be unrealistic, the goal of nondiscriminatory assessment should be viewed to reduce bias to the maximum extent possible (see Ford & Whiting, 2006; Whiting & Ford, 2006).

How Do Personal Biases Affect Testing of CLDE Learners?

While educators may recognize the limits of intelligence tests in general, but particularly with CLDE individuals, they seldom have formal training in understanding their own personal and professional biases (Banks, 2006; Snyderman & Rothman, 1987). Was this the case with Ms. Johnson and her views about the usefulness, accuracy, and power of tests? How much experience did she have with tests and how did this influence the credibility she gave to Darnel's test scores or performance? Has she ever considered the difference between test bias and test fairness? Has she ever thought about the limitations of tests in general, but especially when used with CLDE students?

Educators who hold stereotypes about CLDE individuals will impact the test performance of these students, and such views will influence how they interpret test results. This concept is called *confirmative bias*. Confirmative bias exists when educators consciously or unconsciously administer and interpret tests in the light of stereotypes or preconceived ideas about learners. Ortiz (2001) noted that confirmative bias can occur in both the type of data collected and the manner in which the data are interpreted (Matsumoto, 1994; Sandoval et al., 1998). For example, confirmative bias can occur if standardized test data are supplemented only by rating scale results completed by the teacher who made the referral on the student. Chances are that the referring teacher will likely reflect the same concerns about the student on a rating scale that is to determine whether the student has special needs (disability and/or gifted). Collecting subjective data or lack of sufficient data contributes to interpretation bias. Bias at the interpretation level can also occur when the evaluator(s) fails to note the significant strengths or weaknesses of students' performance on assessment measures, perhaps because the evaluator gives too much weight to test performance. Additionally, bias in interpreting results can occur if all the assessment data gathered are not interpreted and reported, or when some data are weighted more heavily than other data, as was evident with Darnel's teacher.

Educators can reduce confirmative bias by trying not to confirm their presumptions or preexisting deficits and, instead, testing their hypotheses (Ortiz, 2001; Ford & Joseph, 2006; Ford & Whiting, 2006). The process of assessment should begin with the hypothesis that the student's performance, particularly if low, is *not* intrinsic in nature, but a function of environment and external factors (e.g., unequal opportunity to learn, poor educational experiences, lack of access to reading, test anxiety, etc.). In other words, *the assumption of normality* should guide the assessment process. When the process of assessment or evaluation is guided with the presumption of normality, it reduces the tendency to search for data or "see" patterns of dysfunction where none may exist. In essence, educators who lack formal preparation to work with and evaluate CLDE students might need to seek such training. This may help to reduce stereotypes and other preconceived notions about CLDE students and, in turn, increase the validity of interpretations and the overall assessment process.

Interestingly, the educational community's reliance on standardized tests has not diminished; instead, testing is flourishing, as evidenced by the number of school districts that require students to pass proficiency or achievement tests and the importance placed on tests promoted by federal legislation, such as No Child Left Behind (2001). Given this obvious commitment to testing students, no time is better than the present to find ways to increase the educational and diagnostic usefulness of tests. As discussed later in the chapter, one such recommendation is applying culturally responsive assessment (also referred to here as *nondiscriminatory* or *nonbiased* assessment).

> **TEACHING TIPS**
>
> **The Wise Selection of Tests**
>
> **Below, we present a few questions for you to consider when using tests and other instruments (such as checklists) with CLDE students.**
>
> Standardized tests are here to stay and they are increasingly being used with all students. Recognizing their advantages and disadvantages for CLDE learners, educators must give careful consideration to selecting the instruments. Refer to CLDE students with whom you have worked when considering these questions and think about Darnel.
>
> 1. What is the purpose of the test? What types of information does the test provide?
> 2. On whom was the test normed or standardized?
> 3. Is the test/instrument valid and reliable for use with CLDE students? Has bias been reported for the test/instrument?
> 4. What are the advantages and disadvantages of using the test with CLDE students?
> 5. What happens when CLDE students do not perform well on the test? Are there negative consequences for scoring poorly?
> 6. Is there a pattern in which CLDE students consistently perform lower than other students on the test/instrument?
> 7. Who will interpret the scores/results? Does this person have much knowledge about using tests with CLDE students? Is he or she culturally sensitive, aware, and competent?
> 8. How will the results inform instruction?
> 9. What other instruments will be used to assist with interpreting test scores in a comprehensive manner? Will both formal and informal tools be used? Will both objective and subjective information be gathered?

The Bigger Picture: What Is Assessment and How Does Assessment Differ from Testing?

Professionals and laypersons alike appear to use the words *testing* and *assessment* interchangeably. We contend that the two terms and practices are not synonymous. Assessment is a broad, comprehensive process of which testing is but one component. Specifically, assessment is a process through which information reflecting the behavior, performance, or functions of an individual is collected, analyzed, interpreted, and summarized (Dent, 1996). Assessment involves gathering a variety of information from many sources to create a *comprehensive* profile of the individual based on the data. Such comprehensiveness makes it possible for teachers and other educators to diagnose needs, strengths, and weaknesses, and to prescribe appropriate educational services. Indeed, the primary purpose of assessment is to obtain information to facilitate effective decision making. In schools and other educational settings, then, assessment is used to make decisions about students in the areas of (a) screening; (b) classification and placement; (c) student progress; (d) instruction; and (e) program effectiveness (Salvia & Ysseldyke, 1995; Spinelli, 2002). Each type of decision requires the collection of a variety of data on students' specific and unique contexts—their background, health, interests, educational experiences, learning styles, and strengths and shortcomings.

Although assessment is broad and comprehensive, testing refers to the administration of a test in a systematic, prescribed manner. Tests, therefore, are *one* component of the assessment process. A test is a standardized procedure for sampling behavior and describing

Special precautions need to be taken when testing children from culturally and linguistically different backgrounds.

behavior according to categories or scores (Gregory, 2004). In reality, a test is a limited sample of behavior, as was shown with Darnel; however, the results of a "good" test help educators make tentative or initial inferences about relevant behaviors. Gregory stated:

> The purpose of the vocabulary test is not to determine the examinee's entire word stock by requesting definitions of a very small but carefully selected sample of words. Whether the examinee can define the particular 35 words from a vocabulary subtest is of little direct consequence, but the indirect meaning of such results is of great importance because it signals the examinee's general knowledge of vocabulary (p. 31).

An implicit assumption of tests is that they measure individual differences in traits or characteristics that exist in all people, but in varying amounts. Therefore, the purpose of testing is to estimate the amount of that characteristic within an individual. However, due to their limited scope, we must note two cautions about tests: (1) Testing is imprecise—every test score reflects some degree of measurement error, and it is important to make the error as small as possible in order to increase precision and inferences drawn from the scores; and (2) educators must be careful of reifying the characteristics being measured. In essence, test scores do not represent a "thing" with physical reality; they portray an abstraction that is considered useful in predicting non-test behaviors (e.g., grades in school). Hence, "in discussing a person's IQ score, psychologists are referring to an abstraction that has no direct, material existence but that is, nonetheless, useful in predicting school achievement and other outcomes" (Gregory, 2004, p. 32).

Despite the broad and comprehensive nature of assessment, concerted effort must still focus on potentially unfair or discriminatory instruments and results. "Non-discriminatory assessment is not a single procedure or test, but a wide range of approaches that collectively seek to uncover as fairly as possible relevant information and data upon which decisions regarding individuals can be equitably based" (Ortiz, 2001, p. 1321). Further, nondiscriminatory assessment—culturally responsive assessment—is not a search for an unbiased test, but rather a process that ensures that every individual, not just those who are different in some way, is evaluated in the least discriminatory manner possible.

TEACHING TIPS

Testing versus assessment: Some considerations

Testing	Assessment
Unidimensional—One instrument used to draw inferences and to make decisions.	Multidimensional—Multiple instruments used to draw inferences and to make decisions.
Tests students' knowledge of specific facts and isolated skills.	Assesses students' broader knowledge base.
Provides limited information, often in the form of multiple-choice responses, restricting students to a single way of demonstrating their knowledge and skills.	Provides comprehensive, more thorough information. Information is gathered from multiple sources and in different formats, giving students different ways to demonstrate their knowledge and skills.
Treats testing as independent of curriculum and instruction.	Aligns assessment with curriculum and instruction.
Goal is to identify a need.	Goal is to diagnose, prescribe, and design appropriate interventions and services.
Compares students' performance with others.	Compares students' performance with established criteria.
Demonstrates knowledge in laboratory, artificial ways and settings.	Demonstrates learning in authentic ways.
Uses tests to sort students.	Uses assessment tools to address individual student needs.
Regards testing as sporadic and conclusive.	Regards assessment as ongoing and dynamic.
Little regard to biases and cultural issues.	Attends to biases, cultural issues, fairness, and equity.

Also see Regional Educational Laboratories, February, 1998, *Improving Classroom Assessment: A Toolkit for Professional Developers* (Toolkit 98), Portland, OR: Northwest Regional Educational Laboratory.

Having presented an overview of concerns regarding both testing and standardized tests themselves (test bias, cultural loadings, and test fairness), we now turn to a discussion of features of culturally responsive assessment.

What Are Some Key Features of Culturally Responsive Assessment?

Culturally responsive assessment (CRA, i.e., nondiscriminatory assessment) includes much more than considering which instruments should be used and which should not. It is more than simply eliminating tests that may contain bias (Ortiz, 2001). Although educators must strive to conduct completely culturally responsive assessments—assessments that are nondiscriminatory or nonbiased—some scholars contend that "completely unbiased assessment is an illusion because it is impossible to eliminate every single instance of bias or every potentially discriminatory aspect of assessment" (Ortiz, 2001, p. 1321). Nondiscriminatory assessment is concerned with fairness in all aspects of evaluating individuals. It includes selecting the least biased instruments, seeking to avoid confirmatory biases (having preconceived notions or stereotypes about diverse individuals), and ensuring that policies and procedures are fair or nondiscriminatory. CRA is a collection of approaches, each designed to systematically reduce bias within the broader framework. Regardless of whether one is using curriculum-based assessment (discussed in other chapters), designing tests to assess learning after lessons have been taught, or using formal traditional measures, the following principles are helpful. CRA is guided by several promising procedures and recommendations:

1. Assess and evaluate the learning ecology (context or environments).
2. Assess and evaluate language proficiency.
3. Assess and evaluate opportunity for learning as well as whether limited, inappropriate, or no instruction has occurred.
4. Assess and evaluate educationally relevant cultural and linguistic factors.
5. Evaluate, revise, and retest hypotheses.
6. Determine the need for and language of assessment.
7. Reduce bias in traditional testing practices.
8. Utilize authentic and alternative assessment procedures.
9. Evaluate and interpret all data within the context of the learning ecology.
10. Link assessment data to selecting or designing interventions.
11. Intervene by providing opportunities for learning and appropriate instruction.
12. Assess and evaluate the effectiveness of interventions.

Assess and Evaluate the Learning Ecology. The reasons any given student scores low on an intelligence test are difficult to quantify. CRA begins with directing initial assessment efforts toward an exploration of the extrinsic or external factors that might be related to the student's performance. Hypotheses should be developed around a student's unique experiential background within the context of the learning environment. When assessment is conducted on culturally or linguistically diverse students, we must keep in mind that factors associated with culture and experiences can affect (adversely) test performance.

Assess and Evaluate Language Proficiency. An evaluation of a student's language proficiency is crucial to nondiscriminatory assessment. It provides the required context within which poor test scores (and academic performance) can be properly evaluated and forms the basis for the development of instructional interventions that are linguistically appropriate.

Assess and Evaluate Opportunity for Learning. While it is clear that learning takes place at home, much of it is informal; it is not grounded in formal training on the part of parents and caregivers. Rather, the school setting, as noted by Ortiz (2001), provides the most significant context for formal learning. The curriculum, personnel, policies, and instructional setting must be evaluated to determine whether diverse students have been provided with adequate "opportunity to learn." Data can be collected from evaluations of the classroom environment and teaching methods, direct observation of students' academic performance, review of educational records and progress reports, attendance records, review of the content and level of the curriculum, analysis of the match between the students' needs and the curriculum and the match between students' language and the language of instruction, the cultural relevance of the curriculum, teaching strategies and styles, teacher attitudes and expectations, interviews with students and their families, peer relationships and pressures, and more.

Assess and Evaluate Educationally Relevant Cultural and Linguistic Factors. Learning takes place not only in school but also in the broader scope of a student's social and cultural milieu. With diverse individuals in particular, it is important to assess and evaluate these milieu and their influences on school learning, language development, and educational process. Language assessments, observations of the individual, home visits, and interviews with family members can shed light on these factors.

Evaluate, Revise, and Retest Hypotheses. All reasonable and viable factors that could be related to a student's test performance should be evaluated and ruled out. Information for testing hypotheses should be collected and used to revise original hypotheses. The relevant data to collect has been described in the previous recommendations (e.g., learning opportunities, etc.). All effort must be made to reduce or eliminate potentially discriminatory attributions regarding the test performance of CLDE students.

Determine the Language Need. As we have already noted, when a student is not proficient in English, test performance may be significantly suppressed. To address this issue, CLDE learners should be assessed in their primary language or native mode of communication. Students should be evaluated by an assessor who is knowledgeable regarding the factors relevant to the student's unique experiences and how they may affect—especially hinder—performance.

Reduce Bias in Traditional Testing Practices. This may be accomplished by administering tests in a nondiscriminatory manner or modifying the testing process in a way that is less discriminatory. Some suggestions include bilingual administration of tests, extending or eliminating time constraints when appropriate, accepting alternative response formats (e.g., gestures, a different language, additional probing and querying of incorrect responses, etc.). Like Ortiz (2001), we recognize that these changes and others should not be used to the extent that they compromise the measures by which the tests were standardized.

Utilize Authentic and Alternative Assessment Procedures. Nonstandardized assessment instruments and strategies can provide valuable information about students. Curriculum-based assessments, performance-based assessments, portfolio assessments, nonverbal reasoning tests, metacognitive awareness inventories (e.g., Mokhtari & Reichard, 2002) should be included in the assessment process. Additionally, observing the strategies that CLDE students are using while completing items on tests may provide insights as to how they are reasoning about information. The data derived from these types of assessment procedures provide the evaluator with an opportunity to view performance through a qualitative lens. Every effort must be made to avoid using single scores, interpreting only the results from quantitative sources of data, and unduly favoring certain data over other data, as this can lead to discriminatory inferences and outcomes (Ortiz, 2001). Moreover, educators should keep in mind that direct, curriculum-based, and performance-based assessments offer a more direct link to intervention than cognitive ability tests (Canter, 1997), as discussed earlier in this chapter.

Evaluate and Interpret All Data Within the Context of the Learning Ecology. All data collected over the course of CRA should be evaluated in an integrated manner, utilizing information obtained about CLDE learners' unique experiences and background as the appropriate context. Thus, the influence of culture, language, exceptional needs, and academic experiences must be considered.

Link Assessment to Intervention. Testing and assessment are not interventions. Assessment, even the most comprehensive assessment and the most nondiscriminatory assessment, is of little value unless it can be used to target or develop intervention options. It should be noted that there is inadequate data to suggest that many standardized intelligence tests have treatment utility (Braden, 1997, Sternberg, 2000), and this consideration must be addressed, as it contributes, in part, to the overall validity of an instrument (American Educational Research Association [AERA], American Psychological Association [APA] & National Council on Measurement in Education [NCME], 1999).

Intervene by Providing Opportunities for Learning and Appropriate Instruction. Vygotsky (1978) defined intelligence as the zone of proximal development, which is considered to be what a student can accomplish if provided appropriate mediational or "cultural" tools. Many educators today use the term *scaffolding* when they refer to providing appropriate types of assistance to students. When CLDE students score low, it may be necessary to scaffold their learning by modifying instructional programs and providing students with test-taking skills, language-based skills, opportunities to receive corrective feedback and practice, and other relevant interventions. These students may not have had opportunities to perform cognitive/academic tasks, such as inductive and deductive reasoning. They may need to be exposed to tasks that demand these ways of thinking and to have particular ways of thinking modeled for them through, for example, teacher vocalizations of thought processes while solving problems. For instance, most of us learned to solve verbal analogies by having the solutions to these types of analogies demonstrated to us. Before many of us learned to apply the scientific method to science fair projects, scientific inquiry procedures were demonstrated to us with opportunities to practice through simulated or lab experiments in class before completing the science fair project. Thus, providing insufficient opportunities to learn and inappropriate instruction can be considered biased educational practices (Canter, 1997), and bias is created when individuals are excluded from receiving opportunities.

Assess the Effectiveness of Interventions. The effectiveness of targeted interventions should be assessed to determine if alternative interventions or modifications to existing interventions need to be made. In other words, the assessment-to-intervention link is not linear but rather circular and continuous. As CLDE learners acquire skills as observed through assessment data, instruction on more advanced skills is provided and assessed, and so forth.

How Can We Address High-Stakes Testing of CLDE Learners?

What Are High-Stakes Tests?

Large-scale tests that are administered by the states are often referred to as high-stakes tests due to the consequences that are attached to them. The consequences may have implications for student promotions, teacher salaries, or district finances and rankings. Two major pieces of national legislation (i.e., IDEA 1997/2004 and NCLB 2001) have caused students with disabilities to be included in this testing. The recent reauthorizations of IDEA stipulate that students with disabilities would be tested on state- or district-level assessments in the given or in altered forms. Additionally, NCLB specified that school systems must disaggregate the test data so that results are reported by subgroups, such as disability, race, and ethnicity. Schools are expected to establish baseline scores against which adequate yearly progress (AYP) is to be monitored for students in Grades 3 through 8 (Altshuler & Schmautz, 2006). The goal is to have all students proficient by 2014. Failure to show consistent progress could result in various penalties, such as monetary fines or the takeover of the school by the state.

Including students with disabilities or exceptional needs in this testing is viewed as providing an additional measure of accountability in special education. The beneficial effects of special education have long been debated, and some authorities contend that the continued exclusion of special education students from these assessments may call into question the legitimacy of educational reform (Schulte & Villwock, 2004). Another consideration is that the inclusion of students with disabilities will suppress the tendency to place low-performing students in special education in order to avoid including their scores in the general education test data.

The concern over the lack of accountability for students with disabilities must be measured against the real and potential deleterious effects of large-scale testing, particularly for CLDE students, to which much attention has been given. Much of the worry centers on the impact these tests have on students with and without disabilities from culturally and linguistically diverse backgrounds. Researchers and other authorities have frequently noted that CLD students are demoralized by these tests, which often result in their being held back, dropping out, or being pushed out of school (Fine, 2005; Nichols, Glass, & Berliner, 2006; Tuerk, 2005). A particularly controversial issue is the relationship between instruction and test performance. Research by Tuerk shows an inverse relationship between poverty and highly qualified teachers. That is, as poverty increases, particularly in urban areas, the likelihood of having highly qualified teachers decreases (Barton, 2003). This situation is directly linked to poorer test performance, leading authorities to complain that students are being penalized for inadequate instruction. Other issues for poor-performing students are the fear that the curriculum will be so narrowed that class instruction will focus almost exclusively on material related to the test or that the use of one test may keep a student from being placed in advanced classes (Ford & Joseph, 2006; International Reading Association, 1999).

How Do We Help CLDE Students Perform on High-Stakes Tests?

Although many authorities emphasize the shortcomings of high-stakes testing (e.g., Nichols et al., 2006), researchers offer evidence of improved performance in states that attached consequences to their testing compared to those that did not (Rosenshine, 2003). Furthermore, there is little question that there must be educational accountability for exceptional learners.

In some cases, existing large-scale tests have been modified for students with disabilities (e.g., Schulte & Villwock, 2004; Shaftel, Yang, Glasnapp, & Poggio, 2005). However, a key means of assisting students in these testing situations is through accommodations (Bolt & Thurlow, 2004; Fletcher et al., 2006). Based on their review of the research, Fletcher et al. concluded that accommodations during testing should be specific to the disability of the learner. In a study of the accommodations during a state test for students with decoding reading problems and those without disabilities, Fletcher et al. accommodated the students by giving them more time to take the test, reading proper nouns to the students, and reading the comprehension questions to the students. The researchers found that the accommodations helped only the students with disabilities, thereby validating these procedures.

Accommodations for students with disabilities are widely used but have not been found universally effective. Bolt and Thurlow (2004) have offered a set of guidelines for employing test accommodations, which are summarized in the following list:

1. Accommodations should be specified according to the skill being measured. If the skill is to assess rate of performance, such as the number of problems that a student

can calculate or reading-word fluency within a certain time frame, then extended time should not be given. On the other hand, if the goal is to assess the child's ability to calculate specific problems without a time dimension, then the extended time might be given.
2. Use the accommodation that is closest to the expected response for the test. For example, if the student is unable to complete a paper-and-pencil test but is able to use a computer, it is better to let the student use the computer rather than to have the student dictate the response.
3. Make certain students have been instructed in the assessment accommodations prior to testing. Students need to be familiar with the type of responses expected, such as dictating answers, so that they can respond with ease during testing.
4. Make sure those who are to administer testing accommodations have prior training. For example, interpreters should have test items prior to the testing to develop skill in giving the items to students. They also should be trained in how to give all the necessary information to the learner without prompting or giving clues to the learner.
5. Prepare for possible additional challenges. If technology is being used, make sure it is operating properly prior to test taking.
6. Monitor the effects of accommodations for individual students. There are occasions when accommodations have not been helpful to students. Monitor student performance with and without accommodations.

What Are Some Additional High-Stakes Testing Considerations for CLDE Students?

High-stakes tests are in conflict with the collectivist orientation of many CLDE students (Altshuler & Schmautz, 2006; Cartledge & Milburn, 1996; LaRoche & Shriberg, 2004). Altshuler and Schmautz, for example, maintain that U.S. schools are dominated by an *idiocentric* view, which emphasizes the individual and competition. Other cultures, such as that of Hispanics, value *allocentrism*, which emphasizes interdependence and seeing one's worth in relation to others, not according to the individual. These authorities argue that cultural values such as *allocentrism* are barriers to academic endeavors such as test taking because a competitive and individualistic orientation provides an advantage. Teachers and schools need to become better informed about the cultural backgrounds and values of their CLDE students (Altshuler & Schmautz, 2006; LaRoche & Shriberg, 2004; Townsend, 2002). Instead of blaming the students and their parents for the students' poor academic performance, teachers should use cultural knowledge as a means of involving the student's family in the child's schooling, inform the family of the school's academic goals, and collaborate on ways to achieve those goals.

A history of doing poorly on high-stakes tests can have negative psychological effects on CLDE learners, creating states of high anxiety and even poorer performance (LaRoche & Shriberg, 2004; Townsend, 2002). Educators need to devise strategies that will help to minimize student anxiety, such as giving students practice sessions with the type of responses required on the tests, providing frequent and meaningful learning experiences where student successes are highlighted, identifying and emphasizing individual and group strengths, making certain that the skills, concepts, and higher-level understandings are well taught, and making students aware of their successes to help them become more confident in their ability to succeed.

Decisions based on one statewide test are extremely problematic for CLDE students. CLDE students with or without exceptionalities are not likely to be the benefactors of higher-level or rigorous curriculums. LaRoche and Shriberg (2004) stated, "Holding students who have not had exposure to specific concepts to the same standard as students who have had extensive exposure to these topics is very problematic, if not outright discriminatory" (pp. 211–213). Sloane and Kelly (2003) pointed out that high-stakes tests are designed to find out what students know but that it is equally, if not more, important to assess students to determine what they need to know and how to teach them. To avoid penalizing students, they need to have access to the instructional material. Sloane and Kelly advised that "the task for teachers is to know and understand their state's standards, and then translate this knowledge to continuously help students learn and self-assess to meet those standards" (p. 15).

A related issue is the types of assessments used with CLDE learners. Administrators and teachers would be wise to use multiple measures, such as formative assessments and portfolios, as well as standardized tests. The International Reading Association (1999) recommended that teachers administer well-developed, rigorous, classroom tests and make the effort to educate parents and others on the ways these assessments can be used to improve the learner's reading performance. As noted earlier in this chapter and discussed further in chapters 10 and 13, curriculum-based assessments/measures (CBA/M) and progressive monitoring are particularly useful for this purpose with CLDE learners. The assessments are easily interpreted, even to non-English-speakers. Noting the progress that their children are making can be an effective way of engaging the family in the schooling process. In contrast, standardized tests are typically administered at the end of the school year and are of limited value in determining how to address learning needs.

Teachers—all educators—are advised to use ethical practices in assessment so that, for example, they teach students how to take the test but avoid devoting instructional time to students most likely to perform well to the detriment of lower-performing students. They must also resist the temptation to teach a very narrow curriculum related strictly to the test while overlooking equally valuable content material. These practices are particularly problematic with regard to CLDE learners (e.g., LaRoche & Shriberg, 2004; Townsend, 2002). The focus in CLDE classrooms needs to be on academic engagement and achievement. Rosenshine (2003) speculates that the improved test performance observed in certain states is probably due to the academic focus in the classrooms rather than to the consequences attached to test performance or to the possibility that teachers were teaching to the tests.

Assessment conditions for culturally and linguistically diverse students with disabilities need to be accommodating and fair.

Where Do We Go from Here? Assessment Principles

At the heart of CBM is nondiscriminatory assessment. Nondiscriminatory or culturally responsive assessment is guided by a set of principles, a few of which are described here.

Nondiscriminatory Assessment Principles

The overall goal of nondiscriminatory assessment, as we see it, is to eliminate or reduce as much as possible biases in instruments, policies, and procedures. When interpreting the test scores of CLDE students, educators must gather two important and interrelated pieces of information: (1) the student's level of acculturation, and (2) the degree to which performance on any given test is contingent upon culture-specific knowledge.

Principle 1. Intelligence tests measure a limited range of abilities, and a large number of variables considered "intelligent" are beyond the scope of most intelligence tests. No test or battery of tests can ever give a complete picture; they can only assess certain areas of present functioning (Groth-Marnat, 2003). Even though tests proclaiming to measure intelligence are limited, it is well known that interindividual differences exist within the construct of intellectual abilities (Braden, 1997; Sternberg, 2000). Some children learn at faster rates and can generalize knowledge across various contexts better than other children, despite similar types and amounts of instruction. Thus, intelligence test scores should never be used rigidly as part of any decision-making process (Ford & Joseph, 2006; Gregory, 1999; National Association for Gifted Children, 2001).

Principle 2. All tests have some degree of cultural and linguistic loading. In other words, as stated earlier, no test is culture free. In all probability, no test can be created that will entirely eliminate the influence of learning and cultural experiences. The test and materials, the language in which the questions are phrased, the test directions, the categories for classifying the responses, the scoring criteria, and the validity criteria are all culture bound (Sattler, 1992). Thus, educators must search for and use instruments containing the least amount of cultural loadings, as well as collect information from multiple sources and in various ways.

Principle 3. Whenever standardized tests are used with students from CLD backgrounds, the possibility exists that what is actually being measured is acculturation or English proficiency, rather than ability. The structure and design of intelligence tests and the construction of representative norm groups are based on the notions of equivalency in levels of acculturation for both the individuals on whom the test was standardized and on whom the test will be used (Ortiz, 2001). Thus, an in-depth analysis of the student's level of acculturation (e.g., language proficiency, cultural values and styles, etc.) should be conducted and used when administering tests and interpreting results.

Principle 4. When cultural differences are limited to examining linguistic differences, this leads to neglect of factors that are extremely important in understanding the nature of test results (Flanagan & Ortiz, 2001), for example, conceptions of time, competitiveness, field dependence and field independence, etc. Thus, educators must have an understanding of the concept of "culture," including values, beliefs, customs, traditions, communication styles, and more (Ford & Harris, 1999), and how these dimensions of culture affect test performance (see Helms, 1992, 2005). It may also be important to have at least one member of the assessment team who has formal training in cross-cultural or multicultural assessment and/or is from the same culture as the CLDE students being assessed.

Principle 5. The cultural and linguistic demands of a test can differentially affect the performance of CLDE learners. Namely, the more the cultural and linguistic demands of the test, the more adverse the impact on the test scores of culturally and linguistically diverse students (Flanagan & Ortiz, 2001). Practitioners, therefore, must strive to adopt tests that have the least amount of linguistic demands and to make interpretations of the test scores of diverse students based on knowledge of their language skills (Ortiz, 2001).

Principle 6. Cultural and linguistic differences serve to artificially *depress* the scores of CLDE learners. Thus, the less acculturated the test taker or student, the lower the test score is likely to be. Further, the higher the cultural and linguistic demands of the test, the greater the probability that CLDE students will have lower test scores than mainstream students. It is necessary, therefore, when making group comparisons, to consider the differences between the groups relative to cultural background and language skills. Hypotheses regarding the nature and extent of group differences should include considerations of culture and language (Ortiz, 2001). Further, CLDE learners must not be penalized for their cultural and linguistic differences by being denied access to challenging curriculum and gifted education programs. Likewise, these differences should not be misinterpreted as deficits or disadvantages such that inappropriate referrals are made to special education.

Principle 7. The greater the difference between a student's cultural or linguistic background and the cultural or linguistic background of individuals comprising the norm group, the more likely the test will measure lower performance as a function of this *experiential* difference as opposed to being due to actual lower ability (Flanagan & Ortiz, 2001). The very purpose of assessment should be to enhance learning rather than simply to diagnose the causes of poor performance (Ortiz, 2001). Thus, to close the performance gap between CLDE and mainstream groups, and to improve the test performance of CLDE students, educators will need to improve the quality of the schooling and educational experiences. Such experiences include, for example, providing students assistance in test-taking skills, study skills, listening skills, and language-based or literacy-based instruction.

Principle 8. The test scores of CLDE students may reflect the impact of different experiences and "social inequality." In the face of inadequate cultural and educational opportunity, unbiased tests provide an accurate estimate not only of individual capability but also of the inhospitable conditions that depress that capability (Skiba, Knesting, & Bush, 2002). As discussed in the previous principle, test performance is influenced by the nature and quality of one's experiences. To interpret the test scores of students without considering this reality is to contribute to a biased assessment; this renders the information collected unusable. Every effort must be made to interpret results according to the effects of social injustices as a fundamental consideration.

Principle 9. A test that is considered nonbiased technically or statistically can still contain low to high degrees of cultural and linguistic demands (Flanagan & Ortiz, 2001). Thus, all instruments, including those considered technically sound, should be evaluated for their degree of cultural and linguistic demands. When the linguistic demands of a test are low or reduced, the cultural loadings must still be considered. When the cultural loadings of a test are low or reduced, the linguistic demands must still be considered. Essentially, if cultural and educational considerations are overlooked in terms of the depressed scores of diverse individuals, those scores will become biased estimates of individual potential by misattributing the effects of inadequate educational opportunity to a lack of individual aptitude or ability (Skiba, Knesting, & Bush, 2002, p.70).

Principle 10. Proper and systematic consideration of the relevant cultural and linguistic characteristics of tests provides a framework for interpretation that is more valid and reliable than what is ordinarily obtained using traditional methods (Flanagan & Ortiz, 2001). Appropriate assessment must involve a determination of how well any particular assessment situation matches the practices individuals experience as part of culturally contextualized activities (Miller-Jones, 1989). In this regard, practitioners must consider ways to accommodate differences (e.g., translated tests, language interpreter, nonverbal tests, authentic assessments, etc.).

Principle 11. No matter how much a test developer might want to emphasize the fairness of a given test by illustrating the inclusion of culturally and linguistically diverse individuals, claims about equity are highly misleading and inaccurate (Valdez & Figueroa, 1994). Teachers should thus be careful not to fall prey to the assumption that stratification in the norm sample on the basis of race is equivalent to stratification on the basis of culture. If different groups have different group norms on intelligence tests, then those subgroup norms should be considered when making decisions (e.g., placement).

Principle 12. The assumption of normality should guide the assessment process. When the process of assessment or evaluation is guided by the presumption of normality, it reduces the tendency to search for data or "see" patterns of dysfunction where none may exist (Ortiz, 2001).

Principle 13. Nondiscriminatory assessment should be multifaceted, collaborative, and guided by a comprehensive framework that "integrates efforts to reduce bias in a cohesive and systematic manner" (Ortiz, 2001, p. 1327).

Taken together, these principles suggest practitioners must consider the possibility that the research that overwhelmingly supports the notion that intelligence tests are not biased is based on definitions of bias that are either untenable or inaccurate. Bias is not simply a function of item content, factor structure, or racial differences. "Bias is more a function of differences in experience that are due to factors involving many variables, including culture and language" (Flanagan & Ortiz, 2001, p. 266). Thus, "the absence of technical bias in intelligence tests in no way absolves those who administer and make decisions based on those tests from socially responsible decision making" (Skiba, Knesting, & Bush, 2002, p. 75). In the final analysis, culturally competent assessment is much more than ensuring that tests are unbiased; rather, "culturally competent assessment represents a commitment to data collection . . . [and] assists in identifying and eliminating sources of bias throughout the educational process" (Skiba, Knesting, & Bush, 2002, p. 62).

Where Do We Go from Here? Educational Implications

Tests are used extensively, and sometimes exclusively, to screen, identify, and place students in special education and gifted education programs (Council of State Directors of Programs for the Gifted and The National Association for Gifted Children, 2003). Despite cautions and precautions against the exclusive use of tests for identifying gifted and special education students (e.g., Ford, 1996, 2004; National Association for Gifted

TEACHING TIPS

A Few Strategies for Making Assessment Culturally Responsive

1. Make sure that you establish rapport and gain the trust of CLDE students.
2. Make sure that the student understands the directions and format of the test.
3. Provide opportunities for taking practice tests so that students can get comfortable and familiar with the test.
4. Allow the student to respond in his or her native language.
5. Assess the student in both English and his or her native language.
6. Allow the student to use a language/bilingual dictionary.
7. Teach the student the language of academic testing.
8. Use a translator throughout the assessment process.
9. Take into account language differences when scoring tests.
10. Allow students opportunities to demonstrate knowledge and mastery in different ways—oral, projects, written, etc.
11. Use reinforcers that are tailored to individual students.
12. Teach test-taking skills.
13. Select and use tests that are valid and reliable for culturally and linguistically diverse exceptional learners.
14. Never ignore, minimize, or trivialize the powerful influence of culture on learning and test performance.

Back to Darnel ...

- How might you establish rapport with Darnel?
- What questions might you ask Darnel to make sure that he understands the test directions?
- What can you do in your class to improve Darnel's test-taking skills and strategies?

Children, 1997; Raymond, 2004), many districts are using one test, along with strict cutoff scores, to identify gifted students, according to data collected from state departments of education (Council of State Directors, 2003). We believe that this practice is indefensible and serves to keep gifted and special education programs very much in the midst of controversy. So many variables affect test performance. Prior to drawing conclusions, we need to consider all of these issues—and others that are relevant. (Also see Spinelli, 2002 and the sample assessment resources in Figure 7–3 for a detailed analysis of testing and assessing students with different exceptionalities.)

In addition to these concerns, other issues must be considered when students are culturally and/or linguistically diverse and have exceptional needs. Educators and others who administer, interpret, and use tests must consider how (and the extent to which) tests are contributing to the overrepresentation in special education and underrepresentation of CLDE students in gifted education. Here is one question worth considering: *If culturally and linguistically diverse exceptional learners consistently perform poorly on a test or tests, why do we continue to use the test(s)?* Gregory and Lee (1986) asserted that tests have been (mis)used to deny CLDE students opportunities to fully participate in society. They summarize litigation and legislation detailing how problems in testing have contributed to unequal or unfair educational opportunities for diverse students, such as

FIGURE 7–3 Teacher tools: Sample assessment resources

Cohen, L. G. & Spenciner, L. J. (2003). *Assessment of children and youth with special needs*. Boston: Allyn & Bacon.

Elliott, J., Thurlow, M., & Ysseldyke, J. (1996). *Assessment guidelines that maximize the participation of students with disabilities in large-scale assessments: Characteristics and considerations*. (Synthesis Rep. 25). National Center on Educational Outcomes (ERIC Document Reproduction Service No. ED 404 799). Minneapolis, MN: University of Minnesota.

King-Sears, M. E. (1998). *Curriculum-based assessment in special education*. San Diego, CA: Singular Publishing Group, Inc.

McLoughlin, J. A. & Lewis, R. B. (2001). *Assessing special students* (5th ed.). Upper Saddle River, NJ: Merrill/Prentice Hall.

Oosterhof, A. (2003). *Developing and using classroom assessments* (3rd ed.). Upper Saddle River, NJ: Merrill/Prentice Hall.

Overton, T. (2003). *Assessment in special education* (4th ed.) Upper Saddle River, NJ: Merrill/Prentice Hall.

Pierangelo, R., & Giuliani, G. A. (2002). *Assessment in special education: A practical approach*. Boston, MA: Allyn & Bacon.

Salvia, J. & Ysseldyke, J. E. (1999). *Assessment* (7th ed). Boston, MA: Houghton Mifflin.

Spinelli, C. S. (2002). *Classroom assessment for students with special needs in inclusive settings*. Upper Saddle River, NJ: Merrill/Prentice Hall.

Tindal, G. A., & Marston, D. B. (1990). *Curriculum-based assessment: Evaluating instructional outcomes*. Upper Saddle River, NJ: Merrill/Prentice Hall.

Witt, J. C., Elliott, S. N., Daly E. J., Gresham, F. M., & Kramer, J. J. (1998). *Assessment of at-risk and special needs children* (2nd ed). Boston, MA: McGraw-Hill.

---

overrepresentation in special education and underrepresentation in gifted education. Specifically, they state: "Psychological assessment is an area of professional practice that has been particularly subject to complaints about the differential treatment of racial and ethnic minorities" (p. 635). As discussed throughout this chapter, educators must carefully consider not only the tests but also policies and procedures that are used in the decision-making process. We propose that culturally responsive assessment holds much promise for increasing the representation of CLDE students in gifted education and decreasing their participation in special education. With this last point in mind, we offer several final recommendations.

First, educators must develop hypotheses to study and explain group differences on the test performance of gifted diverse students. What factors account for their test scores? How does stereotype threat, as proposed by Steele (1997), for example, explain their test scores? According to Steele, too many Black students have internalized the belief that they are either not good test takers or that they are genetically inferior to White students when it comes to intelligence. Therefore, when asked to take some type of intelligence or aptitude test, Black students lose confidence; as a result, they test poorly.

Second, tests, other instruments (e.g., checklists, nomination forms, referral forms, etc.), policies, and procedures (e.g., teacher referrals) must be examined for possible disparate impact (Office for Civil Rights, 2005). For instance, if teachers underrefer CLDE students for gifted education screening and overrefer them for special education services, what is the efficacy of continuing this practice (Ford, 1996; Ford, Harris, Tyson, & Frazier Trotman, 2002; Raymond, 2004)?

Third, the notion of "assessment"—being comprehensive and thorough in collecting information—must replace that of "testing"—using information from one instrument (recall Ms. Johnson). We caution educators against making identification decisions (e.g., labeling) and placement decisions based on a single test score. This practice, we believe, is indefensible given that information gleaned from a single test is too limited.

Fourth, the concept of fairness and access should be at the forefront of discussions regarding culturally and linguistically diverse exceptional students. Every effort must be made to help or support diverse students (all students) in testing and assessment situations. For linguistically diverse learners specifically, such support or advocacy can come in the form of bilingual test administrators and using interpreters, as well as adopting tests and instruments translated in their language.

Fifth, educators administering, interpreting, and using tests must be trained to do so taking into account cultural and linguistic diversity. We cannot test in a "culture-blind" fashion. The test results are only as good as the testing situation (Kaufman, 1994), which includes educators acknowledging and considering the examinee's cultural and linguistic background as well as level of acculturation (Sattler, 1992). This understanding goes a long way in helping educators to interpret test scores and using the results for the benefit of the student. Stated another way, tests should be used to benefit, not harm, students (Ford & Frazier Trotman, 2000; Ford & Joseph 2006; Kaufman, 1994; Naglieri & Ford, 2005; Sattler, 1992).

Sixth, school districts need to examine the demographics of their gifted programs and special education programs relative to cultural and linguistic diversity. These data should then be used to conduct studies on variables that contribute to underrepresentation and overrepresentation. For instance, current and former CLDE students and their families can be interviewed about their experiences in gifted education and special education. This information can be used to improve, if and where necessary, education services. Other areas of study might consist of (a) exploring the number or percentage of CLDE students referred for both gifted education and special education screening compared to mainstream students; (b) exploring the number or percentage of CLDE students referred for gifted education screening but who failed to meet criteria, and conversely, those who are referred for special education with limited justification; (c) examining the profiles of CLDE students who score high on achievement indices (grades and achievement tests), but low on intelligence tests, and vice versa; and (d) examining if high-SES (socioeconomic status) CLDE learners are disproportionately being identified as gifted or in need of special education services compared to low-SES CLDE students.

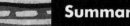

Summary

The use of traditional tests, especially intelligence tests, with students who are culturally and linguistically diverse has always been controversial and hotly debated (e.g., Fish, 2002; Gould, 1996; Helms, 1992, 2005; Jencks & Phillips, 1998). Opponents argue that tests are biased and place CLDE learners at a disadvantage. Opponents focus on the underrepresentation of these students in gifted programs and their overrepresentation in special education in support. Proponents offer a different perspective and consider the tests to be fair, valid, and reliable.

As stressed in this chapter, when tests are used to make important decisions about students, all cautions must be heeded, particularly with high-stakes tests. While we do not advocate discarding tests completely, we do recommend that they be used with caution and with other corroborating information, as seen in Darnel's case. Essentially, the more information we collect, the better informed educators will be and the more effective will be academic services and interventions.

All school districts face issues specific to their context as they endeavor to identity and serve culturally and linguistically diverse students with exceptional needs. Whatever the circumstances and constraints, every effort must be made to ensure that belief systems, tests, policies, and procedures do not shut the door of opportunity for exceptional learners who are culturally and linguistically diverse.

Related Learning Activities

1. In your school building, locate two or more students from culturally and linguistically diverse backgrounds with exceptional needs (gifted or LD, MR, etc.). Browse school records to see when these students were identified as gifted or special education learners. What measures were used? What other information was gathered? After gathering this information, observe the students. Do they seem to be appropriately identified and placed? What concerns, if any, do you have? Share your perceptions with teachers and/or administrators.

2. Talk with a special education administrator about the percentage of CLDE students in gifted education or special education. Do you find/observe any discrepancies? If so, how large are these discrepancies? What explanation(s) is offered? What role do tests play in the identification and assessment and decision-making process? Do the tests that are used for making these decisions have high linguistic and/or cultural demands? Share your observations or concerns, along with alternative measures.

3. Locate two or more CLDE students who have been identified as gifted or as students with disabilities. Examine their test scores. How do the students perform on the verbal subscales versus the nonverbal subscales?

4. Interview the school psychologist about observations on how CLDE students tend to perform on traditional intelligence tests. What training does this person have in cross-cultural assessment? What modifications does he or she make when testing and assessing CLDE students? Does the psychologist believe that tests are biased or unfair in any way? How does this person try to reduce biases?

References

Altschuler, S. J., & Schmautz, T. (2006). No Hispanic student left behind: The consequences of "high stakes" testing. *Children & Schools, 28,* 5–14.

American Educational Research Association (AERA), American Psychological Association (APA), and National Council on Measurement in Education (NCME). (1999). *Standards for educational and psychological testing.* Washington, DC: American Psychological Association.

Banks, J. A. (2006). *Diversity in American education: foundations, curriculum and teaching.* Boston, MA: Allyn & Bacon.

Barton, P. (2003). *Parsing the achievement gap.* Washington, DC: Educational Testing Service.

Bolt, S. E., & Thurlow, M. L. (2004). Five of the most frequently allowed testing accommodations in state policy: Synthesis of research. *Remedial and Special Education, 25,* 141–152.

Braden, J. (1997). The practical impact of intellectual assessment issues. *School Psychology Review, 26*(2), 242–248.

Canter, A. (1997). The future of intelligence testing in the schools. *School Psychology Review, 26*(2), 255–261.

Cartledge, G., & Milburn, J. F. (2006). *Cultural diversity and social skill instruction: Understanding ethnic and gender differences.* Champaign, IL: Research Press.

Cole, M., & Cole, S. R. (1993). *The development of children.* New York: Scientific American Books.

Cole, M., Gay, J., Glick, J. A., & Sharp, D. W. (1971). *The cultural context of learning and thinking.* New York: Basic Books.

Cole, N. S., & Moss, P. A. (1989). Bias in test use. In R. L. Linn (Ed.), *Educational measurements* (3rd ed. pp. 201–220). New York: ACE/Macmillan.

Council for Exceptional Children. (2000). High stakes testing: A mixed blessing for special education. *Today, 7*(2), 1–5.

Council of State Directors of Programs for the Gifted and the National Association for Gifted Children. (2003). *State of the states gifted and talented education report, 2001–2002.* Washington, DC: Author.

Cummins, J. C. (1984). *Bilingual and special education: Issues in assessment and pedagogy.* Austin, TX: Pro-Ed.

Davis, G. A. & Rimm, S. B. (2004). *Education of the gifted and talented.* Boston: Allyn & Bacon, 2004.

Dent, H. (1996). Non-biased assessment or realistic assessment? In R. L. Jones (Ed.), *Handbook of tests and measurements for Black populations* (Vol. 2, pp. 103–122). Hampton, VA: Cobb & Henry.

Esters, I. G, Ittenback, R. F., & Han, K. (1997). Today's IQ tests: Are they really better than their historical predecessors? *School Psychology Review, 26*(2), 211–223.

Figueroa, R. A. (1990). Best practices in the assessment of bilingual children. In A. Thomas & J. Grimes (Eds.), *Best practices in school psychology* (Vol. 2, pp. 93–106). Washington, DC: National Association of School Psychologists.

Fine, M. (2005, Summer) High-stakes testing and lost opportunities: The New York State Regents Exams. *ENCOUNTER: Education for Meaning and Social Justice, 18*, 24–29.

Fish, J. M. (2002). *Race and intelligence: Separating science from myth.* Mahwah, NJ: L. Erlbaum.

Flanagan, D. P. & Ortiz, S. (2001). *Essentials of cross-battery assessment.* New York: Wiley.

Fletcher, J. M., Francis, D. J., Boudousquie, A., Copeland, K., Young, V., Kalinowski, S., & Vaughn, S. (2006). Effects of Townsend, B.L. (2002). "Testing while black": Standards-based school reform and African American learners. *Remedial and Special Education, 23*, 222–230.

Ford, D. Y. (1996) *Reversing underachievement among gifted Black students: Promising practices and programs.* New York: Teachers College Press.

Ford, D. Y. (2004). *Intelligence testing and cultural diversity: Cautions, concerns and considerations.* Storrs, CT: National Research Center on the Gifted and Talented, University of Connecticut.

Ford, D. Y., & Frazier Trotman, M. (2000). The Office for Civil Rights and non-discriminatory testing, policies, and procedures: Implications for gifted education. *Roeper Review, 23*, 109–112.

Ford, D. Y., Harris III, J. J. (1999). *Multicultural gifted education.* New York: Teachers College Press.

Ford, D. Y., Harris, J.J., III, Tyson, C. A., & Frazier Trotman, M. (2002). Beyond deficit thinking: Providing access for gifted African American students. *Roeper Review, 24*, 52–58.

Ford, D. Y., & Joseph, L. M. (2006). Non-discriminatory assessment: Considerations for gifted education. *Gifted Child Quarterly, 50*(1), 41–51.

Ford, D. Y., & Whiting, G. W. (2006). Under-representation of diverse students in gifted education: Recommendations for nondiscriminatory assessment (part 1). *Gifted Education Press Quarterly, 20*(2), 2–6.

Glick, J. (1968, February). *Cognitive style among the Kpelle of Liberia.* Paper presented at the meeting on Cross-Cultural Cognitive Studies, American Educational Research Association, Chicago, IL.

Gould, S. J. (1996). *The mismeasure of man.* New York: W.W. Norton.

Greenfield, P. M. (1966). On culture and conservation. In J. S. Bruner, R. R. Olver, & P. M. Greenfield (Eds.), *Studies in cognitive growth* (pp. 225–256). New York: John Wiley & Sons.

Greenfield, P. M. (1997). You can't take it with you: Why ability assessments don't cross cultures. *American Psychologist, 52*, 1115–1124.

Greenfield, P. M. & Bruner, J. S. (1969). Culture and cognitive growth. In D. A. Goslin (Ed.), *Handbook of socialization theory and research* (pp. 633–660). Chicago, IL: Rand McNally.

Gregory, R. J. (1999). *Foundations of intellectual assessment: The WAIS-III and other tests in clinical practice.* Boston, MA: Allyn & Bacon.

Gregory, R. J. (2004). *Psychological testing: History, principles, and applications.* Boston, MA: Allyn & Bacon.

Gregory, S., & Lee, S. (1986). Psychoeducational assessment of racial and ethnic minority groups: Professional implications. *Journal of Counseling and Development, 64*, 635–637.

Groth-Marnat, G. (2003). *Handbook of psychological assessment* (4th ed.). New York: John Wiley & Sons.

Helms, J. E. (1992). Why is there no study of cultural equivalence in standardized cognitive ability testing? *American Psychologist, 47*, 1083–1101.

Helms, J. E. (2005). Stereotype threat might explain the Black-White test-score difference. *American Psychologist, 60*(3), 269–270.

Herrnstein, R. J., & Murray, C. (1994). *The bell curve: Intelligence and class structure in American life.* New York: Free Press.

International Reading Association. (1999). High-stakes assessments in reading: A position statement of the International Reading Association. *The Reading Teacher, 53*, 257–264.

Jencks, C., & Phillips, M. (1998). The black-white text score gap. Washington, DC: Brookings Institution Press.

Kaufman, A. S. (1993). King WISC assumes the throne. *Journal of School Psychology, 31*, 345–354.

Kaufman, A. S. (1994). *Intelligence testing with the WISC-III.* New York: John Wiley & Sons.

Kaufman, A. S., & Lichtenberger, E. O. (2000*). Essentials of WISC-III and WPPSI-R assessment.* New York: John Wiley & Sons.

LaRoche, M. J., & Shriberg, D. (2004). High stakes exams and Latino students: Toward a culturally sensitive education for Latino children in the United States. *Journal of Educational and Psychological Consultation, 15*, 205–223.

Lynn, R. (2006). *Race differences in intelligence: An evolutionary analysis.* Washington, DC: Summit Books.

Matsumoto, D. (1994). *Cultural influences on research methods and statistics.* Pacific Grove, CA: Brooks/Cole.

Miller-Jones, D. (1989). Culture and testing. *American Psychologist, 44*, 360–366.

Mokhtari, K., & Reichard, C. A. (2002). Assessing students' metacognitive awareness of reading strategies. *Journal of Educational Psychology, 94*(2), 249–259.

Naglieri, J. A., & Das, J. P. (1997). *Das-Naglieri Cognitive Assessment System.* Chicago, IL: Riverside Publishing Company.

Naglieri, J. A., & Ford, D. Y. (2005). Increasing minority children's representation in gifted education: A response to Lohman. *Gifted Child Quarterly, 49*(1), 29–36.

Naglieri, J. A., & Jensen, A. (1987). Comparison of Black-White differences on the WISC-R and the K-ABC: Spearman's hypothesis. *Intelligence, 11*, 21–43.

National Association for Gifted Children. (2001). *Position paper: Using tests to identify gifted students*. Washington, DC: Author.

Neisser, U. (2004). Serious scientists or disgusting racists? *Contemporary Psychology*, 49, 5–7.

Neisser, U., Boodoo, G., Bourchard, T. J., Boykin, A. W., Brody, N., Ceci, S. J., Halpern, D. F., Loehlin, J. C., Perloff, R. P., Sternberg, R. J., & Urbina, S. (1996). Intelligence: Knowns and Unknowns. *American Psychologist*, 51, 77–101.

Nicholas, S. L., Glass, G. V., & Berliner, D. C. (2005, September). High-stakes testing and student achievement: Problems for the No Child Left Behind Act. Executive Summary. NEA: National Education Association. Retrieved February 6, 2006, from http://www.org/esea/highstakesepsl.html

Nichols, S. L., Glass, G. V. & Berliner, D.C. (2005). High-stakes testing and student achievement: Problems for the No Child Left Behind Act. *Education Policy Research Unit*. Tempe, AZ: Arizona State University. Retrieved August 6, 2007 from http://epsl.asu.edu/epru/document/EPSL-0509-105-EPRU.pdf

Nichols, S. L., Glass, G. V, & Berliner, D. C. (2006). High stakes testing and student achievement: Does accountability pressure increase student learning? *Education Policy Analysis Archives, 14*(1). Retrieved August 6, 2007 from http://epaa.asu.edu/epaa/v14nl/.

No Child Left Behind Act of 2001, PL 107–110.

Office for Civil Rights (2005). *Annual report to Congress*. Washington, DC: U.S. Department of Education.

Ortiz, S. O. (2001). Best practices in nondiscriminatory assessment. In A. Thomas & J. Grimes (Eds.), *Best practices in school psychology IV* (pp. 1321–1336). Bethesda, MD: National Association of School Psychologists.

Perloff, R., Sternberg, R. J., & Urbina, S. (1996). Intelligence: Knowns and unknowns. *American Psychologist, 51*, 77–101.

Puckett, M. & Black, J. (2000). *Authentic Assessment of the Young Child: Celebrating Development and Learning (2nd Edition)*. New Jersey: Merrill/Prentice Hall.

Raymond, E. B. (2004). *Learners with mild disabilities: A characteristics approach* (2nd ed.). Needham Heights, MA: Allyn & Bacon.

Rogoff, B., & Chavajay, P. (1995). What's become of research on the cultural basis of cognitive development? *American Psychologist, 50*(10), 859–877.

Rosenshine, B. (2003, August 4). High-stakes testing: Another analysis. *Education Policy Analysis Archives, 11*(24). Retrieved February 6, 2006, from http://epaa.asu.

Rosenthal, R., & Jacobson, L. (1992). *Pygmalion in the classroom: Teacher expectation and pupils' intellectual development*. New York: Irvington Publishers.

Rowe, D. C. (Jan 2005). Under the skin: On the impartial treatment of genetic and environmental hypotheses of racial differences. *American Psychologist, 60*(1), 60–70.

Salvia, J., & Ysseldyke, J.E. (2001). *Assessment (8th ed.)*. Boston: Houghton Mifflin.

Sandoval, J., Frisby, C. L., Geisinger, K. F., Scheueneman, J. D. and Grenier, J. R. (Eds.). (1998). *Test Interpretation and diversity: Achieving equity in psychological assessment*. Washington: American Psychological Association.

Sattler, J. (1992). *Assessment of children* (rev. 3rd ed.). San Diego, CA: Author.

Sattler, J. (2001). *Assessment of children: Cognitive applications*. San Diego, CA: Jerome Sattler, Inc.

Scarr, S. (1978). From evolution to Larry P., or what shall we do about IQ tests? *Intelligence, 2*, 325–342.

Schulte, A. C., & Villwock, D. N. (2004). Using high-stakes tests to derive school-level measures of special education efficacy. *Exceptionality, 12*, 107–126.

Scribner, S. (1975). Recall of classical syllogisms: A cross-cultural investigation of error on logical problems. In R. J. Falmagne (Ed.), *Reasoning: Representation and process in children and adults* (pp. 153–273). New York: John Wiley & Sons.

Scribner, S. (1977). Modes of thinking and ways of speaking: Culture and logic reconsidered. In P. N. Johnson-Laird & P. C. Wason (Eds.), *Thinking* (pp. 483–500). Cambridge, England: Cambridge University Press.

Shaftel, J., Yang, X., Glasnapp, D., & Poggio, J. (2005). Improving assessment validity for students with disabilities in large-scale assessment programs. *Educational Assessment, 10*, 357–375.

Skiba, R. J., Knesting, K., & Bush, L. D. (2002). Culturally competent assessment: More than nonbiased tests. *Journal of Child and Family Studies, 11*, 61–78.

Sloane, F. C., & Kelly, A. E. (2003). Issues in high-stakes testing programs. *Theory into Practice, 42*(1), 12–17.

Snyderman, M., & Rothman, S. (1987). Survey of expert opinion on intelligence and aptitude testing. *American Psychologist 42*, 137–144.

Sparrow, S., & Gurland, S. T. (1998). Assessment of gifted children with the WISC-III. In A. Prifitera & D. Saklofske (Eds.), *WISC-III clinical use and interpretation* (pp. 59–72). San Diego, CA: Academic Press.

Spinelli, C.G. (2002). *Classroom assessment for students with special needs in inclusive settings*. Upper Saddle River, NJ: Prentice Hall.

Steele, C. M. (1997). A threat in the air: How stereotypes shape the intellectual identities and achievement of women and African Americans. *American Psychologist, 52*, 613–629.

Sternberg, R. J. (2000). The concept of intelligence. In R. J. Sternberg (Eds.), *Handbook of intelligence* (pp. 3–15). Cambridge, England: Cambridge University Press.

Suzuki, L., & Aronson, J. (2005). The cultural malleability of intelligence and its impact on the racial/ethnic hierarchy. *Psychology, Public Policy, and Law 11*(2), 320–327.

Taylor, R. L., Ziegler, E. W., & Partenio, I. (1984). An investigation of WISC-R Verbal-Performance differences as a function of ethnic status. *Psychology in the Schools, 21*, 437–441.

Townsend, B. L. (2002). "Testing while black": Standards-based school reform and African American learners. *Remedial and Special Education, 23*, 222–230.

Tuerk, P. W. (2005). Research in the high-stakes era: Achievement, resources, and No Child Left Behind. *Psychological Science, 16*, 419–425.

Tyerman, M. J. (1986). Gifted children and their identification: Learning ability not intelligence. *Gifted Education International, 4*, 81–84.

U.S. Department of Education (2002). *Elementary and Secondary School Civil Rights Survey (2002).* Retrieved January 20, 2007 from www.demo.beyond2020.com/ocrpublic/eng

Valdez, G., & Figueroa, R. A. (1994). *Bilingualism and testing: A special case of bias.* Norwood, NJ: Ablex.

Vygotsky, L. S. (1978). *Mind in society: The development of higher psychological processes.* Cambridge, MA: Harvard University Press.

Whiting, G. W., & Ford, D. Y. (2006). Under-representation of diverse students in gifted education: Recommendations for nondiscriminatory assessment (part 2). *Gifted Education Press Quarterly, 20*(3), 6–10.

Chapter 8

Culturally Responsive Community-Based Interventions

Other chapters in this text present culturally responsive inclusive practices for CLDE learners during school hours. Unfortunately, children often have too few opportunities to practice instruction on skills critical for intellectual and personal development beyond the school day. This is especially true for CLDE students with special needs. The school day is only a part of the daily learning experience; children also benefit from community-based instruction. The purposes for including a chapter on community-based interventions within a text on teaching diverse learners with exceptionalities are two-fold. First, CLDE learners often do not have readily available or do not readily access community resources that contribute to their school and long-term success, so one purpose is to identify such resources and discuss how schools might be instrumental in facilitating access. A second purpose is to point out that CLDE learners (like all children) must learn to live successfully in a variety of environments, including the community, which presents unique challenges and opportunities for CLDE learners and their families. This chapter offers rationales and suggestions for community-based inclusion practices. Community-based activities include employment, recreation, cultural activities, specialty programs (e.g., classes for art, music, dance, sports), religious programs, and community-wide resources (e.g., libraries, museums, and special community centers).

After finishing this chapter, readers will be able to answer the following questions:

1. What is community-based inclusion?
2. What is the legal basis for community inclusion?
3. What are the benefits of community-based inclusion for CLDE learners?
4. Why is after-school programming important for CLDE learners?
5. Why is planning necessary for community-based inclusion?
6. What is the role of educators in community-based inclusion for CLDE learners?
7. How might we make community-based programs more culturally responsive?
8. What are some community-based institutions that are important for CLDE learners?

This chapter will describe community-based inclusion and different types of community-based programs, including the primary purpose of each program and how each can address the needs of CLDE children. Specific strategies include:

1. How to include CLDE learners in public facilities such as libraries.
2. How to make community-based recreational activities more culturally responsive.
3. How to support community-based learning programs.
4. How to utilize religious institutions to support the CLDE learner's cognitive and personal development.

What Is Inclusion in a Community Setting?

The term *inclusion* has been used to describe the many different arrangements for children with disabilities relative to their typical peers. The level of involvement for a student with a disability can range from being on the periphery of an activity to being an integral participant, such as a starting player on a sports team. One definition of inclusion is "a place where everyone belongs, is accepted, supports, and is supported" (Stainback & Stainback, 1996, p.3). Inclusion means the meaningful involvement of children with disabilities with their nondisabled peers in activities that are primarily designed for nondisabled children.

At their best, community programs build on lessons learned during the school day or in children's homes to assist families and others to increase the social participation of children with disabilities. Educators know that simply placing children in a general education classroom does not mean the child will learn the academic information presented, become more socially skilled, or be socially included by peers (Division of Learning Disabilities, 2001; Freeman & Alkin, 2000). Inclusion's goal is to have children with disabilities actively participating in environments that are designed for typical children without lessening the quality of the experience for typical peers. In other words, successful inclusion is making the activity meaningful for children with disabilities, without diminishing the positive effects of the experience for typical children. In fact, the inclusion of children with disabilities should enhance the experience for all children.

Inclusion of persons with disabilities does not have to be expensive or require extensive alterations. Block and Zeman (1996) suggest that with minimal modification and little expense, people with disabilities can have access to community-based activities. Such access might include providing a ramp for persons in a wheelchair or modifying games so that persons with physical or sensory disabilities can fully participate.

How Can Inclusive Community Activities for CLDE Learners Be Provided During After-School Hours?

The school dismissal bell does not signal an end to the need for inclusive interventions for children with disabilities. Children with disabilities do not suddenly become nondisabled because they are no longer in classrooms. Nor do typically developing children become more willing to interact with children with disabilities simply because the school day has ended.

The task of including children with disabilities in all environments in which they live is important and carries lifelong ramifications. Successful inclusion during sport and recreation activities can promote positive relationships, improved self-esteem, cooperative skills, and improved on-task behavior (Block, 1998). The fact is that after-school hours are a critical time and provide opportunities for children to either progress toward closing the gap between their performance and that of their typical peers or having the gap increase.

It may not be appropriate to have all children with disabilities included in all activities all the time, since the nature of some disabilities may limit a child's participation. For example, children who have difficulty running or maintaining their balance may not be good candidates for a baseball team using standard rules. However, these children should be able to participate in a modified baseball activity (e.g., batting but having a peer run for them), and they may eventually develop the physical abilities for competitive baseball.

Malik's Story

It is the end of another school day. Malik Jackson is riding the school bus home with his friends. Malik is a seventh grader who spends part of his school day in general education classrooms and part in a resource room for children with learning disabilities. Malik has both academic and social skill deficits. Specifically, Malik is reading at the third-grade level. His science and social studies teachers are concerned because he is not able to read his assignments independently. Malik's teachers are also concerned about his off-task behavior (e.g., talking to peers at inappropriate times, being the class clown).

Malik's academic problems and social problems in school prevent him from participating in the school band despite the fact that he is a skilled drummer and plays for his church. Malik was retained in the second grade prior to his placement in special education. This has resulted in Malik being only one grade level ahead of his brother Rahsaan, who is two years younger. Rahsaan is a typically developing child who maintains a solid "B" average in school. The brothers generally get along well; however, when they do disagree, Rahsaan is quick to point out Malik's reading difficulties. Malik's typical response to his brother's insult is to hit him, something that has frequently gotten Malik in trouble with his parents.

Today, like most days, Malik and Rahsaan will arrive home to an empty house. Both Mr. and Mrs. Jackson work outside the home, and the family lives in a low-income section of the city. After arriving home, Malik and his brother will quickly leave for the local Boys and Girls Club. They are known as "latchkey" children. The phenomenon of latchkey children has become increasingly prevalent as families attempt to meet the economic challenges of the 21st century. Over 7 million school-age children are left alone at home each week (McWhirter, McWhirter, McWhirter, & McWhirter, 2004).

CHAPTER 8 • Culturally Responsive Community-Based Interventions   **191**

Using community members to assist in the classroom can make the environment more welcoming for CLDE learners.

Why should we be concerned about what happens after school to students like Malik? What kinds of experiences would contribute best to Malik's cognitive and social development? What kind of community resources would aid in this effort?

What Are the Benefits of After-School Programs for CLDE Learners?

Although CLDE children live in all areas of America, they are disproportionately located in urban centers. Urban centers often have higher crime rates, partly due to a higher concentration of people within the urban area. Living in neighborhoods where violence is prevalent can have an impact on children even if the children are not directly involved in the violence. Bell (1991) found that inner-city children living in high-crime areas have a higher incidence of sleep disturbances and aggressive behavior that are similar to behavior patterns seen in persons with posttraumatic stress syndrome.

To overcome these types of negative outcomes, programs that can provide positive alternatives to the risky behaviors that are so readily available in poor urban neighborhoods are needed. Risky behaviors may be particularly attractive to children with disabilities. Children with high-incidence disabilities, without guidance, may be easy prey for more streetwise youth. Structured after-school programs engage children in positive activities that reduce the likelihood of their being a victim of crime and of their perpetrating crimes (Cosden, Morrison, Gutierrez, & Brown, 2004). Marshall, Coll, Marx, McCartney, Keefe, and Ruh, (1997) found that the lack of adult supervision has a particularly negative impact on the social development of inner-city children, many of whom are from culturally diverse families.

After-school programs can help fill the void caused when working parents are unable to be home after school. The programs provide valuable opportunities for the children to practice or learn vital academic and social skills that can impact their school success (Cosden, et al., 2004; Gardner, Cartledge, Seidl, Woolsey, Schley, & Utley 2001). Effective after school programs may help some children avoid special education services by giving them the additional boost academically and socially that they require. For children with disabilities, after-school programs provide academic, recreational, and social skill opportunities in a structured, supportive environment. However, finding quality, affordable after-school programming continues to be a challenge for families in impoverished neighborhoods, despite the consistent evidence that such services are needed (Gardner & Talbert-Johnson, 2000; Halpern, 1992; Posner & Vandell, 1994).

Despite the best efforts of teachers, the school day may be insufficient to meet all the needs of children with disabilities. After-school programs can assist these children in practicing the skills that have been taught in school, thereby increasing the potential for mastery, retention, and generalization of the skills. Additionally, after-school programs may promote the development of new skills that teachers are unable to address due to time and curricular restraints. As with academic skills, the social deficits that CLDE children experience may require additional instructional time in order to close the social behavior gap between the children with disabilities and their typical peers. The community program may also provide more cultural continuity for CLDE learners than the school does. After-school programs may also offer activities not available in school (e.g., group counseling sessions, religious services, and community service). Children may discover new activities that they enjoy and at which they experience success.

Miller (2001) identified three categories of after-school programs: (1) those for school-age childcare that are designed to support child development by providing supervision for children of working families; (2) youth development programs like the Boys and Girls Clubs, Boy Scouts, and Girl Scouts that promote youth development and prevent risky behaviors; and (3) educational after-school programs that focus on improving academic achievement and decreasing gaps in academic achievement.

School-Age Childcare

School-age childcare programs, often called *latchkey* programs, are usually designed for elementary-age children whose parent(s) or guardians are at work when the children arrive home from school (Gardner & Talbert-Johnson, 2000; Tinnish, 1995). The primary purpose of these programs is to provide a safe environment for children (particularly young school-age children) while their parents work. Latchkey programs are operated throughout the year and provide a structured routine for children (Gardner & Talbert-Johnson). The programs generally provide the children with a nutritious snack and the opportunity to play and/or do homework under adult supervision. Latchkey programs are an important safety net for families.

Some working-poor families, however, cannot afford the fee associated with latchkey programs. Seventy-seven percent of poor children live in a family where someone has worked in the past year (McWhirter et al., 2004). Poor families are disproportionately minority: Approximately 31% of African American children and 28% of Latino children are poor (McWhirter et al.). Unless the families have help from the extended family or friends in the community, they have few viable options for providing a safe after-school environment for their children. This problem may be exacerbated when English is not the family's first language. In other words, limited English skills may cause a family to be unaware of childcare options, or members in the family may not possess the communication skills to access childcare services. Providing a family written information in their native language is one way to address this concern, but there is no guarantee that the family can read the information. Parents of linguistically diverse children may be illiterate in their native language just as many Americans are functionally illiterate in English.

When families do not have access to childcare options, they have few alternatives for keeping their children safe. Some families choose to leave their children home alone, limiting the children's opportunities to interact with others but possibly protecting them from street crime. Latchkey children are often "babysat" by the television or video games. Parents typically teach their latchkey children how to be safe when home alone and what to do if an emergency occurs. But despite the parents' best training efforts, children, especially those with disabilities, may display impulsive behaviors, such as letting a stranger into the house, inviting other children into the home, engaging in unsupervised cooking activities, or forgetting the emergency plan when accidents occur (e.g., forgetting to call 911). The fact is latchkey children may have difficulty distinguishing between a minor problem (e.g., scraped knee) and a true emergency (e.g., a cut that involves an artery).

Training latchkey children to be safe when home alone is a challenge both for parents of typically developing children and for parents of children with disabilities. It is impossible to prepare children for every problem that could happen when they are alone, so some families try to place their children in situations where other responsible adults are available. Libraries are free public facilities that are generally viewed as safe, and some families use libraries as if they were latchkey programs (Tinnish, 1995)—in fact, many unsupervised children spend after-school hours in libraries (Budziszewski, 1990; Tinnish, 1995), which challenges the libraries to meet the needs of this population. Some libraries have increased security, developed story hours, and invited agencies (e.g., the 4-H Club) to have their meetings in the library in an effort to attract unsupervised children (Dowd, 1992; Tinnish, 1995). The Rolling Meadows Library in Illinois provides refreshments, a film, a craft activity, or a book talk specifically for unsupervised children who have English as a second language (Dowd, 1992).

The difficulties of managing children in this environment may increase when a child has a disability. Many children with disabilities have trouble successfully managing their behavior. Children with mild disabilities (i.e., specific learning disabilities, mild mental retardation, or severe emotional disorders), in addition to their academic deficits, often have social skills deficits that may manifest in noncompliance, short attention, poor self-concept, and unsatisfactory interpersonal skills. These children often are physically indistinguishable from their typical peers, yet their behavior may be significantly different from that of other children under similar circumstances. For example, a child with behavior disorders who is instructed by an unknown adult to be quiet in the library may feel picked on and react inappropriately. Library personnel have few options when dealing with children who exhibit inappropriate behavior: asking the child to leave, having security escort the child from the premises, or, in extreme situations, contacting the police. All of these options remove the child from the relative safety of the library.

What can teachers do to promote positive results for their CLDE students in the library?

- Make sure students know what the behavioral expectations in libraries are by taking them to community or school libraries and explicitly teaching the expectations.
- Teach students how to use the library resources. By helping students identify books that fit their literacy skills, teachers can directly teach, along with the librarian, how to find a book or other resource (e.g., multimedia).
- Require students to apply for a library card. This also provides the library with family contact information.
- Instruct children in appropriate ways to ask for assistance. Who do I ask for help? Where can I find someone to assist me? Students with limited English proficiency or communication disabilities may need to have more practice in seeking assistance. Cue cards to prompt and support language can be used for this purpose.
- Help students develop a list of books, videos, and magazines that are of interest and appropriate for their skill level.

- Assist students in identifying books about culturally and linguistically diverse characters or historical personalities.
- When making specific assignments that require students to use the library, also give the assignment specifics to the library to be held at the front desk or some other designated place so that both the students and the library staff can have access to the teacher's directions as needed.

Libraries are a valuable community resource that, when used appropriately, can supplement school activities. Students should be encouraged to use their neighborhood libraries often, and libraries should seek to expand their appeal to the community. Japzon and Gong (2005) found that African Americans and Latinos underused neighborhood libraries while Whites and Asians tended to be actively engaged in using library resources. They also found that poor people tended to use library resources less frequently than middle-class people. If adults in general do not initiate trips to the library, then it is not likely that parents will take their children there without an additional incentive. As noted previously, teachers of CLDE students should plan regular field trips to neighborhood libraries and libraries could seem more welcoming to CLDE populations by featuring culturally sensitive materials and activities that reflect neighborhood demographics.

In addition to libraries and latchkey programs, other valuable programs include organizations such as the YMCA or the Boys and Girls Club. These have more flexibility than libraries and are better prepared to address children's inappropriate behaviors.

Youth Development Programs

After-school programs can provide structured, positive, and safe environments for children (Cosden et al., 2004; Gardner & Talbert-Johnson, 2000). The Boys and Girls Club, Boy Scouts, Girl Scouts, YMCA, YWCA, and 4-H Clubs focus on developing leadership skills, teamwork, a sense of belonging, and self-confidence in youth through various activities (e.g., organized sports, crafts, nature experiences, and so forth) that might otherwise be inaccessible to the children. Youth development programs strive to meet the needs of all children; however, like most community-based programs, they are a work in progress as they attempt to meet the needs of a growing population of CLD children as well as become more accessible to children with exceptionalities.

What Are Educational After-School Programs for CLDE Learners?

The number of educational after-school programs has been increasing since the late 1990s. These programs have an academic focus and are intended to assist CLD and poor children in closing the achievement gap. The 21st Century Community Learning Centers were initiated in 1998 during the Clinton administration with an appropriation of $40 million. Their purpose is to enhance the development of critical skills (i.e., academic, college preparation, and career development). The Bush administration has continued to expand the program, making it a key component of the No Child Left Behind legislation. Originally designed as school-based after-school programs targeting rural and inner-city schools, the learning centers have maintained their academic focus but now may be housed in nonschool buildings as well as in schools (U.S. Department of Education, 2006). Once a child has achieved grade-level performance, that child graduates from the program.

All three types of after-school programs are important and provide needed supports for children. Sometimes, in an effort to meet the needs of children, the distinctions become blurred. For example, later in this chapter you will read about an academic after-school program housed in the Boys and Girls Club (youth development program).

TEACHING TIPS

Inclusive After-School Programs

1. Identify a safe and convenient facility that is accessible.
2. Compare the after-school program hours to the school hours and calendar. Ideally, the after-school program will be in session when the school is closed.
3. Provide nutritious snacks for children.
4. Provide a variety of activities to meet the interests and needs of diverse participants. Acknowledge and celebrate culturally significant days (e.g., Cinco de Mayo).
5. Make "working together" an ongoing theme of the program. Explicitly teach children how to include others who have physical, cognitive, cultural, and language differences. Adults should model inclusive behavior. Prominently display pictures and artifacts that reflect the culture of the people who live in the neighborhood.
6. Regularly invite CLD professionals to participate in the program.
7. Implement effective instructional practices with ongoing assessment to determine how each participant is progressing.
8. Develop a communication system between the home and the after-school program.
9. Provide information in the native language of the parents.

Revisiting Malik

At the beginning of this chapter, we met Malik, a seventh grader who spends part of his school day in general education classrooms and part in a resource room for children with learning disabilities. Malik has both academic and social skill deficits. He attends the Boys and Girls Club 5 days a week. Ms. Green, the club director, asks Malik if he wants to participate in a new academic program designed to improve children's reading skills.

Malik is reluctant to give up his gym time for reading (something he dislikes). Ms. Green reminds him of his poor grades and that if he does not improve his reading, his grades will not improve. Malik agrees to take the permission letter for the reading program home to his parents. Mr. and Mrs. Jackson are excited about the additional reading help for Malik and make Malik promise to attend regularly. Ms. Green asks Malik to sign an agreement that he will participate in the reading program three times a week for 6 months, and on days when he is scheduled to read, that he will read first before playing in the gym.

The tutor works with Malik for 30 minutes three times a week using explicit phonic instruction, oral reading of books, and fluency training. The tutor also assists Malik with his homework, time permitting. Malik is able to graph his performance after each session and can see he is making progress by looking at the increase in words read correctly per minute on his graph. Malik has improved from 64 words read correctly with five errors in a minute to over 120 words read correctly per minute with only one error, in less than 3 months. He is also beginning to feel more confident in reading orally.

After Malik has been in the program for 2 months, the tutor begins monthly telephone contacts with his teachers to check on Malik's school performance. After 4 months, his teachers indicate that Malik is reading more accurately and seems to have greater confidence when reading orally. The teachers state that Malik still needs academic assistance but is making continuous progress in keeping up with his assignments. His grades should show an improvement in the next grading period. He has also decreased his silly behavior in class.

Malik knows that with improved grades and teacher recommendations he may get his chance to play in the school band. The additional reading instruction made a significant difference in his attitude toward reading as well as in his reading skills. As a result, Malik feels more positive about school and his ability to be successful.

How Can We Serve CLDE Students Through Community-Based Programs?

Malik and his family benefit in several ways from the community after-school program. Mr. and Mrs. Jackson have a safe place to send their boys. There are a variety of activities, so the boys can choose to be together or in different activities. Malik has the opportunity to improve his reading skills that can positively impact his school performance.

The fact is, all families with children face the task of finding community-based programs that can meet their children's unique needs. Families who have children with disabilities must also find programs that have a positive attitude toward including their children in the programs and a willingness to modify activities (when necessary) to allow these children to fully participate. Families from diverse cultures also seek programs that are culturally relevant and inclusive toward their children.

Programs should project positive images of the children's cultures and should provide adult role models. During the day, children with disabilities from diverse cultures typically attend schools that have few, if any, teachers from the same ethnic background (National Clearinghouse for Professions in Special Education, 2002). Often, the authority figures these children encounter throughout a school day are almost entirely from European American backgrounds, a concern especially in poor neighborhoods where there are fewer positive professional role models. As mentioned earlier, poor children tend to be disproportionately minority, and they often attend schools along with other poor children from families who themselves have limited education (Orfield & Kornhaber, 2001).

Community-based programs provide a venue for CLD professionals who are working during school hours to engage in positive relationships with children. Successful minority adult professionals can be role models and help by telling the children how they achieved success in their careers. It is important for CLD children to see successful adults from their cultural and linguistic background. For example, encouraging Native American or Hispanic American professionals to participate in after-school programming by tutoring, coaching, or counseling can send a powerful message to young CLD children who might not be aware of all the opportunities available to them.

Finding inclusive culturally responsive community programs, as we have said, can be a daunting task, even for the most resourceful and supportive family. Yet, effective inclusive community-based programs can make a significant difference in the lives of CLDE children and their families. Inclusive programs let families select activities that allow all of their children (i.e., children with and without disabilities) to fully participate, thereby eliminating the need for separate programs or having to decide which child will have the opportunity to participate in a program. Think how difficult it might be for Mr. and Mrs. Jackson to find two separate after-school programs for Malik and Rahsaan. Community participation in a supportive environment allows children to develop skills, such as making friends, communicating needs, expressing concerns, working with others toward a common goal, handling difficulties, and so forth—all skills important for success in adulthood.

Community-based inclusion is not just a nice idea; it is grounded in U.S. law.

Community-Based Inclusion and the Law

A strongly held belief in American society is that each person deserves an opportunity to pursue happiness. Historically, this opportunity has not been afforded to persons with disabilities or to CLD persons. During the latter part of the 20th century, laws were enacted to assist persons with disabilities to secure the same privileges as nondisabled citizens. Section 504 of the Rehabilitation Act of 1973 expressly prohibits discrimination on the sole basis of a disability in programs and activities that receive federal funding. Federal law recognizes that people not only need access to an "appropriate education" (P.L. 105-17 IDEA, 1997) but to other community opportunities that give added value and substance to our lives.

The requirement to provide access to community resources was stated again in the Americans with Disabilities Act (ADA) (1990). ADA extended civil rights protection to individuals with disabilities in private business and further emphasized their need for access to public services, public accommodations, telecommunication, and transportation. The goal of these federal acts is to provide equal access to community resources (both public and private) for all citizens (see Table 8–1).

Although the goal of equal access for persons with disabilities has not been completely achieved, tremendous progress has been made in the last 40 years. Millions of individuals with disabilities have had access to community resources previously denied to them and their predecessors. Obviously, children with disabilities also need access to community resources, such as employment, libraries, extracurricular programs, after-school programs, religious services, and summer programs. Opportunities for employment, academic

TABLE 8–1 Federal laws and community-based inclusion

Year	Law	Community Implications
1966	Amendments of the Elementary and Secondary Education Act (P.L. 89-313)	Provided monies in various settings for state-supported programs for children with disabilities
1968	Handicapped Children's Early Assistance Act (P.L. 90-538)	Established the experimental programs for preschool children with disabilities called the "first chance network"
1973	Section 504 of the Rehabilitation Act (P.L. 93-112)	Persons cannot be excluded from programs receiving federal funds solely based on a disability
1983	Amendments to the Education of the Handicapped Act (P.L. 98-199)	Funding for schools to work with and for services for preschool children
1986	Rehabilitation Act amendments (P.L. 99-506)	Development of supported employment programs
1990	American with Disabilities Act (P.L. 101-336)	Provided private-sector civil rights protection for persons with disabilities. Provided access to public services, accommodations, transportation, and telecommunication

enhancement, social and spiritual activities, and recreation and sports allow children to develop their abilities, expand their network of friends, increase their independence, and contribute to society. For a complete discussion of community-based transition issues, see Chapter 13.

Why Do CLDE Learners Benefit from Well-Designed Community-Based Programs?

Why is access to community resources so critical for individuals with disabilities? One reason is that there are many essential skills that children learn beyond the school day that better prepare them to be productive adults (Abery, 1991). First, community-based programs, such as after-school programs, Boy Scouts and Girl Scouts, clubs, the YMCA, and academic skill-building programs, can develop skills that will enhance social acceptance, physical activity, goal-seeking behavior, and teamwork skills through sport and recreational activities.

Second, children have the opportunity to learn important emotional skills as they experience both team success and failure. Structured activities with a diverse group permit children with disabilities to acquire important social skills and acceptance across the barriers of cultural, linguistic, and skill differences. Children learn their strengths and weaknesses and those of others in a variety of activities. They can then use this new awareness to play to each other's strengths to achieve a common goal.

Third, academic skill-building programs can supplement school instruction and allow children with disabilities valuable opportunities to practice academic skills. Gardner et al. (2001) reported that urban children with and without disabilities could improve their math and reading skills during an after-school academic enrichment program. Frazier-Trotman (2002) found that inner-city African American children at elementary to secondary grade levels could achieve significant reading improvement through a structured, peer-mediated program using Direct Instruction (DI) materials. Corrective Reading DI is a phonetic based remedial reading intervention that is designed for persons with a history of reading failure (Englemann, Hanner, & Johnson, 1989). The lessons are scripted and students are required to achieve mastery of each lesson prior to moving to the next lesson. Frazier-Trotman (2002) found that children made over a year's gain in their reading achievement during the 6 months they participated in the DI program.

Fourth, the inclusion of children with disabilities in after-school activities allows typically developing children opportunities to interact with them in ways that often do not occur during the school day. Without careful planning, children with disabilities may be included in general education classrooms but have limited interactions with other students in the class. Sometimes the very structure of the classroom does not lend itself to interaction. The most common method of delivering instruction is the teacher-led whole-class arrangement (Woolsey, 2001), which usually limits the number of interactions between children. Children are usually warned not to talk with each other and to respond directly to the teacher instead. Poor-achieving students are frequently those least likely to speak up in class (Wolford, Alber, & Heward, 2001), possibly due to their insecurities.

Even inclusion during nonacademic times does not guarantee interactions between children with and without disabilities. Children with disabilities are often isolated during free-time activities on the playground or in the gymnasium. Chamberlin (1999) found that students with disabilities were "socially isolated" in an inclusive physical education class in an urban school. Place and Hodge (2001) found social isolation and segregated inclusion of children with physical disabilities in an urban middle school. "Segregated inclusion refers to a separation of children/youth with disabilities from peers without disabilities in terms of proximity and social isolation, refers to feelings of discomfort, awkwardness, and isolation of children/youth with disabilities from peers without disabilities" (Hodge, Yahiku, Murata, Von Vange, 2003, p. 23) In other words, segregated inclusion occurs when children with and without disabilities are in the same class or activity but the two groups primarily interact among themselves, creating a physical distance between the groups. Social isolation refers to the emotions that the child with disabilities may feel in regard to the social exclusion. Without intervention, social isolation and segregated inclusion can limit peer interactions and can impede the development of relationships between children with and without disabilities.

Fifth, children with disabilities can experience benefits from effective community-based programs similar to those of their typical peers, including friendships, positive self-images, and the positive use of time (Abery, 1991). People tend to form relationships with people who have similar interests. For example, children who enjoy playing soccer may more readily interact with each other because of their mutual passion for soccer. In order for children to develop an interest in an activity, they must have some exposure to it. Children who are poor and/or culturally diverse may have few opportunities to explore new activities. Similarly, children with disabilities are sometimes limited in their exposure to activities, not by their disabilities, but by the attitudes of other people in positions of authority. Block and Malloy (1998) found that nondisabled peers and parents were more receptive to the idea of including a child with a disability in a regular softball league than were the softball league coaches. If those in charge of activities in the community do not permit children with disabilities access, the opportunity is lost for the child to experience and determine if they are interested. As is the case for nondisabled learners, inclusive community programs provide CLDE learners with positive activity choices. See Table 8–2 for information about the types of after-school activities and their benefits to children.

TABLE 8-2 Benefits of inclusive community programs

Type of Program	Example	Benefit
Library	Summer reading program	Reading for pleasure, improved reading skills
Library	Free access to books, computers, and software	Learn about new computer software and ability to obtain information
After-school programs	Academic skill building or homework-assistance program	Additional opportunities to build important academic skills and improve school grades
After-school programs	Recreational and sport programs	Social and physical skill development
Recreation program	Physical activities, arts and crafts, intramural sports	Team skills (e.g., learning how to work with others toward a common goal), leisure activities
Sport programs	T-ball, football, soccer	Competition skills (e.g., learning how to respond appropriately to winning and losing), team skills
Vocations	Job, career awareness	Establishing and developing positive relationships with others, earning money, following directions, accomplishing goals
Religious	Worship, religious classes, fellowship	Opportunities to build positive family and friend relationships; moral development

Sixth, community-based programs are important because they provide unique opportunities for CLDE children. These programs have some distinct advantages over traditional school programs, including:

- More flexibility than school programs. The lack of specific guidelines allows for more professional discretion. Poor CLDE children often have less exposure to positive opportunities in the community that can nurture important cognitive and social skills.
- Less bureaucracy.
- Potential for closer connection to the parents.
- More freedom for CLDE children to select activities that interest them rather than following a prescribed curriculum.

Community after-school programs have been found to be especially beneficial for poor children living in low socioeconomic communities (Posner & Vandell, 1994). In addition to the benefits, however, they also face some unique challenges:

- Many community programs have staff that has less formal training than school staff. Therefore, the staff may not have been exposed to empirically based inclusive strategies. Or, staff may lack information about characteristics of children with disabilities.
- Community-based programs often have fewer resources than schools to meet the wide range of needs of children with disabilities. Community-based programs may need to use low-cost or no-cost inclusive strategies due to financial constraints.
- Community-based programs often have less information about children's individual needs and usually do not use the same type of formal tracking process found in the school setting (e.g., IEPs) that allows for the effective transfer of information across staff and time.
- Community-based programs are confronted with a wider range of children's ages and skill diversity than is typically found in a classroom, where children are placed according to educational guidelines. These types of institutional requirements are generally not a part of community-based programs.

Despite these challenges, community-based programs can play a valuable role in the development of children with disabilities and should be expected to provide inclusive programs of high quality.

An Example of a Community-Based Program for CLDE Learners: Project D.E.L.T.A.A.

Project D.E.L.T.A.A was a collaborative project between the Boys and Girls Club, the graduate chapter of Delta Sigma Theta Sorority (a predominantly African American sorority), and The Ohio State University. The project was designed to improve the reading and math skills of urban youth who attended the local Boys and Girls Club. The youth came from the surrounding neighborhood, which was an impoverished section of the city with a high crime rate. The club had approximately 300 members, with approximately 70 children attending on a typical day. The majority of the children who attended and all the children who participated in the project were African American and all had significant reading deficits, including youth both with and without designated disabilities.

Members of Delta Sigma Theta sorority and students in the special education program at The Ohio State University volunteered to be the adult tutors for this project. The tutors were trained to use the Corrective Reading Direct Instruction curriculum (Englemann et al., 1989) and provided reading instruction and homework assistance for the children. The club director selected four teenage members of the club to be trained as reading tutors using the DI materials. Tutoring sessions were conducted three evenings a week, from 4:30 to 6:30 P.M.

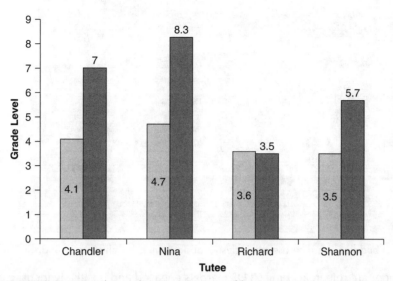

FIGURE 8–1 Reading achievement scores of four tutees in Project D.E.L.T.A.A. as measured on the Slosson Oral Reading Test

The teenage and adult tutors taught the children/tutees one-on-one using the DI materials. All of the children who regularly attended the tutoring made important academic gains in reading; one tutee (Richard) had long absences (e.g., one absence lasted 4 consecutive weeks) and therefore, his reading achievement did not improve. Four tutees were targeted for extensive data collection. Figure 8–1 shows a sampling of their data. There was no difference in the effectiveness of the adult tutors compared to the teenage tutors, who were given adult assistance with their homework. The teenage tutors, like the tutees, demonstrated improved school grades throughout the duration of the project.

The academic activities also included math instruction. The elementary and middle school learners participated in math facts intervention using reciprocal peer tutoring. In groups of two the participants took turns presenting math facts to each other using index cards that had one math fact printed on each card for 5-minute periods. The tutor presented the index cards one at a time to the tutee until the 5 minutes had elapsed. After the practice, the tutee was tested on how many problems he or she could answer correctly in 1 minute. Then the tutor and tutee switched roles and repeated the procedure. Each participant improved in accuracy and fluency in mathematics facts.

How Can We Make Community-Based Interventions More Culturally Responsive?

As we have pointed out many times, the United States is becoming increasingly diverse. Many community programs include children who are from culturally and linguistically diverse populations who represent as well a continuum of abilities, from gifted to severe disabilities. Culturally and linguistically diverse children are at greater risk of dropping out of school. They perform less well than European American students on standardized tests (Orfield & Kornhaber, 2001; Viadero & Johnston, 2000), especially if they come from a poor family (Diaz-Rico & Weed, 2002). Effective community-based programs can play an

Peer buddies can increase the inclusive opportunities for children with disabilities.

important role in keeping CLDE learners engaged and positively focused on socially appropriate goals by providing children with positive experiences within the context of their own community and culture. Recognizing culturally relevant holidays—such as Cinco de Mayo, Chinese New Year, and Kwanzaa—and acknowledging the accomplishments of historical and current members of the community are important ways to respect diverse cultures. If written information is part of an activity, then information needs to be provided in the primary language of the participants. As mentioned earlier, pictures and modeling the activity are good ways to teach the skills needed to participate if communication barriers exist. It is always good to have the participants demonstrate the activity in response to instruction to ensure that all essential aspects of the activity have been communicated.

Culturally responsive teaching is evidence-based instruction that is sensitive to the unique needs of learners from culturally and linguistically diverse families (Tam & Gardner, 1997). Educators increasingly understand the need for instruction that more closely matches the experiences and learning styles of a diverse student population. Culturally responsive instruction uses the abilities that a child has and environmentally familiar information to teach new skills. Instruction that builds on a child's knowledge base should decrease the size of the information gap that a child experiences. These same tactics can be used in after-school programs.

Inclusive Games

Recreation facilities are busy places, with children coming and going at various times. Each child who comes to the facility brings a particular set of skills and experiences. Recreation leaders must provide activities that are flexible enough to include all the children who want to participate. Kasser (1995) suggests using the MAGIC principles for modifying or developing inclusive games:

M = Motivational
A = Age-appropriate
G = Growth oriented
I = individualized
C = Comparable

Motivational.   Activities should emphasize the game rather than the developmental skill. Activities need to be fun to be motivational.

Age-Appropriate.   Allow children to participate in activities similar to those of their peers: "[F]or example, a junior high student with a physical disability should be afforded the opportunity to learn and play in a modified football game and not merely offered wheelchair obstacle courses or throwing to targets" (Kasser, 1995, p. 8).

Growth Oriented.   All activities should promote skill development. Activities should only be modified enough to allow success, while remaining a challenge.

Individualized.   Activities should allow each child to be challenged and feel a significant part of the game.

Comparable.   "Less skilled players should not be assigned only as the scorekeeper or as the turner for the jump rope. Instead, they should have opportunities to develop the skills that would allow them to play a variety of positions or share in many aspects of the activity" (Kasser, 1995, p. 9).

Using the MAGIC principles, adults should select wholesome games and activities that are culturally specific and help build needed skills. As noted elsewhere in this text, CLD learners are more likely to subscribe to collective or peer-based activities where youngsters support each other in a community of learning. Following are examples of peer-focused activities.

Cooperative Teaming

Cooperative teaming is culturally sensitive and allows for inclusion of children with disabilities. Children can be placed in cooperative teams for activities such as treasure hunts or making art collages that allow each member to be invested in the process and make a contribution. Since each member is invested in the task, members must work together to achieve the best results. Members choose topics of personal or cultural interest.

Peer Buddy Systems

Peer buddy systems have proven to be an effective tool in assisting children with disabilities in inclusive settings (Block, 2003). This can be achieved by recruiting typical peers to assist children with disabilities during recreation activities. Typical children either volunteer or are assigned to be a peer buddy, with the understanding that being a peer buddy might compromise some of their practice time. The role of the peer buddy is to ensure that the child with a disability has the opportunity to participate and has supportive feedback. If modifications are needed for inclusion, the peer buddy is made aware of the modification and makes sure that the modifications are in place during the activity. Of course, the peer buddy needs to be carefully trained in how to give social praise for appropriate behavior as well as appropriate corrective feedback. At times, students from the same cultural background might be assigned to each other, if deemed important for mentoring purposes. At other times (if available) cross-cultural assignments might be made for the purpose of promoting cultural understanding and awareness.

> **TEACHING TIPS**
>
> **Including Learners with Sensory and Physical Disabilities**
>
> 1. Recruit typical peer buddies to help peers with disabilities to participate fully in activities.
> 2. Make sure the buddy can perform the designated task and knows how to maximize the special-need student's involvement.
> 3. Teach the peer buddy how to use social praise appropriately to reinforce and encourage effort.
> 4. Rotate peer buddy responsibilities so that they do not always fall on the same peers.
> 5. Identify activities that are of high interest to the child with a disability and that can help the CLDE child's inclusion by peers.

Planning for Individuals with Severe Disabilities

Children with severe disabilities present the most difficult challenge for establishing and maintaining interactions with typical peers beyond the school day. To remove community barriers, professionals need to work effectively with families to help them gain access to resources, including financial support (e.g., waiver programs) (U.S. Department of Health and Human Services, 2002). Professionals working with families to meet the unique needs of each child are essential in achieving more meaningful access to the community for CLDE children. The family and friends of a person with severe disabilities can help by becoming part of a supportive team that can aid in providing age-appropriate and interesting experiences for the child. Offerings from the federal and state governments might prove valuable too, but it is important to note that CLD families might find accessing these resources particularly challenging due to lack of information about what is available or about how to navigate bureaucratic red tape. Professionals should make sure families know their rights and how to access these resources.

Religious Institutions

For many people, religion is an important part of family life, particularly for those from diverse backgrounds (e.g., Gutman & McLoyd, 2000; Kim, Kim, & Kelly, 2006). Parents who attend religious services want to share their beliefs, moral perspectives, and cultural values with their children. They view the transmission of this information as an important part of the parental role. Having a child with a disability may increase the parents' desire for spiritual understanding (Stainton & Besser, 1998). Engaging in religious activities with family members is an important part of the development of children with disabilities. It provides another way for families to bond, increases the child's support network, and assists in social maturation.

Religious institutions (e.g., churches, synagogues, temples, mosques) are increasing their efforts to accommodate individuals with disabilities, not only as spectators but also as participants in various religious experiences (McNair & Swartz, 1995). Schools need to recognize the beneficial role that religious institutions can play in educating CLDE learners. Religious institutions often provide social services and recreational opportunities for their members (Willis, 1992). Religious institutions also often provide informal or formal learning programs that greatly benefit learners (e.g., Gardner et al., 2001). As noted previously, high-achieving, low-socioeconomic African American students were involved in more community and religious activities than their low-achieving African American peers (e.g., Gutman & McLoyd, 2000).

Educators might advise religious institutions on how to overcome barriers, such as making physical facilities more accessible for individuals with disabilities, how to access resources (e.g., sign language interpreters for the deaf) appropriate for individuals with special needs, and how to manage the atypical behaviors of certain children such as those with attention or behavior disorders. Additionally, educators can support these institutions by sharing strategies that are effective in both religious and academic instruction.

Summary

Community-based inclusion is a crucial component in the overall development of CLDE children and youth. Worthwhile community-based activities provide CLDE youth with opportunities to increase their intellectual and social skills, develop friendships, expand their life experiences, and pursue activities of interest. Educators can play a role in this process by sharing information about community resources and assisting families with strategies that might enable their children to fully benefit from the community offerings. All children with disabilities can participate in community-based activities.

Although not every child will be able or want to participate in every activity, meaningful activities should be available in an after-school program to every child regardless of disability. Some children may participate in an academic program while others play table games, read, or do computer activities. CLDE learners need to be able to choose from a full range of activities and not be limited to those designated for those with disabilities. All positively structured activities can help social and/or academic development.

School personnel can help to promote community involvement by introducing CLDE youth and their families to the various options available, such as libraries and museums. They can teach students how to use these facilities and encourage them to access them frequently. Teachers might advise and collaborate with community-based persons who want to reinforce the learner's schooling or personal development.

Community inclusion is more than just a nice idea; it has a legal foundation. Civil rights laws guarantee that individuals cannot be discriminated against because of race, culture, language, or ethnic background. The Americans with Disabilities Act similarly prohibits discrimination based on exceptionalities.

Effective community-based inclusion involves adults with positive attitudes about children with disabilities, typical children that are willing to participate in activities with children who have disabilities, activities that are not diminished in appropriateness for typical children when modified for children with disabilities, cultural sensitivity, and empirically sound intervention.

Related Learning Activities

1. Develop a list of community resources within a 5-mile radius of your school.

2. Survey your students about their interests and their after-school activities. Identify which students participate in after-school or weekend learning activities such as after-school tutoring. Where are these activities located—public schools? local churches? community centers? Which of your CLDE students participate in ethnically specific community activities such as learning a family language like Spanish or Japanese?

3. Visit a community resource—the local library or museum. What services are offered for young people the age of your students? What accommodations are made for students with disabilities? What culturally specific activities are available for students? Does the library, for example, prominently display children and young adult books by and about individuals from CLD backgrounds? Are there CLD books and materials that can be read easily by your students? What activities provided by the library would you recommend for your students?

4. Select a student in your class who, in your opinion, would benefit from some community-based program. Visit the facility and make a list of the offerings that would benefit your student. Interview the staff about their expertise with students with disabilities. Also find out what the staff might provide to make the learner's experience culturally responsive. Explore the family's interest in involving their child in such programs.

References

Abery, B. (1991). Promoting social inclusion beyond the school community. *Impact, 4,* 16–17.

Bell, C. (1991). Traumatic stress and children in danger. *Journal of Health Care for the Poor and Underserved, 2,* 175–188.

Block, M. E. (1998). Don't forget about the social aspects of inclusion. *Strategies, 12,* 30–34.

Block, M. E. (May, 2003). Inclusion: Common problems—practical solutions. *Teaching Elementary Physical Education,* 6–12.

Block, M. E., & Malloy, M. (1998). Attitudes on inclusion of a player with disabilities in a regular softball league, *Mental Retardation, 36,* 137–144.

Block, M. E., & Zeman, R. (1996). Including students with disabilities in regular physical education: Effects on nondisabled children. *Adapted Physical Activity Quarterly, 13,* 38–49.

Budziszewski, M. (July/August, 1990). Latchkey children in the public library now common. *Feliciter, 47,* 2.

Chamberlin, J. L. (1999). *Inclusion in physical education: the students' voice.* Unpublished master's thesis. The Ohio State University, Columbus, Ohio.

Cosden, M. Morrison, G., Gutierrez, L., & Brown, M. (2004). The effects of homework programs and after-school activities on school success. *Theory to Practice, 43*(3), 220–225.

Dalaker, J., & Naifeh, M. (1998). *Poverty in the United States: 1997. Current Populations Report* (Series p.60-201). Washington, DC: Government Printing Office.

Darling-Hammond, L. (1996). The right to learn and the advancement of teaching: Research, policy, and practice for democratic education. *Educational Researcher, 23,* 5–17.

Diaz-Rico, L. T., & Weed, K. Z. (2002). *Cross-cultural language, and academic development handbook: A complete K–12 reference guide* (2nd ed.). Boston: Allyn & Bacon.

Division of Learning Disabilities. (2001). Award-winning researchers raise questions about "inclusion" *DLD Times, 18,* 4.

Dowd, F. S. (1992). Library latchkey children. *ERIC Digest EDO-PS-92-1.* Clearinghouse on Elementary and Early Childhood Education. (Retrieved February, 26, 2006), from http://ceep.crc.uiuc.edu/eecearchive/digests/1992/dowd92.html

Englemann, S., Hanner, S., & Johnson, G. (1989). *Direct instruction: Corrective reading.* Columbus, OH: Macmillan.

Frazier-Trotman, M. (2002). *A model academic after school program in an urban African American community.* Unpublished doctoral dissertation. The Ohio State University, Columbus, OH.

Freeman, F., & Alkin, M. (2000). Academic and social attainments of children with mental retardation in general education and special education settings. *Remedial and Special Education, 21,* 3–18.

Fuchs, D., Fuchs, L. S., Mathes, P. G., & Simmons, D. C. (1997). Peer-assisted learning strategies: Making classrooms more responsive to diversity. *American Educational Research Journal, 34,* 174–206.

Gardner, R., Cartledge, G., Seidl, B., Woolsey, L., Schley, G., & Utley, C. (2001). Mt. Olivet after school program: Peer mediated interventions for at-risk students. *Remedial and Special Education, 22,* 22–33.

Gardner, R., & Talbert-Johnson, C. (2000). School reform and desegregation: The real deal or more of the same? *Education and Urban Society, 33,* 74–87.

Gutman, L. M., & McLoyd, V. C. (2000). Parents' management of their children's education within the home, at school, and in the community: An examination of African-American families living in poverty. *The Urban Review, 32*(1), 124.

Halpern, R. (1992). The role of after-school programs in the lives of inner city children: A study of the urban youth network. *Child Welfare, 7,* 215–230.

Heron, T. E., Villareal, D. M., Yao, M., Christianson, R. J., & Heron, K. M. (2006). Peer tutoring systems: Applications in classrooms and specialized environments, *Reading and Writing Quarterly, 22,* 27–45.

Heward, W. L. (2006). *Exceptional children: An introduction to special education* (8th ed.). Upper Saddle River, NJ: Merrill/Prentice Hall.

Hodge, S. R., Yahihu, K., Murata, N., & Von Vange, M. (January, 2003). Social inclusion or social isolation: How can teachers promote social inclusion for students with disabilities? *Teaching Elementary Physical Education, 14*(3), 29–32.

Japzon, A. C., & Gong, H. (2005). A neighborhood analysis of public library use in New York City. *Library Quarterly, 75,* 446–463.

Kasser, S. L. (1995). *Inclusive games: Movement fun for everyone!* Champaign, IL: Human Kinetics.

Kim, I. J., Kim, L. I. C., & Kelly, J. G. (2006). Developing cultural competence in working with Korean immigrant families. *Journal of Community Psychology, 34*(2), 149–165.

Lieberman, L. J., Dunn, J. M., van der Mars, H., & McCubbin, J. (2000). Peer tutors' effect on activity levels of deaf students in inclusive elementary physical education. *Adapted Physical Activity Quarterly, 15,* 64–81.

Maheady, L., Sacca, M. K., & Harper, G. F. (1988). Classwide peer tutoring with mildly handicapped high school students. *Exceptional Children, 55,* 52–59.

Marshall, N. L., Coll, C. G., Marx, F., McCartney, K., Keefe, N., & Ruh, J. (1997). After-school time and children's behavioral adjustment. *Merrill-Palmer Quarterly, 43,* 497–514.

McNair, J., & Swartz, S. L. (1995). Local church support to individuals with developmental disabilities. *Education and Training in Mental Retardation and Developmental Disabilities,* 304–312.

McWhirter, J. J., McWhirter, B. T., McWhirter, E. H., & McWhirter, R. J. (2004). *At-risk youth: A comprehensive response.* (3rd ed). Toronto, Canada: Brooks/Cole.

Miller, B. M. (2001, April). The promise of after-school programs. *Educational Leadership, 58,* 6–12.

National Clearinghouse for Professions in Special Education. (2002). *Just the facts: Percent of special education teachers by racial group 1999–2000.* Retrieved April 25, 2006, from http://www.specialedcareers.org/pdf/Se_teachers_ethnicity.pdf

Orfield, G., & Kornhaber, M. L. (2001) (Eds.). *Raising standards or raising barriers? Inequality and high stakes testing in public education.* Washington DC: The Century Foundation Press.

PL 105-17: The Individuals with Disabilities Act [IDEA] Amendments (June 4, 1997). The 105 U.S. Congress. Retrieved August 14, 2007 from http://frwebgate.access.gpo.gov/cgi-bin/getdoc.cgi?dbname=105_cong_public_laws&docid=f:publ17.105.pdf

Place, K., & Hodge, S. R. (2001). Social inclusion of students with physical disabilities in general physical education: A behavioral analysis. *Adapted Physical Activity Quarterly, 18,* 389–404.

Posner, J. K., & Vandell, D. L. (1994). Low-income children's after-school care: Are there benefits effects of after-school programs? *Child Development, 65,* 440–456.

Premack, D. (1959). Toward empirical behavior law, I: Positive reinforcement. *Psychological Review, 66,* 219–223.

Robinson, D. R., Schofield, J. W., & Steers-Wentzell, K. L. (2005). Peer and cross-age tutoring in math: Outcomes and their design implications. *Educational Psychology Review, 17,* 357–362.

Rohrbeck, C. A., Ginsburg-Block, M. D., Fantuzzo, J. W., & Miller, T. R. (2003). Peer–assisted learning interventions with elementary school students: A meta-analytic review. *Journal of Educational Psychology, 95,* 240–257.

Stainback, S., & Stainback, W. (Eds.) (1996). *Inclusion: A guide for educators* (2nd ed.). Baltimore, MD: Paul Brookes.

Stainton, T., & Besser, H. (1998). The positive impact of children with an intellectual disability on the family. *Journal of Intellectual and Developmental Disability, 23,* 57–70.

Tam, B., & Gardner, R., III (1997). Multicultural education for students with behavior disorders: Much to do about nothing or a real issue? *Addressing Cultural and Linguistic Diversity in Special Education: Issues and Trends, 2,* 1–11.

Tinnish, D. (1995). Latchkey kids & the library. *Emergency Librarian, 23*(2), 17–19.

U.S. Department of Education (2006). *Guide to U.S. Department of Education programs.* Washington, DC: Office of Communication and Outreach. Retrieved March 14, 2007, from http://www.ed.gov/programs/21stcclc/index.html

U.S. Department of Health and Human Services, (2002). *Delivering on the Promise: Self-evaluation to promote community living for people with disabilities.* Report to the President on Executive Order 13217. Washington DC: Author.

Viadero, D., & Johnston, R. C. (2000). Lifting minority achievement: Complex answers. *Education Week, 19* (30), 14–16.

Willis, W. (1992). Families with African American roots. In E. W. Lynch & M. J. Hanson (Eds.), *Developing cross-cultural competence: A guide for working with young children and their families* (pp. 121–150). Baltimore, MD: Paul Brookes.

Wolford, T., Alber, S. R., & Heward, W. L. (2001). Teaching middle school students with learning disabilities to recruit peer assistance during cooperative learning group activities. *Learning Disabilities Research & Practice, 16,* 161–173.

Woolsey, M. L. (2001). *The use of echobehavioral analysis to identify the critical behavioral variables in two types of residential classrooms for students who are deaf.* An unpublished doctoral dissertation at The Ohio State University, Columbus, OH.

PART 3

Culturally Responsive Instruction

Chapter 9

Understanding Effective Instruction for CLDE Learners

Educators and members of the larger society as well are increasingly concerned that too many culturally and linguistically diverse exceptional (CLDE) learners receive a poorer quality of education within highly restrictive environments, compared to their nonminority peers (National Academy Press, 2002). In addition, the achievement gap between CLD learners and European American students has been well documented (Callins, 2006; Winzer & Mazurek, 1998), pointing to the need for a heightened commitment by schools to appropriate education for all students, largely through effective instruction.

The purpose of this chapter is to present the principles of effective instruction. It describes the research base for the principles of effective instruction and identifies those practices that are effective with children from diverse cultural and linguistic backgrounds. After completing this chapter, readers should be able to answer the following questions:

1. What is effective instruction?
2. How has legislation improved instruction for CLDE learners?
3. How do you measure the effectiveness of instruction for CLDE learners?
4. What is meant by scientifically valid practices?

5. Why is effective instruction so critical for CLDE learners?
6. How do teacher qualifications and expectations affect instruction for CLDE learners?
7. How can culturally responsive components be incorporated into effective instruction?

What Is Effective Instruction?

The effectiveness of instruction is often measured by student performance on a standardized test. High-stakes tests, as discussed in Chapter 7, have become an important part of the education landscape. They provide a snapshot of the overall performance of a school or school district; however, these tests do not provide an assessment of individual teacher effectiveness. As used in this text, *effective instruction* refers mainly to instruction delivered by individual teachers and that promotes desired achievement outcomes for each student. We view effective instruction as a five-step process, which we will discuss here and in Chapter 10.

First, the teacher must assess each child to determine the current academic skill level. Second, the teacher must translate that assessment into school/district curriculum outcomes to determine the instructional needs of the child. That is, the teacher must analyze the student's performance on the assessment so that the student can be given curriculum materials at the appropriate instructional level. Third, the teacher needs to identify the instructional materials and strategies to be used with each student. Not all children enter school at the same skill level. Some will have different entry points to the curriculum and may need different instructional materials and/or strategies. Fourth, teachers must regularly assess or progressively monitor the effectiveness of their instruction. That is, teachers must ensure that children are accurately acquiring the information presented with the proficiency desired. Fifth, teachers need to make sure that the skills taught will be maintained over time and transferred to other skills as appropriate.

Kiwan's Story

Kiwan is an 18-year-old African American high school graduate. He attended an urban high school where the majority of the students were from low-income minority families. He is the youngest of three brothers. Both of his brothers were involved in illegal street activities. A street rival killed one brother as he was coming out of a neighborhood grocery store, and the other brother is in jail on drug-related charges. Kiwan's mother has also been in and out of prison.

Kiwan, like an incarcerated uncle and his deceased brother, is a gifted athlete. At 6 feet and 240 pounds and with the ability to run the 40-yard dash in 4.7 seconds, he proved to be a formidable middle linebacker for his high school football team. Kiwan's gifts on the athletic field were, however, not duplicated in the classroom, where he experienced significant academic difficulties.

Kiwan was diagnosed with a learning disability in elementary school. He was exempted from statewide assessments of academic achievement due to his severe learning disability. Although he graduated from high school reading at a beginning second-grade level, he was accepted at a state university as a partial qualifier (under the National Collegiate Athletic Association rules). In other words, if he paid for school (or received financial aid) during his freshman year and if he was able to be successful in his first year of college, he would be given a football scholarship.

Kiwan's learning disability clearly has had a negative impact on his academic achievement. However, part of Kiwan's academic difficulties appeared to be due to ineffective classroom instruction. For example, Kiwan's reading program during his senior year consisted of listening to books on tape (he was not asked to complete any comprehension assignments related to the books on tape). He says that he was unable to follow along as he listened to the book because he could read so few words that he was not sure if he was looking at the same word that was being read on the tape. All of his tests were read to him, and he was rarely asked to write. Yet, Kiwan demonstrates above-average verbal skills and superior social skills. Kiwan talked wistfully to his postsecondary tutor about how his middle school teacher instructed him in reading using phonics and how he made progress in learning to read. However, that type of instruction stopped when he entered high school. At this point (immediately following high school), he just wants to learn how to read so he can have a chance to be successful in college, possibly make it to the NFL, and read a story to his daughter.

One of the questions to be addressed in this chapter is what more effective instructional strategies might have been employed with Kiwan during his schooling? What are the cultural factors that might play a role in Kiwan's education? What strategies might the professional consultant use now to help Kiwan? We'll return to Kiwan's story later.

What Is the Legislative Impact on Effective Instruction?

Before presenting the research on the principles of effective instruction, we should acknowledge that education law has played a significant role in encouraging the development of empirically based educational practices. Both the No Child Left Behind (2001) and the Individuals with Disabilities Education Improvement acts (2004) call for educators to identify and implement empirically validated instructional strategies. No Child Left Behind (NCLB) requires school districts to provide effective instruction for all children and to demonstrate the effects of instruction by annual testing. As noted elsewhere, an achievement gap exists between European American youth and most subgroups of CLDE learners. NCLB stresses the importance of this issue and mandates that school systems disaggregate the annual test data to show what the yearly progress is for students with disabilities and for those from culturally and linguistically diverse backgrounds. Under these conditions, schools are challenged to use teaching practices that produce the highest returns (i.e., effective instruction). But even though federal laws mandate the implementation of effective instruction in schools, they do not provide clear definitions of what constitutes effective instruction. For a more detailed discussion of special education laws, see Chapter 2.

Educators are required to use student-generated data to guide instructional decisions. In other words, the students' performance in the curriculum must serve as a guide for planning future lessons. Are students learning the content or skill at the appropriate pace? For example, a teacher may design and implement a unit on writing complete simple sentences. The teacher would begin by collecting data on the students' prior knowledge of writing complete simple sentences and then prepare the unit based on an analysis of the students' preinstruction knowledge and on curricular expectations. During the instructional unit, the teacher would constantly examine the effects of instruction by analyzing the students' responses to questions, assignments/project quality, and quizzes/tests performances. The teacher would either reteach the information or move to new content based on the daily performance of the students. This process would continue until the students reach the predetermined mastery level for the content.

Effective Instruction: A Five-Step Process

What Are Effective Assessments for CLDE Learners?

Appropriate assessments are critical to the effectiveness of instruction. Assessments are used to identify the student's current level of performance, how that student compares to others, and whether the student is making appropriate progress in the curriculum or has mastered the skill(s) being taught.

Formal Assessments. Formal assessments usually consist of standardized tests that are used to help identify whether a student has a disability (diagnosis) and/or how the student's skills compare to peers' skills (achievement). Formal assessments—for example, the Woodcock Reading Mastery-III (WJ-III) (Woodcock, McGrew, & Mather, 2001), the Metropolitan Achievement Test (2000), and so on—are norm-referenced instruments, which means they have been normed on a representative sample population so that student performance can be compared to the normed peer group. These assessments typically have strict protocols that must be followed for the results to be valid.

A type of formal assessment that can measure one or more content areas is the achievement test. The data generated from these tests tend to be global, that is, the tests provide an overall rating (e.g., grade level equivalent) of each skill measured. Achievement tests rarely provide information specific enough for teachers to develop effective lesson plans, however.

Diagnostic tests, formal tests designed to be administered individually, provide specific, detailed information on the skill(s) being assessed. For example, a diagnostic reading test will typically assess skills in phonemic awareness, phonics, letter and word identification, oral reading fluency, and comprehension. These tests include several assessment items within each skill area, but the items are only representative, not exhaustive. Thus, a particular reading test, for example, may not include all the phonetic sounds in the English language but would select representative sounds one would expect the learner to know at specific grade levels. The tests are progressive, covering several grade levels in order to assess the general grade level of the learner.

Formal assessments are important to effective instruction. First, they can help identify students who are significantly above or below their peers in content-area knowledge. Second, they allow comparisons to be made across school districts, schools, and classrooms. Nevertheless, with CLDE populations, formal assessments must be used and interpreted with caution. A major limitation is that significant numbers of children with disabilities and/or children from diverse cultures may not have been included in the normative samples. As discussed in Chapter 7, standardized tests are often constructed using typically-developing, majority students as the model. The tests are then used to assess and evaluate CLDE learners who may not have been adequately represented during the test norming process.

Informal Assessments. Informal assessments are teacher-made assessments that are usually tied directly to the classroom curriculum. Teachers use informal assessments to identify instructional objectives for students and to measure student progress. These measures are typically short, quick, and curriculum-based, and thus are a good tool for directly measuring the impact of instruction on learners (Deno, 2006).

Curriculum-based measures (CBM) tend to be the assessment tool most sensitive to changes in students' ability with regard to instruction. CBM can be used frequently, which quickly reveals student learning patterns, and therefore allows teachers to monitor the progress of each student closely. Frequent assessment also provides critical information to both the teacher and the students about the effectiveness of the instruction because there is a direct relationship between content and the assessment tool. The teacher can then make decisions about future instruction based on assessment data.

Students often find it reinforcing to see their own progress as measured by CBM. For example, Gardner, Cartledge, Seedl, Woolsey, Schley, and Utley (2001) assessed the reading performances of urban African American children using CBM. One-minute fluency timings were used to check both accuracy and speed by charting daily performances, and each child was able to see his own progress. Students would make comments like "I really improved today!" or "I can do better." Another common example of frequent assessment is the weekly spelling test, with children held accountable both to improve their scores from week to week and to master words not spelled correctly on the test.

Teachers need to have ongoing data on the effect of instruction if they are to make the appropriate changes, in a timely manner, to instruction based on students' performances. There are numerous ways to track students' performance, for example, line graphs, cumulative graphs, tables, frequency counts, or percentages of accuracy. Data can be recorded by the teacher, student, peers, or through a computer program. Assessments can be short and should focus on the target skill, for example, a 1-minute assessment of reading accuracy, which records correctly and incorrectly read words, or, a 1-minute assessment of math facts. Writing can be assessed using timed (5–10 minutes) writing probes.

Figure 9–1 is an example of assessing the phonemic awareness (phoneme segmentation fluency, PSF, and nonsense word fluency, NWF) and oral reading fluency (ORF) of three kindergarten ELL learners (Klett, 2006), who were assessed two to three times per week. Although the students were receiving instruction in these skills, the baseline data show that Faith and Adam, two of the lower-performing students in the class, were making no progress. Once Faith and Adam started receiving small-group instruction they began, as shown in the intervention data, to make noticeable and consistent progress. It took Faith a little longer to begin to benefit from the small-group instruction, but that provided the trainer the information necessary to make instructional adjustments so that Faith could make the substantial progress noted. Sam, on the other hand, one of the more skilled ELL students, needed the small-group instruction to help him focus on NWF and ORF. The regular assessments helped to target instruction to his specific needs and to monitor the effects of the instruction.

Commercially available materials may be useful for monitoring pupil performance. For example, Klett (2006) used probes from the Early Reading Intervention curriculum (ERI) (Simmons & Kame'enui, 2003) for frequent assessment of PSF and NWF. The Dynamic Indicators of Basic Early Literacy Skills (DIBELS) (Good & Kaminski, 2003) can be used for initial assessments and progressive monitoring of oral reading fluency. DIBELS, a tool that has features of both formal and informal assessments, assesses students' reading skills using 1-minute timing. Like the formal assessments, DIBELS has a strict protocol, can serve as a screening tool to identify both high- and low-functioning students in reading, and is normed for the general school population. Like the informal assessments, it can be given repeatedly, provides teachers with clear, specific information that they can use to develop appropriate lessons, and can be used to monitor the effectiveness of instruction.

In summary, commercial instruments can provide information useful in guiding effective instruction. However, caution needs to be exercised in using these instruments with CLDE learners. Regular curriculum-based assessments and progressive monitoring are probably more beneficial to this population. Such assessments yield a more accurate portrait of skills the student needs to develop, help determine whether instruction is effective, and establish when the learner has achieved the desired skill levels. These assessments may also be used to provide feedback to the learner, which may further motivate the student to achieve.

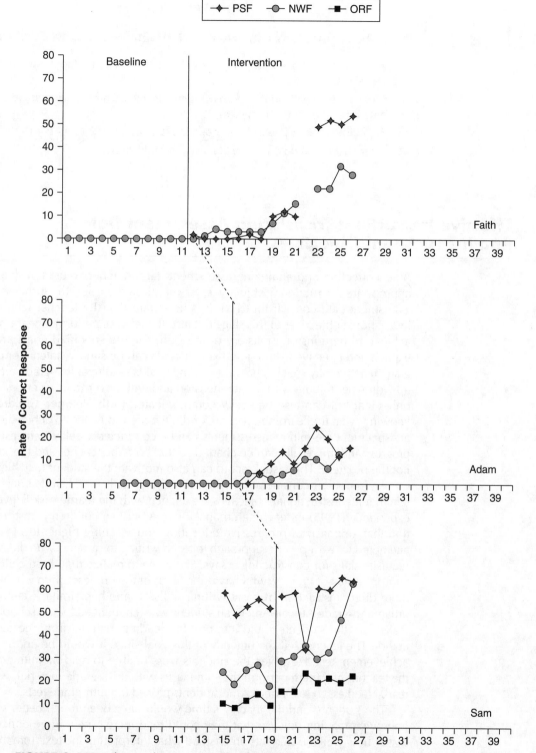

FIGURE 9-1 Baseline and intervention data on phoneme segmentation fluency, nonsense word fluency, and oral reading fluency for Faith, Adam, and Sam

> **TEACHING TIPS**
>
> **Assessments for Instructional Effectiveness with CLDE Learners**
>
> 1. For instructional purposes, emphasize curriculum-based rather than standardized measures.
> 2. Make assessments brief and easy to implement. Commercially available instruments may be useful for this purpose.
> 3. Regularly assess students for academic progress on important skills.
> 4. Graph learners' data and let them see their progress.

Effective Instruction: Translating Assessment Data into Instructional Objectives

After collecting and analyzing assessment data, teachers must translate that data into appropriate instructional objectives. As mentioned earlier, this process is easier if the assessment data come from CBM. It is important that the teacher identify not only the instructional objectives at this stage but also the level of performance the student needs to achieve to demonstrate mastery of the skill. Clearly specified goals are important for explicit and effective instruction. Explicit goals can be simply stated. For example, a first-grade teacher may specify that one reading goal is reading a first-grade reading passage at 40 words per minute with comprehension and with fewer than 10 errors. This goal is not only clear but can also be easily communicated to the learner. Children benefit from knowing what the learning goals are and often are motivated to achieve goals when they are specific. One-minute assessments can be conducted weekly to measure the student's progress and the results can be charted so that both the teacher and the student can monitor the progress. This visual record can also motivate the student to achieve the goal.

An important consideration when specifying goals for CLDE learners is to make certain that the instructional objectives are aligned with the learners' skill levels. Lisa Delpit's experience (1995) in teaching urban African American children is instructive. In a situation that emphasized progressive education and teaching higher-level skills, Ms. Delpit attempted to use a *process* approach to teach writing to students who did not have the prerequisite skills for constructing essays. She came to realize that these children did not suffer from a lack of fluency, which was the focus of the process approach, but rather needed more direct instruction in basic writing skills. In another, similar example, a teacher of urban fifth-grade African American students was challenged by the school's curriculum to make sure the students could interpret the reading material from the perspective of the author. The teacher felt the urgency of this goal since it would be on the end-of-the-year achievement test. However, the students were unable to read the fifth-grade material, so the teacher had them perform the same tasks with third-grade material, which they could read. Needless to say, none of the students passed the fifth-grade tests.

The students' and the teacher's time would have been much better spent focused on improving reading skills so that they could read increasingly more difficult material. No matter how well the students understood what interpreting the text from the perspective of the author meant, if they could not read the fifth-grade material, they would not be able to complete the test item. What we teach students needs to begin with the skills they bring to the situation and then we must systematically move them on to the higher-level skills. It makes little sense to try to start at the top without a foundation of basic skills. Schools often fail to address these critical skill deficits, with the result that CLDE students consistently fall further behind.

Effective Instruction: Standards and Strategies

What Are the Professional Standards for Effective Instruction?

If teachers are to utilize empirically-based instructional practices in their classrooms, then they will need to understand what the quality indicators are for each of the research methodologies. A scientifically validated instructional strategy is one that has been analyzed using rigorous experimental methodology and has been shown to have a strong positive impact on student learning. In January 2003, the Council for Exceptional Children, Division of Research, established a task force to examine the issue of different research methodologies and their relevance in special education (Odom, Brantlinger, Gersten, Horner, Thompson, & Harris, 2005). Four types of research methodologies were identified: (1) experimental group, (2) correlational, (3) single-subject, and (4) qualitative. Research on educational practices may be conducted through these various research designs, which were discussed in a special edition of *Exceptional Children* (Winter, 2005), where Odom et al. pointed out the difficulty of designing evidence-based studies in special education but did identify quality indicators of valid evidence-based practices. For example, if an educational practice (e.g., a particular reading method) were repeatedly studied and validated under rigorous research conditions, then that practice would be considered "evidence based."

Effective Instruction: An Evidence-Based Practice

How does an instructional strategy become one that a teacher can confidently use knowing there is substantial data indicating that the strategy is an effective instructional tool? Let's examine how peer tutoring became empirically validated (Heron, Villareal, Yao,

It is important to determine if each student has the prerequisite skills needed to master the material being taught.

Christianson, & Heron, 2006). In discussing peer tutoring, it is important to first draw a distinction between informal peer-tutoring common to classrooms and peer-tutoring systems. Informal peer tutoring typically involves one student who has successfully completed an assignment (or who has a higher skill level) assisting another student in completing an assignment. Although informal peer tutoring can be of assistance to both teacher and students, it usually involves minimal guidelines, rarely includes data collection, and has minimal supporting empirical data (Wagner, 1990).

Peer-tutoring systems are instructional tools that can be used to teach skills systematically. Peer-tutoring systems have clear, research-based rules that are essential to the success of the instruction. Over the past few decades, peer-tutoring systems have received a great deal of attention from researchers (Robinson, Schofield, & Steers-Wentzell, 2005), whose findings have consistently shown that systemic peer tutoring can improve the academic achievement of students (Franca, Kerr, Reitz, & Lambert, 1990; Greenwood, Delquadri, & Hall, 1984; Heron et al., 2006; Robinson et al., 2005). Considering the vulnerability of many CLDE learners to academic failure, educators should make every effort to use strategies that have been thoroughly validated in the research literature.

Peer-tutoring systems have emanated primarily from four centers across the United States: the University of Kansas Juniper Gardens Children's Project (CWPT—ClassWide Peer Tutoring), Vanderbilt University Peabody College (PALS—Peer Assisted Learning Strategies), SUNY Fredonia (CSTT—Classwide Student Tutoring Teams), and The Ohio State University (Classwide Peer Tutoring). The foundational methodologies of the four systems have important commonalities. Each involves a training component (of teachers, students or both), frequent and active peer-mediated student responding, and an evaluation element. Empirical data have shown these peer-tutoring systems to be effective for learners with and without disabilities, across ages, ethnicities, and socioeconomic status (e.g., Al-Hassan, 2003; Fuchs, Fuchs, Yadian, & Powell, 2002; Gardner, Cartledge et al., 2001; Heron et al., 2006; Robinson et al., 2005). Over 30 years of data indicate that these systems are effective in promoting student achievement (Rohrbeck, Ginsburg-Block, Fantuzzo, & Miller, 2003). Much of the research cited shows them to be highly effective with CLDE learners. These results allow teachers to use any of the peer-tutoring systems knowing that the strategy is validated by empirical data.

What Are Effective Instruction Strategies?

Researchers have studied instructional practices since the early 20th century. John Dewey (1916) wrote that children learn more effectively "by doing," and he advocated actively engaging children in order to improve their skills.

Academic Learning Time (ALT). In the 1970s, there was renewed focus on identifying elements of effective instruction. The concept of Academic Learning Time (ALT) arose during the Beginning Teacher Evaluation Study (BTES) (Berliner, 1979). ALT is defined as "engaged time with materials or activities that produce a high success rate and are related to the outcome measures being used" (Berliner, 1980, p. 305). Academic learning time focuses on the instructional activities that maximize the student's engagement with learning and enhances the student's learning.

Opportunity to Respond (OTR). Researchers who were guided by behavioral principles independently developed another line of research on teaching. Charles Greenwood and his colleagues at Juniper Gardens used ecobehavioral assessments that allowed them to systematically examine the relationship between teacher and student classroom behaviors

(Greenwood, Delquadri, & Hall, 1984; Greenwood, Delquadri, Stanley, Sasso, Whoroton, & Schulte, 1981). Opportunity to respond (OTR) and ALT are similar in that both focus on student activities during instruction and are concerned with increasing the amount of time the student is engaged in academic tasks. There are also differences between OTR and ALT. ALT is more general and does not qualify the type of student behavior except to say that the student should have a high rate of success. OTR emphasizes the frequency of student response to the instructional stimulus so that teachers can provide corrective feedback and social praise, thereby promoting achievement. Teachers can improve academic achievement by increasing the number of opportunities to respond that the students have during instruction (Greenwood, Arreaga-Mayer, & Carta, 1994). One instructional strategy closely associated with the OTR literature is peer tutoring. Classwide peer tutoring allows for a high level of OTR with immediate feedback from the tutors on the quality of the tutee's responses.

Active Student Responding (ASR). Researchers consistently find a positive relationship between active engagement and academic achievement (Gardner et al, 2001; Harrison, 2002; Heward, 2006). Active student responding is an observable response made to instructional stimulus. The student who writes the numeral 4 when asked the sum of 2 plus 2 is making an academic response to an instructional stimulus or task. ASR promotes the efficient use of instructional time to accelerate student achievement. It offers several advantages, in that it permits a teacher to readily assess a pupil's skill acquisition and make subsequent instructional decisions. While observing students write answers to a series of facts, the teacher can quickly assess if they are developing the skills and can continue with the instructional sequence as planned. If numerous errors are noted, on the other hand, and students continue to need extensive prompting, the teacher can immediately make crucial instructional adjustments and limit the possibility that students will practice errors. Additionally, ASR is correlated with increased on-task behavior (Lambert, Cartledge, Lo, & Heward, 2006). Off-task behavior is usually incompatible with ASR. Decreasing off-task behavior allows for more efficient use of instructional time.

Instructional strategies associated with ASR are peer tutoring, response cards, repeated readings, choral responding, and guided notes (see Chapter 10). Each of these strategies promotes high levels of active student engagement with feedback during instruction on the accuracy of student responses. During peer tutoring, the tutors provide the feedback. Teachers provide the feedback when response cards and choral responding are used. During instruction using guided notes, students can compare their written responses to the teacher's lecture key.

Why are ASR strategies important for CLDE learners? As noted previously in this chapter, many CLD students are academically behind their majority or nonminority peers. ASR strategies permit CLD students to be taught more to allow them to catch up with their peers (Kame'enui & Simmons, 1990). Greenwood, Hart, Walker, & Risley (1994) found that the instruction used in inner-city schools tended to promote low rates of student engagement, contrary to what researchers have found to be effective instruction. As we have discussed, active student engagement improves academic achievement (Gardner, Heward, & Grossi, 1994; Heward, 1994). Greenwood et al. (1994), examining over 10 years of research, determined that low student rates of academic responding were a critical factor in the progression of developmental retardation. Developmental retardation, caused by poor instruction, results in children who are significantly behind their chronological peers in mastery of the basic academic skills. Without intervention, the achievement gap between poor/CLDE learners and their affluent peers only increases.

By design, ASR strategies force learners to make many more responses to academic materials, and high response rates are positively correlated with academic achievement. Another advantage of ASR strategies for culturally diverse populations is the increased opportunities they provide for peer-based interventions. Peer tutoring, repeated readings, choral responding, and even response cards lend themselves to peer-mediated formats. Greater peer orientation and preference for collaborative instructional activities have been empirically documented among some CLD learners (e.g., Ellison, Boykin, Tyler, & Dillhunt, 2005). Furthermore, these strategies can foster more positive classroom environments and help create a caring community of learners, considered to be especially critical for CLD students (e.g., Gay, 2000; Ladson-Billings, 1994).

Effective Instruction: Progressive Monitoring

To be effective, it is imperative that teachers closely monitor the performance of CLDE learners. The procedures for regular assessment are the same as noted previously, but we reiterate the important point that these procedures are necessary both for determining what to teach in the beginning and later for assessing whether the instruction has been effective. It is not uncommon for these children to have substantial academic losses within a relatively short time period. Musti-Rao (2005), for example, found that children who performed at benchmark or strategic levels on the DIBELS at the beginning of the school year were performing at strategic or intensive levels by midyear. These children were in classrooms where phonemic awareness skills were being taught, but they were not benefiting from the large-group instruction. They all made pronounced gains when given supplementary small-group instruction and closely monitored for progress. Another consideration is that many CLDE students will not receive close monitoring or assistance at home on their skill development. This is especially true for ELL students like Faith, Adam, and Sam, whose assessment data were shown in Figure 9–1. These children were from Somalia and there was no evidence that their parents spoke or read English. Many U.S.-born parents also have literacy limitations and are unable to monitor or coach their children.

Effective Instruction: Maintenance and Generalization

Maintenance

Teachers must not only teach students to mastery level but must also design instructional environments that promote the maintenance of instructed skills. In order to accomplish this goal of skill maintenance, teachers need to sequence skill instruction so that new skills are connected to previously learned skills and provide multiple opportunities for students to practice previously learned skills. In addition to teacher-directed reviews, classroom activities might be structured so that students are directed to centers, games, computer programs, and other materials (including homework) designed for practice of previously taught skills.

Generalization

Like maintenance, generalization is a critical component in skill instruction. The goal of academic instruction is to provide students with a set of skills that can be utilized in whatever settings the student will need them. For example, children are instructed in reading so that whenever they come across printed materials they are able to use their reading skills to comprehend the printed information. Teachers need to plan for generalization, especially with children who have disabilities. Oftentimes, children with disabilities do not transfer skills learned in school to other environments without purposeful instruction designed to promote skill generalization. Teachers need to teach multiple examples of a skill (e.g., $4 \times 4 = 16$, $4(4) = 16$, $4^2 = 16$, $4 \cdot 4 = 16$, 4 times 4 equals 16, 4 multiplied by 4 equals 16, 4 squared equals 16). It is often impossible to instruct on each possibility, but it is possible to instruct on a number of exemplars so that when the student is faced with untaught examples he or she will have a better opportunity to respond correctly to the stimulus.

What Are Some Special Considerations for Effective Instruction of CLDE Learners?

Teacher Quality

The research literature verifies that high-quality teachers are best equipped to positively impact the achievement of poor and minority students (Ohio Department of Education, 2006). Unfortunately, poor and minority children are least likely to be taught by high-quality, experienced teachers. Children in urban schools and SED classrooms in particular are more likely to have less-experienced teachers, teachers not fully licensed, or teachers from alternative teacher education programs (Billingsley, Carlson, & Klein 2004: Peske & Haycock, 2006). Having the least experienced teachers teach students who represent the more challenging end of the student population creates a potentially disastrous situation. The result is that everyone loses—students do not receive the most effective instruction; teachers become frustrated, disillusioned, and may leave the profession; and school systems struggle to keep qualified teachers in their most difficult schools/classrooms.

Teachers need to be fully prepared (i.e., receive instruction and practice) to implement effective instruction with diverse learners. Poorly prepared teachers often blame the students and their families for lack of academic achievement (Delpit, 1995) and therefore assume little or no responsibility for pupil failure. *Teacher preparation and inservice programs need to provide extensive training and experience with effective instruction practices. This is key to* ensuring that CLDE children receive quality instruction.

Low Expectations

Teachers are key to the academic development of children. They have the capacity to open or shut the doors to new worlds of opportunity for their students. Teacher perceptions of children can be influenced by variables that are not directly related to academic achievement (e.g., internalized values or beliefs) (Winzer & Mazurek, 1998); they need to have high expectations that all children, including CLDE learners, can achieve (Patton, 1997). When teachers have positive expectations for students, they are more apt to provide high-quality instruction (Brophy & Good, 1986). This is especially critical for CLDE learners. Teachers' high expectations for this population lead not only to quality instruction but also to helping CLDE learners believe in themselves, to believe that they are capable of being successful students.

In order to have and maintain high expectations, teachers need to experience success in their teaching, and to be successful in their teaching, teachers need to use effective strategies. If they have a limited instructional repertoire or lack cultural sensitivity, they may become frustrated with students' lack of progress, assume students are incapable of learning, and lower their expectations for their own and the pupils' success. This type of outcome points up the critical need for highly qualified teachers for CLDE populations. Most of these children will not come from homes where parents can make up the difference. If we are to close the achievement gap, then, we must provide CLDE learners with well-prepared teachers skilled in effective instructional practices who are knowledgeable in the subject matter, believe in their students, and know how to get their students to believe in themselves.

Culturally Specific Strategies

Effective instruction includes culturally responsive teaching. Teachers have a responsibility to all of their children to help them achieve to the best of their ability (Richards, Brown, & Forde, 2007). Incorporating culturally sensitive information into the instructional materials is an effective way to do that (Richards et al., 2007; Tam & Gardner, 1997). The standard U.S. curriculum is based on the assumption that most children attending school will have had similar experiences that allow them to readily understand the teacher's lessons. Children from diverse families who come to school with a different set of experiences often have difficulty mastering the standard curriculum. This difficulty has little to do with intelligence and more to do with exposure. Culturally responsive teaching requires that teachers be familiar with the culture(s) of the students in order to integrate students' culture into the content in a manner that maintains the integrity of the content while promoting interest and academic achievement among the students. For example, in the following "Revisiting Kiwan" section, the instructor incorporated both Kiwan's personal interests and his cultural background into his reading instruction.

Culturally sensitive, empirically sound instruction allows teachers to give children new opportunities for knowledge. For example, the Assembly of Alaskan Native Educators (2007) recommends that teachers regularly participate in community events and incorporate the local environment and community resources into their lesson plans, thereby linking the instruction to the everyday lives of their students.

Following are some questions adapted from Grant and Gomez (2001) that a teacher should ask about a culture group.

1. What are the contributions of this cultural group to U.S./world history?
2. What are the important cultural values (including religion)? How are they similar to and different from U.S. middle-class values?

Effective instruction is key to students learning to read.

TEACHING TIPS

Appropriate Educational Programming

1. Believe in and program for the success of CLDE learners.
2. CLDE learners need strategies that are evidenced based and provide for high response rates.
3. Select instructional goals that are aligned with student skill levels.
4. Closely monitor student performance and adjust instruction as needed.
5. Utilize materials and concepts from the learner's cultural background in instructional strategies.

3. Who are some famous individuals from this cultural group?
4. What are the current political concerns of this group? What type of discrimination might members of this group experience?
5. What are the cultural group's special days?
6. How can I incorporate the students' culture into the curriculum?

Revisiting Kiwan

Earlier in this chapter we introduced Kiwan, a graduating senior with a learning disability who was accepted for college. Kiwan was placed in a summer reading and writing program.

Although it was not possible to completely close the achievement gap between Kiwan and his college freshmen peers, a program was designed to accelerate his mastery of reading and writing. The reading program consisted of Corrective Reading DI, level B1 (Engelmann, et al., 2002), which is designed for students who are beyond the third grade but continue to experience difficulty in reading. Scripted DI lessons allow multiple tutors to easily and efficiently participate in Kiwan's instruction. The Corrective Reading series is an accelerated phonics reading program utilizing faultless communication and high levels of ASR. Students do not move on until they master the current skill. Though Kiwan was taught one-on-one, the program is actually developed for group instruction.

In addition to the DI program, the tutor developed flash cards for each DI lesson to provide additional opportunities for sight-word mastery. The sight words on the flash cards were selected based on past lessons and words the tutor believed that Kiwan would have difficulty with in the lesson.

Kiwan was also required to read authentic literature from Goodman's Five Star stories, which are high-interest, low-reading-level stories (Goodman, 1994). The first book that Kiwan read was *Chills: Chilling Tales and Exciting Stories* (Goodman, 1994), which is at the third-grade reading level. Kiwan read the story silently and responded to multiple-choice comprehension questions. Once a week, Kiwan was also asked to read a short (250 words or less) passage from a sports magazine of his choosing. Kiwan was very familiar with both football and basketball sport teams and players, so this activity built on his prior knowledge. Before he read the passage he was instructed on selected sight words using flash cards. Fluency-building activities were used with both the DI and authentic reading materials. One-minute assessments of the number of words that Kiwan read correctly and incorrectly were recorded. Finally, he was asked to read a library book once a week about an influential African American person. His first book was about Booker T. Washington. He was able to read the entire book in one session and respond accurately to the oral questions posed by the tutor.

Kiwan's writing instruction occurred once a week using the Morningside Language Fluency Program (Johnson & Ross, 1997). The student workbook required Kiwan to combine like sentences into one cohesive and comprehensible sentence. In addition to instruction in sentence combining, Kiwan was required to write one essay per week. The resulting product provided Kiwan's tutor with information regarding his specific instructional needs in writing. The tutor chose only two or three correction areas to focus on, i.e., specific writing skills that would then be the only skills assessed in the next writing piece produced. New focus areas were not selected until Kiwan demonstrated mastery of skills previously targeted.

Results indicated that Kiwan became more confident about his reading skills. He improved his reading skills from 76 words read accurately per minute to 140 words a minute read accurately in the first 3 weeks of instruction, despite the increasing difficulty on the text (Hessler & Gardner, 2006).

Summary

Effective instruction is fundamental to the academic success of CLDE learners. It requires the use of curriculum-based measures to determine what skills students need to learn to meet the goals of the curriculum. Effective teachers use thoroughly researched, evidence-based interventions to systematically teach the desired skills. Regular assessments enable teachers to monitor the effects of their instruction to determine if the skills are being developed or, if not, whether they need to employ alternative procedures. CLDE learners especially benefit from strategies that require them to make frequent responses to the instructional material, and they tend to prefer collaborative or peer-mediated instructional formats. Equally important are culturally responsive strategies that build on the student's prior knowledge with the purpose of achieving skill mastery. Effective instruction can serve as a preventive intervention, promoting academic achievement and appropriate student deportment. The more academic success students experience, the more likely they will value their education. The more students value their education, the more likely they are to invest in it. Effective instruction is essential for positive outcomes for CLDE learners.

Related Learning Activities

1. Complete an observation of a classroom with CLDE learners. Record the level of one student's academic responding to instructional stimuli. For example, how much reading (i.e., oral reading) does a student do in the reading group. What happens when the student misreads a word(s)? How would you assess the impact this amount of active reading might have on the student's reading achievement? What modifications would you make to the reading program based on the principles of effective instruction?

2. Observe a classroom and identify the academic accommodations that are used for CLDE learners with disabilities. How does the accommodation improve the student's opportunity for success in the curriculum? What guidelines might you put in place to determine when the accommodation is no longer useful?

3. Select a student from a culturally diverse group with an exceptionality. Identify a specific academic problem that this student is experiencing and design an intervention that includes evidence-based practices and incorporates the student's culture in the instruction. How would you monitor the effectiveness of the intervention?

References

Al-Hassan, S. (2003). *Reciprocal peer tutoring effect on high frequency sight word learning, retention, and generalization of first- and second-grade urban elementary students.* Unpublished doctoral dissertation. The Ohio State University, Columbus, OH.

Assembly of Alaskan Native Educators (2007). *Alaskan Standards for Culturally Responsive Schools.* Retrieved September 13, 2007, from http://www.ankn.uaf.edu/publications/standards.html

Berliner, D. C. (1979). Tempus Educre. In P. L. Peterson & H. J. Walberg (Eds.), *Research on teaching: Concepts, findings, and implications* (pp. 120–135). Berkeley, CA: McCutchen.

Berliner, D. C. (1980). Using research on teaching for the improvement of classroom practice. *Theory into Practice, 19,* 302–308.

Billingsley, B., Carlson, E., & Klein, S. (2004). The Working conditions and induction support of early career special education. *Exceptional Children 70*(3), 333–347.

Brophy, J. E., & Good, T. L. (1986). Teacher behavior and student achievement. In M. Wittrock (Ed.) *Handbook of research on teaching* (3rd ed., pp. 328–375). New York: Macmillan.

Callins, T. (2006). Culturally responsive literacy instruction. *Teaching Exceptional Children, 38*(2), 62–65.

Carnine, D. (1992). Expanding the notion of teachers' rights: Access to tools that work. *Journal of Applied Behavior Analysis,* Monograph No. 7, pp. 7–13.

Carnine, D. (2000). *Why education experts resist effective practices (and what it would take to make education more like medicine).* Thomas B. Fordham Foundation report of April 2000.

Cartledge, G., & Milburn, J. (1998). *Cultural diversity and social skills instruction: Understanding ethnic and gender differences.* Champaign, IL: Research Press.

Chall, J. S. (2000). *The achievement challenge: What really works in the classroom?* New York: Guilford Press.

Delpit, L. (1995). *Other people's children: Cultural conflict in the classroom.* New York: The New Press.

Deno, S. L. (2006). *Curriculum based measurement: Student assessment.* Research Works, University of Minnesota. http://education.umn.edu/research/ResearchWorks/CBM.html

Dewey, J. (1916). *Democracy and education.* New York: Macmillian.

Ellison, C. M., Boykin, A. W., Tyler, K. M., & Dillhunt, M. L. (2005). Examining classroom learning preferences among elementary school students. *Social Behavior and Personality, 33,* 699–708.

Engelmann, S., Meyer, L., Carnine, L., Becker, W., Eisele, J., & Johnson, G. (2002). *Corrective reading: Decoding strategies.* Columbus, OH: SRA McGraw-Hill.

Franca, V. M., Kerr, M. M., Reitz, A. L., & Lambert, D. (1990). Peer tutoring among behaviorally disordered students: Academic and social benefits to tutor and tutee. *Education and Treatment of Children, 13,* 109–128.

Fuchs, L. S., Fuchs, D., Yadian, L., & Powell, S. R. (2002). Enhancing first grade children's mathematical development with peer-assisted learning strategies. *School Psychology Review, 31,* 569–583.

Gardner, R., Cartledge, G., Seidl, B., Woolsey, L., Schley, G., & Utley, C. (2001). Mt. Olivet after school program: Peer mediated interventions for at-risk students. *Remedial and Special Education, 22,* 22–33.

Gardner, R., III, Heward, W. L., & Grossi, T. A. (1994). Effects of response cards on student participation and academic achievement: A systematic replication with inner-city students during whole class science instruction. *Journal of Applied Behavior Analysis, 27,* 63–71.

Gay, G. (2000). *Culturally responsive teaching: Theory, research, & practice.* New York: Teachers College Press.

Good, R. H., III, & Kaminski, R. A. (2003). *DIBELS Dynamic Indicators or Basic Early Literacy Skills* (6th ed). Longmont, CO: Sopris West.

Goodman, B. (1994). *Chills: Chilling tales and exciting stories.* Lincolnwood, IL: Jamestown Publishers.

Grant, C. A., & Gomez, M. L. (2001). *Making schooling multicultural: Campus and classroom* (2nd ed.). Upper Saddle River, NJ: Merrill/Prentice Hall.

Green, E. J., (1997). Guidelines for serving linguistically and culturally diverse young children. *Early Childhood Education Journal, 24*(3), 147–154.

Greenwood, C. R., Arreaga-Mayer, C., & Carta, J. J. (1994). Identification and translation of effective teacher-developed instructional procedures for general practice. *Remedial and Special Education, 15*(3), 140–151.

Greenwood, C. R., Delquadri, J. C., & Hall, R. V. (1984). Opportunity to respond and student academic performance. In W. L. Heward, T. E. Heron, J. Trapp-Porter, & D. S. Hill (Eds.), *Focus on behavior analysis in education* (pp. 58–88). Columbus, OH: Charles Merrill.

Greenwood, C. R., Delquadri, J., Stanley, S. O., Sasso, G., Whoroton, D., & Schulte, D. (1981). Allocating opportunity to learn as a basis for academic remediation: A developing model for teaching. *Monograph in Behavioral Disorders* (Summer) 22–33.

Greenwood, C. R., Hart, B., Walker, D., & Risley, T. (1994). The opportunity to respond and academic performance revisited: A behavioral theory of developmental retardation and its prevention. In R. Gardner, D. Sainato, J. Cooper, T. Heron, W. Heward,

J. Eshleman, & T. Grossi (Eds.), *Behavior analysis in education: Focus on measurably superior instruction.* (pp. 213–224). Pacific Grove, CA: Brooks/Cole.

Hall, R. V., Delquadri, J., & Harris, J. (1977). The opportunity to respond: A new focus for applied behavior analysis. Paper presented at the May 1977 Annual Meeting of the Association for Behavior Analysis, Chicago, IL.

Harrison, T. (2002). The development of a peer-tutoring program to teach sight words to deaf elementary students. Unpublished doctoral dissertation. The Ohio State University, Columbus, OH.

Heron, T. E., Villareal, D. M., Yao, M., Christianson, R. J., & Heron, K. M. (2006). Peer tutoring systems: Applications in classrooms and specialized environments, *Reading and Writing Quarterly, 22,* 27–45.

Hessler, T. & Gardner, R. (May, 2006). Curriculum-based measures (CBM) at the high school level. 32nd Annual National Convention of the Association for Behavior Analysis, Atlanta, GA.

Heward, W. L. (1994). Three "low-tech" strategies for increasing the frequency of active student response during group instruction. In R. Gardner, D. Sainato, J. Cooper, T. Heron, W. Heward, J. Eshleman, & T. Grossi (Eds.), *Behavior analysis in education: Focus on measurably superior instruction* (pp. 283–320). Pacific Grove, CA: Brooks/Cole.

Heward, W. L. (2006). *Exceptional children: An introduction to special education* (8th ed.). Upper Saddle River, NJ: Merrill/Prentice Hall.

Heward, W., Gardner, R., Cavanaugh, R. Courson, F., Grossi, T., & Barbetta, P., (1996). Everyone participates in this class: Using response cards to increase active student response. *Teaching Exceptional Children, 28,* 4–10.

Johnson, K., & Ross, R. (1997). *Morningside language fluency: Sentence-combining fluency student workbook.* Seattle, WA: Morningside Academy.

Kame'enui, E. J., & Simmons, D. C. (1990). *Designing instructional strategies: The prevention of academic learning problems.* Upper Saddle River, NJ: Merrill/Prentice Hall.

Klett, L. (2006). The effects of a secondary early reading intervention on the reading skills of young, urban, English language learners. Unpublished master's thesis. The Ohio State University, Columbus, OH.

Ladson-Billings, G. (1994). *The dreamkeepers: Successful teachers of African American children.* San Francisco, CA: Jossey-Bass.

Lambert, M.C., Cartledge, G, Lo, Y., & Heward, W. L. (2006). Effects of response cards on disruptive behaviors and academic responding during math lessons by fourth-grade students in an urban school. *Journal of Positive Behavior Interventions, 8,* 88–99.

Lee, J. (2002). Racial and ethnic achievement gaps trends: Reversing the progress toward equity? *Educational Researcher, 31,* 3–12.

Metropolitan Achievement Test—Eighth Ed. (2000). San Antonio, TX: Harcourt Assessment.

Musti-Rao, S. (2005). *The effects of an early reading intervention with urban kindergarten and first grade students: A preventive approach.* Unpublished doctoral dissertation. The Ohio State University, Columbus, Ohio.

National Academy Press (2002). Minority students in special education and gifted education. *Executive summary.* http://books.nap.nap.edu/books/0309074398/html#pagetop

Nieto, S. (2000). Affirming diversity: *The sociopolitical context of multicultural education.* (3rd ed.) New York: Addison Wesley Longman.

No Child Left Behind (2001). P.L. 107–110. Reauthorization of the Elementary and Secondary Act of 1965.

Odom, S. L., Brantlinger, E., Gersten, R., Horner, R. H., Thompson, B., & Harris, K. R. (Winter, 2005). *Exceptional Children, 71*(2).

Ohio Department of Education (2006, July). *Ohio's teacher equity plan.* Author. www.ed.gov/programs/teacherqual/hqtplans/ohep.doc

O'Neil, J. (1994/1995). Can inclusion work? A conversation with Jim Kauffman and Mara Sapon-Shevin. *Educational Leadership, 52,* 7–11

Patton, J. M. (1997). Disproportionate Representation in gifted programs; Best practices for meeting this challenge. In A. J. Artiles & G. Zamora-Duran (Eds.), *Reducing disproportionate representation of culturally diverse students in special education and gifted education.* Reston, VA: Council for Exceptional Children.

Peske, H. G., & Haycock, K. (2006). *Teaching inequality: How poor and minority students are shortchanged on teacher quality.* The Education Trust. www.edtrust.org

Richards, H. V., Brown, A. F., & Forde, T. B. (2007). Addressing diversity in schools: Culturally responsive pedagogy. *Teaching Exceptional Children, 39,* 64–68.

Robinson, D. R., Schofield, J. W., & Steers-Wentzell, K. L. (2005). Peer and cross-age tutoring in math: Outcomes and their design implications. *Educational Psychology Review, 17,* 357–362.

Rohrbeck, C. A., Ginsburg-Block, M. D., Fantuzzo, J. W., & Miller, T. R. (2003). Peer-assisted learning interventions with elementary school students: A meta-analytic review. *Journal of Educational Psychology, 95,* 240–257.

Simmons, D. C., & Kame'enui, E. J. (2003). *Scott Foresman early reading intervention.* Glenview, IL: Scott Foresman. Official website: http://www.scottforesman.com/eri/index.cfm

Talbert-Johnson, C. (2001). The quest for equity: Maintaining African American teachers in special education. *Journal of Negro Education, 70*(4), 286–296.

Tam, B., & Gardner, R. (1997). Multicultural education for students with behavior disorders: Much to do about nothing or a real issue? *Addressing Cultural and Linguistic Diversity in Special Education: Issues and Trends, 2,* 1–11.

U.S. Department of Education (2003). No Child Left Behind.

Wagner, L. (1990). Social and historical perspectives on peer tutoring in education. In H. C. Foot, M. J. Morgan, & R. H. Schute (Eds.), *Children helping children* (pp. 21–42). Chichester, England: John Wiley & Sons.

Winzer, M. A., & Mazurek, K. (1998). *Special education in multicultural contexts.* Upper Saddle River, NJ: Merrill/Prentice Hall.

Worsdell, A. S., Iwata, B. A., Dozier, C. L., Johnson, A. D., Neidert, P. L., & Thomason, J. L. (2005). Analysis of response repetition as an error-correction strategy during sight word reading. *Journal of Applied Behavior Analysis, 38,* 511–527.

Woodcock, R. W., McGrew, K. S., & Mather, N. (2001). *Woodcock-Johnson III tests of achievement.* Itasca, IL: Riverside Publishing.

Chapter 10

Implementing Effective Instruction in Inclusive Classrooms for CLDE Learners

Educating children to be productive members of society is the fundamental business of schools. That is, schools are intended to equip children with the cognitive and social skills essential for their success as adults (Schloss, Smith, & Schloss, 2001). Although the policies and regulations that govern school procedures typically emanate from the federal, state, and district levels, the implementation of those policies most often occurs in classrooms. Individual teachers are the agents of change who must apply these policies during their interactions with students. The implementation of effective instruction is a teacher's most important responsibility (Heward & Dardig, 2001). The fact is, the central task of educating all children regardless of cultural, linguistic, or exceptionality differences cannot happen without the daily diligence of teachers.

Understanding the principles of effective instruction presented in Chapter 9 is fundamental to developing an educational environment that will promote student academic achievement. Researchers in general education and special education alike have found that teachers educated in traditional teacher-training programs that promote effective instruction are better prepared to meet the challenges of a classroom (Laczko-Kerr & Berliner, 2001;

Nougharet, Scruggs, & Mastropieri, 2004). The application of effective instruction in classrooms is especially important for culturally and linguistically diverse children with exceptionalities (CLDE). Compared to other students, CLDE learners are more likely to enter schools with fewer of the skills needed for academic success (Peske & Haycock, 2006). Although the skills with which learners begin their education are important, it is not the entry skills of young learners that solely determine their abilities after 12 years of schooling. Teachers interacting positively with their students can create an atmosphere of learning and safety (Nougharet, et al., 2004). Teachers who systematically implement empirically validated instructional strategies, monitor the effectiveness of those strategies on individual learners, and make instructional decisions based on the learners' data are effective teachers. That is, effective teachers are those who can skillfully manage their classroom and promote student learning.

How can teacher education programs prepare effective educators? What is it that teachers must do to meet the instructional needs of an increasingly diverse student population with exceptionalities so that high school graduates will have the skills necessary for occupational and social success in the 21st century?

The purpose of this chapter is to present models and strategies that are empirically valid and culturally responsive to CLDE learners. After completing this chapter, the readers should be able to answer the following questions:

1. What is the essential purpose of schools?
2. What are the most likely skill deficits of CLDE learners?
3. How can teachers most effectively help CLDE learners acquire basic skills (i.e., reading, writing, and mathematics)?
4. How can teachers determine the instructional effectiveness of a strategy?
5. How can a child's culture be used to enhance the classroom instruction?
6. What are instructional strategies that can be used across a variety of academic content areas?

By the end of this chapter, readers will obtain information on strategies to:

1. Teach reading to beginning CLDE readers.
2. Teach reading to older, struggling CLDE readers.
3. Teach writing to CLDE learners
4. Teach math skills to CLDE learners.
5. Use effective teaching strategies to teach skills in other content areas.

Fatima

Fatima is an 8-year-old girl whose parents emigrated from the country of Lebanon in 1989. She has normal intelligence and seems motivated to be successful in school. Fatima lives with her father and grandmother. Her mother died as a result of a severe asthma attack four years ago. Fatima's father is a successful businessman, having established an accounting business during the 1990s. The grandmother does not work outside of the home and is the primary caretaker for Fatima.

Fatima is asthmatic, having been diagnosed when she was 2 years old. She has been absent from school numerous days due to asthma attacks and related complications (e.g., pneumonia, frequent colds, severe headaches) in her short school career. Because of her frequent absences during her first- and second-grade years, her reading, writing, and math skills lag behind those of her peers. Fatima's frequent school absences have also made it more difficult for her to develop friendships with other children in the class. Efforts to assist Fatima in improving her academic skills are further hampered by the fact that the grandmother is unable to assist her with homework, especially reading and writing, since the grandmother speaks and writes only Arabic. Arabic is generally spoken in the home.

How can the school most effectively address Fatima's instructional needs? What role might her culture play in this instruction?

What Should Be Taught?

The three "R's"—reading, writing, and arithmetic—are still the foundation of every child's education and present a hierarchy for acquisition. Reading remains the skill most closely aligned with student success or failure (Moats, 1999). In order for students, especially those with disabilities, to have their best chance for success in middle and high school, these basic academic skills must be effectively taught in elementary school. This can pose a significant challenge for teachers of students who have limited English proficiency (LEP) or students from impoverished backgrounds, even if the students are academically gifted.

Students who do not master the basic skills during elementary school will be faced with the daunting task of trying to keep up with grade-level materials in the general school curriculum while still struggling to master the basic skills. It is not only important for teachers to teach academic skills but, as discussed in Chapter 5, schools also must focus on social skill development. There is a reciprocal relationship between academic and social behavior (Cartledge & Milburn 1995). Skilled teachers will purposefully incorporate teaching strategies (e.g., peer tutoring) that simultaneously build the social and academic repertoire of their students.

In order for students to master the full general education curriculum, they must first become proficient in reading, writing, and math. Further, students must exit schools with the skills necessary for lifelong learning, especially given the rapid changes required for success in a technologically driven society. Unfortunately, far too many U.S. students, especially CLDE learners, have achievement levels below what is expected and needed for their grade levels.

The problem of poor achievement by U.S. students, in particular CLD learners, has not gone unnoticed. In fact, there has been a fierce debate among educators, politicians, and families about the best way to improve academic achievement. One result has been legislation at both the state and national levels (as discussed in previous chapters) designed to improve student achievement through increased accountability for teachers and school districts. Of all of the academic areas, reading instruction has received the most attention from legislators who want to improve the performances of American students.

How Do We Provide Reading Instruction to CLDE Learners?

What Is the Reading Profile of CLDE Learners?

Reading, as stated earlier in this chapter, is the most essential skill for school success. Reading ability serves as the gatekeeper to the general curriculum and higher-level performance for all children. Reading is a complex task that requires students to simultaneously engage in multiple behaviors (e.g., tracking words from left to right, decoding, fluency, vocabulary comprehension, and text comprehension). Approximately 20% of all elementary children experience difficulty learning to read; 37% of fourth graders read below a basic level (Moats, 2000; National Center for Educational Statistics, 2003; 2005); 80% of children with learning disabilities experience problems in learning to read (Lyon & Moats, 1997); and the failure rates for CLD and impoverished learners are reported as high as 60% to 70% (Grigg, Daane, Jinn, & Campbell, 2003). Children who read poorly are at increased risk for school failure (Moats, 2000).

The groups who are consistently identified at the greatest risk for reading failure are minority students (i.e., African, Hispanic, and Native Americans) and students who are poor. Although some would argue that the "issues of poverty are more strongly associated with educational achievement (e.g., beginning reading) than ethnicity or race" (Scott & Kame'enui, 1994, p.373), the poor reading performance of certain CLD groups as well as impoverished children deserves special attention.

Students attending high-poverty or low-performing schools make up a significant fraction of the school-age population at risk for reading failure, with students from minority groups constituting the fastest-growing group of school-aged students in the United States. These schools typically have high teacher turnover, low expectations for both teachers and students, inconsistent leadership, and high rates of student mobility (Foorman & Moats, 2004). Complex environmental and social factors such as neglected, underfunded schools with limited community and parental support place students attending these schools at acute risk for limited academic achievement (Davis, 2003).

Even though educational reforms have focused on addressing the problems of educating low-performing CLD learners, the achievement gap has continued to be of widespread concern in recent decades (Kretovics, Faber, & Armaline, 2004). In 2001, the fourth-grade reading report card showed 63% of African American, 58% of Hispanic American, and 57% of Native American students reading below basic levels compared to 27% of European American students (National Center for Educational Statistics, 2001). African American children showed lower mean achievement scores than other racial/ethnic groups upon entering kindergarten, and the gap continued to grow from the start of kindergarten to the end of third grade (National Center for Educational Statistics, 2003). Many CLD students enter kindergarten without the preliteracy experiences and oral language skills needed to facilitate early classroom learning. The warning signs are apparent very early in their schooling and they systematically fall behind their peers.

The most recent data from the National Center for Educational Statistics (NCES, 2005) is a bit more encouraging, showing a slight narrowing of the reading gap. Test scores were analyzed for students at ages 9, 13, and 17. For all three age groups, Hispanic and African American students achieved higher reading scores in 2004 than in 1975 or 1971, respectively. For example, with 9-year-olds, Hispanic Americans moved from a 34-point gap in 1975 to a 21-point gap in 2004. African Americans progressed from a 44-point gap in 1971 to a 26-point gap in 2004. These gains most likely resulted from the greater emphasis placed on reading over the past decade (Dobbs, 2005). These gains notwithstanding, there are still reading score differences ranging from 25 to 29 points between CLD students and their European American peers. There remains a tremendous need for reading improvement among CLD learners.

The high rate of reading failure explains "much about the poor academic achievement of some minority students and why they are underrepresented in professions that depend on higher education" (Moats, 2000, p. 4). Students who fall behind in reading at the end of first grade tend to continue to lag behind their peers across academic areas (Kame'enui, 1994). The effects of reading failure can be enormous, negatively affecting the child's self-concept, academic performance, and social interactions as well as future employment and adult success.

What Reading Skills Should Be Taught CLDE Learners?

The National Reading Panel lists five areas of reading instruction: phonemic awareness, phonics, fluency, vocabulary development, and text comprehension.

- *Phonemic awareness* refers to the ability to hear and manipulate sounds in the spoken language. When given the word *sat*, for example, the learner is able to isolate sounds such as "s" as the beginning sound. The learner is also able to blend sounds so that /sss/ /aaa/ /ttt/ is sat and the learner can segment the word *sat* as /sss/ /aaa/ /ttt/.
- *Phonics* pertains to teaching letter–sound relationships used to read or spell. The student is able to accurately make the sounds that letters represent and to use that skill in decoding words.
- *Fluency* involves reading accurately, with speed, and with proper expression for the text. Automaticity is developed in the student's reading skill. That is, the student's decoding process becomes so quick that words are read almost immediately upon presentation. Fluency also facilitates comprehension.
- *Vocabulary development* enables the learner to understand and use words presented orally and in print. Vocabulary development fosters comprehension.
- *Comprehension* is the ability to derive meaning from print. The student is able to accurately determine facts from reading and make appropriate inferences from the text. Comprehension is the essence of reading and is dependent upon the development of critical phonemic awareness, phonological, fluency, and vocabulary skills.

Most, if not all, elementary schools have adopted a reading curriculum that is used by all the teachers in the building and/or district. Teachers should examine reading curriculum materials to ensure that the five skill areas recommended by the National Reading Panel are directly taught as a part of the reading curriculum.

How Should We Teach Beginning Reading to CLDE Learners? One means for addressing the high rate of reading failure is to provide differentiated reading instruction according to the individual students' needs. The Three Tier Reading Model is a reading instructional model designed by Good, Kame'enui, Simmons, and Chard (2002) for diverse learners. A dynamic reading program for beginning readers (i.e., kindergarten to third grade), the model proposes three different levels of reading intervention. The expectation is that approximately 80% of all students will be in Tier I. That is, these students are able to make appropriate progress in the school's adopted reading program. The assumption is that the reading curriculum is evidence based with a history of good reading outcomes for the majority of students in the school. All students would receive their basic reading instruction from this curriculum. Tier I involves benchmark testing using programs such as the Dynamic Indicators of Basic Early Literacy Skills (DIBELS) (Good, Kaminski, & Smith, 2003) and curriculum-based measurements (see Figure 10–1).

Tier II is for those students who need supplemental instruction beyond that provided in Tier I. Tier II students receive an additional 30 minutes daily of intensive small-group instruction focused on the prerequisite reading skills (e.g., phonemic awareness, letter–sound development, fluency) that are needed for reading progress. Depending on class structure and resources, this additional instruction might be provided by paraprofessionals (i.e., teacher assistants) or peers in formats such as peer or cross-age tutoring.

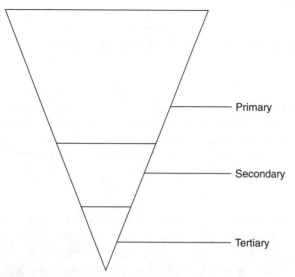

FIGURE 10–1 The three-tier reading model

Under these circumstances, clearly prescribed or scripted instructional sequences are essential.

Despite the additional reading activity time, a few students will continue to have reading difficulty in Tier II and will need more intensive intervention twice daily. This level of instruction is Tier III. These students will need carefully designed, explicit, and systematic instruction in small groups (i.e., 2 to 5 students) or one-on-one instruction, along with progressive monitoring of their learning.

A student's placement in a specific tier is not permanent but is predicated on the student's skills. Students can move up and down the tiers according to their level of progress. Progress should be closely monitored using both curriculum-based assessments/measures (CBA/M) and standardized measures (e.g., DIBELS). Students in Tier III should be assessed most frequently (e.g., including CBM as a part of each lesson along with weekly DIBELS assessments). Teachers should graph and analyze the data to determine if the instruction is effective and whether the student needs to be moved to a more or less intensive tier.

What Are Some Special Reading Instruction Considerations for CLDE Learners? The Three Tier Model (Good et al., 2002) just presented is hypothetical in that many low-performing CLDE students are in schools where far greater than 20% of the pupil population is performing below grade level. This is especially true in low socioeconomic schools, such as many urban or rural schools. In these situations, schools need to structure and train their staff so that they are able to accommodate the special learning needs of greater numbers of students without the requisite reading readiness skills. For example, some studies show that trained paraprofessionals can be used effectively to teach phonemic awareness skills in small-group secondary interventions for CLD/impoverished kindergarten inner-city students (Musti-Rao & Cartledge, in press; Yurick & Cartledge, 2007).

It is important that students at risk be identified and provided interventions as early as possible. (See Chapter 12 in this text for a more detailed discussion of early interventions for at-risk CLD learners.) It is also important to continuously monitor the progress of students who do not initially show risk since there is some evidence that these children are especially vulnerable to falling behind throughout the school year (Yurick & Cartledge,

2007). The importance of learning to read and the precarious nature of CLD students' learning dictate that their instruction be explicit, intensive, and systematic (Mathes & Torgesen, 1998). According to Musti-Rao and Cartledge (2006):

> Explicit instruction refers to teaching specific reading skills such as phonemic awareness, letter–sound correspondence, and so forth, all of which help students acquire the knowledge to decode print. Explicit instruction requires the integration of modeling, guided practice, scaffolding, and independent practice. It is not merely a combination of various activities. Intensive instruction includes providing a greater number of teaching and learning opportunities with increased repetition of previously learned skills. Systematic instruction is the careful structuring of instruction such that one skill builds on a previously taught skill (p. 26).

Much of the instructional curriculum in U.S. schools is Eurocentric in structure and content, as we have mentioned. We need to draw upon the culture of CLD students to make literacy instruction more meaningful to them (Jackson, 2005). Using multicultural literature, authentic stories written by individuals from students' background or about their background, can make reading more relevant. Yurick, Robinson, Cartledge, Lo, and Evans (2006) found that urban African American and poor students preferred stories such as *Scorpions* (Myers, 1988) during repeated reading instruction to improve their fluency. Gay (2002) reports positively on curriculums that used literature of African, Hispanic, Asian, and Native American cultures to teach reading and writing skills to low-achieving students. According to Gay, improved results showed up both on standardized tests and in students' more positive attitudes toward reading.

Sanacore (2004) advises that in addition to providing opportunities to read multicultural literature, we provide interactive experiences for students. That is, we might set up small-group literature circles to discuss the stories, engage students in oral readings with repeated refrains, or even have students participate in dramas, pantomimes, or improvisations. The story *Amazing Grace* (Hoffman & Binch, 1991), for example, might lend itself to a dramatic presentation. This is a popular story of a young girl who wants to be lead actor in the play *Peter Pan* but is discouraged by her classmates because she is neither male nor White. Culturally specific literature may inspire CLD learners to write about their own experiences, which can then be acted out or shared in the form of poems, raps, and so forth.

Other important points are that we need to have high expectations for students' capacity to learn and become efficient readers (Gay, 2002; Sanacore, 2004). The expectations we have for students will determine the effort we put forth in making sure that they learn. We also need to instruct in ways that reflect the culture of the learners. Cooperative learning and peer-mediated activities are often recommended for these students from evidence about their learning preferences (Boykin, Tyler, Watkins-Lewis, & Kizzie, 2006). Role plays, paired reading, puppet plays, story theatre, and games not only allow for peer interactive learning but also may be valuable learning opportunities for English language learners (Flood, Lapp, Tinajero, & Hurley, 1996/1997). The materials used need to be authentic, affirming, and devoid of ethnic or racial stereotypes.

The interactive activities suggested above should be used to supplement the instructional reading program, not in lieu of basic instruction. CLDE learners must be taught to decode and read fluently and with comprehension. Direct Instruction (DI) is one curriculum that has demonstrated success in teaching learners with and without disabilities, including CLDE learners (Carnine, Silbert, Kame'enui, & Tarver, 2004; Forness, Kavale, Blum, & Lloyd, 1997). DI, implemented correctly, systematically instructs to mastery the five critical reading skills recommended by the National Reading Panel.

Fatima's Reading Program

Fatima's reading deficits place her in Tier III of the Three Tier Reading Model. Based on the research data and past experiences, the school professionals determine that the students in the school would make the most progress in a phonics-based reading program. Therefore, the class uses the *Success for All* (Slavin & Madden, 2003) reading series.

Fatima will continue to receive reading instruction in her *Success for All* reading group and supplemental reading activities daily to assist her in developing English reading skills more rapidly. She will engage in 20 minutes of reciprocal peer tutoring of sight words with a student who is also in Tier III, under the supervision of a paraprofessional. This will give Fatima numerous opportunities to practice with immediate feedback the 107 most frequently used words in English.

Additionally, Fatima's teacher determined it would be wise to use a computer-based program that would provide independent practice and would be compatible with the phonics-based basal reading curriculum of *Success for All*. One such computer/Internet-based program is *Headsprout* (http://www.headsprout.com/), an interactive reading program that provides explicit instruction in phonics. The program begins by helping students to correctly identify letter–sound relationships. *Headsprout* was selected because in order for students to progress through the program they must demonstrate mastery of each skill presented. Each of the 80 *Headsprout* lessons takes approximately 30–40 minutes and can be used on any computer with Internet access. This allowed Fatima to use the program at school, home, the library, or wherever there was a computer with Internet access, and to receive some reading instruction at home on those days when she is unable to attend school.

Fatima was assessed weekly using DIBELS (Good, Kaminski, & Smith, 2003) and daily with a curriculum-based measurement. The curriculum-based measurement was a 1-minute oral reading of a passage she had read recently, with the teacher recording the number of words read correctly and incorrectly. Each session of peer tutoring ended with an assessment of sight words correctly identified within 3 seconds. Finally, *Headsprout* provided detailed written feedback that was downloaded after each reading lesson.

How Do We Teach Older Struggling Readers?

Despite teachers' best efforts, too many children beyond the third grade (especially CLDE learners) continue to experience reading difficulties (Moats, 1999). (See Kiwan's story in Chapter 9.) The causes of reading difficulties vary, including learning disabilities, English as a second language, and poor reading instruction. These students often have poor fluency, limited vocabulary, poor comprehension, writing difficulties, and poor self-confidence (Alvermann, 2002). Older students who are experiencing reading problems usually need intensive interventions.

Helping students who have experienced reading failure across the years to read and enjoy reading is one of the difficult challenges that face middle and secondary education teachers. An initial step in helping older struggling readers is to obtain an accurate assessment of the students' reading skills. Using a curriculum-based assessment (e.g., *Corrective Reading: Decoding Strategies* assessment [Engelmann, Meyer, Carnine, Becker, Eisele, & Johnson, 2002]) or a standardized assessment tool (e.g., *Woodcock-Johnson*; Woodcock, McGrew, & Mather, 2001), the teacher needs to match carefully the emerging reading skills of the student to the instructional materials. Second, the teacher needs to develop an aggressive individualized plan for each student. It is critical that the plan allow for high rates of student response with immediate corrective feedback. This is not only important in building skill mastery but also in helping the struggling reader become more self-confident.

Teachers need to use scientifically validated curriculums that follow the guidelines of the National Reading Panel. In other words, the curriculum should emphasize the development of phonemic awareness, phonics, fluency, vocabulary, and comprehension. In some cases, it may be necessary to combine more than one program or strategy to meet the special needs of a learner, as was done with Fatima. The selected curriculum(s) should sequence lessons so that each one builds on previous lessons and provides the necessary redundancy required for skill development. Further, the curriculum should promote mastery learning, requiring students to master one skill before going on to the next skill. With the goal of having students progress as quickly as possible, it is essential to incorporate additional reading opportunities into the school day. Finally, instruction needs to employ culturally responsive materials. It is important for CLDE learners to see images of persons similar to themselves. The reading materials should also be culturally sensitive, providing accurate and positive references to diverse cultures.

Middle and high school teachers must be prepared to meet the reading needs of children with and without disabilities. Strategies exist that are designed to help students improve their basic reading skills (e.g., decoding and comprehension) and others designed to assist students in understanding difficult text.

Corrective Reading. Direct Instruction Corrective Reading (Engelmann et al., 2002) has documented success in assisting older children with reading problems to master both decoding and comprehension skills using systematic instruction. Students are assessed using a curriculum-based test that determines where they should begin based on their present skills. The lessons are scripted, with guidelines for the teacher to follow when children make errors. The program is also mastery based, so students do not progress through the curriculum until they have demonstrated mastery of the current skills. Corrective Reading is designed for students in the fourth grade and above. A research-based application for adolescents was described in Chapter 9 in Kiwan's story.

REWARDS. Archer, Gleason, and Vachon (2000) developed the Reading Excellence: Word Attack & Rate Development Strategies (REWARDS) program to assist older readers in correctly decoding multisyllabic words. The program can be used independently or as a complement to other reading intervention programs. REWARDS is designed to provide students with the skills to successfully read academic content textbooks. The 20 lessons are scripted, with explicit instruction and mastery learning, and can be taught to an entire class, a small group, or an individual student.

Repeated Readings. Repeated reading is a strategy that can be used with struggling readers (as well as younger readers) to build fluency and comprehension (Rasinski, 1990; Sammuels, 1979). Students repeatedly read the same passage until a predetermined level of fluency (i.e., words read correctly per minute) is achieved. The student reads a passage out loud, with the teacher correcting errors and praising accuracy. The teacher then has the student practice reading the passage as quickly and accurately as possible during 1-minute timings or 10-second sprints. The teacher records and graphs the correctly and incorrectly read words. Along with the repeated reading, students are usually asked to do 1-minute retells. During retells, the students tell the teacher as many facts about the story as they can remember in 1 minute. The number of correct facts is also recorded and graphed. When students reach their fluency goal or criteria with comprehension, they are then given a new passage for repeated readings along with a new goal.

This strategy can be used in a peer-mediated format so that students can be trained to serve as each other's teacher (Cartledge & Lo, 2006; Staubitz, Cartledge, Yurick, & Lo,

2005; Yurick, Robinson, Cartledge, Lo, & Evans, 2006). Peer-mediated procedures allow many students to practice reading while the teacher circulates throughout the class providing assistance and reinforcement. Research by Staubitz et al. and Yurick et al. demonstrated the beneficial effects of repeated readings with urban upper-elementary students with and without disabilities. *Teaching Urban Learners* by Cartledge and Lo (2006) provides a detailed procedure for implementing repeated readings in the classroom.

High Interest—Low Reading Level. High interest—low reading level books are important instructional tools for promoting reading success. Two examples are Goodman's *Five Star Stories* (Goodman, 1994) and *Bring the Classics to Life* (Solimene, 1997). High interest—low reading level books allow students to practice independent reading and reading for pleasure. Teachers can include these books in the classroom library. Of course, they should also be included in the school library.

Another rich source of high interest—low reading level materials is parallel texts. These texts provide access to literature that is often difficult, if not impossible, for nonproficient readers to decode or comprehend. Literature such as Shakespeare or early American authors' writings is placed alongside a modern translation, thus giving nonproficient readers the opportunity to read the same content as others in their classes. For example, Abraham Lincoln's Gettysburg Address would appear in its original prose—"Four score and seven years ago our fathers brought forth on this continent, a new nation, etc." (Schumacher, 2000, p. 256)—on one page facing a current translation on the opposite page—"Eighty-seven years ago our ancestors created a new nation on this continent" (p. 257).

High interest—low reading level materials provide struggling readers access to more sophisticated content. Decreasing the decoding difficulties students experience will increase the likelihood that they will comprehend the content. Comprehension (vocabulary and content) is recommended as an essential component of reading programs by the National Reading Panel (University of Texas Center for Reading & Language Arts, 2003).

How Can We Provide Multicultural Reading Materials?

Teachers at all grade levels need to have books in their classrooms that reflect the diversity in the United States. It is important for children to see themselves, as well as others, in literature. Providing multicultural reading materials can create positive experiences for

---

TEACHING TIPS

Building Reading Skills

1. Use evidence-based reading programs with explicit instruction on decoding.
2. Use strategies (i.e., repeated reading) to build reading fluency.
3. Use reading materials that reflect a diverse society.
4. Assess students regularly and graph individual progress.
5. Encourage reading for pleasure with a variety of reading materials reflecting diverse interests and a culturally diverse population.
6. Provide opportunities for supplementary interactive literacy activities such as enactments and role plays.
7. Provide opportunities for students to share their readings with their peers.

children and help in building relationships. For example, Fatima's teacher reads every day to her class for 15 minutes and one of the books she has chosen is *Hosni the Dreamer: An Arabian Tale* (Ben-Ezer, 1997). Fatima occasionally volunteers information about Lebanon (based on stories she has heard from her grandmother). The teacher has even observed other children approaching Fatima during the day and asking about Lebanon and her family. The effective use of multicultural materials can help build understanding, acceptance, and tolerance among students. Books written by minority authors are a rich source of culturally sensitive reading materials (Callins, 2006). Table 10–1 provides of list of multicultural resources.

TABLE 10–1 Web sources for multicultural books and resources

African American literature
http://www.edchange.org/multicultural/sites/aframdocs.html

Arab American culture
http://www.spl.org/default.asp?pageID=audience_children_readinglist&cid=1066163185578

Asian children
http://www.comeunity.com/adoption/books/0children-asianfaces.html

Celebrating diversity through children's literature
http://www.multiculturalchildrenslit.com/

Chinese American culture
http://www.spl.org/default.asp?pageID=audience_children_readinglist&cid=1126729543992

Correta Scott King Award Books
http://www.spl.org/default.asp?pageID=audience_children_readinglist&cid=1133196707257

Hispanic American children's literature
http://www.geocities.com/Heartland/Estates/4967/hispanic.html

Japanese American culture
http://www.spl.org/default.asp?pageID=audience_children_readinglist&cid=1066163398171

Jewish American culture
http://www.spl.org/default.asp?pageID=audience_children_readinglist&cid=1126734753195

Multicultural children's books
http://www.willesdenbookshop.co.uk/

Multicultural education
http://www.edchange.org/multicultural/sites1.html

Multicultural education
http://www.mhhe.com/socscience/education/multi_new/

Multicultural literature
http://members.aol.com/mcsing29/books.htm

Native American culture
http://www.spl.org/default.asp?pageID=audience_children_readinglist&cid=1066163506234

Native American literature
http://www.edchange.org/multicultural/sites/nat-amlit.html

The Hmong: Children's books
http://library.uwsuper.edu/hmong/childbooks.html

Young children's books about disabilities
http://catnet.ksu.edu/subguides/specialed/disability.htm

Source: T. Callins (2006), "Culturally Responsive Literacy Instruction," *Teaching Exceptional Children, 39*(2), 62–65. Copyright © 2006 by The Council for Exceptional Children. Reprinted with permission.

How Do We Help CLDE Students Develop Writing Skills?

Writing is a skill closely associated with reading. Often, children with learning disabilities have not only deficits in reading but writing as well. Writing, however, does not attract the same level of attention as reading (Bridge & Hiebert, 1985). Students with learning disabilities tend to write very little and less maturely (i.e., stories lack cohesiveness) than their peers (Nodine, Barenbaum, & Newcomer, 1985). Sentence combining can be an effective place to begin for extremely poor writers, who can then build the sentences into stories (Johnson & Ross, 1997).

It is important that writing be relevant to students (Nicolini, 1994). Nicolini used the device of autobiographies to motivate inner-city at-risk students to increase and improve writing skills. By their very nature autobiographies are culturally sensitive. Using them sends a clear message that students' lives are important and should be recorded. Because the students are the experts on the subject, writing autobiographies can also allow students to feel more comfortable. Howard (1996) used journal writing with a poor writer and reader and saw across a 2-year period progress in that student's ability to write clearly. This student was able to do an autobiography.

Graham and Harris (2005) recommend making the writing environment more enjoyable and supportive for students with special needs. For example:

1. Establish an exciting mood during writing time.
2. Create a writing environment where students feel free to take risks when writing.
3. Develop writing assignments that are compatible with students' interests.
4. Provide opportunities for students to arrange their own space.
5. Encourage students to help each other as they plan, write, revise, and edit their work.
6. Hold conferences with students about goals, advances, and setbacks on current projects.
7. Ask students to share work in progress and completed papers with each other.
8. Praise students for their accomplishments, effort, and use of strategy.
9. Reinforce students' writing by displaying their best work in prominent places.
10. Model and promote an "I can do" attitude. (p. 161)

Explicit regular instruction in writing is important to help students develop written-language skills.

Success in learning is essential to effective instruction.

CLDE students who have had limited writing experiences would benefit from guided assistance through writing prompts. Hessler (2005) developed a series of writing prompts that increased the amount and quality of writing by secondary African American students with learning disabilities. The prompts were a series of questions that if answered would guide the student in developing a paper (see Figure 10–2).

Teachers have to be careful to provide sufficient instruction and corrective feedback without going overboard to the extent that students with writing deficits are discouraged from continuing their writing efforts (Graham & Harris, 2005; Mercer, 1997). One way to avoid overwhelming students with corrective feedback is "by focus correcting," that is, focusing on correcting one skill at a time (e.g., comma use in a series or the appropriate use of quotation marks with dialogue) (Heward, Heron, Gardner, & Prayzer, 1991).

Teachers might also use computer software programs that predict words so that as the student writes, the program will provide the student with possible words that would make

FIGURE 10–2 Writing prompt

Time Capsule

Writing Prompt #5

A time capsule is a container (usually metal) that is filled with items that represent that period of time. A time capsule from the 1960s might contain a picture and article about John F. Kennedy (because he was president at the beginning of the decade) and a model of a rocket (because the government spent a lot of time, effort, and money to get a man into space and then to the moon).

What 3 items would you put in a time capsule to represent you during your high school years? Each paragraph you write should be about one of those items. Name and explain the items and then tell how they represent you in your high school years. The best essays will contain stories that illustrate your points.

Good writers plan what they are going to write. You can start by using this page to brainstorm a list of items, things you use every day, for example, brush, nail file, fork, etc. You could also list food and drinks you enjoy and favorite clothing and games.

Source: T. Hessler (Summer, 2005), *The Effects of a Writing Template on the Writing Behaviors of High School Students with Learning Disabilities*. Unpublished dissertation. The Ohio State University, Columbus, OH.

> **TEACHING TIPS**
>
> **Developing Writing Skills**
>
> 1. Make the writing relevant to the learners (e.g., autobiographical stories, a favorite activity).
> 2. Use journal writing.
> 3. Use writing prompts. Provide students with two or three prompts, then ask them to choose one.
> 4. Use brainstorming strategies to prompt ideas.
> 5. Provide 1 to 3 minutes of thinking time before writing.
> 6. Have learners write multiple times during the week.
> 7. Integrate writing with other academic activities.

sense for the sentence based on the words the student wrote at the beginning of the sentence. For example, the student writes "I love walking _____" and the computer presents "home." The student has the opportunity to accept or reject the word. The current generation of predictive software, however, does not always ensure that the sentences in the writing are cogent. Therefore, teachers must directly teach students how to develop connectivity between sentences in order to convey linear thoughts.

Another strategy for working within an inclusive setting is "brainstorming," or having the students generate one-word ideas on a particular topic such as "hurricane." The teacher then writes each idea on the board and leaves them there as the students begin to write essays on the topic. Providing a list of correctly spelled words associated with the topic can be particularly helpful to students who have reading and writing problems, especially English language learners who might still be developing skills in letter–sound associations in English. Most people's verbal skills exceed their ability to write words correctly. For poor writers, this can be especially frustrating since their spelling attempts may not be close enough to the actual spelling to benefit from computer spell checks and/or they may not have the skill or perseverance to find the word in a dictionary. Many students will become so frustrated that they will stop writing. Teachers can build both classwide and individual word banks that help students express their thoughts better.

One way to help CLDE learners maintain interest is by having them write about subjects with which they are familiar. This type of strategy is by its very nature culturally sensitive because it allows the students to share information from their culture, activities, or other experiences.

How Do We Help CLDE Students Develop Math Skills?

Although mathematics has not received the level of attention that reading has over the last few decades, it remains one of the essential skills for success in everyday life. Math skills such as counting, telling time, estimating distance, money skills, and so forth are used multiple times throughout each day. Children with disabilities frequently experience difficulties mastering math skills. Students with high-incidence disabilities frequently have difficulty remembering math facts, completing calculations, and solving word problems (Bryant 2005).

Mathematics is sometimes called the universal language, but it is hardly language independent. It uses highly compressed communication—each word or symbol can represent an entire concept or idea (Garrison, Amaral, & Ponce, 2006). To solve a problem, learners are often required to understand every, or nearly every, word. The need to understand language and math symbols precisely can be particularly challenging to ELLs (Garrison et al., 2006).

One of the critical issues in math education is how to eliminate the mathematics achievement gap among races and other groups (Clarkson & Taylor, 2006). The research literature repeatedly shows CLD learners (i.e., African and Hispanic American) performing less well than their European American counterparts (Edwards, Kahn, & Brenton, 2001; Hall, Davis, Bolen, Chia, 1999; Ryan & Ryan, 2005). Andrews and Slate (2002) found that, although the discrepancies were small, African American prekindergarten students were consistently behind their European American peers. In their review of the relevant literature, Hall et al. report that African and Hispanic American students begin to perform below grade level in math in the second grade and that during the same period European and Asian American students begin to advance in math. Another finding was that as students progressed through the grades, Asian and European American students reported greater enjoyment of math, whereas the reverse was the case for African and Hispanic American students. Although African and Hispanic American students tend to test below their European and Asian American classmates, there have been continuous improvements (Hall et al.). The 2005 NCES national report card on math reported that fourth- and eighth-grade European, African, and Hispanic Americans averaged higher math scores in 2005 than in any previous year. Higher scores also were reported for low-income students and females.

A particularly interesting and puzzling observation is that certain groups (i.e., African Americans and females) consistently score lower on math tests despite comparable backgrounds and indications of similar abilities (Ryan & Ryan, 2005; Steele, 2003; Steele & Aronson, 1995). Steele and Aronson found that African American students tested less well than their European American counterparts if they believed they were being compared to their race peers. On the other hand, if the African American students believed they were simply assessing the validity of the tests (not themselves), they performed at a level commensurate with their European American peers. This phenomenon was subsequently tested with other groups, such as females, and was labeled *psychological threat*. That is, when certain groups experience pervasive stereotypes (e.g., African Americans and females do not perform well in math), the accompanying pressure serves to suppress the students' performance (Ryan & Ryan, 2005). There have been attempts to determine the entry points of psychological threat in public education and the factors that might moderate its effects (Aronson, 2004; Steele, 2003). Authorities point out that such school practices as high-stakes testing may have a debilitating effect on certain subgroups who are vulnerable to the effects of psychological threat.

What are some basic principles of teaching important mathematic concepts? Learners experiencing math difficulties may have deficits in "number sense" (Bryant, 2005; Gersten, Jordan, & Flojo, 2005). Theoretically, number sense links mathematical relationships, principles, and procedures. In other words, number sense guides how learners think about numbers. For young children there are two components of number sense: counting/simple computation and sense of quantity (Gersten et al., 2005). For example, a young child may be able to count from 1 to 10 without error, but the child does not know that 8 is larger than 5. Griffin, Case, and Siegler (1994) found that 96% of beginning kindergarten children from high socioeconomic status (SES) families were able to answer questions about which number is bigger, compared to only 18% of children from low SES families.

Explicit instruction in quantity discrimination, counting skills, and computational skills (i.e., addition and subtraction) can be used to improve the number sense of learners. The skills associated with number sense assist learners in understanding the meaning of numbers, and having an understanding of what numbers mean is fundamental to success in mathematics. If children from low SES groups (which are disproportionally minority) are more likely to enter school without understanding what numbers mean, then it is imperative that teachers directly instruct this important skill. Students must not only improve their ability to understand numbers must also develop automaticity in counting and computing. Teachers might use an instructional strategy such as peer tutoring or self-correction materials to increase student accuracy in math facts. Both strategies provide students with immediate feedback so that they do not practice errors. As students increase their accuracy with math facts, teachers can begin to build fluency using 1- to 2-minute timed assessments of math facts.

As they work with students, educators must be careful to make sure that students not only can do the math skill, but that they understand the underlying math concept. Miller and Hudson (2006) provide five guidelines for assisting students with disabilities to understand math concepts:

1. Use various modes of representation.
2. Consider appropriate structures for teaching specific concepts.
3. Consider the language of mathematics.
4. Integrate real-world applications.
5. Provide explicit instruction (p. 29).

Various modes of representation can be implemented through using the concrete, semiconcrete, abstract teaching progression (Miller & Hudson, 2006). For example, when teaching addition, begin by using manipulatives (concrete) to illustrate the concept. Once students are successful in completing the task using manipulatives, then provide similar problems with pictures (semiconcrete) to cue the students. When students are successful in responding to problems at the semiconcrete level, have them work problems at the abstract level or use number symbols only.

Teachers should be careful to match the instruction to the skill. For example, measurement, fractions, or weight can be taught effectively using compare and contrast (National Council of Teachers of Mathematics, 2000). Teachers should always provide both examples and nonexamples of the concept to help students learn to discriminate. A step-by-step structure can be used to teach math operations such as computational skills. Step-by-step instruction can be particularly useful in helping students who have memory or organizational problems (Miller & Hudson, 2006).

In addition to lesson structure, teachers should also be concerned about the language they use to present math content. Students with language learning disabilities or who are ELLs may have difficulty understanding the language of math and subsequently have difficulty mastering and retaining math knowledge (Miller & Hudson, 2006; Williams 2006). It is important that teachers take into account students' vocabulary when planning math lessons; in some cases, teachers may need to directly teach math vocabulary prior to teaching the mathematical concept (Miller & Hudson, 2006) and teachers need to be consistent in language usage when instructing mathematics, especially vocabulary terms.

The fourth of Miller and Hudson's guidelines recommends providing real-world applications. Helping students see how math has everyday application and affects the quality of life can promote understanding and motivate students.

The final guideline is that teachers provide explicit and systematic instruction in mathematics (Miller & Hudson, 2006). Researchers have consistently found that students with disabilities benefit from explicit instruction (Fuchs, Fuchs, Hamlett, & Appleton, 2002).

How Do We Make Math Materials and Instructional Formats Appropriate for CLDE Learners?

Teachers need to carefully review the mathematics materials to make sure that skills are not only presented clearly with appropriate amounts of practice for students but that maintenance and generality are also built in. Sometimes math textbooks are effective at presenting individual skills and providing practice with the skill but then do not build in opportunities for students to continue to practice the skill once that particular chapter has been completed. When that happens, previously learned skills may not be maintained or generalized to other appropriate settings. If the textbook does not build in maintenance and generalization, then the teacher needs to develop lessons or activities to provide these two important components of effective instruction. Teachers also need to examine the textbook for cultural sensitivity. Word problems might draw upon the students' various cultures or use language that incorporates references that are culturally familiar, for example. There is no need to change the math that is required of students in word problems. For example, a word problem might say:

> Mrs. Smith's class is planning a party. There are 15 boys and 10 girls in the class. Each boy will eat two hot dogs and each girl will eat one hot dog. How many hot dogs will the students need to prepare?

The problem can be changed to:

> Mrs. Gonzales's class is planning a party. There are 15 boys and 10 girls in the class. Each boy will eat two tacos and each girl will eat one taco. How many tacos will the students need to prepare?

The changes do not affect the math but do provide a clear message to the CLDE learners that you think their culture is important. People generally like to read things that are somewhat familiar to them.

As noted elsewhere, CLD groups tend to come from collectivist cultures, and many youths from these groups prefer cooperative or peer-mediated learning formats (e.g., Boykin et al., 2006). One highly recommended strategy for teaching math is peer tutoring. In their review of the peer and cross-age tutoring research, Robinson, Schofield, and Steers-Wentzell (2005) found such programs to have positive academic outcomes for African American and other CLD learners. They also observed positive affective findings, such as more favorable attitudes toward school, enhanced self-concept, and a greater sense of academic efficacy.

Other educators have spoken of creating a community of learners where students assume responsibility for their own and others' progress (Gay, 2002; Ladson-Billings, 1997). This concept was the foundation of the summer math camp Edwards et al. (2001) created for inner-city African American learners. The first guiding principle was to create a sense of family. Within this family atmosphere, youths were helped to feel that they belonged to something special. Mentors (college students) and professional staff were selected on the basis of their sense of caring and ability to be sensitive to special needs of this group. Most of the math activities took place in the problem-solving setting of *learning groups*, with students discussing math and helping each other. High school students were used to tutor middle school students; as a result, the tutors gained a deeper understanding of their own math skills as well a heightened sense of self.

Another guiding principle of the program was *high expectations*. The staff established and maintained high standards for academic and social behaviors. No excuses were accepted, for example, for missed homework or being tardy. All students were expected to be successful in their math work. High-math-achieving, same-race peers were included in the program to serve as models. *Math immersion* and *math challenges* were other key guiding principles. In addition to classroom instruction, students were bombarded with math throughout the day in various forms, such as games, competitions, the stock market, and art. Also, within and outside of class, students were continuously challenged to solve increasingly complex math problems. The math instruction was not, therefore, viewed simply as a remedial program.

Although the typical classroom does not have the flexibility or resources of a summer camp, many of these principles can be incorporated. The importance of high expectations, high standards, a community of learners, and caring environments cannot be overstated for CLDE learners in all academic areas, particularly math.

> **TEACHING TIPS**
>
> **Building Mathematics Skills**
>
> 1. Teach for both skill and concept acquisition.
> 2. Use real-world examples that take into account the students' environment.
> 3. Make sure that the students continue to have opportunities to use the instructed skills after the math unit has been completed.
> 4. Use language that students understand during instruction so students can focus on the math problem.
> 5. Create a community of learners with high expectations and group/peer learning opportunities.

Teaching Other Academic Content to CLDE Learners

Health, science, social studies, English, and foreign languages are all important to the academic curriculum. Teachers in these academic areas are concerned about teaching content in an efficient manner. One of the most widely used instructional strategies in schools is the whole-class lecture.

Lectures

Time and resource considerations often make whole-class instruction an attractive option. What can teachers do as lecturers to ensure the likelihood that their students will understand and learn the information being taught? Teachers might begin each lecture by doing the following:

1. Tell students the topic of the lecture.
2. Explain how this topic relates to previous topics.
3. Present key vocabulary that will be a part of the lecture.
4. Make sure that the lecture flows in a logical fashion.
5. Pose questions to students throughout the lecture to make sure they are paying attention and can correctly respond.
6. If giving a transparency or PowerPoint presentation, use systematic disclosure (i.e., present each point just before you discuss it to aid in maintaining student focus).
7. When appropriate, enhance the instructional materials with culturally sensitive materials.
8. Use verbal cues to highlight critical information (e.g., "this is important," "you need to write this down," "you need to remember this").
9. At the end of the lecture, summarize the major points.
10. Provide a review of the lecture by asking questions.
11. Provide opportunities for students to use the information in other instructional tasks.
12. Begin the next lecture with a brief review of the major points from the previous lecture.

This type of structured presentation is particularly beneficial for children with disabilities or for linguistically diverse learners who do better when instructional objectives are clear and the lesson is sequential. One tactic to help teachers immediately assess the effectiveness of their lectures is to examine the quality of student responses to questions covering the content. Asking questions and having one student respond may not provide enough information on the effectiveness of the instruction for all students. Two whole-group strategies that can be used to promote active student responding, allowing all students to respond to teacher-posed questions simultaneously, are choral responding and response cards.

Choral Responding

Choral responding, like all instructional strategies, works best when the teacher begins by instructing the students how and when to respond to teacher-posed questions, that is, teaching students to chorally respond after the question has been asked and the teacher's signal (e.g., vocal signal "class" or hand signal) has been given. Teachers should require that students respond in unison, and students should be praised for responding simultaneously. When students respond in unison, it is easier for the teacher to determine if all of the students are responding correctly. Choral responding can be especially beneficial for children with visual impairments, who will be able to follow the auditory teacher prompts more readily than visual prompts.

Choral responding is similar to the "call-and-response" style frequently used in the African American community and is a method of communication used in its churches, music, and speeches.

> The call-and-response pattern of singing that was the basis for the spiritual is one cultural trait that has flourished everywhere the people of Western and Central African countries have gone. In this pattern the soloist sings something different each time, changing the words and the melody, but the group sings the same response, chorus, or refrain after each solo. (*Making Music*, Silver Burdett, 2005, http://www.sbgmusic.com/html/teacher/reference/styles/spirituals.html)

Foster (2002) recommends using the "call-and-response" style in classrooms with African American students, thereby building on their community linguistic traditions. It is a relatively easy transition from "call-and-response" to choral responding since both are a structured verbal interaction between an individual and a group. Not only is choral responding culturally responsive to African Americans but also to those from many emerging countries (e.g., South America, Africa, the Caribbean), which use choral responding as an essential part of the educational experience. Thus, choral responding can give a sense of familiarity to those students who have experienced it in their communities or native countries.

Response Cards

Response cards are another effective tool for whole-class instruction across a variety of academic content areas. Students should be instructed to listen for teacher prompts when using response cards. The teacher poses a question, waits 1–2 seconds for students to think about the answer, and then says "hold up your cards." With teacher-prepared cards, distinctive colors can be used for the "True" and "False" sides of the cards. Preprinted response cards (e.g., cards that have "Yes/True" on one side and "No/False" on the other) can easily accommodate students with communication problems, including those with augmented communication devices and those who are deaf. If deaf students in the class use a sign language interpreter, the wait time between the teacher question and holding up the response cards should be increased to 4–5 seconds to allow the student with a hearing impairment the opportunity to receive the information from the interpreter and respond at the same time as other students. Students with communication disabilities who have use of their hands and arms can hold up their preprinted response cards just like other students in the class. Those who have communication disabilities and/or limited use of arms and hands can point to one preprinted response card or two response cards on their desktop, one card with "True" facing up and the other with "False" facing up.

Write-on response cards can also increase responding for all students in the class. Write-on response cards involve two teacher prompts after the question, with each student writing one- to three-word responses. The teacher asks a question, then tells students to "write," waits 2–3 seconds, and then says "hold up your cards." Once again, this strategy is effective for students with vocal communication challenges. Response cards allow students with these problems to fully participate in the lesson in the same way other students do.

Peer Tutoring

Peer tutoring is another flexible strategy that can be used with a variety of academic content. Peer tutoring has been used to teach health concepts to learners with developmental disabilities (Utley, Reddy, Delquadri, Greenwood, Mortweet, & Bowman, 2001), sight words to first- and second-grade minority students at risk for reading failure (Al-Hasaan, 2003), musical skills to middle school students with developmental disabilities (Pilewskie, 1995), Spanish vocabulary to secondary students with and without disabilities (Wright, Cavanaugh, Sainato, & Heward, 1995), sight words to students who are deaf (Harrison, 2002), and time-telling skills to elementary students with behavior disorders (Ma, 2006). Peer tutoring has proven to be an effective instructional strategy for CLDE learners (Al-Hassan, 2003; Bargh, & Schul, 1980; Greenwood, Carta, & Hall, 1988; Jenkins & Jenkins, 1985; McKain, 2004; Noble, 2005; Sherman, 1991). Chapter 9 discussed peer-tutoring systems, of which there are several types, such as classwide peer tutoring, cross-age, role-reversal, and reciprocal peer tutoring (Cartledge & Lo, 2006). Peer tutoring has proven to be a strategy that can be modified to address the instructional needs of diverse students across academic subjects.

How Can Teachers Know If Their Instruction Is Effective with CLDE Learners?

If teachers are to achieve success in the classroom, they must consistently monitor the effectiveness of instruction on individual students. Chapter 9 presented information on curriculum-based measurement (CBM), which is an excellent tactic for evaluating instructional effectiveness by measuring individual students' progress in acquiring basic skills (i.e., reading, writing, math, spelling). CBM can provide quick assessments (e.g., 1-minute timing) in oral reading, math completion, and writing with which to measure the student rate of achievement. By assessing frequently and graphing the data, teachers provide for themselves, students, and parents a picture of the students' academic progress on the targeted skills (see Figure 10–3). Graphs are also ways to assist communication between the teacher and students and parents, particularly when the family's native language is not English. Graphic displays of data have much more universal appeal and clarity for non-native English speakers than written or even spoken language.

Return to Fatima

Fatima's third-grade teacher, Ms. McNeil, recognizes that multiple concerns need to be addressed if Fatima is to be successful in her class. First, a more consistent academic program must be put in place that will decrease the effects of her frequent absences. Second, a systematic plan must be developed to help Fatima form friendships with her classmates.

The general education teacher requests a meeting involving the father, grandmother, special education teacher, school nurse, physical education teacher, Arabic language interpreter, bilingual teacher, and a school administrator. During the meeting, a comprehensive plan is devised to improve Fatima's school experience. The teachers will work with the Arabic interpreter to provide regular weekly updates to the grandmother on Fatima's schoolwork and on home activities for Fatima that would help her academically. If the grandmother needs to contact the school during the day, she will contact the interpreter, who will relay the message to

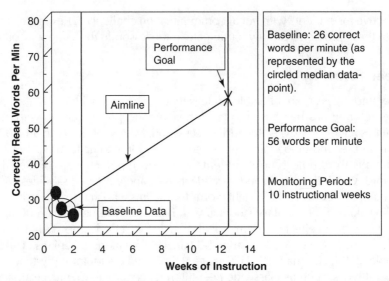

FIGURE 10–3 Jim Wright's workshop manual
Source: Jim Wright's Curriculum-based measurement: A Manual for Teachers. © Jim Wright, Baldwinsville (NY) Central School District. Retrieved August 31, 2007 from http://www.jimwrightonline.com/pdfdocs/cbaManual.pdf

the school. There are two other students in Ms. McNeil's third-grade class who live less than a block from Fatima. Fatima's father or grandmother will be able to pick up homework assignments from either of these students when Fatima is unable to attend school. Ms. McNeil will also send an email to Fatima's father and the parents of the two girls (who live nearby and befriended Fatima) indicating what assignments have been sent to Fatima. The two girls can also explain assignments to Fatima when needed.

When Fatima is able to come to school, she will be provided one-on-one instruction daily in reading and twice a week in math to help her master the third-grade curriculum. The physical education teacher will work with the school nurse and the district's adapted physical education coordinator to develop activities that will allow Fatima to participate without placing undue stress on her respiratory system. For example, during a kickball game Fatima will have the opportunity to kick the ball but another student will actually run the bases for her.

Important actions were also taken in order to build more positive relationships with her peers. First, to help classmates better understand Fatima's disability, the nurse will come to the class and discuss asthma: what it is, how it can be triggered, and some of the challenges that people with asthma face. Second, when Fatima is absent, Ms. McNeil will email Fatima's father to get an update on her condition so that she (Ms. McNeil) can keep classmates informed about Fatima's health. Third, prior to Fatima's return to school, the class will discuss how they can help her to be successful upon her return.

What Are Other Factors Impacting the Inclusive Education Environment?

Teaching in inclusive settings requires even more preplanning than teaching in self-contained classrooms. Both classroom settings require that student academic and social needs be carefully addressed. Both also require that instruction be aligned to the general education curriculum, including instruction for CLDE learners. Meeting the needs of children with exceptionalities in inclusive classrooms requires effective communication between special and general educators. Such collaboration is becoming increasingly prevalent, but not necessarily easier. When two or more educators must work together to provide instruction for a child(ren), both parties must compromise. Thus, tension is a natural part of the collaboration, particularly at the beginning (Heron & Harris, 2001). Each must listen to the other and consider the other's perspective on the situation. If the collaboration is to be successful, there must be honest, clear communication that is focused on what is best for children.

An important aspect of the collaboration is identifying instructional strategies comfortable for both teachers and effective with a variety of children. It is important that these strategies minimize the differences between the children with disabilities and the typically developing children. For example, the teacher could use write-on response cards during whole-class instruction rather than call on one student at a time to answer questions. Or, the teacher could allow a student to use headphones when working on a computer so that additional audio prompts can be given without other students hearing the prompts.

Additionally, teachers need to make decisions about whether adaptations or modifications are needed for the student with a disability, or, for gifted students, decide if enrichment activities are necessary. Adaptations are changes in how the instruction is presented: For example, a student with a severe reading disability might need to have assignments read to him or her. Modifications are changes in what is being taught or how mastery is measured compared to typical students. For example, a grade modification might be appropriate for some students with disabilities, so that rather than achieving 95% on an assignment to earn an "A," the student might need to achieve 80% or a certain level of improvement to earn an "A."

By working together, special and general education teachers can develop inclusive classrooms centered on the principle that all children can succeed and thereby plan for the success of all students. Under these conditions, teachers develop academic schedules that promote a high level of accurate academic responding by each student, establish a classroom environment that demonstrates value for each student, use positive strategies to foster appropriate behaviors, and employ curriculum-based measurements to closely monitor important skills.

How Do We Develop an Academic Schedule? At every school level (i.e., elementary, middle, or high school) teachers must develop an academic schedule prior to the first day of school. If the schedule is based on the Premack Principle (Premack, 1959), the academic effort of that can have a positive impact on student academic achievement. The Premack Principle involves having students do a less reinforcing activity before doing a more reinforcing activity, and is easily incorporated into a classroom schedule. Elementary-level teachers can arrange their classroom schedule to have the students do more challenging activities such as reading and math during the morning prior to more traditionally reinforcing activities such as recess, physical education, and/or art. Middle and high school teachers can structure their classes so that the beginning of the period is more rigorous than the end of the period. For example, in English class, students could write an essay from a writing prompt as the class begins and at the end keyboard their essay into the computer or share their stories with each other. A science class might begin with a lecture and end with a related hands-on activity.

Using the Premack Principle allows the more reinforcing activities to serve as built-in, natural motivation for completing the less reinforcing activities since the consequences are that students cannot do the preferred activity until the less preferred activity is completed satisfactorily. Using the Premack Principle as a foundation, the next step is to employ instructional tactics that promote the understanding of the content and the development of the targeted skill. To accomplish this objective, teachers need to employ the most effective instructional strategies, as discussed in this and other chapters.

Summary

Academic achievement remains the primary goal of schooling. Students with disabilities, particularly those from culturally and linguistically diverse families, are at greater risk for poor academic achievement than those who are developing normally. For both, reading is the most critical skill for school success. If more positive outcomes are to occur for CLDE learners, they need effective instruction in reading and other content areas.

Instructional curricula need to be empirically validated and their effectiveness systematically measured if students are to maximize their academic potential. To meet the instructional needs of CLDE learners, teachers need to use culturally responsive materials along with effective instruction. Culturally responsive teachers will purposely incorporate their students' cultures into the school curriculum.

Related Learning Activities

1. Use a CBM to assess a student who needs instruction. Based on the data, determine the next steps in instruction. For example, conduct 1-minute assessments of the students' oral reading, recording the number of correctly read and incorrectly read words, for three consecutive days.

2. Incorporate culturally responsive materials into an academic lesson. Identify the different cultures represented in your classroom. Learn about each culture by reading books by authors from that culture or talking to adult members of the culture. Decide how you can systematically include in the lesson the information that you are learning.

3. Review the math program in your class or the class where you are observing. How are the principles of effective instruction being employed? How can that class provide for a community of learners? How are the principles of caring and high expectations being communicated to the learners? How are the students being challenged in their studies? How are the students responding to this learning climate?

4. Read literature from culturally diverse authors, and read books to your students from culturally diverse authors. Have students write the author after reading or listening to you read the book.

References

Al-Hassan, S. (2003). *Reciprocal peer tutoring effect on high frequency sight word learning, retention, and generalization of first-grade and second grade urban elementary school students.* Unpublished doctoral dissertation, The Ohio State University, Columbus, OH.

Alvermann, D. E. (2002). Effective literacy instruction for Adolescents. *Journal of Literacy Research, 34*, 189–208.

Andrews, S. P., & Slate, J. R. (2002). Public and private prekindergarten programs: A comparison of student readiness. *Educational Research Quarterly, 25*(3), 59–74.

Archer, A., Gleason, M. M., & Vachon, V. (2000). *Rewards: The multisyllabic word reading program.* Longmont, CO: Sopris West.

Aronson, J. (November, 2004). The threat of stereotype. *Educational Leadership, 62*, 14–19.

Bargh, J. A., & Schul, Y. (1980). On the cognitive benefits of teaching. *Journal of Educational Psychology, 72*, 593–604.

Ben-Ezer, E. (1997). *Hosni the dreamer: An Arabian tale.* New York: Farrar, Straus, & Giroux/HarperCollins.

Boykin, A. W., Tyler, K. M., Watkins-Lewis, K., & Kizzie, K. (2006). Culture in the sanctioned classroom practices of elementary school teachers serving low-income African American students. *Journal of Education for Students Placed At Risk, 11*, 161–173.

Bridge, C. A., & Hiebert, E. H. (1985). A comparison of classroom writing practices, teachers' perceptions of their writing instruction, and textbook recommendations on writing practices. *The Elementary School Journal, 86*, 155–172.

Bryant, D. P. (2005). Commentary on early identification and intervention for students with mathematics difficulties. *Journal of Learning Disabilities, 38*, 340–345.

Callins, T. (2006). Culturally responsive literacy instruction. *Teaching Exceptional Children, 39*(2), 62–65.

Carnine, D. W., Silbert, J., Kame'enui, E. J., & Tarver, S. G. (2004). *Direct instruction reading* (4th ed.). Upper Saddle River, NJ: Merrill/Prentice Hall.

Cartledge, G., & Lo, Y. (2006). *Teaching urban learners: Culturally responsive strategies for developing academic and behavioral competence.* Champaign, IL: Research Press.

Cartledge, G., & Milburn, J. F. (1995). *Teaching social skills to children and youth.* Boston, MA: Allyn & Bacon.

Cawley, J. F., & Miller, J. H. (1989). Cross-sectional comparisons of mathematics performance of children with learning disabilities: Are we on the right track toward comprehensive programming? *Journal of Learning Disabilities, 23,* 250–254.

Clarkson, L. M. C., & Taylor, R. (2006). Mathematics leadership needed to close the achievement gaps. *National Council of Supervisors of Mathematics Journal 8*(2), 4–5.

Czarnecki, E., Rosko, D., & Fine, E. (1998). How to CALL UP note taking skills. *Teaching Exceptional Children, 30,* 14–19.

Davis, J. E. (2003). Early schooling and academic achievement of African American males. *Urban Education, 38*(5), 515–537.

Dobbs, M. (2005, July 15). Black, Latino elementary students closing achievement gap, study says. *The Columbus Dispatch,* p. A3.

Edwards, T., Kahn, S., & Brenton, L. (2001). Math corps summer camp: An inner city intervention program. *Journal of Education for Students Placed At Risk, 6*(4), 411–426.

Engelmann, S., Meyer, L., Carnine, L., Becker, W., Eisele, J., & Johnson, G. (2002). *Corrective reading: Decoding strategies.* Columbus, OH: SRA McGraw-Hill.

Flood, J., Lapp, D., Tinajero, J. V., & Hurley, S. R. (1996/1997). Literacy instruction for students acquiring English: Moving beyond the immersion debate. *Reading Teacher, 50,* 356–359.

Foorman, B. R., & Moats, L. C. (2004). Conditions for sustaining research-based practices in early reading instruction. *Remedial and Special Education, 25*(1), 51–60.

Forness, S. R., Kavake, K. A., Blum, I. M., & Lloyd, J. W. (1997). Mega-analysis of meta-analyses. *Teaching Exceptional Children, 29*(6), 4–9.

Foster, M. (2002). Using call-and-response to facilitate language mastery and literacy acquisition among African American students. *Educational Resources Information Center (ERIC) Digest.* http://www.cal.org/ericcll/digest/0204foster.html

Fuchs, L. S., Fuchs, D., Hamlett, C. L., & Appleton, A. C. (2002). Explicitly teaching for transfer: Effects on the mathematical problem-solving performance of students with mathematics disabilities. *Learning Disabilities Research and Practice, 17,* 90–106.

Garrison, L., Amaral, O., & Ponce, G. (2006). Unlatching mathematics for English language learners. *National Council of Supervisors of Mathematics, 9*(1), 14–24.

Gay, G. (2002). Culturally responsive teaching in special education for ethnically diverse students: Setting the stage. *Qualitative Studies in Education, 15*(6), 613–629.

Gersten, R., Jordan, N. C., & Flojo, J. R. (2005).Early identification and intervention for students with mathematics difficulties. *Journal of Learning Disabilities, 38,* 293–304.

Good, R. H., Kame'enui, E. J., Simmons, D. S., & Chard, D. J. (2002). *Focus and nature of primary, secondary, and tertiary prevention: The CIRCUITS model* (Tech. Rep. No. 1). Eugene, OR: University of Oregon, College of Education, Institute for the Development of Educational Achievement.

Good, R. H., Kaminski, R. A., & Smith S. (2003). *DIBELS: Dynamic indicators of basic early literacy skills* (6th ed.). Longmont, CO: Sorpris West.

Goodman, B. (1994). *Goodman's five star stories.* Lincolnwood, IL: Jamestown Publishers.

Graham, S., & Harris, K. R. (2005). *Writing better: Effective strategies for teaching students with learning difficulties.* Baltimore, MD: Paul Brookes.

Greenwood, C. R., Carta, J. L., & Hall, V. (1988). The use of peer tutoring strategies in classroom management and educational instruction. *School Psychology Review, 17,* 258–275.

Griffin, S. A., Case, R., & Siegler, R. S. (1994). Rightstart: Providing the central conceptual prerequisites for first formal learning of arithmetic to students at risk for school failure. In K. McGilly (Ed.), *Classroom lessons: Integrating cognitive theory and classroom practice* (pp. 24–49). Cambridge, MA: MIT Press.

Grigg, W. S., Daane, M. C., Jinn, Y., & Campbell, J. R. (2003). The nation's report card: Reading 2002. Washington, DC: National Center for Statistics. Retrieved February 11, 2007, from http://nces.ed.gov/nationsreportcard/pubs/main2002/2003521.asp

Hall, C. W., Davis, N. B., Bolen, L. M., & Chia, R. (1999). Gender and racial differences in mathematical performance. *The Journal of Social Psychology, 139*(6), 677–689.

Hamilton, S. L., Seibert, M. A., Gardner, R., III, & Talbert-Johnson, C. (2000). Using guided notes to improve the academic achievement of incarcerated adolescents with learning and behavior problems. *Remedial and Special Education, 21,* 133–140.

Harrison, T. (2002). The development of a peer tutoring program to teach sight words to deaf elementary students. Unpublished doctoral dissertation, The Ohio State University, Columbus, OH.

Heron, T. E., & Harris, K. C. (2001). *The educational consultant: Helping professionals, parents, and students in inclusive classrooms* (4th ed.). Austin, TX: Pro-Ed.

Hessler, T. (Summer, 2005) *The Effects of a writing template on the writing behaviors of high school students with learning disabilities.* Unpublished doctoral dissertation, The Ohio State University, Columbus, OH.

Heward, W. L., & Dardig, J. C. (Spring, 2001). What matters most in special education. *Education Connection,* 41–44.

Heward, W. L., Heron, T. E., Gardner, R., III, & Prayzer, R. (1991). Two strategies for improving students' writing skills. In G. Stoner, M. R. Shinn, & H. M. Walker (Eds.), *A school psychologist's interventions for regular education* (pp. 379–398). Washington DC: National Association of School Psychologists.

Hoffman, M., & Binch, C. (1991). *Amazing grace*. New York: Dial Books for Young Readers.

Howard, G. (1996). Heart. *English Journal, 85*(2), 67–70.

Jackson, Y. (2005). Unlocking the potential of African American students: Keys to reversing underachievement. *Theory Into Practice, 44*(3), 203–210.

Jenkins, J. R., & Jenkins, L. M. (1985). Peer tutoring in elementary and secondary programs. *Focus on Exceptional Children, 17*, 12.

Johnson, K. R., & Ross, L. (1997). *Morningside language fluency: Sentence-combining fluency*. Seattle, WA: Morningside Academy.

Kame'enui, E. (1994). Measurably superior instructional practices in measurably inferior times: Reflections on Twain and Pauli. In R. III, Gardner, D. M., Sainato, J. O. Cooper, T. E. Heron, W. L. Heward, J. Eshleman, & T. A. Grossi (Eds.), *Behavior analysis in education: Focus on measurably superior instruction* (pp. 149 –159). Pacific Grove, CA: Brooks/Cole.

Kiewra, K. A. (2002). How classroom teachers can help students learn and teach them how to learn. *Theory Into Practice, 41*, 71–80.

Kretovics, J., Faber, K. S., & Armaline, W. D. (2004). It ain't brain surgery: Restructuring schools to improve the education of children placed at risk. *Educational Horizons, 82*(3), 213–225.

Laczko-Kerr, I., & Berliner, D. C. (2001). The effectiveness of "Teach for America" and other under-certified teachers on student academic achievement: A case of a harmful policy. *Education Policy Analysis Archives, 10*, 37. Retrieved February 8, 2007, from http://epaa.asu.edu/epaa/v10n37/

Ladson-Billings, G. (1997). The dreamkeepers: *Successful teachers of African American Children*. San Francisco, CA: Jossey-Bass Inc.

Lambert, M. C., Cartledge, G., Lo, Y., & Heward, W. L. (in press). Effects of response cards on disruptive behaviors and academic responding during math lessons by fourth-grade students in an urban school. *Journal of Positive Behavior Interventions*.

Lyon, G. R. & Moats, L. C. (1997). Critical conceptual and methodological considerations in reading interventions research. *Journal of Learning Disabilities, 30*, 578–588.

Ma, Y. (2006). Effects of a computer-assisted peer-tutoring program on the acquisition, maintenance, and generalization of time-telling skills of elementary students with behavior disorders. Unpublished doctoral dissertation, The Ohio State University, Columbus, OH.

Mathes, P. G., & Torgesen, J. K. (1998). All Children can learn to read: Critical care for the prevention of reading failure. *Peabody Journal of Education, 73*, 317–340.

McKain, K. N. (2004). Effects of computer-assisted peer tutoring on acquisition, maintenance, and generalization of time telling with primary students with developmental delays. Unpublished master's thesis, The Ohio State University, Columbus, OH.

Mercer, C. (1997). *Students with learning disabilities*. Upper Saddle River, NJ: Merrill/Prentice Hall.

Miller. S. P., & Hudson, P. J. (2006). Helping students with disabilities understand what mathematics means. *Teaching Exceptional Children, 39*, 28–35.

Moats, L. (1999). *Teaching reading is rocket science: What expert teachers of reading should know and be able to do*. Washington DC: Union of Professionals: AFT Teachers.

Moats, L. (2000). *Speech to print: Language essential for teachers*. Baltimore, MD: Paul Brookes.

Musti-Rao, S., & Cartledge, G. (2006). Beginning reading instruction. In G. Cartledge & Y. Lo (Eds.), *Teaching urban learners: Culturally responsive strategies for developing academic and behavioral competence* (pp. 21–35). Champaign, IL: Research Press.

Musti-Rao, S., & Cartledge, G. (in press). Effects of a supplemental early reading intervention with at-risk urban learners. *Topics in Early Childhood Special Education*.

Myers, W. D. (1988). *Scorpions*. New York: Harper & Row.

National Center for Educational Statistics (April 2001). *The national assessment of educational progress (NAEP)*. Washington, DC: Institute of Education Sciences, U.S. Department of Education. http:/ /nces.ed. gov/ nationsreportcard/

National Center for Educational Statistics (2003). *The nation's report card: Reading highlights 2003*. Washington, DC: U.S. Department of Education, National Center for Education Statistics: Author.

National Center for Educational Statistics. (October, 2005). *National assessment of educational progress reading 2005*. Washington, DC: U.S. Department of Education, Institute of Education Sciences NCES 2006-451.www.nationsreportcard.gov.

National Center for Educational Statistics. (October 2005). *National assessment of educational progress math 2005*. Washington, DC: U.S. Department of Education, Institute of Education Sciences NCES 2006-451. www.nationsreportcard.gov.

National Council of Teachers of Mathematics (2000). *Principles and standards for school mathematics*. Reston, VA: Author.

Nicolini, M. B. (1994). Stories can save us: A defense of narrative writing. *English Journal, 83*, 56–61.

Noble, M. M. (2005). *Effects of peer tutoring on the acquisition, maintenance, and generalization of science vocabulary words for seventh grade students with learning disabilities and/or low achievement*. Unpublished doctoral dissertation, The Ohio State University, Columbus, OH.

Nodine, B. F, Barenbaum, E., & Newcomer, P. (1985). Story composition by learning disabled, reading disabled, and normal children. *Learning Disability Quarterly, 8,* 167–179.

Nougharet, A., Scruggs, T. E., & Mastropieri, M. A. (2004). The effects of teacher licensure on teachers' pedagogical competence: Implications for elementary and secondary teachers of students with learning and behavioral disabilities. In T. E. Scruggs & M. A. Mastropieri (Eds.), *Research in secondary schools: Advances in learning and behavioral disabilities* (Vol. 17, pp. 301–318). Oxford, UK: Elsevier Science/JAI Press.

Peske, H. G., & Haycock, K. (June, 2006). Teaching inequality: How poor and minority children are shortchanged on teacher quality. Report from Educational Trust. Retrieved February 8, 2007, from http://www2.edtrust.org/EdTrust/Press+Room/teacherquality2006.htm

Pilewskie, A. A. (1995). *Effects of peer tutoring on the percussion instrument performance of a student with moderate developmental disabilities.* Unpublished master's thesis, The Ohio State University, Columbus, OH.

Point-Counterpoint. (1997). Literacy instruction for students acquiring English: Moving beyond the immersion debate. *The Reading Teacher, 50*(4), 356–359.

Premack, D. (1959). Toward empirical behavior laws: Positive reinforcement. *Psychological Review, 66,* 219–233.

Rasinski, T. V. (1990). Effects of repeated reading and listening-while-reading on reading fluency. *Journal of Educational Research, 83,* 147–150.

Robinson, D. R., Schofield, J. W., & Steers-Wentzell, K. L. (2005). Peer and cross-age tutoring in math: Outcomes and their design implications. *Educational Psychology Review, 17*(4), 327–362.

Ryan, K. E., & Ryan, A. M. (2005). Psychological processes underlying stereotype threat and standardized math test performance. *Educational Psychologist, 40*(1), 53–63.

Samuels, S. J. (1979). The method of repeated reading. *The Reading Teacher, 32,* 403–408.

Sanacore, J. (2004). Genuine caring and literacy learning for African American children. *The Reading Teacher, 57*(8), 744–753.

Schloss, P. J., Smith, M. A., & Schloss, C. N. (2001). *Instructional methods for secondary students with learning problems.* Boston, MA: Allyn & Bacon.

Schumacher, J. A. (2000). *A parallel text: Early American literature.* Logan, IA: Perfection Learning.

Scott, B. K., & Kame'enui, E. J. (1994). Beginning reading: Educational tools and diverse learners. *School Psychology Review, 23*(3), 372–392.

Sherman, L. W. (1991). Cooperative learning in post secondary education: Implications from social psychology for active learning experiences. Paper presented at the annual meeting of the American Educational Research Association, 1991, Chicago, IL.

Silver Burdett: Making music (2005). Pearson Education: Scott Foresman. Retrieved August 30, 2007 from http://www.sbgmusic.com/html/teacher/reference/styles.html.

Slavin, R. E., & Madden, N. A. (2003). *Success for all/Roots & wings: 2003 summary of research on achievement outcomes.* Baltimore, MD: Johns Hopkins University, Center for Research on the Education of Students Placed at Risk.

Solimene, P. (1997). *Bringing the classics to life.* Long Island, NY: EDCON.

Staubitz, J., Cartledge, G., Yurick, A., & Lo, Y. (2005). Repeated reading for students with emotional or behavioral disorders: A full classroom application. *Behavioral Disorders, 3,* 51–64.

Steele, C. M. (2003). Through the back door to theory. *Psychological Inquiry, 14*(3&4), 314–317.

Steele, C. M., & Aronson, J. (1995). Stereotype threat and the intellectual test performance of African-Americans. *Journal of Personality and Social Psychology, 69,* 797–811.

University of Texas Center for Reading & Language Arts (2003). *Meeting the needs of struggling readers: A resource for secondary English language arts teachers.* Austin, TX: University of Texas/Texas Educational Agency.

Utley, C. A., Reddy, S. S., Delquadri, J. C., Greenwood, C. R., Mortweet, S. L., & Bowman, V. (2001). Classwide peer tutoring: An effective teaching procedure for facilitating the acquisition of health education and safety facts with students with developmental disabilities. *Education and Treatment of Children, 24,* 1–27.

Vaughn Gross Center for Reading and Language Arts (2006). *Scientifically based research,* University of Texas at Austin. http://www.texasreading.org/3tier/levels.asp

Williams, H. (2006). Math in the grammar classroom. *ELT Journal, 61,* 23–33.

Woodcock, R. W., McGrew, K. S., & Mather, N. (2001). *Woodcock-Johnson III Tests of Achievement.* Itasca, IL: Riverside.

Wright, J. Cavanaugh, R. A., Sainato, D. M. & Heward, W. L. (1995). Somos todos ayudantes y estudiantes: A demonstration of a classwide peer tutoring program in a modified Spanish class for secondary students identified as learning disabled or academically at-risk, *Education and Treatment of Children, 18*(1), 33–52.

Yurick, A., & Cartledge, G. (2007). Reducing reading failure for kindergarten urban students: A study of phonemic awareness instruction, treatment quality, and treatment duration. Unpublished manuscript. The Ohio State University, Columbus, OH.

Yurick, A.L., Robinson, P.D., Cartledge, G., Lo, Y., & Evans, T. (2006) Using Peer-mediated repeated readings as a fluency-building activity for urban learners. *Education and Treatment of Children, 29,* 1–38.

Chapter 11

Creating Self-Directed CLDE Learners

The purpose of this chapter is to present strategies to help exceptional learners become more self-regulated and successful students. Through teacher-directed, systematic instruction, students can acquire the critical skills needed to become more efficient learners. Although these strategies can be adapted for students at all age levels, the importance of self-regulated learning perhaps is most salient for middle and high school students. By the end of this chapter, readers should be able to answer the following questions:

1. What are the characteristics of a self-directed or self-regulated learner?
2. What are the special challenges CLDE students encounter in becoming self-regulated learners?
3. How can teachers help students increase their class preparedness?
4. How can teachers help students improve their homework performance?
5. How can teachers involve parents in helping their children become more self-directed students?
6. How can teachers help students set high but realistic academic goals?
7. How can teachers help students to devise plans to achieve their goals?
8. How can teachers help students to self-monitor and evaluate their academic-related behaviors?

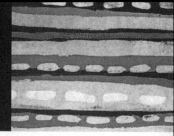

By the end of this chapter, readers will have obtained information on strategies to:

1. Increase student class preparedness.
2. Increase student homework production.
3. Develop study skills for content comprehension.
4. Improve note-taking skills.
5. Set realistic goals.
6. Monitor progress toward goals.

Chris

Chris is a middle school student identified with mild disabilities. Chris's difficulties have persisted since the elementary grades. Academically, he has the most trouble with reading. He has always been at the bottom of his class in reading and now at the age of 14 he is reading at only the fourth-grade level, four grade levels below his assigned class of eighth grade. In other subjects, he often performs at or above grade level. This is especially true in math, where he is often at the top of his class. His teachers view him as a bright youngster who could be a much better student if he managed to improve his reading. They feel his reading problems are limiting his potential in all of his subjects, including math.

To make matters worse, Chris tends to exhibit a few behavior problems. Typically, he is rather quiet and compliant; however, he occasionally displays a temper during which he becomes argumentative with the teacher and refuses to participate in classroom activities. Although infrequent, these episodes are most likely to occur when he is frustrated by some academic task, especially one that involves reading.

Chris has been diagnosed with a learning disability and is receiving instruction in the LD resource classroom for one period per day. The resource teacher focuses on helping Chris develop his reading skills, but he still is having difficulty with some of his mainstreamed classes such as English and social studies. In these classes, Chris is often sullen, frequently fails to participate, and typically does not complete assignments or homework. Chris is in jeopardy of failing both of these classes.

In addition to math, a particular area of strength for Chris is sports. He has special gifts in both basketball and football. He says he wants to become a professional football player in adulthood. Chris knows that in order to achieve his goal he must do better in reading and some of his academic subjects. He does not see himself making much progress and he becomes frustrated and angry.

Chris is an African American male with mixed heritage. Although he identifies primarily with the African American culture, he takes pride in his Native American background and enjoys learning about that culture. Chris's mom, who is a single parent, wants to encourage her son but is not sure what to do. Chris has an older sister who does very well in school. She tries to help Chris with his homework but does not know how to help him become a better reader.

What are some critical academic-related behaviors that Chris must acquire? How might Chris's teachers help him develop these skills? These and other such questions are addressed in this chapter.

How Do We Help CLDE Students Become More Effective Learners?

Self-directed or self-regulated learners evidence higher academic achievement and are characterized as being organized, focused on the subject matter, and engaged in the instructional process (Cooper, Horn, & Strahan, 2005; Harris, Friedlander, Saddler, Frizzelle, & Graham, 2005; Ruban, McCoach, McGuire, & Reis, 2003). Zimmerman (2002) further defines the self-reliant student as one who learns to acquire and employ various processes according to the demands of the task. These processes include setting goals, utilizing strategies effective in attaining the goals, monitoring one's performance, evaluating one's performance, arranging conditions conducive to the goals, and managing one's time. That is, self-regulated learners are expected to be motivated to identify a strategy that will enable them to accomplish a goal, to have the self-discipline to employ the identified strategy, and then to reflect on their efforts in order to evaluate their level of success. According to Zimmerman, teachers and other significant individuals in the learner's life can teach self-regulatory behaviors.

The poor academic persistence and school failure of CLD groups (i.e., African, Hispanic, and Native American) are well documented (Bailey & Paisley, 2004; Caldwell & Siwatu, 2003; Griffin, 2002; Hassinger & Plourde, 2005). In contrast to their European and Asian American peers, these students present a profile of being much more likely to experience academic failure, disproportional special education and disciplinary assignments, early school leaving, and postsecondary marginality. As noted in Chapter 13, these poor outcomes are even greater for CLD students with disabilities. An obvious solution to reversing these trends is to find ways to keep these students engaged in the schooling process until successful graduation. Griffin offers that an important predictor for retaining a student in school is the student's ability to identify with the academic program. Some of the most obvious reasons for lack of identification include poor academic self-confidence, perceived racism, psychological alienation, limited resourcefulness, low self-expectations and goals, and poor academic self-management.

How Do We Help CLDE Students Develop Self-Directed Preparedness Skills?

Why Teach Organization and Preparedness Skills?

The importance of class organization and preparedness increases as students move through the grades. In the higher grades, students not only need to be attentive but also are responsible for materials in multiple classes and for different assignments in each of these classes. Although students are expected to act responsibly and independently, many students will need direct instruction and support in order to acquire the required preparation skills. This is particularly true for students with disabilities and this becomes most critical as they attempt to matriculate in inclusive settings.

Needless to say, classroom preparation is situation specific. That is, the subject matter and conditions in class A may give rise to different expectations for class preparation than in class B. In one study of high school survival skills, for example, Schaeffer, Zigmond, Kerr, and Farra (1990) observed that survival skills meant that students went to class every day, arrived on time, brought pencils, paper, and books to class, submitted work on time, refrained from talking back to teachers, and followed directions. In another study with middle school students with severe cognitive disabilities within an inclusive setting, Gilberts, Agran, Hughes, and Wehmeyer (2001) listed the teacher-specified classroom survival skills as: (1) in class when bell rings, (2) in seat when bell rings, (3) brings appropriate materials to class, (4) greets the teacher, (5) greets other students, (6) asks questions, (7) answers questions when addressed by the teacher, (8) sits up straight, (9) looks at the teacher, (10) acknowledges the teacher, and (11) records class work in planner. A third example provided by Williams (1987) suggests that being prepared means the student comes to class with the class book, homework, notebook, paper, and pencil. Williams suggested that the notebook be a three-ring binder with lined paper, dividers for each class, and an assignment notebook and that pencils and highlighting pens be kept in plastic pencil cases. Thus, with variations, it is generally acknowledged that the prepared student comes to class possessing the requisite materials, task-related social skills, and a positive attitude toward learning.

Bailey and Paisley (2004) devised Project: Gentlemen on the Move (PGOTM), a comprehensive program for African American high school males designed to increase school connectedness and success. Participants in the program were expected to:

1. Attend school daily, with the admonition that they could not learn if they were not in school.
2. Come to class prepared. It was their responsibility to themselves and to their peers. They were to be respectful to their teachers and to treat each class as if it was their future.
3. Show respect for all school personnel; that's being a gentleman.
4. Strive to be above average; being average was not the goal of the program.

An important component of this model was the involvement of gender- and culturally specific mentors who advised the youth on daily living issues such as race, manhood, and academic performance. Participating youth met weekly to discuss program rules and principles. Participation in the program was voluntary, and the authors report that although some students "fell through the cracks," others went on to successful and distinguished careers.

Another program with a similar orientation toward increasing academic persistence among African and Hispanic American high school students is The Educational

Culturally and linguistically diverse students benefit from mentoring programs that help them to think of themselves as competent learners and to be successful students.

Navigating Skills Seminar (TENSS) (Caldwell & Siwatu, 2003). Although designed to promote college orientation among high school students, the principles and procedures could be adapted for students with disabilities for whom college may or may not be a realistic goal. The authors assert that to persist academically, CLD students need both strong cognitive and affective functions, "to be equipped with skills that allow them to persist academically even in unwelcoming environments" (p. 34). For example, students participate in seminars that begin with affirmations of the positive aspects of their cultural diversity in the midst of ongoing challenges to their sense of self. Along the same lines, students are engaged in discussions intended to refute stereotypes and have them think about themselves as capable learners. The authors report using visual imagery to help students think more positively about their own learning potential as well as of those from the students' cultural and socioeconomic group.

Addressing racial and identity issues as described in the PGOTM and TENSS models is extremely important in helping CLDE students become self-directed learners. It is also important to provide explicit instruction in specific self-direction skills. As noted in the following sections, discussions alone are often inadequate, particularly for students with disabilities.

How Do We Teach for Student Organization and Preparedness?

Leinweber (1991) compared a series of strategies to increase the organization and preparedness of four urban middle school students with learning disabilities. These strategies consisted of individual discussions with the students, daily prompts, specific preparation training, self-monitoring, and peer assistance. During the discussions, students acknowledged the need to improve their classroom preparation behavior and generally stated that they needed to try harder to be prepared. The researcher followed discussions with daily prompts to remind students to be prepared, but the data showed that discussions and daily prompting had little or no effect on student preparation. It did, however, improve when preparation training accompanied by self-monitoring and peer assistance were added. During preparation training, the researcher presented and modeled the notebook students were to prepare for each day's class. They were shown how to organize the notebooks so that the assignment papers and materials were visible and readily accessible. Students also were taught how to head their papers according to the classroom teacher's expectations. Students practiced these skills during the training.

To increase the likelihood that the students would employ these steps on a daily basis, the researcher taught the students to self-monitor. Self-monitoring training took the following pattern:

1. Students received a self-monitoring form listing all the materials they needed to be prepared for class. (see Figure 11–1).
2. Students were shown how to complete the card and how to calculate points and a grade for completing their homework.
3. Students were given directions on when they would receive the card and when they were to turn it in to the classroom teacher.
4. Students were advised that they would receive one point for turning in the card, one point for completing the card accurately, and one point for having at least four of the five items for class. Homework must be one of the four items. Students received one-half point if homework was not one of the four items completed, and they got two points if they had all five items.

FIGURE 11-1 Self-monitoring class preparedness card

Name _____			Date _____
	Yes	No	
Pencil	___	___	Homework Percentage _____ %
Text book	___	___	
Folder	___	___	Points Earned _____
Paper	___	___	
Homework	___	___	_____

Source: Leinweber, M. (1991). *Effects of preparation training self-monitoring, and peer-assistance on the daily class preparation of low-achieving middle-school students.* Unpublished master's thesis. The Ohio State University, Columbus, OH. Used with permission.

5. The researcher discussed with the students rewards that they could earn with the points and the number of points needed for each item.
6. Individual contingency contracts were devised for each student.

As a result of the self-monitoring, all four students showed substantial improvements in their class preparedness once they were trained to monitor their own behavior. In addition to the checklist that probably served as a cue for preparedness, the reinforcement component most likely helped to motivate students to be more compliant in classroom preparation.

Nickel (2005) used similar procedures to improve the organization and class preparedness skills of six middle school students with emotional and behavior disorders. The training package consisted of a combination of instruction, prompts, self-monitoring, and rewards. Students were taught how to organize their notebooks and to monitor their behavior at the same time. Once the students were trained, the teacher verbally prompted the students daily and then gradually faded the prompts over a period of 5 weeks. Students then were prompted by a mnemonic graphic posted in the classroom (see Figure 11–2). All six of Nickel's middle school students improved considerably in classroom preparedness in both their special and general education classes.

How Do We Help Improve Homework Performance?

The homework studies observe the difficulties in improving homework preparation (e.g., Cosden, Morrison, Gutierrez, & Brown, 2004; Leinweber, 1991; Nickel, 2005). It appears that more powerful interventions to improve homework preparation are warranted (e.g., more assistance with the homework subject matter, a stronger home–school connection, or more attractive rewards for completing homework). Teachers have traditionally assigned students homework ostensibly to increase academic skill proficiency and to maximize learning opportunities that are limited by the typical school day. Although the beneficial effects of homework completion may be debated (Krashen, 2005), there is evidence that homework can have desirable returns. For example, data on the after-school study habits of Asian American (Krashen) and Asian (Yoo, 2005) students strongly point to the beneficial effects of homework on academic achievement. Krashen cites research showing that Hmong students from Laos reported spending nearly twice as much time on homework as their peers and achieved the highest grades compared to their peers who

FIGURE 11-2 Poster for classroom preparedness
Source: Copyright © E. L. Nickel. Used with permission.

TEACHING TIPS

Organization and Classroom Preparedness

1. Teach students how to organize class materials for daily use.
2. Teach students how to use a daily self-monitoring form to track their preparedness for class every day.
3. Devise and administer reinforcing contingencies for class preparedness.
4. Use classroom prompts such as posters to remind students of steps for class preparedness.

---

spent less time on homework. In this research, students who spent 1 hour or less on homework averaged grade point averages of 2.3, whereas those who spent 4 or more hours achieved grade point averages of 3.1. Other research with at-risk students shows that homework programs can lead to improvements in students' academic self-confidence and study skills as well as serve as a protective mechanism preventing students from losing any academic gains (Cosden et al., 2004).

Along with evidence supporting the value of homework, authorities in the field also note that students with learning problems often experience more difficulty meeting homework expectations (Margolis, 2005). Margolis gives several suggestions for helping "struggling learners" with homework, including (1) providing after-school assistance,

(2) providing peer models, (3) developing organization/self-management skills, and (4) working with parents.

After-School Programs. One means of helping at-risk students with homework has been after-school programs. Under these conditions, students typically are assigned to work one-on-one or in small groups with tutors, who provide assistance with homework. In their review of existing research on such programs, Cosden et al. (2004) found positive effects, especially for English language learners (ELL). Compared to their English-proficient peers, teachers rated ELL students more favorably in terms of academic effort and study skills. Increases in homework performance appeared to lead to more favorable perceptions of students by teachers as well as by students toward themselves. Both conditions led to better grades (Cosden et al.; Krashen, 2005).

Peer Assistants. In her efforts to increase student preparedness, including homework, Leinweber (1991) speculated that students were failing to complete these assignments because they did not completely understand them or how to do them. Therefore, she assigned more competent peers to be peer assistants. During the last 10 minutes of school each day, the target student was to meet with the peer assistant and begin the homework assignment. This gave the student the opportunity to ask questions about the work and a head start on that day's homework assignment. Target students and peer assistants were trained how to participate in these sessions. The student being helped was told to (1) make sure the assignment was written down, (2) ask the peer assistant any questions the student might have about the assignment, (3) begin working together, (4) try to work individually for a while, and (5) get additional clarification from the peer assistant if there were more questions. The peer assistant was trained in these same steps, with an emphasis on helping the student to do his or her own work and not doing the work for the student. Peer assistants were encouraged to be positive and to find out if the student had more questions before they left school.

Leinweber found peer assistance to be particularly effective for two of the four students she studied. As other research has found (e.g., Cosden et al., 2004), peer-assistant interventions can benefit some students, but the mitigating factors are not always entirely clear.

Parents. Parents are an important factor in students' homework performance. For all parents, homework can be extremely stressful, and especially for those with limited academic or English skills. Assisting students with their homework during or after school can reduce some of this stress, but Cosden et al. (2004) point out that such assistance removes parents from the homework "loop" and "may reduce parental opportunities to communicate with the child about school" (p. 225). Students do need to see their parents engaged in literacy activities and they need to know that their parents value their academic competence. Parents of youth in the PGOTM program, for example, attend monthly meetings, where they discuss their child's academic and social performance.

If parents are not sufficiently skilled to assist their children with school assignments, they can learn to create home environments that foster academic performance (Margolis, 2005). Teachers and other school personnel can supply parents with useful strategies. For example, they can either provide information directly or show parents how to access websites like the Family Education Network that offer suggestions on how to change homework behavior. One example is the Homework Behavior Plan, which essentially consists of a parent-child contract in which the parties (parent and student) specify what homework behavior they wish to change, the strategy that will be used, and how the student

FIGURE 11–3 Homework tips.

Homework Tips

1. Make homework routine. Have a set time and place for homework each day.
2. Be positive about homework; it is not something to dread.
3. Let the child do the homework. Help with understanding, if necessary, but the child needs to demonstrate understanding of the material.
4. Help your child decide the order in which to do homework. Find the order that is most comfortable for the child.
5. Set a time limit for homework. If the child does not understand a problem, communicate this to the teacher so that the teacher can provide additional instruction.
6. Talk with your child's teacher about homework expectations and the district's policy about homework. Find out how much time the teacher expects your child to spend on homework.
7. Notice correct problems first. Focus on strengths first, then needs.
8. Be prepared. Have the supplies, assignments, and an uncluttered space for the child.
9. Recognize frustration. Let your child take a break and have a chance to refocus.
10. Reward the work. Let your child know you are proud of his or her hard work.

Source: Adapted from "Homework Doesn't Need to Create Stress for Students and Parents." *Speakout: Colorado's Information Newsletter for Children with Disabilities*, Fall 2003, Peak Parent Center.

will be rewarded. The contract is signed and dated by both parties. This website also has suggestions from parents on how they helped to improve their children's homework behavior. One such suggestion follows:

> The best way to get my child to be motivated and goal oriented is to use a timer. We set the timer for a mutually agreed upon time frame and this helps him to focus. He feels a sense of accomplishment upon achieving this goal. If he doesn't make the time goal, we just adjust it for the next task and discuss why this didn't work. He has participated in his success!

Some parents will need considerable help in devising strategies that will be successful with their children. Teacher investment of time and effort in helping these families is extremely important, especially for culturally diverse students with disabilities, whose families are less likely to have the resources or skills to devise these interventions on their own. In such cases, teachers and other school staff might access or develop simple guidelines for the parents, put the guidelines in the parents' reading language, and demonstrate to parents how they might implement the steps. Figure 11–3 shows such a list, which was adapted from the Peak Parent Center newsletter. Teachers need to review each item with parents to make sure the points are clear and that the parents are able to follow through. The newsletter provides the same listing in Spanish for Spanish-speaking parents.

How Do We Help CLDE Students Develop Study Skills?

Why Teach Study Skills?

If students are to be successful learners, they need to acquire various study skills. Gettinger and Seibert (2002) observe that one key difference between good and poor students is that good students are active learners whereas poor students tend to display a passive learning style. Active learners are inclined to scan the material before reading, try to identify the most important information, draw upon previous knowledge to try to understand the material, and switch strategies if the current strategy is not working. Passive learners, on the other hand, tend to rely on their teachers or others to supply them with the needed information and seem to be unaware that they need to exert effort in order to learn the material. According to Gettinger and Seibert, poor learners tend to rely on rote memorization, are not inclined to set goals, and allocate insufficient time to studying. All students need to be motivated to study. Additionally, learning must be active and students need a supportive home environment.

What Are Study Skills?

Gettinger and Seibert (2002) note four basic types of study strategies: (1) repetition or rehearsal-based, where the learner repeatedly rehearses information, which may be enhanced with the use of mnemonics; (2) procedural or organization-based, which involves learning to organize time or assignments to facilitate learning; (3) cognitive-based, which requires the learner to connect new material to previous knowledge and employ a schemata to help learn new information; and (4) metacognitive-based, which focuses on the way the student thinks about the material. For example, the student will ask questions such as "Why am I studying this passage?"

Numerous studies conducted on teaching study skills indicate that cognitive and metacognitive strategies are effective and the combination of these strategies is superior to either one in isolation (Gettinger & Seibert, 2002). In helping students acquire these skills, the authors point out the need to model rather than simply tell students how to perform them. Teachers first demonstrate how to use a study strategy, followed by giving the student an opportunity to imitate the teacher's behavior. The next step is to provide practice with many varied opportunities. Over time, as the student displays increasing skill, the student gradually transitions from teacher guidance to being self-regulated in using these study strategies.

A Sample Study Skill

One commonly used cognitive study skill strategy is SQ3R, which stands for Survey, Question, Read, Recite, and Review. Students are taught to use these five steps to increase their understanding and retention of the material they read, particularly in the content areas.

Survey. Have the student reflect on what is already known about the topic. Have students review the table of contents, headings, subheadings, and visuals such as maps and charts to get an idea of what is being discussed in the material to be read.

Question. Have students formulate questions before they begin to read and ask themselves these questions while reading. One way to form questions is to turn the chapter headings and subheadings into questions. If the chapter in a historical novel is entitled "The Camp by the River," related questions might be "Who is in the camp by the river?," "Where is the camp?," "What is the river?," and "Why are they by the river?"

Read. Students should read to answer the questions. Have students break the reading material into brief segments, according to their skill. As they read, students may want to formulate additional questions. Encourage students to read everything in the assigned segment, including maps, charts, and graphs.

Recite. Students may stop at the point where they are able to answer each question. Students recite the information gained, how they would answer their questions, and make connections with previously read sections.

Review. Students attempt to recall what they have read, putting the material in a logical and meaningful context. While reading or following reading, students should write down the answers to their questions and other important notes about the section. These notes are used for review immediately after reading the section and can serve as future study notes in preparing for quizzes or essays.

Although SQ3R is widely known, some students may have difficulty using it because it is rather time-consuming. Students should be coaxed to use variations that might work well for them. For example, the student might generate a sentence or phrase that captures each subheading. These could be listed on the computer, easily corrected with reviews,

---

APPLICATION

Mr. Thomas, Chris's resource room teacher, decided it would be helpful to teach Chris the SQ3R study skill to use in his content-area classes, especially English and social studies, where he was less successful. He decided to teach Chris using the historical novel *Sacajawea* (Bruchac, 2000) because this was one of the novels recommended in his English class, and dealt with the American history period of President Jefferson and Lewis and Clark that were currently being studied in his social studies class. Another attraction was that Chris had Native Americans in his ethnic background and Sacajawea was a Native American guide for the Lewis and Clark expedition. Finally, Mr. Thomas speculated that the content of this story would be attractive to a middle school male and that the short chapters would not greatly tax Chris in reading. Mr. Thomas also planned to use this novel in the resource room for the repeated reading strategies designed to improve Chris's overall reading.

Mr. Thomas presented the book to Chris, pronounced the name, and asked Chris what he thought the book might be about. They looked at the chapter titles and Mr. Thomas asked Chris if he had any more ideas, and what he knew about President Jefferson, the Louisiana Purchase, and the Lewis and Clark expedition.

After a brief discussion, Mr. Thomas directed Chris to read the first chapter, "The Camp by the River." Before reading, Mr. Thomas helped Chris specify questions, such as "Who was in the camp?," "Where is the river?," and "What happened at the camp?" Chris wrote down the questions.

As Chris read, he stopped periodically to discuss the answers to one of the questions. Due to his reading problems, Mr. Thomas helped Chris with any words that he did not know. Chris wrote down the answers to his previously listed questions and was encouraged to read the map in the book as well as the text to get the answers to some of his questions (e.g., the name of the river).

At the end of the chapter, Chris reviewed with Mr. Thomas the main ideas of what he got from that chapter. He also corrected his notes and put them in a notebook to be used for this book. The next day, Chris reviewed the previous day's notes before using the SQ3R procedure to read the next chapter.

As Chris developed skill in using this study strategy, Mr. Thomas encouraged Chris to work more and more independently. Chris shared daily with Mr. Thomas the questions he developed, the answers he identified, and his summaries of each chapter. Chris was encouraged to apply this strategy as he worked with other tutors on his content area subjects.

and then printed and filed for future review. A notebook could be developed for each subject area.

How Do We Help CLDE Students Develop Note-Taking Skills?

Why Teach Note-Taking Skills?

In order to be successful in school, especially at the middle school and secondary levels, students need to acquire effective note-taking skills. It is especially important for students with disabilities to learn to take notes in mainstreamed classes, where they are expected to be more independent learners. Some research shows a positive relationship between note taking and test scores (Boyle, 2001), and other studies underscore the role of active student responding during note taking and subsequent higher achievement (Heward, 2001).

Note taking is a multidimensional process. Boyle (2005) points out that note taking involves listening, cognitive processing of information received, writing the information, and then reviewing one's notes with understanding. A related subset of abilities noted by Boyle involves sustained and focused attention so that students are able to select out the most important information to record. If students attempt to take verbatim notes, they undoubtedly would miss important information and probably would become frustrated. Students also need to be able to evidence an understanding of what was said and to personalize the information so that they can connect it to previous experiences or their own background knowledge. Additionally, according to Boyle, students need to be able to organize information and to write fluently.

Students with disabilities have characteristic writing problems (Graham, Schwartz, & MacArthur, 1993). Boyle advises that when taking notes these students will have difficulty organizing the information, writing fast, writing neatly, and spelling. Difficulties in spelling often slow down the note-taking process because students often spend precious minutes trying to figure out how to spell a word or set of words. Even if they master the spelling in time, often too much information has been shared for them to complete that set of notes. Thus, their notes are incomplete and often meaningless.

What Are Specific Note-Taking Strategies?

Strategic Note Taking. All of these difficulties need to be taken into consideration when helping students improve their note-taking skills. One strategy recommended by Boyle is *strategic note taking*. Students are given note-taking paper containing specific cues. The cues are intended to help students organize their thoughts about the lecture, which will promote comprehension. The steps involve (1) finding out what the student knows about the topic, (2) periodically during the lecture asking clusters of students to identify three to seven main points and to summarize the information, and (3) requiring students at the end of the lecture to write five main points with descriptions of each point. An example of the Strategic Note-Taking Form is given in Figure 11–4.

Note Taking with AWARE. Hughes and Suritsky (1993) provide another model for helping students with disabilities to develop note-taking skills. They recommend teaching students how to take notes using the AWARE strategy, which is outlined as follows:

1. Arrange to take notes by arriving early, take a seat in clear view of the instructor/ board/visual materials. Note and date paper.

FIGURE 11-4 An abbreviated strategic note taking form

Strategic Note-Taking Form

Fill this portion before the lecture begins.
What is today's topic?
Describe what you know about the topic.

As the instructor lectures, use these pages to take notes of the lecture.
Today's topic?
Name three to seven main points with details of today's topic as they are being discussed.
Summary—Quickly describe how the ideas are related
New Vocabulary or Terms:
Name three to seven new main points with details as they are being discussed.
New Vocabulary or Terms:
Summary—Quickly describe how the ideas are related.
Name three to seven new main points with details as they are being discussed.
New Vocabulary or Terms:
Summary—Quickly describe how the ideas are related.

At End of Lecture
Write five main points of the lecture and describe each point.
1.
2.
3.
4.
5.

Source: From "Enhancing the Note-Taking Skills of Students with Mild Disabilities," 2001, *Intervention in School and Clinic, 36,* 221. Copyright © 2001 by PRO-ED, Inc. Reprinted with permission.

2. Write quickly using shorthand. Students are taught to use abbreviations (e.g., abbreviating by using the first three or four letters of a long word) and symbols.
3. Attend to cues (e.g., when the instructor says, "The three most important reasons for . . ." the learner knows this is important information to note and highlight).
4. Review notes. Review notes as soon as possible after lecture.
5. Edit. Fill in any missing information, include personal information, and clarify/elaborate as needed. Numbers 4 and 5 are done simultaneously.

Note Taking Through Technology. Technology also can be used to aid students with disabilities in note taking. Technology may contribute to motivation, increased productivity, and a sense of belonging for students with disabilities within an inclusive class (Quenneville, 2001). According to Quenneville, various types of assistive technology can benefit the writing and note taking of students with disabilities if they are effectively taught. One such technical tool is the portable note taker, a simple machine that requires only turning on and off. The student is able to take notes quickly with little attention to the device. In addition to writing quickly, this tool enables the learner to edit, check spelling, and automatically save the text.

Note Taking Through Guided Notes. Guided notes provide even more structure to aid in students' note taking. Heward (2001) defines guided notes as "instructor-prepared handouts that provide all students with background information and standard cues with specific spaces to write key facts, concepts, and/or relationships during the lecture" (p. 1). Among the various advantages of guided notes, an important point is that they help students with disabilities to organize the information, eliminate the need for them to guess at what is most important about the instructor's lecture, help keep students engaged in the class, and perhaps help them achieve better academic performance (Austin, Lee, & Carr, 2004; Lazarus, 1993). Heward's (2001) guidelines for developing guided notes advise instructors to streamline the course content to emphasize the most important information, cue students where to fill in key points, project lectures through PowerPoint slides or transparencies, and minimize the amount of writing required. Heward recommends using a fairly standard set of symbols to aid students in their understanding of lecture information:

---

(1) ❶☆ A star or circled numeral might be used to signal a definition, concept, key point, or procedure.

(2) _____ Fill-in blank lines are used for the student to complete a definition, concept, key point, or procedure.

(3) ☞ A pointing finger is used in reviewing or studying notes. The student is expected to think of and write in his or her own example(s) of a concept or idea for applying a particular strategy.

(4) ✎ **Big Idea** ✎ Big ideas are statements or concepts with wide-ranging implications for understanding and/or applying course content. (p.4)

Taken from Heward, W. L. (2001). *Guided notes: Improving the effectiveness of your lectures.* Columbus, OH: The Ohio State University Partnership Grant for Improving the Quality of Education for Students with Disabilities.

Prompting students with disabilities to write their own examples to explain a lecture concept can be a particularly effective means of helping them to apply and synthesize the instructional information. If they are unable to generate their own examples, students then realize that they do not understand the material and need to seek out additional assistance. A sample guided note instructional page might be like the one in Figure 11–5. Words in parentheses would be omitted on the student's sheet; the student would fill in the blanks as the teacher lectured.

FIGURE 11–5 Example of guided notes

Sample Guided Notes

(An (expedition) is a trip made by a group of people to explore an unknown territory.

Sacajawea was a Native American woman who served as a (guide) for the Lewis and Clark expedition.

☞ Lewis and Clark explored unknown territories. Can you name another example of explorers?

> **TEACHING TIPS**
>
> **Note Taking**
>
> 1. Provide students with structured note-taking forms such Strategic Note-Taking Forms or Guided Notes.
> 2. Teach students how to identify the most important information in lectures.
> 3. Teach students how to use lecture notes to assess their understanding of lecture content.
> 4. Teach students how to use abbreviations and how to edit notes.
> 5. When necessary, teach students how to use assistive technology for taking notes.

How Do We Help CLDE Students Improve Their Academic Self-Management Skills?

How Do We Teach CLDE Students to Set Goals?

The ability to set and systematically pursue realistic goals is an important factor in becoming a competent learner. Goal-setting studies indicate good beneficial effects for secondary (Troia & Graham, 2002) as well as elementary-aged students (Palmer & Wehmeyer, 2003). There also is evidence that student-set goals may produce greater returns than teacher-set ones (Swain, 2005) and that goal attainment may lead students to express greater confidence in their learning ability (Cooper, Horn, Strahan, 2005).

There are some important considerations when attempting to set goals with CLD learners. Caldwell and Siwatu (2003) point out, for example, that African American students often have an unrealistic idea of their competence and of expectations within an academic setting. They recommend that school personnel first present these youth with an

Culturally and linguistically diverse students would benefit from special strategies to assist in taking lecture notes.

accurate appraisal of the skills needed for a particular goal (e.g., college), and then follow up with a session in which students are encouraged to do a self-assessment, taking a personal inventory of their existing skills and the skills they will need to achieve a particular educational goal.

Griffin (2002) cautions that these realistic assessments not concentrate on deficits, which may discourage students, but rather on setting realistic goals that students can achieve. It is important to encourage students, create a sense of belonging within the school setting, and foster positive teacher relationships, which are important to CLDE students especially during the assessment process. Hassinger and Plourde (2005) observed that high expectations, a caring attitude, and good relationships with their students were teacher characteristics that contributed greatly to the academic success of Hispanic American students. Also related to positive relationships is student support. Directors of the PGOTM program provided student support through individual and group counseling sessions during which they set short- and long-term academic and social goals (Bailey & Paisley, 2004).

What Are Some Specific Goal-Setting Strategies? Goal setting is often described as a multistep, problem-solving process in which the learner identifies the goal, generates options to determine the method for achieving the goal, and evaluates the effects of these efforts. Palmer and Wehmeyer (2003) describe the Self-Determined Learning Model of Instruction in which the problem-solving steps are labeled as *What is my goal? What is my plan? What have I learned?* Each step involves a series of four student questions and teacher objectives designed to help the learner be successful in this process. The first step is enabling the learner to set a goal. The first two student questions are *What do I want to learn? and What do I know about it now?* Related teacher supports include helping students to identify interests and understand what they already know about the topic. The second step requires the student to take action, with questions such as *What can I do to learn what I don't know? and What could keep me from taking action?* Teachers support students by helping them assess their current status relative to the goal and what they need to do to bridge the gap. The final step of adjusting the goal or plan involves questions such as *What actions have I taken?* and

---

TEACHING TIPS

Goal Setting with CLDE Students

1. Help students to explore their interests, background knowledge, and current status in order to identify specific goals to accomplish. Make sure students have a realistic assessment of their goals.
2. Help students conduct a personal assessment of their skills relative to the desired goals.
3. Conduct goal-setting sessions optimistically, helping students identify achievable goals.
4. Maintain a positive, caring attitude toward students.
5. Identify support systems for students.
6. Help students identify strategies that can be used to achieve these goals.
7. Apply reinforcing contingencies for students acting on these strategies.
8. Help students develop and use recording forms to assess the progress they are making toward their goals and to evaluate their accomplishments.

What barriers have been removed? Teachers help students to evaluate their progress toward the goal and desired outcomes. Although this model was initially designed for adolescents, Palmer and Wehmeyer report success with primary-aged children as young as kindergarten.

Troia and Graham (2002) offer a slightly different version of the problem-solving model for teaching a goal-setting writing strategy to adolescents with learning disabilities. The researchers used the acronym STOP & LIST, which stands for "Stop, Think of Purposes," and "List Ideas, Sequence Them." Using this mnemonic, students were guided in identifying purposes or goals of the essay, generating as many ideas as possible, and organizing and modifying the ideas as appropriate. Students are taught to use this method through instructor modeling over several sessions until they are able to apply the model independently in developing written essays. The authors report qualitatively better essays from students taught by this model compared to students taught the typical process approach of drafting, revising, proofreading, and publishing.

How Do We Teach CLDE Students to Self-Monitor Their Academic Behavior?

Self-monitoring provides a means whereby the student can be actively involved in the learning process; it enables the student to take ownership for academic progress. Additionally, self-monitoring may aid in the generalization of behaviors, and it may provide support in inclusive settings (Daly & Ranalli, 2003; Gilberts, Agran, Hughes, & Wehmeyer, 2001; McConnell, 1999; Prater, Joy, Chilman, Temple, & Miller, 1991). Furthermore, there is good research evidence showing that self-monitoring can increase academic on-task behaviors as well as academic productivity (Levendoski & Cartledge, 2000). Finally, many of the self-monitoring procedures are unobtrusive and easy to implement in an inclusive classroom.

What Are the Guidelines for Helping Students to Use Academic Self-Monitoring Systems? In teaching students to manage their own behavior, McConnell (1999) advises teachers to discuss the behavior with students, to define it, and to model it so that students know exactly what is expected. Additionally, it is important to get students to commit to monitoring the behavior and to set goals of desired performance. The student and teacher then collaborate to determine appropriate reinforcers.

Commitment is a key factor in academic self-monitoring for CLD learners. These youth are not likely to participate in these strategies if they feel alienated from school, if they have low expectations of their ability to perform, or if they do not have school-related goals. Group sessions, as discussed previously in this chapter, may be needed to identify cultural and academic issues before pursuing self-monitoring strategies. School personnel need to make every effort to communicate to CLDE students that they are valued and capable of achieving. Self-monitoring systems can be extremely effective and affirming for CLDE learners. Daily feedback on achieving increasingly higher goals can encourage them about their capabilities and motivate them not only to persist in their school programs but also to pursue even higher goals.

Daly and Ranalli (2003) provide the following guidelines for teaching students to use self-monitoring tools:

1. Define the behavior. Decide if the focus is on increasing positive behavior or on reducing undesired behavior
2. If the latter, determine an incompatible or alternative behavior you would like to depict (e.g., reduce talk-outs versus asking for permission to speak).

3. Collect baseline data for at least 3 days and determine at what level the behavior currently exists (e.g., averages 5 out of 10 completed items on reading practice items each day).
4. Select self-monitoring forms based on the student's ability to count and whether you are focused on reducing behavior or just increasing positive behavior.
5. Set the criterion level for both desired and undesired levels, based on baseline counts. Set criteria for desired behavior slightly above and criteria for undesired behavior slightly below baseline counts. Gradually increase the criteria.
6. Specify the reward for meeting both criteria.
7. Present the self-monitoring tool to the student, get the student's commitment to use the tool, and train the student how to use it. Practice with the student and prompt the student during the initial efforts until the student is responding without prompting.
8. Use the self-monitoring procedure during specific periods when the positive behavior is most desired or when the undesired behavior is most likely to occur.
9. At the end of the period, praise the student for counting, evaluate with the student, and reward the student accordingly.
10. Revisit and revise the self-monitoring form as the student progresses. Involve parents in the use of the self-monitoring form so that some of the strategies might be used at home, enabling parents to reinforce the progress the student is making at school.
11. Gradually fade the use of the self-monitoring form as the student demonstrates more and more ability to manage behavior. Be sure to continue to praise the student for appropriate behavior.

Some accommodations for special populations recommended by these authors might include smiling and unsmiling faces to replace numerals for students without reading skills, color coding (e.g., red and green, representing stop and go) to emphasize depictions of desired and undesired behaviors, student drawings of desired/undesired behaviors, and the use of children's photographs, especially for children with autism, so that they might appropriately associate themselves with the targeted behavior(s).

What Are Some Specific Self-Monitoring Strategies? Daly and Ranalli (2003) have presented a self-monitoring system called "Countoons" that can even be used with nonreaders. The self-monitoring tool is in the form of a simple cartoon strip like that depicted in Figure 11–6 designed to address a specific behavior, such as completing math problems. Two of the frames show the desired behavior (i.e., doing my math work); between the two desired-behavior frames is one frame illustrating the undesired or incompatible behavior (i.e., chatting with friend). Positioned above the desired-behavior frame is a box for counting the desired behaviors, and above the undesired behavior frame is a box for counting the undesired behavior. In this situation, the student is not allowed to have more than 6 instances of chatting with a friend (or other off-task behavior), and is expected to complete at least 10 math problems. The last frame in the cartoon sequence depicts the positive consequence (i.e., 5 minutes with a favorite computer game) for having fewer than 6 chats with friends and completing 10 or more problems.

Levendoski and Cartledge (2000) used relatively simple classroom procedures to increase the on-task behaviors and academic productivity of intermediate-aged urban students with behavior disorders during math seat work. Following small-group math instruction, students were given seat work to practice the skills they had just been taught. They were trained to use the self-monitoring form depicted in Figure 11–7. When the buzzer sounded—every 10 minutes—students recorded whether they were on task at the

FIGURE 11-6 Countoon self-monitoring form
Source: From "Using Countoons to Teach Self-Monitoring Skills" by P. M. Daly and P. Ranalli, *Teaching Exceptional Children, 35*(5), 30–35. Copyright © 2003 by the Council for Exceptional Children. Reprinted with permission.

exact moment they heard the buzzer. Students recorded their behavior twice during each 20-minute seat-work period, on-task behavior under the smiling face and off-task behavior under the frowning face. The authors found these procedures effective in increasing task-related behaviors during independent math seat work. When self-monitoring procedures were faded, students continued to display on-task behaviors, but the level of academic productivity declined. Self-monitoring procedures may need to be kept in place for periods longer than the relatively short length of this study (approximately 6 weeks). The length of time needed before fading completely needs to be determined by the progress of the students in their self-management skills.

McConnell (1999) provided the following example of monitoring academic behavior (Figure 11–8) to help students manage their own behavior and complete their academic assignments.

Several other researchers have described self-monitoring strategies that are effective with students with severe disabilities (e.g., Agran et al., 2005; Gilberts et al., 2001). In one study, Gilberts et al. used typically developing middle school peers to teach five students with severe cognitive disabilities how to self-monitor their behavior within inclusive settings. Using the classroom survival skills noted previously in this chapter, the researchers engaged the typically developing students in helping their classmates with disabilities to self-monitor these skills. The peers were taught to employ the following steps:

1. Tell the student that it is important to pay attention.
2. Show the student how to attend to the teacher; give an example and nonexample.
3. Show the student how to use the self-recording sheet correctly.
4. Ask the student if he or she has performed one of the survival skills correctly. Show the student how to record that response on the recording form.

Name: ____________________

Date: __________

* At this exact second am I doing my work?

	Yes		No	
Day	1st Bell	2nd Bell	1st Bell	2nd Bell

FIGURE 11–7 Self-monitoring form

Source: Reproduced from L. Levendoski and G. Cartledge, 2000. "Self-monitoring for Elementary School Children with Serious Emotional Disturbances," *Behavioral Disorders, 25*(3), 211–224.

5. Praise the student for self-recording.
6. Coach the student to perform the survival skill if the student is not performing it.

Observations showed that all students made progress in these survival skills, with at least three of the five making quite satisfactory adjustments in the general education classes.

Agran et al. (2005) directly taught a similar group of middle school students with moderate to severe cognitive disabilities to self-monitor their direction-following behavior within general education classrooms. During the training, the students were taught how to discriminate when they received a direction, how to acknowledge they had received the direction, how to follow the direction, the importance of monitoring their behavior, and how to complete the self-monitoring forms. Training continued until students achieved 80% consistent correct responding.

These studies provide good evidence that students with moderate to severe disabilities can be taught to be more responsible in managing their own classroom behavior. Some

FIGURE 11–8 Assignment checklist.

```
                    Assignment Checklist
        Name: _____
        Date: _____

        1.  Is my name on the paper?                    Yes   no
        2.  Do all sentences begin with a capital letter?   Yes   no
        3.  Do sentences end with the correct punctuation?  Yes   no
        4.  Did I answer all the questions?             Yes   no
        5.  Do I need extra help?                       Yes   no
        6.  Do I need more time?                        Yes   no
        7.  Do I understand the assignment?             Yes   no
        8.  Did I finish all of my work?                Yes   no
        9.  Did I follow teacher directions?            Yes   no
        10. Did I turn in my assignment?                Yes   no
```

Source: From "Self-Monitoring, Cueing, Recording, and Managing" by M. E. McConnell, *Teaching Exceptional Children, 32*(2), 14–21. Copyright © 1999 by the Council for Exceptional Children. Reprinted with permission.

effort on the part of teachers and students is required, however, and direct training of students with disabilities using peer support might be the most effective strategy.

Self-monitoring strategies can be effective in helping students better manage their class behavior and become more successful, but it is important that the procedures be easy to implement and unobtrusive. It is helpful, for example, if students are able to monitor their behavior with minimal classroom noise or teacher prompting. Lo and Cartledge (2006) used a vibrating signal and a simple self-monitoring sheet to help four African American elementary males with and at risk for behavior disorders to better

---

TEACHING TIPS

Self-Monitoring

1. Clarify cultural/identity issues to make sure students are committed to monitoring academic or social behavior.
2. Select important but realistic goals.
3. Select a behavior that is critical to the student's success in class (e.g., on-task behavior).
4. Devise a simple, unobtrusive, self-monitoring form or device (e.g., MotivAider).
5. Teach students how to use the form or system.
6. Reward students for using the form, for monitoring accurately, and for being academically productive.
7. Continue self-monitoring procedures until the behavior is well established.
8. Gradually fade self-monitoring.
9. To the extent possible, include the student's family in the self-monitoring procedure.

manage their classroom behavior. A device called the MotivAider® (MotivAider, 2002) was clipped to the student's belt or waistband and signaled by means of a brief vibration when it was time for the student to mark his self-recording form. The signals were delivered every 5 or 2 minutes, depending on the special needs of the student. When signaled, students were to record whether they were doing their work, whether they needed the teacher's assistance, and whether they employed the appropriate method for soliciting the teacher's attention. Prior to using the MotivAider, students were taught both how to appropriately gain the teacher's attention and how to use the self-monitoring strategy. Task-related and teacher attention-getting behavior improved for all four students.

A final consideration in effective self-monitoring strategies is home support. Self-monitoring sheets showing progress in classroom compliance can be used as take-home forms for home-based rewards. Hutchinson, Murdock, Williamson, and Cronin (2000) used this procedure to increase the on-task behavior of a 6-year-old student. According to the number of items recorded, the student got to take home the "I am a Great Kid!" sheet, which was redeemed at home.

APPLICATION

Goal Setting and Self-Monitoring

Due to poor reading skills and failing performance in English and social studies, Chris was quick to say that he could not succeed in these classes. He did not believe he could pass these classes, improve in reading, or pursue his dream of a football career through college. Mr. Thomas, his resource teacher, was one of the few persons in his life who encouraged Chris to keep his dreams and to begin to set higher but realistic goals for his classes.

Mr. Thomas got the school counselor to set up a support group that included Chris and other African American males to discuss cultural identity and academic performance issues. Although the counselor was European American, he was successful in getting African American males who presented good models to attend the support sessions periodically. These males discussed the importance of school and why they should believe they could be successful. Due to these sessions, Chris and the other students began to recognize the steps they needed to take to reach their goals.

Determining a goal

For example, in social studies Chris was getting 50% or 60% correct on weekly quizzes and was not turning in his social studies assignments. Mr. Thomas and Chris decided that they should set an initial goal of completing all social studies assignments each day and to achieve at least 75% or better on the weekly quizzes.

Devising a plan

Chris and Mr. Thomas decided on the following plan to make these goals happen:
1. Chris would use the guided notes form daily to take notes from class lecture.
2. During the last 10 minutes of school, Chris would work with his assigned peer partner to review notes and make sure he understood lecture material.
3. Chris would attend the after-school study program to get assistance in reading his social studies chapter and apply his study skills.

> *(continued)*
> 4. Each day Chris would write five sentences to summarize what he learned in that day's social studies lesson.
> 5. Each day Chris would submit his social studies notes and homework to Mr. Thomas and get feedback on their accuracy.
> 6. Each day Chris would carry his self-monitoring form to show that he was prepared for class and that his materials were organized. Chris received one point for having completed his self-monitoring card, one point for having his materials, and an additional point for completing his homework.
> 7. The day before the weekly quiz, Chris would
>   (a) Review the key social study points for that week with his peer partner.
>   (b) Review his study questions with his tutor in the after-school program.
>   (c) Spend at least one-half hour reading his social studies book at home in the evening.
>   (d) Receive points from his mom for reading his text and making some notes on his reading.
>
> **Evaluation**
>
> Chris and Mr. Thomas kept a record of how often and to what extent Chris performed each step in his plan. At the end of the week, they noted whether Chris had followed his plan, and if not, what adjustments were needed. For example, Chris was not getting enough time to participate in the after-school tutoring program because of football practice. Mr. Thomas arranged more time for Chris to work with his peer partner during their study period. Also, Chris's church had an evening tutoring program where Chris could get the same assistance available in the after-school study program.
>
> As Chris met his initial goals, he and Mr. Thomas gradually raised them by 1% or 2% each week, relying less and less on Mr. Thomas to check his homework. The more Chris read his text in tutoring sessions and during reading instruction in the resource room, the better Chris was able to read. Later goals were for Chris to read more and more independently. Chris' confidence in his ability to reach these academic goals increased as he recorded his daily and weekly progress.

Summary

Students who are self-directed and assume responsibility for their learning are more successful than students who rely largely on others to direct their learning experiences. There is good evidence that teachers can help students acquire the skills they need to better manage their academic-related behaviors. Teachers can help students learn to take better notes during class lectures and to apply study skills so that the class content is meaningful and easily retained.

Students with disabilities will need much assistance from others in their environment in order to become competent learners. This is particularly true for students from diverse backgrounds whose families may not have the skills or resources to provide extended assistance. Some CLDE students experience special challenges due to a history of academic underperformance and low expectations. These students often require interventions that address affective components as well as the development of critical cognitive skills. Special mentoring or support groups might be used to help these students develop more positive attitudes toward formal schooling and the strategies they need to be successful. Resourceful teachers might explore other options for diverse exceptional students, such as peer assistants, after-school instructional programs, and community-based programs, such as local churches. Families can be instrumental in helping their students when they are given suggestions from the school on how to monitor and reinforce their children's academic behaviors.

Setting realistic but high goals and then taking action to achieve these goals is the essence of being a responsible and competent student. Students can learn to be confident about their abilities to be successful in managing their academic behaviors. Self-monitoring strategies can enable students to become increasingly independent as they systematically move toward their desired goals.

Related Learning Activities

1. Review various study skills and select one to teach to a student in your classroom or practicum site. For example, select a strategy for practicing weekly spelling words. Prior to teaching the strategy, record the student's spelling test scores for several weeks. Teach the strategy and practice it several times until you are certain the student has mastered the strategy. Prompt the student to use the strategy and observe whether there are improvements in spelling scores. If not, either make sure the student is using the strategy or teach another strategy.

2. Identify one student who is having considerable difficulty with organization skills. Teach the student how to organize class materials and also how to monitor behavior to make sure he or she comes to class with the requisite materials. Check with the student's classroom teachers to determine whether the student is more organized and if this greater organization has had any impact on the student's school success.

3. Interview two or three middle school or high school teachers. Find out what kinds of homework assignments they give and what difficulties, if any, they have with students completing homework assignments. Note what strategies the teachers use to get students to complete and submit homework. What other strategies might you add to the ones the teachers use for increasing homework completion?

4. Get permission to review the class notes of at least five students in one middle school or high school class. Include in this group at least two students diagnosed with disabilities. Note the difficulties the students are having taking lecture notes. Based on your review, what type of note-taking strategies would you recommend for each of the students? Select one student and teach that student one of the note-taking strategies. Observe the student to see if there are improvements in the understanding of the course content and in class performance.

References

Agran, M., Sinclair, T., Alper, S., Cavin, M. Wehmeyer, M., & Hughes, C. (2005). Using self-monitoring to increase following-direction skills of students with moderate to severe disabilities in general education. *Education and Training in Developmental Disabilities, 40,* 3–13.

Austin, J. L., Lee, M., & Carr, J. P. (2004). The effects of guided notes on undergraduate students' recording of lecture content. *Journal of Instructional Psychology, 31,* 314–320.

Bailey, D. F., & Paisley, P. O. (2004). Developing and nurturing excellence in African American male adolescents. *Journal of Counseling & Development, 82,* 10–17.

Boyle, J. R. (2001). Enhancing the note-taking skills of students with mild disabilities. *Intervention in School and Clinic, 36,* 221–224.

Boyle, J. R. (2005, October). Content area note-taking skills for students with LD. Paper presented at the 27th International Conference on Learning Disabilities, Fort Lauderdale, FL.

Bruchac, J. (2000). *Sacajawea.* New York: Harcourt.

Caldwell, L. D., & Siwatu, K. O. (2003). Promoting academic persistence in African American and Latino high school students: The educational navigation skills seminar. *The High School Journal, 87*(1), 18–29.

Cooper, J. E., Horn, S., & Strahan, D. B. (2005, February/March). "If only they would do their homework": Promoting self-regulation in high school English classes. *The High School Journal,* 10–25.

Cosden, M., Morrison, G., Gutierrez, L., & Brown, M. (2004). The effects of homework programs and after-school activities on school success. *Theory Into Practice, 43,* 220–226.

Daly, P. M., & Ranalli, P. (2003). Using countoons to teach self-monitoring skills. *Teaching Exceptional Children, 35*(5), 30–35.

Family Education Network. Retrieved November 25, 2005, from http://myschoolonline.com/printables/jump/04051,23-12006-682,00.html

Gettinger, M., & Seibert, J. K. (2002). Contributions of study skills to academic competence. *School Psychology Review, 31,* 350–365.

Gilberts, G. H., Agran, M., Hughes, C., & Wehmeyer, M. (2001). The effects of peer delivered self-monitoring strategies on the participation of students with severe disabilities in general education classrooms. *JASH, 26,* 25–36.

Graham, S., Schwartz, S., & MacArthur, C. A. (1993). Knowledge of writing and the composing process, attitude toward writing, and self-efficacy for students with and without learning disabilities. *Journal of Learning Disabilities, 26,* 237–249.

Griffin, B. W. (2002). Academic disidentification, race, and high school dropouts. *High School Journal, 85*(4), 71–81.

Harris, K. R., Friedlander, B. D., Saddler, B., Frizzelle, R., & Graham, S. (2005). Self-monitoring of attention versus self-monitoring of academic performance: Effects among students with ADHD in the general education classroom. *The Journal of Special Education, 39,* 145–156.

Hassinger, M., & Plourde, L. A. (2005). "Beating the odds": How bi-lingual Hispanic youth work through adversity to become high achieving students. *Education, 126*(2), 316–327.

Heward, W. L. (2001). *Guided notes: Improving the effectiveness of your lectures.* Columbus, OH: The Ohio State University Partnership Grant for Improving the Quality of Education for Students with Disabilities.

Hughes, C. A, & Suritsky, S. K. (1993). Notetaking skills and strategies for students with learning disabilities. *Preventing School Failure, 38,* 7–12.

Hutchinson, S. W., Murdock, J. Y., Williamson, R. D., & Cronin, M. E. (2000). Self-recording PLUS encouragement equals improved behavior. *Teaching Exceptional Children, 32,* 54–58.

Krashen, S. (2005). The hard work hypothesis: Is doing your homework enough to overcome the effects of poverty? *Multicultural Education, 12,* 18–19.

Lazarus, B. D. (1993). Guided notes: Effects with secondary and post secondary students with mild disabilities. *Education and Treatment of Children, 16*(3), 272–289.

Leinweber, M. (1991). *Effects of preparation training, self-monitoring, and peer-assistance on the daily class preparation of low-achieving middle-school students.* Unpublished master's thesis. The Ohio State University, Columbus, OH.

Levendoski, L., & Cartledge, G. (2000). Self-monitoring for elementary school children with serious emotional disturbances: Classroom applications for increased academic responding. *Behavioral Disorders, 25*(3), 211–224.

Lo, Y., & Cartledge, G. (2006). FBA and BIP: Increasing the behavior adjustment of African American boys in schools. *Behavioral Disorders, 31,* 147–161.

Margolis, H. (2005). Resolving struggling learners' homework difficulties: Working with elementary school learners and parents. *Preventing School Failure, 50,* 5–12.

McConnell, M. E. (1999). Self-monitoring, cueing, recording, and managing: Teaching students to manage their own behavior. *Teaching Exceptional Children, 32,* 14–21.

MotivAider (2002). Thief River Falls, MN: Behavioral Dynamics, Inc.

Nickel, E. L. (2005). *Effects of an organization-training package consisting of prompting, preparation-training, self-monitoring, and rewards on the daily class readiness and homework completion of middle school students with severe emotional disturbance.* Unpublished master's thesis, The Ohio State University, Columbus, OH.

Palmer, S. B., & Wehmeyer, M. L. (2003). Promoting self-determination in early elementary school: Teaching self-regulated problem-solving and goal-setting skills. *Remedial and Special Education, 24,* 115–126.

Peak Parent Center. (2003, Fall). Homework doesn't need to create stress for students and parents. *SpeakOut: Peak Parent Center Newsletter.* Retrieved November 30, 2005, from http://www.peakparent.org/pdf/speakout/speakoutfall_03.pdf

Portes, A., & Rumbaut, R. (2001). *Legacies: The story of the immigrant second generation.* Los Angeles: University of California Press.

Prater, M. A., Joy, R., Chilman, B., Temple, J., & Miller, S. (1991). Self-monitoring of on-task behavior by adolescents with learning disabilities. *Learning Disability Quarterly, 14,* 164–177.

Quenneville, J. (2001). Tech tools for students with learning disabilities: Infusion into inclusive classrooms. *Preventing School Failure, 45,* 167–170.

Ruban, L. M., McCoach, D. B., McGuire J. M., & Reis, S. M. (2003). The differential impact of academic achievement among university students with and without learning disabilities. *Journal of Learning Disabilities, 36,* 270–286.

Schaeffer, A. L., Zigmond, N., Kerr, M. M., & Farra, H. E. (1990). Helping teenagers develop school survival skills. *Teaching Exceptional Children, 23,* 6–9.

Swain, K. D. (2005). CBM with goal setting: Impacting students' understanding of reading goals. *Journal of Instructional Psychology, 32,* 259–262.

Troia, G. A., & Graham, S. (2002). The effectiveness of a highly explicit, teacher-directed strategy instruction routine: Changing the writing performance of students with learning disabilities. *Journal of Learning Disabilities, 35,* 290–305.

Williams, J. M. (1987). *Tips for being a successful student: A handbook for students and teachers.* Paper presented at the International Conference on Learning Disabilities, Louisville, KY. (ERIC Document Reproduction Service No. ED 306 750).

Yoo, J. (2005, November 28). In South Korea, education is king. *The Columbus Dispatch,* p. B6.

Zimmerman, B. J. (2002). Becoming a self-regulated learner: An overview. *Theory into Practice, 41,* 64–70.

Chapter 12

Early Interventions for the CLDE Learner

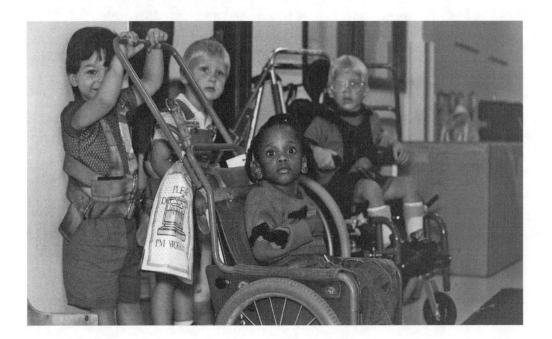

The purpose of this chapter is to present educational and instructional models effective with young children with and at risk for exceptionalities. The targeted population includes infants, toddlers, preschool children, and kindergarteners from culturally and linguistically diverse backgrounds. Conditions that set the occasion for successful schooling begin in the womb. Children from diverse backgrounds are at much greater risk for adverse birthing events and early childhood development. The extensively documented disproportionality of learning and behavior problems among certain CLD groups is more amenable to prevention than to remediation. Prevention for CLD populations begins no later than birth. By the end of this chapter, readers should be able to answer the following questions:

1. Why is early intervention important for culturally diverse learners with or at risk for exceptionalities?
2. Why are some culturally diverse groups disproportionately represented among young children with or at risk for exceptionalities?
3. Which programs have been shown to be most beneficial for culturally diverse young children at risk for exceptionalities?

4. How effective are Head Start programs in providing early intervention for culturally diverse learners at risk for exceptionalities?
5. How effective are preschool programs in reducing special education and school failure for young culturally diverse learners?
6. What competencies should effective early childhood teachers of culturally diverse learners possess?
7. What can we do to prevent early reading failure?

By the end of this chapter, readers will obtain information on strategies for:

1. Effective interventions for CLD infants and toddlers.
2. Effective interventions for CLD three- to five-year-olds.
3. Ways to upgrade early intervention programs for CLD infants, toddlers, and preschoolers.
4. Early interventions to prevent reading failure for CLD at-risk learners.

Why Provide Early Interventions for Young Children With or At Risk for Disabilities?

Professionals and policy makers have come to recognize the critical importance of early intervention and preschool programs for children with and at risk for disabilities. These programs support families by helping them to process the information required to understand the child's special needs; relieving conditions, such as a stressful diagnostic process, that could lead to interpersonal family distress; supplying resources according to the demands of the child's disability; and strengthening parenting by providing self-confidence and a greater sense of control over the situation (Guralnick, 2000). Not only do these programs provide tremendous support to these families but they greatly benefit the cognitive and overall development of the children. There is very good evidence that early interventions can be effective in preventing or reducing intellectual decline in the first five years of life (Campbell, Pungello, Miller-Johnson, Burchinal, & Ramey, 2001; Guralnick, 2000).

Early interventions are important not only to minimize/prevent disabilities but, as James Heckman (2002), Nobel Laureate in Economic Sciences 2000, asserts: "investments made in the young bring a much better return than similar investments in older individuals." This position is based on the reality that young children have more time to recoup this investment and that "learning begets learning." Therefore, the skills acquired early in life will facilitate later learning, thus maximizing learning for a greater number. Heckman also argues that society cannot afford to delay interventions until children reach school age: Children are born ready to learn and interventions need to begin at infancy and continue through adulthood. Additionally, interventions need to be expanded to include the social and emotional domains, which are more predictive of later life success. Figure 12–1 illustrates Heckman's position that it is more beneficial to invest in the very young.

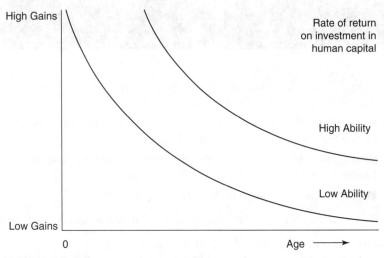

FIGURE 12-1

Source: From Heckman, J. J. (2002). "Invest in the Very Young," ED 467 549, http://www.ounceofprevention.org. Ounce of Prevention Fund and the University of Chicago Harris School of Public Pollicy Studies.

Henry

Henry is a 5½-year-old kindergarten student. He spent the previous two years in preschool, he was in Early Head Start for two years before preschool, and immediately after birth his parents participated in early intervention programs due to his at-risk birth status. Henry is an African American male born prematurely to teen-aged parents whose income fell below the poverty line. Henry weighed a little less than 4 pounds when he was born and had some medical respiratory complications related to his lung development. Henry remained in the hospital for a month after he was born to make certain that his respiratory problems were resolved and that he had made a satisfactory weight gain. Henry was fortunate that his parents received information and had access to early intervention programs that provided valuable services for him for his first 5 years of life.

Physically, Henry made good progress: At age 5 he fell within the 50th percentile for weight and height for his age group, he now is well coordinated and interacts well with his peers, and there is no residual evidence of his health problems at birth. Now that Henry is in kindergarten, it is important to determine whether his cognitive development is sufficient for him to keep pace with his peers and make grade-level progress. Henry knows some of his letters, numbers, and sounds, but apparently not at the levels expected. The initial school assessment showed some prereading and math delays, so the early childhood specialist, Ms. Grey, decided to conduct some additional assessments to determine specific deficits and methods of intervention. At this point, the focus is on determining the type of instruction that would enable Henry to make progress and be maintained in general rather than special education.

Within this chapter, we will review the type of programs that might have been available to Henry during the first 5 years of his life and what might be most beneficial to him at this point.

What Are the Conditions That Place Infants and Toddlers At Risk?

Early interventions for infants and toddlers include those for children diagnosed with disabilities such as cerebral palsy or sensory impairment as well as those for children suspected of developing disabilities due to environmental factors (e.g., extreme poverty) or to birthing conditions (e.g., low birth weight). The importance of early intervention services has increased in recent years due to the improved survival rate of extremely low-birth-weight infants, which includes an increased risk of neurodevelopmental impairment (Freund, Boone, Barlow, Lim, 2005; Nolan, Young, Herbert, & Wilding, 2005; Wilson-Costello, Friedman, Minich, Fanaroff, & Hack, 2005). In the 1980s and the 1990s, Wilson-Costello et al. found that along with an increased survival rate, low-birth-weight infants also were more likely to have disabilities. Among the infants they monitored, for example, there was a 9% increase in cerebral palsy and a 4% increase in the rate of deafness.

Preterm or low-birth-weight infants typically require longer hospital stays and often experience medical complications. These conditions not only create greater needs for the family and infant but also require more services. The conditions that place infants and toddlers at risk are magnified for many children from culturally diverse backgrounds. Infants born into extreme poverty or with special neonatal risk such as low birth weight or fetal alcohol syndrome (FAS) are in considerable jeopardy of significant physical and learning disorders.

Why Is Early Intervention Important for Culturally Diverse Learners With or At Risk for Exceptionalities?

What Is the Impact of Poverty Among CLDE Populations?

The U.S. Census Bureau reports (2006) that the national rate of poverty for 2005 was essentially 12.6%; the rates were the same as the previous year for African and Hispanic Americans but showed a slight decrease for European Americans. Data in Figure 12–2, from the U.S. Bureau of Statistics, show how the numbers of those living in poverty and the rates have fluctuated from 1959 to 2005.

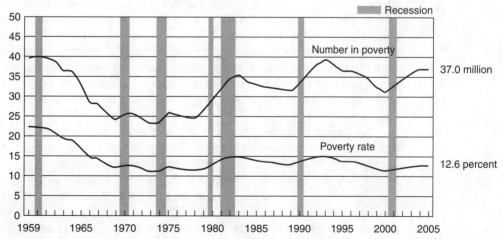

FIGURE 12–2 Number in poverty and poverty rate: 1959 to 2005 (Numbers in millions, rates in percent)

Note: The data points are placed at the midpoints of the respective years.

Source: U.S. Census Bureau, Current Population Survey, 1960 to 2006 Annual Social and Economic Supplements.

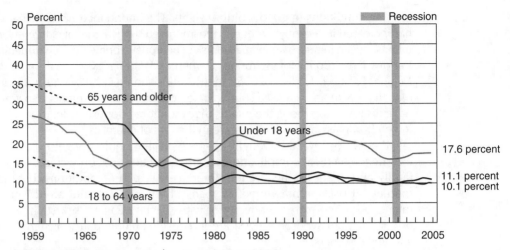

FIGURE 12–3 Poverty rates by age: 1959 to 2005

Note: The date points are placed at the midpoints of the respective years.
Data for people 18 to 64 and 65 and older are not available from 1960 to 1965.
Source: U.S. Census Bureau, Current Population Survey, 1960 to 2006 Annual Social and Economic Supplements.

These data tell us that starting in the mid-1960s, there was a rather pronounced decline in poverty until the 1980s, when the numbers began a rather steady upward trend, remaining above 12.8% until 1993, when there was another reduction to 11.3% by 2000 (National Poverty Center, NPC, 2006). After 2000, poverty began to climb again, reaching 12.7% in 2004 and 12.6% in 2005.

Poverty in the United States has also been studied according to subgroups. Figure 12–3 profiles poverty according to age and shows that over the period of 1959 to 2005 the greatest declines have been among senior citizens, those in the 65 or older age group. At the same time, there were substantial increases in poverty among children, those under 18 years of age. In 2005, the poverty rate for adults (those between the ages of 18 and 64) was 11.1%, but for children (under 18 years of age), it was 17.6%. Even more revealing are the data according to racial/ethnic diversity and age. Table 12–1, taken from the U.S. Bureau of Statistics, gives poverty by race and shows that Native, African, and Hispanic Americans have the highest poverty rates in this country. Compared to the national rate of 12.6%, these groups document poverty rates of 25.3%, 24.7%, and 22.0%, respectively.

The disproportionate representation of children among the poor is evident in the fact that they make up 25% of the general population but 35% of the poor (NPC, 2006). When data are viewed by subgroups, the disproportionality becomes even clearer. In Table 12–2 data from the U.S. Bureau of Statistics and presented by the NPC show that compared to the approximate 10% rate for European and Asian American children living in poverty, nearly or more than 30% of African and Hispanic American children live in poverty. These data support the argument for the potentially greater risk of children in these subgroups having poor outcomes and the greater efforts needed from all segments of society, including the schools, to mitigate the impact of poverty.

The effects of poverty are far-reaching and long-lasting, undermining the cognitive, social, physical, and emotional well-being of children (Hudson, 2005; Park, Turnbull, & Turnbull, 2002; Ramey et al., 2000). Children who live in chronic poverty have less positive

TABLE 12-1 Number in poverty and poverty rates by race and Hispanic origin using 3-year average: 2003 to 2005 (Numbers in thousands. People as of March of the following year)

	3-year average 2003–2005			
	Number		Percentage	
Race and Hispanic origin	Estimate	90-percent confidence interval (±)	Estimate	90-percent confidence interval (±)
All races	36,617	494	12.6	0.2
White	24,824	399	10.6	0.2
White, not Hispanic	16,346	329	8.4	0.2
Black	8,988	242	24.7	0.6
American Indian and Alaska native	573	65	25.3	2.5
Asian	1,335	98	10.9	0.8
Native Hawaiian and Other Pacific Islander	79	24	12.2	3.6
Hispanic origin (any race)	9,180	252	22.0	0.6

Source: U.S. Census Bureau, Current Population Survey, 2004 to 2006 Annual Social and Economic Supplements.

cognitive and social development than children living under less severe economic conditions (National Institute of Child Health and Human Development Early Child Care Research Network, NICHD, 2005). Chronic poverty is considered to produce stressors that undermine the quality of parenting and home environments. In a study of the relative effects of poverty according to children's ages, NICHD speculated that brief periods of poverty would be more debilitating to younger children (i.e., before age 4) than for older children (i.e., between ages 4 and third grade). Interestingly, the researchers found that children encountering later poverty (i.e., after 4 years of age) received more negative cognitive and behavioral evaluations than children who had transitory poverty experiences before the age of 4. Consistent with previous research on children in poverty, they found that children in chronic poverty situations evidenced the poorest school performance as measured by more reports of externalizing and internalizing behavior problems. On a long-term basis, children of poverty, particularly those from diverse backgrounds, are more likely to be incarcerated and less likely to be college graduates than non-CLD youth growing up under more affluent conditions (NPC, 2006).

TABLE 12-2 Children under 18 living in poverty, 2004

Category	Number (in thousands)	Percent
All children under 18	13,027	17.8
White only, non-Hispanic	4,507	10.5
Black	4,049	33.2
Hispanic	4,102	28.9
Asian	334	9.8

Source: National Poverty Center, University of Michigan, Gerald R. Ford School of Public Policy.

Children with disabilities are more vulnerable to the conditions of poverty than their typically developing peers. Parish and Cloud (2006) reason that this is due to the fact that (1) it costs more to raise children with disabilities, (2) parental employment is often reduced by limited childcare services and work-leave policies, and (3) governmental support through vehicles such as supplemental Social Security Insurance (SSI) is often inadequate.

What Are the Special Birth Risks of CLD Populations?

Birthing conditions related to poverty are highly predictive of later development. Infants of certain CLD groups are subjected to much higher levels of birth risk than others (Boyle & Cordero, 2005). African Americans have much higher rates of infant mortality and low-birth-weight babies than European Americans or other U.S. ethnic groups (David & Collins, 1997; Hessol & Fuentes-Afflick, 2005). Low-birth-weight babies may be either premature (less than 37 weeks of gestation) or full term but have a low birth weight (less than 2500 grams, or 5.5 pounds) (BDPH; David & Collins, 1997). Low birth weight is associated with immediate health disorders and later learning and adjustment problems (Berkeley Division of Public Health, BDPH, 2002; Hack et al. 2002). David and Collins, using birth records from 1980 through 1995, documented the incidence of low birth weights to be 13.2% for African American mothers compared to 4.3% for European American mothers. The low-birth-weight risks are even greater among adolescent mothers (BDPH), especially African Americans. A 10-year study at Johns Hopkins revealed that African American adolescents were twice as likely to deliver low-birth-weight infants compared to African American mothers of all ages (Chang, O'Brien, Nathanson, Mancini, & Witter, 2003). Some of the risk factors associated with these teenage girls included low maternal body weight and poor prenatal care.

Another adverse birth condition is fetal alcohol syndrome (FAS), which has significantly higher rates among Native American and African American infants due to higher rates of alcohol consumption by the mothers during pregnancy (Castor et al., 2006; Lucas, Goldschmidt, & Day, 2003; Ma, Toubbeh, Cline, & Chisholm, 1998; Ryan & Ferguson, 2006). According to Ma et al., in the general population there are 1.9 children with FAS per 1,000 births; the rate is 0.3 for Asian Americans, 0.8 for Hispanic Americans, 0.9 for European Americans, but 6.0 for African Americans and 29.9 for Native Americans—six times the national average. Some of the characteristics associated with FAS include lower birth weight, facial abnormalities, severe neurobehavioral impairments, feeding difficulties, speech and hearing delays, coordination deficits, learning disabilities, and attention deficit hyperactivity disability. Significantly, FAS is one of the leading causes of mental retardation (Ma et al.).

Following birth, CLD infants continue to be at considerable risk. In a study of well-child care, researchers found that compared to 58% of European American children, only 37% of Hispanic American and 35% of African American children received well-child care (Ronsaville & Hakim, 2000). Other medical studies have shown the dangers of high blood lead levels (BLL), which disproportionately affect children who are poor and from CLD backgrounds. Lead absorbed into the body is highly toxic. "Lead is most harmful to children under age six because it is easily absorbed into their growing bodies and interferes with the developing brain and other organs and systems. Pregnant women and women of child-bearing age are also at increased risk, because lead ingested by the mother can cross the placenta and affect the unborn fetus" (Alliance for Healthy Homes, AHH, ND). Elevated levels of lead in the blood can lead to damage to the brain and nervous system, behavior and learning problems, slowed growth, hearing problems, headaches, anemia, and seizures (New York Presbyterian Hospital, 2003). A 2005 report from the Centers for Disease Control (CDC) indicates that BLL for U.S. children dropped to 1.6% from a previous high of 2% in 1994 (see Figure 12–4). Nevertheless, the report shows that 3% of African American children in the 1- to-5 age range have elevated levels of lead. That is, these children are twice as likely as their European American peers to have dangerous BLLs. Furthermore, other data from the CDC show that nearly 20% of African American children living in houses built before 1946 have elevated BLLs.

An obvious implication of this discussion of adverse birthing and postnatal conditions is the importance of providing education to families prior to pregnancy, during pregnancy, and following birth. Young people need to understand the health risks to their babies and to themselves of factors such as teenage pregnancies, substance use (alcohol and drugs), poor health/prenatal care, and absorbing toxins such as lead. Ma et al. (1998), for example, observing that most sixth-grade Native American middle school students did not know the relationship between alcohol and FAS, recommended educating the students on this topic and teaching them to resist the pressure of peers to drink.

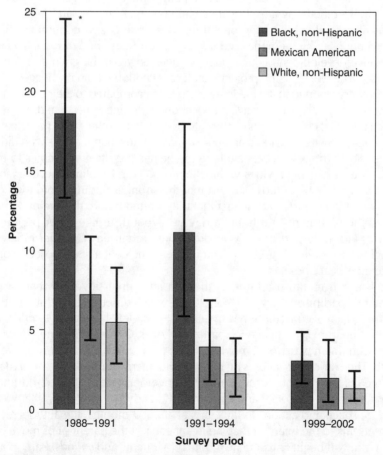

FIGURE 12–4 Percentage of children aged 1–5 years with blood lead levels ≥ 10 µg/dL, by race/ethnicity and survey period—National Health and Nutrition Examination Surveys, United States, 1988–1991, 1991–1994, and 1999–2002

Note: *95% confidence interval.

Source: Centers for Disease Control and Prevention, MMWR 2005: 54.

What Interventions Are Available for Infants to Three-Year-Old Children?

Intervening with At-Risk Infants and Toddlers

An important feature of early intervention programs for infants and toddlers is the prevention as well as the remediation or minimization of disabilities. Prevention is a principal focus for infants born prematurely, with low birth weight and special neonatal risks such as fetal alcohol syndrome or within extreme poverty. One of the most extensive and encouraging studies of this population is the research reported by Campbell and Ramey and their colleagues at the Abecedarian Project in North Carolina (e.g., Campbell, Pungello, Miller-Johnson, Burchinal, & Ramey, 2001; Campbell & Ramey, 1994, 1995; Campbell, Ramey, Pungello, Sparling, & Miller-Johnson, 2002; Ramey & Campbell, 1984). Recognizing the deleterious effects of poverty on children's cognitive development and school success, the Abecedarian Project targeted impoverished families and their children. Participating families were primarily African American (98%), with 76% of the children born to single parents or living in multigenerational households. The mothers averaged slightly less than 20 years of age and 10th-grade education at the time of the target child's birth.

Unlike other programs for young children, the Abecedarian Project conducted interventions at its childcare center, beginning with infants and continuing through age 5. The interventions, which emphasized language, were designed to foster social, emotional, and cognitive development. Educational activities engaged the children in "games" throughout the day. The effects of the project were evaluated longitudinally at ages 12, 15, and 21. The researchers reported that experimental students, compared to their controls, had higher academic achievement, more years of education, including college, and, on average, were older when their first child was born. They also found that mothers who participated in the program achieved higher educational and employment status than mothers who did not participate in the project. The researchers attribute the higher cognitive test scores to the enhanced language development provided within the project (The Carolina Abecedarian Project, 2005).

Campbell et al. (2001) suggest that the stronger findings from their early intervention program might be due to the fact that they started before the age of 3 and that they intensified the treatment to 8 hours a day year-round, unlike other programs that provided services for only part of the year or for only a half day. Another difference was that the program was child-focused and within a learning center, as opposed to programs based on parent visits at home.

The curriculum used in the Abecedarian Center involved learning "games," developed by Sparling and Lewis (1979; 2001), which emphasized adult-child interactions. The learning games curriculum has five levels, each level designed to address one year of the child's life from birth to age 5 (Sparling & Lewis, 2001). Level one, for example, is for children from infancy up to 12 months of age; the next level is from 1 to 2 years of age, and so forth. The curriculum focuses on parent-child interactions and uses everyday events/activities as means for parents to advance the development of their children. Developmental themes include (1) social and emotional, (2) early literacy, (3) oral language, (4) cognitive, and (5) space and action. To illustrate, at about 3 months, the authors recommend that the parents talk to the infant so that the infant can see the parent's lips move while speaking, so the child will begin to associate mouth movements and sounds. Parents are advised to cup the child's head in their hands while speaking so that the child is looking at them. Parents are to talk "happily" to the infant and then pause to see if the infant responds with utterances. If so, the parent repeats the infant's sounds and lets the child know that the parent likes this. These actions, according to Sparling and Lewis, foster speech and relate to both social/emotional as well as oral language development.

An activity for a toddler at 17 months that relates to both of these developmental areas is "Singing Together." Parents and caretakers are encouraged to sing with children throughout such everyday activities as dressing and walking. Songs with refrains—"Amen," "Kum Ba Ya," "Mockingbird"—are especially recommended because they are simple and give children the opportunity to repeat words. Children in multilingual homes could learn songs in more than one language, for example, the Hispanic song "Palomita Blanca" ("Little White Pigeon") . If songs are sung regularly and with enthusiasm, children will begin to enjoy them and try out some of the words in the song. Over time, they will sing the songs from beginning to end. Among other things, this activity encourages both social and language development. Curriculum activities are developmental so that by the end of the series (i.e., ages 4 and 5), activities focus on recognizing letters, hearing sounds in words, and early numeracy. The simply written curriculum is equally appropriate for the structured setting of a childcare center or the informal setting of the home. Motivated and supported parents can easily use these activities daily with their children. In their introduction to the curriculum, Craig and Sharon Ramey (2001) note that empirical evidence has validated the program's effectiveness in improving school readiness and in reducing special education placements. The expanded curriculum versions of the program have been widely adopted.

Given our understanding of the plasticity of the human infant brain (Ramey & Ramey, 1992), recent findings on the impact of developmental practices on brain development (McMullen, 1999), and evidence that early childhood programs yield greater effects when they start earlier in the child's life (Campbell & Taylor, 1996), the importance of starting interventions at infancy cannot be overstated. Such interventions appear to be especially important and beneficial for young children born in homes with limited economic and intellectual resources (Ramey & Ramey). In a discussion of "essential daily ingredients" to promote the development of these children, Ramey and Ramey recommend:

- helping the children to explore their environment,
- developing basic cognitive skills such as labeling, celebrating, and reinforcing developmental accomplishments,
- rehearsing and further developing newly acquired skills,
- minimizing harsh and aversive adult interactions, and
- providing rich, interactive language.

The authors also noted greater gains for those children whose families had high levels of participation in the activities than for those whose families had lower participation.

Freund et al. (2005) describe a service system for these children that coordinates health care, early intervention, and family support. Shortly after the birth, project staff initiate a program designed to provide *social-emotional support* to the family by connecting the family to other individual families or groups of families that have had similar experiences. By helping families identify and build informal networks, the project attempts to provide social-emotional support. A second means of support is providing families with *resource-material support*, that is, assisting families with basic needs such as housing or food stamps as well as with obtaining specialized equipment needed for the infant. The third major form of support is *informational-services*, which is intended to help the parents understand critical information such as the child's development and medical needs or how to participate in developing the individualized family service plan (IFSP) that is specified for infants and toddlers under Part C of IDEA 2004. Although the program is in its early stages and initial responses from consumers have been quite positive, the authors report that subsequent efforts are needed to give more attention to educating families about child development, to facilitate child development during the hospital stay, and to make services more culturally sensitive, including supports for Spanish-speaking families.

Culturally diverse families of young children with disabilities do appear to have greater and different needs compared to their non-CLD counterparts. In a study of European American urban and rural families and African American urban and rural families, Darling and Gallagher (2004) found that parents who reported the greatest need also reported the least amount of family support, specifically, African American urban families. European American rural families reported the greatest family support and European American urban families reported the least need. The greater financial need reported by African Americans is consistent with their higher levels of poverty in this society. But the differences within as well as across groups point to a need for individualized services and for greater cultural sensitivity.

How Can Early Head Start Best Serve CLD Learners?

Head Start is designed to provide educational, social, medical, and nutritional services to young impoverished children in order to compensate for their limited experiences and opportunities and to give the students a head start in school. The goal is to enable the children to compete academically and behaviorally with their more privileged peers. As noted previously, most of the early childhood programs are for children beyond the age of 3, despite the fact that a greater impact on the child's development can apparently be made if interventions start at an earlier age. The most widespread government-supported program for preschool children is Head Start, initiated in 1965 as part of the War on Poverty programs. More recently, in 1994, this early childhood program was extended as Early Head Start (EHS) to children from birth to 3 years (Barnett & Hustedt, 2005).

As noted previously in this chapter, poor children are at greater risk for disabilities and developmental delays, and they are less likely to receive early intervention services compared to children from more affluent families, especially CLD families (Wall et al., 2005). In a longitudinal study conducted by the U.S. government of preschoolers receiving preschool education, only 11% of the children were African American compared to 22% Hispanic American and 67% European American (Markowitz et al., 2006). Furthermore, Hispanic and African American children were more likely to have moderate to severe disorders compared to the milder disorders of speech and language impairments of European

Research shows early intervention programs for culturally and linguistically diverse infants and toddlers to be effective in minimizing learning problems.

American children. Assessments showed European American children performing better than Hispanic or African American children in the preschool settings. It should be noted, however, that the CLD children came from the lowest income groups, their parents had the lowest education levels, and the African American children had the lowest birth weights. Given these considerations, early childhood programs such as EHS need to be more accessible and "family friendly" toward CLD families (Wall et al., 2005), but a case can also be made for intensifying the instructional programs serving at-risk CLD children.

One extremely important early intervention activity is reading to children from infancy throughout the preschool years. Upon examining the mother-child book-reading patterns of low-income African, Hispanic, and European American parents of children enrolled in EHS programs, Raikes et al. (2006) found a relationship between daily readings and children's cognitive and language development. The characteristics associated with reading daily to children included the mother's being European American, having more education, and the child being the mother's first born.

APPLICATION

Henry in Preschool

Henry was not diagnosed with a disability, but he did evidence some language delays. At 3 years of age, he was enrolled in a preschool program in his local school district. This class contained 12 children (ages 3 to 5), one general education teacher, one special education teacher, and two teacher assistants. Eight of the children were typically developing and four had special needs. Three of the special needs children had diagnosed disabilities. The fourth child was Henry, with language delays.

The class day began at 9:15 A.M. and ended at 2:30 P.M. for all of the children. The day was divided into large-group, small-group, and individualized activities, according to student needs. The activities included morning introductory activities, circle time for stories and songs, free play, language and cognitive skill development, and meals. In order to promote language and social interaction skills for their students with special needs, the teachers decided to use peer-mediated procedures. Four- and five-year-old typically developing children were trained to prompt their special needs peers to interact with them. The peer trainers were taught individually and the teacher directed them to

1. Stand close to your partner. Look at him/her.
2. Tell your partner you want to play with him/her.
3. Show your partner two or three toys and ask which toy he/she wants to play with.
4. Talk while you are playing with the toy (e.g., "We are throwing the ball. It is fun to throw the ball.")
5. Thank your partner for playing with you.

Peer trainers changed each week so that the students with special needs got the opportunity to be "trained" by each of the children in the class. The peer-mediated training took place for approximately 15 minutes during the designated free play period. The teachers observed the students closely during this period, prompting both trainers and trainees in appropriate behaviors. Teacher assistants supervised the remaining typically developing children in their free play activities.

To assess the effectiveness of their peer-mediated strategy, the teachers targeted two of the students with disabilities who had extremely low peer interaction rates. For 10 minutes, three times per week, one of the teachers would record the number of peer initiations and responses these students made to their peers. Over a period of 10 weeks, the teachers recorded dramatic increases for both of the targeted students. They also observed over this time period that Henry was making more and longer utterances to both peers and adults.

> **TEACHING TIPS**
>
> **Infant and Toddler Programs**
>
> 1. Intervene early to achieve the greatest possible returns in student development.
> 2. Develop important language and cognitive skills through the purposeful structuring and adapting of everyday activities, such as labeling objects or singing about events and objects.
> 3. Intensify instruction for those children showing the poorest skill development and lowest parent involvement.
> 4. Involve families in early childhood interventions. Teach parents how to conduct daily readings with their children.
> 5. Use curriculums that address social-emotional, literacy, language, cognitive, and mobility development.

Cultural factors were possible explanations for lower levels of readings among the CLD mothers according to Raikes et al. (2006). Hispanic American mothers, for example, might be more inclined to resort to oral storytelling, as typical in their culture, than to story reading. Furthermore, non-English-speaking mothers may have difficulty finding books in their language to read to their children. In terms of African American parents, Slaughter-Defoe (2000) recounted the example of the researcher working with African American parents of young children in Louisiana. The parents were confused by the directive to read to their children, so the researcher created a 21-page booklet to teach them how. According to Slaughter-Defoe, teachers needed to understand that many of the parents could be either illiterate or poor readers and that parents might need help in interpreting teachers' directions. Slaughter-Defoe compared Japanese and African American parents. Japanese parents are expected to teach their children to read before the children begin school; they also are expected to prepare their children for social relations. African Americans, on the other hand, tend to believe that teachers are responsible for teaching children basic skills and traditionally have not assumed responsibility for their children's reading readiness.

Early childhood programs need to account for these cultural differences. Interventions need to be intensified for those groups at the greatest risk (i.e., African, Hispanic, and Native American children), and their parents need to be taught and encouraged to provide home-based activities such as daily readings.

What Interventions Are Available for 3- to 5-Year-Old CLD Children?

How Can Head Start Best Serve CLD Learners?

Head Start is designed to serve low-income children from ages 3 to 5. Although some have questioned the beneficial effects of the program, the research findings have generally indicated positive outcomes for participants, particularly in terms of lower levels of grade retentions and special education placements (Barnett, 1998; Barnett & Hustedt, 2005). Barnett and Hustedt further note that some preschool programs, such as the Abecedarian program, have better student outcomes than Head Start, possibly due to the fact that these other programs tend to have better-qualified teachers, smaller classes, more resources, and more effective supervision than Head Start. Other key factors appear to be providing early intervention services before the age of 3 and focusing these services on the child rather than the

An extremely important early intervention activity is to read to infants and toddlers.

family (Campbell & Taylor, 1996). In their review of early childhood programs, Campbell and Taylor observed that in addition to the schooling advantages for the children, the support provided in these programs enabled parents to make positive changes in their work and parenting lives.

Preschool programs can vary widely, but a particular focus in quality programs is to prepare young children for school success. Accordingly, many of the activities will focus on reading and writing skills, which are taught in individualized, small-group, and whole-group formats. A special challenge for large-scale preschool programs such as Head Start or those found in large school systems is to provide the type of quality control characteristic of many model preschool programs (Conyers, Reynolds, & Ou, 2003). Markers of successful early childhood intervention include eventual academic achievement as well as reductions in special education placements. In a study of the early childhood preschool programs in the Chicago public schools, Conyers et al. found that children who participated in the half-day program for 4 and 5 year olds had 32% fewer special education placements than their nonparticipating peers. In addition to lower special education rates, these students also spent fewer years in special education. The special education discrepancies between the two groups were noted as early as first grade, strongly suggesting a cognitive advantage from the preschool program. These findings are encouraging and further confirm the beneficial effects of early interventions for young children, particularly poor minority (i.e., African American) children. The fact that large programs such as those provided by Head Start and urban school districts do not report reductions in special education placements as large as those in model programs (Conyers et al.) suggests a need for more specialized investment in early childhood programs in order to achieve greater returns.

How Do We Upgrade Early Childhood Programs?

Improving early childhood programs might best be accomplished by investing in personnel preparation. Teachers of preschool children often have less educational preparation than do teachers of school-age children. Horm (2003) argues that there is a critical need to upgrade the preparation of preschool teachers, particularly those who teach children at greatest educational risk (i.e., children who are poor, urban, recent immigrants, of color, and with disabilities). Horm notes that children under the age of 6 in our society are more likely to be poor, that changes in family structure will make home–school partnership challenging, and that differences between the cultural background of the teacher and the child are increasingly common. As the diversity and corresponding needs of our student population increase, the competence of our preschool teaching corps must increase accordingly. In a discussion of teacher preparation for diverse, urban, early childhood populations, Horm points out that many teachers have no coursework in teaching children with disabilities, from diverse backgrounds, or with limited English proficiency.

An especially important issue is poverty. Horm (2003) draws from the research of Hart and Risley (1995) to show the dramatic differences in school readiness between poor and more affluent children. Children from welfare families, for example, enter school at age 6 with a vocabulary of about 4,000 words compared to about 20,000 words for children from professional families. Additionally, low-income children tend to be in early childhood programs of such poor quality that their overall developmental progress may be undermined. Poor children need to be enrolled in programs with highly qualified teachers who are skilled in helping their students develop the language and reading skills that will result in academic success.

Teachers of young children need to be aware that explicit, intensive, and systematic instruction is key to preventing school failure. Teachers also need to know how to identify children who are at risk of failure and how to support learning gains (Mathes & Torgesen, 1998). Explicit instruction refers to teaching specific skills, such as phonological processing or recognizing the letters of the alphabet. Equally important is recognizing when children are failing to grasp the skills and concepts presented to them. Teachers need to learn how to progressively monitor their students' development and to apply intensive instruction as needed. This requires providing a greater number of teaching and learning opportunities with increased repetitions of previously learned skills, preferably in small groups of two or three so that students will have many opportunities to respond to and acquire skills critical for subsequent learning. Finally, teachers need to learn how to be systematic in their instruction. That is, they need to learn how to carefully structure their lessons so that one skill builds upon a previously taught skill. Using good, scientifically validated curriculum programs is extremely important. Teachers are not expected to develop their own curriculum, but they need to be prepared to teach from sound programs and to recognize when programs lack internal validity. Curriculums such as *Learning Games* (Sparling & Lewis, 2001) might be used for early literacy, oral language, and early numeracy. Teacher preparation programs could instruct teachers how to use this and other curricula (e.g., *Early Reading Intervention*, ERI, Simmons & Kame'enui, 2003) to systematically develop these skills in children.

Horm (2003) also stressed attitude as a point to be addressed in preparing teachers for young urban learners. She proposed that teachers learn to respect individuals from diverse backgrounds and refrain from viewing differences as deficits. Other attitude problems Horm described include nonproductive anger toward families and blaming children for their difficulties. Teachers of hard-to-teach children often externalize their lack of success to the families or the child. A significant portion of the problem may arise from the fact that teachers have been prepared to teach middle-class children, who do not present as many learning challenges. When poor CLD children do not respond as expected, teachers often find fault with the child or the family rather than recognize the need to explore alternative instructional approaches.

Horm (2003) recommended expanding the teacher preparation program to include other disciplines, such as special education, health, and social services. Since so many poor and CLD young children present special learning needs, Horm recommended that

1. All preschool, kindergarten, and primary teachers in schools of targeted (poor and minority) populations have strong professional preparation in special education as well as early childhood education.

> **TEACHING TIPS**
>
> **Key Features of Preschool Programs for CLDE 3- to 5-Year-Olds**
>
> 1. Preschool programs for 3- to 5-year-olds are beneficial, but programs that begin interventions with infants and toddlers have even greater returns.
> 2. Provide high-quality early childhood programs for poor and CLD children.
> 3. Make certain school programs have highly qualified staff, lower staff–child ratios, close supervision, and good resources.
> 4. Use scientifically validated curricula to provide explicit and systematic instruction.
> 5. Develop skill in identifying children at risk of failure in order to intensify instruction for these children.
> 6. For poor CLD children, professionals need competence in early childhood general *and* special education.

2. All preschool, kindergarten, and primary teachers in schools of targeted populations have strong professional preparation in scientifically-based literacy instruction.
3. All preschool, kindergarten, and primary teachers in schools of targeted populations have strong professional preparation in scientifically-based behavioral interventions.

How Can We Reduce Special Education Placements of CLDE Learners Through Early Intervention?

The decade between 1990 and 2000 saw a 30.3% increase in special education enrollments, which greatly exceeded the 13.7% growth in overall school enrollments (Conyers et al., 2003). The greatest growth occured in the categories of learning disabilities (50.5%), speech or language impairments (19.2%), mental retardation (10%), and emotional disturbance (8%). Given this dramatic increase in special education enrollments, educators and public officials have become concerned that too many children are being identified, that too many of the children are victims of ineffective instruction in general education, that the discrepancy between IQ and achievement is an ineffective tool for LD identification, and that the present identification rate is too costly (Fuchs & Fuchs, 2005).

The issue of overidentification is particularly pertinent to CLD children, especially African Americans and ELLs, who show the most disproportionality for learning disabilities, emotional disturbance, and mild mental retardation (Harry & Klingner, 2006; Skiba, Poloni-Staudinger, Gallini, Simmons, & Feggins-Azziz, 2006). Mild disabilities (i.e., learning disabilities, educable mental retardation, and behavior disorders) have greater relevance within an academic context. The special education model has been to wait until the third or fourth grade before special education intervention. Recently, authorities have referred to this as the "wait-until-fail" model, contending that specialized attention at this point is often too late to make a difference (Fuchs & Fuchs, 2005; Hettleman, 2003).

How Can We Prevent Special Education Placements Through Early Reading Intervention?

What Are the Reading Needs of CLDE Learners? Prevention and early intervention are considerably more effective and efficient than later intervention and remediation for ensuring reading success (Institute for the Development of Educational Achievement,

2002). Nearly 80% of all special education referrals are for problems in reading, and this is particularly true of CLD children (International Reading Association, 2003). The research on the reading performance of children in U.S. schools indicates there is considerable room for improvement. Data reported by the National Center for Educational Statistics (NCES, 2001) show that nearly 40% of fourth-grade students are reading below basic levels. As noted in Chapter 10, a bleaker picture in reading exists for CLD learners (i.e., African, Hispanic, and Native American). The slight narrowing of the reading gap observed in recent years may be partly attributed to the greater availability of early childhood programs. Still, there is a tremendous need for continued growth, particularly among underachieving diverse populations.

Since reading is fundamental to overall school success, reading acquisition should be emphasized early in the child's schooling, with a special urgency for certain CLD groups. Decades of reading research have given us much information about the prevention of reading difficulties in children at risk for reading and school failure. All students, including students with mild disabilities, can become competent readers when provided with appropriate instruction (Mathes and Torgesen, 1998). The key factors appear to be intervening sufficiently early and with scientifically validated strategies.

When early intervention should begin is not entirely clear. Considering the achievement gap between many CLD and European American children, it appears wise to start formal instruction as early as Head Start or preschool, but certainly no later than kindergarten. Farkas (2003) reports, for example, that African American students are 1 year behind European Americans at first grade but are 4 years behind by 12th grade. Rather than view this situation as a demand for intensive instruction, schools often respond to it as evidence of low ability with limited promise and proceed to school the students accordingly.

Although some would argue that only "developmentally appropriate" practices should be employed in early childhood classrooms, several decades of evidence have revealed that the reading skills of many children, particularly minorities (i.e., African, Hispanic, and Native Americans), will not easily emerge from "appropriate practices" (Hettleman, 2003). The International Reading Association (IRA) and the National Association for the Education of Young Children (NAEYC) issued a joint position statement on developmentally appropriate practices in reading (1998). Learning to read, they stated, is a process that occurs across developmental stages:

1. *Awareness and exploration*—Preschool. Children explore their environment to acquire the basic foundations for reading and writing such as identifying labels and signs in their environment.
2. *Experimental reading and writing*—Kindergarten. Children begin to engage in reading and writing such as matching spoken words with written ones.
3. *Early reading and writing*—First grade. Children begin to read and write about simple stories.
4. *Transitional reading and writing*—Second grade. Children read and write more fluently and more extensively.
5. *Independent and productive reading and writing*—Third grade. Children extend reading and writing so that they demonstrate, for example, the ability to enjoy reading and edit their own work.

The "developmentally appropriate" practices formula is valid and functions most smoothly for children who enter school with rich literary experiences, have effective instruction, and do not present special learning needs. For purposes of prevention, children need to be monitored closely and instruction intensified when expected abilities fail to emerge.

What Is Early Reading Intervention? Early reading intervention actually starts with home-based activities such as mother-child reading or learning games, as discussed previously in this chapter. The position taken by the authors of this text is that as CLD children approach school age (i.e., ages 3 to 6), early reading interventions require more formal and systematic instruction. Although opinions about formal early reading intervention vary, the general consensus based on current research indicates that phonemic awareness undergirds beginning reading (National Institute of Child Health and Human Development, 2000) and that phonemic awareness, alphabetic understanding, fluency with text, vocabulary, and comprehension provide the framework for beginning reading instruction (Bishop, 2003; Coyne, Kame'enui, & Simmons, 2001). These are considered the most important, core skills, which must be thoroughly taught.

Phonemic/phonological awareness plays a critical role in early intervention for young children. Phonological awareness is considered to have a causal relationship to acquiring reading skills and to differentiate between poor and good readers. It can be reliably assessed in children and can be taught effectively (Smith, Simmons, & Kame'enui, 1998). The critical role of phonological awareness in an early reading intervention program has been well substantiated in the existing research (Bursuck et al., 2004; King & Torgesen, 2000; Simmons et al., 2003).

Phonological processing and alphabetic understanding skills also are key to the early reading development of English language learners (ELLs) (Geva, 2000). In a review of the related research literature, Geva found that phonological skills, such as the analysis of nonsense words or the rapid naming of letters, was significant for both native English speakers and ELLs. Geva concluded that phonological processing skills along with rapid basic naming would be better predictors of basic reading skills than oral language proficiency. In other words, for ELLs, oral language proficiency did not have to precede the development of phonological skills.

What Should We Do to Prevent Reading Failure? Existing reading studies underscore the technical or scientific nature of teaching reading (Moats, 1999). Teachers of beginning readers need to have a good understanding of phonological awareness and the structure of the English language in order to be effective teachers (Mather, Bos, & Babur, 2001). Young children who are struggling beginning readers will not automatically catch up

Early intervention in reading instruction can help to prevent reading problems for young culturally diverse learners.

(Simmons & Kame'enui, 2003). According to Moats, many children "never learn to read unless they are taught in an organized, systematic, efficient way by a knowledgeable teacher using a well-designed instructional approach" (p. 7). She proposes that reading instruction include direct teaching of phonemic awareness, decoding, the code system of written English, vocabulary instruction, and comprehension. Additionally, children should be exposed to a variety of texts and should be encouraged to write to promote a greater understanding of reading. Unfortunately, most teachers have not been prepared for this type of teaching of reading, and research shows that many teachers do not have a basic understanding of the structure of the English system (Mather et al.; Moats). To

APPLICATION

Henry in Kindergarten

Henry made progress in his preschool program but still displayed some risk in terms of reading readiness. The assessment at the beginning of kindergarten, DIBELS (*Dynamic Indicators of Basic Early Literacy Skills*, Good & Kaminski, 2002) revealed that Henry was fluent in only 2 initial sounds and 10 letters. This placed him at the intensive level, meaning he needed intensive instruction to be ready for first-grade reading.

His kindergarten teacher thought perhaps Henry would catch up as a result of instruction in the kindergarten curriculum, which was heavily based on phonological awareness skills. When assessed again by the intervention specialist in January, the specialist found that Henry, along with seven other students (30% of the class), did not meet the benchmarks for that point in kindergarten. Henry, for example, was now fluent in 6 initial sounds and 24 letter names. However, he scored zero in phoneme segmentation fluency and nonsense word fluency. Henry still needed intensive instruction.

The specialist organized the eight students into groups of two and three for more intensive instruction. She used the *Early Reading Intervention* (ERI, Simmons & Kame'enui, 2003) curriculum, which is designed to complement DIBELS. Each group received 30 minutes of instruction per day, 5 days per week, until the end of the school year. The specialist monitored the students closely, assessing them weekly to ensure that they were mastering the skills taught. Because the curriculum was scripted, the specialist decided to train the assistant teacher to teach one of the more skilled groups that needed additional instruction.

At the end of the school year, Henry had reached benchmark on the DIBELS on the letter naming, phonemic segmentation, and nonsense word fluency. Additionally, reading assessments showed Henry to be on grade level and ready for first grade. The intervention specialist planned to continue with Henry and the other seven students in first grade to make sure that they maintained these skills.

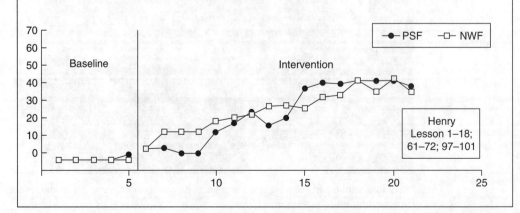

> **TEACHING TIPS**
>
> **Early Reading Intervention**
>
> 1. Special education referrals disproportionately are for children with problems in reading.
> 2. A substantial gap in reading continues between white and minority (i.e., African, Hispanic, and Native American) children.
> 3. Provide early reading intervention with an emphasis on phonological processing and alphabetic principles, which are basic to eventual reading success.
> 4. Begin formal early literacy instruction in the preschool years and no later than kindergarten.
> 5. Assess early literacy skills with validated assessment instruments such as DIBELS.
> 6. Provide intensive instruction daily in phonemic and phonological awareness for young children experiencing difficulty with early literacy.
> 7. Use a research-validated curriculum that provides explicit systematic and intensive instruction.

prevent reading failure, researchers (e.g., Simmons & Kame'enui) make the following recommendations:

- Identify students early and intervene strategically.
- Emphasize the most important areas of reading instruction.
- Teach the critical skills thoroughly.
- Teach a skill before expecting the student to produce it.
- Hold instruction time sacred.
- Differentiate instruction according to student groupings and the amount of instruction needed by individual students.
- Closely monitor student learning.

Summary

High-quality early childhood programs can be effective in minimizing the impact of disabilities or in preventing disabilities for children with at-risk markers. Federal legislation has authorized early childhood services, starting in infancy for children with disabilities and their families. In the latest reauthorization of IDEIA (2004), emphasis is placed on preventing the need for special education services through early intervention, especially for low socioeconomic, culturally diverse populations. Children from some culturally diverse groups are disproportionately impoverished and are more likely to experience at-risk conditions, such as low birth weight. These factors predispose children to learning problems and increase the probability of special education referral and placement.

Over the past two decades, researchers have validated certain programs and approaches effective for young children with and at risk for disabilities. Systematic exposure to a well-defined curriculum of developmental activities has proved effective. Early childhood programs with qualified staff using evidence-based practices that begin in infancy appear to produce the best results. Head Start documents favorable findings for its participants, but its impact on reducing special education referrals and school failure is not as great as that of model early childhood programs. There is a need to further upgrade many of the early childhood programs for poor, culturally diverse children.

The preparation of early childhood teachers needs to be improved. Educational standards need to be raised so that early childhood teachers are skilled in identifying children at risk for failure, implementing scientifically verified curriculums, intensifying instruction when needed, and monitoring pupil performance. Since reading failure is a principal reason for special education referral, teachers of young children need to be highly skilled in teaching early literacy skills, such as phonemic and phonological awareness.

Related Learning Activities

1. Observe a local preschool program that includes CLD students with diagnosed disabilities. Try to make several visits to this class. Specify the social, language, cognitive, and physical needs of one child with disabilities. Review the curriculum being used in the class to address each of these areas. How is this student progressing compared to classmates? Describe the strategies being used to help the child develop skill in each of these areas. How might the instruction be intensified to meet the student's needs? Indicate whether peers are being used to facilitate skill development. What suggestions might you have, if any, to augment the curriculum for this particular child?

2. Observe a Head Start center in your community. Target a CLDE child who may have some special risk factors, such as low birth weight, FAS, or living in a foster home. Complete the assignment described in activity 1.

3. Obtain a copy of the *Dynamic Indicators of Basic Early Literacy Skills* (6th ed.)—DIBELS from the website http://dibels.uoregon.edu/. Identify a local kindergarten with a significant enrollment of children from low socioeconomic or culturally diverse backgrounds. With the classroom teacher, identify two or three children who present the greatest academic need in this class and get permission to assess them on DIBELS. What skill strengths and deficits are revealed? What instructional plan is indicated for these children?

4. Review an early literacy curriculum such as *Learning Games*—48 to 60 months (Sparling & Lewis, 2001) or *Early Reading Intervention* (Simmons & Kame'enui, 2003). Design a lesson for one of the students you assessed in the kindergarten (activity 3). Also design an assessment procedure for progressively monitoring the student's acquisition and maintenance of this skill. Get permission to teach this skill to the targeted student.

References

Alliance for Healthy Homes. (ND). Lead poisoning. Retrieved December 14, 2006, from http://www.afhh.org/chil_ar/chil_ar_lead_poisoning.htm.

Barnett, W. S. (1998). Long-term cognitive and academic effects of early childhood education on children in poverty. *Preventive Medicine, 27*, 204–207.

Barnett, W. S., & Hustedt, J. T. (2005). Head Start's lasting benefits. *Infants & Young children, 18*, 16–24.

Berkeley Division of Public Health (2002). *Health status report, 2002: Low birth weight.* Retrieved December 13, 2006, from http://www.ci.berkeley.ca.us/publichealth/reports/2002lowbirthweight.html.

Bishop, A. G. (2003). Prediction of first-grade reading achievement: A comparison on fall and winter kindergarten screenings. *Learning Disability Quarterly, 26*, 189–200.

Boyle, C. A., & Cordero, J. F. (2005). Birth defects and disabilities: A public health issue for the 21st century. *American Journal of Public Health, 95*(11), 1884–1886.

Bursuck, W. D., Smith, T., Munk, D., Damer, M., Mehlig, L., & Perry, J. (2004). Evaluating the impact of a prevention-based model of reading on children who are at-risk. *Remedial and Special Education, 25,* 303–313.

Campbell, F. A., Pungello, E. P., Miller-Johnson, S., Burchinal, M., & Ramey, C. T. (2001). The development of cognitive and academic abilities: Growth curves from an early childhood educational experiment. *Developmental Psychology, 37,* 231–242.

Campbell, F. A., & Ramey, C. T. (1994). Effects of early intervention on intellectual and academic achievement: A follow-up study of children from low-income families. *Child Development, 65,* 684–698.

Campbell, F. A., & Ramey, C. T. (1995) Cognitive and school outcomes for high-risk African-American students at middle adolescence: Positive effects of early intervention. *American Educational Research Journal, 32,* 743–772.

Campbell, F. A., Ramey, C. T., Pungello, E. P., Sparling, J., & Miller-Johnson, S. (2002). Early childhood education: Young adult outcomes from the Abecedarian Project. *Applied Developmental Science, 6,* 42–57.

Campbell, F. A., & Taylor, K. (1996, May). Early childhood programs that work for children from economically disadvantaged families. *Young Children,* 74–80.

Cartledge, G. (2005, February 3). Individuals with Disabilities Education Act (IDEA) 2004 Hearings. The Ohio State University, Columbus, Ohio.

Castor, M. L., Smyser, M. S., Taualii, M. M., Park, A. N., Lawson, S. A., & Forquera, R. A. (2006). A nationwide population-based study identifying health disparities between American Indians/Alaska Natives and the general populations living in select urban counties. *American Journal of Public Health, 96*(8), 1478–1484.

Centers for Disease Control and Prevention. (2005). Blood lead-levels United States, 1999–2002. MMWR 2005: 54: 513–516. Retrieved December 14, 2006, from http://0-www.cdc.gov.mill1.sjlibrary.org/ MMWR/PDF/wk/mm5420.pdf.

Chang, S., O'Brien, K. O., Nathanson, M. S., Mancini, J., & Witter, F. R. (2003). *The Journal of Pediatrics, 143*(2), 250–257.

Conyers, L. M., Reynolds, A. J., & Ou, S.-R. (2003). The effect of early childhood intervention and subsequent special education services: Findings from the Chicago Child-Parent Centers. *Educational Evaluation and Policy Analysis, 25,* 75–95.

Corsello, C. M. (2005). Early intervention in autism. *Infants & Young Children, 18,* 74–85.

Council for Exceptional Children. (2000). The individual family service plan (IFSP). Information Center on Disabilities and Gifted Education. Retrieved January 18, 2006, from http://evicec.org/digests/e605.html.

Coyne, M. D., Kame'enui, E. J., & Simmons, D. C. (2001). Prevention and intervention in beginning reading: Two complex systems. *Learning Disabilities Research & Practice, 16*(2), 62–73.

Darling, S. M., & Gallagher, P. A. (2004). Needs of and supports for African American and European American caregivers of young children with special needs in urban and rural settings. *Topics in Early Childhood Special Education, 24,* 98–109.

David, R. J., & Collins, J. W. (1997). Differing birth weight among infants of U.S.-born Blacks, African-born Blacks, and U.S.-Born Whites. *The New England Journal of Medicine, 337*(17), 1209–1214.

Delprato, D. J. (2001). Comparisons of discrete-trial and normalized behavioral language intervention for young children with autism. *Journal of Autism and Developmental Disorders, 31,* 315–325.

Dobbs, M. (2005, July 15). Black, Latino elementary students closing achievement gap, study says. *The Columbus Dispatch,* p. A3.

Farkas, G. (2003). Racial disparities and discrimination in education: What do we know, how do we know it, and what do we need to know? *Teachers College Record, 105,* 1119–1146.

Freund, P. J., Boone, H. A., Barlow, J. H., & Lim, C. I. (2005). Healthcare and early intervention collaborative supports for families and young children. *Infants & Young Children, 18,* 25–36.

Fuchs, D., & Fuchs, L. (2005, April). *Curriculum Based Measures (CBM): Role in Responsiveness to Intervention.* Paper presented at the meeting of the Council for Exceptional Children, Baltimore, MD.

Fuchs, L. S., Fuchs, D., Safer, N., & McInerny, M. (2005, April). *Progress Monitoring: What It Is And How It Can Benefit You.* Presentation at the meeting of the Council for Exceptional Children, Baltimore, MD.

Geva, E. (2000). Issues in the assessment of reading disabilities in L2 children—beliefs and research evidence. *Dyslexia, 6,* 13–28.

Good, R. H., & Kaminski, R. A. (Eds.). (2002). *Dynamic indicators of basic early literacy skills* (6th ed.). Eugene, OR: Institute for the Development of Educational Achievement. Available: http://dibels.uoregon.edu/.

Guralnick, M. J. (2000). Early childhood intervention: Evolution of a system. *Focus on Autism and Other Developmental Disabilities, 15,* 68–79.

Hack, M., Flannery, D. J., Schluchter, M, Cartar, L., Borawski, E., & Klein, N. (2002). Outcomes in young adulthood for very-low-birth-weight infants. *New England Journal of Medicine, 346*(3), 149–157.

Harry, B., & Klingner, J. (2006). *Why are so many minority students in special education? Understanding race and disability in schools.* New York: Teachers College Press.

Hart, B. M., & Risley, T. R. (1968). Establishing use of descriptive adjectives in the spontaneous speech of disadvantaged preschool children. *Journal of Applied Behavior analysis, 1,* 109–120.

Hart, B., & Risley, T. R. (1974). Using preschool materials to modify the language of disadvantaged children. *Journal of Applied Behavior analysis, 7,* 243–256.

Hart, B., & Risley, T. R. (1995). *Meaningful differences in the everyday experiences of young American children.* Baltimore, MD: Paul Brookes.

Heckman, J. J. (2002). Invest in the very young. (ED 467 549). Retrieved December 6, 2006, from http://www.ounceofprevention.org.

Hessol, N. A., & Fuentes-Afflick, E. (2005). Ethnic differences in neonatal and postneonatal mortality. *Pediatrics, 115*(1), e44–e51.

Hettleman, K. R. (2003). *The invisible dyslexics: How public school systems in Baltimore and elsewhere discriminate against poor children in the diagnosis and treatment of early reading difficulties.* Baltimore, MD: The Abell Foundation. (Hyperlink "http://www.abell.org" www.abell.org)

Horm, D. M. (2003). Preparing early childhood educators to work in diverse urban settings. *Teachers College Record, 105,* 226–244.

Hudson, C. G. (2005). Socioeconomic status and mental illness: Tests of the social causation and selection hypotheses. *American Journal of Orthopsychiatry, 75*(1), 3–18.

IDEA (2004). Individuals with Disabilities Education Act of 2004. Retrieved May 3, 2005 from http://thomas.loc.gov/cgi-bin/query/z?c108:h.1350.enr.

Institute for the Development of Educational Achievement. (2002). How do I teach the BIG IDEAS in beginning reading. Retrieved August 11, 2004, from http://reading.uoregon.edu/instruction/instruc_2.php.

International Reading Association. (2003). The role of reading instruction in addressing the overrepresentation of minority children in special education in the United States. Retrieved January 18, 2006, from www.reading.org/downloads/positions/ps1063_minorities.pdf.

International Reading Association and the National Association for the Education of Young Children. (1998). Learning to read and write: Developmentally appropriate practices for young children. *Young Children, 53*(4), 30–46.

Juel, C. (1998). Learning to read and write: A longitudinal study of 54 children from first through fourth grade. *Journal of Educational Psychology, 80,* 437–447.

King, R., & Torgesen, J. K. (2000). Improving the effectiveness of reading instruction in one elementary school: A description of the process (FCRR Technical Report No. 3). Retrieved March 14, 2005, from http://www/fcrr.org/science/technicalreports.htm.

Koegel, R. L., O'Dell, M., & Koegel, L. K. (1987). A natural language teaching paradigm for nonverbal autistic children. *Journal of Autism and Developmental Disorders, 17,* 187–200.

Koegel, R.L., Schreibman, L., Good, A., Cerniglia, L., Murphy, C., & Koegel, L. K., (1989). *How to teach pivotal behaviors to children with autism: A training manual.* Santa Barbara, CA: University of California, Santa Barbara.

Lin, C. (1996). The effects of curriculum-based peer-mediated social skills training on the positive peer interactions of preschool children with special needs. Unpublished doctoral dissertation, The Ohio State University, Columbus, OH.

Lucas, E. T., Goldschmidt, L., & Day, N. I. (2003). Alcohol use among pregnant African American women: Ecological considerations. *Health and Social Work, 28*(4), 273–283.

Ma, G. X., Toubbeh, J., Cline, J., & Chisholm, A. (1998). Native American adolescents' views on fetal alcohol syndrome prevention in schools. *Journal of School Health, 68,* 131–137.

Markowitz, J., Carlson, E., Frey, W., Riley, J., Shimshak, A., Heinzen, H., Strohl, J., Lee, H., & Klein, S. (2006). *Preschoolers' characteristics, services, and results: Wave 1 overview report from the pre-elementary education longitudinal study (PEELS).* Rockville, MD: Westat. Available at www.peels.org.

Mathes, P. G., & Torgesen, J. K. (1998). All children can learn to read: Critical care for the prevention of reading failure. *Peabody Journal of Education, 73,* 317–340.

Mather, N., Bos, C., & Babur, M. (2001). Perceptions and knowledge of preservice and inservice teachers about early literacy instruction. *Journal of Learning Disabilities, 34,* 472–482.

McMullen, M. B. (1999, July). Achieving best practices in infant and toddler care and education. *Young Children,* 69–76.

Mellard, D. (2005). Understanding responsiveness to intervention in learning disabilities determination. Retrieved July 11, 2005 from http://www.nrcld.org/publications/papers/mellard.shtml.

Moats, L. (1999). Teaching reading is rocket science: What expert teachers of reading should know and be able to do. Retrieved July 14, 2005, from http://www.aft.org/pubs-reports/downloads/teachers/rocketsci.pdf.

National Association for the Education of African American Children with Learning Disabilities. Retrieved August 13, 2006, from http://www.charityadvantage.com/aacld/HomePage. asp.

National Center for Educational Statistics (2001, April). *The national assessment of educational progress (NAEP).* Washington, DC: Institute of Education Sciences, U.S. Department of Education. Retrieved July, 6, 2005 from http://nces.ed.gov/nationsreportcard/.

National Center for Educational Statistics (2005, July). Trends in average reading scale scores by race/ethnicity. Washington, DC: Institute of Education Sciences, U.S. Department of Education. Retrieved July 15, 2005, from http://nces.ed.gov/nationsreportcard/ltt/results2004/natsubgroups.asp.

National Institute of Child Health and Human Development. (2000). *Report of the National Reading Panel. Teaching children to read: An evidence-based assessment of the scientific research literature on reading and its implications for reading instruction: Reports of the subgroups* (NIH Publication No. 00-4754). Washington, DC: U.S. Government Printing Office.

National Institute of Child Health and Human Development Early Child Care Research Network (2005). Duration and development timing of poverty and children's cognitive and social development from birth through third grade. *Child Development, 76* (4), 795–810.

National Poverty Center (2006). University of Michigan, Gerald R. Ford School of Public Policy. Retrieved December 10, 2006, from http://www.npc.umich.edu/poverty/#4.

National Research Center on Learning Disabilities. (2005). Core concepts of RTI. Retrieved July 11, 2005, from http://www.nrcld.org/research/rti/concepts.shtml.

New York-Presbyterian Hospital. (2003). Lead poisoning. Retrieved December 14, 2006, from http://wo-pub2.med.cornell.edu/cgi-bin/WebObjects/PublicA.woa/6/wa/viewHContent?website=nyp&contentID=848&wosid=MRhbpgXzBE9lnKI22DywFg.

Nolan, K. W., Young, E. C., Herbert, E. B., & Wilding, G. E. (2005). Service coordination for children with complex healthcare needs in an early intervention program. *Infants & Young Children, 18,* 161–170.

Parish, S. L., & Cloud, J. M. (2006). Financial well-being of young children with disabilities and their families. *Social Work, 51*(3), 223–232.

Park, J., Turnbull, A. P., & Turnbull, H. R. (2002). Impacts of poverty on quality of life in families of children with disabilities. *Exceptional Children, 68*(2), 151–170.

Pierce, K., & Schreibman, L. (1997). Using peer trainers to promote social behavior in autism: Are they effective at enhancing multiple social modalities? *Focus on Autism & Other Developmental Disabilities, 12*, 207–219.

Pollard-Durodola, S. (2003). Wesley Elementary: A beacon of hope for at-risk students. *Education and Urban Society, 36*, 94–117.

Raikes, H., Luze, G., Brooks-Gunn, J., Raikes, H. A., Pan, B. A., Tamis-LeMonda, C.S., Constantine, J., Tarullo, L. B., & Rodrigues, E. T. (2006). Mother-child bookreading in low-income families: Correlates and outcomes during the first three years of life. *Child Development, 77*(4), 924–953.

Ramey, C. T., & Campbell, F. A. (1984). Preventive education for high-risk children: Cognitive consequences of the Carolina Abecedarian Project. *American Journal of Mental Deficiency, 88*, 515–523.

Ramey, C. T., Campbell, F. A., Burchinal, M., Skinner, M. L., Gardner, D. M., & Ramey, S. L. (2000). Persistent effects of early childhood education on high-risk children and their mothers. *Applied Developmental Science, 4*(1), 2–14.

Ramey, C. T., & Ramey, S. L. (1992). Effective early intervention. *Mental Retardation, 30*, 337–345.

Ramey, C., & Ramey, S. (2001). Introduction. In J. Sparling & I. Lewis *Learning games: The Abecedarian curriculum.* Chapel Hill, NC: Mindnurture.

Ronsaville, D. S., & Hakim, R. B. (2000). Well child care in the United States: Racial differences in compliance with guidelines. *American Journal of Public Health, 90*(9), 1436–1443.

Ryan, S., & Ferguson, D. L. (2006). On, yet under, the radar: Students with fetal alcohol syndrome disorder. *Exceptional Children, 72*(3), 363–379.

Shapiro, B. J., & Derrington, T. M. (2004). Equity and disparity in access to services: An outcomes-based evaluation of early intervention child find in Hawaii. *Topics in Early Childhood Special Education, 24*, 199–212.

Simmons, D. C., & Kame'enui, E. J. (2003). Early reading intervention. Pearson Scott Foresman official website: http://www.scottforesman.com/eri/index.cfm.

Simmons, D. C., Kame'enui, E. J., Harn, B. A., Thomas-Beck, C., Edwards, L. L., Coyne, M. D., & Peterson, K. (2003). *A summary of the research findings of Project Optimize: Improving the early literacy skills of kindergarteners at-risk for reading difficulties using effective design and delivery principles.* Retrieved May 6, 2004, from http://reading.uoregon.edu/curricula/opt_research.pdf.

Skiba, R. J., Poloni-Staudinger, L., Gallini, S., Simmons, A. B., & Feggins-Azziz, R. (2006). Disparate access: The disproportionality of African American students with disabilities across educational environments. *Exceptional Children, 72*, 411–424.

Slaughter-Defoe, D. T. (2000). *Early childhood development and school readiness: Some observations about "homework" for new century working parents.* Paper presented at the Annual Meeting of the Voices for Illinois Conference, Chicago, IL., September 22, 2000. (ED 447 952).

Smith, S. B., Simmons, D. C., & Kame'enui, E. J. (1998). Phonological awareness: Research bases. In D. C. Simmons & E. J. Kame'enui (Eds.), *What reading research tells us about children with diverse learning needs: Bases and basics* (pp. 61–128). Mahwah, NJ: Lawrence Erlbaum.

Smith, T. E. C., Gartin, B. C., Murdick, N. L., & Hilton, A. (2006). *Families and children with special needs.* Upper Saddle River, NJ: Merrill/Prentice Hall.

Sparling, J., & Lewis, I. (1979; 2001). *Learning games: The Abecedarian curriculum.* Chapel Hill, NC: Mindnurture.

Stahmer, A. C. (1995). Teaching symbolic play skills to children with autism using pivotal response training. *Journal of Autism and Developmental Disorders, 25*, 123–141.

Stahmer, A. C., & Ingersoll, B. (2004). Inclusive programming for toddlers with autism spectrum disorders: Outcomes from the children's toddler school. *Journal of Positive Behavior Interventions, 6*, 67–82.

The Carolina Abecedarian Project (2005). http://www.fpg.unc.edu/~abc/summary.cfm.

Umansky, W., & Hooper, S. R. (1998). *Young children with special needs.* Upper Saddle River, NJ: Merrill.

Wall, S.M., Taylor, N.E., Liebow, H., Sabatino, C. A., Mayer, L.M., Farber, M.Z., & Timberlake, E.M. (2005). Early heard start and access to early intervention services: A qualitative investigation. *Topics in Early Childhood Special Education, 25*(4), 218–231.

Wilson-Costello, D., Friedman, H., Minich, N., Fanaroff, A. A., & Hack, M. (2005). Improved survival rates with increased neurodevelopmental disability for extremely low birth weight infants in the 1990s. *Pediatrics, 115*, 997–1003.

Chapter **13**

Effective Postsecondary Transitions for CLDE Learners

The purpose of this chapter is to provide information about the unique transition needs and instructional strategies for students with disabilities, particularly those from culturally diverse backgrounds. By the end of this chapter, the reader should be able to answer the following questions:

1. What are the postsecondary outcomes for students with disabilities compared to their nondisabled peers?
2. How do postsecondary CLD students with exceptionalities fare compared to their non-CLD peers with exceptionalities?
3. What are the special transition needs of CLDE students?
4. What are self-determination skills?
5. How do we help CLDE students become more self-directed in transitioning to postsecondary environments?
6. What are some of the transition barriers typically faced by CLDE students?
7. What cultural understandings are needed by school personnel to facilitate the transition of CLDE students?

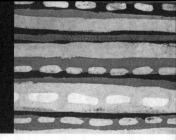

8. Why is person-centered planning important for CLDE students?
9. How important is career/vocational education to the successful transition of CLDE students?

By the end of this chapter, readers will have obtained information on strategies relative to:

1. Self-determination skills.
2. Person-centered planning for postsecondary transitions.
3. Career/vocational transitional skills.

Alma Moon

Alma Moon is a 15-year-old Native American female freshman in a high school in the northwest United States. Alma was born on an Indian reservation, but when she was 5 years of age her family moved 100 miles to the largest city in their state. Her father works as a groundskeeper on some of the business properties in the area but earns little more than the minimum wage. Alma's mother works as a housekeeper at one of the local hotels, but the combined salaries of both parents does not elevate the family above the poverty level. Alma is the second of three children; she has an older brother, who dropped out of high school and is now unemployed, and she has a younger sister, who is still in school in the fifth grade.

Alma is very close to her family. She enjoys being with them and participating in many traditional Native American activities. She especially misses her grandparents and many cousins who still live on the reservation. The family often travels back to the reservation for visits. Although there are many Native American students in her school whom Alma likes and is friendly with, she considers her siblings and her cousins to be her best friends.

Alma gets along well in school. She is compliant and socially appropriate. Alma's teachers like her but express concern over her academic performance. Alma has been diagnosed with a learning disability in reading. She is reading on the fifth-grade level and has made little or no progress over the past year.

Alma is a star in her school. She is six feet tall, strong, and athletic. She is an outstanding basketball player. She is the best female player in the state at her grade level and there is little question that she could become a star college athlete if she could become academically eligible.

How should the school proceed in planning for Alma's high school transition?

What Are the Transition Needs of Special Populations?

Transition services have been specified for students with disabilities since the early 1980s and the federal government has included key provisions on transition with each subsequent authorization of IDEA (i.e., 1990, 1997, and 2004). The purpose of transition services, according to IDEA 2004, is "to ensure that all children with disabilities have available to them a free appropriate public education that emphasizes special education and related services designed to meet their unique needs and prepare them *for further education*, employment, and independent living" (National Center on Secondary Education and Transition, 2005, p. 1. Emphasis added). This means that schools need to provide students with the instruction and experiences that would prepare them for success in the appropriate educational, work, or independent living environment once they have completed high school. The 2004 authorization included for the first time preparation for further education. In addition to work and independent living, schools must now make sure that, where appropriate, students with disabilities are also prepared to access programs of additional learning, including colleges and universities.

What Are the Transition Needs of Students with Disabilities?

The poor postsecondary outcomes for students with disabilities compared to their general education peers have been detailed in the research literature (Kohler & Field, 2003; Thoma, Baker, & Saddler, 2002; Tomblin & Haring, 1999). In the 1980s and 1990s, researchers found that students with disabilities were less likely to graduate from high school, to be employed, or to be living independently compared to their nondisabled peers. One of the most extensive and thorough studies on the transitional status of students with disabilities was the National Longitudinal Transition Study (n.d.) from 1987 through 1993, as contracted by the U.S. Department of Education. Students with disabilities fared poorly on several critical indexes. For example, students with disabilities had a 38% high school dropout rate compared to 25% for their general education classmates. Prior to dropping out, these students had considerably higher absenteeism rates (nearly one-fourth were absent for 4 or more weeks) and course failure (two-thirds failed a course). Absenteeism and course failure were found to be predictive of dropping out of school. Course failure was more likely to occur early in the student's secondary career, so that the more academically successful students were those that remained in high school.

The NLTS study also found that compared to their nondisabled peers students with disabilities were more likely to be enrolled in vocational education classes, less likely to be in general education, and less likely to take college preparation classes. Fewer than 27% of students with disabilities were enrolled in postsecondary education compared to 68% of the general education population. Three to five years after graduation, the researchers found that about one-half of the students with disabilities were competitively employed, but only at average annual wages, in 1990, of $12,000; and just a little over one-third were living independently compared to 60% of the general population.

A more recent national longitudinal study (NLTS2) revealed mixed results for students with disabilities (Wagner & Cameto, 2004; Wagner, Cameto, & Newman, 2003; Wagner, Newman, & Cameto, 2004; Wagner, Newman, Cameto, & Levine, 2005). Dropout rates declined by 17 percentage points and absenteeism was at a level commensurate with the general education population. However, the number of these students suspended or expelled from school increased substantially. Although enrollment in academic courses increased, there was no substantial change in courses passed, employment, or independent living.

What Are the Transition Needs According to Gender?

Special attention needs to be given to transition planning and interventions based on gender. Females with disabilities are found to have special issues in transitioning to postsecondary environments due to their greater tendency for premature pregnancy (NLTS, n.d.; Unruh & Bullis, 2005). Lindstrom and Benz (2002) note that females are likely to receive less vocational training than males or to be programmed into low-wage occupations. In a study of female juvenile offenders with disabilities, Unruh and Bullis observed that females are particularly vulnerable to sexual abuse, depression, running away, and lowered self-esteem. They also found that these females were more likely to be parents and to risk suicide. On the other hand, males were more likely to be diagnosed with a learning disability, to have been retained in a grade, to be diagnosed with ADD/ADHD, and less likely to have had stable employment before incarceration. Males also were less likely than females to have married and to be living independently following high school (NLTS, n.d). The higher rate of independent living among females was attributed to their higher marriage rate.

These gender differences suggest differential attention to transitional programming. Females, for example, need to be taught how to navigate the mental health, child-rearing, and employment agencies to get support for their unique needs (Unruh & Bullis, 2005). Females also should be exposed to the full range of vocational options so that they can make intelligent decisions about career opportunities (Lindstrom & Benz, 2002) and select occupations most likely to provide a living wage. The transition programs for males and females should be individualized to address their special needs. Lindstrom and Benz recommend providing individualized support through the use of transition specialists.

What Are the Transition Needs According to Cultural and Linguistic Diversity?

Transition issues are further complicated for students from cultural and linguistically diverse backgrounds with disabilities. The existing data indicate that CLD students with disabilities receive little help in transitioning to the world of work and have unemployment rates two to three times those of European Americans (Wentling & Waight, 1999). Those who are employed are likely to be earning lower wages (NLTS, n.d.; NLTS2). Because CLD students are less likely to be employed with adequate salaries, they are also less likely to be living independently (NLTS; NLTS2). Another major transitional impediment for CLD students with disabilities is poverty (NLTS, n.d.; Wentling & Waight, 1999). The NLTS study reported greater poverty for students with disabilities and that these students were less likely to have parents who were high school graduates, less likely to enroll in postsecondary education, and spent less time in general education classes. Wentling and Waight rank poverty the number-one transitional barrier for minority youth, noting that minority youth from middle-income backgrounds do not experience the same problems as impoverished youth. African and Native American CLD students are disproportionately represented in special education programs—that is, their proportion in special education is twice that of their proportion in the overall student population (NLTS, n.d.; NLTS2)— they also are disproportionately impoverished.

Investigations into the transitional barriers for CLD students with disabilities highlight the lack of cultural understanding on the part of school and community personnel (Frankland, Turnbull, Wehmeyer, & Blackmountain, 2004; Jeffries & Singer, 2003; Rueda, Monzo, Shapiro, Gomez, & Blacher, 2005; Trainor, 2005; Wentling & Waight, 1999). Wentling and Waight cite the example of Hispanic parents tending to turn the education of their children over to the schools and very rarely questioning the school's authority. These parents are therefore less likely to become involved with the school, and the school may interpret this as lack of interest in the child's education. A similar observation has been made about African American parents (Paratore, 2001).

Many CLD students with disabilities have the highest dropout rates. As Sinclair, Christenson, and Thurlow (2005) suggest, dropping out of school is a process of withdrawal and disengagement that begins long before the ninth grade, and the contributing factors need to be studied more closely. Sinclair, Christenson, and Thurlow note that only 28% of African Americans with BD graduate compared to 42% of all students with BD, 56% of all students with disabilities, and 79% of the general education population. Even after intervention, Sinclair et al. found that African American males were more likely to drop out than their white male counterparts. Jeffries and Singer contend that American Indian/Alaska Native students have the highest dropout rates of all groups.

An extremely important school-based factor identified by Wentling and Waight (1999) was *teacher resistance.* In their national study, work partnership directors reported that teachers often refused to adapt their instruction according to the learning needs of CLD students and continued to teach as they had always taught. A related school-based concern is the lack of integrated or relevant curriculum (NLTS, n.d.; Wentling & Waight). The researchers found vocational and academic curriculums were typically segregated, and although CLDE students were equally likely to take vocational training, they were less likely to take comprehensive vocational training (NLTS) or were often placed in the lowest academic tracks (Wentling & Waight). Students placed in low-level classes typically experience low teacher expectations and, accordingly, low-level instruction.

Communication problems also emerged as major transition impediments for CLD students with disabilities. Many CLD students and their families lack English proficiency, and these families feel that they do not receive sufficient information from the schools regarding transition services available to their children (Rueda et al., 2005). Additionally, there is a communication breakdown between the schools and the business world. Work partnership directors reported that schools are often unaware of the expectations of the business world and fail to prepare their students accordingly (Wentling & Waight, 1999). This is particularly problematic for low-income CLDE students, because they are less likely to have knowledgeable adults in their lives to provide direction along these lines. Other school-based factors that undoubtedly contribute to the special transition problems of CLDE students are the higher rates of absenteeism and failing grades among African Americans compared to other students, and the fact that African and Hispanic Americans spend less time in general education classes than European Americans (NLTS, n.d.; NLTS 2).

Finally, there are barriers that are largely the responsibility of the CLDE student, for example, placing greater importance on education and striving to improve the requisite academic and work-related skills. An understanding of the importance of schooling and training to postsecondary success is likely to motivate some students to remain in school. The NLTS (n.d.) study found that students who had specific work-related goals and initiated that training in high school were more likely to complete school and secure employment following graduation. However, although described here as the responsibility of the individual, as discussed in Chapter 11, students are not likely to make much progress toward valuing school without considerable assistance from school personnel. The impersonal high school climate with its emphasis on rules and academic performance is likely to further alienate and disengage minority students with disabilities (Gillock & Reyes, 1996). It is also true that many of the barriers described here are also present among poor whites, but these conditions impact CLDE students more negatively.

How Do We Prepare CLDE Students to Make Successful Transitions?

The experiences and instruction that students have in school play a major role in their postsecondary outcomes. Research findings such as those from the NLTS (n.d.) and NLTS2 indicate that students with the most successful transitions are those who had clearly specified goals, vocational education, work experiences, advanced academic courses, access to general education classes, participation in school or community groups, and parent support.

TEACHING TIPS

Transition Needs by Population

Students with Disabilities	Special Needs of Females	Greater Needs of CLDE Students
1. Improved graduation rates 2. Reduced absenteeism 3. Greater access to general education 4. Higher levels of competitive employment and wages 5. Fewer suspensions	1. Assistance with premature parenting 2. Access to full array of vocational options 3. Mental health interventions for depression and abuse	1. Paid employment 2. Improved high school graduation 3. Greater access to general education 4. Concentrated vocational training 5. Reduced absenteeism 6. Greater academic success 7. Access to full range of vocational options 8. Alternative, constructive measures to suspensions and expulsions 9. Supportive school personnel 10. Supportive and nurturing adults 11. Community resources

What Are Self-Determination Skills?

Self-determination has been defined in various ways, but essentially it refers to the ability to be self-directed and to act autonomously to achieve one's goals. Some specific self-determination skills include goal setting and attainment, choice making, decision making, problem solving, self-regulation (e.g., self-observation, self-evaluation, self-reinforcement), self-instruction, self-advocacy, self-awareness, self-efficacy, life skills, planning, acting on plans, and minimizing risks (Field, Hoffman, & Posch, 1997; Hoffman & Field, 1995; Wood, Karvonen, Test, Browder, & Algozzine, 2004). All of these concepts may not appear in every self-determination instructional program, but their main intent is to help students develop self-awareness and self-management skills so they can become more self-directed and transition successfully to post–high school environments. Wehmeyer, Agran, and Hughes (1998) divided the concept of self-determination into the four basic components of autonomy, self-regulation, psychological empowerment, and self-realization. The skills taught should thus enable students to act independently, regulate their behavior according to the demands of the situation, have a realistic assessment of their traits, and believe in their ability to achieve desired goals. Explicit examples of self-determination goals of self-advocacy and self-awareness are described by Wood et al.:

Self-advocacy: ability to advocate on one's own behalf; whereas leadership skills are those needed for a person to lead, guide, or direct.
Self-awareness or self-knowledge: refers to a comprehensive and reasonably accurate knowledge of one's strengths and limitations.

Alma Moon Continued

In terms of Alma Moon's situation, as described at the beginning of this chapter, she would have to learn to assume a leadership role in her transition meetings in school. Alma already had assumed considerable responsibility at home, so she needed to be prompted to use a variation of these leadership skills at school. With the assistance of her teachers, Alma identified the persons who should be at her meetings and would be instrumental in helping her to reach her long-range goals of successfully completing high school, remaining a top athlete, improving her academic skills, passing her college entrance exams, and being accepted at a college or university that would enable her to remain connected to her family and culture. In addition to taking a leadership role in planning these meetings, Alma also had to take the lead in speaking out during the meetings and keeping the discussions and actions focused on helping her to achieve immediate objectives and long-term goals. Alma needed to commit to weekly practice sessions with her teachers so that she could learn to speak out and advocate for herself.

Self-awareness is important for students in learning how to utilize their strengths and address their weaknesses in order to achieve their goals. In Alma's case, at a minimum, she knew she would need to:

a. Improve her school attendance.
b. Participate more fully in remedial programs to improve her reading skills.
c. Increase her self-confidence and self-advocacy skills.
d. Adjust her schedule in order to meet the demands of schooling while continuing to contribute to her family/community.

Student goals and objectives need to be based on assessments, which may be either formal or informal. Two examples of formal assessment instruments are the AIR Self-Determination Scale (Wolman, Campeau, DuBois, Mithaugh, & Stolarski, 1994) and the Choicemaker Self-Determination Transition Assessment (Martin & Marshall, 1995). Wood, Karvonen, et al. point out that these two instruments are structured to provide information on developing goals and objectives for instruction. The authors also suggest how teachers might assess students informally. For example, if the objective is helping students develop problem-solving skills, the teacher might ask a series of questions: Does the student know how to define a problem? Does the student know how to identify possible alternatives for this problem? Does the student know how to identify alternatives that are most likely to meet his goals? Does the student know how to identify consequences for each alternative? Does the student know how to select the best possible solution? More elementary assessments might begin with having students specify their likes and dislikes.

These assessments need to be adapted for the special needs of CLDE learners. As noted previously, many more CLDE students are likely to drop out of school, to be subjected to school suspensions or expulsions, and to have limited access to comprehensive vocational and general education programs. Assessments might be adapted to determine the extent to which these students:

a. Understand the consequences of dropping out of school.
b. Are able to identify high school and postsecondary alternatives for themselves, such as technical schools.
c. Recognize the importance of being in a comprehensive vocational program and what they need to do to enroll and become vocationally successful.
d. Are having difficulties in general education programs.
e. Understand the problems associated with improving their academic skills and how they might be instrumental in increasing their achievement.
f. Understand factors contributing to disciplinary problems and how they might circumvent these negative outcomes.

How Do We Prepare CLDE Students to Assume Leadership Roles in Transition Planning?

Goal-setting and transition plans will be most valuable if students not only are part of the planning but also if they are helped to develop skills that will allow them to take the lead in carrying out these plans and advocating for themselves. In their research, Thoma, Rogan, and Baker (2001) observed that professionals did most of the talking, often used technical jargon, tended to focus on deficits, saw themselves as the providers of information, and minimized input from students and parents. These researchers saw a need to teach self-determination skills and to have meetings be student-centered and led by the student.

One of the first steps in helping students with disabilities become more self-regulated and independent is to involve them in planning for transition. The planning should focus on the students' preferences and interests and they should assume the lead in the planning process (Thoma, Rogan, & Baker, 2001). Student leadership is not likely to happen, however, unless there is a corresponding change in the way that team members (i.e., parents and teachers) respond to the learner (Thoma, 1999). Thoma lists nine strategies useful in supporting students with disabilities in the transition process:

1. Hold high expectations for students.
2. Prepare students for their transition planning meeting. Prior to the meeting, meet individually with the student to discuss possible goals, possible rebuttals, and ways to redefine goals. Role-play interactions so that the learner will be prepared for the meeting.
3. Allow students to make important decisions about the IEP/ITP planning meeting, including who should participate, where the meeting should be held, and at what time.
4. Expand your own ideas about what is possible; for example, a student with Down Syndrome had a successful experience at a university campus even though her parent and teacher did not envision this as a possibility.
5. Involve community members as participants on transition planning teams (e.g., persons who have positions in or expertise about the areas where the learner wishes to become involved or work).
6. Encourage students to attend transition fairs or other information-gathering events and help them to prepare for their participation.
7. Use a portfolio-based assessment process to document student achievement.
8. Focus on supports rather than programs. One example is the student who wanted to be an auto mechanic, deviating substantially from typical programs of fast food or retail offered these students. The team determined that the learner's disability did not hinder his work as a mechanic and he was assisted with modifications to the written materials that enabled him to enter the auto mechanics program.
9. Provide opportunities for students to explore their communities and career interests.

This list is appropriate for non-CLDE students as well as CLDE students, but there are some special considerations for CLDE populations. First, school personnel especially need to avoid the pitfall of low expectations for CLDE students. Messages of low expectations are often communicated throughout their schooling so that by the time CLDE students reach secondary school they also have internalized the belief that vocational or academic success is beyond their reach. Encourage these students to try out some of the more challenging programs and provide reinforcement for progress, no matter how minor. Related to this is providing supports from the community, people that the learner can identify with culturally and who can provide extended psychological as well as vocational support. Since CLDE students, especially from low socioeconomic backgrounds, come from communities with limited vocational opportunities, they will need more time for community exploration, moving through a variety of communities with the understanding that working in these environments is a viable option for them. School personnel need to seek out culturally specific agencies, organizations, or churches to assist in this process. For example, in the African American community, possible resources might include 100 Black Men of America (www.100Blackmen.org) or the Urban League (222.nul.org). A national organization with chapters throughout the United States, 100 Black Men of America provides mentoring and training programs to aid CLD youth. Its job readiness, program targeting at-risk high school youth, is a 10-week course with at least one half-hour session per week. Instruction focuses on developing a work ethic, personal appearance, work awareness, and securing employment. The organization also offers a mentoring program, either one-on-one or group, that targets work- or college-bound high school students and is designed to emphasize the development of academic, career, and social skills. Although the organization serves males and females as well as young people from other diverse backgrounds, it is a particularly valuable resource for African American males, given their poor high school and postsecondary prognosis. The Urban League, founded in 1910, is a well-established organization that provides many of the same work-related and educational services as 100 Black Men of America. These and other such community resources can be instrumental in helping to reinforce or develop critical transition skills through culturally specific experiences not easily provided within the schools.

Teaching students to lead IEP meetings can involve several steps, including (1) teaching students about their disabilities; (2) preparing scripts for the students to use during the IEP meetings; (3) conducting mock IEP meetings; and (4) collaborating on an ongoing basis with families, students peers, colleagues, and administrators (Myers & Eisenman, 2005). The National Information Center for Children and Youth with Disabilities (NICHCY) provides detailed information for teachers and students on how to get ready for this process, how to prepare students for this leadership role, how to introduce and write the IEP, how to get ready for the IEP meeting and to conduct the meeting, and what to do after the meeting. One of the NICHCY documents for students is entitled *A student's guide to the IEP* (McGahee-Kovac, 2002). It is designed to be used by students to prepare them for participating in and leading their own IEP meetings. The workbook covers the following topics:

1. What is an IEP?
2. How do I develop my IEP?

Students with exceptionalities can be helped to assume leadership roles in their own transition planning.

3. What do I do before the IEP meeting?
4. Writing the IEP.
5. Getting reading for the IEP meeting.
6. Participating in the IEP meeting.
7. After the IEP meeting.

The 12-page guide can be obtained online at http://www.nichcy.org/pubs/stuguide/st1book.htm. It requires students to think through and plan the entire IEP process, with assistance from teachers and parents. Some students may be able to complete the steps fairly independently, but most students with disabilities would need the teacher to sensitively explain the guide and help plan each step. This process would lead into more extensive discussions about disabilities, with perhaps some audiovisual presentations about disabilities, as recommended in the guide.

Teaching students to take an active and leading role in their IEPs is an extensive and time-consuming process but can be an effective means for helping them become more engaged in schooling and assume more responsibility for their education. This is especially important for CLDE students, who, as noted elsewhere in this text, tend to be underinvolved in school and to have the poorest postschool outcomes. Therefore, school personnel need to place special emphasis on teaching CLDE students to assume leadership roles in this planning, particularly those whose parents are less involved in the school program.

An important first step in facilitating the transition of CLDE youth is to acquire an understanding of their culture (Test, Aspel, & Everson, 2006). One way to do this is to make every effort to meet with the family and to talk at length with the student to determine cultural values, interests, and preferences. School personnel must exercise caution to avoid imposing their values on the youth and the family, and keep in mind that they are to help the youth and the family articulate their desires as goals and objectives for the student's instructional program. For example, as noted, some CLD families may not see their children with mild disabilities as having a disability. Additionally, some CLD families may not subscribe to self-assertion for their children and may tend to distrust service providers (Rueda et al., 2005). Because CLDE families tend to be underinvolved in the IEP process and the preferences of students are often overlooked, transition planning for CLDE students especially may be misguided and ineffective. As noted in the NLTS findings, African American students most in need of help were least likely to receive it. Therefore, professionals need to recognize the importance of establishing relationships and building trust in order to make progress in transition planning. A series of informal meetings where the families and students are the information givers rather than just receivers should take place. Their information should be accepted nonjudgmentally and respectfully. When these meetings begin early in the child's schooling, no later than middle school, trust and mutual respect around transition issues have been established when the student reaches high school. These meetings need to be well planned and conducted thoughtfully. In addition to parents and the student, someone who represents the culture of the student, who enjoys the trust of the family, and who can provide translations, if needed, should be invited to participate.

How Do We Teach Self-Determination Skills?

Taking a leadership role in IEP/transition meetings is only one small part of self-determination. Wood, Karvonen, Test, Browder, and Algozzine (2004) assert that in addition to leading meetings, students need to be taught specific self-determination skills that should be specified on the student's IEP. Students assessed to be high in self-determination skills evidenced better financial, employment, and independent living outcomes than their peers with lower self-determination scores (Wehmeyer & Palmer, 2003), differences found even when controlling for IQ.

Once skills to be taught are specified, the instructional methods are similar to those used to teach any other cognitive or social skill. The basic strategies include *modeling*, where students are shown how to perform the skill; *student responding*, often in the form of role-playing, where students are given opportunities to imitate the model; and *performance feedback*, where the student is helped to understand whether or not the response was correct (Field, Hoffman, & Posch, 1997; Hoffman & Field, 1995). To illustrate, one of the self-management skills that students with disabilities often have to master is basic grooming. That is, coming to school or work having completed certain minimal tasks, such as washed face, washed hands, brushed teeth, combed hair, and changed clothes. The first step is to specify which grooming skills the teacher feels need to be taught. Each subskill would be taught individually, involving the teacher modeling each behavior, prompting student responses, and evaluating student progress. Verbal prompts could be supplemented with a personal listing of grooming steps for each student. The student takes the list to the lavatory each morning to check if he or she has completed each step. Where possible, corrections are made at that time. Students would be reinforced and taught to monitor their own behavior as they make progress on each subskill.

Prior to embarking on teaching a particular skill, Hughes and Carter (2000) advise verifying the significance of the problem through observations and consultations with other important persons in the learner's environment. It also is important to determine the acceptability of teaching the behavior and whether there will be persons in the learner's environment to support the skill. It would be most helpful in the example above if the learner's family could be engaged in supporting the grooming goals. In teaching self-determination skills, it is important to include cooperative learning, simulations, and community-based instructions so that the instruction is active and the learner has the opportunity for many applied and real-life experiences.

Several commercial curricula exist for teaching self-determination skills (e.g., *Choices in Transition,* Balcazar, Cantu, Melo, & Garate, 2004; *The Transition Handbook,* Hughes & Carter, 2000; *Choicemaker Self-Determination Curriculum,* Martin, Marshall, Maxson, & Jerman, 1996; *Take Charge For The Future,* Powers, Turner, Westwood, Matuszewski, Wilson, & Phillips, 2001). Test, Karvonen, Wood, Browder, and Algozzine (2000) in an extensive review found 60 programs designed to teach some aspect of self-determination. The programs varied so that some taught specific self-determination skills, others focused on self-awareness, and still others emphasized learning how to take leadership in the IEP process. Test et al. list the following eight components of a self-determination curricula:

1. Choice/decision-making
2. Goal setting/attainment
3. Problem-solving
4. Self-evaluation, observation, and reinforcement
5. Self-advocacy
6. Inclusion of student-directed IEP
7. Relationships with others
8. Self-awareness

To help teachers determine which curriculum programs would be best for their students, Test et al. offer a curriculum review checklist designed to assess instructional utility through questions about developmental appropriateness, practice opportunities, field-testing, and attractiveness of the materials. Wood, Test, Browder, Algozzine, and Karvonen (2004) list the 60 curriculum programs and describe relevant selection information.

How Do We Develop Self-Determination Skills with CLDE Learners?

A major problem for CLDE students in generating realistic transition goals is their limited exposure to a full range of occupations. CLD students with disabilities are not likely to get extensive vocational exposure or work experiences outside of the school. Therefore, the school needs to not only provide vocational exploration but ensure that CLDE students receive a concentrated sequence of vocational instruction.

As a result of their limited exposure, many minority youth often specify goals that emulate high-profile figures, such as athletes or entertainers. Although they may seem somewhat far-fetched, these aspirations should not be discouraged. Rather, students should be helped to analyze the related academic and social goals and objectives, which can then be embedded in the learner's instructional plan. Although the attainment of the goal may be remote, the process of developing the requisite skills might help the student develop critical skills and possibly expose the student to more realistic career options, such as technician, mechanic, or retailer, that may be associated with the original goal. *Choices in Transition* (Balcazar et al., 2004), which was written with a focus on CLD students, provides step-by-step instructions to help students with effective goal setting as well as other critical skills, such as determining strengths, networking, self-advocacy, obtaining support, and moving toward independence.

The traditional culture of some CLD students may put them at odds with the larger society and deemphasize goals for independent living. Some Hispanic or Native American families, for example, expect their children to remain in the family and contribute to its support according to the student's levels of functioning (Frankland et al., 2004; Rueda et al., 2005). Therefore, teachers would be wise to connect with the child's culture to determine how self-determination skills can be reinforced or what skills might be discouraged. Frankland et al. (2004) point out that traditional Diné (Navajo) culture encourages self-management and decision making on the part of children but, in contrast to the larger society, decisions in this culture must be made in the interest of the family and community. Children's accomplishments and autonomy are celebrated, but children are expected to use these skills within the context of family and community responsibilities. Therefore, when teaching self-determination skills, teachers need to be prepared to help the learner understand how developing these skills will contribute to the learner's family and community. The teacher also needs to be prepared to alter or reassess instruction in some self-determination skills depending on the needs or desires of the family.

How Can Teachers Become More Flexible in Teaching for Transitions?

Another critical factor in helping CLDE students transition successfully to postsecondary environments is the willingness of teachers to adjust their curriculum to the learning needs of these students (Wentling & Waight, 1999). CLDE students who are poor will present significantly more skill deficits than their nonimpoverished and non-CLD classmates. As a result of their limited exposure to the legitimate world of work, CLDE students may have "extraordinary" (e.g., professional athlete) or no career goals. This means teachers will have to intensify their instruction on vocational options to provide more direct, real-life experiences in the various occupations and exposure to a wide array of work settings, making certain that workers of the same cultural background as the students are represented in the workplace. Such persons could be brought into the classroom as guest speakers to generate interest in their work and to encourage students to pursue these and other goals. Students from diverse backgrounds need to see their cultural group represented in the full range of vocational options and to understand that, commensurate with their skills and interests, these are viable opportunities for them, as well.

Flexibility is also called for because the significant skill deficits of CLDE students require more instruction, not less. The research findings show that CLDE students have more school failure than non-CLD students (e.g., NLTS, n.d.; NLTS2; Ryan, Reid, & Epstein, 2004), and that reading is the principal area of difficulty, often resulting in dropping out of school, delinquency, and other forms of marginality (Marchand-Martella, Martella, Bettis, & Blakely, 2004). High school curriculums and instructional programs need to be adjusted to address these greater needs. For example, adolescent struggling readers would benefit from explicit and intensive reading instruction. Programs for the adolescent skill-deficient reader, such as the Corrective Reading Program (Engelmann, Hanner, & Johnson, 1999; Grossen, 1999), might be useful.

How Can We Mentor Students for Transitions?

Caring, nurturing adults can have a powerful and positive effect on the lives of young people. As Benz, Lindstrom, and Yovanoff (2000) state, ". . . . what adolescents with disabilities appear to want, *and what many adolescents desperately need,* is a personal relationship with a trusted adult who will be available to encourage their efforts, validate their fears, and celebrate their accomplishments" (p. 525). Mentors can be especially important to low-socioeconomic CLD youth with disabilities. Jongyeun (1999) points out that successful students typically have a vision about their future, but unsuccessful students often believe that their success is dependent on others. Furthermore, successful students will have long-range goals toward which they are systematically working. According to Jongyeun, the lack of goal orientation is predictive of failure among some CLD youth (i.e., Hispanic and African American). In a study on mentoring, Jongyeun matched low-income African American youth with adult mentors. The mentors and the students jointly set goals, which varied from improving school attendance to performing better in a particular subject. The mentors committed to spending at least 2 hours per month with the students with the possibility of additional hours outside of school. Research findings showed that students who had been mentored for at least a year showed higher aspirations than those students who had not been assigned mentors. Jeffries and Singer (2003) reported success with American Indian students also by creating student learning teams and mentoring groups.

Sinclair et al. (2005) used a "check and connect" model to reduce the dropout rate of students with disabilities, who were disproportionately African American males. *Check* was a monitoring system to continuously assess the student's level of engagement in school, and *connect* was a procedure for providing timely individualized intervention as needed. Project staff routinely monitored students' absenteeism, out-of-school suspensions, and accrual of credits. The features of this program included:

1. Weekly or bi-weekly problem-solving sessions designed to help students make constructive life choices.
2. Emphasis on relationship building.
3. "Persistence Plus" where staff let it be known that they were not going to give up on students.
4. Involvement of students in extracurricular activities.
5. Weekly contacts with students that continued through the summer, stressing the importance of summer school to make up lost credits.

The researchers found that students who participated in the "check and connect" program had significantly lower dropout rates than the controls. The African American males dropped out less in year 4 of the program, although they still dropped out more than their same-group peers.

Some of these findings are promising, suggesting that CLDE students will benefit from close monitoring by persistent and caring adults. Unfortunately, these findings also suggest that some subgroups (i.e., African American males) may need even more intensive interventions to promote their school success. These youngsters may need, for example, same-race and same-gender mentors who are able to meet with them on a more frequent basis. The contingencies for compliance might have to be made more powerful, and the point of intervention probably should begin long before high school or even middle school (Kunjufu, 1986).

How Can We Provide CLDE Students Person-Centered Planning?

Person-centered planning (PCP) is one means of addressing the unique needs of CLDE learners. Some evidence indicates that PCP may result in better outcomes for students with disabilities (Bui & Turnbull, 2003; Menchetti & Garcia, 2003), and it is particularly attractive for these learners because it attempts to move the individual from a subservient to a dominant role. Various models of PCP exist but all share the theme of emphasizing the preferences and desires of the individual with the collaboration of those who truly care about the individual (Bui & Turnbull). Other basic features are creating supports for the individual, placing the individual in a respected and leadership role, and aiming for community participation (Test et al., 2006). Keyes and Owens-Johnson (2003) provide some guidelines, pointing out the importance of gathering basic information, such as the person's history, talents, dreams, nightmares, goals, and present levels of performance. The PCP individualized education plan is then designed to avoid the nightmares (e.g., being arrested or failing to graduate) and figure out the steps needed to achieve the goals/dreams and the support persons needed. Students are given responsible roles so that they must specify their desires, strong preferences, who should be part of their support system, and what will have to happen in order to

Students with exceptionalities can benefit greatly from culturally specific mentors who can help the youth explore viable employment options.

achieve the goals. Keyes and Owens-Johnson's (2003) specific suggestions for conducting PCP-based meetings include:

1. Begin each meeting pointing out the student's gifts and talents and give examples of such.
2. Prepare students for the meeting. Give them specific responsibilities with written plans to follow during the meeting.
3. Provide a checklist to help meeting participants to understand the interrelatedness of the various goals, desires, needs, and so forth.
4. As appropriate, involve other relevant persons in the student's meeting, including peers, family members, and individuals from the community that might help to support the student in these goals.

Traditional transition goals are those that reflect the dominant culture; they may not be consistent with the goals of those from culturally diverse backgrounds (Keyes & Owens-Johnson, 2003). PCP methods offer advantages in this situation because professionals can concentrate on the interests of the individual and family rather than being bound by those of the institution. Bui and Turnbull (2003) advise incorporating cultural understanding into the PCP process. In an analysis of traditional Asian culture, for example, the authors observed some possible conflicts, such as a tendency not to include community members in planning due to the cultural tradition of being extremely private about family matters. Another point of resistance may be the focus on the individual, for within Asian culture the needs of the individual often are subjugated to the interests of the group. Similar cultural understandings should be applied to the process for each cultural subgroup using the information provided throughout this text as well as from other sources.

How Can We Use Culturally Specific Literature in Teaching for Transitions?

Literature, both fiction and nonfiction, written by and for CLD learners can be redemptive, providing models and experiences that can lead the reader to a more positive life definition. For some CLD youth, these readings can be transformative (e.g., see *The Freedom Writer's Diary* by Erin Gruwell, 1999), especially for adolescents with disabilities. Typically, these youth are trying to define themselves but may feel alienated from their own cultural peer group as well as the larger society. *Willy's Summer Dream* by Kay Brown (1990) is a story about a 14-year-old African American male with a learning disability who is aware of his differences and becomes disillusioned after being assigned to special education. A young visiting neighbor befriends Willy and helps him to develop his talents and overcome his feelings of worthlessness. The book ends with Willy achieving greater self-awareness and taking control of his life. Three other books for middle to high school African American males are set within the urban basketball culture: *Slam* by Walter Dean Myers (1998), *Danger Zone* by David Klass (1998), and *The Squared Circle* by James Bennett (2002). These authentic stories take young men through difficult problem-solving episodes, but they eventually emerge, taking charge of their lives in a positive direction. *The Eagles Who Thought They Were Chickens: A Tale of Discovery* by Mychal Wynn (1993) is an inspiring story that could lead youth to greater self-awareness and worthwhile goals. *Monster*, another compelling real-life story by Walter Dean Myers (2001), focuses on a young man's self-development within the criminal justice system.

Everyday problems of Latino youth growing up in central California are the themes of the stories in *Baseball in April and Other Stories* by Gary Soto (2000). The situations involve sports, peer relations, families, and the opposite sex—themes young people can easily identify with. Harsher realities are depicted in books such as *The Circuit: Stories from the Life of a Migrant Child* by Francisco Jimenez (1997) and *Parrot in the Oven: mi vida* by Victor Martinez (1996). Both books tell stories of growing up poor within a Mexican American family. In the midst of a migrant life style, the stressors of the larger society, and the difficulties of an impoverished family, the stories show the main characters' personal development and emergence of self. Coming of age and the Latino culture are the themes of *Cool Salsa: Bilingual Poems on Growing Up Hispanic in the United States* by Lori Marie Carlson (1994) and *Spirits of the High Mesa* by Floyd Martinez (1997). Martinez tells the story of a young, maturing Mexican American male who is caught between the attractive progressiveness of the mainstream culture and the cultural traditions of family and village. Carlson presents a collection of poems that depicts an array of experiences and emotions relative to growing up Hispanic in the United States. The cultural differences and stressors for Puerto Rico teens told from the perspective of the teen is the essence of *An Island Like You: Stories of the Barrio* by Judith Ortiz Cofer (1996). The series of stories, set in New Jersey, is narrated by teens struggling with the dichotomy between the attractive American dream and the desire to respect the culture of their family.

Females are the protagonists or central figures of several coming-of-age books on Native Americans. Even though the basketball court is the setting, Larry Colton (2000) provides a true story of a young Crow Indian woman in *Counting Coup: A True Story of Basketball and Honor on the Little Big Horn*. The author narrates the life and struggles of Sharon LaForge, the main character, over several years, through high school, college, abuse, parenting, racism, alcoholism, and other problems. The book gives an intimate view of her ability to persevere and the drive needed to survive. *The Place at the Edge of the Earth* by Bee Faas Rice (2002) and *Walk Two Moons* by Sharon Creech (1996) emphasize personal ancestry and the Native American culture. Both books feature Native American females who emerge more self-aware and empowered as a result of their ancestral journeys. An exciting, award-winning book about the adventures and trials of a Native American male is *Meely LaBauve* by Ken Wells (2001). This engaging novel realistically depicts a young man in the Cajun culture who manages to evolve from this harsh life with a greater sense of purpose and wisdom.

Teachers would be well advised to read and discuss these books with students as part of the curriculum on self-determination. The goal setting, decision making, problem solving, and so forth employed by the characters in these stories could serve as a springboard for students to discuss and carry out similar actions in their own lives. The reading levels of many students may make it necessary to read parts or all of the books to them or, when appropriate or possible, use books on tape.

How Can We Help CLDE Students Transition to Postsecondary Environments?

Successful transitioning to postsecondary environments for most students with disabilities means the immediate or eventual entry into the world of work. Along with high school completion, some of the most important factors for post high school employment appear to be paid employment, vocational training, and a supportive relationship with an adult during high school (Benz et al., 2000; Eisenman, 2003; Harvey, 2001; NLTS, n.d.). Prior to

> **TEACHING TIPS**
>
> **Teaching CLDE Students Self-Determination Skills**
>
> 1. Prepare students to take a leadership role in transition planning and meetings.
> 2. Specify self-determination skills, such as goal setting, problem solving, decision making, and self-regulation, in the IEP. Encourage students to set high goals and not put limits on themselves based on cultural/ethnic differences.
> 3. Consult others and observe the student to assess the student's current competence in self-determination skills. Build on skills the student may have already developed within the family or community.
> 4. Study the student's culture to determine any conflicts about self-determination skills between the school and the family's values.
> 5. Expose students to the full range of occupational/career options. Support student aspirations and interests.
> 6. Explore ways that skills can be supported within the student's culture. Involve family members, extended family members, and, as appropriate, community members.
> 7. Be flexible. Intensify or alter instruction for students with limited career goals. Help students identify with a variety of work options.
> 8. Provide direct instruction on self-determination skills and monitor student progress.
> 9. Provide direct instruction on critical basic skills (i.e., reading and math) and on academic subjects. Intensify instruction as needed.
> 10. Access culturally specific agencies and organizations that might reinforce and extend classroom instruction.
> 11. Provide culturally specific adult models from the work world.
> 12. Provide culturally specific, nurturing adult mentors.
> 13. Provide culturally specific models through authentic literature.

engaging students directly in work experiences, school programs typically provide students with instruction on career education.

How Do We Provide Career Education for CLDE Learners?

Test et al. (2006) describe the stages of career education as *career awareness, career exploration, career preparation, and career assimilation*. Information on careers and planning for a career is to be infused into the learner's curriculum from the earliest point of school entry. From the beginning of formal schooling, all members of the child's educational team, including teachers, parents, and other relevant professionals, need to help identify and support career-related content in the child's educational program.

The first stage of career education is *career awareness*, which is initiated in the elementary grades. The focus at this point is to help children understand the concepts of work, what a worker is, the value of work, and to view themselves as workers, even in their role as students. Also during this stage students begin to learn about their own strengths and interests as future workers. Students need to develop an appreciation for the full range of work, from unskilled occupations to professions. Instructional emphasis is also placed on work-related social skills such as punctuality, task completion, task perseverance, and cooperation. These skills can be taught on a daily basis, relating work as a student to future work as wage earners. Teachers need to be careful to avoid presenting

APPLICATION

The school decided to take a PCP approach with Alma. Although her parents rarely came to school to discuss Alma's school progress, school personnel learned that Alma had a close and very supportive family. The family helped her to celebrate her successes, but at this point in her life they felt that Alma was sufficiently mature to make her own decisions. They did not consider Alma to have a disability, especially since she displayed so many competencies in the home and her community. Her mother depended on Alma to assume many of the domestic responsibilities, including care for her younger sister.

Alma indicated that her number-one goal was to pursue her basketball career by playing basketball in college and eventually playing on a professional female team. Because of her family traditions and a desire to be close to home, Alma wanted to attend college within her state. Another long-term career goal was to be a basketball coach either at the high school or college level.

Alma's teachers worked with her to identify specific objectives she had to accomplish in order to reach her goal. The most important objective pertained to Alma's reading progress. Other related goals focused on the need to reduce Alma's school absenteeism and to increase her wholesome social activities. It was important for Alma to avoid some common pitfalls, such as addictions or premature parenting, in order to achieve these goals.

Alma and her teachers identified special support persons. One was Dr. Sheryl Franklin, a Native American professor at the local university who specialized in teaching reading to adolescents. She agreed that she and a graduate assistant would provide weekly tutorial sessions to Alma, with reinforcement and practice activities to be implemented by Alma's teachers. Dr. Franklin used direct instruction and progressive monitoring (as discussed in Chapter 10) so that Alma was constantly aware of her progress. Working with Dr. Franklin also gave Alma the opportunity to regularly visit the college campus and begin to see herself as a student in this setting. Alma was enrolled in a peer tutoring after-school program, which gave her extra support in her reading and academic classes. One of the 12th-grade high-achieving students agreed to be Alma's special tutor. Alma also was assigned a Native American college student from Alma's reservation, who met with Alma two or three times a month to discuss Alma's goals, choices, decision making and social activities. She was able to relate to Alma's experiences and to share with her some of the steps she took to help her remain focused and achieve her goals. She also read and discussed with Alma books about other Native American females. Alma's basketball coach was enlisted to "coach" Alma in her school attendance. Additional basketball opportunities were made contingent on school attendance and accomplishments.

Alma and her teachers developed an explicit record-keeping system for each of these forms of intervention and met monthly to discuss her progress. For example, Alma kept a notebook for each class. She recorded daily each assignment she had, whether or not she completed it, and the evaluation she received. She also recorded quiz and test scores. These data were used to evaluate Alma's progress and to adjust parts of her plan, where needed. Alma was being trained to assume more and more responsibility for her school performance and success.

---

careers in stereotypical ways so that occupations in construction, for example, are not depicted as solely male domains. Similarly, all professions should be presented as the prerogative of every cultural and racial group. As noted previously, greater effort will be needed to expose CLDE students to a full array of work options.

Career exploration is stressed from middle school through high school. At this second stage, students are encouraged to explore their personal interests and skills relative to work. Explorations are often campus based; students might receive assignments to work in the school office, school cafeteria, school landscaping, or tutoring other students as a means of exploring occupations related to clerical work, horticulture, food service, or teaching. One effective means for simulating the work world and training related skills is through school-based enterprises (Test et al., 2006). These projects are sponsored by the school but are designed to be operated primarily by the students to give them supervised real-life work experiences. One high school special education department, for example, operated a bagel shop where faculty and students daily purchased bagels, breakfast rolls, and beverages from the special education students who operated the shop. Test et al. give details for setting up and operating such enterprises and advise that the service or product should be relevant to the community, be meaningful and beneficial to the students, increase the students' marketability and inclusion in the larger society, and be produced with minimal teacher input.

It is also at this stage that teachers help students understand how their classroom instruction fits with their work and daily living experiences. This is especially important for CLDE learners, who are more likely to drop out of school and see less relevance in schooling to their present or future lives. In their discussion of educating American Indian students, Jeffries and Singer (2003) note that a major feature of their program was to help students understand how academic courses fit into their daily lives. The instruction focused on applications so that concepts learned in the classroom in the mornings were then applied in the afternoons. For example, a student like Alma preparing to go to college not only needs to master the course content but also needs to develop the study skills that will be useful in higher education.

High school is the period during which *career preparation* is stressed. Instruction emphasizes the development of job-seeking and job-specific skills. Students are helped to engage in decision making around certain career interests and options and receive specific training in vocational education courses that concentrate on their specific career interests. Students also may have the opportunity for paid work experiences to further develop or refine their job and job-related skills. This is a critical stage for many CLD students with disabilities, since many of them may come from neighborhoods where unemployment is relatively high and the full range of occupational options is not readily evident. Transportation also may be an important factor for these students. Even though substantial numbers of African and Hispanic American students with disabilities have moved into suburban areas, these students continue to have relatively few resources in their communities (Wagner, Newman, & Cameto, 2004). They need apprenticeships with others representing their cultural background, and they need assurances that such occupations can become a reality for them. Supportive programs can increase the transition success of at-risk students (e.g., Benz, et al., 2000; Sinclair et al., 2005).

Career assimilation is the final stage where students finalize their plans in high school for post–high school careers. This most likely occurs during the last two years of high school, with school professionals and community agencies making certain the student is well prepared to achieve the specified goals.

What Is the Role of Vocational Training for CLDE Learners?

Vocational education or career-technical education (Test et al., 2006) is extremely important for the postsecondary work life of students with disabilities (Benz, Lindstrom, Unruh, & Waintrup, 2004; Eisenman, 2003; Harvey, 2001; Lindstrom & Benz, 2002). Students with disabilities have assurances of access to the full range of vocational training with equal rights and protections within the least restrictive environment as provided in the Carl Perkins Act (Test et al.). In order to access vocational education programs, students with disabilities often need special supports, such as curriculum, equipment, and classroom modifications.

Students may also need special support personnel, such as special education coordinators and counselors, as well as special instructional aids, such as augmentative communication devices (Test et al.).

Many CLDE learners will also need culturally specific mentors/coaches. Because of these special needs, vocational and special educators need to collaborate and maintain continuous communication to make sure vocational professionals have the requisite assistance and understandings and that CLD students with disabilities are well served. As noted previously in the transition studies, CLDE students have less successful vocational outcomes than their non-CLD peers with disabilities, partly due to inadequate vocational training. Every effort needs to be made to enroll CLDE youth in comprehensive vocational programs early in their high school studies. With the requisite training and support and realistic options, these students should emerge prepared for either entry-level positions or additional training within apprenticeships or postsecondary technical schools.

How Can We Promote Independent Living for CLDE Learners?

An important IDEA mandate is to prepare youth with disabilities for independent living beyond high school. The specific competencies for independent living may vary somewhat, but as a rule, they minimally require that the individual is able to secure and maintain shelter, manage finances, take care of health, grooming, and safety needs, effect healthy family and social relationships, participate in recreation and leisure activities, participate in community activities, and effectively travel within the environment. The skills

---

TEACHING TIPS

CLDE Students' Transition to Work and Independent Living

1. Begin career awareness in elementary grades. Help students to see themselves as workers and to identify with many forms of work. Expose students to work opportunities outside their immediate communities.
2. Provide students with on-campus work opportunities and systematically develop work-related skills.
3. Connect coursework to real-life work and postsecondary experiences. Help students utilize coursework through applied work-related activities.
4. Provide community paid work experiences and supports that could lead to postsecondary careers.
5. Ensure that CLDE students have concentrated sequences of vocational training within general education settings.
6. Provide supports to assure basic skills and academic course success. Intensify instruction where needed.
7. Provide direct instruction in daily living skills.
8. Use PCP strategies so that students' interests and preferences are highlighted. Identify school, personal, and community resources that would enable students to achieve employment and independent living goals.
9. Continue with culturally specific models in the world of work to help CLDE students pursue appropriate work options.
10. Continue with culturally specific nurturing models to help students remain in school and pursue postsecondary training as needed.

APPLICATION

Over the course of high school, Alma assumed increasingly more responsibility for her transitional plan and the related activities. The record-keeping system she developed with Dr. Franklin helped her to see the progress she was making in her reading, and she began to realize that she could become eligible for college. Her tutors helped her prepare for and become eligible through college entrance exams.

During the last 2 years of high school, much of Alma's program focused on preparing for college. All of her academic courses were in general education and she received assistance from the special education teachers and her tutors. The special education coordinator accompanied Alma to the state university, which she planned to attend, to learn what supports she could expect through the university's offices for students with disabilities. She also got information about the tutoring services that the university provided their athletes.

While in high school, Alma was taught many skills that would be useful to her as a college student, such as how to advocate for herself with her professors and how to use tape recorders to help her take notes. She also was advised on how to use other sources of support, such as university writing labs to get feedback on her papers and how to access private tutors and mentors, if needed.

needed by CLD students with disabilities will vary according to the planned level of independence, ranging from total independence for those with mild disabilities to assisted living for those with moderate to severe disabilities. For all students there needs to be extensive planning and skill development long before completing high school.

The national longitudinal studies of student outcomes show that within 2 years following high school, nearly 75% of the students continued to live at home, with only about 1 in 8 students living independently. Another 1% to 3% lived in a facility or institution (NLST, n.d.; NLST2; Wagner, Newman, Cameto, & Levine, 2005). The more recent study found that African American youth continued to lag greatly behind European American youth in independent living and had higher rates of school suspension/expulsion, job firings, and arrests (Wagner, Cameto, & Newman, 2003). School personnel need to come up with more constructive options for behavior management than relying so extensively on school suspensions and expulsions. These excessively punitive actions apparently exacerbate rather than minimize the poor outcomes for CLDE learners. More attention needs to be paid to teaching the desired social skills and self-discipline behaviors, as discussed in Chapters 4 and 5. Although, as noted previously, many CLDE youth come from backgrounds where they are expected to live permanently within the care of the family, not independently, their lower levels of independent living may be substantially due to employment and skill deficits, which reflect inadequate transition education and planning.

Summary

Students with disabilities typically have had less postsecondary vocational, career, education, financial, independent living, and higher education success than their general education peers. CLDE students have had even less transitional success than their non-CLD counterparts with disabilities. Although some improvements have been noted in recent years, positive changes are found mostly for European American and more affluent students. Students with disabilities continue to need more effective planning for employment and careers that will support independent living. CLDE students have special needs related to support systems and community resources.

Students with disabilities need to learn how to become more self-directed. Teachers need to teach these skills directly so that, to the extent possible, students will assume responsibility and become self-advocates. Person-centered planning may be one effective tool for accommodating cultural differences among CLDE learners. School personnel need to understand how the institution's values might clash with those of the learner's culture and adjust goals accordingly.

CLDE students need as many paid and applied vocational experiences as possible to make their learning meaningful to them and to motivate them to complete school. They should be encouraged and empowered to believe in their dreams and in their ability to achieve them.

Related Learning Activities

1. Get permission to review the IEP for one high school student in the school where you are teaching or having a practicum experience. List the self-determination goals and objectives that you find on this plan. Through direct observations, review of progress reports, and interviews with the teacher and student, assess the type of progress the student is making toward achieving these goals. If progress is minimal, what additional instructions or plans would you suggest? If no goals and objectives for self-determination exist in the student's plans, what self-determination goals and objectives would you recommend based on the information provided and your discussion with the student?

2. In your practicum situation, get permission to attend an IEP meeting where the student is taking a leadership role. Make note of how the student was prepared beforehand to conduct this meeting, how the student led the meeting, and how other team members responded to the meeting. Do you feel the student was able to articulate his or her wishes? What, in your opinion, were the strengths of this meeting? What is the likelihood that the team will be able to carry out the plan as specified? What recommendations do you have, if any, to strengthen the meeting and the overall plan for this student?

3. Interview a secondary teacher or special education coordinator. Find out what they consider to be their greatest challenges in educating secondary students with disabilities. What do they consider to be the unique problems of students from culturally diverse backgrounds? What do they recommend that schools can do to remedy these unique needs or special problems?

4. Read a culturally specific book like *Counting Coup: A True Story of Basketball and Honor on the Little Big Horn* by Larry Colton. Note the particular stressors, setbacks, and triumphs of the main character. Detail ways in which understandings from this real-life story could be used to help a student like Alma develop her own self-determination skills.

References

Balcazar, F., Cantu, C., Melo, X., & Garate, T. (2004). *Choices in transition*. Chicago: University of Illinois at Chicago.

Bennet, J. (2002). *The squared circle*. New York: Scholastic Signature.

Benz, M. R., Lindstrom, L., Unruh, D., & Waintrup, M. (2004). Sustaining secondary transition programs in local schools. *Remedial and Special Education, 25*, 39–50.

Benz, M. R., Lindstrom, L., & Yovanoff, P. (2000). Improving graduation and employment outcomes of students with disabilities: Predictive factors and student perspectives. *Exceptional Children, 66*, 509–529.

Brown, K. (1990). *Willy's summer dream*. New York: Harcourt Brace Jovanovich/Gulliver.

Bui, Y. N., & Turnbull, A. (2003). East meets west: Analysis of person-centered planning in the context of Asian American values. *Education and Training in Developmental Disabilities, 38*, 18–31.

Carlson, L. M. (Ed.). (1994). *Cool salsa: Bilingual poems on growing up Hispanic in the United States*. New York: Henry Holt.

Cofer, J. O. (1996). *An island like you: Stories of the Barrio*. New York: Puffin.

Colton, L. (2000). *Counting coup: A true story of basketball and honor on the Little Big Horn*. New York: Warner Books.

Creech, S. (1996). *Walk two moons*. New York: Harper Trophy.

Eisenman, L. T. (2003). Theories in practice: School-to-work transitions for youth with mild disabilities. *Exceptionality, 11*, 89–102.

Engelmann, S., Hanner, S., & Johnson, G. (1999). *Corrective reading series guide*. New York: Macmillan/McGraw-Hill.

Field, S., Hoffman, A., & Posch, M. (1997). Self-determination during adolescence: A developmental perspective. *Remedial and Special Education, 18,* 285–293.

Field, S., Sarver, M., & Shaw, S.F. (2003). Self-determination: A key to success in postsecondary education for students with learning disabilities. *Remedial and Special Education, 24,* 339–349.

Frankland, H. C., Turnbull, A. P., Wehmeyer, M. L., & Blackmountain, L. (2004). An exploration of the self-determination construct and disability as it relates to the Diné (Navajo) culture. *Education and Training in Developmental Disabilities, 39,* 191–205.

Gillock, K. L., & Reyes, O. (1996). High school transition-related changes in urban minority students' academic performance and perceptions of self and school environment. *Journal of Community Psychology, 24,* 245–261.

Grossen, B. (1999). *The research base for SRA.* DeSoto, TX: Science Research Associates.

Gruwell, E./The Freedom Writers (1999). *The freedom writer's diary: How a teacher and 150 teens used writing to change themselves and the world around them.* New York: Main Street Books Doubleday.

Harvey, M. W. (2001). Vocational-technical education: A logical approach to dropout prevention for secondary special education. *Preventing School Failure, 45,* 108–113.

Hoffman, A., & Field, S. (1995). Promoting self-determination through effective curriculum development. *Intervention in School & Clinic, 30,* 131–141.

Hosp, M. K., Griller-Clark, H., & Rutherford, R. B. Jr. (2001). Incarcerated youth with disabilities: Their knowledge of transition plans. *Journal of Correctional Education, 52,* 126–130.

Hughes, C., & Carter, E. W. (2000). *The transition handbook: Strategies high school teachers use that work!* Baltimore, MD: Paul H. Brookes.

Jeffries, R. B., & Singer, L. C. (2003). Successfully educating urban American Indian students: An alternative school format. *Journal of American Indian Education, 42,* 40–57.

Jimenez, F. (1997). *The circuit: Stories from the life of a migrant child.* Albuquerque, NM: University of New Mexico Press.

Jongyeun, L. (1999). The positive effects of mentoring economically disadvantaged students. *Professional School Counseling, 2*(3), 172–179.

Keyes, M. W., & Owens-Johnson, L. (2003). Developing person-centered IEP's. *Intervention in School and Clinic, 38*(3), 145–152.

Klass, D. (1998). *Danger zone.* New York: Scholastic Paperbacks.

Kohler, P. D., & Field, S. (2003). Transition-focused education: Foundation for the future. *The Journal of Special Education, 37,* 174–183.

Kunjufu, J. (1986). *Motivating and preparing Black youth for success.* Chicago: African American Images.

Lindstrom, L. E., & Benz, M. R. (2002). Phases of career development: Case studies of young women with learning disabilities. *Exceptional Children, 69,* 67–83.

Marchand-Martella, N., Martella, R. C., Bettis, D. F., & Blakely, M. R. (2004). Project pals: A description of a high school-based tutorial program using corrective reading and peer-delivered instruction. *Reading & Writing Quarterly, 20,* 179–201.

Martin, J., & Marshall, L. (1995). Choicemaker: A comprehensive self-determination transition program. *Intervention in School and Clinic, 30,* 147–156.

Martin, J. E., Marshall, L. H., Maxson, L., & Jerman, P. (1996). *Choicemaker self-determination curriculum: Self-directed IEP.* Longmont, CO: Sopris West.

Martinez, F. (1997). *Spirits of the high mesa.* Houston, TX: Arte Publico Press.

Martinez, V. (1996). *Parrot in the oven: mi vida.* New York: Harper Collins.

Mastropieri, M. A., Scruggs, T. E., Spencer, V., & Fontana, J. (2003). Promoting success in high school world history: Peer tutoring versus guided notes. *Learning Disabilities Research & Practice, 18,* 52–65.

McGahee-Kovac, M. (2002). *A student's guide to the IEP* (2nd ed.). Washington, DC: National Information Center for children and Youth With Disabilities (Document available online at http://www.nichcy.org/pubs/stuguide/st1book.htm)

Menchetti, B. M., & Garcia, L. A. (2003). Personal and employment outcomes of person-centered career planning. *Education and Training in Developmental Disabilities, 38,* 145–156.

Myers, A., & Eisenman, L. (2005). Student-led IEPs: Take the first step. *Teaching Exceptional Children, 37,* 52–58.

Myers, W. D. (1998). *Slam!* New York: Scholastic Paperbacks.

Myers, W. D. (2001). *Monster.* New York: Amistad.

National Center on Secondary Education and Transition. (2005). *Key provisions on transition: IDEA 1997 compared to H. R. 1350 (IDEA 2004).* Minneaplois, MN: University of Minnesota.

National Longitudinal Transition Study (n.d.) *A summary of findings.* Retrieved August 15, 2005, from http://www.sri.com/policy/cehs/publications/dispub/nlts/nltssum.html.

NLTS2 (2001–2005). Reports from the National Longitudinal Transition Study. Retrieved from www.nlts2.org. Reports produced by National Center on Secondary Education and Transition, Minneapolis, MN: University of Minnesota.

Paratore, J. R. (2001). *Opening doors, opening opportunities: Family literacy in an urban community.* Needham Heights, MA: Allyn & Bacon.

Powers, L. E., Turner, A., Westwood, D., Matuszewski, J., Wilson, R., & Phillips, A. (2001). Take charge for the future: A controlled field-test of a model to promote student involvement in transition planning. *Career Development for Exceptional Individuals, 24,* 89–103.

Rice, B. F. (2002). *The place at the edge of the earth.* New York: Clarion Books.

Rueda, R., Monzo, L., Shapiro, J., Gomez, J., & Blacher, J. (2005). Cultural models of transition: Latina mothers of young adults with developmental disabilities. *Exceptional Children, 71,* 401–414.

Ryan, J. B., Reid, R., & Epstein, M. H. (2004). Peer-mediated intervention studies on academic achievement for students with EBD: A review. *Remedial and Special Education, 25,* 330–341.

Sinclair, M. F., Christenson, S. L., & Thurlow, M. L. (2005). Promoting school completion of urban secondary youth with emotional or behavioral disabilities. *Exceptional Children, 71,* 465–482.

Soto, G. (2000). *Baseball in April and other stories.* New York: Harcourt Paperbacks.

Test, D. W., Aspel, N. P., & Everson, J. M. (2006). *Transition methods for youth with disabilities.* Upper Saddle River, NJ: Pearson.

Test, D. W., Karvonen, M., Wood, W. M., Browder, D., & Algozzine, B. (2000). Choosing a self-determination curriculum. *Teaching Exceptional Children, 33,* 48–54.

Thoma, C. A. (1999). Supporting student voice in transition planning. *Teaching Exceptional Children, 31,* 4–9.

Thoma, C. A., Baker, S. R., & Saddler, S. J. (2002). Self-determination in teacher education: A model to facilitate transition planning for students with disabilities. *Remedial and Special Education, 23,* 82–89.

Thoma, C. A., Rogan, P., & Baker, S. R. (2001). Student involvement in transition planning: Unheard voices. *Education and Training in Mental Retardation and Developmental Disabilities, 36,* 16–29.

Todis, B., Bullis, M., Waintrup, M., Schultz, R., & D'Ambrosio, R. (2001). Overcoming the odds: Qualitative examination of resilience among formerly incarcerated adolescents. *Exceptional Children, 68,* 119–139.

Tomblin, M. J., & Haring, K. A. (1999). Vocational training for students with learning disabilities: A qualitative investigation. *Journal of Vocational Education and Training, 51,* 357–370.

Trainor, A. A. (2005). Self-determination perceptions and behaviors of diverse students with LD during the transition planning process. *Journal of Learning Disabilities, 38,* 233–249.

Unruh, D., & Bullis, M. (2005). Female and male juvenile offenders with disabilities: Differences in the barriers to their transition to the community. *Behavioral Disorders, 30,* 105–117.

Wagner, M., & Cameto, R. (2004). *NLTS2 data brief: The characteristics, experiences, and outcomes of youth with emotional disturbances. A report from the National Longitudinal Transition Study-2.* Available at www.ncset.org/publications/default.asp#nlts2.

Wagner, M., Cameto, R., & Guzmán, A. *NLTS2 data brief: Who are secondary students in special education today? A report from the National Longitudinal Transition Study-2.* Available at www.ncset.org/publications/default.asp#nlts2

Wagner, M., Cameto, R., & Newman, L. (2003). *Youth with disabilities: A changing population. A special topic report of findings from the National Longitudinal Transition Study-2 (NLTS2).* Available at www.nlts2.org/pdfs/execsum_changepop.pdf.

Wagner, M., Newman, L., & Cameto, R. (2004). *Changes over time in the secondary school experiences of students with disabilities. A special topic report of findings from the National Longitudinal Transition Study-2 (NLTS2).* Menlo Park, CA: SRI International, Available at www.nlts2.org/pdfs/changestime_exec_sum_stanalone.pdf.

Wagner, M., Newman, L., Cameto, R., & Levine, P. (2005). *Changes over time in the early postschool outcomes of youth with disabilities. A report from the National Longitudinal Transition Study-2 (NLTS2).* Menlo Park, CA: SRI International Available at www.nlts2.org/pdfs/str6_execsum.pdf.

Wehmeyer, M. L., Agran, M., & Hughes, C. (1998). *Teaching self-determination to students with disabilities: Basic skills for successful transition.* Baltimore: Paul H. Brookes.

Wehmeyer, M. L., & Palmer, S. B. (2003). Adult outcomes for students with cognitive disabilities three years after high school: The impact of self-determination. *Education and Training in Developmental Disabilities, 38,* 131–144.

Wells, K. (2001). *Meely LaBauve.* New York: Random House.

Wentling, R. M., & Waight, C. L. (1999). Barriers that hinder the successful transition of minority youth into the workplace. *Journal of Vocational Education Research, 24,* 165–183.

Wolman, J. M., Campeau, P. L., DuBois, P. A., Mithaugh, D. E., & Stolarski, V. S. (1994). *AIR self-determination scale and user guide.* Palo Alto, CA: American Institutes for Research.

Wood, W. M., Karvonen, M., Test, D. W., Browder, D., & Algozzine, B. (2004). Promoting student self-determination skills in IEP planning. *Teaching Exceptional Children, 36,* 8–16.

Wood, W. M., Test, D. W., Browder, D., Algozzine, B., & Karvonen, M. (2004). UNC Charlotte Self-Determination Synthesis Project. Self-Determination Technical Assistance Centers Project. www.uncc.edu/sdsp/sd_curricula.asp.

Wynn, M. (1993). *The eagles who thought they were chickens: A tale of discovery.* Marietta, GA: Rising Sun Publishing.

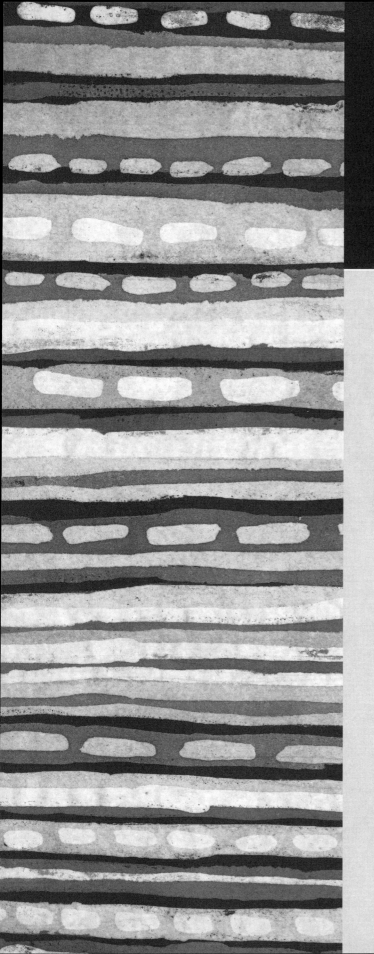

PART 4

Special Issues for Special Populations

Chapter 14

Gifted and Talented CLDE Learners

In previous discussions, we stated that students who are gifted and talented receive limited attention in special education literature and research and that these students, despite having exceptional needs, are not protected by federal laws and mandates. In this chapter, we focus on a subset of this population who are underidentified and underrepresented in gifted programs: African American, Hispanic American, and Native American students. After reading this chapter, readers will be able to answer the following questions:

1. How does the federal government define gifted and talented?
2. What are some characteristics of students who are gifted and talented?
3. What does "underrepresentation" mean, and how severe is underrepresentation among CLDE learners?
4. Why are culturally and linguistically diverse students underrepresented in gifted education?
5. Why is it important to focus on recruitment and retention with gifted students?
6. How can educators more effectively recruit and retain CLDE learners in gifted education?
7. What are some promising instruments and practices for assessing giftedness among underrepresented learners?
8. What are some promising intervention strategies and programs and services for underrepresented gifted learners?

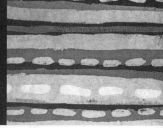

Maxwell: A Case in Point

Maxwell Billingsley is a third grader who loves to read, draw, and play practical jokes. He is also very inquisitive and insightful. His teacher, Ms. Lane, comments that Maxwell asks lots of questions in class, especially when the material is interesting to him. The more interesting the lesson topic, the more questions Maxwell asks. Sometimes, Ms. Lane thinks Maxwell asks too many questions, or primarily asks these questions to get attention from classmates or to irritate her. Maxwell does enjoy being popular with classmates. Ms. Lane often sends letters home to Maxwell's mother about his "poor" behavior; Mrs. Billingsley does not respond directly to Ms. Lane, but she does talk with Maxwell. Maxwell's mother believes that it is the teacher's responsibility to take care of what goes on in the class; she takes care of what goes on at home. Besides, every time she hears from Ms. Lane, it is "bad news." Maxwell's father holds the same sentiments. He proudly works two jobs, keeps the bills paid, and has limited time after catching up on his rest.

Not only is Maxwell inquisitive, he is one of the most creative students in his class; he thrives on projects that are open-ended, leaving room for his imagination, playful ideas, and risk taking. On a recent class assignment in which students were required to write a biography of one of their heroes, every student, except Maxwell, wrote about a cartoon character or parent or friend. Maxwell chose Martin Luther King, Jr. as his hero, even though Dr. King had not been discussed in any of his classes. Rather than write a paper, he wrote a skit in which he interviewed his subject. Although Ms. Lane thought Maxwell's work was very original and far beyond her expectations and requirements, he received a C because he did not follow directions—the assignment was to write a biography, not a play. This was not unusual; Maxwell often changed the assignments because he found them too boring, structured, and predictable. As a result, he often gets low grades from Ms. Lane. In previous grades, teachers encouraged and nurtured Maxwell's imagination, creativity, initiative, and risk taking. They thought he was a great writer. Until this year, Maxwell earned mostly As in all school subjects; now, he earns Bs and Cs.

A look at Maxwell's school records indicates that he has an IQ score of 126, high achievement test scores in language arts and science (both in the 97th percentile), and above-average scores in social studies and math (80th and 85th percentiles, respectively).

In this particular district, the identification process for gifted education begins in the third grade. To be identified as gifted, students must first be referred by their teachers, and then achievement and intelligence tests scores are examined. Students are identified as gifted if they earn a composite score at the 95th percentile on the achievement test or have an IQ score of 130 or higher. Although Maxwell shows many of the characteristics of giftedness (e.g., inquisitive, insightful, creative, independent worker, strong language skills) and has high achievement and intelligence test scores, Ms. Lane has not referred Maxwell for screening because of his low grades (from not following directions) and his "challenging" attitude and behaviors.

Questions to Consider

1. What strengths (social, academic and cognitive) do you see in Maxwell?
2. What appear to be his shortcomings? Should these shortcomings exclude him from gifted education referral and placement?

3. What behaviors displayed by Maxwell would trouble you if he were a student in your class? For example, do you value a sense of humor? Do you like risk taking? Do you value creativity? Do you penalize or praise students who march to the beat of a different drum?
4. Why do you think Maxwell has not been identified as gifted?
5. Do you think Maxwell should receive gifted education services? Explain your response.
6. In what ways do Maxwell and Ms. Lane appear to be culturally different? Do you agree with his parents' views about the role of teachers and the role of parents in the educational process?

Decades of reports indicate that culturally and linguistically diverse exceptional learners are underrepresented in gifted education. Because gifted education is not federally mandated, it is difficult to acquire updated statistics on the demographics of these programs and services. Nonetheless, Ford's (1998b) examination of trends in the demographics of gifted programs between 1978 and 1992 (see Figure 14–1) indicated that African American, Native American, and Hispanic American students have always been underrepresented in gifted education. The most recent statistics available indicate that culturally diverse students were underrepresented by 50 to 60% in gifted programs during the 2002 school year (Office for Civil Rights Survey, 2002). As reflected in Figure 14–2, gifted African American students were the most underrepresented group (60%), followed by Hispanic American (50%), and American Indian students (approximately 20%). Interestingly, Asian American students are the only CLD students who are well represented in gifted education.

In this chapter, we consider why this problem exists and persists. The statistics raise at least two questions: Why are CLDE learners underrepresented—consistently and grossly—in gifted education programs? What factors contribute to difficulties in recruiting and retaining CLDE learners in gifted education?

FIGURE 14–1 Special Education Data on Trends in the Representation of Diverse Students in Gifted Education Programs, 1978 to 1992

Student Population	1978	1980	1982	1984	1992
Hispanic American	6.8 / 5.15 (U = 25%)	9.0 / 5.4 (U = 40%)	8.6 / 4.0 (U = 53%)	13.2 / 7.2 (U = 45%)	13.7 / 7.9 (U = 42%)
American Indian	.8 / .3 (U = 62%)	.7 / .3 (U = 57%)	.5 / .3 (U = 40%)	.8 / .3 (U = 62%)	1.0 / .5 (U = 50%)
Asian American	1.4 / 3.4 (O = 59%)	2.2 / 4.4 (O = 50%)	2.6 / 4.7 (O = 45%)	3.7 / 6.8 (O = 46%)	4.0 / 7.0 (O = 43%)
African American	15.7 / 10.3 (U = 33%)	20.1 / 11.1 (U = 45%)	25.8 / 11.0 (U = 57%)	24.5 / 12.9 (U = 47%)	21.1 / 12.0 (U = 41%)

Notes: Top number indicates the percentage of total student population; middle number represents percentage of gifted education; U = underrepresented; O = overrepresented.
Source: From "The Underrepresentation of Minority Students in Special Education" by D. Y. Ford, 1998, *The Journal of Special Education, 32*(1), 4–14, Copyright © 1998 by PRO-ED, Inc. Reprinted with permission.

FIGURE 14-2 Gifted Education Demographics by Race/Ethnicity and Gender

Sex	Male		Female		Total	
Students Race/Ethnicity	Number of Students	Percentage of Students	Number of Students	Percentage of Students	Number of Students	Percentage of Students
American Indian/Alaskan Native	11,966	0.42	12,890	0.45	24,856 (1.1%)	0.87
Asian/Pacific Islander	90,541	3.17	96,706	3.39	187,247 (4.0%)	6.57
Hispanic	117,954	4.14	128,239	4.50	246,193 (14.3%)	8.63
Black (Not of Hispanic Origin)	104,717	3.67	134,999	4.73	239,716 (17.0%)	8.40
White (Not of Hispanic Origin)	1,058,865	37.13	1,095,279	38.40	2,154,144 (63.7%)	75.53
Total	1,384,044	48.53	1,468,114	51.47	2,852,158	100.00

Source: U.S. Department of Education, Office for Civil Rights (2002). Elementary and Secondary School Civil Rights Survey.

In this chapter, we first provide an overview of gifted education and then discuss the underrepresentation of CLDE students. Two central issues are addressed: (1) a "deficit perspective" about culturally and linguistically diverse populations and (2) educators' lack of understanding and appreciation of cultural diversity, as discussed in Chapter 1. These issues effectively prevent educators from recognizing the gifts and talents of students who are different from the dominant or mainstream culture.

Who Are Gifted and Talented Students?

We use the terms *gifted* and *talented* interchangeably. We recognize that others may have very different definitions. For example, talented students may be viewed as creative, and gifted students may be viewed as smart. Having said this, it is worth noting that five types of gifts and talents are recognized by the federal government. According to the most recent federal definition in 1993:

> Children and youth with outstanding talent perform or show the potential for performing at remarkably high levels of accomplishment when compared with others of their age, experience, or environment. These children and youth exhibit high performance capacity in intellectual, creative, and/or artistic areas, possess an unusual leadership capacity, or excel in specific academic fields. They require services or activities not ordinarily provided by the schools. Outstanding talents are present in children and youth from all cultural groups, across all economic strata, and in all areas of human endeavor. (U.S. Department of Education, 1993, p. 3)

Note that the definition does not contain the term *gifted*, but instead uses *talent*. The definition also urges considering factors other than age in determining who is gifted or talented. It asks us to consider how experiences and environment affect the development of potential gifts and talents. For example, children who live in poverty may have fewer opportunities, at home and school, to develop their academic and cognitive skills and interests. Therefore, it may be unfair to ask such a student to take a test and then "compete" with a student who is wealthy for a place in gifted education (and Advanced Placement) classrooms. To reduce unfairness, only students who come from similar economic status backgrounds should be compared to each other, as discussed in the assessment chapter. A third feature of the definition is the acknowledgement that no group has a monopoly on gifts and talents. Essentially, regardless of race, socioeconomic status, and so on, all groups have gifted and talented students in them.

The five types of gifts and talents differ, as do the different types of special education categories. Intellectually gifted students often have high IQ scores—scores of 130 or higher. Their strengths are in the cognitive areas, they are inquisitive and thoughtful, they prefer complexity in learning, they make connections quickly, and they often have an extensive vocabulary. Academically gifted students tend to have high achievement test scores and grades and show strengths in one or more subject areas. Creatively gifted students tend to be flexible and original; they also elaborate and are fluent in their thinking, as E. Paul Torrance describes. In the visual and performing arts, these students are excellent artists, musicians, actors, and so on. Those who have leadership gifts demonstrate them by participating in committees, taking initiative, and showing strong social skills. These brief descriptions of the five areas of gifts and talents are not comprehensive; readers should consult the works of Robert Sternberg and Howard Gardner for more specifics, and the many texts on gifted and talented education (e.g., Colangelo & Davis, 2003; Davis & Rimm, 2004).

Despite this culturally sensitive federal definition and its inclusion of five different areas or types of gifts and talents, Black, Hispanic, and American Indian students are poorly represented in gifted education. Several scholars have devoted their careers to finding ways to recruit and retain culturally diverse students in these programs. For example, Alexinia Baldwin, Mary Frasier, and Donna Ford have focused decades of work on Black students; Stuart Tonemah has done the same with American Indian students; Margie Kitano has studied Asian American students; and Ernesto Bernal has focused on Hispanic American students. At the heart of their efforts is the recognition that the potential gifts and talents of CLDE students will atrophy if unrecognized and undeveloped.

Gifted and talented students are found among all racial and socioeconomic groups.

Underrepresentation: What Are the Contributing Factors Associated with Recruitment and Retention?

To more fully understand the underrepresentation of culturally and linguistically diverse students in gifted education, we must consider, and then go beyond blaming test scores (see Chapter 7 for a discussion of assessment). Ford (2004) introduced the concept of "recruiting and retaining" those who are culturally and linguistically diverse in gifted programs as one way to meet this challenge. She argued that these students continue to be underidentified and underserved because past efforts to resolve the problem have myopically focused only on testing issues. Because of this limited and narrow focus, educators have addressed only one barrier (testing and assessment), thereby limiting opportunities to adequately address the underrepresentation problem in a proactive, comprehensive, and systemic way. Stated another way, educators have been using a band-aid to fix a gaping wound.

Those scholars (e.g., E. Paul Torrance, Harry Passow, Alexinia Baldwin, Mary Frasier, Joe Renzulli, Ernesto Bernal, Sally Reis, Margie Kitano, James Borland, Nicholas Colangelo, and Tarek Grantham) who have devoted much of their careers to exploring these issues of underidentification and underrepresentation have been seeking ways to correct the problem. Their individual and collective efforts indicate that the major barriers can be categorized as (1) recruitment barriers and (2) retention barriers. Recruitment barriers are those associated with identification and placement that keep diverse students from being screened, identified, and placed (Ford, Moore, & Whiting, 2006; Moore et al., 2006; U.S. Department of Education, Office for Civil Rights, 2005). Recruitment barriers, described in more detail in the next section, include the following:

1. ***Teacher referral***—teachers seldom refer Black, Hispanic, and Native American students for gifted education screening (e.g., Elhoweris, Kagendo, Negmeldin, & Halloway, 2005).
2. ***Testing issues***—school districts tend to adopt and use tests that may not be appropriate for use with culturally diverse students (as discussed in Chapter 7 on culturally responsive assessment).
3. ***Policies and practices***—some school policies and practices have the adverse effect of limiting the presence of CLDE students in gifted education, as described in several reports by the U.S. D.O.E. Office for Civil Rights (OCR).
4. ***Student choice***—some CLDE students do not want to participate in gifted education classes and AP classes, primarily due to negative peer pressures and social-emotional reasons.
5. ***Lack of family awareness and involvement***—CLDE families tend not to be aware that gifted education programs and services exist; and while they do care about their children's education and achievement, they tend to be less involved physically at their children's schools.
6. ***Community pressures and politics***—middle-class European American communities may not support the inclusion of diverse students in gifted education classes; schools appear to succumb to these pressures by making minimal changes to criteria for gifted education, measures, policies, and procedures (Ford, 2006; OCR, 2005).

Retention barriers, also described in more depth later, represent the other half of the underrepresentation problem. Those factors that contribute to CLDE learners leaving—withdrawing from—gifted education programs and services, include:

1. ***Lack of culturally responsive support services***—few educators are formally trained to work with and teach culturally and linguistically diverse students (Banks, 2006); and

few school counselors and psychologists are trained to understand the unique and/or specific needs of this student population (Ford & Joseph, 2006).
2. *Underachievement*—CLDE learners who do not perform well in school or gifted programs may be "unidentified" regardless of the reason for underachievement (e.g., health problems, family issues, low income, low-quality instruction, transitional issues, etc.) (Barton, 2003; Tomlinson, Ford, Reis, Briggs, & Strickland, 2004).
3. *Lack of multicultural education*—CLDE students who do not consider the curriculum to be personally meaningful and relevant may lose interest in learning (Banks, 2006).
4. *Social-emotional needs*—CLDE learners often confront negative peer pressures, and they complain that the lack of diversity in gifted education and AP classes keeps them from wanting to participate in these classes and services.

What Are Some Barriers to Recruiting and Retaining CLDE Learners in Gifted Education?

Educators often explain the underrepresentation of CLDE learners in gifted education in one of two ways. The first explanation involves issues related to cultural misunderstanding; the second relates to testing and assessment. We discussed issues associated with cultural diversity in Chapter 1 and those regarding testing in Chapter 7, so we will only highlight some points here.

Most publications point to problems related to testing and assessment as the cause of underrepresentation.

Although the tests can be problematic if they are biased and unfair in any way, they are not totally to blame. Issues surrounding testing and assessment are a symptom of the problem. Specifically, the primary cause is the pervasive perception of deficit existing in society and in our schools. Negative stereotypes and prejudices, for example, inhibit the ability of teachers to see strengths in students who are different from them.

Cultural Misunderstanding

The body is the hardware. Culture is the software. —Hofstede (2003)

Attitudes about differences among students have a powerful influence in educational settings, particularly on how students are perceived and how their behaviors are interpreted. (See Figure 14–3.) A common folk saying among African Americans is "the less we know about each other, the more we make up." For instance, if a teacher does not understand how some cultural groups value cooperation or communalism over competition (see Boykin, 1994; Cartledge & Loe, 2001; Ogbu, 2003; Shade, Oberg, & Kelly, 1997), the culturally and linguistically diverse child who prefers cooperation may be perceived as being "too social" or lacking in independence. Communalism is a commitment to social relationships and social learning (e.g., working in groups, helping others, etc.). It is a "we, us, our" philosophical orientation. Therefore, students like Maxwell may have a strong need to be liked and accepted; they may have a strong preference for social approval, especially from their peers. Thus, some may become class clowns to gain attention. Similarly, teachers who do not understand that some students come from cultures that value the oral tradition may neither recognize nor appreciate the strengths of those who prefer speaking over writing and reading. They may not recognize that students who speak non-standard English can still have strong verbal skills, that they are somewhat bilingual. Thus, teachers may not refer culturally and linguistically diverse students for gifted education services if they equate giftedness with verbal, reading, and/or writing proficiency.

FIGURE 14–3 Cultural Styles/Strengths of African Americans

Spirituality

A conviction that nonmaterial, religious forces influence people's everyday lives; acceptance of a nonmaterial higher force that pervades all of life's affairs.

Harmony

The notion that one's fate is interrelated with other elements in the scheme of things so that humankind and nature are harmonically conjoined; harmony—one's functioning is tightly linked to nature's order; sensitive to rhythm.

Movement

An emphasis on the interweaving of movement, rhythm, music, and dance, which are considered central to psychological health. A need to move—physical overexcitability; expresses self nonverbally.

Verve

A propensity for relatively high levels of stimulation, to action that is energetic and lively.

Affect

An emphasis on emotions and feelings, together with a special sensitivity to emotional cues and a tendency to be emotionally responsive.

Communalism

A commitment to social connectedness—social bonds and responsibilities transcend individual privileges; a commitment to the fundamental interdependence of people and to the importance of social bonds and relationships; need for affiliation and social acceptance/approval.

Oral Tradition

A preference for oral modes of communication—speaking and listening are treated as performances. Oral virtuosity—use metaphorically colorful, graphic forms of spoken language. Speaking is a performance. Enjoy oral traditions—storytelling, embellishments, jokes, etc.

Expressive Individualism

Seeks and cultivates a distinctive personality; a proclivity for spontaneity, and genuine personal expression; denotes the uniqueness of personal expression, personal style; risk taker, independent, impulsive.

Social Time Perspective

The event is more important than the time; the here and now is important. May not adhere to time limitations imposed by others.

Source: Adapted from Boykin (1994).

The matrix in Figure 14–4 is a cultural filter that uses Boykin's (1994) framework to help educators see that the characteristics and strengths of African Americans can become a liability in schools that have little understanding of and respect for cultural differences. In their report entitled *A New Window for Looking at Gifted Children,* Frasier and colleagues (1995) came to a similar conclusion—we must learn more about cultural diversity in order to effectively identify and serve students who are different from us (also see Frasier & Passow, 1996). Essentially, the matrix indicates that ideas about cultural diversity influence definitions, policies, and practices. Too often, differences are equated with deficits. Herrnstein and Murray (1994) gave support to the deficit orientation in *The Bell Curve.* Among other grievous errors (e.g., equating IQ with actual intelligence, viewing intelligence as static and almost totally inherited, misinterpreting correlation as causation, etc.),

FIGURE 14–4 Giftedness in Cultural Context: Problems Related to Identifying and Serving Gifted Black Students

Characteristics of Giftedness	Cultural Filter	Manifestations of Giftedness Based on Cultural Filters	Possible Interpretations of Gifted Black Student Characteristics
Large memory; acquires and retains information quickly	Harmony—adept at reading verbal and nonverbal behaviors, observant and reads environment well Affective—sensitive; sense of justice	Quick to see discrepancies, inconsistencies, injustices Remembers negative events more than positive events	Overly sensitive; overly preoccupied with negative events; difficult to please or appease
Inquisitive—searches for significance and meaning	Social time perspective—needs a context, a reason for learning Harmony—adept at reading the environment	Quick to note lack of relevance in assignments, rules, and so forth Frustrated by irrelevance and lack of context and meaning	Questions perceived as a challenge; feedback and concerns are perceived as too critical and judgmental
Intrinsic motivation; Task commitment	Social time perspective—social, seeks relevance, valence	Most engaged when tasks are personally rewarding and meaningful	Extrinsically motivated
Seeks cause-effect relations	Harmony—seeks order and logic; traditions are important	Sees things that others do not; insightful, perceptive; asks "why" as much as "why not"	Rude, stubborn, arrogant, too demanding
Heightened sensitivity; concerned about equity and justice	Affective—worries about humanitarian concerns, primarily immediate social issues in home, neighborhood, and school	Confronts rather than accepts inequities (i.e., questions, resists, protests, refuses to accept the status quo)	Defensive, overly sensitive; narrow-sighted, self-centered (personal concerns outweigh larger social issues)
Advanced, large vocabulary; verbal proficiency	Oral tradition—expresses self with openness and honesty; forthright	May use words to manipulate, to present double messages May use words and language considered inappropriate in school settings Talkative	Verbal skills, advanced vocabulary, and content (what) of messages not recognized due to delivery mode (how statements are made)
Creative, inventive, divergent thinkers	Expressive individualism—wants to be seen as an individual within group; creative; innovative	Dislikes structure, routine Dares to be different; risk taker, enjoys challenges Sees things that others do not; sees many alternatives; resourceful	Disruptive, troublemaker, class clown; nonconforming, weird; indecisive
Empathetic, strong interpersonal skills	Affective—feelings influence thoughts and behaviors	Sensitive to rejection, fear of isolation, strong need for positive social relations and student-centered classrooms	Too social, too emotional and needy

(continued)

Characteristics of Giftedness	Cultural Filter	Manifestations of Giftedness Based on Cultural Filters	Possible Interpretations of Gifted Black Student Characteristics
Interpersonal; desire for social acceptance and approval	Harmony—self and one's environment are one (interconnected)	Sensitive to negative feedback or unconstructive criticism Strong desire to belong; to fit in	Socially incompetent (too social, too emotional and needy) Follower rather than leader; overly dependent
Independent, prefer to rely on self or to work alone	Communal, family-oriented Cooperative; social, group-oriented ("we" rather than "I")	Less motivated in competitive situations; more engaged in cooperative situations	Lacks independence and initiative, too dependent on others; overly conforming
Strong sense of humor	Expressive individualism Oral tradition	Likes to play with words and ideas; enjoys puns; clever Uses humor to improve social relations Metaphorically colorful, graphic language used	Cruel, sarcastic, insensitive, class clown, attention seeker
Diverse interests	Verve—energetic, eclectic, multipotential	Inquisitive, willing to take risks and flirt with temptations May not show strengths in one area Attention easily diverted	Unfocused, disorganized, easily distracted; flat profile—major strengths not recognized
Intense concentration	Social time—time is expended and measured by relevance and meaning; time not measured by hands on a clock	May not want to be disturbed or interrupted May have difficulty managing and allocating time Likes to take time rather than be ruled by schedules	Stubborn or single-minded; disorganized
High energy	Movement and verve (intense)	Frustrated and bored by inactivity Highly engaged during active learning and experiential activities Physical	Hyperactive, out of control, aggressive; behavioral problem

Herrnstein and Murray overinterpreted and misinterpreted results of studies on the intelligence of African American children. They ultimately drew the fatalistic conclusion that African Americans are intellectually and culturally inferior to other cultural and ethnic groups. This premise is harmful and unsound, and has no place in educational settings.

Back to Maxwell...

The less we know about each other, the more we make up. At this point in the chapter, two major topics have been discussed: (a) culture in general and (b) African American culture in particular. Reread Maxwell's story. Now, how do your earlier responses change when you recall Maxwell and Ms. Lane?

- If you were another teacher in his school, what suggestions and advice would you give Ms. Lane about Maxwell?
- If you were the principal or school psychologist, what steps would you take to advocate for Maxwell, and what steps would you take to get Ms. Lane the support that she needs to work effectively with Maxwell and other students who are culturally and linguistically diverse?
- What training does she need to become more culturally sensitive and competent?
- Do you believe that formal training in gifted education would be effective in helping Ms. Lane to understand and work with gifted students? What might this training or coursework include in terms of topics?

How Does Deficit Thinking Influence Assessment, Policy, and Practice?

A person's color is the first thing we see, but the last thing we talk about (Lynch, 1992b).

Menchaca (1997) wrote an interesting book that traced the history of deficit thinking. Deficit thinking carries connotations of genetic inferiority, and one group is held up as being either superior or inferior to another group. Groups that are perceived as different from the evaluator (teacher, counselor, etc.) are deemed inferior in some way or another. The focus is on students' shortcomings rather than strengths, as may be the case with Ms. Lane and Maxwell. In the following sections, we apply our previous discussions of deficit orientations to gifted and talented education with the intent of showing how deficit thinking can limit CLDE students' access to gifted and talented programs.

Extensive Reliance on Tests

In other chapters, we have discussed how test scores play a central and predominant role in identification and placement decisions. Over 90% of school districts use intelligence or achievement test scores for identification and placement decisions (Colangelo & Davis, 2003; Davis & Rimm, 2004). This nearly exclusive reliance on test scores for identification and placement decisions keeps the demographics of gifted programs primarily European American and middle class. Unfortunately, educators frequently justify their use of tests because of their purported objectivity.

Students who score at the requisite level in terms of IQ (often 130 is the minimum) or achievement (often 95th percentile is the minimum) tend to qualify for gifted education services. Unfortunately, CLDE learners tend to score lower than White students on traditional standardized intelligence and achievement tests for many reasons, as discussed in Chapter 7. Data indicate that African and Hispanic American students score at least 1 deviation below European American students on standardized intelligence tests (e.g., Barton, 2003; Gould, 1991; Jencks & Phillips, 1998; Sattler, 1998). More specifically, on the Weschler tests, the mean IQ for Black students is 86.4; it is 91.9 for Hispanic students, and 102.3 for White students (see Mercer, 1979; Samuda, Feuerstein, Kaufman, & Sternberg, 1998). On the *Kaufman-Assessment Battery for Children* (K-ABC), the mean IQ score for African American students is 95.0; it is 95.8 for Hispanic students and 102.0 for European American students (see Kaufman & Kaufman, 1983; Figures 14–5 and 14–6). Further, when socioeconomic status (SES) is controlled, the gap in test scores continues, although it decreases by almost half. That is, research by Naglieri and Hill (1986) and Krohn and Lamp (1989) indicates that when SES is similar, the traditional standard deviation gap decreases on the *WISC-R* and *K-ABC*. On the *K-ABC*, African American children

FIGURE 14–5 African American–White Differences on the *K-ABC* and *WISC-R*

	African Americans		White Americans		
	N	Mean	N	Mean	Difference
K-ABC	807		1,569		
• Sequential Processing		98.2		101.2	−3.0
• Simultaneous Processing		93.8		102.3	−8.5
• Mental Processing Composite		95.0		102.0	−7.0
WISC-R	305		1,870		
• Verbal		87.8		102.0	−14.2
• Performance		87.2		102.2	−15.0
• Full Score		86.4		102.3	−15.9

Source: Adapted from A. S. Kaufman and N. L. Kaufman, 1983, *Interpretive Manual for the Kaufman Assessment Battery for Children (K-ABC)*, Circle Pines, MN: American Guidance Service; also see R. J. Samuda, R. Feuerstein, A. S. Kaufman, J. E. Lewis, and R. J. Sternberg, 1998, *Advances in Cross-Cultural Assessment*. Thousand Oaks, CA: Sage. K-ABC data are for children ages 2.5 through 12.5. WISC-R data are for children ages 6 through 16. © 1983 NCS Pearson, Inc. Reproduced with permission.

score 6 IQ points lower than European American students; and on the *WISC-R*, Black students score 9 points lower than European American students.

Given the persistent gaps in the intelligence test scores of African, Hispanic, and European American students (Jencks & Phillips, 1998), one must question why educators continue to rely extensively or exclusively on such tests for recruitment purposes. One instrument must not dictate identification and placement decisions, as we have already emphasized in Chapter 7. The National Association for Gifted Children (1997) published a position statement urging educators to use more than one test to make educational and placement decisions about gifted students and to seek equity in their identification and

FIGURE 14–6 Hispanic–White Differences on the *K-ABC* and *WISC-R*

	Hispanic		White Americans		
	N	Mean	N	Mean	Difference
K-ABC	106		1,569		
• Sequential Processing		98.7		101.2	−2.5
• Simultaneous Processing		99.5		102.3	−2.8
• Mental Processing Composite		95.8		102.0	−3.1
WISC-R	520		640		
• Verbal		87.7		102.0	−14.3
• Performance		97.9		103.8	−5.9
• Full Score		91.9		101.9	−11.2

Source: K-ABC data are adapted from A. S. Kaufman and N. L. Kaufman, 1983, *Interpretive Manual for the Kaufman Assessment Battery for Children (K-ABC)*, Circle Pines, MN: American Guidance Service; p. 151; WISC-R data are from J. R. Mercer, 1979, *System of Multicultural Pluralistic Assessment*, San Antonio, TX: The Psychological Corporation; also see Samuda, Feuerstein, Kaufman, Lewis, and R. J. Sternberg, 1998, *Advances in Cross-Cultural Assessment*. Thousand Oaks, CA: Sage. © 1983 NCS Pearson, Inc. Reproduced with permission.

assessment instruments, policies, and procedures. And the standards of the American Psychological Association (1999) call for the use of more than one instrument when making educational decisions, especially decisions that have lifelong implications.

Why do we continue to use these tests so exclusively and extensively, particularly when they have negatively affected CLDE learners' representation in gifted education? There are at least three explanations for the continued use of tests even when they appear to be barriers: (1) the fault for underrepresentation rests with particular tests (e.g., test bias); (2) the fault rests with the educational environment (e.g., poor instruction and lack of access to high-quality education contributes to poor test scores); or (3) the fault rests with (or within) the student (e.g., he or she is cognitively inferior or "culturally deprived").

The first two viewpoints consider the influence of environmental or external forces on test performance. If a test is suspect, alternative tests and assessment tools will be considered and adopted. If the quality of the instruction and resources are poor or inadequate, then educators recognize that students' test scores are likely to be low (Ford, 2006). The last explanation is based on deficit thinking; it points to shortcomings within the students. Educators who support this view abdicate any responsibility for minority students' lower test scores because they believe that genetics exclusively or primarily determines intelligence and that intelligence is unchangeable. They are also likely to believe that the environments (e.g., families) in which culturally and linguistically diverse students are reared are inferior to those of other groups. Both beliefs support a deficit-oriented philosophy that hinders educators from seeing the potential of diverse students and prohibits them from working effectively with such students.

Psychometric-Based Definitions and Theories

Despite the shortcomings of tests, educators continue to define giftedness psychometrically—as a function of test scores. Thus, definitions and theories are extensively based on the results of intelligence or achievement tests. With respect to the underrepresentation of CLDE learners in gifted education, IQ-based or test-driven definitions often ignore the strengths of students who are culturally diverse, who are linguistically diverse, who live in poverty, and/or who are poor test takers. These students may very well be capable but lack experiences deemed necessary for school success, as explained earlier. According to Helms (1992), cultural styles affect test performance (see Figure 14–7). For example, verve (as conceptualized by Boykin, 1994) can make it difficult for students to sit through and maintain attention during lengthy assessments; harmony can contribute to poorer performance if the assessor is perceived by the student as uncaring or hostile; and communalism may contribute to students wishing to help others and, therefore, being distracted by their friend's progress and performance on the test.

Achievement-Based Definitions and Theories

Along with high intelligence and intelligence test scores, giftedness is often defined in terms of high achievement or productivity, as measured by grades or school performance. Gifted students are expected to *demonstrate* their ability. Such definitions and theories ignore the reality that gifted students can and do underachieve (Ford, 1996, 2006). Gifted underachievers may be teachers' greatest "nightmare" because the students have the ability and potential to excel but do not. Sylvia Rimm, who has spent several decades working with gifted students who underachieve, has suggested that as many as 20% of gifted students do not reach their potential (Davis & Rimm, 2004).

When giftedness is equated with achievement we ignore an important reality—gifted and talented students may lack academic motivation, may have a conflict between need

FIGURE 14–7 The Influence of Culture During Testing Situations

Characteristics	Sample Behaviors
Movement	Rocking, leg(s) swinging, moving around, playing with pencil, stretching, etc. Physical responses to test items (e.g., laugh); request breaks.
Verve	Energetic, excited, stimulated (appear distracted, inattentive, daydreaming, unconcerned). May not extend great deal of attention to test items, thus, may miss relevant information and details.
Harmony	Sensitive to directions, test-taking conditions. May refuse to take test if upset.
Affect	Passionate, sensitive. May react negatively to test items. May refuse to respond to offensive items.
Spirituality	Have much faith; optimistic; feels "lucky." Therefore, may not study or exert effort in preparation for test and during test. May need a pep talk before taking test.
Expressive individualism	Sense of humor, creative, clever. May be drawn to and select unique and humorous responses and questions; may be impulsive.
Communalism	Social, need for affiliation. May want to know how friends and classmates are doing; may want to share answers; may want to take test in groups.
Oral tradition	Prefer to respond orally. May look for blatant, obvious answers; may respond/react verbally to items (laughs, groans, talks out loud).
Social time perspective	May lose track of time; may mismanage time (e.g., start late; may not want to stop if enjoying test; may want to stop early if not enjoying test).

Source: Adapted from J. E. Helms, 1992, "Why Is There No Study of Cultured Equivalence in Standardized Cognitive Ability Testing," *American Psychologist, 47*(9), 1083–1101.

for achievement and need for affiliation, and may have personal problems that hinder their productivity and interest in school (Whiting, 2006; Whiting, in press). Compounding these realities is another reality—school performance is influenced by the quality of students' learning experiences at home and school (Barton, 2003; Ford, 2006). If expectations and standards are low for diverse students (e.g., due to cultural misunderstanding and/or deficit thinking), the quality of curriculum and instruction will suffer. Therefore, students are not likely to do as well as they could in school (see Harmon, 2002).

Inadequate Policies and Practices

Procedural and policy issues also contribute to the underrepresentation of CLDE learners in gifted education. For instance, there may be a policy that gifted education screening must first begin with a teacher referral. Because teachers (including culturally diverse teachers) underrefer CLDE learners for gifted education services (Elhoweris et al., 2005; Saccuzzo, Johnson, & Guertin, 1994), this policy is problematic. Ford (1996) found many Black students with high test scores who were underrepresented in gifted education because teachers did not refer them for screening. A more recent study confirmed this pattern (Elhoweris et al., 2005). Thus, when teacher referral is the first (or only) recruitment step, CLDE students are likely to be underrepresented. Teacher, counselor, and other referrals are subjective; they rest heavily on our expectations and perceptions of students.

An additional policy may be that students must have a certain grade point average to be referred to the gifted program or AP classes or to remain in such courses. The implications and impact of this policy are clear; since a disproportionate percentage of CLDE students underachieve, their opportunities to be identified as gifted and to remain in gifted education classes are diminished.

What Changes Should Be Made for Recruitment and Retention Interventions?

Schools must eliminate barriers to the participation of economically disadvantaged students in services for students with outstanding talents . . . and must develop strategies to serve students from underrepresented groups (U.S. Department of Education, 1993, p. 28).

Increasing the participation of CLDE learners in gifted education requires more than finding the "right" test. To effectively recruit and retain these students, educators must

FIGURE 14–8 A Comparison of Traditional vs. Contemporary Beliefs and Practices

Traditional Beliefs and Practices	Contemporary Beliefs and Practices
Identification—focus is on a convergent answer. Is the child gifted? (yes/no response required)	Assessment—focus is on a divergent answer. How is the child gifted and what are his/her needs? This is diagnostic and prescriptive.
Identification—focus is on students earning a certain number on an intelligence or achievement test.	Assessment—focus in on developing a profile of students' strengths and shortcomings.
Giftedness—represented by a high IQ score or achievement percentile.	Giftedness—viewed as multidimensional
Measurement—the best (most valid and reliable) measure of giftedness is a test(s).	Measurement—giftedness must be assessed in multiple ways due to its multimodal nature.
Measurement—one measure/test is sufficient.	Measurement—multiple sources are essential to develop a profile.
Ability is rewarded.	Effort and achievement are rewarded.
Ability must be demonstrated.	Talent development and potential are recognized.
Etiology—genetics primarily determines giftedness.	Etiology—the environment and genetics determine giftedness. We must look at characteristics.
Students are in a gifted program. Gifted education is a place.	Students receive gifted education services. Gifted education is not a place.
Excellence vs. equity debate.	Excellence and equity are not mutually exclusive.
Gifted education is a privilege.	Gifted education is a need.

shed deficit thinking. As Einstein once said, "The world we have created is a product of our thinking. We cannot change things until we change our thinking." Figure 14–8 illustrates the pragmatic and philosophical changes needed to begin recruiting and retaining CLDE students in gifted education.

Adopt Contemporary Definitions and Theories

Since 1970, there have been five definitions of giftedness. The U.S. Department of Education's (1993) most recent definition of gifted broadens the concept to include potential and talent development. Further, it acknowledges that giftedness is a social and relative construct. Educators are urged to carefully make comparisons based on similar experiences and backgrounds. Unlike other definitions, the USDE definition recognizes that giftedness also exists among children living in ghettos, barrios, and hollows. Unfortunately, as with other definitions and theories, practical, valid, and reliable instruments have yet to be developed to assess these proactive and contemporary theories of intelligence. Our hope is that this will be rectified in the near future.

Among the theories of intelligence and giftedness, two appear to capture the strengths, abilities, and promise of gifted diverse learners, particularly Sternberg's (1985) Triarchic Theory of Intelligence and Gardner's (1983) Theory of Multiple Intelligences (see Figure 14–9). These two comprehensive, flexible, and inclusive theories contend that giftedness is a social construct that manifests itself in many ways and means different things to different cultural and linguistic groups. The theorists acknowledge the multifaceted, complex nature of intelligence and how current tests (which are too simplistic and static) fail to do justice to this construct. Sternberg's Triarchic Theory of Intelligence, for example, includes the following ideas:

a. **Contextual/Practical**—Intelligence is the ability to adapt to the environment (not measured by IQ tests). Street smart, socially competent, practical, pragmatic (may not do well in school, but is a survivor, is able to apply and use their abilities).
b. **Experiential/Synthetic**—Intelligence is a function of insight. Creativity and the ability to deal with novelty are important. Do not necessarily do well on conventional tests in intelligence; able to see more in the problem/item than the test constructor; reads many things into it; divergent thinker; contrarian. May not be the one with the highest IQ, but may make the greatest contribution.
c. **Componential/Analytic**—Analytical and abstract thinker (similar to psychometric theory). Does well on standardized tests. Does well in school. Has the ability to dissect a problem and understand its parts.

Adopt Culturally Sensitive Instruments

To date, the most promising instruments for assessing the strengths of culturally diverse students are such nonverbal tests of intelligence as the *Naglieri Non-Verbal Abilities Test* and *Raven's Matrix Analogies Tests*, which are considered less culturally loaded than traditional tests (Saccuzzo, Johnson, & Guertin, 1994). Accordingly, these are likelier to capture the cognitive strengths of culturally diverse students. Saccuzzo et al. identified substantively more Black and Hispanic students as gifted using the *Raven* than using a traditional test, and reported that "50% of the non-White children who had failed to qualify based on a *WISC-R* qualified with the *Raven*" (p. 10). They went on to state that "the *Raven* is a far better measure of pure potential than tests such as the *WISC-R*, whose scores depend heavily on acquired knowledge" (p. 10).

Educators should understand that the "nonverbal" term in the test title does not mean that students are "nonverbal" (e.g., cannot talk). Rather, the tests give students opportunities

FIGURE 14-9 Gardner's Multiple Intelligences Theory

Intelligence	End-States	Core Components
Logical-mathematical	Scientist, Mathematician, Physicist	Sensitivity to, and capacity to discern, logical or numerical patterns; ability to handle long chains of reasoning. *Concept oriented*.
Linguistic	Poet, Journalist, Storyteller, Writer, Actor	Sensitivity to the sounds, rhythms, and meanings of words; sensitivity to the different functions of language; strong in oral and written expression and understanding. *Word oriented*.
Musical	Composer, Violinist	Ability to produce and appreciate rhythm, pitch, and timbre; *rhythm and melody oriented* (an appreciation of the forms of musical expressiveness). Becomes animated and may study better when music is playing.
Spatial	Navigator, Sculptor, Artist, Designer, Inventor, Daydreamer, Engineer, Mechanic, Chess Player	Capacities to perceive the visual-spatial world accurately. *Visually oriented* (attracted to visual media and creates visual patterns).
Bodily-kinesthetic	Dancer, Athlete, Mime, Surgeon	Abilities to control one's body movements and to handle objects skillfully; excels in fine-motor activities and crafts; *physically oriented*; achieves self-expression through body action; touches things to learn about them.
Interpersonal	Teacher, Therapist, Salesman, Religious, or Political Leader	Capacities to discern and respond appropriately to the moods, temperatures, motivations, and desires of other people. *Socially oriented*; strong leadership skills; enjoys group games and cooperative learning; mediates disputes.
Intrapersonal	Person with detailed, accurate self-knowledge	Understanding of self. Has access to one's own feelings and the ability to discriminate among them, and to guide behavior; knowledge of one's own strengths, weaknesses, desires, emotions, and intelligences. *Intuitively oriented*.

to demonstrate their intelligence without the confounding influence of language, vocabulary, and academic exposure. Gardner, Sternberg, and others argue that some gifted individuals do not have strong verbal or linguistic skills, as may be the case with musically gifted students, creatively gifted students, spatially gifted students, and those having a great deal of practical or social intelligence. Thus, we must find ways to assess the strengths, the gifts, of these capable students. At this time, nonverbal tests hold much promise for identifying such students, although one test and one type of test cannot possibly measure the many types of intelligences that exist.

In addition to adopting culturally sensitive instruments, educators must consider the following when interpreting test results:

a. subgroup norms (e.g., Does the test manual report differences in test performance for diverse groups? Do groups who are CLDE perform differently than European American students on the tests?)
b. trends in test scores (e.g., Are early test scores higher than later test scores? Are achievement test scores significantly different from intelligence test scores for groups who are CLDE?)
c. differences in subtests within the tests (e.g., Do certain groups score higher on performance versus verbal subscales?)

The most recent testing standards provide more detailed precautions and recommendations regarding culturally sensitive, equitable assessment (APA, 1999).

How Do We Identify and Serve Underachievers and Low-Socioeconomic-Status Students?

Underachievement is learned; children are not born underachieving (Ford, 1996). Yet, when giftedness is equated with high achievement, gifted underachievers, many of whom are CLDE, will be underreferred for gifted education. Under the leadership of Joyce VanTassel-Baska, former president of the National Association for Gifted Children, a special conference was convened in 2006 to discuss the status of identifying and educating gifted students who live in poverty. A common thread of the published proceedings (VanTassel-Baska and Stambaugh, 2006b) is that when designing programs and services to address underachievement, educators must tailor them to the needs of culturally and linguistically diverse students and students who are low income and include supportive strategies, intrinsic strategies, and remedial strategies. Supportive strategies, which affirm the identity and worth of CLDE students, include:

1. providing opportunities for students to discuss concerns with teachers, administrators, and counselors;
2. addressing issues of motivation, self-perception, and self-efficacy;

Gifted and talented students from culturally and linguistically diverse groups often require more equitable and alternative assessment instruments and procedures.

3. accommodating learning styles; modifying teaching styles (e.g., abstract, concrete, visual, auditory);
4. using mastery learning or diagnostive-prescriptive teaching (VanTassel-Baska & Stambaugh, 2006a);
5. decreasing competitive, norm-referenced learning environments;
6. using cooperative learning and group work;
7. using positive reinforcement and praise;
8. seeking affective and student-centered classrooms;
9. setting high expectations of students;
10. using multicultural education and counseling techniques and strategies;
11. involving mentors and role models; and
12. involving family members in substantive ways, as collaborators and equal partners.

Intrinsic strategies help students develop internal motivation; they are designed to increase academic engagement and self-efficacy (Whiting, 2006). Thus, we must

1. provide students constructive and consistent feedback; feedback they can learn from to change their behaviors and improve academically;
2. give choices by focusing on students' interests (VanTassel-Baska & Stambaugh, 2006a);
3. provide for active and experiential learning (e.g., role plays, simulations, case studies, projects, internships);
4. use bibliotherapy and biographies to motivate and inspire students (Ford & Harris, 1999);
5. use mentorships and role models to show students that they can succeed (Whiting, 2006); and
6. adopt an education that is multicultural; this is an education that is culturally relevant and personally meaningful; it is an education that provides insight and self-understanding (Banks, 2006).

Finally, we must provide remedial strategies, when necessary, as a way to support students. These strategies include implementing academic counseling (e.g., tutoring, study skills, test-taking skills), teaching time management and organization, using individual and small-group instruction, and using such devices as learning contracts and learning journals.

Recruitment and Retention of Maxwell and Other Diverse Students

We have defined and given examples of the concept of recruitment and retention. How can we not only recruit students like Maxwell into gifted education but also retain him and others? What are the key issues to consider in recruitment? Even if ultimately identified as gifted and talented, Maxwell may not do well. What are some additional issues to consider in retention so that Maxwell and other CLDE students will experience success in gifted education? What supportive, intrinsic, and/or remedial strategies seem relevant to adopt with Maxwell? What considerations should be given to his parents as we think about recruitment and retention of Maxwell?

Where Do We Go from Here?

Addressing underrepresentation takes more than testing. Some substantive recommendations for addressing this problem include:

1. increasing the participation of CLDE students in challenging courses, including AP classes;
2. investing in professional development for teachers and other school personnel;
3. implementing comprehensive research-based models for school improvement;
4. focusing on prevention (i.e., expanding high-quality preschool programs and opportunities);
5. addressing inequities and discrepancies in curriculum, instruction, resources, and facilities;
6. raising educators' expectations of CLDE students;
7. providing extended learning time and intensive support for struggling students;
8. strengthening family–educator relationships for increased family involvement; and
9. increasing the number and percent of highly qualified teachers in diverse settings.

In the following sections, we examine these recommendations more closely.

Provide Multicultural Preparation for Educators

With forecasts projecting a growing minority student population, teachers will have to take greater responsibility for multicultural competence (Ford, Grantham, & Harris, 1998; Ford & Harris, 1999, 2000; Ford et al., 2000). Multicultural education preparation of all school personnel may increase the recruitment and retention of diverse students in gifted education. Lynch (1992b) noted that "achieving cross-cultural competence requires that we lower our defenses, take risks, and practice behaviors that may feel unfamiliar and uncomfortable. It requires a flexible mind, an open heart, and a willingness to accept alternative perspectives. It may mean changing the way we think, what we say, and how we behave" (p. 35).

To become more culturally competent, educators must, at minimum, (1) engage in critical self-examination that explores their attitudes and perceptions concerning cultural diversity, and the influence of these attitudes and perceptions on diverse students' achievement and educational opportunities; (2) acquire and use accurate information about culturally and linguistically diverse or CLDE groups (e.g., histories, cultural styles, norms, values, traditions, customs, etc.) to inform teaching and learning; (3) learn how to infuse multicultural perspectives and materials into curriculum and instruction so as to maximize the academic, cognitive, social-emotional, and cultural development of all students; and (4) build partnerships with diverse families, communities, and organizations. In teacher education programs and staff development initiatives, we must prepare future and current teachers to work with culturally and linguistically diverse or CLDE students. Theories, models, and strategies proposed by Banks (1999, 2006), Ford and Harris (1999), Ford and Milner (2005), Shade, Kelly, & Oberg (1997), Tomlinson et al. (2004) and others should be shared with school personnel so that they can create multicultural learning environments—classrooms and schools that are culturally responsive.

Provide a Multicultural Education for Gifted Students

Just as gifted students are gifted 24 hours of the day, culturally diverse students are culturally diverse 24 hours of the day. With this in mind, many scholars emphasize the need for all students to have a multicultural education (e.g., Banks, 1999, 2006; Ford, 2006; Ford,

Grantham, & Harris, 1998; Ford & Harris, 2000). Students have the right to see themselves reflected (and affirmed) in the curriculum. Minimally, this means that teachers must expose students to high-quality multicultural books and materials, create lesson plans that focus on multicultural themes and concepts, and expose students to culturally diverse role models (e.g., using biographies and videos, and having speakers visit classrooms). What resources accurately and effectively teach about slavery? What materials and resources offer multiple perspectives on the Trail of Tears? How can we ensure that all subject areas (including math and science) have a multicultural focus?

Banks (1999, 2006) has proposed four approaches to infusing multicultural content into the curriculum: the contributions approach, the additive approach, the transformation approach, and the social action approach. Teachers must try to teach at the highest levels so that students have a substantive understanding and appreciation of diverse populations.

Bloom's (1985) taxonomy is often used in gifted education as a model for designing curriculum that promotes higher-level thinking in students. As shown in Figure 14–10, the six levels, from the lowest-level thinking to highest-level thinking, are knowledge,

FIGURE 14–10 Bloom's Taxonomy: Levels, Definitions, Verbs, and Student Products

	Category	Definition	Action Verbs	Products
Most Complex	Evaluation	Judges value of something using certain criteria; can support belief, judgment, opinion, perspective, point of view	Appraise, compare, conclude, contrast, criticize, describe, discriminate, explain, justify, interpret, relate, summarize, support	Critique, decision, debate, editorial
	Synthesis	Changes, (re)forms, remakes, rebuilds parts to make a new whole	Categorize, combine, compile, compose, create, design, devise, rewrite, summarize, tell, write	Invention, lesson plan, poem, song, story
	Analysis	Understands how parts relate to the whole; understands structure and motive	Break down, diagram, differentiate, discriminate, distinguish, identify, illustrate, infer, outline, point out, relate, select, separate, subdivide	Plan, prospectus, questionnaire, report
	Application	Transfers knowledge learned in one situation to another	Change, compute, demonstrate, discover, manipulate, modify, operate, predict, prepare, produce, relate, show, solve, use	Demonstration, model, recipe
	Comprehension	Demonstrates basic understanding of concepts and curriculum; can translate to other words	Convert, defend, distinguish, estimate, explain, extend, generalize, give examples, infer, paraphrase, predict, rewrite, summarize	Diagram, drawing, revisions
Least Complex	Knowledge	Ability to remember something previously learned	Define, describe, identify, label, list, match, name, outline, select, state	Exams/tests, isolated facts

comprehension, application, analysis, synthesis, and evaluation. The model is often presented as a triangle or pyramid to show that, proportionally, for gifted students, more of curriculum and instruction should be at the analysis, synthesis, and evaluation levels.

Ford and Harris (1999) extended the Banks model by incorporating Bloom's taxonomy in a matrix designed to challenge gifted students as gifted individuals and cultural beings at the highest level of Bloom's taxonomy and Banks's model. Using the Ford-Harris matrix (also known as the Bloom-Banks matrix), illustrated in Figure 14–11, it is possible for every teacher in every subject area to create lesson plans that challenge students cognitively and multiculturally.

Develop Home–School Partnerships

In theory, school districts consider family involvement central to student achievement. In practice, few schools consistently and aggressively build partnerships with diverse families (Harry, Kalyanpur, and Day, 1999). During the first week of school and throughout the school year, teachers and administrators must make sure that diverse families know that the school district offers gifted education services, that they understand referral and screening measures and procedures, and that they know how placement decisions are made. Just as important, CLDE families must understand the purpose and benefits of gifted and talented education. Efforts by schools must be aggressive and proactive; school personnel will need to go into diverse communities (e.g., visit homes), attend minority-sponsored events, and seek the support of minority churches and corporations in order to build home–school partnerships. Equally important is family education—holding workshops and meetings designed to educate diverse parents on how to meet the needs and advocate for their gifted children. As Ford (2004) and Harry, Kalyanpur, and Day (1999) have noted, culturally diverse parents need strategies for helping their children to cope with peer pressures and social injustices, for maintaining achievement, and for staying motivated and goal-oriented in the face of social injustices.

Conduct Ongoing Evaluation

There are no easy or quick fixes to increasing access opportunities for diverse students to gifted education services. Educators at all levels (e.g., teachers, administrators) and in all positions (e.g., counselors, psychologists) must constantly evaluate and reevaluate their efforts to recruit and retain diverse students in gifted education. They must focus on instruments, definitions, policies and procedures, curriculum and instruction, and staff development (VanTassel-Baska & Stambaugh, 2006a). Armed with information and data, schools can be proactive in opening doors that have been historically closed to diverse students. The success schools achieve at diversifying or "desegregating" gifted education depends heavily on critical self-examination and on a willingness to move beyond the equity versus excellence debate and beyond deficit thinking. As Borland (1996) suggested, gifted education must question and examine its fundamental premises and practices to see if they remain (or ever were) valid. Students in the gifted program should closely represent the community's demographics. The reasons for disparities must be evaluated and rectified.

Remembering Maxwell: Changing His Story to Success

Maxwell's case is all too familiar. Relying upon the work of Boykin (1994), one can see that Maxwell displays the following characteristics: verve, orality, and communalism. Within these various characteristics his sense of humor and risk taking are evident. Sadly, Ms. Lane seems unfamiliar with these cultural characteristics. Hence, rather than build upon these

FIGURE 14–11 Ford-Harris Matrix Using Bloom-Banks Model: Definition/Description of Categories

	Knowledge	Comprehension	Application	Analysis	Synthesis	Evaluation
Contributions	Students are taught and know facts about cultural artifacts, events, groups, and other cultural elements.	Students show an understanding of information about cultural artifacts, groups, etc.	Students are asked to and can apply information learned on cultural artifacts, events, etc.	Students are taught to and can analyze (e.g., compare and contrast) information about cultural artifacts, groups, etc.	Students are required to and can create a new product from the information on cultural artifacts, groups, etc.	Students are taught to and can evaluate facts and information based on cultural artifacts, groups, etc.
Additive	Students are taught and know concepts and themes about cultural groups.	Students are taught and can understand cultural concepts and themes.	Students are required to and can apply information learned about cultural concepts and themes.	Students are taught to and can analyze important cultural concepts and themes.	Students are asked to and can synthesize important information on cultural concepts and themes.	Students are taught to and can critique cultural concepts and themes.
Transformation	Students are given information on important cultural elements, groups, etc., and can understand this information from different perspectives.	Students are taught to understand and can demonstrate an understanding of important cultural concepts and themes from different perspectives.	Students are asked to and can apply their understanding of important concepts and themes from different perspectives.	Students are taught to and can examine important cultural concepts and themes from more than one perspective.	Students are required to and can create a product based on their new perspective or the perspective of another group.	Students are taught to and can evaluate or judge important cultural concepts and themes from different viewpoints (e.g., minority group).
Social Action	Based on information on cultural artifacts, etc., students make recommendations for social action.	Based on their understanding of important concepts and themes, students make recommendations for social action.	Students can apply their understanding of important social and cultural issues; they make recommendations for and take action on these issues.	Students are required to and can analyze social and cultural issues from different perspectives; they take action on these issues.	Students create a plan of action to address a social and cultural issue(s); they seek important social change.	Students critique important social and cultural issues, and seek to make national and/or international change.

Note: Actions taken on the social action level can range from immediate and small scale (e.g., classroom and school level) to moderate (e.g., community or regional level) to large scale (state, national, and international levels). Likewise, students can make recommendations for action or actually take social action.
Source: Reprinted by permission of the Publisher. From Donna Y. Ford and J. John Harris, III. *Multicultural Gifted Education.* New York: Teachers College Press, © 1999 by Teachers College, Columbia University. All rights reserved.

cultural strengths and Maxwell's personality, she seems to view them as weaknesses, perhaps even deficits. She does not seem to honor or reward Maxwell's creativity, verve, orality, and communalism and seems to be more concerned with structure and control than with getting to know Maxwell and working with these strengths. Ms. Lane wants Maxwell to follow directions and to suppress his creativity and risk taking, and she ignores the actual quality of Maxwell's work and ideas. For these reasons, she may not have referred him for gifted education screening.

Maxwell has not been identified as gifted. He does not have consistently high test scores compared to other students who have been identified as gifted; he scores high in some areas and average or above average in other areas. This has also been a barrier to his being identified as gifted. In addition to such cultural misunderstandings and testing issues, it appears that Ms. Lane does not have a good rapport and working relationship with Ms. Billingsley.

How can Maxwell be helped? First, Ms. Lane needs training in both gifted education and urban/multicultural education. Training in gifted education would help Ms. Lane to understand the characteristics and needs of gifted students. She would learn more about creatively gifted students, for example, and their tendency to be risk takers who may dislike following rules, routine, and predictability. Given that gifted students are not a homogeneous group—they have different needs and learning styles, for example—Ms. Lane would learn to vary her assignments, using the options listed in Figure 14–10. Some students enjoy writing papers, while others enjoy creating plays. Just as important, Ms. Lane would also learn that some gifted students do not test well, but still require the challenge of gifted education and AP classes. And she would learn that test scores should not be the only criteria for assessing giftedness.

If gifted education courses and degrees are not offered at local colleges and universities, educators can attend conferences hosted by the National Association for Gifted Children and Council for Exceptional Children (TAG division). These workshops (or professional development sessions hosted in schools) would focus on the following areas to help Ms. Lane and other teachers:

1. Flexibility in accepting the student's creative products.
2. Providing peer-mediated activities, such as cooperative groups, to develop class projects.
3. Providing peer tutoring so that advanced students might aid the less skilled students.
4. Presenting the student positively to the family and encouraging family members to reinforce and nurture the student's gifts and talents.
5. Providing the student with the opportunity to work with older, academically advanced students.
6. Helping the student secure scholarships to community-based programs, such as the Saturday Science Forum conducted at the local museum.
7. Helping to identify an adult mentor with similar talents (preferably one of the same gender and cultural group) who could help to nurture gifts and talents (Whiting, 2006).

Further, courses and workshops in urban/multicultural education would provide Ms. Lane and other teachers with more insight into issues of testing culturally and linguistically diverse students. She would understand why some CLDE students do not score well on tests. She would also become familiar with the cultural styles of CLDE students and, ideally, view these as strengths rather than weaknesses. Likewise, Ms. Lane would be better prepared to use the cultural styles of her students as a basis for teaching and curricular planning. Finally, such courses may help Ms. Lane to learn how to build relationships with culturally and linguistically diverse students and their families.

Training in gifted education would help teachers understand the needs of gifted students and how to identify culturally and racially diverse gifted learners.

Maxwell also needs support, particularly those actions recommended toward the end of this chapter. He seems to require support in test-taking skills to help improve his test scores. He also needs to learn that some rules have to be followed; if he wishes to do assignments differently than requested by teachers, he should talk with them about his different ideas. Maxwell is an energetic, intelligent, creative child. School practices should not kill this spirit.

Recognizing that the gifts and talents of too many CLDE learners have not been developed, Tomlinson et al. (2004) sought out programs that have been successful and found, among others, AVID, A Better Chance, and Minority Student Achievement Network. Readers are encouraged to examine these programs and places where educators are making a positive and meaningful difference for students like Maxwell.

Summary

There is a wealth of talent and intelligence in this field [of gifted education], but I worry that we are using it to defend yesterday, not to imagine and build tomorrow.

—Borland (1996, p. 145)

Underrepresentation of CLDE students in gifted and talented education has gone on for many decades. The persistent and pervasive underrepresentation of diverse students in gifted education is likely to have devastating, long-lasting effects. As discussed in this chapter, there is controversy regarding why CLDE students are underrepresented, focusing on whether the causes are deficiencies in the children and their families or discriminatory practices of schools and society that restrict the search for, and discovery of, gifts and talents among CLDE groups. Much of the problem can be attributed to deficit thinking, which limits access and opportunity, and to extensive attention—misguided attention—paid to testing issues only.

Efforts to increase the participation of CLDE students in gifted education must be proactive, comprehensive, systemic, and systematic. Changes must focus on examining recruitment and retention barriers and then finding ways to both recruit and retain CLDE learners in gifted education. Some promising practices addressing both issues have been suggested in this chapter.

Related Learning Activities

1. Interview several CLDE students about their experiences in gifted classes and AP courses. What are their likes and dislikes or concerns? What trends and themes emerge from their comments? What changes can be made to address their concerns?

2. Interview teachers about their views of gifted education. Do they support gifted programs? What are their concerns about gifted programs? What factors do they consider when referring students for gifted education screening and identification? What other concerns and considerations do they express about CLDE students?

3. Interview CLDE families about their views of and experiences in gifted education. What trends and themes do you see? What changes can be made to address their concerns? What can schools do to knock down barriers and to increase their involvement in education?

4. Talk with the gifted education coordinator in your school district. Are CLDE students underrepresented in gifted education? If so, why? What is being done to address this problem?

5. Find out which colleges and universities in your area offer gifted education training; locate institutions that offer training in multicultural education.

6. Visit the websites of the National Association for Gifted Children and Council for Exceptional Children to gain information and resources on gifted education and gifted students. Search the Internet websites on multicultural education (e.g., National Association for Multicultural Education, Education Pavilion at the University of Virginia, and Teaching for Tolerance).

7. Visit the website of the department of education in your state. What formal training is required to teach gifted students? What information and resources are available on gifted education? How are gifted students identified? What programs and services are available? Are CLDE students underrepresented in gifted education? What efforts are being implemented to address this?

8. Read about programs like AVID, A Better Chance, Minority Student Achievement Network and others described by Tomlinson et al. (2004) and VanTassel-Baska and Stambaugh (2006b). Which aspects of these programs can be adopted in your classroom, school, and district?

References

American Educational Research Association (AERA), American Psychological Association (APA), and National Council on Measurement in Education (NCME). (1999). *Standards for educational and psychological testing.* Washington, DC: American Psychological Association.

Banks, J. A. (1999). *Introduction to multicultural education* (2nd ed.). Boston, MA: Allyn & Bacon.

Banks, J. A. (2006). *Diversity in American education: Foundations, curriculum and teaching.* Boston, MA: Allyn & Bacon.

Barton, P. (2003). *Parsing the achievement gap.* Washington, DC: Educational Testing Service.

Begoray, D., & Slovinsky, K. (1997). Pearls in shells: Preparing teachers to accommodate gifted low-income populations. *Roeper Review, 20*(1), 45–50.

Bloom, B. L. (Ed.). (1985). *Developing talent in young people.* New York: Ballantine.

Borland, J. H. (1996). Gifted education and the threat of irrelevance. *Journal for the Education of the Gifted, 16,* 129–147.

Boykin, A. W. (1994). Afrocultural expression and its implications for schooling. In E. R. Hollins, J. E. King, & W. C. Hayman (Eds.), *Teaching diverse populations: Formulating a knowledge base* (pp. 225–273). New York: State University of New York Press.

Cartledge, G., & Loe, S. (2001). Cultural diversity and social skill instruction. *Exceptionality, 9,* 33–46.

Colangelo, N. & Davis, G. A. (2003). *Handbook of gifted education.* Boston, MA: Allyn & Bacon.

Davis, G. A. & Rimm, S. B. (2004). *Education of the gifted and talented.* Boston, MA: Allyn & Bacon.

Educational Policies Commission. (1950). *Education of the gifted.* Washington, DC: National Education Association and American Association of School Administrators.

Elhoweris, H., Kagendo M., Negmeldin A., & Halloway, P. (2005). Effect of children's ethnicity on teachers' referral and recommendation decisions in gifted and talented programs. *Remedial and Special Education, 26*(1), 25–31.

Ford, D. Y. (1996). *Reversing underachievement among gifted Black students: Promising practices and programs.* New York: Teachers College Press.

Ford. D. Y. (1998a). *Factors affecting the career decision making of minority teachers in gifted education.* Storrs, CT: The University of Connecticut, National Research Center on the Gifted and Talented.

Ford, D. Y. (1998b). The underrepresentation of minority students in special education: Problems and promises in recruitment and retention. *The Journal of Special Education, 32*(1), 4–14.

Ford, D. Y. (2004). A challenge for culturally diverse families of gifted children: Forced choices between affiliation or achievement. *Gifted Child Today, 27*(3), 26–29.

Ford, D. Y. (2004). Recruiting and retaining culturally diverse gifted students from diverse ethnic, cultural, and language groups. In J. Banks & C. A. Banks (Eds.), *Multicultural education: Issues and perspectives* (5th ed.). (pp. 379–397). Hoboken, NJ: John Wiley & Sons, Inc. (reprinted in 2005, 5th ed. Update).

Ford, D. Y. (2005). *Intelligence testing and cultural diversity.* Storrs, CT: National Research Center on the Gifted and Talented.

Ford, D. Y. (2006). Diamonds in the rough: Recognizing and meeting the needs of gifted children from low SES backgrounds. In J. VanTassel-Baska & T. Stambaugh (Eds.), *Overlooked gems: A national perspectives on low-income promising learners. Conference proceedings from the National Leadership Conference on Low-Income Promising Learners.* Washington, DC: National Association for Gifted Children, Jack Kent Cooke Foundation, College of William and Mary.

Ford, D. Y., Grantham, T. C., & Harris, J. J., III. (1998). Multicultural gifted education: A wakeup call to the profession. *Roeper Review, 19,* 72–78.

Ford, D. Y., & Harmon, D. A. (2001). Equity and excellence: Providing access to gifted education for culturally diverse students. *Journal of Secondary Gifted Education, 12*(3), 141–147.

Ford, D. Y., & Harris, J. J., III. (1999). *Multicultural gifted education.* New York: Teachers College Press.

Ford, D. Y., & Harris, J. J., III. (2000). A framework for infusing multicultural curriculum into gifted education. *Roeper Review, 23*(1), 4–10.

Ford, D. Y., Harris, J. J., III, Tyson, C. A., & Frazier Trotman, M. (2002). Beyond deficit thinking: Providing access for gifted African American students. *Roeper Review, 24*(2), 52–58.

Ford, D. Y., Howard, T. C., Harris, J. J., III, & Tyson, C. A. (2000). Creating culturally responsive classrooms for gifted minority students. *Journal for the Education of the Gifted, 23*(4), 397–427.

Ford D. Y. & Joseph, L. M. (2006). Non-discriminatory assessment: Considerations for gifted education. *Gifted Child Quarterly, 50*(1), 41–51.

Ford, D. Y. & Milner, H. R. (2005). *Teaching culturally diverse gifted students.* Waco, TX: Prufrock Press.

Ford, D. Y., Moore, J. L., III, & Whiting, G. W. (2006). Eliminating deficit orientations: Creating classrooms and curriculums for gifted students from diverse cultural backgrounds. In M. G. Constantine & D. W. Sue (Eds.), *Addressing racism: Facilitating cultural competence in mental health and educational settings.* Hoboken, NJ: Wiley.

Ford, D. Y., & Webb, K. (1995). Desegregating gifted education: A need unmet. *Journal of Negro Education, 64,* 52–62.

Frasier, M. M., Martin, D., Garcia, J., Finely, V. S., Frank, E., Krisel, S., & King, L. L. (1995). *A new window for looking at gifted children.* Storrs, CT: The University of Connecticut, National Research Center on the Gifted and Talented.

Frasier, M. M., & Passow, A. H. (1996). *Toward a new paradigm for identifying talent potential.* The University of Connecticut: National Research Center on the Gifted and Talented.

Gardner, H. (1983). *Frames of mind: The theory of multiple intelligences.* New York: Basic Books.

Gould, S. J. (1991). *The Mismeasure of Man.* New York: W. W. Norton & Co.

Hall, E. T. (1989). Unstated features of the cultural context of learning. *Educational Forum, 54,* 21–34.

Harmon, D. (2002). They won't teach me: The voices of gifted African American inner-city students. *Roeper Review, 24,* 68–75.

Harry, B., Kalyanpur, M., & Day, M. (1999). *Building cultural reciprocity with families: Case studies in special education.* Baltimore: Paul Brookes.

Helms, J. E. (1992). Why is there no study of cultural equivalence in standardized cognitive ability testing? *American Psychologist, 47*(9), 1083–1101.

Herrnstein, R. J. & Murray, C. (1994). *The bell curve.* New York: Free Press.

Jencks, C., & Phillips, M. (Eds.). (1998). *The Black-White test score gap.* Washington, DC: Brookings.

Kaufman, A. S., & Kaufman, N. L. (1983). *Interpretative manual for the Kaufman Assessment Battery for Children (K-ABC).* Circle Pines, MN: American Guidance Service.

Krohn, E. J., & Lamp, R. E. (1989). Concurrent validity of the Stanford-Binet Fourth Edition and K-ABC for Head Start children. *Journal of School Psychology, 27,* 59–67.

Lynch, E. W. (1992a). From culture shock to cultural learning. In E. W. Lynch & M. J. Hanson (Eds.), *Developing cross-cultural competence: A guide for working with young children and their families* (pp. 19–34). Baltimore, MD: Paul Brookes.

Lynch, E. W. (1992b). Developing cross-cultural competence. In E. W. Lynch & M. J. Hanson (Eds.), *Developing cross-cultural competence: A guide for working with young children and their families* (pp. 34–64). Baltimore, MD: Paul Brookes.

Menchaca, M. (1997). Early racist discourses: The roots of deficit thinking. In R. Valencia (Ed.), *The evolution of deficit thinking* (pp. 13–40). New York: Falmer.

Mercer, J. R. (1979). *System of multicultural pluralistic assessment*. San Antonio, TX: The Psychological Corporation.

Moore, J. L., III, Ford, D. Y., Owens, D., Hall, T., Byrd, M., Henfield, M., & Whiting, G. W. (2006). Recruitment of African Americans in gifted education: Lessons learned from higher education. *Mid-Western Educational Research Journal, 19*(2), 3–12.

Naglieri, J. A., & Hill, D. S. (1986). Comparison of WISC-R and K-ABC regression lines for academic prediction with Black and White children. *Journal of Clinical Child Psychology, 15*(4), 352–355.

Nobles, W. W. (1990, January). *Infusion of African and African American culture*. Keynote address at the annual conference, Academic and Cultural Excellence: An Investment in Our Future, Detroit Public Schools, Detroit, MI.

Ogbu, J. U. (2003). *Black American students in an affluent suburb: A study of academic disengagement*. New Jersey: Lawrence Erlbaum.

Passow, A. H., & Frasier, M. M. (1996). Toward improving the identification of talent potential among minority and disadvantaged students. *Roeper Review, 18*, 198–202.

Saccuzzo, D. P., Johnson, N. E., & Guertin, T. L. (1994). *Identifying underrepresented disadvantaged gifted and talented children: A multifaceted approach* (vols. 1 & 2). San Diego, CA: San Diego State University.

Samuda, R. J., Feuerstein, R., Kaufman, A. S., Lewis, J. E., & Sternberg, R. J. (1998). *Advances in cross-cultural assessment*. Thousand Oaks, CA: Sage.

Sattler, D. N. (1998). The need principle in social dilemmas. *Journal of Social Behavior and Personality, 13*, 667–678.

Shade, B. J., Kelly, C., & Oberg, M. (1997). *Creating culturally responsive classrooms*. Washington, DC: American Psychological Association.

Sternberg, R. J. (1985). *Beyond IQ: A triarchic theory of human intelligence*. Cambridge, MA: Cambridge University Press.

Tomlinson, C. A., Ford, D. Y., Reis, S. M., Briggs, C. J., & Strickland, C. A. (Eds.). (2004). *In search of the dream: Designing schools and classrooms that work for high potential students from diverse cultural backgrounds*. Washington, DC: National Association for Gifted Children.

U.S. Department of Education. (1993). *National excellence: A case for developing America's talent*. Washington, DC: Author.

U.S. Department of Education, Office of Civil Rights (1978). *1978 elementary and secondary school survey*. Washington, DC: Author.

U.S. Department of Education, Office for Civil Rights. (2002). Elementary and Secondary School Civil Rights Survey 2002, retrieved September 1, 2007 from www.demo.beyond2020.com/ocrpublic/eng.

U.S. Department of Education. Office for Civil Rights. (2005). *Annual report to Congress*. Washington, DC.

VanTassel-Baska, J., & Stambaugh, T. (2006a). *Comprehensive curriculum for gifted learners* (3rd ed.). Boston, MA: Pearson.

VanTassel-Baska, J., & Stambaugh, T. (Eds.). (2006b). *Overlooked gems: A national perspective on low-income promising learners. Conference proceedings from the National Leadership Conference on Low-Income Promising Learners*. Washington, DC: National Association for Gifted Children, Jack Kent Cooke Foundation, College of William and Mary.

Whiting, G. (2006). Enhancing culturally diverse males' scholar identity: Suggestions for educators of gifted students. *Gifted Child Today, 29*(3), 46–50.

Whiting, G. (in press). From at risk to at promise: Developing a scholar identity among Black male adolescents. *Journal of Secondary Gifted Education*.

Name Index

Abbate, J., 31
Abery, B., 198, 199
Agran, M., 256, 270, 271, 273, 309
Alber, S. R., 198
Alberto, M., 103
Algozzine, B., 78, 309, 313, 314
Al-Hassan, S., 66, 146, 147, 218, 247
Alkin, M., 189
Altschuler, S. J., 174, 176
Alvermann, D. E., 235
Amaral, O., 241
Andersonn, G., 106
Anthony, S., 75
Antrop-Gonzalez, R., 32
Appleton, V., 81, 138, 243
Archer, A., 236
Armaline, W. D., 231
Armento, B., 18
Aro, H. M., 106
Aronson, J., 158, 242
Arreaga-Mayer, C., 219
Artiles, A. J., 31, 32, 37, 47, 57, 63
Aspel, N. P., 313
Atkinson, S. E., 140
Austin, J. L., 267

Babur, M., 297
Baca, L. M., 31, 63, 64
Bailey, D. F., 256, 257
Baker, S. R., 306, 311
Balcazar, F., 314, 315
Baldwin, A., 334, 335
Banks, J. A., 18, 19, 58, 168, 335, 336, 348, 349, 350
Barenbaum, E., 239
Bargh, J. A., 247
Barkley, R. A., 40
Barlow, J. H., 283
Barnett, D., 104
Barnett, W. S., 290, 292
Barton, P., 175, 336, 340, 343
Battle, D. E., 40
Bauer, A. M., 135
Becker, W., 235
Bell, C., 191
Ben-Ezer, E., 238
Bennett, J., 318

Benz, M. R., 306, 316, 319, 322
Berliner, D. C., 175, 218, 228
Bernal, E., 334, 335
Bernhard, J. K., 137
Besser, H., 204
Bettis, D. F., 316
Billingsley, B. S., 33, 221
Binch, C., 234
Bishop, A. G., 297
Blacher, J., 307
Black, E., 134
Black, J., 161
Blackmountain, L., 307
Blake, C., 116, 117
Blakely, M. R., 316
Block, M. E., 189, 190, 199, 203
Bloom, B. L., 350
Blue-Banning, M., 102
Blum, I. M., 234
Bolen, L. M., 242
Bolt, S. E., 175
Bond, M., 15
Bonds, M., 124
Boone, H. A., 283
Borland, J., 335, 351, 354
Bos, C. S., 45, 59, 297
Bowman, V., 247
Boykin, A. W., 73, 74, 117, 220, 234, 336, 337, 342, 351
Boyle, C. A., 286
Boyle, J. R., 265
Braden, J., 174
Bradley, R. H., 143
Bransford, J., 18
Brantlinger, E., 217
Brendtro, L. K., 78
Brenton, L., 242
Bridge, C. A., 239
Briggs, C. J., 336
Brophy, J. E., 221
Browder, D., 309, 313, 314
Brown, A. F., 222
Brown, M., 191, 259
Brown, R., 318
Brusca-Vega, R., 145
Bryant, D. P., 241, 242
Budziszewski, M., 193
Bui, Y. N., 317, 318

Bullis, M., 115, 306
Burchinal, M., 281, 288
Burford, H., 121
Bursuck, W. D., 297
Bush, L. D., 179, 180

Calderon, R., 43
Caldwell, L. D., 256, 258, 268
Callins, T., 210, 238
Camarota, S. A., 65, 66
Cameto, R., 306, 322, 324
Campbell, F. A., 281, 288, 289, 293
Campbell, J. R., 231
Campeau, P. L., 310
Canter, A., 173, 174
Cantu, C., 314
Carlson, E., 221
Carlson, L. M., 319
Carnine, D. W., 234
Carnine, L., 235
Carr, J., 267
Carta, J. J., 219, 247
Carter, E. W., 314
Carter, M., 107
Carter, W. J., 140
Cartledge, G., 17, 73, 74, 75, 76, 77, 78, 82, 94, 102, 103, 104, 106, 108, 110, 111, 113, 116, 118, 121, 137, 139, 143, 149, 176, 191, 214, 218, 219, 230, 232, 234, 236, 237, 247, 271, 273, 274, 336
Case, R., 242
Castor, M. L., 286
Cavanaugh, R. A., 247
Cervantes, H. T., 31, 63, 64
Chamberlain, C., 43
Chamberlin, J. L., 198
Chang, S., 286
Chard, D. J., 232
Chavajay, P., 164
Chen, M., 133
Chia, R., 242
Childes, K. E., 84
Chilman, B., 270
Chinn, P. G., 32, 44, 47, 60
Chisholm, A., 286
Choudhury, I. M., 12

Christenson, S. L., 307
Christianson, R. J., 218
Chud, G., 137
Chung, C.-G., 76
Clark, R., 104, 142
Clarke, S., 84
Clarkson, L. M. C., 242
Clemmer, J. T., 76
Cline, J., 286
Cochran, L., 106
Cofer, J. O., 319
Colangelo, N., 335, 340
Cole, S. R., 164
Cole, W., 73, 76
Coll, C. G., 191
Colle, M., 164
Collins, J. W., 286
Colton, L., 319
Colvin, G., 37, 115
Connor, D. J., 74
Conyers, L. M., 293, 295
Cooke, N. L., 107, 143
Cooley, J. J., 122
Cooper, J. E., 256, 268
Cordero, J. F., 286
Corso, R. M., 30
Cortez, J. D., 31
Cosby, B., 109
Cosden, M., 191, 194, 259, 260, 261
Coster, W. J., 106
Coyne, M. D., 297
Craft, S. A., 133
Crawley, J. E., 34
Creech, S., 319
Cronin, M. E., 275
Cullinan, D., 37
Cummins, J. C., 165
Curran, M., 73, 110, 111

Daane, M, C, 231
Dalaker, J., 33
Daly, P. M., 270, 271
D'Andrade, R., 11
Dardig, J. C., 228
Darling, S. M., 290
Darling-Hammond, L., 18, 19
David, R. J., 286
Davis, G. A., 161, 340, 342
Davis, G. Y., 143
Davis, J. E., 231
Davis, N. B., 242
Day, N. I., 286
Day-Hairston, B. O., 81
Day-Vines, N. L., 81
Deal, A. G., 141

DeBose, C. E., 40
Delpit, L., 65, 73, 108, 216, 221
Delquadri, J. C., 218, 219, 247
Deno, S. L., 213
Dent, H., 161, 169
Derzon, J. H., 37
Dewey, J., 218
Diaz-Rico, L. T., 201
Digiovanni, L. W., 73
Dillhunt, M. L., 74, 117, 220
Dillon, C., 75
DiSalvo, C.A., 107, 116
Dobbs, M., 231
Doorlag, D. H., 43
Dowd, F. S., 193
Downey, D. G., 76
Dresser, N., 13
DuBois, P. A., 310
Duda, M. A., 83, 93
Dunlap, G., 84
Dunst, C. J., 141, 142
Dykeman, C., 81, 138, 139

Earle, A., 135
Edwards, T., 242
Eisele, J., 235
Eisenman, L. T., 319, 322
Elhoweris, H., 343, 344
Ellis, R., 64
Ellison, C. M., 74, 117, 220
Engelmann, S., 198, 235, 236, 316
Epstein, J. L., 132
Epstein, M. H., 316
Esters, I. G., 162
Evans, T., 234, 237
Everson, J. M., 313

Faber, K. S., 231
Fall, A., 33
Fan, X., 133
Fanaroff, A. A., 283
Fantuzzo, J. W., 143, 218
Farkas, G., 296
Farmer, T. W., 76, 77, 78
Farra, H. E., 256
Feggins-Azziz, R., 76, 295
Feil, E., 124
Feinberg, D., 106
Feng, H., 103, 104, 108
Ferguson, A. A., 78
Ferri, B. A., 74
Fessler, D. M. T., 103
Feuerstein, R., 340
Field, S., 306, 309, 314
Figueroa, R. A., 165, 180
Fillmore, W., 65

Findlay, P., 143
Fine, M., 175
Finn, J. D., 32
Flanagan, D. P., 162, 163, 165, 166, 178, 179, 180
Fletcher, J. M., 175
Flojo, J. R., 242
Flood, J., 234
Foley, L., 121
Foley, T. E., 34
Ford, D. Y., 18, 19, 57, 158, 161, 164, 168, 175, 178, 180, 182, 183, 332, 334, 335, 336, 342, 343, 347, 348, 349, 350, 351
Forde, T. B., 222
Forness, S. R., 106, 234
Foster, M., 246
Franca, V. M., 218
Frankel, F., 106
Frankland, H. C., 307, 315
Franklin, C., 139
Frasier, M., 334, 335, 337
Frazier Trotman, M., 182, 183, 198
Freeman, F., 189
Freilich, M., 11
Freund, P. J., 283, 289
Friedlander, B. D., 256
Friedman, H., 283
Frizzelle, R., 256
Fuchs, D., 74, 218, 243, 295
Fuchs, L. S., 218, 243, 295

Gallagher, P. A., 290
Gallini, S., 295
Garate, T., 314
Garcia, L. A., 317
Gardner, R., III, 37, 44, 59, 66, 116, 146, 147, 191, 192, 194, 198, 202, 205, 214, 218, 219, 222, 240, 346
Garrett, T., 32
Garrison, L., 241
Garrity, C., 115, 124
Gartin, B.C., 28
Gause, C. P., 112
Gavin, K., 132
Gay, G., 18, 19, 73, 74, 76, 79, 80, 81, 93, 220, 234, 244
Gay, J., 164
Gaylord-Ross, R., 106
Gersten, R., 217, 242
Gettinger, M., 262, 263
Geva, E., 297
Gibbons, J. L., 102
Gilberts, G., 143
Gilberts, G. H., 256, 270, 271

Gilkey, B., 143
Gillock, K. L., 308
Ginsburg, M. D., 143
Ginsburg-Block, M. D., 218
Glasnapp, D., 175
Glass, G. V., 175
Gleason, M. M., 236
Glick, J. A., 164
Goforth, J. B., 76
Goldschmidt, L., 286
Goldstein, A. P., 111, 124
Gollnick, D. M., 32, 44, 60
Golly, A., 124
Gomez, J., 307
Gomez, M. L., 222
Gong, H., 194
Good, R. H., III, 214, 232, 235, 298
Good, T. L., 221
Goodman, B., 223, 237
Gould, S. J., 161, 163, 340
Graham, S., 34, 239, 240, 256, 265, 268, 270
Grant, C. A., 222
Grant, M., 57
Grantham, T., 335, 349, 350
Gray, C. D., 106
Greenfield, P. M., 164, 167
Greenwood, C., 74, 218, 219, 247
Gregory, R. J., 166, 167, 170, 178, 181
Gresham, F. M., 107, 111, 114, 115
Griffin, B. W., 256, 269
Griffin, S. A., 242
Grigg, W. S., 231
Grossi, T. A., 219
Grossman, D., 124
Grossman, H., 38
Groth-Marnat, G., 161, 162, 166, 167, 178
Gruwell, E., 112, 318
Guertin, T. L., 343, 345
Guralnick, M. J., 281
Gutierrez, L., 191, 259
Gutman, L. M., 133, 142, 204, 205

Hack, M., 283, 286
Hagan-Burke, S., 82
Hakim, R. B., 286
Hakuta, K., 30
Hale, J., 18
Hall, C. W., 242
Hall, E. T., 15
Hall, M., 15
Hall, R. V., 218, 219
Hall, V., 247
Hallahan, D. P., 33, 34, 37, 39, 45

Halpern, R., 192
Haltiwanger, J., 106
Hamilton, V., 109
Hamlett, C. L., 243
Hammond, W. R., 124
Han, K., 162
Handler, M. W., 77
Hanner, S., 198, 316
Harden, B., 138, 139
Haring, K. A., 306
Harmon, D., 19, 343
Harper, W., Jr., 141, 143, 145
Harris, J. J., III, 18, 178, 182, 348, 349, 350, 351
Harris, K. R., 34, 217, 239, 240, 256
Harris, K.C., 249
Harrison, T., 44, 219, 247
Harry, B., 47, 135, 136, 137, 295, 351
Hart, B., 133, 219, 294
Harvey, M. W., 319, 322
Hassinger, M., 256, 269
Haycock, K., 33, 221, 229
Heckaman, K., 113
Heckman, J. J., 281, 282
Hedgpeth, D., 138, 139
Heflin, L. J., 107, 116
Heller, L. R., 143
Helms, J. E., 167, 178, 342, 343
Herbert, E. B., 283
Herbst, M., 76
Heron, K. M., 218
Heron, T. E., 143, 217–218, 218, 240, 249
Herrnstein, R. J., 57, 158, 161, 337, 339
Hessler, T., 34, 240
Hettleman, K. R., 295, 296
Heward, W. L., 30, 31, 35, 44, 143, 198, 219, 228, 240, 247, 267
Hewstone, M., 20
Heyman, S. J., 135
Hiebert, E. H., 239
Higareda, I., 32
Hill, D. S., 340
Hill, N. E., 133
Hilliard, A. G., 39
Hilton, A., 28
Hodge, S. R., 199
Hoffman, A., 309, 314
Hoffman, M., 234
Hofmeister, A., 143
Hofstede, G., 12, 15, 336
Hooper, S. R., 27
Horn, D. M., 293, 294
Horn, S., 256, 268
Horne, E. B., 103, 107

Horner, R. H., 93, 114, 217
Hosie, J. A., 106
Hosp, J. L., 32, 33
Howard, G. R., 18, 239
Huang, G., 136, 137
Hudson, C. G., 284
Hudson, P. J., 243
Hughes, C., 256, 265, 270, 309, 314
Hunter, N., 106
Hurley, S. R., 234
Hustedt, J. T., 290, 292
Hutchinson, S. W., 275
Huurre, T. M., 106

Irvine, J., 18, 19, 73, 104
Ishii-Jordan, S. R., 31, 37, 56
Ittenback, R. F., 162

Jackson, D., 44
Jackson, Y., 234
Jacobson, L., 11
Japzon, A. C., 194
Jean, R. E., 137
Jefferson, G. L., 77
Jefferson, T., 5
Jeffries, R. B., 307, 316, 322
Jencks, C., 340, 341
Jenkins, J. R., 247
Jenkins, L. M., 247
Jens, K., 115, 124
Jensen, A., 164
Jenson, W. R., 73
Jerman, P., 314
Jimenez, F., 319
Jinn, Y., 231
Johnson, C. C., 122
Johnson, G., 198, 235, 316
Johnson, K. A., 122, 224
Johnson, N. E., 343, 345
Johnston, R. C., 201
Jones, C. W., 136
Jongyeun, L., 316
Jordan, N. C., 242
Joseph, L. M., 158, 161, 168, 175, 178, 183, 336
Joy, R., 270
Jung, D. I., 102

Kahn, S., 242
Kalyanpur, M., 351
Kame'enui, E. J., 214, 219, 231, 232, 234, 294, 297, 298, 299
Kaminski, R. A., 214, 232, 235, 298
Karvonen, M., 309, 313, 314
Kasser, S. L., 202, 203
Katsiyannis, A., 76

Name Index

Kauffman, J. M., 33, 34, 37, 39, 45
Kaufman, A. S., 183, 340
Kaufman, N. L., 340
Kavale, K. A., 106, 115, 234
Kavanagh, K., 124
Kay, P., 78
Kea, C., 139, 154
Keefe, N., 191
Kelly, A. E., 177
Kelly, C., 336, 349
Kelly, J. G., 148, 204
Kemp, C., 107
Kern, L., 84
Kerr, M. M., 116, 218, 256
Kessler, C., 64, 65
Keyes, M. W., 317, 318
Kiarie, M., 110
Kilburide, K. M., 137
Kim, I. J., 148, 204
Kim, L. I. C., 148, 204
King, R., 297
Kitano, M., 334, 335
Kizzie, K., 73, 117, 234
Klass, D., 318
Kleefeld, J., 111, 118
Klein, S., 221
Klett, L., 214
Klingner, J., 295
Knesting, K., 179, 180
Knoff, H. M., 75
Kohler, K. R., 32
Kohler, P. D., 306
Koonce, D. A., 141, 143, 145
Kopelowicz, A., 102
Kornhaber, M. L., 196, 201
Kozol, J., 42
Kraft, B. L., 143
Krashen, S., 31, 32, 65, 259, 261
Kretovics, J., 231
Krohn, E. J., 340
Kunjufu, J., 317
Kuykendall, C., 149

Laczko-Kerr, I., 228
Ladson-Billings, G., 18, 19, 220, 244
LaForge, S., 319
Lambert, D., 218
Lambert, M. C., 117, 219
Lamp, R. E., 340
Lampe, J. R., 103
Lange, R., 137
Lapp, D., 234
Larney, P. S., 139
LaRoche, M. J., 176, 177
Larsen, H. C., 106
Laushey, K. M., 107, 116

Lazarus, B. D., 267
Ledlow, S., 73
Lee, G., 136, 139, 145
Lee, M., 267
Lee, R. S., 136
Lee, S., 108, 181
Lefebvre, M. L., 137
Leinweber, M., 258, 259, 261
Lesson-Hurley, J., 58
Leung, C. B., 103, 107
Levendoski, L., 271
Levine, P., 306, 324
Lewis, I., 288, 294
Lewis, J. E., 341
Lewis, R. B., 43
Lewis, T. J., 85, 88, 93, 115
Lewis-Palmer, T., 82
Liang, C. T. H., 108
Lian-Thompson, S., 137
Lim, C. I., 283
Lindsey, J. D., 46
Lindstrom, L. E., 306, 316, 322
Lines, P. M., 131
Lipsey, M. W., 37
Litvak-Miller, W., 121
LL Cool J, 109
Lloyd, J. W., 234
Lo, Y., 76, 77, 78, 82, 94, 143, 219, 234, 236, 237, 247, 274
Loe, S., 110, 111, 336
Long, N. J., 78
Lopez, G. R., 142
Losen, D. J., 58, 62
Lucas, E. T., 286
Lucas, T., 18, 19
Luiselli, J. K., 77
Lynch, E. W., 340, 349
Lynn, R., 158
Lyon, G. R., 231

Ma, G. X., 286
Ma, Y., 247
MacArthur, C. A., 265
Madden, N. A., 235
Mahitivanichcha, K., 142
Majel-Dixon, J., 139, 145
Major, J., 143
Malloy, M., 199
Mancini, J., 286
Manning, M. L., 136, 139, 145
Marchand-Martella, N., 316
Margolis, H., 260, 261
Markowitz, J., 290
Marshall, L., 310, 314
Marshall, N. L., 191
Martella, R. C., 316

Martin, J., 310, 314
Martinez, A. C., 109, 111, 112
Martinez, F., 319
Martinez, V., 319
Marx, F., 191
Mastropieri, M. A., 229
Mather, N., 213, 235, 297
Mathes, P. G., 234, 294, 296
Matsumoto, D., 165
Maude, S. P., 30
Mauszewski, J., 314
Maxson, L., 314
Mayberry, R. I., 43
Mazurek, K., 210, 221
McCabe, K. M., 104
McCarnes, K., 124
McCartney, K., 191
McCoach, D. B., 256
McCollin, M. J., 31
McConnell, M. E., 83, 84, 85, 270, 271, 274
McField, G., 31, 32
McGahee-Kovac, M., 312
McGinnis, E., 111, 124
McGrew, K. S., 213, 235
McGuire, J. M., 256
McKain, K. N., 247
McLoyd, V. C., 133, 142, 204, 205
McMullen, M. B., 289
McNair, J., 204
McWhirter, B. T., 190
McWhirter, E. H., 190
McWhirter, J. J., 192
McWhirter, R. J., 190
Meadows, D., 3, 4
Melo, X., 314
Menchaca, M., 340
Menchetti, B. M., 317
Mendez, L. M. R., 75
Mercer, C., 240
Mercer, J. R., 340, 341
Meyer, L., 235
Michael, R. S., 75
Milburn, J. G., 73, 74, 111, 121, 137, 139, 176, 230
Miller, M. C., 107, 192
Miller, S. P., 243, 270
Miller, T. R., 218
Miller-Johnson, S., 281, 288
Miller-Jones, D., 167, 180
Milner, H. R., 18, 19, 349
Minaya-Rowe, L., 31
Minich, N., 283
Miranda, A. H., 37
Misra, A., 78

Mithaugh, D. E., 310
Moats, L. C., 34, 230, 231, 235, 297
Mokhtari, K., 173
Monroe, C. R., 73, 76, 81
Montecel, M. R., 31
Monzo, L., 307
Moore, J. L., 335
Moore, R., 113
Moran, C. E., 30
Morrell, E., 112
Morrison, G., 191, 259
Morrisson, G. M., 75, 77
Morse, J., 73, 76
Mortweet, S. L., 247
Moses, K., 134
Mostert, M. P., 106, 115
Murata, N., 199
Murdick, N. L., 28
Murdoch, J. Y., 275
Murray, C., 57, 158, 161, 337, 339
Musti-Rao, S., 220, 232, 234
Myers, W. D., 109, 234, 318

Naglieri, J. A., 158, 164, 183, 340
Nakamura, K. K., 116
Nardo, A. C., 75
Nathanson, M. S., 286
Neisser, U., 161, 163
Nelson, C. M., 83
Nelson, J. R., 81, 82, 132, 138
Nelson, K., 124
Newcomer, P., 239
Newman, L., 306, 322, 324
Nguyen, A., 65
Nichols, S. L., 175
Nickel, E. L., 259
Nicolini, M. B., 239
Nieto, S., 18, 31
Nixon, E., 106
Noble, M. M., 247
Nodine, B. F., 239
Nolan, K. W., 283
Norwood, P. M., 140, 141
Nougharet, A., 229

Oberg, K., 13, 349
Oberg, M., 336
Obiakor, F., 32, 33, 57
O'Brien, K. O., 286
Odom, S. L., 217
Oertzel, J. G., 11, 14, 15
Ogbu, J. U., 336
Olsson, E., 106
Orfield, G., 58, 62, 196, 201
Ortiz, A. A., 31, 63, 110

Ortiz, S. O., 32, 162, 163, 165, 166, 168, 170, 171, 172, 178, 179, 180
O'Shea, D. J., 31
Oswald, D. P., 107, 116
Ou, S.-R., 293
Owens, R. E., 40
Owens-Johnson, L., 317, 318

Paisley, P. O., 256, 257
Palmer, J., 57, 269
Palmer, S. B., 268
Paratore, J. R., 136, 307
Park, E., 136
Park, J., 92, 284
Parmar, R. S., 34
Parrish, T., 33
Parsons, R. D., 18
Partenio, I., 164
Passow, A. H., 335, 337
Patton, J. M., 58
Paul, P. V., 44, 106
Payne, K. T., 40
Pereira, L., 102, 108
Perozzi, J. A., 65
Peske, H. G., 33, 221, 229
Peterson, R., 75
Phillips, A., 314
Phillips, J., 138
Phillips, M., 340, 341
Pilewskie, A. A., 247
Place, K., 199
Plourde, L. A., 256, 269
Poggio, J., 175
Poloni-Staudinger, L., 76, 295
Ponce, G., 241
Porter, W., 115, 124
Posch, M., 309, 314
Posner, J. K., 192
Powell, S. R., 218
Powers, L. E., 314
Prater, M. A., 116, 270
Prayzer, R., 240
Premack, D., 249
Pribesh, S., 76
Proctor, B. D., 33
Puckett, M., 161
Pungello, E. P., 281, 288
Purnell-Hall, T., 132
Putnam, R. F., 77

Qi, S., 137, 145
Quenneville, J., 266

Ragland, E. U., 116
Raikes, H., 292

Ramey, C. T., 133, 281, 288
Ramey, S. L., 133, 288
Ramsey, E., 37, 111
Ranalli, P., 270, 271
Rapp, A. J., 45
Rapp, D. W., 45
Rasinski, T. V., 236
Raymond, E. B., 158, 159, 181, 182
Reavis, H. K., 73
Redden, D., 133
Reddy, S.S., 247
Reichard, C. A., 173
Reid, R., 82, 316
Reis, S. M., 256, 335, 336
Reitz, A. L., 218
Renzulli, J., 335
Reschly, D. J., 32, 33, 47
Reyes, O., 308
Reyes-Wasson, P., 145
Reynolds, A. J., 293
Reynolds, C. D., 152
Rhode, C., 73
Rice, B. F., 319
Richards, H. V., 222
Ridsdale, J., 106
Riggins-Newby, C. G., 142
Rimm, S. B., 161, 340, 342
Risley, T. R., 133, 219, 294
Ritter, S., 32
Robinson, D. R., 218, 244
Robinson, N. M., 133
Robinson, P. D., 234, 237
Robinson-Zanartu, C., 139, 145
Rogan, P., 311
Rogoff, B., 164
Rohrbeck, C. A., 218
Rollins, P., 121
Rondal, J. A., 65
Ronsaville, D. S., 286
Rooze, G. E., 103
Rosario, K., 121
Rosenshine, B., 175, 177
Rosenthal, R., 161
Ross, R., 224
Rothman, S., 168
Rowe, D. C., 158
Roy, S., 34
Ruban, L. M., 256
Rueda, R., 32, 39, 307, 308, 313, 315
Ruh, J., 191
Russell, P. A., 106
Ryan, A. M., 242
Ryan, J. B., 316
Ryan, K. E., 242
Rydell, A., 106

Saccuzzo, D. P., 343, 345
Sacks, S., 106
Saddler, B., 256
Saddler, S. J., 306
Sager, N., 115, 124
Sainato, D. M., 247
Saladana, D. C., 140
Salazar, J., 32
Salmon, S., 34
Salvia, J., 169
Samuda, R. J., 340
Samuels, S. J., 236
Sanacore, J., 234
Sanchez, M. L. C., 65
Sanders, D., 102, 103
Santos, R. M., 30
Sasso, G., 219
Sattler, J., 178, 183, 340
Scarr, S., 164
Schaeffer, A. L., 256
Scharp, D. W., 164
Schley, G., 191, 214
Schloss, C. N., 228
Schloss, P. J., 228
Schmautz, T., 174, 176
Schneider, B. H., 73, 74, 102, 103
Schofield, J. W., 218, 244
Schul, Y., 247
Schulte, A. C., 175
Schulte, D., 219
Schumacher, J. A., 237
Schumm, J. S., 45, 59
Schwartz, S., 265
Scott, B. K., 231
Scott, C., 106
Scott, T. M., 83, 85, 88
Scribner, J. D., 142
Scribner, S., 164
Scruggs, T. E., 229
Seibert, J. K., 262, 263
Seidl, B., 191, 214
Serna, L., 116
Severson, H., 124
Shade, B., 18, 336, 349
Shaftel, J., 175
Shapiro, J., 307
Shea, T. M., 135
Sheridan, S., 124
Sherman, L. W., 247
Shin, F., 65
Shkodriani, G. M., 102
Short-Camilli, C., 115, 124
Shriberg, D., 176, 177
Shriner, J. G., 77
Siegler, R. S., 242
Silbert, J., 234

Simmons, A. B., 32, 76, 219, 295
Simmons, D. C., 214, 294, 298, 299
Simmons, D. S., 232
Simmons-Reed, E., 139
Simpson, R. L., 140
Sinclair, M. F., 307, 316, 322
Singer, L. C., 307, 316, 322
Siwatu, K. O., 256, 258, 268
Skiba, R. J., 32, 75, 76, 77, 179, 180, 295
Skrtic, T. M., 32
Slaughter-Defoe, D. T., 143, 292
Slavin, R. E., 235
Sleeter, C. E., 58
Sloane, F. C., 177
Smith, M. A., 78, 228
Smith, S., 232, 235
Smith, T. E. C., 28
Snyderman, M., 168
Sosik, J. J., 102
Soto, G., 319
Sparling, J., 288, 294
Spinelli, C. G., 158, 159, 169, 181
Spradlin, L. K., 18
Sprague, J. R., 115
Stainback, S., 189
Stainback, W., 189
Stainton, T., 204
Stambaugh, T., 347, 348, 351
Stanley, S. O., 219
Staubitz, J., 236
Steele, C. M., 182, 242
Steers-Wentzell, K. L., 218, 244
Sternberg, R. J., 162, 174, 340, 341, 346
Stiller, B., 124
Stoker, S., 124
Stolarksi, V. S., 310
Storino, M., 75
Storti, C., 13, 15, 17, 19, 20
Strahan, D. B., 256, 268
Strain, P. S., 116
Strickland, C. A., 336
Sugai, G., 82, 85, 88, 93, 114, 115
Summers, J. A., 132, 133, 136, 140
Surat,. M. M., 109
Suritsky, S. K., 265
Suzuki, L., 158
Swain, K. D., 268
Swartz, S. L., 204

Talbert-Johnson, C., 75, 102, 103, 104, 121, 192, 194
Talbott, E., 37
Tallent-Runnels, M., 103
Tam, B., 59, 202, 222

Tarver, S. G., 234
Taylor, G. R., 124
Taylor, K., 289, 293
Taylor, L. S., 136, 138, 139
Taylor, O., 40
Taylor, R., 242
Taylor, R. L., 164
Tellez, K., 140
Temple, J., 270
Test, D. W., 107, 309, 313, 314, 317, 320, 322, 323
Thao, Y. J., 136, 137, 138
Thiede, K., 37
Thoma, C. A., 311
Thomas, A., 58
Thomas, C. A., 306
Thomas, D. D., 136
Thompson, B., 217
Thompson, G. L., 136, 145
Thompson, J. H., 76, 106
Thurlow, M. L., 175, 307
Tidwell, N., 152
Tillman, L. C., 75
Tinajero, J. V., 234
Ting, M. P., 108
Ting-Toomey, S., 11, 13, 14, 15
Tinnish, D., 192, 193
Tomblin, M. J., 306
Tomlinson, C. A., 336, 349, 354
Tomlinson-Clarke, S., 73
Tonemah, S., 334
Torgesen, J. K., 234, 294, 296, 297
Torrance, E. P., 335
Torres-Burgo, N. T., 145
Torrez-Guzman, M. E., 31
Toubbeh, J., 286
Townsend, B. L., 136, 139, 176, 177
Trainor, A. A., 307
Trent, S. C., 57
Tressell, P. A., 136
Triandis, H. C., 102
Trivette, C. M., 141
Troia, G. A., 268, 270
Tuerk, P. W., 175
Turnbull, A. P., 92, 93, 102, 108, 134, 140, 141, 145, 146, 151, 152, 284, 307, 317, 318
Turnbull, H. R., 92
Turnbull, R., 134, 140, 141, 145, 146, 151, 152, 284
Turner, A., 314
Tyler, K. M., 73, 74, 117, 220, 234
Tyson, C. A., 182

Umansky, W., 27
Unger, D. G., 136

Unruh, D., 306, 322
Utley, C. A., 33, 83, 93, 191, 214, 247

Vachon, V., 236
Valdez, G., 165, 180
Vandell, D. L., 192
Vang, C. T., 108
Van Keulen, J. E., 40
VanTassel-Baska, J., 347, 348, 351
Vaughn, S., 45, 59, 106
Velez, W., 32
Venn, J. J., 31, 39
Viadero, D., 201
Villareal, D. M., 217–218
Villegas, A. M., 18, 19
Villwock, D. N., 175
Von Vange, M., 199

Wagner, L., 218
Wagner, M., 306, 322, 324
Waight, C. L., 307, 308, 315
Waintrup, M., 322
Walker, D., 219
Walker, H. M., 37, 111, 115, 124
Wall, S. M., 290, 291
Wang, W., 116, 117
Watkins, N., 152
Watkins-Lewis, K., 73, 117, 234
Waukechon, J., 139

Weddington, G. T., 40
Weed, K. Z., 201
Wehmeyer, M., 256, 268, 269, 270, 307, 309
Weinberg, R. A., 133
Weinstein, C., 73, 79, 80, 81
Wells, K., 319
Wentling, R. M., 307, 308, 315
Westwood, D., 314
White, R., 107
White-Bradley, P., 108
Whiting, G. W., 168, 335, 343, 348
Whittaker, C. R., 136, 138, 139
Whoroton, D., 219
Wilding, G., 283
Williams, H., 243
Williams, T. O., Jr., 33
Williams, V., 149
Williamson, R. D., 275
Willis, W., 204
Wilson, R., 314
Wilson-Costello, D., 283
Winzer, M. A., 210, 221
Witter, F. R., 286
Witty, J. P., 136
Wolford, T., 198
Wolman, J. M., 310
Wood, J. W., 30
Wood, W. M., 309, 313, 314

Woodcock, R. W., 213, 235
Woolsey, L. M., 44, 191, 214
Woolsey, M. L., 198
Wren, D. J., 73
Wright, J., 247
Wu, F., 137, 145
Wu, T. C., 32
Wynn, M., 95, 318

Yadian, L., 218
Yahiku, K., 199
Yang, X., 175
Yao, M., 217–218
Yates, J. R., 110
Yell, M. L., 77
Yoo, J., 259
Young, E. C., 283
Yovanoff, P., 316
Ysseldyke, J. E., 169
Yurick, A. L., 232, 234, 236, 237

Zamora-Duran, G., 32, 37
Zeman, R., 189
Zhan, D., 76
Zhou, M., 139
Ziegler, E. W., 164
Zigmond, N., 256
Zimmerman, B. J., 256
Zolotow, C., 109

Subject Index

A-B-C (Antecedent-Behavior-Consequence) form, 88, 89–90
Academically gifted students, 334
Academic Learning Time (ALT), 218
Academic schedules, developing, 249
Accommodations, 26
Accountability, in special education, 175
Achievement tests, 213
Active student responding (ASR), 219–220
ADHD (attention deficit/hyperactivity disorders), 41–42
Advocacy, parental, 151–154
  history of, 151–152
  resources for, 152–153
African American children, using traditional culture for social skill instruction, 108
African Americans
  cultural styles/strengths of, 337
  parenting practices of, 137
  social behaviors of, 104–105
  special birth risks of, 286–287
  2000 census data profiles, 6
After-school programs, 191–195. *See also* Community-based programs
AIR Self-Determination Scale, 310
Allocentrism, 176
ALT (Academic Learning Time), 218
American Association on Mental Retardation (AAMR), 38
American Speech-Language-Hearing Association (ASHA), 39
Antisocial behaviors, reducing, 124
Asian Americans
  parenting practices of, 137–138
  social behaviors of, 103–104, 104–105
  2000 census data profiles, 7
Asian Americans children, using traditional culture for social skill instruction, 108
Asperger syndrome, 46
ASR. *See* Active student responding (ASR)

Assessment. *See also* Functional assessments
  culturally responsive, 171–174
  for effective instruction, 213–215
  formal, 213
  informal, 213–215
  nondiscriminatory principles of, 178–180
  testing *vs.*, 169–171
Attention deficit/hyperactivity disorders (ADHD), 41–42
Autism, 46–47
Autism disorder, 46
AWARE strategy, for note taking, 265–266

Beach Center on Families and Disability, 147
Behavior, social
  culture and, 72
  culture of schools and, 72–74
Behaviorally disordered, 37
Behavior disorders, 35–37
Bilingual education, 30–31
Birth risks, of CLD populations, 286–287
Blindness, 45. *See also* Vision impairments
Bloom's taxonomy, 350–351
Boys. *See* Gender
Brainstorming, 241
Brown v. the Board of Education of Topeka, Kansas, 25, 55
Bullying, 124

Career education, for CLDE learners, 320–322
Career preparation, 322
Carolina Abecedarian Project, 288
Center for Applied Linguistics, The, 147
Childhood disintegrative disorder, 46
Children with disabilities, social skill needs of, 106–107
Children with learning disabilities (CLD), 31
Choicemaker Self-Determination Transition Assessment, 310

Choral responding, 246
CLD children
  cultures of schools and behavior of, 73–74
  interventions for 3- to 5-year old, 292–295
  role of families in schooling of, 134–136
  techniques for enhancing learning of, 74
CLDE learners
  affirming, 95–96
  with autism, 46–47
  with behavior disorders, 37–38
  being proactive in disciplinary issues for, 82–96
  benefits of community-based programs for, 198–201
  career education for, 320–322
  with communication disorders, special concerns for, 40–41
  curriculum for, 230
  developing self-determination skills with, 315–319
  developing self-directed preparedness skills of, 256–258
  developing writing skills and, 239–241
  disability distribution for/ by race/ethnicity, 34
  discipline *vs.* punishment for, 78–79
  early interventions for, 281–282
  educational after-school programs for, 194
  effective discipline for, 81
  family involvement for, 134–136
  gifted education and, 48
  with hearing impairments, 44–45
  high-incidence, 42
  high-incidence disabilities, 32–33
  inclusive community activities for, 190–194
  increasing effectiveness of, 256

367

instructional strategies for teaching other academic content to, 245–247
interventions for reducing special education placements of, 295–299
learning second language and, 64–65
with mental retardation, special concerns for, 38–39
monitoring of teacher instruction with, 247–249
peer-mediated interventions for, 116–121
with physical disabilities, 46
planning for, 204
preparing, to assume leadership roles in transition planning, 311–313
preparing, to make successful transitions, 308–314
promoting independent living for, 323–324
providing peer-mediated interventions for, 116–120
reading instruction for, 230–238
reading needs of, 295–296
religious instruction and, 204–205
setting goals with, 268–270
social behaviors of, 102–105
social skill needs of, 106–107
special placement issues for, 31–32
standardized testing for, 160–169
teaching self-determination skills to, 320
teaching tips for affirming, 96
CLDE learners (cont.)
transitioning to postsecondary environments, 319–324
with visual impairments, 45
vocational training for, 322–323
CLDE populations
impact of poverty among, 283–286
special birth risks of, 286–287
CLD families of children with disabilities
cultural discontinuities for, 139
economic issues, 138–139
effective communication with parents, 145–151
family adaptation, 136–137
family perceptions, 136
federal legislation for, 135–136
goals of, 137
parenting issues, 137–138
reaction of, 134–135

trust issues, 136
CLD parents, communication with, 145–151
Clearinghouse for Immigrants Education (CHIMME), 147
Collaboration, in inclusive settings, 249
Collectivist view, of self, 16
Communication, styles of, 17–18
Communication disorders, 39
Community activities, inclusive, for CLDE learners, 189–190
after-school hours for, 190–191
benefits of, 191–194
Community-based inclusion, federal laws and, 197–198
Community-based programs. *See also* After-school programs
for CLDE students, 196–197
culturally responsive, 201–204
example of, 200–201
reasons CLDE learners benefit from, 198–201
Comprehension, 232
Conductive hearing loss, 43–44
Confirmative bias, 168
Content integration, 59
Control, locus of, 17
external, 17
internal, 17
Cooperative groups, 74
Cooperative teaming, 203
Corrective reading, 236
Countoons (self-monitoring system), 271, 272
CRA. *See* Culturally responsive assessment (CRA)
Creatively gifted students, 334
Cultural competence, model of, 19–20
Culturally and linguistically diverse (CLD) children. *See* CLD children
Culturally and linguistically diverse exceptional (CLDE) learners. *See* CLDE learners
Culturally responsive assessment (CRA), 171–174, 173
Culturally responsive discipline, 79–82
Culturally responsive lessons, implementing, 61–62
Culturally shared beliefs, 13
Culturally shared traditions, 12–13
Cultural norms, 13
Cultural understanding, defined, 79–80

Culture. *See also* Diversity; School culture
defined, 11–12
dimensions of, 15–18
disciplined environments and, 71–74
functions of, 14–15
Iceberg analogy for, 12, 13
role of, in schooling, 55–56
social behavior and, 72
traditional, using, for social skill instruction, 107–108
Culture shock, 13–14
Curriculum
for CLDE learners, 230
hidden, 73
for social skill instruction, 124–125
Curriculum-based measures (CBM), 213–214, 247

Deafness. *See* Hearing impairments
Deficit thinking, 340–344
Diagnostic tests, 213
Difficult situations, handling, 150–151
Direct cultures, 18
Direct Instruction Corrective Reading, 236
Disabilities
high-incidence, 32–42
low-incidence, 43–47
Discipline
caring classroom environments and, 80
culturally appropriate management strategies for, 81
culturally responsive, 79–82
fairness and, 80
Discipline, punishment *vs.,* 78–79
Discipline gap, 76
Discipline issues, 75–79
being proactive in, for CLDE learners, 82–96
race/gender concerns and, 75–77
students with disabilities and, 77–78
Disproportionality, defined, 32–33
Diversity. *See also* Culture
appreciating classroom, 60–61
impact of, on education, 56–58
student, 9–10
teacher, 7–9
in United States, 3–5
Due process principle, of IDEA, 28
Dynamic Indicators of Basic Early Literacy Skills (DIBELS), 214

Early childhood programs, 293–295
Early Head Start (EHS), 290–292
Early reading intervention, 295–297, 299
Early Reading Intervention curriculum, 214
Education, impact of diversity on, 56–58. *See also* Multicultural education
Educational after-school programs, 194
Education of All Children Act (1975), 25
Educators. *See* Teachers
Effective instruction
  assessment and, 213–215
  CLDE learners and, 229
  considerations for, of CLDE learners, 221–223
  defined, 211
  as evidence-based practice, 217–218
  generalization, 220–221
  legislative impact on, 212
  maintenance and, 220
  professional standards of, 217
  progressive monitoring of, 220
  standards for, 217
  strategies, 218–220
  teacher monitoring of, 247
  teacher quality and, 221
  translating assessment data into instructional objectives for, 216–217
Effective schools, 71
EHS. *See* Early Head Start (EHS)
ELL. *See* English Language Learners (ELL)
Emotionally disturbed, 37
Empowerment, 59
  of families, 142–145
  of parents, 141–142
  schools and, 140–141
English Language Learners (ELL), 31
  family involvement and, 66
  immigration and, 65–66
  providing culturally responsive education for, 63–66
Equity pedagogy, 59
ESL teachers, learning disability resources for, 36
Ethnicity
  race and, 3–5
  in United States, 5–6
Expulsions, 75
  students with disabilities and, 77

Fairness, discipline and, 80
Families. *See* CLD families of children with disabilities; Family involvement
Family-centered empowerment, 142
Family Education Network, 261
Family involvement
  for CLDE learners, 134–136
  for English Language Learners, 66
  promoting, in schools, 140–145
  special issues, for CLDE learners, 136–139
  student achievement and, 133–134
Family Network on Disabilities of Florida, Inc., 147
Fetal alcohol syndrome (FAS), 283, 286
504 Plans, 25–27
Fluency, 232
Focus correcting, 240
Formal assessments, 213
Free, appropriate public education (FAPE) principle, of IDEA, 28
Functional assessments, 82–92. *See also* Assessment
  compile assessment information for, 83–90
  drawing hypothesis about problem behavior, 91–92
  interview forms for, 83, 84–85
  multidisciplinary teams for, 82–83
  for problem behaviors, 82

Gay youth
  social skill needs of, 122–124
  teaching tips for, 123
Gender
  discipline issues and, 75–77
  social skill instruction and, 121–122
  transitions needs and, 306–307
Generalization, effective instruction and, 220
Gifted education, 33
  barriers to recruiting/retaining CLDE learners in, 336–339
  influence of deficit thinking on, 340–344
  recruiting/retaining CLDE learners to, 335–336
  suggested changes for recruitment/retention for, 344–347
Gifted students, 48, 333–334
  academically, 334
  creatively gifted, 334

  intellectually, 334
  leadership, 334
  multicultural education for, 349–352
  race and, 334
Girls. *See* Gender
Goal setting, CLDE learners and, 268–270
Grief cycle, 136–137
Guide notes, for note taking, 267
Gun Free Schools Act (1994), 77

Head Start, for CLD learners, 290–293
Hearing impairments, 43–45
Hidden curriculum, 73
High-context cultures, 18
High-incidence disabilities, 32–42
High-interest–low reading level books, 237
High-stakes tests. *See also* Assessment; Standardized testing; Testing
  considerations for, 176–177
  defined, 174–175
  helping CLDE students perform on, 175–176
HIPPY (Home Instructional Program for Preschool Youngsters), 143
Hispanic/Latino Americans
  social behaviors of, 102–103, 104–105
  special birth risks of, 286–287
  2000 census data profiles, 6
Home-based learning, 142–144
Home Instructional Program for Preschool Youngsters (HIPPY), 143
Home-school partnerships, 351
Home-school relationships, 131–134
Homework Behavior Plan, 261–262
Homework performance. *See also* Study skills
  after-school programs for improving, 261
  improving, 259–262
  parents and, 261–262
  peer assistants for, 261
  tips for, 262

IDE. *See* Individuals with Disabilities Education Improvement Act (IDEIA) (2004)
IDEA. *See* Individuals with Disabilities Education Act (IDEA) (2004)

IDEIA. *See* Individuals with Disabilities Education Improvement Act (IDEIA) (2004)
Idiocentric view, 177
IEP. *See* Individualized Education Programs (IEP)
Immigration, U.S., 65–66
Inclusion, 189
  community-based, 197–198
  defined, 30
  segregated, 199
Inclusive education environments, factors impacting, 248–249
Inclusive games, MAGIC principles for developing, 202–203
Independent living, promoting, for CLDE learners, 323–324
Indirect cultures, 18
Individualism, self and, 15–16
Individualized Education Programs (IEP), 28
Individualized Family Service Plan (IFSP), 28–29
Individuals with Disabilities Education Act (IDEA) (2004), 25, 27–29, 55
  principles of, 28
  qualification process for, 31
Individuals with Disabilities Education Improvement Act (IDEIA) (2004), 131
Infants with disabilities
  Early Head Start for, 290–292
  early interventions for, 282–283
  legislation for, 28–29
  types of interventions for, 288–290
Informal assessments, 213–215
Informal peer tutoring, 218
Informational-services support, 289
Instruction. *See* Effective instruction; Reading instruction; Religious instruction; Social skill instruction
Intellectually gifted students, 334
Intelligence tests, 161–163
  criticisms of, with CLDE groups, 163–168
  issues and concerns about, 161–163
Intertribal Deaf Council, 45
Introductory letters, for communication with CLD parents, 146–148

Knowledge construction, 59

Language, social skill development and, 109–110
Language development, 40–41
Language disorders, 39–40
Latchkey programs, 192–193
Latino Americans. *See* Hispanic/Latino Americans
Lau v. Nichols, 30, 63
Least restrictive environment (LRE), 28, 29–30, 71
Lectures, 245
Lesbian youth
  social skill needs of, 122–124
  teaching tips for, 123
Lessons, culturally responsive, implementing, 61–62
Libraries, for after-school programs, 194
Locus of control, 17
  external, 17
  internal, 17
Low-context cultures, 18
Low-incidence disabilities, 43–48
  hearing impairments, 43–45
  physical disabilities, 45–46
  vision impairments, 45
Low-socioeconomic-status students, identifying and serving, 347–348
LRE. *See* Least restrictive environment (LRE)

MAGIC principles, for developing inclusive games, 202–203
Maintenance, effective instruction and, 220
Manifestation Determination, 77–78
Math challenges, 244
Mathematics achievement gap, 242
Math immersion, 244
Math skills, developing, CLDE learners and, 241–245
Mekye Center, 152
Mental retardation
  CLDE learners with, special concerns for, 38–39
  defined, 38
  definition of level of support for persons with, 38
Minding the Village (MTV), 152
Monochronic orientation, to time, 16–17
Morphology, 39
MotivAider, 275
Multicultural education, 58
  content integration dimension of, 59

  empowering school culture dimension for, 59
  equity pedagogy dimension of, 59
  knowledge construction dimension of, 59
Multiculturalism, 62
Multicultural reading materials, 237–238
Multifactored evaluation, 31–32
Multiple Intelligences, Theory of (Gardner), 345, 346

Naglieri Non-Verbal Abilities Test, 345
National Asian Deaf Congress, 45
National Association of the Education of African American Children with Learning Disabilities (NAEAACLD), 152
National Black Deaf Advocates, 45
National Clearinghouse for Bilingual Education (NCBE), 147
National Council on Disability, 147
National Information Center for Children and Youth with Disabilities (NICHCY), 312–313
Native Americans
  parenting practices of, 138
  social behaviors of, 103, 104–105
  special birth risks of, 286–287
  2000 census data profiles, 6
Native Americans children, using traditional culture for social skill instruction, 107–108
Native Hawaiians, 2000 census data profiles, 7
NCLB. *See* No Child Left Behind (NCLB) (2001)
No Child Left Behind (NCLB) (2001), 20, 25, 75, 131, 212
Nondiscriminatory principle, of IDEA, 28
Nonverbal communication, 74
Northwest Regional Resource Center, 147
Note-taking skills
  reasons for teaching, 265
  strategies for, 265–268

Office of Bilingual Education and Minority Languages Affairs, 147
100 Black Men of America, 312
Opportunity to Respond (OTR), 218–219

Organization skills
  reasons for teaching, 256–258
  teaching, 258–259

Pacer Center, 152
Pacific Islander populations, 2000 census data profiles, 7
Parent Advocacy Coalition of Educational Rights (PACER), 147
Parental advocacy, 151–154
  history of, 151–152
  resources for, 152–153
Parenting practices, of CLD families, 137–138
Parent involvement. *See* Family involvement
Parent-teacher conferences, 148
Particularlism, 16
PBIS. *See* Positive behavior intervention supports (PBIS)
Peer assistants, for homework, 261
Peer-based lessons, for social skill instruction, 117
Peer buddy systems, 203
Peer-mediated interventions, for CLDE learners, 116–121
Peer-peer aggression, 124
Peer tutoring, 218, 247
Personal Responsibility and Work Opportunity Reconciliation Act (PRWORA) (1996), 135
Pervasive developmental disorder, 46
PGOTH (Project: Gentlement on the Move) program, 257–258
Phonemic awareness, 232
Phonics, 232
Phonology, 39
Polychronic orientation, to time, 17
Positive behavior intervention supports (PBIS), 93–95
  primary level, 93–94
  secondary level, 94
  tertiary level, 93–95
Poverty, impact of, on CLDE populations, 283–286
Pragmatics, 39
Predictive software, for writing skills, 241
Premack Principle, 249
Preparedness skills
  reasons for teaching, 256–258
  teaching, 258–259
Preschool programs, 293
Problem Behavior Questionnaire, 85–88

Problem behaviors, functional assessments for, 82–96
Project: Gentlemen on the Move (PGOTH) program, 257–258
Project D.E.L.T.A.A., 200–201
Punishment, discipline *vs.*, 78–79
Pupil diversity, 9–10

Race
  ethnicity and, 3–5
  gifted students and, 334
  mathematics achievement gap and, 242
  in United States, 5
Rainbow Alliance of the Deaf, 45
Raven's Matrix Analogies Test, 345
Reading Excellence: Word Attack & Rate Development Strategies (REWARDS), 236
Reading failure, preventing, 297–298
Reading instruction
  to CLDE learners, 230–238
  early, to prevent special education placements, 295–299
  teaching tips for, 237
Reading materials, multicultural, 237–238
Regional Resource and Federal Centers (RRFC), 147
Religious instruction, CLDE learners and, 204–205
Repeated readings, 236–237
Resource-material support, 289
Response cards, 245–251
REWARDS (Reading Excellence: Word Attack & Rate Development Strategies), 236
Rhett syndrome, 46
Rolling Meadows Library, Illinois, 193

Scaffolding, 174
School-age childcare programs, 192–194
School culture, children's social behavior and, 72–74
School environments, creating positive, 92–95
  positive behavior intervention supports (PBIS), 93–95
  teaching tips for, 95
Schooling, role of culture in, 55–56
Schools
  changes in, 55
  culture of, children's social behavior and, 72–74

  discipline issues in, 75–79
  empowered, 140–141
  promoting CLD family involvement in, 140–145
Second language development
  concurrent, 64
  sequential, 64
Second Step Curriculum, 148–149
Section 504 of Rehabilitation Act (1974), 25–27
Segregated inclusion, 199
Self, concept of, 15–16
Self-advocacy, 309
Self-awareness, 309
Self-determination skills, 309–310
  developing, with CLDE learners, 315–319
  teaching, 313–314
Self-directed learners, 256
Self-knowledge, 309
Self-monitoring
  defined, 270
  strategies, 271–276
  tools for, 270–271
  training, 258–259
Self-regulated learners, 256
Self-reliant learners, defined, 256
Semantics, 39
Sensorineural hearing loss, 44
Sexual orientation, social skill needs according to, 122–124
SLD. *See* Specific learning disabilities (SLD)
Social behavior
  culture and, 72
  culture of schools and, 72–74
Social-emotional support, 289
Social skill development, language and, 109–110
Social skill instruction, 102–103
  culturally responsive, 111–114
  curriculum programs for, 124–125
  gender and, 121–122
  guidelines for selecting books for, 110
  model for culturally responsive, 111–114
  sexual orientation and, 122–124
  teaching tips for, 115–116
  using culturally specific literature for, 109
Specific learning disabilities (SLD), 34–35
SSS (stroke, stifle, and stroke) strategy, 81

Standardized testing, 160–169. *See also* Assessment; High-stakes tests; Testing
  criticism of, for CLDE groups, 163–168
  intelligence tests, 161–163
  personal biases and, 168
  questions to consider for, 169
Strategic note taking, 265, 266
Student diversity, 9–10
Study skills. *See also* Homework performance
  defined, 263
  reasons for teaching, 262–263
  sample, 263–265
Suspensions, pupil, 75
  students with disabilities and, 77
Syntax, 39

Talented students. *See* Gifted students
Teacher diversity, 7–9
Teacher resistance, 308
Teachers
  caring, 80
  culturally responsive, 18–21
  multicultural preparation for, 349
  quality of, effective instruction and, 221
Teaching tips
  for affirming CLDE students, 96
  for building reading skills, 237
  for culturally response positive school environments, 95
  for culturally responsive functional behavior assessments, 91
  for culturally responsive punishment and discipline, 82
  for culture and social behavior, 74
  for gay and lesbian youth, 122–124
  for high-incidence CLDE learners, 42
  for home-based instruction, 145
  for low-incidence CLDE learners, 47
  for note taking, 268
  for self-determination skills, 320
  for self-monitoring, 274
Technical Assistance Alliance for Parent Centers, 147
TENSS. *See* The Educational Navigating Skills Seminar (TENSS)
Testing. *See also* Assessment; High-stakes tests; Standardized testing
  assessment *vs.*, 169–171
  educational implications of, 180–183
The Educational Navigating Skills Seminar (TENSS), 258
Three Tier Reading Model, 232–233
Time
  monochronic orientation to, 16–17
  polychronic orientation to, 17
Toddlers with disabilities
  Early Head Start for, 290–292
  early interventions for, 282–283
  legislation for, 28–29
  types of interventions for, 288–290
Transition needs
  according to cultural and linguistic diversity, 307–318
  gender and, 306–307
  of students with disabilities, 306
Transition planning, 311–313
Transitions
  mentoring students for, 316–317
  using culturally specific literature in teaching for, 318–319
Transition services, 305–306
Triarchic Theory of Intelligence (Sternberg), 345
Trust issues, for families of CLDE learners, 136
Tutoring, peer, 218

Underachievers, identifying and serving, 347–348
United States
  African American population of, 6
  Alaska native population of, 6
  American Indian population of, 6
  Asian population of, 7
  diversity in, 3–5
  ethnic diversity in, 5–6
  Hispanic/Latino population of, 6
  Native Hawaiian and other Pacific Islander population of, 7
  pupil diversity in, 9–10
  race in, 5–6
  teacher diversity in, 7–9
  White population of, 6
Universal design assistive technology, 46
Universalism, 16

Vision impairments, 56
Visual acuity, 45
Vocabulary development, 232
Vocational training, for CLDE learners, 322–323

Warm demanders, 80
"We-us-our" orientation, 16
White population, 2000 cenus data profiles, 6
Writing prompts, 240
Writing skills, developing, for CLDE learners, 239–241

Youth development programs, 194

Zero reject principle, of IDEA, 28
Zero-tolerance policies, 75, 77